# Pseudorandom recursions

Laszlo Hars[1*] and Gyorgy Petruska[2]

**Abstract**

We present our earlier results (not included in Hars and Petruska due to space and time limitations), as well as some updated versions of those, and a few more recent pseudorandom number generator designs. These tell a systems designer which computer word lengths are suitable for certain high-quality pseudorandom number generators, and which constructions of a large family of designs provide long cycles, the most important property of such generators. The employed mathematical tools could help assessing the bit-mixing and mapping properties of a large class of iterated functions, performing only non-multiplicative computer operations: SHIFT, ROTATE, ADD, and XOR.

**Keywords:** pseudorandom number generator, recursive function, invertible functions, matrix, binary modular polynomial, extended GCD algorithm

## 1. Introduction

Security applications, simulations, randomized algorithms, gambling, etc. need good quality random numbers. They can often be substituted with pseudorandom numbers, which are generated by software and behave like true random numbers in many statistics. When these pseudorandom numbers are generated in embedded microprocessors, speed and memory requirements pose constraints, limiting the choice of algorithms.

The quality of the generated sequences is crucial. Randomness tests can verify desired statistical properties for the targeted applications. One of the desired properties of such sequences is the length of the unavoidable cycles. The main point of our investigations is the invertibility of the generator function of such pseudorandom sequences, which can ensure very long cycles in certain operation modes.

Many more characterizations of the generated sequences are possible, like the distribution of blocks of bits. Our corresponding results in this regard have to be deferred to a future publication. This article represents the first step in the investigations of random properties of the sequences generated by a large class of iterated functions, performing only non-multiplicative computer operations: SHIFT, ROTATE, ADD, and XOR.

### 1.1 Prior work

In our original study [1], we presented many small and fast pseudorandom number generators, which pass the most common randomness tests. They repeatedly call simple bit-mixing functions that perform only a few non-multiplicative operations for each generated number, and require very little memory. Therefore, they are ideal for embedded- or time-critical applications. In [1], we also presented general methods to ensure very long cycles in repeated calls of the mixing functions, and showed how to use these algorithms as cryptographic building blocks.

In 2005 (unpublished submission to the CHES'06 workshop), we proved that a necessary condition for the invertibility of a rotate-XOR chain is that the *number of rotations is odd*. This result later appeared in [1]. In this article, we presented our previously unpublished results of 2005/2006, together with some newer results and useful tools, which would help resolving the invertibility in concrete general cases.

A similar class of functions turned out to be very useful in cryptography and pseudorandom number generation, the T-functions. They have been extensively studied [2-11]. A T-function is a mapping from $n$-bit input to $n$-bit output in which each bit $i$ of the output depends only on bits $0,1,..., i$ of the input. All the logical operations, such as XOR, AND, OR, NOT, and most of the arithmetic operations modulo $2^n$, such as addition, multiplication, subtraction, negation, as well as left shift

* Correspondence: lhars@cputech.com
[1]CPU Technology, Pleasanton, CA 94588, USA
Full list of author information is available at the end of the article

and their compositions, are T-functions. However, rotations and right shift operations are not.

### 1.2 This work

The most important property of the considered bit-mixing functions is long period length, related to the invertibility of their generating function. For invertible functions, a counter can be included in the input, assuring that no output value repeats before the counter wraps around. Even when the output is truncated or its bits are mixed together, there will still be no short cycle. A large part of this study below deals with this invertibility, which is present in many pseudorandom number generator modes we have proposed.

In the era of synthesizable processor cores unusual word lengths are easy to implement. Our results tell a systems designer which ones allow efficient pseudorandom number generators, and which constructions could work. It can save design and experimentation work. The employed mathematical tools are easy to use and powerful, and they can aid investigating large classes of iterated functions.

This article comprises three major sections. In Section 2, we describe and analyze several recent random number generator designs, and include some characteristic code segments. In Sections 3 and 4, we discuss the existence of inverses of rotate-add functions and rotate-XOR functions, respectively. Our experience shows that rotate-add methods are usually inferior to rotate-XOR methods.

### 2. New random number generator modes

Recall our notation in [1]: Counter mode (of pseudorandom number generators) is defined as $x_i = f(i)$, where the counter $i$ is incremented before each call of the function $f$. Hybrid counter mode uses a function of several variables, one of them is a similar counter as above: $x_i = f(i, x_{i-1}, x_{i-2},..., x_{i-k})$. Multi-stage generators are based on this kind of iterations, but several calls are performed to such type of functions for one set of output values.

The apparent pseudo-randomness of the counter mode and hybrid counter mode can be improved by incrementing the counter by a large odd constant $c$ (instead of 1), because many more bits change at such addition than at incrementing by 1, most of the time. Although a (loop) counter $i$ is sometimes available for free, and this number $c$ needs extra storage, we found that the pseudo-randomness improves significantly, and so ultimately computation can be saved. We call these new modes offset counter mode and offset hybrid counter mode.

Note that the function $f$ could compute the modified counter $k$ from a regular one $i$, as $k = i \cdot c \bmod 2^{32}$ (in case of 32-bit machine words), but we excluded

multiplication from the admissible operations (because they need large hardware cores and multiple clock cycles at high clock frequencies).

### 2.1 MIX permutations

It is an intriguing idea to design some small additional hardware to embedded processors for rearranging the bits of a register. With the help of a few extra gates (or just wires) the performance of our pseudorandom number generator might be improved.

A MIX operation has to be a permutation of bits, not to reduce the range of the outputs. At repeated application of the MIX permutation a bit gets back to an already occupied position after at most 32 steps. Odd rotations are maximal permutations in every bit position (when the machine word is $2^w$ bits). This is advantageous for random number generation, where we must not have short cycles.

Bit or byte reversals are sometimes available as CPU operations, but they are not very good mixers, as they define permutations with short cycles. Similarly, bit-swap, byte swap, or a rotation followed by swapping neighbor bits all proved to be less effective mixers, than simple rotations. This explains why our best constructions are based on rotations, not on complicated MIX permutations.

### 2.2 MIX-XOR circuits

As compared to our earlier designs, a little more complex bit mixing hardware still proved to be advantageous. It could be implemented with very few gates and wires. For example, in such operations each output bit can be the XOR of two (or more) different input bits. An example is the offset hybrid counter mode generator, which passes all Diehard tests:

$$x = \text{rot}(x, 5) \ ^\wedge \ \text{rot}(x, 24) \ ^\wedge \ (k \mathrel{+}= 0x37798849)$$

where $(x, k)$ represent the state of the random number generator, updated during each invocation of the mixing function. The output, the generated random number, is $x$.

In hardware, the rotations need not actually be performed, only the corresponding bits of the machine word $x$ are XOR-ed, so one iteration can provide 32 bits output in 2 clock cycles.

### 2.3 Statistical randomness tests

We wrote simple C programs for creating 10 MB binary data files for every variant of our pseudorandom number generators and applied statistical tests to them, to assess their quality. Many randomness tests have been published, for example [12-14]. In [15], there is a survey. A recent test suite for testing randomness of sequences for cryptographic applications is the NIST 800-22 Randomness tests

[14], provided as C-99 source code. Unfortunately, it contains errors (acknowledged by its publisher), which were not fixed at the time of this writing.

We found the classic Diehard test suite the most stable and reliable. It was published by Marsaglia [12] and performs 15 different groups of statistical randomness tests. Many different properties are tested and the protocol of the results is 17 pages long. The randomness measures are 250 $p$-values. We employed the standard way for accepting a single $p$-value: checked if it was in a certain interval, like [0.001, 0.999].

### 2.4 Offset hybrid counter mode

We assume 32-bit machine words. The smallest case is of stage-2: These random number generators have two parameters (which can be treated as two internal state variables), one is recursively updated by a mixing function, while the other one (an offset counter) is incremented by a large, odd constant before each call.

Surprisingly, for satisfying the Diehard randomness tests, loading an operand with its bits rotated by a fixed amount proved to be sufficiently random.

$$x = \text{rot}(x, 9) \,{}^\wedge\, (k \mathrel{+}= 0x37798849).$$

This generator passes all Diehard tests, with one near fail of $p$-value = 0.9995. Rotation by 7 works, too, with one $p$-value = 0.9998.

Rotation to the right works even better (because the carry propagation is better utilized):

$$x = \text{rot}(x, 23) \,{}^\wedge\, (k \mathrel{+}= 0x49A8D5B3).$$

(Rotate by 23 to the left is the same as rotate by 9 to the right.) This generator passes all Diehard tests, with no $p$-value > 0.999. Rotation by 25 bits (or 7 bits to the right) is equally good.

Because these generators are already good enough with the minimum number of operations, there is no need for considering more stages (stored in more internal variables).

### 2.5 Offset counter mode

Offset counter mode is the one-stage version of the above-discussed offset hybrid counter mode, that is, there is no state variable, except the counter $k$ to be incremented by a large odd constant before each call. It can be supplied as input, and the output is computed directly from $k$. This mode can be used as a component for data scrambling, hashing, and encryption. Note that invertible functions are needed to map the input to the full range of machine words as output.

We use the notation ROL/ROR$(x, k)$ for rotation of the unsigned integer $x$ to the left/right, respectively, by $k$ positions.

### 32-bit words

The generators are defined as

$(L, R) = (4, 9)$, no Diehard test fails, or nearly fails (rotate left).

$x = (k \mathrel{+}= 0x37798849)$.

$x = (x \,{}^\wedge\, \text{ROL}(x, L) \,{}^\wedge\, \text{ROL}(x, R)) + 0x49A8D5B3$.

$x = (x \,{}^\wedge\, \text{ROL}(x, L) \,{}^\wedge\, \text{ROL}(x, R)) + 0x6969F969$.

$x = (x \,{}^\wedge\, \text{ROL}(x, L) \,{}^\wedge\, \text{ROL}(x, R))$;

$(L, R) = (4, 9)$, no Diehard test fails, or nearly fails (rotate right).

$x = (k \mathrel{+}= 0x37798849)$.

$x = (x \,{}^\wedge\, \text{ROR}(x, L) \,{}^\wedge\, \text{ROR}(x, R)) + 0x49A8D5B3$.

$x = (x \,{}^\wedge\, \text{ROR}(x, L) \,{}^\wedge\, \text{ROR}(x, R)) + 0x6969F969$.

$x = (x \,{}^\wedge\, \text{ROR}(x, L) \,{}^\wedge\, \text{ROR}(x, R))$.

Here $x$ is the output, used also for storing intermediate values. Its value is not retained between calls. These generators work even with structured constants for both adders (e.g., 0x55555555, with only one near fail), so we can safely replace these constants with parameters, to diversify the generators.

### 64-bit Words

One could think that 64-bits need more iterations to get full distribution of bits, but the process above proved to have enough reserve that it still works adapted for long machine words.

The direct dispersion of any bit is to $3 \times 3 \times 3 = 27$ positions. With the two long added constants, most of the time, the carry makes the majority of the 64 bits changed when a single bit is flipped in the counter. Of course, when two initial values are close (e.g., $k = 0$ and 1, or generally at small counter increments), this 1-to-27 dispersion effect is not sufficient. That is why we increment $k$ with a large odd value, ensuring that many input bits change between consecutive calls.

If these increment values (considered as 64-bit keys), have no blocks of 20 identical bits, the scheme was found to work well, so we are reasonable safe against accidental weak keys. Nevertheless, these keys should be tested for blocks of more than 12 zeros or 12 ones, and reject such numbers.

The generators are defined as

$(L, R) = (4, 9)$, no fail, no near fail in Diehard (rotate left).

$x = (k \mathrel{+}= 0x3779884922721DEB)$.

$x = (x \,{}^\wedge\, \text{ROL}(x, L) \,{}^\wedge\, \text{ROL}(x, R)) + 0x49A8D5B369$ $69F969$.

$x = (x \,{}^\wedge\, \text{ROL}(x, L) \,{}^\wedge\, \text{ROL}(x, R)) + 0x6969F96949A$ $8D5B3$.

$x = (x \,{}^\wedge\, \text{ROL}(x, L) \,{}^\wedge\, \text{ROL}(x, R))$.

$(L, R) = (4, 9)$, no fail, no near fail in Diehard (rotate right).

$x = (k \mathrel{+}= 0x3779884922721DEB)$.

$x = (x \wedge \mathrm{ROR}(x,L) \wedge \mathrm{ROR}(x,R)) + 0x49A8D5B3696$
$9F969$.

$x = (x \wedge \mathrm{ROR}(x,L) \wedge \mathrm{ROR}(x,R)) + 0x6969F96949A$
$8D5B3$.

$x = (x \wedge \mathrm{ROR}(x,L) \wedge \mathrm{ROR}(x,R))$.

If we set both other additive constants in the rotate-left version to the structured $0x3333333333333333$ or $0x7777777777777777$, only one Diehard test fails. With $0x7E7E7E7E7E7E7E7E$ all tests pass (with one near fail). Experiments with many similar values show that we have a safety margin for weak constants, therefore these numbers can serve as further 64-bits keys.

### 2.6 Data expansion

For ciphers, e.g., of unbalanced Feistel networks [16,17], we often need to scramble and to expand short, e.g., 32-bit numbers to long values. We can do this really fast in hardware: perform several of these offset counter mode mix operations with different additive constants, in parallel, maybe with varying rotate directions and distances. To get the expanded data just concatenate the results.

If the additive constants are treated as secret keys, or they are derived from a secret key, we get a primitive cipher. With sufficiently many iterations of varying constants, it could be secure.

### 3. Invertibility of rotate-add functions

Since we observed thorough mixing properties in the offset counter mode generators, we could be tempted to simplify the generator function by tweaking their code lines. In [1], we showed that XOR-ing two (instead of three) rotated entries breaks the invertibility of the function, so we tried this idea with addition instead of XOR: $x \leftarrow x + \mathrm{ROT}(x,k)$. (It represents a reduction from two rotates and two XOR operations to one rotate and one addition.) The Diehard tests still pass with a rotation by 7 or 11, in either a left- or the right-rotating variant.

The rationale of investigating this function is that adding to the input its rotated version causes larger changes in the output than a rotate-XOR operation had: a flipped bit in the input influences at least two output bits, but usually much more, dependent on the carry propagation. In this sense the *dispersion* of input changes is larger than at the rotate-XOR type functions, so better mixing properties are expected.

Unfortunately, most of the time this simplified function cannot be inverted, that is, we cannot solve the equation $y = x + \mathrm{ROL}(x, k) = \mathrm{floor}(x \cdot (1 + 2^k + 2^{k-32}))$ mod $2^{32}$ for $x$ (assuming 32-bit machine words). For many $y$ values, there is no solution, or there are more than one possible $x$ values. Therefore, we should better *avoid these functions in counter mode, in hybrid counter mode of random number generators, or in ciphers*.

The problems are easily seen by computing $x + \mathrm{ROL}(x, k)$ for all values of $x$, and sorting the results. For example, for $w = 16$-bit machine words, and rotation by $k = 3$, the sequence of the sorted $y$ values starts as:

0, 2,2,2, 5,5,5, 8,8, 9, 11,11,11, 14,14,14, 17,17, 18, 20,20,20, 23...

To the best of the authors' knowledge, the corresponding general problem has not been addressed in the literature.

**Claim**: *the Rotate-Add functions defined below do not attain all $y$ values*, with any fixed $k$: $0 < k < w$, when $x$ goes over all possible values in $[0, 2^w - 1]$.

$$y(x) = x + \mathrm{ROL}(x, k) = \mathrm{floor}(x \cdot (1 + 2^k + 2^{k-w})) \bmod 2^w.$$

In the rest of this section, we are going to validate this claim. We will use a little more convenient way to write $y(x)$, by first partitioning $x$ into its least significant $k$ bits $(v)$, and the remaining bits $(u)$, such that $x = 2^{w-k} \cdot u + v$, (with $0 \le u < 2^{w-k}$ and $0 \le u < 2^k$). Our rotate-add function now expressed as

$$y(x) = (2^k + 1)u + (2^{w-k} + 1)v \bmod 2^w.$$

### 3.1 Word lengths of $2^w$

#### 3.1.1. Common factors

For the ordinary sizes of machine words, the coefficients of $u$ and $v$ are not relative primes. Below we list their common factors as $k$ ranges through 0 to $w$:

$w = 16$:

1, 3, 5, 3, 17, 3, 5, 3, 257, 3, 5, 3, 17, 3, 5, 3, 1

$w = 32$:

1, 3, 5, 3, 17, 3, 5, 3, 257, 3, 5, 3, 17, 3, 5, 3, 65537, 3, 5, 3, 17, 3, 5, 3, 257, 3, 5, 3, 17, 3, 5, 3, 1

$w = 64$:

1, 3, 5, 3, 17, 3, 5, 3, 257, 3, 5, 3, 17, 3, 5, 3, 65537, 3, 5, 3, 17, 3, 5, 3, 257, 3, 5, 3, 17, 3, 5, 3, 4294967297, 3, 5, 3, 17, 3, 5, 3, 257, 3, 5, 3, 17, 3, 5, 3, 65537, 3, 5, 3, 17, 3, 5, 3, 257, 3, 5, 3, 17, 3, 5, 3, 1

As we can see, there is no proper rotation of $0 < k < w$ distance, which does not suffer from common factors. It is a remarkable experience, that all the common factors are Fermat numbers, that is integers of form $F_n = 2^{2^n} + 1$. There are deep and age old open problems concerning Fermat numbers. Computational evidence supports the following conjecture, which is important, because the length of machine words in all practical cases is a power of 2 (8, 16, 32, 64...).

**Conjecture 1**: If $w$ is a power of two and $0 < k < w$, then $\mathrm{GCD}(2^k + 1, 2^{w-k} + 1)$ is a Fermat number $2^{2^n} + 1$.

**Notes**:

• The first few Fermat numbers are $F_0 = 3$, $F_1 = 5$, $F_2 = 17$, $F_3 = 257$, $F_4 = 65537$, $F_5 = 4294967297$, $F_6 = 18446744073709551617$,

$F_7 = 340282366920938463463374607431768211457$.

- Only the first five Fermat numbers $F_0$, $F_1$, $F_2$, $F_3$, $F_4$ are known to be prime. The next three we listed are products of two primes:

$4294967297 = 641 \times 6700417$

$18446744073709551617 = 274177 \times 67280421310721$

$340282366920938463463374607431768211457 = 59649589127497217 \times 5704689200685129054721$

- Conjecture 1 has been numerically verified for $w = 2^2$, $2^3$..., $2^{20}$. Up to $w = 2^{18}$ just minutes of PC computing time was used, $w = 2^{19}$ took 3 h, and verifying the conjecture for $w = 2^{20}$ needed 22 h at light CPU load. The cases $w = 16, 32, 64$ are demonstrated by the tables presented above.

Though Conjecture 1 eludes a rigorous proof, we can prove a somewhat weaker statement, sufficient for our investigations: the GCD in question is at least divisible by a Fermat number:

**Theorem 3.1**: If $W$ is a power of two, then $GCD(2^K + 1, 2^{W-K} + 1)$ is divisible by a Fermat number for any $K$ integer, $0 < K < W$.

**Proof:** We change the notation showing that the exponents are symmetrically positioned around $w = W/2$, again a power of 2 say, $w = 2^p$. Also, we denote $k = w - K$ and using the new notations we are to show that GCD $(2^{w+k} + 1, 2^{w-k} + 1)$ is a multiple of a Fermat number. We put $k = 2^q \cdot r$, $0 \le q < p$ integer, and $r$ is an odd number. Now we obtain

$w + k = 2^p + 2^q r = 2^q \cdot (2^{p-q} + r) = 2^q a$ for the first, and

$w - k = 2^p - 2^q r = 2^q \cdot (2^{p-q} - r) = 2^q b$ for the second exponent, where $a$ and $b$ are odd integers.

With the notation $u = 2^{2q}$ we have $GCD(2^{w+k} + 1, 2^{w-k} + 1) = GCD(u^a + 1, u^b + 1)$. Since $a$ and $b$ are odd, $u + 1$ (that is Fermat number $F_q$) is a divisor of both numbers $u^a + 1$ and $u^b + 1$. $\square$

**Corollary 3.2**: If Conjecture 1 holds true, then the Fermat number $F_q$ we found in the above proof is the greatest common divisor in question.

Indeed, it is well known that the Fermat numbers are pair-wise relative primes, thus a Fermat number cannot be the divisor of another Fermat number. Note that for $q = 0$ we have $F_q = 3$, which explains the occurrence of 3 in every second position in the above tables of common divisors. $\square$

### 3.1.2. Overflow

If the addition of $x$ to $ROL(x, k)$ does not cause overflow, we have $y(x) = (2^k+1)u + (2^{w-k} + 1) \cdot v$. For the investigated word lengths of $2^w$, $y(x)$ is a multiple of one of the common factors granted by Theorem 3.1, and so $y(x)$ does not take all possible values.

The situation is not much more complicated when there is an overflow (which can only be 1):

$$y(x) = (2^k + 1)u + (2^{w-k} + 1)v - 2^w$$

In this case, dividing $y(x)$ by the above discussed common factor the remainder is determined by $2^w$.

Note that when we divide by the Fermat number we found above as a common factor, the remainder is always 1. This is explained by the well known and fairly obvious product formula of Fermat numbers:

$$F_{p+1} - 2 = F_0 \cdots F_p.$$

### 3.1.3. Missing words

As we just saw, $y(x)$ is a multiple of a Fermat number 3, 5, 17, 257, 65537, 4294967297...; or 1 less than such a multiple, in all practical computing systems. Thus, numbers in at least one residue class modulo a Fermat number (at least a third of the possible output values $[0, 2^w - 1]$) never get generated.

## 3.2 Uncommon word lengths

There are machine word lengths, which do give relative prime coefficients of $u$ and $v$, for certain rotation lengths. These machine words are almost never used in real-life computing systems, but in the age of synthesizable processor cores special hardware could easily be built for them, if they were advantageous. Unfortunately, as our negative results show below, they are not much better regarding invertibility than the more common word sizes. This knowledge can save a lot of futile work.

### 24-bit words

We can list the common factors of the coefficients of $u$ and $v$, as $k$ goes from 0 to $w$:

$w = 24$: 1, 3, 5, 9, 17, 3, 65, 3, **1**, 9, 5, 3, 4097, 3, 5, 9, **1**, 3, 65, 3, 17, 9, 5, 3, 1

Here, rotations by 8 and 16 could be good candidates for mixing functions, but when there is an overflow, many $y$ values get repeated. With a simple PC program we counted the number of missing words: at rotation by 8 or 16 there are 4,210,688 missing words, which represents over 25% of all 24-bit words.

### 25-bit words

The odd word length 25 makes *each* pair of the coefficients of $u$ and $v$ relative prime, and still all rotation-add options leave out many words. The best cases are with rotations by 12 or 13 (0.024%: 8191 missing words), the worst cases are with rotations by 1 or 24 (one-third of the words: 11,184,811 are missing).

### 31-bit words

One can drop one bit of the most common 32 bit machine words. All the pairs of multipliers become relative primes, and still every rotation-add option leaves out many words. A PC program found the best cases at rotations by 15 or 16 (65,535 = 0.003% missing words), and the worst cases at rotations by 1 or 30 (one third of the words: 715,827,883 are missing).

Note that the relatively few missing words at rotations by 15 or 16 do make this scheme useable for Feistel-style encryption, but other constructions (like rotate-XOR) are still better.

### 3.3 Arbitrary word sizes

We can show in general that *no* rotate-add function is invertible:

**Theorem 3.3:** At any word length $w$ and rotation distance $k$ the corresponding rotate-add function repeats at least one word (and so at least one output word is always missing).

**Proof:** (a) If there is a common factor $d > 1$ dividing both the coefficients of $u$ and $v$ in $(2^k + 1) \cdot u + (2^{w-k} + 1) \cdot v$, it is odd, therefore at least 3. Thus, $y(x) \equiv 0$ or $-2^w$ mod $d$, hence numbers in the remaining (at least one) mod $d$ residue classes are not generated.

(b) If $GCD(2^k + 1, 2^{w-k} + 1) = 1$, the extended GCD algorithms find $u'$ and $v'$ integers (one of them negative), such that $(2^k + 1) \cdot u' + (2^{w-k} + 1) \cdot v' = 1$. Multiplying this equation with $2^w$ we obtain $(2^k + 1) \cdot (u' \cdot 2^w) + (2^{w-k} + 1) \cdot (v' \cdot 2^w) = 2^w$, thus the Diophantine equation $(2^k + 1) \cdot u + (2^{w-k} + 1) \cdot v = 2^w$ admits a solution.

Note that for any integer $m$, $u = u' + m \cdot (2^{w-k} + 1)$, and $v = v' - m \cdot (2^k + 1)$ represent another solution for the equation above. At a suitable $m$ value there is a solution $(u'', v'')$, such that $0 < u'' < 2^{w-k}$.

Because of the symmetry, we may assume that $k \leq w - k$. Substituting the minimum and maximum $u''$ values into the equation $(2^k + 1) \cdot u + (2^{w-k} + 1)v = 2^w$ we find that $0 < v'' < 2^k$. These $(u'', v'')$ values, therefore, can be concatenated to form a machine integer $x \neq 0$, of length $w$. Our mod $2^w$ rotate-add function transforms this $x$ into 0. Because 0 is a fix point, we found two machine integers ($x$ and 0), which are both transformed to 0. $\square$

## 4. Invertibility of rotate-XOR functions

For many applications of random number generator constructions presented in Section 2 of this article (and of the ones in [1]) we needed the recursions to be invertible. In [1], we proved the following

**Lemma:** The determinant of $M$, the sum of $k$ powers of unit circulant matrices is divisible by $k$.

Its corollary is that even number of rotations XOR-ed together does not define invertible recursions.

In the rest of the article, we investigate the invertibility problem in more details. Two (equivalent) models of the iterated functions are employed, namely, matrix and binary polynomial representations.

### 4.1 Elementary results

Let $N$ denote the length of the machine word where we perform rotate-XOR computations. We denote by $C$ the corresponding unit circulant matrix of size $N \times N$ (all entries are 0, except the 1s above the main diagonal and in the lower left corner). $C$ is the cyclic permutation matrix performing a circular left-shift (rotation) on the elements of an $N$-vector. Its $k$th power $C^k$ performs a rotation by $k$ places.

The parity of the determinant of the $N \times N$ (composite circulant) matrix $M = C^{k_1} + C^{k_2} + \ldots + C^{k_m}$ decides the solvability of the linear system of equations on the individual bits in the recursions defined by rotations (by $k_1, k_2 \ldots, k_m$ positions) and bitwise XOR (with possibly a known number added to the result). Therefore, the matrix entries can be taken modulo 2 (0 or 1). Adding a matrix of all even entries to $M$ does not change the parity of $\det(M)$.

Note that $C^N = I$, and $\det(C^k) = 1$. By $M = C^{k_1} (I + C^{k_2 - k_1} + \ldots + C^{k_m - k_1})$ we may always assume $0 = k_1 < k_2 < \ldots < k_m < N$. Since the system of parameters $\{k_1, k_2 \ldots, k_m; N\}$ fully determines the invertibility of the recursion represented by the corresponding circulant matrix $M$, we may call the system $\{k_1, k_2 \ldots, k_m; N\}$ itself *regular* for $\det(M) = 1$, or *singular* for $\det(M) = 0$. We state the result mentioned in the introductory remark of this section as

**Theorem 4.1** [1]. If for a system $\{k_1, k_2 \ldots, k_m; N\}$ $m$ is an even number, then the system is singular. That is, for regular systems $m$ is necessarily odd. $\square$

It is well known that a matrix **A** has an inverse over any field *iff* (if and only if) its determinant is non-zero ($\det(\mathbf{A}) \neq 0$). The inverse $\mathbf{A}^{-1}$ can be explicitly written as a matrix of cofactors.

Note that the determinant is multiplicative in general: $\det(AB) = \det(A) \det(B)$, and hence $\det(M) \equiv \det^k(M) \equiv \det(M^k)$ mod 2, for any integer $k > 0$.

**The case N = $2^n$**

If we expand $M^2 = (C^{k_1} + C^{k_2} + \ldots + C^{k_m})^2$, the double products contribute only even ($\sim 0$) entries:

$$M^2 \equiv C^{2k_1} + C^{2k_2} + \ldots + C^{2k_m} \text{ mod } 2.$$

If $N = 2^n$, squaring matrix $M$ $n$-times gives $M^N \equiv C^{Nk_1} + C^{Nk_2} + \ldots + C^{Nk_m}$ mod 2. Because $C^{Nk_1} = (C^N)^{k_1}$, and $C^N = I$ (the unit matrix), $M^N \equiv m \cdot I$ mod 2. This proves the following

**Theorem 4.2:** If $N = 2^n$, $M$ is invertible mod 2, that is the system $\{k_1, k_2 \ldots, k_m; N\}$ is regular *iff* $m$, the number of non-zero diagonals is an odd number. $\square$

Theorem 4.2 is important because it covers almost all practical cases in computer systems, where the word length is 8, 16, 32, or 64 bits, even the extended precision of 128 and 256 bits.

**The case N = q·$2^n$, with odd q**

After $n$ squaring operations, two terms become equal: $C^{u2^n} = C^{v2^n}$, *iff* the exponents are congruent mod $N$: $2^n u \equiv$

$2^n v \bmod q \cdot 2^n$, or equivalently $u \equiv v \bmod q$. These terms cancel each other; therefore, it is enough to consider those $M = C^{k_1} + C^{k_2} + \ldots + C^{k_m}$ matrices, where $k_1, k_2, \ldots, k_m$ are all different mod $q$. In particular, the following cancellation law holds true: if we add (or remove) $C^u + C^v$ where $u \equiv v \bmod q$, the parity of $\det(M)$ does not change. Thus we obtain the following useful

**Corollary 4.3**: If $N = q \cdot 2^n$ and $u \equiv v \bmod q$, then replacing $C^u$ by $C^v$ in M does not change the parity of $\det(M)$. In particular, we can restrict our investigations to systems $\{k_1, k_2, \ldots, k_m; q \cdot 2^n\}$ such that $0 \leq k_i < q$, or $-(q-1)/2 \leq k_i \leq (q-1)/2$. □

Now the construction of a regular system $\{k_1, k_2, \ldots, k_m; q \cdot 2^n\}$ ($q$ odd) is easy as shown in

**Corollary 4.4**: The system $\{k_1, k_2, \ldots, k_m; q \cdot 2^n\}$ ($q$ odd) is regular, if $k_1, k_2, \ldots, k_m$ are chosen such that one residue class mod $q$ contains an odd number of $k_i$ values, and every other residue class contains an even number of $k_i$ values. In this case $\det(M)$ is odd. □

We remark that if with the above notations $N = q$ (that is, $n = 0$) the statement of Corollary 4.3 reduces to a triviality: $\det(M)$ is odd if it is derived from a single rotation.

*The sub-case $N = 3 \cdot 2^n$*

This case has practical relevance for digital systems with a word length of 12, 24, 48... bits.

**Theorem 4.5**: If $N = 3 \cdot 2^n$ and $M = C^{k_1} + C^{k_2} + \ldots + C^{k_m}$ is an $N \times N$ matrix, then $\det(M)$ is odd *iff* one of the three residue classes mod 3 contains an odd number of $k_i$ values, and each of the other two residue classes contains an even number of $k_i$ values.

**Proof**: Corollary 4.4 shows that these determinants are indeed odd. As for the other direction, according to the cancellation law in Corollary 4.3, the following systems are to be considered:

$\{0; 3 \cdot 2^n\}$, $\{1; 3 \cdot 2^n\}$, $\{2; 3 \cdot 2^n\}$, $\{0,1; 3 \cdot 2^n\}$, $\{0,2; 3 \cdot 2^n\}$, $\{1,2; 3 \cdot 2^n\}$, $\{0,1,2; 3 \cdot 2^n\}$.

The first three are regular (obvious), the next three are singular (Theorem 4.1). In order to verify Theorem 4.5 we have to show that the last system is also singular. For this we manipulate the corresponding matrix. We do not change the determinant, if we add all the rows of index 4, 7..., $(4 + 3k)$,... to the first row, and add all the rows 5, 8..., $(5 + 3k)$,... to the second row. We obtain a matrix such that all the entries in the first two rows are 1, and hence the determinant is 0. □

### 4.1.1. Consecutive diagonals

In practice, the most important non-trivial invertible recursions (the fastest to compute) have *three* rotations. We can fully characterize the cases, when the rotation displacements are next to each other. We will revisit this case later, and prove a more general theorem with the help of binary polynomials.

**Theorem 4.6**: $\det(C^0 + C^1 + C^2) = 0 \bmod 2$ *iff* N is divisible by 3. That is, the system $\{0,1,2; N\}$ is singular *iff* $N = 3n$.

**Proof**: For $N \geq 6$: The top and bottom rows of the matrix look like:

1 1 1 0 0 0...
0 1 1 1 0 0...
0 0 1 1 1 0...
........
**1 0 0 0** $x$...
**1 1 0 0 0**...

We add rows 1 and 2 to the second but last row, and rows 1 and 3 to the last row, and obtain

0 0 0 1 $x$...
0 0 0 1 1...

in the last two rows. The first column of the matrix has now only a single leading 1 entry, so we can remove it together with the first row (Laplace's formula). In the new matrix the first column still has just a single leading 1, so this row/column removal can be done, all together 3 times. The result is a matrix of the original type, only its dimension decreased by 3. Repeat these reduction steps until the size of the matrix is reduced to $\leq 5$. The result is one of three small matrices, and their determinants $D_3$, $D_4$, and $D_5$ are easily computed, completing the proof:

$$D_3 = 0, \quad D_4 = 3, \quad D_5 = 3.$$

**Note:** The above described reduction method works for *any* number ($m \geq 3$) of consecutive cyclic diagonals. We assume $N \geq 2m$ and, as usual, we can suppose $k_1 = 0$. We denote the sum of row 1 and row $j$ of the matrix by $s_j$, we obtain the following modified rows:

$$S_2 = 1\,\underbrace{0 \ldots 0}_{m-1}\,10 \ldots, \quad S_3 = 11\,\underbrace{0 \ldots 0}_{m-2}\,110 \ldots, \quad \ldots, \quad S_m\,\underbrace{1 \ldots 1}_{m-1}0\,\underbrace{1 \ldots 1}_{m-1}0 \ldots$$

When each of these rows is added to the corresponding row of index $N - m + 2$, $N - m + 3$,..., $N$, respectively, in the bottom section of the matrix the 1 entries in the leftmost $m$ columns are effectively moved $m$ positions to the right. We can apply Laplace's formula for column 1, then for column 2,... up to column $m - 1$, to reduce the matrix to an $m$-diagonal matrix of size $N - m$. The reduction process does not change the determinant.

These steps can be repeated until the matrix becomes too small for any further reduction. In the end $m$ small matrices of size $m \times m$,..., $(2m - 1) \times (2m - 1)$ remain to be evaluated. The smallest one is of size $m \times m$. This matrix, having all its entries = 1, has 0 determinant. The other determinants can easily be computed and their parity may vary. The exact characterization of consecutive diagonals will be completed in Section 5, Theorem 5.2.

## 4.2 Modular binary polynomials

Using a polynomial model and arithmetic, we may obtain better insight to the problem of inverses and prove more general results.

### 4.2.1. Polynomial representation of circulant matrices

There is a one-to-one correspondence between mod 2 circulant matrices of size $n \times n$, and binary polynomials mod $x^n + 1$: Replace the unit circulant matrix $C$ in the matrix equation with $x$, and replace the $(+, \times)$ matrix operations with their polynomial counterparts. The unit matrix $I$ corresponds to the polynomial identically 1, and the matrix equation $C^n = I$ translates to the polynomial equation $x^n = 1 \mod x^n + 1$ (note that $x^n - 1 = x^n + 1 \mod 2$).

**Proposition 4.7**: If $M^{-1}$, the inverse of the circulant matrix $M$ over a finite field exists, it is also a circulant matrix.

**Proof**: For the given size $n \times n$, there are only a finite number of circulant matrices over a finite field, so $M^a = M^b$ for some $a > b \geq 0$ integers. Multiply this equation $(b + 1)$-times with $M^{-1}$ to get $M^{a-b-1} = M^{-1}$. The left-hand side is a non-negative power of a circulant matrix, so it is circulant. □

**Corollary 4.8**: A circulant matrix is mod 2 invertible *iff* the corresponding binary polynomial has an inverse, such that

$$p(x) \cdot q(x) = 1 \mod x^n + 1.$$

The following lemma is well known.

**Lemma 4.9**: The inverse polynomial $q(x)$ of $p(x)$ exists *iff* $GCD(p(x), x^n + 1) = 1$.

**Proof**: (a) The extended Euclidean algorithm computes the inverse $q(x)$ if $GCD(p(x), x^n + 1) = 1$.

(b) If $GCD(p(x), x^n + 1) = h(x) \neq 1$, then $p(x) = p_1(x) \cdot h(x)$ and $x^n + 1 = u_1(x) \cdot h(x)$ with some $p_1(x)$ and $u_1(x)$ polynomials. If there was an inverse, $q(x)$, then there is $u(x)$ polynomial such that $p_1(x) \cdot h(x) \, q(x) = 1 + u(x) \cdot h(x)$. It is equivalent to the impossible equation $[p_1(x) \cdot q(x) - u(x)] \cdot h(x) = 1$. □

The following result shows that the singularity of systems is "stable" for multiplied dimensions. Unfortunately no such stability holds for regular systems, even under stronger conditions.

**Theorem 4.10**: If the system $\{k_1, k_2, ..., k_m; N\}$ is

(i) singular, then for all integer $j > 0$ the system $\{k_1, k_2, ..., k_m; j \cdot N\}$ is also singular

(ii) regular and $d > m$ is a divisor of $N$, then $\{k_1, k_2, ..., k_m; d\}$ is also regular.

**Proof**: Note that (i) and (ii) are equivalent. Let $p(x)$ be the polynomial representation of the system. By Corollary 4.8 and Lemma 4.9, we have $GCD(p(x), x^N + 1) \neq 1$.

Since $x^N + 1$ divides $x^{j \cdot N} + 1$, $GCD(p(x), x^{j \cdot N} + 1) \neq 1$ and statement (i) follows. □

**Note**: Even if both systems $\{k_1, k_2, ..., k_m; N_1\}$ and $\{k_1, k_2, ..., k_m; N_2\}$ are regular, the system $\{k_1, k_2, ..., k_m; N_1 \cdot N_2\}$ is not necessarily regular. We find the following counterexample: $\{0, 1, 6; 7\}$ and $\{0, 1, 6; 9\}$ are regular systems, however $\{0, 1, 6; 63\}$ is singular. Indeed,

$$GCD(x^6 + x + 1, x^7 + 1) = GCD(x^6 + x + 1, x^9 + 1) = 1,$$

but $x^6 + x + 1$ divides $x^{63} + 1$. □

**Theorem 4.11** [18]. Every irreducible binary polynomial of degree $k$ divides $x^{2^k} + x \mod 2$. If $k > 1$ then $p(x) \neq x$, so $p(x)$ has a constant term, and we have $p(x) | x^{2^k-1} + 1 \mod 2$. □

**Corollary 4.12**: For any $p(x)$ binary polynomial with a constant term, there exists an exponent $t$, such that $p(x) \mid x^t + 1 \mod 2$.

**Proof**: Write the polynomial $p(x)$ (not divisible by $x$) as a product of powers of irreducible factors. Each irreducible factor has a corresponding multiple of form $x^u + 1$.

$x^u + 1$ and $x^v + 1$ both divide $x^{u \cdot v} + 1$ (where $u = v$ allowed), from an elementary identity. Because $x^{2u \cdot v} + 1 = (x^{u v} + 1)^2 \mod 2$, $(x^u + 1) \cdot (x^v + 1)$ divides $x^{2u \cdot v} + 1$. Repeating this for all the factors of $p(x)$, we see that there always exists an exponent $t$, such that $p(x) \mid x^t + 1 \mod 2$. □

**Definition**: We call the smallest of such $t$ values the *characteristic exponent* of $p$.

Note that if $p(x) \mid x^u + 1 \mod 2$, then $u$ is a multiple of the characteristic exponent $t$. Indeed, we write $u = kt + r$ ($r < t$) and we get $x^{kt+r} + 1 = ((x^t)^k - 1)x^r + x^r + 1$, and hence $p(x) \mid x^r + 1 \mod 2$, a contradiction to the minimum choice of $t$.

**Theorem 4.13**: Given a $p(x)$ binary polynomial, let $t > 0$ denote its characteristic exponent. Then, $p(x)$ is invertible mod $x^n + 1$ *iff* it is invertible mod $x^{n+t} + 1$, or assuming $n > t$, *iff* it is invertible mod $x^{n-t} + 1$.

**Proof**: Since $p(x)$ divides $x^t + 1 \mod 2$, it also divides $x^{t+n} + x^n \mod 2$. Adding this to $x^n + 1$, we get $x^{t+n} + 1$, which is relative prime to $p(x)$ *iff* $x^n + 1$ is relative prime to $p(x)$. Suppose $n > t$, then we can apply the first part of Theorem 4.13 for $n - t$ in place of $n$, which completes the proof. □

Theorem 4.13 plays a fundamental role in testing the regularity of systems.

**Corollary 4.14**: Let $p$ denote the polynomial associated to the system $\{0 = k_1, k_2, ..., k_m; N\}$, and $t$ the characteristic exponent of $p$. If $N_1 = N_2 \mod t$, the systems $\{k_1, k_2, ..., k_m; N_1\}$ and $\{k_1, k_2, ..., k_m; N_2\}$ are both regular or both singular. That is, the regularity of a system depends on the mod $t$ residue class of the dimension. □

Note that by the above corollary, the notion of regularity/singularity of a system $\{0 = k_1, k_2, ..., k_m; N\}$ is meaningful for any dimension $N$, even if the $N$-dimensional matrix is too small to accommodate the rotations in the system: the dimension is to be considered mod $t$, that is if $N$ is too small we may always replace it by $N + t$.

### 4.2.2. Testing procedure

Based upon Corollary 4.14 above, we established the following testing procedure: if we want to know if a circulant matrix of a fixed set of diagonals, but of arbitrary size $N$, is invertible, we determine the characteristic exponent $t$, and the residue class $q = N$ mod $t$. Now we have to compute the determinant of the circulant matrix of size $q$. In particular, if we know the "regular" residue classes mod $t$, we know every dimension numbers for which the system is regular or singular. Also, rather than computing determinants, we can deal with GCD($p$ $(x)$, $x^q + 1$) to check regularity.

**Corollary 4.15**: A system is singular if the dimension is the characteristic exponent $t$, or any of its multiples. In greater generality, if $q$ is a singular residue class mod $t$, then the system is singular in any dimension $nq$ ($n = 1,2,...$). If $q$ is regular residue class mod $t$ and $d > m$ is a divisor of $q$, then the system is regular in dimension $d$ as well. □

**Lemma 4.16.** For any binary polynomial $p(x)$, $x + 1 \mid p(x)$ mod 2 holds *iff* $p$ has an even number of terms.

**Proof:** Indeed, adding pair-wise the terms of $p$, each such sum $x^a + x^b = x^a(x^{b-a} + 1)$ is divisible by $x + 1$. In case of even number of terms these pairs add up to the polynomial, making it a multiple of $x + 1$, while for an odd number of terms there remains a single term $x^a$, clearly not a multiple of $x + 1$. □

**Theorem 4.17**: Let $p(x)$ be the polynomial associated to a system $\{0 = k_1, k_2,..., k_m; N\}$ and let $t$ denote the characteristic exponent.

(i) If $x + 1 \mid p(x)$ mod 2 then the system is completely singular, that is singular for any dimension $N$.

(ii) If $x + 1$ is not a divisor of $p(x)$ mod 2, then $t - 1$ and $t + 1$ are regular dimensions (in particular, the system is not completely singular). Moreover, if $t$ happens to be a prime number, then the system is completely regular, that is regular for any dimension except the multiples of $t$.

**Proof**: Since $x + 1$ divides $x^n + 1$ mod 2 for any $n$, GCD $(x^n + 1, p(x)) = 1$ cannot hold true, verifying (i). Next consider $x^{t+1} + 1 - (x^t + 1) = x^t(x + 1)$ mod 2 and we obtain GCD($x^{t+1} + 1, x^t + 1$) = GCD($x^{t-1} + 1, x^t + 1$) = $x + 1$. Since $p \mid x^t + 1$ and $x + 1$ is not a divisor of $p$, GCD($x^{t+1} + 1, p$) = GCD($x^{t-1} + 1, p$) = 1, showing that $t - 1$ and $t + 1$ are indeed regular. If, in addition, $t$ is a prime number, then the multiples of a non-zero residue class run through all the residue classes' mod $t$, thus a single singular dimension would imply complete singularity which cannot be the case, proving (ii) and the theorem. □

Note that by Lemma 4.16 above, statement (i) is the polynomial version of Theorem 4.2. By the lemma and Theorem 4.17, the following corollary is immediate.

**Corollary 4.18:** The statements below are equivalent:

(i) A system is completely singular
(ii) A system has an even number of rotations
(iii) $x + 1$ is a divisor of the associated polynomial. □

Several examples are given below illustrating the frequent case of complete regularity.

## 5. Examples

### 5.1 Three non-zero diagonals

For certain fixed sets of diagonals (-polynomial coefficients, corresponding ultimately to the rotation distance in a rotate-XOR bit mixing function) we determined with a computer algebra system, at which word sizes $n$ are the function invertible. We call $n$ "invertible" or "regular".

The computation takes two steps. First, with a search loop we determine the smallest $t$, such that the corresponding binary polynomial $p(x)$ divides $x^t + 1$ mod 2 (the smallest characteristic exponent). Then, we check for which $n < t$, $p(x)$ is invertible. The computation for each case takes only a fraction of a second. (Recall, that we can transform the system to have $k_1 = 0$, that is, $p(x)$ to have a constant term 1.)

(1) For $p(x) = x^2 + x + 1$, $t = 3$. Only $0 = n$ mod 3 is singular.

(2) For $p(x) = x^3 + x + 1$, $t = 7$. Only $0 = n$ mod 7 is singular.

(3) For $p(x) = x^3 + x^2 + 1$, $t = 7$. Only $0 = n$ mod 7 is singular.

(4) For $p(x) = x^4 + x + 1$, $t = 15$. Only $0 = n$ mod 15 is singular.

(5) For $p(x) = x^4 + x^2 + 1 = (x^2 + x + 1)^2$, $t = 6$. The 0 and 3 residue classes mod 6 are singular.

(6) For $p(x) = x^5 + x^4 + 1 = (1 + x + x^2)(1 + x + x^3)$, $t = 21$. The singular residue classes mod 21: 0, 3, 6, 7, 9, 12, 14, 15, 18; (not the ones relative prime to 21).

(7) For $p(x) = x^6 + x + 1$, $t = 63$. Only $0 = n$ mod 63 is singular.

### 5.2. Consecutive non-zero diagonals

The above techniques work for any number of nonzero matrix diagonals:

For $p(x) = x^6 + x^5 + x^4 + x^3 + x^2 + x + 1 = (1 + x + x^3)(1 + x^2 + x^3)$, $t = 7$. Only $0 = n$ mod 7 is singular.

The sum of $k$ (odd) consecutive powers like the above case can be fully characterized. The degree of the polynomial is $k - 1$, thus multiplying the sum with $(x + 1)$ gives $x^k + 1$, and we have $t = k$ for the characteristic exponent. Hence, $k$ is a singular dimension. In general, there can be other singular cases, like

$GCD(x^3 + 1, x^8 + x^7 + x^6 + x^5 + x^4 + x^3 + x^2 + x + 1) = x^2 + x + 1 \bmod 2$

$GCD(x^6 + 1, x^8 + x^7 + x^6 + x^5 + x^4 + x^3 + x^2 + x + 1) = x^2 + x + 1 \bmod 2$.

Having multiplied $p(x)$ with $(x + 1)$ the condition of invertibility is $GCD(x^n + 1, x^k + 1) = x + 1$, because $x + 1 \mid x^n + 1$.

**Lemma 5.1**: If $d = GCD(n, k)$ then $GCD(x^n + 1, x^k + 1) = x^d + 1$.

**Proof:** We assume $k < n$ and put $n = q\,k + r$. Since $x^n + 1 = (x^k)^q \cdot x^r + 1 = [(x^k)^q - 1] \cdot x^r + x^r + 1$, and the term in the brackets is divisible by $x^k + 1 \bmod 2$, we have $GCD(x^n + 1, x^k + 1) = GCD(x^k + 1, x^r + 1)$. This is the $(n, k) \to (k, r)$ reduction the Euclidean algorithm performs in computing $GCD(n, k)$, and the algorithm ends at $d$ and $x^d + 1$, respectively. □

**Theorem 5.2**: Let $k$ be odd and $p(x) = 1 + x +...+ x^{k-1}$.
(i) $p(x)$ is regular mod $x^n + 1$ *iff* $GCD(n, k) = 1$. Or, equivalently, the system $\{0, 1..., k - 1; n\}$ is regular *iff* $GCD(n, k) = 1$.
(ii) If $p(x)$ is irreducible then the characteristic exponent $k$ is a prime number and the system is completely regular.

**Proof**: (i) If $p(x)$ is regular mod $x^n + 1$ then $GCD(p(x), x^n + 1) = 1$, therefore $GCD((1 + x) \cdot p(x), x^n + 1) = GCD(x^k + 1, x^n + 1) = 1 + x$. By Lemma 5.1 we have $GCD(n,k) = 1$.

As for (ii), suppose $k = ab$, where $a > 1$, $b > 1$. Now $p(x) \mid x^{ab} + 1 = (x^a)^b + 1 = (x^a + 1)((x^a)^{b-1} +...+ 1)$ and $p(x)$ must be a divisor of one of the factors on the right hand side. This cannot hold, since for the degrees: $a < k - 1$, and $k - a < k - 1$. □

This Theorem settles the procedure left open in the Note following Theorem 4.6.

Note that the statement in (ii) cannot be reversed as we have seen the counterexample above:

$p(x) = x^6 + x^5 + x^4 + x^3 + x^2 + x + 1 = (1 + x + x^3)\ (1 + x^2 + x^3)$,
$t = k = 7$, prime number.

### 5.3. Further notes

(1) If $p(x) = q^k(x)$, and $q(x)$ is an irreducible binary polynomial, the singular residue classes are 0 mod $t_q$, or 0, $k$, $2k...$ mod $t_p$ (we have $t_p = k \cdot t_q$).

(2) For the computations we needed a polynomial irreducibility test. There have been several such tests published. One of them is the Ben-Or test: a polynomial $p(x)$ of degree $d$ is reducible if $GCD(x^{2^k} + x) \bmod p(x)$; $p(x)) \neq 1$ for any $k < d/2$ (see [19]).

(3) There are a huge number of irreducible binary polynomials available (see [19]). For example:

$d = 32$: 134,215,680; $d = 40$: 27,487,764,474

This number is roughly doubling when $d$ is incremented by 1. More precisely, for large degrees $d$ the

probability that a randomly chosen polynomial is irreducible is about $1/d$. These show that for machine word size $n \geq 32$, one has a very large choice of sets of diagonals to get an invertible binary circulant matrix.

(4) Irreducible binary *trinomials* of the form $1 + x^k + x^d$ can be listed with a computer algebra system:

$k = 1$: The primitive trinomials of the form $1 + x + x^d$ for $d \leq 400$ are those with $d = 2, 3, 4, 6, 7, 15, 22, 60, 63, 127, 153$

$k = 2$: $1 + x^2 + x^d$, $(d > 2)$ is irreducible for the following:

$d = 3, 5, 11, 21, 29, 35, 93, 123, 333, 845, 4125$

$k = 3$: $1 + x^3 + x^d$, $(d > 3)$ is irreducible for the following:

$d = 4, 5, 6, 7, 10, 12, 17, 18, 20, 25, 28, 31, 41, 52, 66, 130, 151, 180, 196, 503, 650, 761, 986$

$k = 4$: $1 + x^4 + x^d$, $(d > 4)$ is irreducible for the following:

$d = 7, 9, 15, 39, 57, 81, 105$

$k = 5$: $1 + x^5 + x^d$, $(d > 5)$ is irreducible for the following:

$d = 6, 9, 12, 14, 17, 20, 23, 44, 47, 63, 84, 129, 236, 278, 279, 297, 300, 647, 726, 737$

(5) Let $q(x)$ be an irreducible polynomial of degree $d > 1$ over a prime field $F_p$. The order of $q$ is the smallest positive integer $n$ such that $q(x)$ divides $x^n - 1$. It is also the multiplicative order of any root of $q$, and a divisor of $p^d - 1$. $q$ is called a <u>primitive polynomial</u> if $n = p^d - 1$.

The smallest degree non-primitive binary irreducible polynomial is $x^4 + x^3 + x^2 + x + 1$. Its order is 5.

There is no degree 5 non-primitive binary irreducible polynomial, because $2^5 - 1 = 31$, a prime.

There are three degree six non-primitive binary irreducible polynomials:

$Ord(x^6 + x^3 + 1) = 9$
$Ord(x^6 + x^4 + x^2 + x + 1) = 21$
$Ord(x^6 + x^5 + x^4 + x^2 + 1) = 21$

There is no degree 7 non-primitive binary irreducible polynomial, because $2^7 - 1 = 127$, a prime.

There are 14 degree 8 non-primitive binary irreducible polynomials.

## 6. Conclusion

We proposed new pseudorandom number generator modes of iterative algorithms built from non-multiplicative computer operations: the offset counter mode and offset hybrid counter mode. They are somewhat better than simple counter- or hybrid counter-mode generators described in [1]. Long cycle lengths of these and some other generators can be assured when the generator function is invertible. We showed that two-term rotate-add functions are never invertible, but many classes of rotate-XOR functions are. In particular, when the length of the computer word is a power of 2 (8, 16, 32, 64...), any rotate-XOR function of an odd number of terms is invertible. For other word lengths, we presented simple algorithms that decides the invertibility of any given set of rotate-XOR terms, and listed the full answers for many classes of fixed terms. These pieces of information could help a system designer.

**Author details**
[1]CPU Technology, Pleasanton, CA 94588, USA [2]Purdue University, Fort Wayne, IN, USA

**Competing interests**
The authors declare that they have no competing interests.

**References**
1. Hars L, Petruska G: **Pseudorandom recursions-small and fast pseudorandom number generators for embedded applications.** *EURASIP J Embed Syst* 2007, Article ID 98417, 13 (2007). doi:10.1155/2007/98417.
2. Anashin V: **Uniformly distributed sequences of p-adic integers.** *Math Notes* 1994, **55**:109-133.
3. Anashin V: **Uniformly distributed sequences of p-adic integers, II.** *Discrete Math Appl* 2002, **12**:527-590.
4. Anashin V: **Pseudorandom number generation by p-adic ergodic transformations.** *arXiv: Cryptography and Security* 2004 [http://arxiv.org/abs/cs/0401030/].
5. Anashin V: **Wreath products in stream cipher design.** *arXiv: Cryptography and Security* 2006 [http://arxiv.org/abs/cs/0602012/].
6. Anashin V, Khrennikov A: In *Applied Algebraic Dynamics. De Gruyter Expositions in Mathematics. Volume 49.* Walter de Gruyter, Berlin; 2009.
7. Klimov A, Shamir A: **A new class of invertible mappings.** *Workshop on Cryptographic Hardware and Embedded Systems 2002* 2003, **2523**:470-483, Lecture Notes in Computer Science.
8. Klimov A, Shamir A: **Cryptographic applications of T-functions.** *Selected Areas in Cryptography (SAC) 2003* 2004, **3006**:248-261, Lecture Notes in Computer Science.
9. Klimov A, Shamir A: **New cryptographic primitives based on multiword T-functions.** *Fast Software Encryption 2004* 2004, **3017**:1-15, Lecture Notes in Computer Science.
10. Klimov A, Shamir A: **New applications of T-functions in block ciphers and hash functions.** *Fast Software Encryption 2005* 2005, **3557**:18-31, Lecture Notes in Computer Science.
11. Klimov A: **Applications of T-functions in cryptography.** *Thesis for the degree of Ph.D., Weizmann Institute of Science* 2005.
12. Marsaglia G: **A current view of random number generators.** *Computer Science and Statistics: The Interface* Elsevier Science; 1985, 3-10.
13. Maurer U: **A universal statistical test for random bit generators.** *J Cryptogr* 1992, **5(2)**:89-105.
14. NIST Special Publication 800-22: **A statistical test suite for random and pseudorandom number generators for cryptographic applications.** 2008 [http://csrc.nist.gov/groups/ST/toolkit/rng/documents/SP800-22b.pdf].
15. Ritter T: **Randomness tests: a literature survey.** 1996 [http://www.ciphersbyritter.com/RES/RANDTEST.HTM].
16. Menezes A, van Oorschot P, Vanstone S: *Handbook of Applied Cryptography* CRC Press; 1996.
17. Morris B, Rogaway P, Stegers T: **How to encipher messages on a small domain.** *Advances in Cryptology. CRYPTO* 2009 [http://www.cs.ucdavis.edu/~rogaway/papers/thorp.pdf].
18. Koblitz N: **A Course in Number Theory and Cryptography.,** 238, Proposition II.1.8 (Springer, Graduate Text in Mathematics 114, 1994), ISBN-13: 978-0387942933.
19. Arndt J: **Matters Computational: Ideas, Algorithms, Source Code.,** (Springer, 2010), ISBN: 3642147631.

# 2

# Real time simultaneous localization and mapping: towards low-cost multiprocessor embedded systems

Bastien Vincke[1*], Abdelhafid Elouardi[1] and Alain Lambert[2]

**Abstract**

Simultaneous localization and mapping (SLAM) is widely used by autonomous robots operating in unknown environments. Research community has developed numerous SLAM algorithms in the last 10 years. Several works have presented many algorithms' optimizations. However, they have not explored a system optimization from the system hardware architecture to the algorithmic development level. New computing technologies (SIMD coprocessors, DSP, multi-cores) can greatly accelerate the system processing but require rethinking the algorithm implementation. This article presents an efficient implementation of the EKF-SLAM algorithm on a multi-processor architecture. The algorithm-architecture adequacy aims to optimize the implementation of the SLAM algorithm on a low-cost and heterogeneous architecture (implementing an ARM processor with SIMD coprocessor and a DSP core). Experiments were conducted with an instrumented platform. Results aim to demonstrate that an optimized implementation of the algorithm, resulting from an optimization methodology, can help to design embedded systems implementing low-cost multiprocessor architecture operating under real-time constraints.

## Introduction

Autonomous robots must be able to localize themselves. Simultaneous localization and mapping (SLAM) algorithms aim to build an environment map while estimating the robot pose. Many researches were conducted to develop SLAM algorithms like extended Kalman filter for SLAM (EKF-SLAM) [1,2], FAST SLAM [3], GRAPH SLAM [4], DP-SLAM [5] which aim to improve consistency, accuracy or robustness. Other algorithms derivate from the EKF-SLAM, such as algorithms using unscented Kalman filter (UKF) [6] which increases the localization accuracy against the classical EKF algorithm based on a linearized model. Only few works deal with the implementation of low-cost SLAM embedded systems.

Most of SLAM implementations rely on the use of accurate and dense measurements provided by expensive sensors like laser rangefinder sensors [7] or time of flight cameras [8]. High-priced smart sensors are not suitable to be integrated in most of embedded systems in commercial objectives or industrial applications.

Simultaneous localization and mapping systems using low-cost sensors have been recently designed. Abrate et al. [9] provide an implementation of the EKF-SLAM algorithm on a Khepera robot. The robot hosts limited range, sparse and noisy IR sensors. Experimental results have shown the importance of the sensor characteristics, the primitives (lines) extraction and data association. Yap and Shelton [10] use cheap, noisy and sparse sonar sensors embedded in a P3-DX robot. To cope with these low-cost sensors, the implemented SLAM algorithm uses a multi-scan approach and an orthogonality assumption to map indoor environments.

Classical SLAM algorithms are too computationally intensive to run on an embedded computing unit. They require at least laptop-level performances. Gifford et al. [11] present a low-cost approach to autonomous multi-robot mapping and exploration for unstructured environments. The robot hosts a Gumstix computing unit (600 Mhz), 6 IR scanning range arrays, a 3-axis gyroscope and odometers. Running DP-SLAM alone on the Gumstix with 15 particles takes on average 3 s per update. While

---

*Correspondence: bastien.vincke@u-psud.fr
[1] Univ Paris-Sud, CNRS, Institut d'Electronique Fondamentale, F-91405 Orsay, France
Full list of author information is available at the end of the article

using 25 particles, it takes more than 10 s per update. Authors have underlined the difficulty to find the right SLAM parameters to fit within the available computing power and the real-time processing. Magnenat et al. [12] present a system based on the co-design of a low-cost sensor (a slim rotating scanner), a SLAM algorithm, a computing unit, and an optimization methodology. The computing unit is based on an ARM processor (533 Mhz) running a FASTSLAM 2.0 algorithm [13]. Magnenat et al. [12] use an evolution strategy to find the best configuration of the algorithm and setting of the parameters.

As pointed out by [11,12], the first improvement of a SLAM algorithm is an efficient setting of the various parameters of the algorithm. Other modifications were investigated to reach real-time constraints. These modifications are necessary due to the low computing power and limited memory resources available on embedded systems. Features restriction for EKF-SLAM algorithm has been implemented to decrease the processing time [14]. Schroter et al. [15] focused on reducing the memory footprint of particle-based gridmap SLAM by sharing the map between several particles.

Robust laser-based SLAM navigation has long existed in robot applications, but systems implement sensors that, in some cases, are more expensive than the final product. Neato Robotics has developed a vacuum cleaner that implements a navigation system using a SLAM algorithm. The approach is based on a low-cost system implementing a designed laser rangefinder [16].

This article presents an efficient implementation of the EKF-SLAM algorithm on a multi-processor architecture. The approach is based on an algorithm implementation adequate to a defined architecture. The aim is to optimize the implementation of the SLAM algorithm on a low-cost and heterogeneous architecture implementing an SIMD coprocessor (NEON) and a DSP core. The hardware includes several low-cost sensors. As [17], we chose to use a low-cost camera (exteroceptive sensor) and odometers (proprioceptive sensors). Following [12], we efficiently tune the parameters of the SLAM algorithm. We improve on previous works by proposing an adequate implementation of the EKF-SLAM algorithm on a multiprocessing architecture (ARM processor, SIMD NEON coprocessor, DSP core). The specifications related to the NEON coprocessor and the DSP core improve the processing time and the system performance. Results aim to demonstrate that an optimized implementation of the algorithm, resulting from an evaluation methodology, can help to design embedded systems implementing low-cost multiprocessor architecture operating under real-time constraints.

Section "EKF-SLAM algorithm" introduces the EKF-SLAM algorithm. Section "Multiprocessor architecture and system configuration" presents the embedded multiprocessor architecture and the system configuration.

Section "Evaluation methodology and algorithm implementation" details the evaluation methodology, provides a first algorithm implementation and analyzes this implementation in terms of processing time. A Hardware–software optimization is proposed and analyzed in Section "Hardware–software optimization and improvements". It presents SIMD optimizations and DSP parallelization. A performance comparison is then performed between the optimized and non-optimized instances. Finally, Section "Conclusion" concludes this article.

## EKF-SLAM algorithm

### Overview

Extended Kalman filter for SLAM estimates a state vector containing both the robot pose and the landmark locations. We consider that the robot is moving on a plane. The algorithm uses 3D points as landmarks. It uses proprioceptive sensors to compute a predicted vector and then corrects this state using exteroceptive sensors. In this article, we consider a wheeled robot embedding two odometers (attached to each rear wheel) and a camera.

### State vector and covariance matrix

With $N$ landmarks, the state vector is defined as:

$$\mathbf{x} = (x, z, \theta, x_{a_1}, y_{a_1}, z_{a_1}, \ldots, x_{a_N}, y_{a_N}, z_{a_N})^T \quad (1)$$

where:

- $x, z$ are the ground coordinates ($x$-axis, $z$-axis) of the robot rear axle center. We suppose that the robot is always moving on the ground, so $y = 0$ (no elevation) and $y$ does not appear in Equation (1).
- $\theta$ is the orientation of a local frame attached to the robot with respect to the global frame.
- $x_{a_1}, y_{a_1}, z_{a_1}, \ldots, x_{a_N}, y_{a_N}, z_{a_N}$ are the 3D coordinates of the $N$ landmarks in the global frame.

The state covariance matrix is defined as:

$$\mathbf{P} = \begin{bmatrix} P_{xx} & P_{xz} & P_{x\theta} & P_{xx_{a_1}} & \cdots & P_{xz_{a_N}} \\ P_{zx} & P_{zz} & P_{z\theta} & P_{zx_{a_1}} & \cdots & P_{zz_{a_N}} \\ P_{\theta x} & P_{\theta z} & P_{\theta\theta} & P_{\theta x_{a_1}} & \cdots & P_{\theta z_{a_N}} \\ P_{x_{a_1}x} & P_{x_{a_1}z} & P_{x_{a_1}\theta} & P_{x_{a_1}x_{a_1}} & \cdots & P_{x_{a_1}z_{a_N}} \\ \cdots & \cdots & \cdots & \cdots & \cdots & \cdots \\ P_{z_{a_N}x} & P_{z_{a_N}z} & P_{z_{a_N}\theta} & P_{z_{a_N}x_{a_1}} & \cdots & P_{z_{a_N}z_{a_N}} \end{bmatrix} \quad (2)$$

### Prediction

The prediction step relies on the measurements of the proprioceptive sensors, the odometers, embedded on our experimental platform. A non linear discrete-time state-space model is considered to describe the evolution of the robot configuration $\mathbf{x}$:

$$\mathbf{x}_{k|k-1} = \mathbf{f}(\mathbf{x}_{k-1|k-1}, \mathbf{u}_k) + \mathbf{v}_k \quad (3)$$

where $\mathbf{u}_k$ is a known two-dimensional control vector, assumed constant between the times indexed by $k-1$ and $k$, and $\mathbf{v}_k$ is an unknown state perturbation vector that accounts for the model uncertainties. $\mathbf{x}_{k-1|k-1}$ represents the state vector at time k-1, $\mathbf{x}_{k|k-1}$ represented the state vector after the prediction step, $\mathbf{x}_{k|k}$ represents the state vector after the estimation step. The classical evolution model, described in [18], is considered:

$$\mathbf{f}(\mathbf{x}_{k-1|k-1},\delta s,\delta\theta) = \begin{pmatrix} x_{k-1} + \delta s \cos\left(\theta_{k-1} + \frac{\delta\theta}{2}\right) \\ z_{k-1} + \delta s \sin\left(\theta_{k-1} + \frac{\delta\theta}{2}\right) \\ \theta_{k-1} + \delta\theta \\ x_{a_1,k-1} \\ y_{a_1,k-1} \\ z_{a_1,k-1} \\ .. \\ .. \\ x_{a_N,k-1} \\ y_{a_N,k-1} \\ z_{a_N,k-1} \end{pmatrix} \tag{4}$$

where $\mathbf{u}_k = (\delta s,\delta\theta)$; $\delta s$ is the longitudinal motion and $\delta\theta$ is the rotational motion [19]:

$$\begin{pmatrix} \delta s \\ \delta\theta \end{pmatrix} = \mathbf{g}(\varphi_l,\varphi_r) = \begin{pmatrix} \frac{w_r\delta\varphi_r + w_l\delta\varphi_l}{2} \\ \frac{w_r\delta\varphi_r - w_l\delta\varphi_l}{e} \end{pmatrix} \tag{5}$$

where:

- $w_r$ and $w_l$ are respectively the radius of the right and left wheel.
- $e$ is the length of the rear axle.
- $\delta\varphi_i = \delta p_i \frac{2\pi}{\rho}$ with $i \in \{r,l\}$ ($r$=right, $l$=left), $\delta p_i$: number of steps, $\rho$: odometer resolution. $\delta\varphi_i$ is the angular movement of the right/left wheel.

The state covariance matrix is defined as:

$$\mathbf{P}_{k|k-1} = \frac{\partial\mathbf{f}}{\partial\mathbf{x}}\mathbf{P}_{k-1|k-1}\frac{\partial\mathbf{f}}{\partial\mathbf{x}}^T + \mathbf{Q}_k \tag{6}$$

where

- $\frac{\partial\mathbf{f}}{\partial\mathbf{x}} = \begin{bmatrix} 1 & 0 & -\delta s \sin\left(\theta_{k-1|k-1} + \frac{\delta\theta}{2}\right) & 0 & .. & 0 \\ 0 & 1 & \delta s \cos\left(\theta_{k-1|k-1} + \frac{\delta\theta}{2}\right) & 0 & .. & 0 \\ 0 & 0 & 1 & & 0 & .. & 0 \\ 0 & 0 & 0 & & 1 & .. & 0 \\ .. & .. & & & & .. & .. \\ 0 & 0 & 0 & & 0 & .. & 1 \end{bmatrix}$

- $\mathbf{Q}_k$ is the covariance matrix of the process noise.

### Estimation

The estimation of the state is made using the camera which returns the position in the image $(u_i, v_i)$ of the $i$-th landmark.

*The innovation and its covariance matrix:* The pinhole model is used to project a known landmark position into the image:

$$\begin{aligned} \begin{pmatrix} u_i \\ v_i \\ 1 \end{pmatrix} &= \text{pinhole}(x_{a_i}^{\text{cam}}, y_{a_i}^{\text{cam}}, z_{a_i}^{\text{cam}}) \\ &= \begin{bmatrix} fk_u & s_{uv} & c_u \\ 0 & fk_v & c_v \\ 0 & 0 & 1 \end{bmatrix} \begin{pmatrix} \frac{x_{a_i}^{\text{cam}}}{z_{a_i}^{\text{cam}}} \\ \frac{y_{a_i}^{\text{cam}}}{z_{a_i}^{\text{cam}}} \\ 1 \end{pmatrix} \end{aligned} \tag{7}$$

where:

- $(u_i, v_i)$ is the position of the $i$-th landmark in the image.
- $(x_{a_i}^{\text{cam}}, y_{a_i}^{\text{cam}}, z_{a_i}^{\text{cam}})$ is the position of the $i$-th landmark in the camera frame.
- $f$ is the focal length.
- $(k_u, k_v)$ is the number of pixels per unit length.
- $s_{uv}$ is a factor accounting for the skew due to non-rectangular pixels. In our case, we take $s_{uv}$=0.

Equation (7) can be written as the predicted observation equation for a single landmark:

$$\mathbf{h}^i(\mathbf{x}_{k|k-1}) = \begin{pmatrix} u_i \\ v_i \end{pmatrix} = \begin{pmatrix} c_u + fk_u \frac{x_{a_i}^{\text{cam}}}{z_{a_i}^{\text{cam}}} \\ c_v + fk_v \frac{y_{a_i}^{\text{cam}}}{z_{a_i}^{\text{cam}}} \end{pmatrix} \tag{8}$$

The pose of a landmark in the camera frame is defined from its pose $(x_{a_i}, y_{a_i}, z_{a_i})$ in the global frame:

$$\begin{pmatrix} x_{a_i}^{\text{cam}} \\ y_{a_i}^{\text{cam}} \\ z_{a_i}^{\text{cam}} \end{pmatrix} = \left( \begin{bmatrix} \cos\theta & 0 & \sin\theta \\ 0 & 1 & 0 \\ -\sin\theta & 0 & \cos\theta \end{bmatrix} \begin{pmatrix} x_{a_i} - x \\ y_{a_i} \\ z_{a_i} - z \end{pmatrix} \right) - \begin{pmatrix} 0 \\ 0 \\ D \end{pmatrix} \tag{9}$$

Where $D$ is the length between the camera and the robot rear axle center.

During the observation step, the algorithm matches $M$ landmarks ($M <= N$) whose observations are added in

$$\mathbf{h}_k = \begin{pmatrix} \mathbf{h}^0 \\ .. \\ \mathbf{h}^{M-1} \end{pmatrix}.$$

Thus, the innovation is:

$$\mathbf{Y}_k = \hat{\mathbf{z}}_k - \mathbf{h}_k(\mathbf{x}_{k|k-1}) \tag{10}$$

where $\hat{\mathbf{z}}_k$ is the measurement for all the $M$ predicted observations.

The innovation covariance $\mathbf{S}_k$ is:

$$\mathbf{S}_k = \mathbf{H}_k\mathbf{P}_{k|k-1}\mathbf{H}_k^T + \mathbf{R}_k \tag{11}$$

where $\mathbf{H}_k$ is the Jacobian of $\mathbf{h}_k$ and $\mathbf{R}_k$ is the observation noise covariance.

*State estimation:* The state is updated using the classical EKF equations:

$$\begin{aligned}
\mathbf{K}_k &= \mathbf{P}_{k|k-1}\mathbf{H}_k\mathbf{S}_k^{-1} \\
\mathbf{x}_{k|k} &= \mathbf{x}_{k|k-1} + \mathbf{K}_k\mathbf{Y}_k \\
\mathbf{P}_{k|k} &= (\mathbf{I} - \mathbf{K}_k\mathbf{H}_k)\mathbf{P}_{k|k-1}
\end{aligned} \tag{12}$$

## Visual landmarks

The landmarks used in the observation equation are extracted from images. Landmark initialization defines the initial coordinates and the initial covariance of landmarks localization (also called interest points or features). In [20], we have evaluated the processing time of corner detectors like Harris, Shi-Tomasi or FAST. Harris and Shi-Tomasi detectors were more time consuming than the FAST detector and do not provide significantly better localization results than FAST. Consequently, there is no need to implement more sophisticated algorithms such as Harris or Shi and Tomasi. FAST [21] (Features from Accelerated Segment Test) corner detector relies on a simple test performed for a pixel p by examining a circle of 16 pixels (a Bresenham circle of radius 3) centered on p. A feature is detected at p if the intensities of at least 12 contiguous pixels are all above or all below the intensity of p with a threshold t. Even if this detector is not highly robust to noises and depends on a threshold it produces stable landmarks and is computationally very efficient [21].

The FAST detector [21] is related to the wedge-model style of detector evaluated using a circle surrounding a candidate pixel. To optimize the detector processing-time, this model is used to made a decision classifier which is applied to the image (Figure 1).

## Matching based on zero-mean sum of squared differences

The EKF-SLAM matches the previously detected feature with a new one using zero-mean sum of squared differences (ZMSSD).

The covariance of the projected feature localization defines a searching area $\tau$. This area includes the robot localization uncertainty and the landmarks localization uncertainty. We use the ZMSSD to find the best candidate

point inside $\tau$. For each candidate point $p : (p_x, p_y)$, the $N_p$ value of the weighted ZMSSD is:

$$N_p = w(p_x, p_y) \times \text{ZMSSD} \tag{13}$$

and

$$\text{ZMSSD} = \sum_{i,j}\left( (d(i,j) - m_d) \right.$$
$$\left. - \left(\text{im}\left(p_x + i - \frac{\text{des}}{2}, p_y + j - \frac{\text{des}}{2}\right) - m_i\right)\right)^2 \tag{14}$$

where:

- $w(p_x, p_y)$ is the Gaussian weights defined by the landmark covariance.
- $i \in [0; \text{des} - 1]$ and $j \in [0; \text{des} - 1]$ and des is the descriptor size.
- $d$ is the feature descriptor.
- $m_d$ and $m_i$ are respectively the means of the pixel values in the descriptor and in the image window.
- $im$ is the image.

The observation $p_{\text{obs}}$ will be selected using $p = (p \in \tau \mid N_p = \min(N_{p_j}), \forall p_j \in \tau)$.

The descriptor, used to identify the landmark during the matching, is classically a small image window of $9 \times 9$ pixels to $16 \times 16$ pixels around the interest point. Davison [22] claims that this sort of descriptor is able to serve as long-term landmark feature.

## Landmark initialization based on davison method

Landmark initialization consists of defining the initial coordinates and the initial covariance of landmarks (interest points). Various methods exist and can be classified as an undelayed or delayed method. Undelayed method adds landmarks with only one measurement whereas the delayed method needs two or more frames. We chose to use the widely spread delayed method proposed by [2] which is both efficient and adequate to implement.

**Figure 1** Image (320 × 240 Pixels) of the embedded camera and result of the FAST detector.

Furthermore the work of Munguia and Grau [23] shows that the delayed method have the same performance as the undelayed method.

In order to compute the 3D depth of a newly detected landmark, as [2], we initialize a 3D line into the map along which the landmark must lie. This line starts at the estimated camera position and heads to infinity along the feature viewing direction. The line is composed of 100 particles which represent depth hypothesis. The prior probability used is uniform and the range is 0.5 to 15 m. At subsequent time, each particle (a feature depth hypothesis) is projected into the image, matched and its probability is re-weighted.

When the ratio of the standard deviation of depth to the expected value is below a threshold, the distribution is approximated as a Gaussian and the landmark is initialized. The landmark pose $A_i = (x_{a_i}, y_{a_i}, z_{a_i})$ is added to $\mathbf{x}$ and the $A_i$ covariance is added into $\mathbf{P}$.

## Multiprocessor architecture and system configuration

In order to test and validate the EKF-SLAM algorithm, experiments were conducted with an instrumented mobile robot called Minitruck [24]. The platform was tele-operated during the experiments. For our first evaluation, the experiment consists to operate inside a large corridor of our research lab (see Figure 2).

We have developed a system architecture on the top of a multi-processor board (Gumstix Overo) based on the OMAP3530 chip (see Figure 3). The OMAP chip integrate a RISC processors (ARM Cortex A8 500 Mhz) with an SIMD NEON coprocessor, a DSP (TMS320C64x + 430 Mhz) and a graphical processor unit (POWERVR SGX). This board communicates with an additional processor for control and data acquisition (Atmega168 16 Mhz).

Multiple sensors (odometers and a camera) are interfaced to this architecture (Figure 2). The variety of sensors enables us to evaluate the SLAM algorithms with different types of sensor data and take advantage of the information complementary of these sensors. Our objective is to

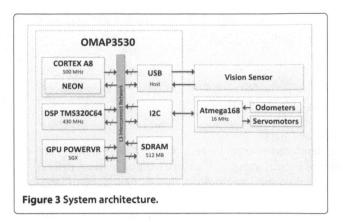

**Figure 3** System architecture.

evaluate the implementation of SLAM algorithms using land vehicles and sensors, like steering encoders and a camera.

The use of wheel and steer encoders is obvious in robotics and navigation. Simple kinematic motion models can be used to integrate velocity and heading measurements from wheel and steer encoders to provide an estimation of the mobile robot location and orientation. Estimations are regularly subject to considerable errors due to misalignment, offsets and wheels slippage. It is possible to implement basic models to approximate and correct offset and slippage errors on-line leading to significant improvement of performances. We chose two HEDS 5540 odometers for our experimental vehicle.

The feature detection in SLAM application relies on the embedded sensors. We chose to achieve this extraction using a vision sensor (a cheap USB webcam, Philips SPC530NC, delivering 30 fps). We chose to use all possible images (30 fps) because it is much easier to perform point matching if the movement is small. Conventional approaches for vision systems design are usually based on general purpose computers interfaced with cameras. The new computing technologies (SIMD, DSP, multi-cores) can greatly accelerate algorithm processing, but require rethinking these algorithms by optimizing the parallelism. This parallel processing is pushed to integrate near the sensors parallel computing units [25]. We have used a Gumstix processing module based on OMAP3530 architecture. It is an heterogeneous architecture (ARM Cortex-A8 500 Mhz processor with power consumption less than 300 mW, SIMD NEON integrated coprocessor, DSP C64x processor and a 3D graphics accelerator) that communicates via a WLAN connection (802.11 g).

The WLAN connection is used only to control speed and direction of the vehicle. In the future, a dedicated algorithm to autonomous navigation will be implemented

**Figure 2** Minitruck in action embedding a multi-sensor system.

and thus the WLAN connection will be used to achieve only the system monitoring. A coprocessor (ATMega168) takes care of data acquisition. It controls the robot speed and its direction using two pulse-width modulation (PWM) signals. It decodes signals coming from the odometers embedded in the rear wheels. It communicates with the main board using an I2C interface. This interface allows the main processor to retrieve odometers data and to send instructions corresponding to speed and direction.

To evaluate the designed system, an experiment was achieved in a corridor of our lab. Frames have been grabbed at 30 fps with 320×240 resolution. Odometer data were sampled at 30 Hz. During the experiment, references are periodically drawn on the ground by an embedded marker.

## Evaluation methodology and algorithm implementation

Our evaluation methodology is based on the identification of the processing tasks requiring a significant computing time. It is based on several steps: we analyze first the execution time of tasks and their dependencies on the algorithm's parameters. A threshold is fixed for each parameter. The algorithm is then partitioned in order to have functional blocks (FBs) performing defined calculations. Each block is then evaluated to determine its processing time. Function blocks that require the most important execution time are then optimized to reduce the global processing time.

Algorithm 1 summarizes the main tasks of EKF-SLAM. The algorithm is composed of two process: Prediction and Correction. The correction process implements three tasks: matching, estimation and initialization.

### Algorithm 1 EKF-SLAM

1: $\chi \leftarrow \emptyset$ ▷List of Landmarks for initialization
2: Robot pose initialization
3: **while** localization is required **do**
4:   DATA $\leftarrow$ Sensors Data acquisition
5:   **if** DATA $= (\varphi_l, \varphi_r)$ **then** ▷Odometer's data
6:     PREDICTION
7:     $(\delta s, \delta \theta) \leftarrow \mathbf{g}(\varphi_l, \varphi_r)$ (see Eq (5))
8:     $\mathbf{x}_{k|k-1} \leftarrow \mathbf{f}(\mathbf{x}_{k-1|k-1}, \delta s, \delta \theta)$ (see Eq (4))
9:     $\mathbf{P}_{k|k-1} \leftarrow \frac{\partial \mathbf{f}}{\partial \mathbf{x}} \mathbf{P}_{k-1|k-1} \frac{\partial \mathbf{f}}{\partial \mathbf{x}}^T + \mathbf{Q}_k$ (see Eq (6))
10:   **else if** DATA = Camera **then**
11:     FAST detector applied on the image
12:     MATCHING:
13:     **for Each** Landmark $\mathbf{N_i} \in \mathbf{x}_{k|k-1}$ **do**
14:       $u_i, v_i, \tau_i \leftarrow$ pinhole$(\mathbf{x}_{k|k-1}, \mathbf{N_i})$ (see Eq (8))
15:       **if** $(u_i, v_i) \in$ Camera Frame **then**
16:         $\hat{\mathbf{z}}_k \leftarrow$ ZMSSD$(\tau_i, \mathbf{N_i})$ (see Eq (13))
17:         $\mathbf{h}_k \leftarrow (u_i, v_i)$
18:         $\mathbf{Y}_k \leftarrow \hat{\mathbf{z}}_k - \mathbf{h}_k$
19:         $\mathbf{H}_k \leftarrow \frac{\partial \mathbf{h}_k}{\partial \mathbf{x}}\big|_{\mathbf{x}_{k|k-1}}$
20:       **end if**
21:     **end for**
22:     ESTIMATION:
23:     $\mathbf{S}_k \leftarrow \mathbf{H}_k \mathbf{P}_{k|k-1} \mathbf{H}_k^T + \mathbf{R}_k$ (see Eq (11))
24:     $\mathbf{K}_k \leftarrow \mathbf{P}_{k|k-1} \mathbf{H}_k \mathbf{S}_k^{-1}$ (see Eq (11))
25:     $\mathbf{x}_{k|k} \leftarrow \mathbf{x}_{k|k-1} + \mathbf{K}_k \mathbf{Y}_k$ (see Eq (12))
26:     $\mathbf{P}_{k|k} \leftarrow (\mathbf{I} - \mathbf{K}_k \mathbf{H}_k) \mathbf{P}_{k|k-1}$ (see Eq (12))
27:     INITIALIZATION:
28:     **for Each** $\mathbf{L} \in \chi$ **do** ▷**L**: Aspiring new Landmark
29:       $\mathbf{L}_{\text{obs}} \leftarrow ZMSSD(\mathbf{L})$ (see Eq (13))
30:       Update the particles weight according $\mathbf{L}_{\text{obs}}$ (see [2])
31:       Compute $\sigma_{\text{depth}}$, *depth*
32:       **if** $\frac{\sigma_{\text{depth}}}{\text{depth}} < \epsilon$ **then**
33:         Compute $\mathbf{L}, \mathbf{P_L}$
34:         append$(\mathbf{x_{k|k-1}}, \mathbf{L})$; append$(\mathbf{P_{k|k-1}}, \mathbf{P_L})$
35:         remove$(\chi, \mathbf{L})$
36:       **end if**
37:     **end for**
38:     **if** Lack of Landmark **then** ▷see [8]
39:       append$(\chi, \text{New\_Landmarks})$
40:     **end if**
41:   **end if**
42: **end while**

### Prediction process

This phase updates the mobile robot position $(\mathbf{x}_{k|k-1})$ according to its proprioceptive data acquired from odometers $(\varphi_l, \varphi_r)$. The processing time of the prediction process is constant. It just updates the 3D vector containing the robot pose and its 3×3 covariance matrix. During the prediction step, the landmarks localization and uncertainties do not change: landmarks are defined in the global frame.

### Correction process

The processing time of the correction process is not constant. The following of this section studies the processing time of each task of the process and their dependencies.

**Matching task** Each landmark in the state vector must be projected in the camera frame using the pinhole model (see L. 2). The computing time of these projections depends only on the number of landmarks in the state vector (L. 2). For each projected landmark on the focal plane, ZMSSD matches an observation. Both the size of the descriptor and the size of the searching area $\tau$ will affect the computing time (see Equation (13)).

The processing time of the matching task depends on several parameters:

- The number of landmarks in the state vector.
- The number of visible landmarks on the focal plane.
- The size of the descriptor.
- Both the localization uncertainty of the mobile robot and the landmarks.

In practice, all the previously defined parameters should be set in order to bound the computing time. The first three parameters can be set by the users. The uncertainty depends on the followed path and cannot be bounded.

**Estimation task** The estimation task uses the classical Kalman equations to update both the robot and landmarks uncertainties. The processing time of the estimation task is time-consuming and depends on:

- The number of landmarks in the state vector.
- The number of landmarks observed.

The size of the matrix and thus the computing cost of the matrix multiplication in the Equations (11) and (12) depend on the number of landmarks in the state vector. Moreover, Equation (11) depends on the number of landmarks observed. As for the matching process, these parameters (size of the state vector and number of observations) should be bounded in order to achieve this estimation task in a constant computing time.

**Initialization task** For each landmark under initialization, each particle (a feature depth hypothesis) is projected into the image, matched and its probability is re-weighted. If there is a lack of landmarks under initialization, we add aspiring new landmarks. The processing time of the initialization task depends on:

- The number of landmarks being initialized.
- The size of the descriptor.
- Both the localization uncertainty of the mobile robot and the landmark.

The number of landmarks being initialized and the size of the descriptors can be bounded. For each landmark being initialized, we have to update the probability of each localization hypothesis using a matching process. As for the matching task, the computing time depends on the localization uncertainty of the mobile robot and the landmarks.

**Thresholds definition**
Previous section shows that the computation time of each task of the EKF-SLAM algorithm depends on many variables. For real-time implementation, it is important to get a constant, or at least a bounded computation time. To solve this constraint we have to:

- set the maximum number of landmarks in the state vector. The size of the state vector will be fixed. Therefore, no dynamic memory allocation will be needed.
- set the maximum number of landmarks observed. This keeps the computation time of the estimation task constant using a fixed size matrix multiplication.
- set the maximum number of landmarks being initialized in order to bound the computation time of the initialization task. Unfortunately, it will not be sufficient to keep the computation time of the initialization task constant due to its internal matching step.
- bound the computing time induced by the uncertainties. The only solution to get a bounded global-processing-time is to set a maximum execution time for the matching task. Due to the constant processing time of the prediction and the estimation task, the execution time of both the matching and initialization task can be bounded ($33$ ms - ($t_{prediction}$ + $t_{estimation}$)). We chose to use all possible images ($30$ fps). We set a maximum execution time for the matching task. The algorithm proceeds in a way to match a maximum of landmarks in a bounded time. The initialization task has a dynamic execution time depending on the real processing time of the matching task and the number of landmarks being initialized. The lower bound of this dynamic execution allows at least a minimum number of landmarks to be initialized.

**Map management**
To keep the size of the state vector constant, we need to delete some landmarks when inserting new ones. The new state vector includes new landmarks (whose initialization has just been performed) and previously used landmarks. Auat Cheein and Carelli [26] proposes an efficient method to select landmarks for the estimation task. It is based on the evaluation of the influence of a given feature on the convergence of the state covariance matrix. The method matches all possible landmarks and computes $(\mathbf{I} - \mathbf{K}_k\mathbf{H}_k)$ from Equation (12). Unfortunately, we cannot implement it exactly as proposed by [26] due to the high computing time. We chose to add the landmarks, based on the previous estimation step, by selecting the previous landmarks which have the best previous influence on the convergence of the state covariance matrix. At time $k$, we select the landmark which had the smallest $(\mathbf{I} - \mathbf{K}_{k-1}\mathbf{H}_{k-1})$.

**Table 1 Functional block partitioning**

| | Functional block (FB) | Description | Line |
|---|---|---|---|
| 1 | Prediction | The entire prediction process | 7, 8, 9 |
| 2 | FAST | The FAST corner detector application | 11 |
| 3 | Landmark projection | The projection of one landmark on the camera plane | 14 |
| 4 | ZMSSD-M | The correlation computation between one candidate point of the image and one descriptor during the Matching Task | 16 |
| 5 | $\mathbf{H}_i$ | $\mathbf{H}_i$ computation for one observation | 19 |
| 6 | Estimation | The entire estimation task | 23 to 26 |
| 7 | ZMSSD-I | The correlation computation between one candidate point of the image and one descriptor during the Initialization Task | 29 |
| 8 | Weight updating | The update of the particle weight for the initialization step | 30, 31 |
| 9 | Addition of a new landmark | The insertion of a new landmark under initialization | 39 |

## Functional block partitioning

All the previously defined tasks do not have a fixed computing time, their computing time depends on the experiment. We have defined FBs which have a fixed computing times to optimize the implementation. The computing time of the FB do not depend on the experiment. Experiments will only affect the number of iterations of some FBs(3,4,5,6,7,8 and 9). From the previous algorithm, we have defined 9 FBs and their runtimes are studied in below Table 1.

Each FB has a fixed computing time and some FB can occur more than one time (Landmark projection, ZMSSD, $\mathbf{H}_i$, Weight updating, Addition of a new landmark).

## Processing time evaluation

As an application scenario, the robot moves over a square of 6 m side. At the end of the trajectory, it joined the initial starting position. Using only odometers, the final localization has an error of 1.6 m. With the EKF-SLAM algorithm, the localization has been significantly improved. The final error is approximately 0.4 m. EKF-SLAM includes all viewed landmarks in the state vector. Indeed, the localization result depends on the number of landmarks but the size of the state vector and the number of observations must be bounded to achieve a bounded computing time. The overall accuracy of the EKF-SLAM depends on the number of the landmarks in the state

vector and the matched observations. The accuracy of the localization depends monotonically on the number of processed landmarks.

The given EKF-SLAM (Algorithm 1) is processed sequentially on the embedded ARM processor operating at 500 MHz (no coprocessor is implemented). In the following, all times given correspond to times evaluated on the embedded system using the ARM processor. The data acquisition time is constant:

- The odometer data acquisition is achieved in 0.7 ms (this processing time is due to the I2C communication with the Atmega168 processor).
- Each image acquisition takes 1.8 ms (due to USB data transfer).

The prediction step does not require significant processing time, it takes only 0.093 ms per iteration. As for the matching task, the estimation task cannot be achieved in a constant processing time. Estimation task processing time depends on the total number of landmarks and the number of matched landmarks. Figure 4 shows the processing time of the estimation task according to the number of landmarks in the state vector. The estimation task is entirely processed on the ARM processor (no use of coprocessor). Obviously it will be impossible to take into account all the landmarks detected when the algorithm is processed: the computation time will be

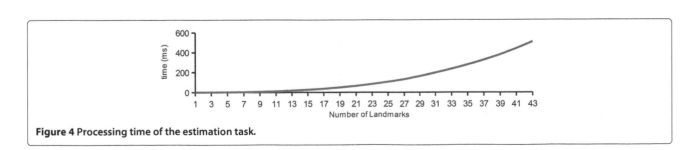

**Figure 4** Processing time of the estimation task.

higher than the 33 ms allowed. It is necessary to find a compromise between the number of landmarks and the processing time.

### Experimental results

An experiment was conducted to evaluate the processing time of the different blocks of the algorithm (including tasks with unboundable processing time). For this experiment, we set the size of the descriptor to $16 \times 16$ pixels and we set the thresholds as follows:

- Maximum number of landmarks in the state vector: 25.
- Maximum number of observed landmarks: 25.
- Maximum number of landmarks being initialized: 20.

First, we can analyze the runtime of the 8 previously defined FBs of the algorithm. We have used the integrated cycle counter register (CCNT) of the ARM processor to compute the processing time of each FB. The prediction process (FB1) occurs in 0.093 ms. Table 2 summarizes, for the other FBs, the processing time per iteration, the mean of the number of iterations and the mean of the processing time per correction process. The estimation task could not be processed in some iterations of the correction process, especially when there is no matched landmark.

The mean processing time by frame is approximately 80.8 ms which corresponds to the sum of all processing times: prediction process (FB1) and correction process (FB2 to FB9). The processing time of the estimation task (FB6) is approximately 70.5 ms and it represents about 87% of the global processing time. The FAST detector (FB2) represents 3.4 ms. The ZMSSD-M task (FB4) takes 2.63 ms per correction process. Finally, the initialization task (FB7, FB8 and FB9) takes 3.9 ms. These six FBs represent 99.6% of the global processing time. We focused on an efficient implementation of these FBs to enhance the global processing time.

### Hardware–software optimization and improvements

#### OMAP3530 architecture description

The OMAP3530 is an heterogeneous architecture designed by TI (Texas Instruments) and implements an ARM Cortex-A8 500 MHz processor, a NEON coprocessor with SIMD instructions, a DSP C64x processor and a 3D graphics accelerator.

The NEON unit is similar to the MMX and SSE extensions existing on an X86 processor. It is optimized for Single Instruction Multiple Data (SIMD) operations. The NEON unit has two floating point pipelines, an integer pipeline and a 128 bits load/store/permute pipeline. An efficient implementation on the SIMD NEON architecture improves the processing time. NEON instructions perform "Packed SIMD" processing as follows:

- Registers are considered as vectors of the same data type elements
- Data types can be: signed/unsigned 8, 16, 32, 64-bits or single precision floating point
- Instructions perform the same operation on multiple data simultaneously as shown in Figure 5. The number of simultaneous operations depends on the data type: NEON supports up to 16 operations at the same time using 8-bits data.

#### SIMD optimization results

In the Algorithm 1, the time-consuming FBs are: the estimation block (FB6), the initialization blocks (FB7, FB8 and FB9), the FAST detector block (FB2) and the ZMSSD-M block (FB4). FAST detector is already an optimized instance using machine learning [21]. Moreover, FAST has been already implemented on an FPGA based architecture [27]. We chose to optimize the other FBs. The matching task computes ZMSSD which computes the image correlation. It performs the same operation (addition, subtraction, multiplication and comparison) on

**Table 2 Processing time of the correction process FBs on the main processor (ARM)**

| Functional block (FB) | Processing time per iteration ($\mu s$) | Mean of the number of iterations per correction process | Mean of the processing time per correction process ($\mu s$) |
|---|---|---|---|
| 2. FAST | 3400 | 1 | 3400 |
| 3. Landmark projection | 9 | 19 | 180 |
| 4. ZMSSD-M | 11.29 | 233 | 2630 |
| 5. $\mathbf{H}_i$ | 14.5 | 4.5 | 66 |
| 6. Estimation | 88845 | 0.8 | 70568 |
| 7. ZMSSD-I | 11.29 | 123 | 1388 |
| 8. Weight updating | 638 | 4.0 | 2586 |
| 9. Addition of a new landmark | 103 | 0.18 | 18 |

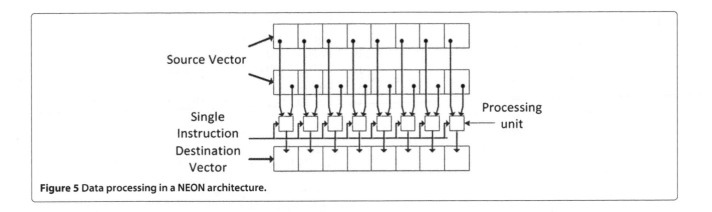

**Figure 5** Data processing in a NEON architecture.

8 bits data. The computation of the ZMSSD can be optimized using the SIMD NEON architecture. The estimation task is based on floating point matrix multiplication, it could efficiently be optimized using the SIMD NEON coprocessor (the ARM Cortex A8 does not include any floating point unit (FPU)). The initialization FBs will be studied at Section "Parallel implementation on a DSP processor".

### ZMSSD (FB4)

The EKF-SLAM matches features using ZMSSD. ZMSSD is computed for each landmark using Equation 2. We chose to use a descriptor with $16 \times 16$ 8-bits pixels size due to the efficiency of SIMD NEON architecture to deal with 128/64 bits vectors.

**Basic implementation** The basic implementation of the ZMSSD function block computes the means of the pixel values in a window $m_i$ ($m_d$ can be precalculated when the landmark is detected). Then the ZMSSD ($ZMSSD$) is computed using loops (Algorithm 2).

### Algorithm 2 Basic ZMSSD

1: $m_i \leftarrow 0$
2: $ZMSSD \leftarrow 0$
3: **for Each** $i \in [0; des - 1], j \in [0; des - 1]$ **do**
4: $\quad m_i \leftarrow m_i + im(p_x + i - \frac{des}{2}, p_y + j - \frac{des}{2})$
5: **end for**
6: $m_i \leftarrow m_i / (des \times des)$
7: **for Each** $i \in [0; des - 1], j \in [0; des - 1]$ **do**
8: $\quad ZMSSD \leftarrow ZMSSD + \sum_{i,j}((d(i,j) - m_d) - (im(p_x + i - \frac{des}{2}, p_y + j - \frac{des}{2}) - m_i))^2$
9: **end for**

This implementation takes 12.60 $\mu s$ on the ARM processor.

**Efficient scalar implementation** The second implementation aims to modify the calculation of ZMSSD in order

to avoid the use of two loops. Formally the ZMSSD is written as:

$$ZMSSD = \sum_{i,j}((d - m_d) - (im - m_i))^2 \tag{15}$$

where $d = d(i,j)$ and $im = im(p_x + i - \frac{des}{2}, p_y + j - \frac{des}{2})$
By expanding the ZMSSD, we obtain:

$$ZMSSD = \sum_{i,j}((d - m_d)^2 - 2(d - m_d)(im - m_i) + (im - m_i)^2) \tag{16}$$

$$= \sum_{i,j}(d^2 - 2d.m_d + m_d^2 - 2d.im + 2d.m_i + 2m_d.im \tag{17}$$

$$- 2m_d.m_i + im^2 - 2im.m_i + m_i^2) \tag{17}$$

Using $m_d = \sum_{kl} \frac{d(k,l)}{des \times des}$ and $m_i = \sum_{kl} \frac{im(p_x + k - \frac{des}{2}, p_y + l - \frac{des}{2})}{des \times des}$, we simplify the sum:

$$\sum_{i,j} m_d = \sum_{i,j} \sum_{kl} \frac{d(k,l)}{des \times des} \tag{18}$$

$$= \sum_{kl} d(k,l) \tag{19}$$

$$\sum_{i,j} m_i = \sum_{i,j} \sum_{kl} \frac{im(p_x + k - \frac{des}{2}, p_y + l - \frac{des}{2})}{des \times des} \tag{20}$$

$$= \sum_{kl} im\left(p_x + k - \frac{des}{2}, p_y + l - \frac{des}{2}\right) \tag{21}$$

The equation becomes:

$$ZMSSD = \left[2\sum_{i,j} dim - \left(\sum_{i,j} d\right)^2 - \left(\sum_{i,j} im\right)^2\right]$$

$$/(des \times des) + \sum_{i,j} d^2 + \sum_{i,j} im^2 - 2\sum_{i,j} dim \tag{22}$$

Using the notation:

- Sd $= \sum_{i,j} d(i,j)$ the sum of the descriptor pixels (this sum can be precalculated).
- Si $= \sum_{i,j} \text{im}(p_x + i - \frac{\text{des}}{2}, p_y + j - \frac{\text{des}}{2})$ the sum of the image pixels.
- SSi $= \sum_{i,j} \text{im}(p_x + i - \frac{\text{des}}{2}, p_y + j - \frac{\text{des}}{2}) \times \text{im}(p_x + i - \frac{\text{des}}{2}, p_y + j - \frac{\text{des}}{2})$ the sum of squared image pixel values.
- SSd $= \sum_{i,j} d(i,j) \times d(i,j)$ the sum of the squared descriptor pixel values (this sum can be precalculated).
- Sdi $= \sum_{i,j} d(i,j) \text{im}(p_x + i - \frac{\text{des}}{2}, p_y + j - \frac{\text{des}}{2})$ the sum of the product of the descriptor pixels and the image pixels.

The final equation is:

$$\text{ZMSSD} = [\,((2Sd \times Si) - Sd^2 - Si^2)/(\text{des} \times \text{des})]$$
$$+ SSi + SSd - 2Sdi \qquad (23)$$

The implementation of Algorithm 2 becomes Algorithm 3:

**Algorithm 3 Efficient scalar ZMSSD**
1: $Si \leftarrow 0$
2: $SSi \leftarrow 0$
3: $Sdi \leftarrow 0$
4: **for Each** $i \in [\,0; \text{des} - 1], j \in [\,0; \text{des} - 1]$ **do**
5: $\quad Si \leftarrow Si + \text{im}(p_x + i - \frac{\text{des}}{2}, p_y + j - \frac{\text{des}}{2})$
6: $\quad SSi \leftarrow SSi + \text{im}(p_x + i - \frac{\text{des}}{2}, p_y + j - \frac{\text{des}}{2})$
$\quad \times \text{im}(p_x + i - \frac{\text{des}}{2}, p_y + j - \frac{\text{des}}{2})$
7: $\quad Sdi \leftarrow Sdi + \text{im}(p_x + i - \frac{\text{des}}{2}, p_y + j - \frac{\text{des}}{2}) \times d(i,j)$
8: **end for**
9: $\text{ZMSSD} \leftarrow$
$(((2Sd \times Si) - Sd^2 - Si^2)/(\text{des} \times \text{des})) + SSi + SSd - 2Sdi$

In this instance, we use only one loop. This reduces memory access. Using this implementation, the computing time decrease from $12.60\mu s$ to $11.29\mu s$.

Vector implementation SIMD NEON architecture allows vector processing and performs the same operation on all the vector processing-units. We have implemented a vectorized instance of the ZMSSD functional block as follows (Algorithm 4):

**Algorithm 4 SIMD vectorized ZMSSD**
1: $V8x8\ V\text{image} \leftarrow 0$ $\qquad \triangleright$ V8x8: $8 \times 8$ bits vector
2: $V8x8\ V\text{descriptor} \leftarrow 0$
3: $V16x8\ VSi \leftarrow 0$ $\qquad \triangleright$V16x8: $8 \times 16$ bits vector
4: $V32x4\ VSSi \leftarrow 0$ $\qquad \triangleright$V32x4: $4 \times 32$ bits vector
5: $V32x4\ VSdi \leftarrow 0$
6: **for Each** $i \in [\,0; \text{des} - 1], j = 0, 8$ **do**
7: $\quad V\text{image} \leftarrow \text{load}_8(im(p_x + i - \frac{\text{des}}{2}, p_y + j - \frac{\text{des}}{2}))$
$\quad \triangleright$load 8 pixels

8: $\quad V\text{descriptor} \leftarrow \text{load}_8(d(i,j))$
9: $\quad VSi \leftarrow VSi + V\text{image}$
10: $\quad VSSi \leftarrow VSSi + V\text{image} \times V\text{image}$
11: $\quad VSSi \leftarrow VSSi + V\text{image} \times V\text{image}$
12: **end for**
13: $Si \leftarrow \text{sum}(VSi)$ $\quad \triangleright$Sums the component of a vectors
14: $SSi \leftarrow \text{sum}(VSSi)$
15: $Sdi \leftarrow \text{sum}(VSdi)$
16: $\text{ZMSSD} \leftarrow$
$(((2Sd \times Si) - Sd^2 - Si^2)/256) + SSi + SSd - 2Sdi$

This instance uses 8 pixels at time. SIMD NEON architecture allows computing eight addition or eight multiplication simultaneously. The processing time of the vector implementation decreases to $1.27\ \mu s$.

**Computation time results** Table 3 summarizes the processing time of the three different implementations of the ZMSSD functional block. The SIMD implementation is approximately 10 times faster than a basic implementation.

*Estimation (FB6)*
ARM Cortex A8 do not integrate a FPU. That's why the processing time of the estimation FB is significant (Figure 4). To optimize the matrix multiplication, we have used the EIGEN3 library [28] which provides SIMD NEON optimized functions. Figure 6 presents the results of the processing-time of the estimation task implemented on the ARM processor (non-optimized task) and those using the SIMD NEON coprocessor (optimized task). The processing time of the optimized task is approximately eight times faster than those of the non-optimized one. This gain is due to the lack of the FPU in the Cortex A8 and to the efficiency of the NEON to evaluate a multiply and accumulate instruction in only one CPU cycle.

**Parallel implementation on a DSP processor**
Digital signal processors (DSP) are usually used in vision systems [29]. They integrate a number of resources that serve to enhance image processing versatility. The use of digital signal processing with data sharing ensures that image processing will be achieved in parallel. With a DSP based image processing, it is possible to parallelize the

**Table 3 ZMSSD processing time**

|  | Processing time | Percentage of the basic implementation |
| --- | --- | --- |
| Basic implementation | 12.60 | 100 |
| Scalar implementation | 11.29 | 89.6 |
| SIMD implementation | 1.27 | 10.8 |

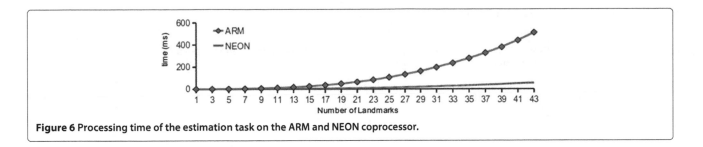

**Figure 6** Processing time of the estimation task on the ARM and NEON coprocessor.

EKF-SLAM algorithm on the multiprocessor architecture (ARM, NEON and DSP processors). This allows enhancing the global processing time especially when we consider to operate in real-time constraints. The landmarks matching (FB3 to FB5) and the robot position estimation (FB6) tasks must be processed sequentially. Fortunately, the initialization tasks (FB7, FB8 and FB9) can run simultaneously with the matching and estimation tasks.

Rethinking the implementation to obtain a parallel implementation, the instance of Algorithm 1 with block partitioning leads to the Algorithm 5.

**Algorithm 5 Multiprocessed EKF-SLAM**
1: Robot pose initialization
2: **while** localization is required **do**
3:   **if** DATA = Odometers **then**
4:     PREDICTION
5:   **else if** DATA = Camera **then**
6:     FAST detector
7:     **ARM Processor** MATCHING and ESTIMATION (FB 3, 4, 5 and 6)
8:     **DSP Processor** INITIALIZATION (FB 7, 8 and 9)
9:   **end if**
10: **end while**

The architecture of the OMAP3530 can interface the ARM and DSP processors using a shared memory. Figure 7 shows the data transfer mechanism using a shared DDR memory area. For each acquired image, the ARM processor writes the image (320×240 pixels), the robot position and its uncertainty on the shared memory. Data transfer between the ARM processor and DSP processor for a 320×240 gray image is done in one millisecond. When the initialization of a landmark is completed, the DSP processor returns the position and the uncertainty of possible new landmarks.

**Global results**

We have improved the EKF SLAM implementation using the SIMD NEON coprocessor and the DSP processor. We have implemented the matching and estimation tasks on a NEON coprocessor and the initialization tasks on a DSP processor. FAST corner detector is already an optimized algorithm using machine learning [21]. For the latest experiment, we set the same thresholds as Section "Experimental results".

Table 4 summarizes the processing time per iteration and the mean processing time per Frame of each FB. The computing time of the initialization task (blocks 7, 8 and 9) implemented on the DSP processor is approximately 4.0 ms. The DSP processor computes the initialization task while the ARM-NEON processors compute the prediction, FAST detection, matching and estimation tasks.

With this implementation and since the processing-time of the initialization task (4.0 ms) is smaller compared to the sum of the processing times of the matching and estimation tasks (13.0 ms for blocks 3, 4, 5 and 6), the overall computing time is reduced to the sum of the processing-times of the prediction process (0.093 ms),

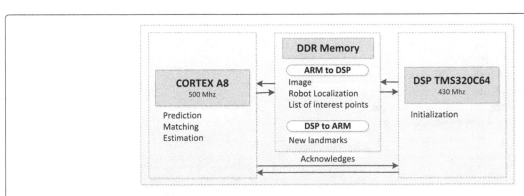

**Figure 7** ARM-DSP interface with a shared memory.

**Table 4 FBs processing times on ARM, NEON and DSP processors**

| Functional bloc (FB) | Nonoptimized implementation ($\mu s$) ARM only | | Optimized implementation ($\mu s$) | | |
|---|---|---|---|---|---|
| | Processing time per iteration | Mean processing time per frame | Processing time per iteration | Mean processing time per frame | Processing unit |
| 1. Prediction | 93 | 93 | 93 | 93 | ARM |
| 2. FAST | 3400 | 3400 | 3400 | 3400 | ARM |
| 3. Landmark projection | 9 | 180 | 9 | 180 | ARM |
| 4. ZMSSD-M | 11.29 | 2630 | 1.27 | 295 | NEON |
| 5. $\mathbf{H}_i$ | 14.5 | 66 | 14.5 | 66 | ARM |
| 6. Estimation | 88845 | 70568 | 15690 | 12552 | NEON |
| Initialization task (FB7, 8 and 9) | 3992 | 3922 | 4025 | 4025 | DSP |
| Total | – | 80859 | – | 16586 | – |

the FAST detector (3.4 ms), the matching and estimation tasks (13.0 ms). The mean processing time per frame with the optimized implementation is 17.6 ms (we add 1 ms for the ARM/DSP data transfer) whereas the nonoptimized implementation has a processing time of 80.85 ms. The optimized processing time represents 22% of the nonoptimized one. The processing time has been reduced by 78%.

## Conclusion

This article proposed an efficient implementation of the EKF-SLAM algorithm on a multiprocessor architecture. The overall accuracy of the EKF-SLAM depends on the number of the landmarks in the state vector and the matched observations. Both are linked to the time allowed to the embedded architecture to compute the robot pose. Based on the application constraints (real-time localization) and an evaluation methodology, we have implemented the algorithm in consideration of the underlying hardware architecture. A runtime analyses shows that the FBs and the initialization task represents 99.6% of the global processing time. We have used an optimized instance of the FAST detector. Two FBs (in matching and estimation tasks) have been optimized on an SIMD NEON architecture. The initialization task has been parallelized on a DSP processor. This optimization required a modification of the algorithm implementation. Using the optimized implementation, the global processing time was reduced by a factor equal to 4.7. The results demonstrate that an embedded systems (with a low-cost multiprocessor architecture) can operate under real-time constraints, if the software implementation is designed carefully. To scale with larger environment, we are going to include an approach of local/global mapping as proposed by [30]. Using this approach, we will be able to map larger environment. The map joining system will be implemented on the GPU coprocessor integrated on the OMAP3530.

Other future developments will be centered around a Hardware–software co-design to improve the system performances implementing a system-on-chip with a field programmable gate array (FPGA). The use of a configurable architecture accelerates greatly the design and validation of a proof of real-time and system-on-chip concept.

**Competing interests**
The authors declare that they have no competing interests.

**Author details**
[1] Univ Paris-Sud, CNRS, Institut d'Electronique Fondamentale, F-91405 Orsay, France. [2] IFSTTAR, IM, LIVIC, F-78000 Versailles, France.

**References**
1. M Dissanayake, P Newman, S Clark, H Durrant-Whyte, M Csorba, A solution to the simultaneous localization and map building (SLAM) problem. IEEE Trans. Robot. Autom. **17**, pp. 229–241 (2001)
2. A Davison, I Reid, N Molton, O Stasse, MonoSLAM: real-time single camera SLAM. IEEE Trans. Pattern Anal. Mach. Intell. **29**, pp. 1052–1067 (2007)
3. M Montemerlo, S Thrun, D Koller, B Wegbreit, in *National Conference on Artificial Intelligence*, FastSLAM: a factored solution to the simultaneous localization and mapping problem. Orlando, Florida, USA, 2002, pp. 593–598
4. J Folkesson, HI Christensen, in *IEEE International Conference on Robotics and Automation*, Graphical SLAM-a self-correcting map. LA, New Orleans, USA, 2004, pp. 383–390
5. A Eliazar, R Parr, in *International Joint Conference on Artificial Intelligence*. DP-SLAM: fast, robust simultaneous localization and mapping without predetermined landmarks. vol. 18. Acapulco, Mexico, 2003, pp. 1135–1142
6. S Thrun, Probabilistic robotics. Assoc. Comput. Mach. **45**(3), pp. 52–57 (2002)
7. C Brenneke, O Wulf, B Wagner, in *IEEE/RSJ International Conference on Intelligent Robots and Systems*, Using 3d laser range data for slam in outdoor environments. Las Vegas, Nevada, USA, 2003, pp. 188–193
8. A Prusak, O Melnychuk, H Roth, I Schiller, Pose estimation and map building with a time-of-flight-camera for robot navigation. Int. J. Intell. Syst. Technol. Appl. **5**(3), pp. 355–364 (2008)
9. F Abrate, B Bona, M Indri, in *European Conference on Mobile Robots*, Experimental EKF-based SLAM for mini-rovers with IR sensors only. Freiburg, Germany, 2007
10. T Yap, C Shelton, in *IEEE International Conference on Robotics and Automation*, SLAM in large indoor environments with low-cost, noisy, and sparse sonars. Kobe, Japan, 2009, pp. 1395–1401

11. C Gifford, R Webb, J Bley, D Leung, M Calnon, J Makarewicz, B Banz, A Agah, in *IEEE International Conference on Technologies for Practical Robot Applications*, Low-cost multi-robot exploration and mapping. Woburn, Massachusetts, USA, 2008, pp. 74–79

12. S Magnenat, V Longchamp, M Bonani, P Rétornaz, P Germano, H Bleuler, F Mondada, in *IEEE International Conference on Robotics and Automation*, Affordable SLAM through the co-design of hardware and methodology, Anchorage, Alaska, 2010, pp. 5395–5401

13. M Montemerlo, S Thrun, D Koller, B Wegbreit, in *International Joint Conference on Artificial Intelligence*, FastSLAM 2.0: An improved particle filtering algorithm for simultaneous localization and mapping that provably converges. Acapulco, Mexico, 2003, pp. 1151–1156

14. S Rezaei, J Guivant, E Nebot, in *IEEE/RSJ International Conference on Intelligent Robots and Systems*, Car-like robot path following in large unstructured environments. Las Vegas, Nevada, USA, 2003, pp. 2468–2473

15. C Schröter, H Böhme, H Gross, in *European Conference on Mobile Robots*, Memory-efficient gridmaps in Rao-Blackwellized particle filters for SLAM using sonar range sensors. Freiburg, Germany, 2007, pp. 138–143

16. K Konolige, J Augenbraun, N Donaldson, C Fiebig, P Shah, in *IEEE International Conference on Robotics and Automation*, A low-cost laser distance sensor. Pasadena, California, USA, 2008, pp. 3002–3008

17. P Pirjanian, N Karlsson, L Goncalves, E Di Bernardo, Low-cost visual localization and mapping for consumer robotics. Indust. Robot. **30**(2), pp. 139–144 (2003)

18. E Seignez, M Kieffer, A Lambert, E Walter, T Maurin, Real-time bounded-error state estimation for vehicle tracking. IEEE Int. J. Robot. Res. **28**, pp. 34–48 (2009)

19. R Siegwart, I Nourbakhsh, *Introduction to Autonomous Mobile Robots* (The MIT Press, London, 2004)

20. B Vincke, A Elouardi, A Lambert, in *IEEE/SICE International Symposium on System Integration*, Design and evaluation of an embedded system based SLAM applications. Sendai, Japan, 2010, pp. 224–229

21. E Rosten, R Porter, T Drummond, Faster and better: a machine learning approach to corner detection. IEEE Trans. Pattern Anal. Mach. Intell. **32**, pp. 105–119 (2009)

22. A Davison, in *IEEE International Conference on Computer Vision*, Real-time simultaneous localisation and mapping with a single camera. Nice, France, 2003, pp. 1403–1410

23. R Munguia, A Grau, in *European Conference on Mobile Robots*, Freiburg, Germany, 2007, pp. 1–6

24. E Seignez, A Lambert, T Maurin, in *IEEE International Conference On Information And Communication Technologies: From Theory To Application*, An experimental platform for testing localization algorithms. Damascus, Syria, 2006, pp. 748–753

25. A Elouardi, S Bouaziz, A Dupret, L Lacassagne, JO Klein, R Reynaud, in *International Journal on Computer Science and Applications*, A smart architecture for low-level image computing. 2008, pp. 1–19

26. F Auat Cheein, R Carelli, Analysis of different feature selection criteria based on a covariance convergence perspective for a SLAM algorithm. Sensors. **11**, pp. 62–89 (2010)

27. M Kraft, A Schmidt, A Kasinski, in *International Conference on Computer Vision Theory and Applications*, High-speed image feature detection using FPGA implementation of fast algorithm. Funchal, Madeira, Portugal, 2008, pp. 174–179

28. Eigen, (2012). http://eigen.tuxfamily.org/

29. K Gunnam, D Hughes, J Junkins, N Kehtarnavaz, A vision-based DSP embedded navigation sensor. IEEE Sens. J. **2**(5), pp. 428–442 (2002)

30. P Piniés, J Tardós, Large-scale slam building conditionally independent local maps: application to monocular vision. IEEE Trans. Robot. **24**(5), pp. 1094–1106 (2008)

# 3

# A space-time coding approach for RFID MIMO systems

Feng Zheng* and Thomas Kaiser

## Abstract

This paper discusses the space-time coding (STC) problem for RFID MIMO systems. First, a mathematical model for this kind of system is developed from the viewpoint of signal processing, which makes it easy to design the STC schemes. Then two STC schemes, namely Scheme I and Scheme II, are proposed. Simulation results illustrate that the proposed approaches can greatly improve the symbol-error rate (SER) or bit-error rate (BER) performance of RFID systems, compared to the non space-time encoded RFID system. The SER/BER performance for Scheme I and Scheme II is thoroughly compared. It is found that Scheme II with the innate real-symbol constellation yields better SER/BER performance than Scheme I. Some design guidelines for RFID-MIMO systems are pointed out.

## Introduction

Radio frequency identification (RFID) is a contactless, usually short distance, wireless data transmission and reception technique for identification of objects. It is believed that RFID can substitute, in the not-far future, the widely used optical barcode technology due to the limitations of the latter in i) the barcode cannot read non-line-of-sight (NLOS) tag; ii) each barcode needs personal care to be read; and iii) limited information-carrying ability of the barcode. Currently, a single antenna is usually used at the reader and tag of RFID in the market. However, RFID research community recently started to pay attention on using multiple antennas at either the reader side or the tag side [1,2]. The reason is that using multiple antennas is an efficient approach to increasing the coverage of RFID, solving the NLOS problem, improving the reliability of data communications between the reader and tag, and thus further extending the information-carrying ability of RFID. Besides, some advanced technology in multiple transmit and receive antennas (MIMO) can be used to solve the problem of detecting multiple objects simultaneously, see e.g., [3].

There have been several studies about RFID-MIMO. In general, these studies are somehow scattered in different topics. It is difficult to find the logical relationship among these studies. Therefore, the state of the art of the

studies will be reviewed in a large degree in a chronological order. The work [4] first showed the idea of using multiple antennas at the reader for both transmission and reception. In [1], the authors first proposed to use multiple antennas at the tag and showed the performance gain by equipping multiple antennas at the reader (for both transmission and reception) and the tag. In [5], the multipath fading for both single-antenna based RFID channel and RFID-MIMO channel was measured and compared. The improvement on the fading depth by using MIMO can be clearly seen from the measured power distribution (see, e.g., Figure Ten therein). In [6], the authors first proposed to apply the Alamouti space-time coding (STC) technique, which is now popularly used in wireless communication systems, to the RFID systems. The reference [6] presented a closed-form expression for the bit-error rate (BER) of the RFID system with the nonecoherent frequency shift keying modulation and multiple transmit antennas at the tag and single transmit/receive antenna at the reader, where the double Rayleigh fading is assumed at the forward and backward links. In [7], the interrogation range of ultrahigh-frequency-band (UHF-band) RFID with multiple transmit/receive antennas at the reader and single antenna at the tag was analyzed, where the forward and backward channels are assumed to take the Nakagami-$m$ distribution. In [3], the blind source separation technique in antenna array was used to solve the multiple tag identification problem, where the reader is equipped with multiple antennas. The work

*Correspondence: feng.zheng@uni-due.de
Institute of Digital Signal Processing, University of Duisburg-Essen, 47057 Duisburg, Germany

[8] applied the maximal ratio combining technique to the RFID receiver, where the channel of the whole chain, including forward link, backscattering coefficient, and backward link, was estimated and used as the weighting coefficient for the combining branches. In [9], a prototype for the RFID-MIMO in the UHF-band was reported. In [10], both MIMO-based zero-forcing and minimum-mean-square-error receivers were used to deal with the multiple-tag identification problem, where the channel of the whole chain was estimated, similar to the approach in [8]. It is reported in [11] that four antennas are fabricated in a given fixed surface at the reader. The measurement results showed that an increase of 83% in area gave a 300% increase in available power to turn on a given tag load and the operational distance of the powered device is increased to 100 cm by the four-antenna setup from roughly 40 cm for the single-antenna setup. The result in [11] suggests that the MIMO technique can be very promising to the RFID technology.

In the aforementioned reports, the Alamouti STC technique has been shown to be able to extend to RFID-MIMO systems. However, it can only apply to the case where the tag has two antennas. Since implementing four antennas at the tag have been shown to be possible in experiments, it is necessary to investigate the possibility of applying other STC techniques to RFID-MIMO systems. In this paper, we will study how to apply the real orthogonal design (ROD) technique, proposed by Tarokh et al. in [12], to RFID-MIMO systems. This technique is suitable for the case where the tag is equipped up to eight antennas, which should be sufficient for the RFID technology in the near future.

The paper is organized as follows. A modified MIMO-RFID channel model will be developed in Section "Channel Modeling of RFID MIMO Wireless Systems". The ROD in [12] and the companion of the ROD (CROD) proposed in [13] are briefly introduced in Section "A Space-Time Coding Scheme for RFID MIMO Systems". Two space-time decoding approaches for RFID MIMO systems will be discussed in Section "Two Space-Time Decoding Approaches for RFID MIMO Systems". Section "Simulation Results" presents the simulation results and discussions, and Section "Conclusions" concludes the paper.

## Channel Modeling of RFID MIMO Wireless Systems

In this paper our discussion is confined only on narrowband RFID systems. The block diagram of the RFID MIMO system is illustrated in Figure 1, where both the reader and tag are equipped with multiple antennas.

In terms of equation (1) of [1], the narrowband RFID MIMO wireless channel can be expressed as

$$\mathbf{y}(t) = \mathbf{H}^b \mathbf{S}(t) \mathbf{H}^f \mathbf{x}(t) + \mathbf{n}(t), \tag{1}$$

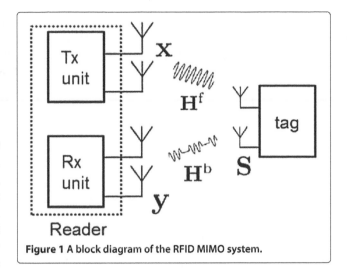

**Figure 1** A block diagram of the RFID MIMO system.

where the reader and tag are equipped with $N_{\rm rd}$ and $N_{\rm tag}$ antennas, respectively, $\mathbf{x}$ (an $N_{\rm rd} \times 1$ vector) is the transmitted signal at the reader, $\mathbf{y}$ (an $N_{\rm rd} \times 1$ vector) is the received signal at the reader, $\mathbf{n}$ is the receiver noise, $\mathbf{H}^f$ (an $N_{\rm tag} \times N_{\rm rd}$ matrix) is the channel matrix from the reader to the tag, $\mathbf{H}^b$ (an $N_{\rm rd} \times N_{\rm tag}$ matrix) is the channel matrix from the tag to the reader, and $\mathbf{S}$ is the backscattering matrix, which is also called signaling matrix. It is assumed that the $N_{\rm rd}$ antennas at the reader are used for both reception and transmission. This assumption is just for brevity of the notation. It is straightforward to extend the approach presented in this paper to the case where the reader has different numbers of antennas for reception and transmission. The channels $\mathbf{H}^f$ and $\mathbf{H}^b$ are assumed to be complex Gaussian distributed, $\mathbf{H}^f$ and $\mathbf{H}^b$ are mutually independent, and all the entries of either $\mathbf{H}^f$ or $\mathbf{H}^b$ are independent of each other. It is also assumed that $\mathrm{Re}(\mathbf{H}^f)$, $\mathrm{Im}(\mathbf{H}^f)$, $\mathrm{Re}(\mathbf{H}^b)$, $\mathrm{Im}(\mathbf{H}^b)$ are mutually independent and of the same distribution.

In most general case where the modulated backscatter signals at the tag are transferred between the antennas, the signaling matrix $\mathbf{S}$ is a full matrix [1]. However no application of the full signalling matrix has been identified up to now [1]. Therefore, we will consider the situation where the RF tag antennas modulate backscatter with different signals and no signals are transferred between the antennas. In this case, the signaling matrix is a diagonal matrix [1]

$$\mathbf{S}(t) = \mathrm{diag}\left\{\Gamma_1(t), \Gamma_2(t) \ldots, \Gamma_{N_{\rm tag}}(t)\right\} \quad \text{with} \quad |\Gamma_i(t)| \leq 1,$$

where $\Gamma_i(t)$ is the backscattering coefficient of $i$th antenna at the tag. The $i$th tag identity (ID) is contained in the coefficient $\Gamma_i(t)$.

Note that in the RFID system, the transmitted signal $\mathbf{x}$ is mainly used to carry the transmit power, while the information data (i.e., tag ID) is carried out by $\mathbf{S}$. Therefore, the central issue for the RFID is to decode $\Gamma_1, \ldots, \Gamma_{N_{\text{tag}}}$ from the received signal. Next we transform equation (1) to the conventional form in signal processing. Let us define

$$
\boldsymbol{\gamma}(t) = \begin{bmatrix} \Gamma_1(t) \\ \Gamma_2(t) \\ \vdots \\ \Gamma_{N_{\text{tag}}}(t) \end{bmatrix}, \quad \mathbf{H}^{\text{f}} = \begin{bmatrix} \mathbf{H}_1^{\text{f}} \\ \mathbf{H}_2^{\text{f}} \\ \vdots \\ \mathbf{H}_{N_{\text{tag}}}^{\text{f}} \end{bmatrix}. \tag{2}
$$

Then equation (1) can be rewritten as

$$
\begin{aligned}
\mathbf{y}(t) &= \mathbf{H}^{\text{b}} \text{diag}\left\{\Gamma_1(t), \ \Gamma_2(t) \ldots, \Gamma_{N_{\text{tag}}}(t)\right\} \mathbf{H}^{\text{f}}\mathbf{x}(t) + \mathbf{n}(t) \\
&= \mathbf{H}^{\text{b}} \text{diag}\{1, \ 0, \ \ldots, \ 0\} \mathbf{H}^{\text{f}}\mathbf{x}(t)\Gamma_1(t) \\
&\quad + \mathbf{H}^{\text{b}} \text{diag}\{0, \ 1, \ \ldots, \ 0\} \mathbf{H}^{\text{f}}\mathbf{x}(t)\Gamma_2(t) + \cdots \\
&\quad + \mathbf{H}^{\text{b}} \text{diag}\{0, \ 0, \ \ldots, \ 1\} \mathbf{H}^{\text{f}}\mathbf{x}(t)\Gamma_{N_{\text{tag}}}(t) + \mathbf{n}(t) \\
&= \mathbf{H}^{\text{b}} \begin{bmatrix} \mathbf{H}_1^{\text{f}} \\ \mathbf{0} \\ \vdots \\ \mathbf{0} \end{bmatrix} \mathbf{x}(t)\Gamma_1(t) + \mathbf{H}^{\text{b}} \begin{bmatrix} \mathbf{0} \\ \mathbf{H}_2^{\text{f}} \\ \vdots \\ \mathbf{0} \end{bmatrix} \mathbf{x}(t)\Gamma_2(t) + \cdots \\
&\quad + \mathbf{H}^{\text{b}} \begin{bmatrix} \mathbf{0} \\ \mathbf{0} \\ \vdots \\ \mathbf{H}_{N_{\text{tag}}}^{\text{f}} \end{bmatrix} \mathbf{x}(t)\Gamma_{N_{\text{tag}}}(t) + \mathbf{n}(t) \\
&= \mathbf{H}^{\text{b}} \begin{bmatrix} \mathbf{H}_1^{\text{f}}\mathbf{x}(t) & 0 & \cdots & 0 \\ 0 & \mathbf{H}_2^{\text{f}}\mathbf{x}(t) & \cdots & 0 \\ \vdots & \vdots & \ddots & \vdots \\ 0 & 0 & \cdots & \mathbf{H}_{N_{\text{tag}}}^{\text{f}}\mathbf{x}(t) \end{bmatrix} \\
&\quad \times \begin{bmatrix} \Gamma_1(t) \\ \Gamma_2(t) \\ \vdots \\ \Gamma_{N_{\text{tag}}}(t) \end{bmatrix} + \mathbf{n}(t) \\
&= \mathbf{H}^{\text{b}} \check{\mathbf{H}}(t) \boldsymbol{\gamma}(t) + \mathbf{n}(t), \tag{3}
\end{aligned}
$$

where

$$
\check{\mathbf{H}}(t) := \begin{bmatrix} \mathbf{H}_1^{\text{f}}\mathbf{x}(t) & 0 & \cdots & 0 \\ 0 & \mathbf{H}_2^{\text{f}}\mathbf{x}(t) & \cdots & 0 \\ \vdots & \vdots & \ddots & \vdots \\ 0 & 0 & \cdots & \mathbf{H}_{N_{\text{tag}}}^{\text{f}}\mathbf{x}(t) \end{bmatrix}.
$$

Equation (3) converts the original system model (1) to the conventional form in signal processing: the signal to be estimated or decoded is packed in a vector, whose entries are independent of each other.

## A Space-Time Coding Scheme for RFID MIMO Systems

Let us first review the real orthogonal design proposed by Tarokh et al. in [12].

**Definition 1.** [12] A real orthogonal design $\mathcal{G}$ of size $m$ is an $m \times k$ matrix with entries $0, \pm \mathcal{S}_1, \pm \mathcal{S}_2, \ldots, \pm \mathcal{S}_k$ such that $\mathcal{G}\mathcal{G}^T = \mathbf{D}$, where $\mathbf{D}$ is a diagonal matrix with diagonal entries being $\mathbf{D}_{ii} = l_{i1}\mathcal{S}_1^2 + l_{i2}\mathcal{S}_2^2 + \cdots + l_{ik}\mathcal{S}_k^2$, $i = 1, 2, \ldots, m$, and the coefficients $l_{i1}, l_{i2}, \ldots, l_{ik}$ are strictly positive integers.

In some cases, we need to explicitly specify the arguments of $\mathcal{G}$. In these cases, the ROD will be denoted as $\mathcal{G}(\mathcal{S}_1, \mathcal{S}_2, \ldots, \mathcal{S}_k)$, where $\mathcal{S}_1, \mathcal{S}_2, \ldots, \mathcal{S}_k$ are the arguments of $\mathcal{G}$.

The construction of general RODs can be found in [12]. For completeness, the RODs for the cases of $m = 2, 3, 4$, denoted as $\mathcal{G}^{(2)}, \mathcal{G}^{(3)}, \mathcal{G}^{(4)}$ respectively, are listed as follows:

$$
\mathcal{G}^{(2)} = \begin{bmatrix} \mathcal{S}_1 & -\mathcal{S}_2 \\ \mathcal{S}_2 & \mathcal{S}_1 \end{bmatrix}, \tag{4}
$$

$$
\mathcal{G}^{(3)} = \begin{bmatrix} \mathcal{S}_1 & -\mathcal{S}_2 & -\mathcal{S}_3 & -\mathcal{S}_4 \\ \mathcal{S}_2 & \mathcal{S}_1 & \mathcal{S}_4 & -\mathcal{S}_3 \\ \mathcal{S}_3 & -\mathcal{S}_4 & \mathcal{S}_1 & \mathcal{S}_2 \end{bmatrix}, \tag{5}
$$

$$
\mathcal{G}^{(4)} = \begin{bmatrix} \mathcal{S}_1 & -\mathcal{S}_2 & -\mathcal{S}_3 & -\mathcal{S}_4 \\ \mathcal{S}_2 & \mathcal{S}_1 & \mathcal{S}_4 & -\mathcal{S}_3 \\ \mathcal{S}_3 & -\mathcal{S}_4 & \mathcal{S}_1 & \mathcal{S}_2 \\ \mathcal{S}_4 & \mathcal{S}_3 & -\mathcal{S}_2 & \mathcal{S}_1 \end{bmatrix}. \tag{6}
$$

For the construction of $\mathcal{G}^{(5)}, \ldots, \mathcal{G}^{(8)}$, readers are referred to [12].

To formulate the decoding algorithm for the ROD, let us define the companion of the ROD as follows.

**Definition 2.** A companion of a real orthogonal design $\mathcal{G}(\mathcal{S}_1, \mathcal{S}_2, \ldots, \mathcal{S}_k)$, denoted as $\mathcal{G}_c(\alpha_1, \alpha_2, \ldots, \alpha_m)$, is a matrix satisfying the following equation

$$
[\alpha_1 \ \alpha_2 \ \cdots \ \alpha_m] \mathcal{G}(\mathcal{S}_1, \mathcal{S}_2, \ldots, \mathcal{S}_k) = [\mathcal{S}_1 \mathcal{S}_2 \cdots \mathcal{S}_k] \\ \times \mathcal{G}_c(\alpha_1, \alpha_2, \ldots, \alpha_m).
$$

For the RODs as shown in equations (4)-(6), their CRODs are

$$
\mathcal{G}_c^{(2)} = \begin{bmatrix} \alpha_1 & \alpha_2 \\ \alpha_2 & -\alpha_1 \end{bmatrix}, \tag{7}
$$

$$
\mathcal{G}_c^{(3)} = \begin{bmatrix} \alpha_1 & \alpha_2 & \alpha_3 & 0 \\ \alpha_2 & -\alpha_1 & 0 & \alpha_3 \\ \alpha_3 & 0 & -\alpha_1 & -\alpha_2 \\ 0 & -\alpha_3 & \alpha_2 & -\alpha_1 \end{bmatrix}, \tag{8}
$$

$$\mathcal{G}_c^{(4)} = \begin{bmatrix} \alpha_1 & \alpha_2 & \alpha_3 & \alpha_4 \\ \alpha_2 & -\alpha_1 & -\alpha_4 & \alpha_3 \\ \alpha_3 & \alpha_4 & -\alpha_1 & -\alpha_2 \\ \alpha_4 & -\alpha_3 & \alpha_2 & -\alpha_1 \end{bmatrix}. \tag{9}$$

For a given ROD, the calculation of its CROD is given in [13].

For the CRODs as defined in equations (7)-(9), it can be easily shown that the following equality

$$\mathcal{G}_c[\mathcal{G}_c]^T = \sum_{j=1}^{m} \alpha_j^2 \cdot \mathbf{I} \tag{10}$$

holds true, where the superscript $^T$ stands for the transpose (*without conjugate!*) of a matrix or vector. As can be seen from the discussion in Section "Simulation Results", one can remove the inter-symbol interference (ISI) by using the above property of CROD, but the diversity gain thus obtained from the multiple channels is limited when the channel is complex instead of real.

To find the decoding scheme, let us consider the property of $\mathcal{G}_c[\mathcal{G}_c]^H$, where the superscript $^H$ stands for the *conjugate* transpose of a matrix or vector. We have

$$\mathcal{G}_c^{(2)}[\mathcal{G}_c^{(2)}]^H = \begin{bmatrix} \sum_{i=1}^{2}|\alpha_i|^2 & \alpha_1\alpha_2^H - \alpha_1^H\alpha_2 \\ \bigstar & \sum_{i=1}^{2}|\alpha_i|^2 \end{bmatrix}, \tag{11}$$

$$\mathcal{G}_c^{(3)}[\mathcal{G}_c^{(3)}]^H = \begin{bmatrix} \sum_{i=1}^{3}|\alpha_i|^2 & \alpha_1\alpha_2^H - \alpha_1^H\alpha_2 & \alpha_1\alpha_3^H - \alpha_1^H\alpha_3 & -\alpha_2\alpha_3^H + \alpha_2^H\alpha_3 \\ \bigstar & \sum_{i=1}^{3}|\alpha_i|^2 & \alpha_2\alpha_3^H - \alpha_2^H\alpha_3 & \alpha_1\alpha_3^H - \alpha_1^H\alpha_3 \\ \bigstar & \bigstar & \sum_{i=1}^{3}|\alpha_i|^2 & -\alpha_1\alpha_2^H + \alpha_1^H\alpha_2 \\ \bigstar & \bigstar & \bigstar & \sum_{i=1}^{3}|\alpha_i|^2 \end{bmatrix} \tag{12}$$

where the entry marked with $\bigstar$ means that its value can be inferred from the value of its corresponding symmetric entry. It can be checked that the structural property as shown in equations (11)-(13) also holds true for higher dimensional CRODs.

Using RODs and the corresponding CRODs, a general space-time encoding scheme and two decoding approaches for RFID-MIMO systems can be developed as follows.

Consider the equivalent RFID-MIMO channel (3). Denote by $T_f$ a symbol period. Suppose that the channels of both forward and backward links do not change with time during a coding block period $KT_f$. The transmit signal $\mathbf{x}$ at the reader is also fixed during one coding block period $KT_f$. Therefore, the equivalent composite channel $\mathbf{H}^b\check{\mathbf{H}}$ will not change with time when we only consider the signal processing for one coding block. Let us define

$$\mathbf{A} = \mathbf{H}^b\check{\mathbf{H}}.$$

Let $\mathcal{G}$ (of dimension $N_{\text{tag}} \times K$) be a ROD in variables $\mathcal{S}_1, \mathcal{S}_2, \ldots, \mathcal{S}_K$, where $\mathcal{S}_1, \mathcal{S}_2, \ldots, \mathcal{S}_K$ are the symbols to be transmitted at the $N_{\text{tag}}$ transmit antennas in one STC frame. Define

$$\mathbf{w}(t) = \begin{bmatrix} w(t) \\ w(t - T_f) \\ \vdots \\ w(t - (K-1)T_f) \end{bmatrix},$$

where $w(t)$ is the baseband waveform of the transmit signal at the tag. The transmitted signal across the $N_{\text{tag}}$ transmit antennas at the tag can be expressed as

$$\boldsymbol{\gamma}(t) = \sqrt{\frac{E_0}{N_{\text{tag}}}}\, \mathcal{G}(\mathcal{S}_1, \mathcal{S}_2, \ldots, \mathcal{S}_K)\mathbf{w}(t), \tag{14}$$

where $E_0$ is the total power used for the transmission of one symbol per time slot. The scaling coefficient $\sqrt{\frac{E_0}{N_{\text{tag}}}}$ is to normalize the overall energy consumption per time slot

$$\mathcal{G}_c^{(4)}[\mathcal{G}_c^{(4)}]^H = \tag{13}$$

$$\begin{bmatrix} \sum_{i=1}^{4}|\alpha_i|^2 & \alpha_1\alpha_2^H - \alpha_1^H\alpha_2 - \alpha_3\alpha_4^H + \alpha_3^H\alpha_4 & \alpha_1\alpha_3^H - \alpha_1^H\alpha_3 + \alpha_2\alpha_4^H - \alpha_2^H\alpha_4 & \alpha_1\alpha_4^H - \alpha_1^H\alpha_4 - \alpha_2\alpha_3^H + \alpha_2^H\alpha_3 \\ \bigstar & \sum_{i=1}^{4}|\alpha_i|^2 & \alpha_2\alpha_3^H - \alpha_2^H\alpha_3 - \alpha_1\alpha_4^H + \alpha_1^H\alpha_4 & \alpha_2\alpha_4^H - \alpha_2^H\alpha_4 + \alpha_1\alpha_3^H - \alpha_1^H\alpha_3 \\ \bigstar & \bigstar & \sum_{i=1}^{4}|\alpha_i|^2 & \alpha_3\alpha_4^H - \alpha_3^H\alpha_4 - \alpha_1\alpha_2^H + \alpha_1^H\alpha_2 \\ \bigstar & \bigstar & \bigstar & \sum_{i=1}^{4}|\alpha_i|^2 \end{bmatrix},$$

at the tag side to be $E_0$ no matter how many antennas are deployed at the tag.

## Two Space-Time Decoding Approaches for RFID MIMO Systems

The received signal after sampling can be expressed as

$$\vec{\mathbf{y}} = \sqrt{\frac{E_0}{N_{\text{tag}}}} \mathbf{A}\mathcal{G}(\mathcal{S}_1, \mathcal{S}_2, \dots, \mathcal{S}_K) + \vec{\mathbf{n}}, \tag{15}$$

where $\vec{\mathbf{n}}$ is the receiver noise (a matrix) at the corresponding time instant. Notice that $\vec{\mathbf{y}}$ is of dimension $N_{\text{rd}} \times K$, since one frame of the transmitted signal contains the pulses of $K$ time slots.

Denote by $[\mathbf{M}]_j$ the $j$th row of a matrix $\mathbf{M}$. Let us consider the $j$th row of the matrix $\vec{\mathbf{y}}$ which is the received signal at the $j$th antenna of the reader for the time instants $1, \dots, K$ respectively. Let

$$[\mathbf{A}]_j = [\alpha_{j1} \ \alpha_{j2} \ \cdots \ \alpha_{jN_{\text{tag}}}].$$

Since the transmitted signal is space-time coded, the entries in $[\mathbf{y}]_j$ should be related with each other somehow. Right-hand multiplying both sides of equation (15) with the matrix $[\mathcal{G}_c(\alpha_{j1}, \alpha_{j2}, \dots, \alpha_{jN_{\text{tag}}})]^T$, we have

$$\mathbf{z}_j := [\vec{\mathbf{y}}]_j \, [\mathcal{G}_c(\alpha_{j1}, \alpha_{j2}, \dots, \alpha_{jN_{\text{tag}}})]^T \tag{16}$$

$$= \left\{ \sqrt{\frac{E_0}{N_{\text{tag}}}} [\mathbf{A}]_j \, \mathcal{G}(\mathcal{S}_1, \mathcal{S}_2, \dots, \mathcal{S}_K) + [\mathbf{n}]_j \right\}$$

$$\times \left[ \mathcal{G}_c (\alpha_{j1}, \alpha_{j2}, \dots, \alpha_{jN_{\text{tag}}}) \right]^T$$

$$= \left\{ \sqrt{\frac{E_0}{N_{\text{tag}}}} [\mathcal{S}_1 \ \mathcal{S}_2 \cdots \mathcal{S}_K] \, \mathcal{G}_c(\alpha_{j1}, \alpha_{j2}, \dots, \alpha_{jN_{\text{tag}}}) + [\vec{\mathbf{n}}]_j \right\}$$

$$\times \left[ \mathcal{G}_c (\alpha_{j1}, \alpha_{j2}, \dots, \alpha_{jN_{\text{tag}}}) \right]^T$$

$$= \sqrt{\frac{E_0}{N_{\text{tag}}}} \sum_{k=1}^{N_{\text{tag}}} [\alpha_{jk}]^2 \, [\mathcal{S}_1 \ \mathcal{S}_2 \ \cdots \ \mathcal{S}_K] + [\vec{\mathbf{n}}]_j$$

$$\times \left[ \mathcal{G}_c (\alpha_{j1}, \alpha_{j2}, \dots, \alpha_{jN_{\text{tag}}}) \right]^T. \tag{17}$$

From equation (17) we can see that the transmitted symbols $\mathcal{S}_1, \mathcal{S}_2, \dots, \mathcal{S}_K$ are decoupled from each other in the processed signal $\mathbf{z}_j$ through the processing algorithm (16). However, it is not efficient to decode the symbols $\mathcal{S}_1, \mathcal{S}_2, \dots, \mathcal{S}_K$ directly from (17) since the complex channel makes the phase of $\sum_{k=1}^{N_{\text{tag}}} [\alpha_{jk}]^2$ randomly change over $[0, 2\pi]$. Define

$$\beta_j = \sum_{k=1}^{N_{\text{tag}}} [\alpha_{jk}]^2. \tag{18}$$

Multiplying both sides of (17) by $\beta_j^H$ will remove the phase ambiguity of the equivalent channel. This gives

$$\bar{\mathbf{z}}_j := \beta_j^H \mathbf{z}_j = |\beta_j|^2 \, [\mathcal{S}_1 \ \mathcal{S}_2 \ \cdots \ \mathcal{S}_K] + \bar{\mathbf{n}}_j, \tag{19}$$

where

$$\bar{\mathbf{n}}_j = \beta_j^H \, [\vec{\mathbf{n}}]_j \, [\mathcal{G}_c(\alpha_{j1}, \alpha_{j2}, \dots, \alpha_{jN_{\text{tag}}})]^T.$$

To collect all the diversities provided by multiple receive antennas at the reader, we sum up all $\bar{\mathbf{z}}_j$'s. This gives

$$\bar{\mathbf{z}} := \sum_{j=1}^{N_{\text{rd}}} \bar{\mathbf{z}}_j = \sum_{j=1}^{N_{\text{rd}}} |\beta_j|^2 \, [\mathcal{S}_1 \ \mathcal{S}_2 \ \cdots \ \mathcal{S}_K] + \sum_{j=1}^{N_{\text{rd}}} \bar{\mathbf{n}}_j. \tag{20}$$

The symbols $\mathcal{S}_1, \mathcal{S}_2, \dots, \mathcal{S}_K$ can be easily decoded from equation (20).

For the convenience of exposition in next section, we call the encoding and decoding scheme discussed above as Scheme I.

Another decoding scheme (hereafter it is referred to as Scheme II) is to exploit the property of the matrix $\mathcal{G}_c(\mathcal{G}_c)^H$, as shown in equations (11)-(13). Right-hand multiplying both sides of equation (15) with the matrix $[\mathcal{G}_c(\alpha_{j1}, \alpha_{j2}, \dots, \alpha_{jN_{\text{tag}}})]^H$, we have

$$\mathbf{u}_j := [\vec{\mathbf{y}}]_j \, [\mathcal{G}_c(\alpha_{j1}, \alpha_{j2}, \dots, \alpha_{jN_{\text{tag}}})]^H$$

$$= \left\{ \sqrt{\frac{E_0}{N_{\text{tag}}}} [\mathcal{S}_1 \ \mathcal{S}_2 \cdots \mathcal{S}_K] \, \mathcal{G}_c(\alpha_{j1}, \alpha_{j2}, \dots, \alpha_{jN_{\text{tag}}}) + [\vec{\mathbf{n}}]_j \right\}$$

$$\times \left[ \mathcal{G}_c (\alpha_{j1}, \alpha_{j2}, \dots, \alpha_{jN_{\text{tag}}}) \right]^H$$

$$= \sqrt{\frac{E_0}{N_{\text{tag}}}} [\mathcal{S}_1 \ \mathcal{S}_2 \cdots \mathcal{S}_K] \cdot [\mathcal{G}_c (\alpha_{j1}, \alpha_{j2}, \dots, \alpha_{jN_{\text{tag}}})]$$

$$\times \left[ \mathcal{G}_c (\alpha_{j1}, \alpha_{j2}, \dots, \alpha_{jN_{\text{tag}}}) \right]^H + [\vec{\mathbf{n}}]_j$$

$$\times \left[ \mathcal{G}_c (\alpha_{j1}, \alpha_{j2}, \dots, \alpha_{jN_{\text{tag}}}) \right]^H. \tag{21}$$

From equations (21) and (11)-(13) we can see that, if the symbols $\mathcal{S}_1, \mathcal{S}_2, \dots, \mathcal{S}_K$ are real, the symbol to be decoded, say $\mathcal{S}_k$ for some $k$, and the ISI caused by other symbols, are projected into different subspaces in the complex plane: the desired signal is in the real subspace, while the ISI is in the imaginary subspace. Therefore, a very simple decoding method for this case works in the following way: From $k$th entry of $\mathbf{u}_j$ (denoted as $\mathbf{u}_{j,k}$), get the real part of $\mathbf{u}_{j,k}$ [denoted as $\text{Re}\,(\mathbf{u}_{j,k})$], and then decode $\mathcal{S}_k$ in terms of $\text{Re}\,(\mathbf{u}_{j,k})$.

The diversities provided by multiple receive antennas at the reader can be collected in the following way:

$$\bar{\mathbf{u}}_k := \sum_{j=1}^{N_{\text{rd}}} \text{Re}\,(\mathbf{u}_{j,k}). \tag{22}$$

Then $\mathcal{S}_k$ can be decoded in terms of $\bar{\mathbf{u}}_k$.

## Simulation Results

In this section, we investigate the symbol-error rate (SER) or bit-error rate (BER) performance of both Schemes I and II. In Scheme I, the quadrature phase shift keying (QPSK) modulation is used and the constellation of transmitted symbols is $\frac{\pm 1 \pm j}{\sqrt{2}}$. In Scheme II, the binary phase shift keying (BPSK) modulation is used and the constellation of transmitted symbols is $\pm 1$. Therefore, the SER in Scheme II reduces to BER. At the transmitter of the reader, the signal $\mathbf{x}$ takes the form of a random vector whose entry is uniformly distributed among $\pm \frac{1}{\sqrt{N_{rd}}}$. It is seen that $\mathbf{x}$ is of unity power. Each entry of the channels $\mathbf{H}^f$ and $\mathbf{H}^b$ is of mean zero and variance unity.

In the figures to be shown, the signal-to-noise power ratio (SNR) is defined as the $\frac{E_0}{\sigma_{\vec{\mathbf{n}}}^2}$, where $\sigma_{\vec{\mathbf{n}}}^2$ is the variance of the each entry of noise vector $\vec{\mathbf{n}}$.

Figure 2 shows the SER of Scheme I for different cases: Figures 2(a) and (b) illustrate how the SER changes with $N_{tag}$ for fixed $N_{rd}$, i.e., when $N_{rd} = 1$ and 4 respectively; while Figures 2(c) and (d) demonstrate how the SER changes with $N_{rd}$ for fixed $N_{tag}$, i.e., when $N_{tag} = 1$ and 4 respectively.

Figure 3 shows the BER of Scheme II for different cases: Figures 3(a) and (b) illustrate how the BER changes with $N_{tag}$ for fixed $N_{rd}$, i.e., when $N_{rd} = 1$ and 4 respectively; while Figures 3(c) and (d) demonstrate how the BER changes with $N_{rd}$ for fixed $N_{tag}$, i.e., when $N_{tag} = 1$ and 4 respectively.

From Figures 2 and 3 the following phenomena can be observed:

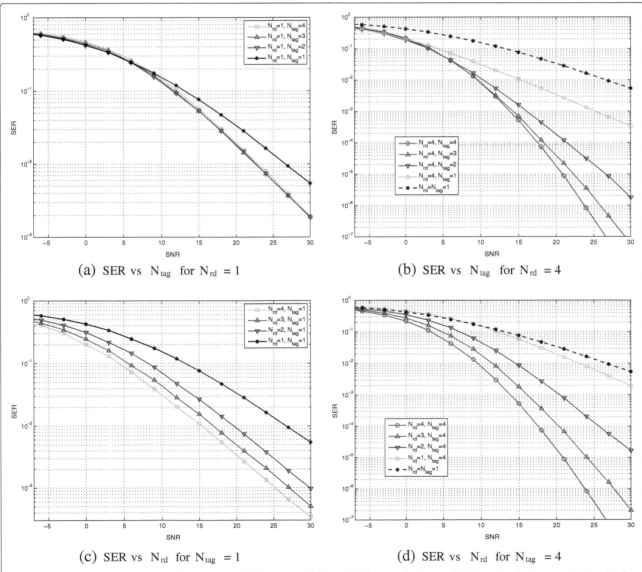

(a) SER vs $N_{tag}$ for $N_{rd} = 1$

(b) SER vs $N_{tag}$ for $N_{rd} = 4$

(c) SER vs $N_{rd}$ for $N_{tag} = 1$

(d) SER vs $N_{rd}$ for $N_{tag} = 4$

**Figure 2 SER of RFID MIMO systems for Scheme I with QPSK modulation. (a)**SER vs $N_{tag}$ for $N_{rd} = 1$ **(b)**SER vs $N_{tag}$ for $N_{rd} = 4$ **(c)**SER vs $N_{rd}$ for $N_{tag} = 1$ **(d)**SER vs $N_{rd}$ for $N_{tag} = 4$.

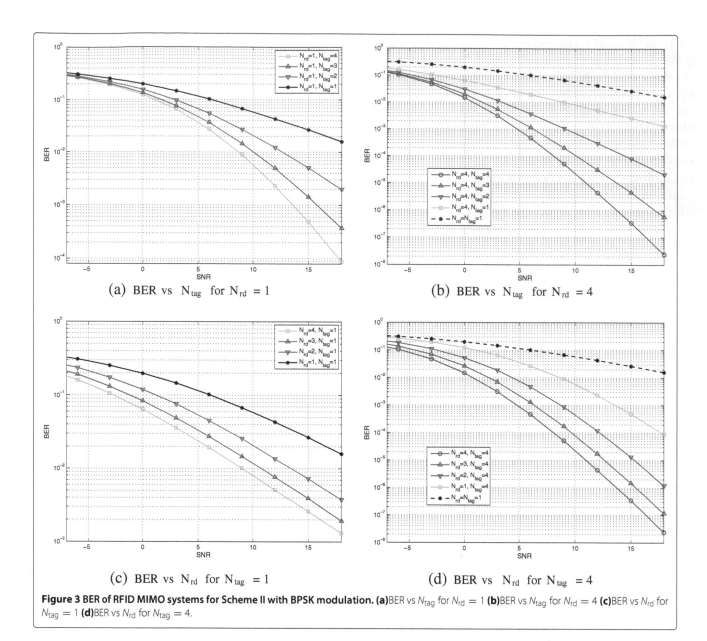

**Figure 3** BER of RFID MIMO systems for Scheme II with BPSK modulation. **(a)** BER vs $N_{tag}$ for $N_{rd} = 1$ **(b)** BER vs $N_{tag}$ for $N_{rd} = 4$ **(c)** BER vs $N_{rd}$ for $N_{tag} = 1$ **(d)** BER vs $N_{rd}$ for $N_{tag} = 4$.

**Claim 1.** Comparing the dashed curves, which corresponds to the performance of the non space-time encoded RFID system with single antenna at both reader and tag sides, and the solid curves in Figures 2(b), (d), and Figures 3(b), (d), we see that deploying multiple antennas at both reader and tag can greatly improve the SER/BER performance of RFID systems.

**Claim 2.** When $N_{rd}$ is fixed to be one, increasing $N_{tag}$ *considerably* decreases the BER of the system in Scheme II, but only *marginally* decreases the SER of the system in Scheme I. For example, when SNR=18 dB and $N_{rd} = 1$, the BER of Scheme II decreases from $1.6 \times 10^{-2}$ at $N_{tag} = 1$ to $2.0 \times 10^{-3}$ at $N_{tag} = 2$ and $8.8 \times 10^{-5}$ at $N_{tag} = 4$, respectively. For the same SNR and $N_{rd}$, the SER of Scheme I decreases from $4.7 \times 10^{-2}$ at $N_{tag} = 1$

to $2.9 \times 10^{-2}$ at $N_{tag} = 2$ and $3.0 \times 10^{-2}$ at $N_{tag} = 4$ respectively. The reason for this phenomenon is that the channel diversity provided by $N_{tag}$ antennas at the tag side is harvested by Scheme II [as seen from equations (11)-(13)], but not harvested by Scheme I [as seen from equation (17)].

**Claim 3.** When $N_{tag}$ is fixed to be one, increasing $N_{rd}$ *noticeably* and *monotonically* decreases the SER or BER of the system. This phenomenon can be clearly seen from Figure 2(c) and Figure 3(c). The reason is that only the array gain is provided by the system when $N_{tag} = 1$ and it is indeed collected by both Scheme I and Scheme II. Due to the double Rayleigh fading channel, the system performance cannot be improved conspicuously by only exploiting this array gain.

**Claim 4.** When $N_{rd}$ (or $N_{tag}$) is fixed and greater than one, increasing $N_{tag}$ (or $N_{rd}$) *greatly* decreases the SER or BER of the system, especially for Scheme II. For example, when SNR=18 dB and $N_{tag} = 4$, the SER of Scheme I decreases from $3.0 \times 10^{-2}$ at $N_{rd} = 1$ to $2.7 \times 10^{-3}$ at $N_{rd} = 2$ and $7.5 \times 10^{-5}$ at $N_{rd} = 4$, respectively. For the same SNR and $N_{tag}$, the BER of Scheme II decreases from $8.8 \times 10^{-5}$ at $N_{rd} = 1$ to $1.2 \times 10^{-6}$ at $N_{rd} = 2$ and $2.4 \times 10^{-8}$ at $N_{tag} = 4$ respectively. To achieve the BER=$8.8 \times 10^{-5}$ for the case of Scheme II and $N_{tag} = 4$, the SNR gain is about 7.5 dB and 10 dB, respectively, by deploying $N_{rd} = 2$ and $N_{rd} = 4$ antennas at the reader, compared to the single-antenna setup at the reader. On the other side, to achieve the BER=$1.3 \times 10^{-3}$ for the case of Scheme II and $N_{rd} = 4$, the SNR gain is about 9 dB and 13.5 dB, respectively, by deploying $N_{tag} = 2$ and $N_{tag} = 4$

antennas at the tag, compared to the single-antenna setup at the tag. This is dramatic improvement for the system performance.

**Claim 5.** Scheme II yields much better SER performance than Scheme I. There are two reasons. The first reason, which is obvious, is that different symbol constellations are used in Schemes I and II. In the above simulations, one symbol in Scheme I actually carries two bit information, while one symbol in Scheme II carries only one bit information. The second reason, which is somewhat subtle to see, is that the diversity gain harvested by Scheme I is lower than that harvested by Scheme II, even though Scheme II throw away the signal in another half signal space. This observation can be seen by comparing equations (11)-(13) and (22) (for Scheme II) and equations

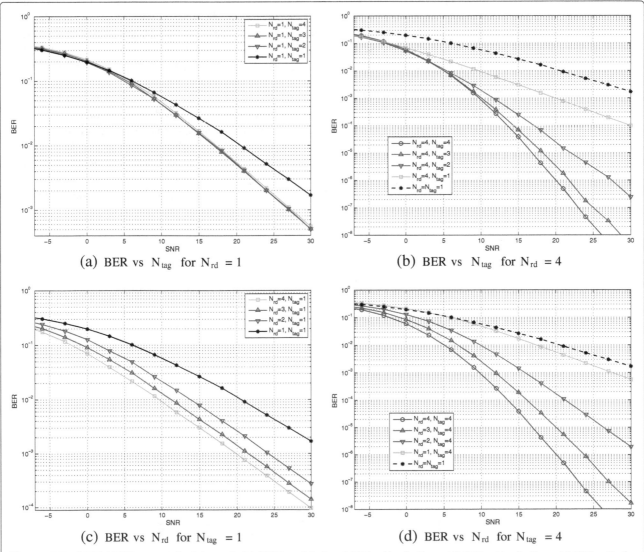

(a) BER vs $N_{tag}$ for $N_{rd} = 1$

(b) BER vs $N_{tag}$ for $N_{rd} = 4$

(c) BER vs $N_{rd}$ for $N_{tag} = 1$

(d) BER vs $N_{rd}$ for $N_{tag} = 4$

**Figure 4 BER of RFID MIMO systems for Scheme I with BPSK modulation. (a)**BER vs $N_{tag}$ for $N_{rd} = 1$ **(b)**BER vs $N_{tag}$ for $N_{rd} = 4$ **(c)**BER vs $N_{rd}$ for $N_{tag} = 1$ **(d)**BER vs $N_{rd}$ for $N_{tag} = 4$.

(17), (18) and (20) (for Scheme I). For Scheme I, it is seen from (17) and (18) that the $N_{tag}$ independent channels are not coherently summed. In (20), the $N_{rd}$ independent summed-channels are further summed. Thus Scheme I yields a diversity order of $N_{rd}$ and the system-inherited diversity order $N_{tag}$ is sacrificed. For Scheme II, it is seen from (11)-(13) that the $N_{tag}$ independent channels are first coherently summed, yielding a diversity order of $N_{tag}$. From (22), the $N_{rd}$ independent summed-channels are further summed, yielding a diversity order of $N_{rd}$. Thus a total diversity order of $N_{rd} \times N_{tag}$ is obtained in Scheme II.

**Claim 6.** Comparing Figure 2 and Figure 3, we can conclude that it is better to deploy as many antennas as possible at the reader. At least the number of antennas at the reader side should be not less than the number of antennas at the tag side. In this way, the full channel diversity generated by multiple antennas at the tag can be maximally exploited.

It may be argued that it is not fair to compare the SER performance of Scheme I and Scheme II, since the former uses QPSK modulation, while the latter uses BPSK modulation. To make the comparison complete, the BER performance of Scheme I with BPSK modulation is shown in Figure 4 for the corresponding cases. Figure 2, Figure 4 and Figure 3 show that the BER performance of Scheme I is much worse than that of Scheme II, even though the BER of Scheme I with BPSK modulation is lower than the SER of Scheme I with QPSK modulation for the same

configuration of antenna numbers at the reader and tag. By comparing Figure 4 and Figure 3 we can see that Claims 1-6 obtained based on the comparison between Figure 2 and Figure 3 also holds true qualitatively.

From the above phenomena, the following conclusions can be drawn: if the required data rate is not high, it is better to use real-symbol constellation for the transmitted symbols at the tag and correspondingly to use Scheme II decoding policy at the reader receiver; by keeping the cost of the system under constraint, it is better to deploy multiple tag antennas and reader antennas, and the number of reader antennas should be at least equal to the number of tag antennas.

It is interesting to compare the ROD based STC and Alamouti STC. Figure 5 shows the comparison. It can be seen that Scheme II and Alamouti STC yield the same BER performance, both are better than Scheme I. This is due to the fact that both Scheme II and Alamouti STC collect all the available channel diversities, while Scheme I does not.

Finally, let us compare the complexity of Scheme I and Scheme II. Both Scheme I and Scheme II perform the same processing, as shown in equations (4)-(6), for the transmitted symbols at the tag. As seen from (4)-(6), the symbol processing at the tag is quite simple: only the sign of the symbols to be transmitted needs to be changed at some time slots for some antennas. For the processing of a block of space-time decoding at the reader , Scheme I needs $N_{rd}(K^2 + K + N_{tag})$ complex multiplications and $N_{rd}K(K-1) + (N_{rd}-1)K + N_{rd}(N_{tag}-1) = N_{rd}(K^2 + N_{tag} - 1) - K$ complex additions, and Scheme II needs

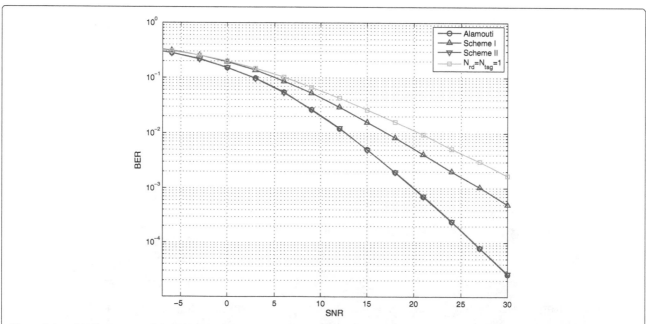

**Figure 5 A comparison among Scheme I, Scheme II and the Alamouti STC.** For the curves marked with "Scheme I", "Scheme II" and "Alamouti", $N_{tag} = 2$ and $N_{rd} = 1$.

$N_{rd}K^2$ complex multiplications, $N_{rd}K(K-1)$ complex additions, and $(N_{rd}-1)K$ real additions. Therefore, the computational burden of Scheme II is a little less than that of Scheme I. With regard to the hardware cost of the proposed STC technique, the main increase in the cost arises from the deployment of multiple antennas. The cost increase for the involved signal processing unit is negligible at either tags or readers, since the space-time encoding is very simple, which can be easily dealt with by the embedded chip at tags, and the required computational burden for the space-time decoding at readers is also negligible compared to the relatively strong computation power of readers.

## Conclusions

In this paper, we have discussed the space-time encoding and decoding problem for RFID MIMO systems. First, a mathematical model for this kind of system is developed from the viewpoint of signal processing, which makes it easy to design the STC schemes. Two STC schemes, namely Scheme I and Scheme II, are proposed. Simulation results illustrate that the proposed approaches can greatly improve the SER/BER performance of RFID systems, compared to non space-time encoded RFID systems. Besides, the SER/BER performance for Scheme I and Scheme II is thoroughly compared and it is found that Scheme II with the innate real-symbol constellation yields better SER/BER performance than Scheme I.

As is commonly assumed in the STC technique, the channel state information (CSI) is required to be available at the receiver side of the reader to adopt the technology of Scheme I and Scheme II. The channel estimation problem for RFID systems has been discussed in [8,10], where a method for estimating the channel of the whole chain, including forward link, backscattering coefficient, and backward link, is presented. However, to estimate the forward and backford channels $\mathbf{H}^f$ and $\mathbf{H}^b$ separately remains an open issue. On the other hand, if the CSI is also available at the transmitter side of the reader, we can combine the design for the reader transmit signal and STC for the tag to further improve the system performance. For the first step towards the optimal transmit signal design at the reader side, readers are referred to the reference [14].

**Competing interests**
The authors declare that they have no competing interests.

**References**
1. JD Griffin, GD Durgin, Gains for RF tags using multiple antennas. IEEE Trans. Antennas Propag. **56**, 563–570 (2008)
2. NC Karmakar (ed.), *Handbook of Smart Antennas for RFID Systems*. (Wiley, New Jersey, 2010)
3. AF Mindikoglu, A-J van der Veen, in *Proc. IEEE Int. Conf. Acoustics, Speech and Signal Processing 2008*. Separation of overlapping RFID signals by antenna arrays, Las Vegas, USA), pp. 2737–2740. 31 Mar. - 4 Apr. 2008
4. MA Ingram, MF Demirkol, D Kim, in *Int. Symp. Signals, Systems, and Electronics*. Transmit diversity and spatial multiplexing for RF links using modulated backscatter, (Tokyo, Japan). 24-27 July 2001
5. JD Griffin, GD Durgin, in *Proc. 2009 IEEE Int. Conf. RFID*. Multipath fading measurements for multi-antenna backscatter RFID at 5.8 GHz, (Orlando, USA), pp. 322–329. 27-28 Apr. 2009
6. C He, ZJ Wang, in *Proc. 23rd Canadian Conf. Electrical and Computer Engineering*. Gains by a space-time-code based signaling scheme for multiple-antenna RFID tags, (Calgary, Canada), 2-5 May 2010
7. D-Y Kim, H-S Jo, H Yoon, C Mun, B-J Jang, J-G Yook, Reverse-link interrogation range of a UHF MIMO-RFID system in Nakagami-m fading channels. IEEE Trans. Industrial Electronics. **57**, 1468–1477 (2010)
8. C Angerer, R Langwieser, G Maier, M Rupp, in *IEEE 2009 Int. Microwave Workshop on Wireless Sensing, Local Positioning, and RFID*. Maximal ratio combining receivers for dual antenna RFID readers, (Cavtat, Croatia), 24-25 Sept. 2009
9. R Langwieser, C Angerer, AL Scholtz, in *Proc. IEEE 2010 Radio and Wireless Symp*. A UHF frontend for MIMO applications in RFID, (New Orleans, USA), pp. 124–127. 10-14 Jan. 2010
10. C Angerer, R Langwieser, M Rupp, RFID reader receivers for physical layer collision recovery. IEEE Trans. Commun. **58**, 3526–3537 (2010)
11. M Mi, MH Mickle, C Capelli, H Switf, RF energy harvesting with multiple antennas in the same space. IEEE Antennas Propagation Mag. **47**(5), 100–106 (2005)
12. V Tarokh, H Jafarkhani, AR Calderbank, Spacetime block codes from orthogonal designs. IEEE Trans. Inform. Theory. **45**, 1456–1467 (1999)
13. T Kaiser, F Zheng, *Ultra Wideband Systems with MIMO*. ((Wiley, Chichester, 2010)
14. F Zheng, T Kaiser, in *4th Int. EURASIP Workshop on RFID Technology (RFID 2012)*. On the transmit signal design at the reader for RFID MIMO systems, Turin, Italy), 27-28 Sept. 2012

# 4

# An advanced physiological data logger for medical imaging applications

Tareq Hasan Khan and Khan A Wahid[*]

## Abstract

The interest of physiological data sensing and recording using wireless body sensor network has increased in recent years due to the advancement of miniature and portable electronic devices. In this study, the design of a portable and rechargeable data logger with high data rate multiple wireless connectivity (Bluetooth and 2.4-GHz radio frequency) is discussed. The data are logged in micro secure digital (SD) cards and can be transferred to PC or Smartphone using SD card reader, USB interface, or Bluetooth wireless link. Analog signals can also be logged through an 8-channel analog-to-digital interface. A graphical LCD with touch screen is added for control and diagnosis. The hardware is generic and targeted for various medical imaging and data collection applications. The functionality of the prototype is later tested for wireless capsule endoscopy and skin temperature logging application.

**Keywords:** Data logger, Bluetooth, Wireless link, Capsule endoscopy, Analog-to-digital

## Introduction

Recent advances in miniature and portable bio-sensors, embedded processors, and wireless technologies have caused a rapid growth in sensing and recording physiological signals for medical applications. Bio-sensors convert body signals such as temperature, blood pressure, breathing [1], heartbeat [2-4], etc., to electrical signals to be processed, transmitted, and recorded in electronic devices [5]. Data coming from implanted or external body sensors can be transmitted wirelessly to a portable and wearable data logger unit, thus giving the patient the freedom to do household works during continuous data recording without the hassle of cumbersome wired devices. After logging is completed, the data are transferred to a personal computer (PC) or Smartphone which may be later examined by physicians. In this article, a portable, battery-operated data logger unit having wireless connectivity with the bio-sensor is discussed. The design of the data logger is general and can be used for several medical applications. In this article, the prototype is demonstrated for video wireless capsule endoscopy (WCE) [6] and skin temperature logging application.

Several works are found in the literature related to data logging for medical applications. In [7], a data logger unit for storing galvanic skin response for autistic patients is discussed. The data logger receives data using RS232 interface and stores it in a 16-MB EEPROM. In [2], the design of a data logger is discussed for electrocardiogram (ECG) signals. The design converts the analog ECG signals to digital and stores them in 20-MB flash memory cards. An ECG signal data logger with custom-designed ASIC controller for multimedia card (MMC) is discussed in [3]. In [8], a fetal and maternal heart beat signal recorder is discussed which detects signals using skin electrodes, converts them to digital, and stores in temporary SRAM for later transfer to PC by RS232 interface. A portable data logger with three body-fixed inertial sensors for monitoring the physical activities of Parkinson's disease patients is proposed in [9]. In [10], the design of a microcontroller-based portable data logger for medical application is described which contains three-electrode ECG circuit, three accelerometers, a pressure sensor, and a temperature sensor. The module can store data in 4-Mb flash memory in real-time or can send data to PC by a wired serial interface. A low power and small size design of an ECG signal recorder is described in [11] for the purpose of long-term portable recording. Data are stored in secure

* Correspondence: khan.wahid@usask.ca
Department of Electrical and Computer Engineering, University of Saskatchewan, Saskatoon, SK S7N5A9, Canada

digital (SD) card and can be transferred to PC by an isolated RS232 interface. In [12], fetal movements are recorded continuously on several pregnant patients using fetal movement acceleration measurement recorder to study its suitability in long-term home monitoring application. The work in [13] presents an IP core for FPGA-based ECG data transmission using wired telephone line through modem interface. Note that, the above-discussed data loggers receive data from body sensors using wired connections which is not comfortable for patients. In [14], a microcontroller-based data logger is implemented by using a four-channel analog-to-digital converter (ADC) to measure sweat activity. Data are stored in an EEPROM with the capability of storing data for over 2 days when one measurement is taken per minute. An RF transceiver is used to export the data to a monitoring host PC. A wireless data logger for recording human movements is discussed in [15]; however, the data logger is not portable as it takes power from house AC line supply, thus restricts the patient's movement near to the data logger. In [16], an ARM microcontroller-based wearable heart rate monitor system is described. It gathers ECE data and sends the data to a nearby PC wirelessly using Bluetooth. It does not have internal storage memory and thus the patient's movements are restricted near the host PC. In [17], a Java2-based software for cell phone is developed to store laboratory data, such as blood pressure, blood urea nitrogen, creatinine, Hb A1c (glycosylated hemoglobin), and other pertinent comments, into a cell phone memory. However, the cell phone does not have any sensor connected with it for automatic data acquisition.

The data logger presented in this study is portable and has high data rate of 2 Mbps wireless connectivity with implantable or externally attached body sensors which eliminated the need for wires. It also has high memory capacity of 4 GB micro SD card, graphical display for showing images, graphs, charts in real time, keypad, and touch screen-based user interface. After logging, the data can be transferred to PC using an SD card reader at a speed of up to 25 MB/s or using an USB interface. Optionally, the data can also be transferred to PC or Smartphone wirelessly using Bluetooth technology. An illustration of a data logging system of a wireless body sensor system using the proposed data logger is shown in Figure 1.

## Design requirements

In order to make an advanced data logger that is useful to various medical image and video application, we consider the following design requirements.

- The data logger must have both wired and wireless input connectivity so that it can be connected with various in-body sensors. For example, for accelerometer or heart monitoring system, it uses wired analog interface, whereas for applications like WCE, it uses wireless RF interface.
- The data logger must have high storage capacity for data intensive application. For example, in WCE, to store QVGA (320 × 240) color, 24 bits-per-pixel images transmitted at 2 frames-per-second (FPS) having 80% compression ratio (CR) for 10 h, at least 3.1 GB memory space is required as calculated using (1).

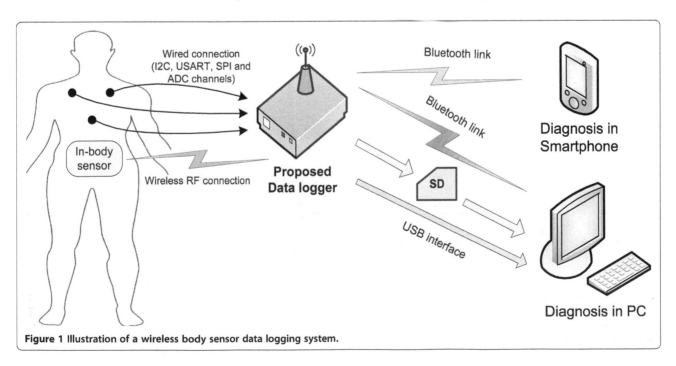

**Figure 1 Illustration of a wireless body sensor data logging system.**

$$
\begin{aligned}
Store\,capacity = {} & Width \times Height \\
& \times Bits\,Per\,Pixel \times (1 - CR) \\
& \times FPS \\
& \times Logging\,time\,(in\,hour) \\
& \times 3600 \quad\quad\quad\quad\quad\quad\quad (1)
\end{aligned}
$$

- The logger must consume low power so that the battery runs for longer time. For example, in WCE, it must run continuously for at least 10 h.
- The data rate of the wireless transceiver and the writing speed of the data logger must be high enough to support storing color video. For example, for QVGA resolution at 2 FPS and 80% CR, the required data rate of the wireless transceiver is at least 720 kbps. The writing speed in storage memory must be higher than 90 kB/s in this case.
- The data logger should be able to communicate with the bio-sensor in real-time during logging and control various features of the sensor, such as, changing image resolution, data rate, data types, etc. The interface used for this interactive control operation must be easy to use.
- Real-time viewing (RTV) of the data (i.e., images, charts, etc.) is another important feature. It will assist a physician performing diagnosis in real-time.
- After data logging is completed, there must be easy and fast way to transfer the data to workstation PC or Smartphone for diagnostics. As a result, we propose to have multiple wired and wireless output (or transfer) connectivity such as, USB interface, micro SD, and Bluetooth.
- To be wearable and easily portable, the physical size and weight of the data logger must be as less as possible.

## Methods

The data logger is designed to have four layers as shown in Figure 2. Each layer completes its functionality by using the resources of its lower layers. By only changing the application layer firmware, the data logger can be used in several applications, without modifying the lower

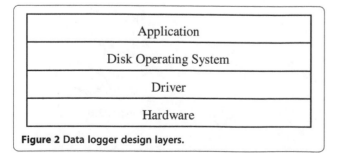

**Figure 2 Data logger design layers.**

level driver and hardware layers. A brief description of each layer is given in the following sections.

### Hardware

The overall block diagram of the hardware is shown in Figure 3. The design consists of a microcontroller (MCU) and several peripherals connected with it. Each major component of the design is briefly described below.

#### Microcontroller

A microcontroller from the XMEGA-A1 [18] family is chosen for this design. A comparison of XMEGA with other microcontrollers is given in Table 1. To increase the data sample rate and writing speed in the storage device, a high-speed MCU is required. Moreover, several peripherals are connected with the MCU using SPI and USART protocols. The XMEGA microcontroller has more hardware SPI and USART units than others which is an advantage. It has 78 programmable I/O lines, 128-kB flash for program storage, 8-kB SRAM, and 2-kB EEPROM to store user defined variables temporarily and permanently namely.

#### Graphical LCD with touch screen

To enable RTV of images, graphs, charts, texts, etc., during data logging, a 2.4″ graphical LCD [21] capable of displaying 320 × 240 pixels (QVGA) using 262,144 colors is chosen. The display also contains resistive touch area, enabling advanced and interactive user interface. The LCD connects with the MCU using hardware

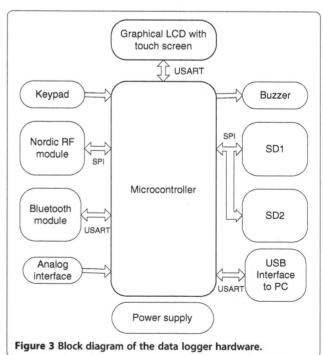

**Figure 3 Block diagram of the data logger hardware.**

**Table 1 Comparison of several MCU**

| | Clock (MHz) | SRAM (kB) | Hardware SPI | Hardware USART | Core power (mW) | Unit price (USD) |
|---|---|---|---|---|---|---|
| PIC (PIC16F1947) [19] | 32 | 1 | 2 | 2 | 11.8 | $3.20 |
| ARM Cortex M3 (LPC1316FBD48) [20] | 25[a] | 8 | 2 | 1 | 13.2 | $4.50 |
| AVR (ATMEGA644P) [18] | 20 | 4 | 1 | 2 | 87.5 | $7.39 |
| XMEGA-A1 (ATXMEGA128A1) [18] | 32 | 8 | 4 | 8 | 66 | $10.20 |

[a]can be increased using PLL up to 72 MHz.

USART and it receives command from the MCU at a baud rate of 2 Mbps.

### Data storage device

In Table 2, the comparisons of different permanent memory storage device in a single chip are shown [18]. Parallel EEPROMs need significant number of I/O lines to interface with MCU. Serial EEPROMs need relatively lesser I/O lines; however, their memory capacity is low and cascading several EEPROMs for increasing capacity, needs significant area, and more I/O lines. Micro SD card [22] seems to be the best choice as it has high memory capacity and needs only few I/O lines. Moreover, its defect and error management unit promises reliable data read/write. In the data logger design, two 2-GB SD card are connected with the MCU using hardware SPI at a 16-MHz clock speed. Note that, several SD cards may be connected as shown in Figure 4 and the storage capacity can be increased significantly. When one SD becomes full, data are written in another SD card automatically, and thus data logging can continue without the interruption of replacing SD card. Moreover, data can be transferred from SD card to PC using SD/MMC card reader at high speed such as 25 MB/s.

### Wireless transceiver

The characteristics of several wireless transceiver units are shown in Table 3. The major challenge of any wireless link is the data corruption in the transmission channel. Nordic transceiver [23] contains cyclic redundancy check (CRC)-based error detection and retry with auto acknowledgement (i.e., resend data packet until success)

feature which makes the link promisingly reliable, though several retry may decrease the overall data transmission rate in a noisy environment [15]. We selected Nordic for our application and it is connected with the MCU using hardware SPI at 8 MHz speed.

### Bluetooth

A Bluetooth transceiver [28] is also connected with the MCU using hardware USART at 230-kbps baud. Data transmitted from wireless body sensor can be captured either by Nordic or by Bluetooth in the data logger and then can be uploaded wirelessly to personal computer or Smartphone using Bluetooth.

### USB interface

The design also contains an USB interface (as shown in Figure 5) that has 1-Mbps data rate to connect with PC using wired link. This wired interface can optionally be used to transfer data to workstation PC after data logging.

### Analog interface

Analog data can also be taken in the data logger using the wired analog interface. The analog interface consists of multiplexed eight programmable ADC channels, eight analog comparators, and two digital-to-analog converter channels of the microcontroller. Analog data such as body temperature, blood pressure can be taken using the ADC channels and then the data can be saved in SD

**Table 2 Comparison of different permanent memory storage device**

| | EEPROM | | | | Micro SD |
|---|---|---|---|---|---|
| | Parallel | Serial | | | |
| | | I2C | SPI | 3 WIRE | |
| Capacity | 512 kB | 64 kB | 64 kB | 2 kB | 2 GB[a] |
| Clock (MHz) | 5 | 0.4 | 20 | 2 | 25[b] |
| Pins required | 30 | 2 | 4 | 4 | 4 |
| Error correction | No | No | No | No | Yes |

[a]Maximum capacity for FAT16 file-system for a single SD.
[b]In standard SPI mode.

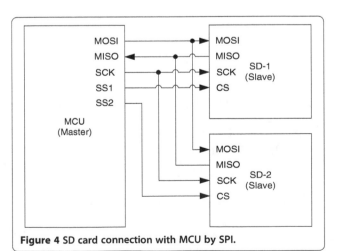

**Figure 4 SD card connection with MCU by SPI.**

**Table 3 Comparison of different wireless transceivers**

|                   | Zarlink [24] | Linx [25] | Micrel [26] | Zigbee [27] | Nordic [23] |
|-------------------|--------------|-----------|-------------|-------------|-------------|
| Frequency band    | 402 MHz      | 433 MHz   | 915 MHz     | 2.4 GHz     | 2.4 GHz     |
| Data rate         | 800 kbps     | 10 kbps   | 115 kbps    | 250 kbps    | 2 Mbps      |
| Retry and auto ack. | Yes        | No        | No          | Yes         | Yes         |
| TX current (mA)   | 5            | 3.4       | 25          | 250         | 11.3        |
| RX current (mA)   | 5            | 5.2       | 13.5        | 55          | 13.5        |

card and its real-time graphical plot can be displayed on LCD.

### Power supply

As the power source of the data logger, three 3.7V polymer lithium-ion battery, each having 2000-mAh rating are used in parallel, thus making total battery rating of 6000-mAh. The design also contains a 200-mA having 3.3–V output voltage boost converter [29] and an under voltage protection of 2.6 V. A 500-mA constant current battery charging circuit [30] using PC's USB port is also included in the design so that recharging can be done without removing the batteries from the hardware. To indicate and monitor the charging level, the battery voltage is sampled using a potentiometer and fed to an ADC channel of the microcontroller.

### Other peripherals

To interact with the user, the design contains four push button switches. The button press is signaled to the MCU as interrupt. A buzzer is included in the design to generate small beep sounds.

### Driver firmware and disk operating system (DOS)

The driver layer consists of low-level firmware for accessing different hardware peripherals. They are briefly described below.

### Graphical LCD and touch screen

The driver for graphical LCD contains functions for initializing the LCD, drawing pixels at any position by providing the co-ordinate and color information, setting background color and brightness, taking the LCD in low-power sleep and wake-up modes, etc. The touch screen driver functions provide the co-ordinate when a touch is made on the screen.

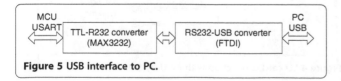

**Figure 5 USB interface to PC.**

### Keypad

When any of the four keys (*Up*, *Down*, *Enter*, and *Escape*) is pressed, the program jumps to its corresponding interrupt routine and sets a flag for that particular key. By executing a *get_key ()* function, the last key pressed is detected by reading the flags.

### Wireless RF transceiver

It contains functions for reading and writing data to the configuration registers of Nordic RF module using SPI, setting the RF module as transmitter or receiver, flashing, and checking the status of internal Fast in, Fast out (FIFO) buffers, sending and receiving data packets to/from other RF module, taking the module to power down and up mode, etc.

### Bluetooth

These functions initialize the Bluetooth device as *slave*, connect with nearby Bluetooth *master* devices (such as Smartphone or PC) when request is made, then send and receive data to/from master Bluetooth device using USART. It also contains functions to take the module in low-power sleep and wake-up modes.

### Buzzer

To generate a "*beep*" sound, square pulses of 1 kHz are sent for the duration of 500 ms to the buzzer.

### SD card and DOS

It contains functions for checking whether any SD card is present in the slot, selecting and initializing the SD card, checking the available memory space, etc. A DOS for embedded system [31] is implemented which handles file operations. Using DOS, data files can be created, read, written, and deleted. The DOS implements FAT16 file system and the maximum writing speed in SD card is found to be 115 kB/s when the MCU is running at 32 MHz.

### USB interface

This driver sends and receives data to/from PC. Data are transferred from the MCU using USART protocol and through an RS232-USB converter chip, data are packed according to USB protocol to transmit to PC through USB port.

### Analog interface

It configures the ADC resolutions (such as 8, 10, 12 bit), reference voltage, channel gain, etc. It provides functions using which the corresponding digital data of an analog channel can be read and processed. It also contains functions to check battery voltages in the *Power Supply* module.

### Application firmware

This layer contains the firmware designed for a specific data logging application. The proposed data logger is generic that encompasses many different medical applications such as ECG, heartbeat, capsule endoscopy, blood pressure, etc. In this study, we have implemented the firmware for capsule endoscopy application [6].

### User interface

In order to set different settings such as image size, imaging mode, enable/disable real-time view, etc., a menu-based graphical user interface is designed in the data logger as shown in Figure 6. User can use either four keys (*Up*, *Down*, *Enter*, and *Escape*) or touch to select different menu options. Additional features may easily be added to the interface if needed.

### Data logging

In order to receive data from the bio-sensor (i.e., capsule in this case study), a command is sent wirelessly to the capsule from the data logger containing information of required image size and imaging mode. After receiving command, the capsule starts to send the data packets of an image frame in compressed from. The data logger reads the packets and stores them in SD card. A timer is also used to add time stamp for each image frame. The end of a frame is detected by a pattern of consecutive four zero bytes. The overall data logging procedure is shown in Figure 7.

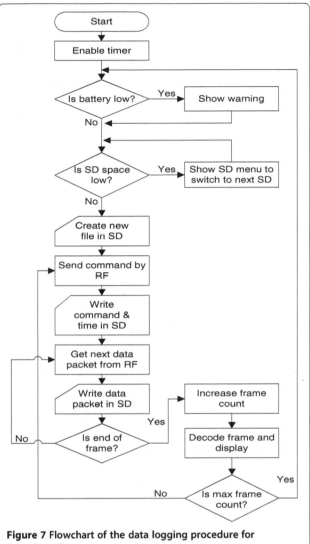

**Figure 7** Flowchart of the data logging procedure for capsule endoscopy.

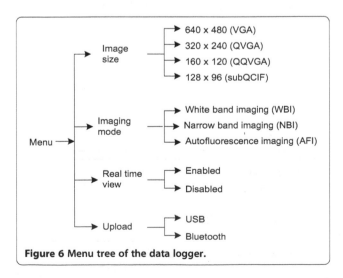

**Figure 6** Menu tree of the data logger.

### Image decoding algorithm

In capsule endoscopy, image data are transmitted wirelessly from the ingested capsule in compressed form. Our proposed compression algorithm consists of a novel color space, YEF [32], which is designed by analyzing the unique properties of endoscopic images for better compression. After converting RGB pixels to YEF color space, the compressor takes the difference of consecutive pixels (left pixel prediction) and then encodes the differences in variable length coding such as in Golomb-rice code. Based on the nature of endoscopic images,

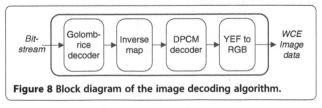

**Figure 8** Block diagram of the image decoding algorithm.

```
1. q := the number of 0 in the code until a 1 is reached
2. if q < (g_limit – log_2 I – 1) then
3.      r := next k bits in binary
4.      m_dx := q × M + r
5. else
6.      m_dx := next 8 bits in binary
```

**Figure 9** Pseudo code for Golomb-rice decoder.

several sub-sampling schemes (such as YEF812) on the chrominance (E and F) components are applied. YEF812 sub-sampling means Y is not sub-sampled, E is sub-sampled after every 8 pixels, and V is sub-sampled after every 4 pixels. The sub-sampling is performed in horizontal direction only. A customized corner clipping scheme is also implemented to remove uninteresting corner area of the image to increase CR [33]. The proposed algorithm works in raster scan fashion and can directly be interfaced with commercial image sensors, eliminating the need of buffer memory. The compressor has an average CR of 80.4% and reconstructed image quality have peak signal-to-noise ratio (PSNR) index of about 43 dB.

In the data logger, the decoder for the above discussed compression algorithm is implemented for RTV of images. The overall image decoding algorithm is shown in Figure 8.

In the compressed bit stream, the first pixel component is stored in raw 8-bit format. This is read in $X$, where $X$ is the actual pixel value. In YEF color space, $X$ corresponds to $Y$, $E$, and $F$ components. $Xp$ is the next predicted pixel value. Initially

$$Xp = X \qquad (2)$$

Next we define

$$I = 2^8 = 256 \qquad (3)$$

$$M = 2^k, \qquad (4)$$

where $k$ is Golomb-rice code parameter. The maximum length of Golomb-rice code ($g_{\text{limit}}$) is chosen as 32. The pseudo code for Golomb-rice code decoder is shown in Figure 9.

The decoded $m\_dx$ is then inversely mapped to signed integer as shown in the pseudo code in Figure 10.

The differential pulse coded modulation decoder then calculates the next actual pixel value using (5) and sets the prediction for next pixel using (2).

$$X = Xp + dX \qquad (5)$$

After the actual component values of a pixel are calculated, they are converted to RGB color space using (6).

$$\begin{bmatrix} R \\ G \\ B \end{bmatrix} = \begin{bmatrix} 1 & 3.33 & 2.67 \\ 1 & -2 & 0 \\ 1 & 0.67 & -2.67 \end{bmatrix} \begin{bmatrix} Y \\ E - 128 \\ F - 128 \end{bmatrix} \qquad (6)$$

The $R$, $G$, $B$ pixels are sent to graphical LCD for displaying the image frame. In order to display VGA images in QVGA size show, the VGA image is sub-sampled by 4. In Figure 11, the original and reconstructed images of an endoscopic image are shown.

### Data uploading

After data logging, data can be uploaded to PC or Smartphone using any of the following three methods: (1) by removing the SD cards from data logger, (2) using USB interface, and/or (3) using wireless Bluetooth link. When using USB or Bluetooth link, a file transfer protocol is implemented which sends at first the filename, then the file size, and then its data bytes. A PC software is developed to receive the data from the data logger by USB or by Bluetooth. After receiving compressed data, the PC software can decode and display the images as video at any given FPS.

```
1. If m_dx mod 2 = 0 then
2.      dx := m_dx / 2
3. else
4.      dx := -((m_dX+1) / 2)
```

**Figure 10** Pseudo code for inverse mapping.

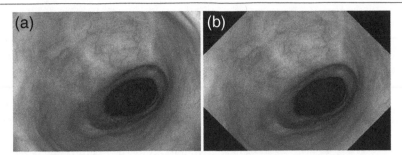

**Figure 11 Comparison between original and reconstructed image (a) Original image. (b) Reconstructed image (PSNR is 43 dB).**

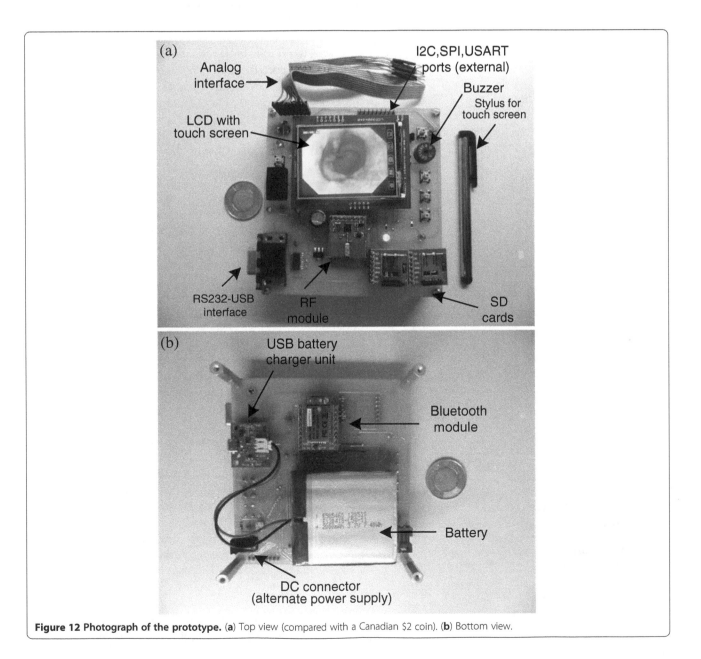

**Figure 12 Photograph of the prototype. (a)** Top view (compared with a Canadian $2 coin). (**b**) Bottom view.

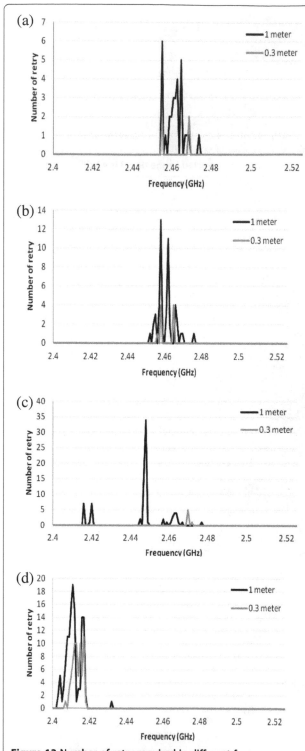

**Figure 13** Number of retry required in different frequency channels; (a) in home environment, (b) in home environment near Smartphone in use, (c) in hospital environment near medical imaging department, (d) in hospital environment near cancer department.

## Results
### Specification of data logger prototype
The proposed data logger for capsule endoscopy application is prototyped in our laboratory as shown in Figure 12. The size of the prototype is $10 \times 10 \times 2$ cm. The weight of the PCB is 114 g; each battery weighs 37 g, making the total weight of the prototype 151 g with one battery. With three batteries, the total weight is $114 + (3 \times 37) = 225$ g. Note that, for capsule endoscopy application, minimum 10-h battery life is required. If we use one battery instead of three batteries then the hardware can run for $35.3/3 = 11.8$ h, which meets the design requirement for capsule endoscopy application. As the design of the proposed data logger is general, three batteries are used to meet other applications which may require more data logging time.

### Experimental results for RF channel selection
We have conducted experiments to observe the interference of other frequencies (such as Wi-Fi, Smartphone, medical instruments, etc.) in both hospital (Royal University Hospital, Saskatoon, SK, Canada) and home environment [15] on the Nordic transceiver in its different frequency channels. Several experiments showed that using duck antenna [34] instead of chip antenna improves the RF transmission quality. In Figure 13, the number of retry required by the transceiver to send 100 data packets (each packet contains 32 bytes) in different frequency channels in several environments using duck antenna is shown. As the data logger is wearable, the distance between the sensor and the logger should be less than 1 m (taking a conservative approach).

From Figure 13, we see that several retries are required from 2.4 to 2.48 GHz channels due to interference in different environments. So, we have decided to operate the transceiver in a clear channel at 2.5 GHz which will cause minimum number of retries during data transmission. Note that, the Bluetooth device will not have any interference effect on Nordic transceiver as they work in a mutually exclusive way.

It is possible to select the best channel dynamically during data logging. The procedure is as follows.

1. The data logger will go to *channel selection mode* after a configurable time (for instance, every after 30 min) or by user at anytime from selecting a menu option.
2. The data logger will send a command to the bio-sensor to set its transceiver at the first channel and the data logger will also set its transceiver to the first channel. Then the data logger will send some data-packets to the bio-sensor and log the number of retry required for that channel. This step will be done for all the available channels (in Nordic

transceiver, a total of 126 channels starting from 2.4 to 2.526 GHz are available).

3. Then the channel which has minimum retries will be selected and the data logger will send a command containing the channel number to the bio-sensor so that both data logger and bio-sensor communicates at the same channel.

## Experimental results simulating capsule endoscopy scenario

An MCU-based capsule emulator hardware as shown in Figure 14 is developed for testing the data logger prototype. The compression algorithm proposed in [32,33] is implemented in a PC software and compressed bit-stream data for several endoscopic images are generated using the software. Then the compressed bit-stream data are downloaded in the program-memory of the MCU of the capsule emulator. When the capsule emulator receives a command from the data logger through the RF interface, it starts to send compressed image data to the data logger wirelessly.

In order to test the data logger for a capsule endoscopy scenario, the capsule emulator hardware is inserted inside a turkey and the data logger is placed 0.3–m away from the capsule as shown in Figure 15. The data logger received images wirelessly through the turkey's skin and flesh successfully from the capsule. As the data logger is wearable and it is generally worn at one side of the belly, the distance between a swallowed capsule and data logger will be near 0.3–m for human endoscopy. The data logger is also placed about 1 m apart from the inserted capsule and images transmitted successfully.

## Experiment results for multiple body sensors

In order to test the wired analog interfaces of the data logger prototype, two temperature sensors [35] are connected with two analog ADC channels. The temperature sensor gives analog voltage output proportional to its surface temperature (0.01 V/°C). The sensors are placed on two places of a human hand as shown in Figure 16. The data logger is programmed to sample data at 10 Hz. It converts the sampled analog data to digital, stores them in SD card along with time stamp,

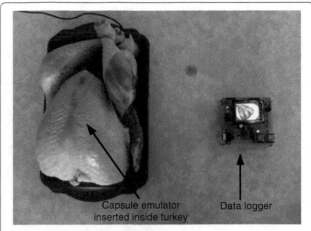

**Figure 15** Experimental setup: capsule emulator is placed inside a turkey and the data logger is placed outside.

and plots the data on graphical LCD for real-time display as shown in Figure 16. The logged data can be transferred to PC or Smartphone and further analysis can be done. By using the analog channels, blood pressure, ECG, heartbeat signals can also be logged and displayed.

## Power consumption

The power consumption of the data logger in different modes is shown in Table 4. When RTV is disabled, the graphical LCD is taken to sleep mode to save power. In Figure 17, the percentage power consumption of different hardware components during data logging (using Nordic RF link, in RTV enabled mode) is shown. We see that the LCD consumes the majority of power (54%) if the RTV is enabled. It should be noted that the RTV mode is not a normal mode of operation, rather a special feature that a physician may use if desired. After the data logging is completed, it can be transferred to PC by removing the SD card, which costs no power for the data logger. When transferring data using Bluetooth, the LCD and Nordic RF are taken to sleep mode to save power. During data transfer by USB interface, the Bluetooth is also taken to sleep mode.

## Comparison with other works

The overall specification of the designed data logger and its comparison with other works are shown in Table 5. Comparing with other works on data loggers in the literature, the proposed data logger has high-speed wireless connectivity including Bluetooth, contains graphical LCD for real-time data viewing, and touch screen. The storage space is sufficient for many other medical applications; moreover, it can be increased easily by connecting more SD cards as shown in Figure 4 or implementing FAT32 file system in the firmware which

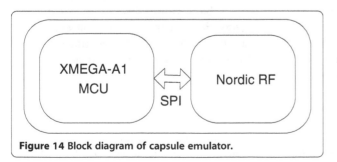

**Figure 14** Block diagram of capsule emulator.

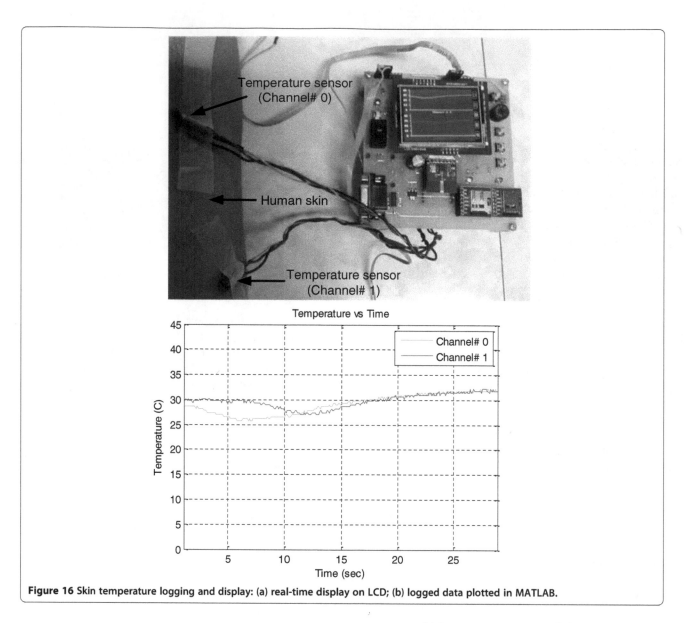

**Figure 16** Skin temperature logging and display: (a) real-time display on LCD; (b) logged data plotted in MATLAB.

can support higher capacity SD card (8 GB or higher) than FAT16. The writing speed and RF bandwidth of the data logger is sufficiently high to capture and store data at high sampling rate. Thus, the proposed data logger fulfills all the design requirements as discussed in Design requirements section for capsule endoscopy application. The data logger is designed for capturing images and images need more RF bandwidth, disk space, writing speed, etc., than recording other physiological signals such as heart beat, blood pressure, temperature, etc. So, the proposed data logger can be used efficiently in other medical applications.

## Discussion

### Wireless data transmission

The medical implantable communication service (MICS) compatible RF transceiver, which works at 402–405

**Table 4 Power consumption in different modes**

| Mode | Current (mA) | Power (mW) @ 3.3 V |
|---|---|---|
| Display menu | 160 | 528 |
| Data logging in SD card | | |
| RTV enabled | 170 | 561 |
| RTV disabled | 90 | 297 |
| Data transfer to PC | | |
| Using SD card reader | 0 | 0 |
| Bluetooth | 140 | 462 |
| USB interface | 93 | 307 |

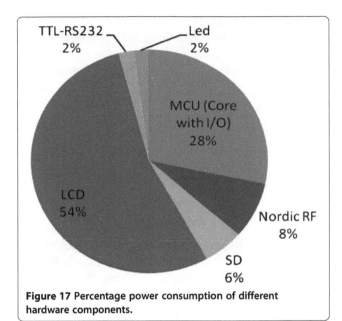

**Figure 17** Percentage power consumption of different hardware components.

**Table 6 Engineering cost of the data logger**

| Task | Time required (hours) | Personnel qualification | Number of personnel |
|---|---|---|---|
| Requirement analysis | 40 | Researcher (graduate student) | One |
| Specification and system design | 24 | | |
| Hardware/software partitioning | 16 | Embedded system engineer (or similar) | One |
| Purchasing components, tools, and compilers | 5 | | |
| Hardware design | 40 | | |
| Firmware design | 48 | | |
| Prototyping, debugging, and testing | 40 | | |
| PCB design and testing | 40 | Technician | One |

MHz frequency, is the most suitable for transmitting data through the human body [36]. However, the MICS RF transceiver vendor, Zarlink [24], sells a low data rate (effective data rate around 500 kpbs [37]) transceiver (ZL70102) which is not sufficient even for 2 FPS capsule endoscopy application. Zarlink has a custom transceiver (ZL70081) having a data rate of 2.7 Mbps which is not available for public purchase. So, we used the RF transceiver by Nordic [23], which works at 2.4 GHz frequency band and having a data rate of 2 Mbps. However, the effective data rate with minimum header information is 1.68 Mbps. The studies in [37,38] show that 2.4 GHz transceivers, such as Nordic, can effectively be used to get data wirelessly through animal body.

In this design, the Nordic transceiver was configured in *auto acknowledgement* mode. In auto acknowledge mode, after receiving a data packet, the receiver checks the CRC bits and detects whether there was any error during the transmission of the packet. If there was any error, then it requests the transmitter to resend the data

packet again. This process goes on until the packet is transmitted successfully. So, in *auto acknowledgement* mode, no data loss happens, though the number of retries will decrease the overall data rate or application throughput. If the receiver is unable to detect error using CRC, then depending upon which bits get corrupted, the reconstructed image will have different distortions. The image compression algorithm [32,33] used here is line-based differential coding (i.e., works row-by-row in raster scan fashion). In some cases, one row (or part of a row) of the image pixels may get corrupted if undetectable errors occurs in data packets. In worst case, the entire image frame may get corrupted.

Commercial capsule endoscopy products [6] such as *PillCam SB*, *EndoCapsule*, and *MiroCam* send images of size 256 × 256, 256 × 256, and 320 × 320, respectively. VGA (640 × 480) images are difficult to sent at 2 FPS because it requires very high data rate custom design RF transmitter. Though, some research works are available in the literature [39,40] on high data rate (as high as 15

**Table 5 Comparison with other data loggers**

| | Memory capacity | Sampling rate (writings speed) | Wireless | Analog interface | Graphical LCD | Touch input | Battery life (hour) |
|---|---|---|---|---|---|---|---|
| [7] | 16 MB | 13.2 kHz | No | Yes | No | No | 50 |
| [2] | 20 MB | 200 Hz | No | Yes | No | No | – |
| [8] | – | 500 Hz | No | Yes | No | No | 24 |
| [15] | – | 60 Hz | 250 kbps | No | No | No | –[a] |
| [3] | 512 MB | 33 kS/s | No | Yes | No | No | 72 |
| [30] | 512 kB | – | No | Yes | No | No | 0.23 |
| [11] | 512 MB | – | No | Yes | No | No | 93.6 |
| This study | 4 GB[b] | 192 k pixel/s[c] (115 kbps) | 2 Mbps link and Bluetooth | Yes | Yes | Yes | 35.3 |

[a]not battery operated, [b]expandable, [c]for 80% CR.

**Table 7 Manufacturing cost of the data logger**

| Item | Price (USD) |
|---|---|
| Hardware components (LCD, MCU, RF unit, Bluetooth unit, misc) | $180 |
| Programmer unit (one-time cost) | $40 |
| PCB fabrication | $40 |
| Total | $260.00 |

Mbps) transmitter for capsule endoscopy, however, they are not commercially available yet. So, the bottleneck of sending VGA images at 2 FPS is the RF transmitter. However, VGA images can be sent at lower FPS using the limited available bandwidth of the commercially available RF transmitters. In order to send VGA color images at 1 FPS, having 80% CR for 10 h, the memory space, the RF data rate, and the writing speed should be at least 6.2 GB, 1440 kbps, and 180 kB/s, respectively. To increase the size of memory capacity, the number of SD cards as shown in Figure 4 can be increased to more than 2. The *MISO*, *MOSI*, and *SCK* pins of the additional SD cards will be connected directly with the MCU's *MISO*, *MOSI*, and *SCK* pins and extra SS pin from the MCU needs to connect with the additional SD cards SS pins. Moreover, memory capacity can be also increased without changing any hardware design. Secure Digital High Capacity (SDHC) cards can be used instead of SD cards which have a capacity of 32 GB and have higher writing speed than SD cards [41]. In order to read/write data in SDHC, FAT32 file system needs to be implemented in the firmware instead of FAT16.

### Cost of developing the data logger prototype

The engineering cost of the proposed data logger is approximately around 260 h. The task list, tentative time required for each task, qualification, and number of personnel are shown in Table 6. This approach can easily be adapted by other researchers interested in similar development. The manufacturing cost of the data logger is shown in Table 7. It should be noted that the cost of programmer module is one-time. For bulk manufacturing, the cost will significantly be lower.

### Future works

A small size FPGA-based capsule prototype is now under development where a novel image compression algorithm proposed in [32,33] is implemented. After the final capsule prototype is developed, it will be inserted in pigs intestine [42] due to its relatively similar gastrointestinal functions in comparison to human and live images will be captured for more rigorous animal testing.

Testing the data logger with capsule endoscopy prototype in several human patients faces several challenges. A number of capsule prototypes need to be manufactured which

requires significant amount of time, money, and human resource. Then the permission from Food and Drug Administration [43] needs to be taken for swallowing the prototype capsules in human. Moreover, it requires approval from hospital, managing a number of patients having gastrointestinal diseases, and involvement of gastroenterologist to evaluate the performance [44] and measuring the accuracy of their decision (fraction of correct decisions, false positives, false negatives, etc.) using statistical tools such as receiver operating characteristics analysis [45]. These tasks are beyond the scope of the article and left for future exploration.

### Conclusion

In this article, the design of a microcontroller-based portable data logger is presented that is targeted for general medical imaging and data collection application. It has high data rate wireless connectivity including Bluetooth, graphical display for real-time data viewing with state-of-the-art touch screen technology. The data are logged in micro SD cards and can be transferred to PC or Smartphone using card reader, USB interface, or Bluetooth wireless link. The features of the prototype are demonstrated for a WCE and skin temperature logging application.

**Competing interests**
The authors declare that they have no competing interests.

**Acknowledgments**
This study was supported by the Natural Science and Engineering Research Council of Canada (NSERC) and the Canada Foundation for Innovation (CFI). The authors would like to give thanks to Mohammad Shamim Imtiaz for helping in collecting data from hospital environment and to Serge Nazerenko for his technical assistance in making the prototype.

**References**
1. P. Corbishley, E. Rodriguez-Villegas, Breathing detection: towards a miniaturized, wearable, battery-operated monitoring system. IEEE Trans. Biomed. Eng. **55**(1), 196–204 (2008). doi:10.1109/TBME.2007.910679
2. G. Cybulski, A. Ksiazkiewicz, W. Lukasik, W. Niewiadomski, T. Palko, Ambulatory monitoring device for central hemodynamic and ECG signal recording on PCMCI flash memory cards. Comput. Cardiol. **1995**, 505–507 (1995). doi:10.1109/CIC.1995.482712
3. R. Rieger, Y.R. Huang, A custom-design data logger core for physiological signal recording. IEEE Trans. Instrum. Meas. **60**(2), 532–538 (2011). doi:10.1109/TIM.2010.2051609
4. T. Deniz, A. Yilmaz, Design and implementation of a digital ambulatory ECG recorder based on flash MultiMediaCard memory, in *Proceedings of the IEEE 46th Midwest Symposium on Circuits and Systems*, 2003, vol. 1, pp. 368–371. doi:10.109/MWSCAS.2003.1562295. Cairo
5. U. Anliker, J. Ward, P. Lukowicz, G. Tröster, F. Dolveck, M. Baer, F. Keita, E. Schenker, F. Catarsi, A. Coluccini, A. Belardinelli, D. Shklarski, M. Alon, E. Hirt, R. Schmid, M. Vuskovic, AMON: A wearable multi parameter medical monitoring and alert system. IEEE Trans. Inf. Technol. Biomed. **8**(4), 415–427 (2004). doi:10.1109/TITB.2004.837888
6. J.L. Toennies, G. Tortora, M. Simi, P. Valdastri, R.J. Webster, Swallowable medical devices for diagnosis and surgery: the state of the art. Proc. IMechE C: J. Mech. Eng. Sci. **224**, 1397–1414 (2009). doi:10.1243/09544062JMES1879
7. R. Luharuka, R.X. Gao, S. Krishnamurty, Design and realization of a portable data logger for physiological sensing [GSR]. IEEE Trans. Instrum. Meas. **52**(4), 1289–1295 (2003). doi:10.1109/TIM.2003.816808

8. F. Ahmed, M.A. Mohd Ali, E. Zahedi, Development of a portable fetal and maternal heart rate recorder for 24 hours, in *IEEE Proceedings of the 22nd Annual International Conference on Engineering in Medicine and Biology Society*, 2000, vol. 4, pp. 3044–3047. doi:10.1109/IEMBS.2000.901523. Chicago, IL

9. A. Salarian, H. Russmann, F.J.G. Vingerhoets, P.R. Burkhard, K. Aminian, Ambulatory monitoring of physical activities in patients with Parkinson's disease. IEEE Trans. Biomed. Eng. **54**(12), 2296–2299 (2007). doi:10.1109/TBME.2007.896591

10. B. Hermans, R. Puers, A portable multi-sensor data-logger for medical surveillance in harsh environments. Sens. Actuators A: Physical (Elsevier) **123–124**, 423–429 (2005)

11. F.S. Jaw, Y.L. Tseng, J.K. Jang, Modular design of a long-term portable recorder for physiological signals. Measurement (Elsevier) **43**(10), 1363–1368 (2010)

12. E. Ryo, K. Nishihara, S. Matsumoto, H. Kamata, A new method for long-term home monitoring of fetal movement by pregnant women themselves. Med. Eng. Phys. (Elsevier) **34**(5), 566–572 (2012)

13. R.K. Kamat, S.A. Shinde, P.K. Gaikwad, H. Guhilot, Analog front end and FPGA based soft IP core for ECG logger, in *Harnessing VLSI System Design with EDA Tools, (Springer)*, 2012, pp. 51–91. doi:10.1007/978-94-007-1864-7_3

14. C. Tronstad, S. Grimnes, O.G. Martinsen, E. Fosse, Development of a medical device for long-term sweat activity measurements, in *Proceedings of the IFMBE*. vol. 17 (Springer, Berlin, 2007), pp. 236–239. Graz, Austria

15. C. Chao, C. Pomalaza-Raez, Design and evaluation of a wireless body sensor system for smart home health monitoring, in *Proceedings of the IEEE Global Telecommunications Conference*, 2009, pp. 1–6. doi:10.1109/GLOCOM.2009.5425471. Honolulu, HI

16. P. Augustyniak, Wearable wireless heart rate monitor for continuous long-term variability studies. J. Electrocardiol. (Elsevier) **44**(2), 195–200 (2011)

17. A. Takeuchi, N. Mamorita, F. Sakai, N. Ikeda, Development of a comprehensive medical recorder on a cellphone. Comput. Methods Programs Biomed. (Elsevier) **97**(1), 28–38 (2010)

18. Atmel Corporation, 2012. [Online], http://www.atmel.com/products/ `microcontrollers/avr/default.aspx

19. Microchip Technology Inc, *PIC16F1947 microcontroller*, 2012. http://www.microchip.com/wwwproducts/Devices.aspx?dDocName=en538146

20. NXP Semiconductors, *32 bit ARM Cortex-M3 microcontroller*, 2012. http://www.nxp.com/products/microcontrollers/cortex_m3/LPC1316FBD48.html#overview

21. Smart GPU, *Vizic technologies*, 2012. http://vizictechnologies.com/#/smart-gpu/4554296549

22. SanDisk microSD, 2012. http://www.sandisk.com/products/memory-cards/microsd/

23. Nordic nRF24L01+ transceiver, 2012. http://www.nordicsemi.com/eng/Products/2.4GHz-RF/nRF24L01P

24. Zarlink Semiconductor, *ZL70102 MICS transceiver*, 2012. http://www.zarlink.com/zarlink/hs/82_ZLE70102.htm

25. Linx Technologies, *LR series transmitter, TXM-433-LR*, 2012. http://www.linxtechnologies.com/resources/data-guides/txm-xxx-lr.pdf

26. QwikRadio™ UHF ASK Transmitter, *MICRF103*, 2012. http://www.datasheetcatalog.org/datasheet/Micrel/mXsvvwt.pdf

27. XBee RF modules, 2012. http://www.digi.com/products/wireless-wired-embedded-solutions/zigbee-rf-modules/point-multipoint-rfmodules/xbee-series1-module#overview

28. Roving Networks, *Class 1 Bluetooth Module, RN-41*, 2012. http://www.rovingnetworks.com/products/RN_41

29. Texas Instruments, *TPS61200 boost converter*, 2012. http://www.ti.com/product/tps61200

30. Microchip Technology Inc, *MCP73831/2 Linear charge management controller*, 2012. http://www.microchip.com/wwwproducts/Devices.aspx?dDocName=en024903

31. MCS Electronics, *AVR-DOS*, 2012. http://www.mcselec.com/index.php?page=shop.product_details&flypage=shop.flypage&product_id=31&category_id=6&option=com_phpshop&Itemid=1

32. T.H. Khan, K. Wahid, Low complexity color-space for capsule endoscopy image compression. IET Electron. Lett. **47**(22), 1217–1218 (2011). doi:10.1049/el.2011.2211

33. T.H. Khan, K. Wahid, Low power and low complexity compressor for video capsule endoscopy. IEEE Trans. Circuits Syst. Video Technol. **21**(10), 1534–1546 (2011). doi:10.1109/TCSVT.2011.2163985

34. Chang Hong Technology Co., Ltd, *2.4GHz dipole antenna*, 2012. http://www.sparkfun.com/datasheets/Wireless/Antenna/DA-24-04.pdf

35. Texas Instruments, *LM35 Precision Centigrade Temperature Sensor*, 2012. http://www.ti.com/lit/ds/symlink/lm35.pdf

36. FCC rules and regulations 47 CFR Part 95, *subparts E (95.601-95.673) and I (95.1201-95.1219) Personal Radio Services*, 2002

37. A.R. Kahn, E.Y. Chow, O.A. Latief, P.P. Irazoqui, Low-power, high data rate transceiver system for implantable prostheses. Int. J. Telemed. Appl., Article ID 563903 (2010). doi:10.1155/2010/563903

38. P. Valdastri, A. Menciassi, P. Dario, Transmission power requirements for novel Zigbee implants in the gastrointestinal tract. IEEE Trans. Biomed. Eng. **55**(6), 1705–1710 (2008)

39. S. Diao, Y. Zheng, Y. Gao, C.H. Heng, M. Je, A 7.2mW 15Mbps ASK CMOS transmitter for ingestible capsule endoscopy, in *Proceedings of the IEEE Asia Pacific Conference on Circuits and Systems (APCCAS)*, 2010, pp. 512–515. Kuala Lumpur

40. S. Stoa, R.C. Santiago, I. Balasingham, An ultra wideband communication channel model for capsule endoscopy, in *Proceedings of the International Symposium on Applied Sciences in Biomedical and Communication Technologies (ISABEL)*, 2010, pp. 1–5. Rome

41. SD Card vs SDHC, *Diffen [Online]*, 2012. Available at http://www.diffen.com/difference/SD_Card_vs_SDHC

42. M. Kopáčová, I. Tachecí, J. Květina, J. Bureš, M. Kuneš, S. Spelda, V. Tyčová, Z. Svoboda, S. Rejchrt, Wireless video capsule enteroscopy in preclinical studies: methodical design of its applicability in experimental pigs. Dig. Dis. Sci. **55**(3), 626–630 (2010). doi:10.1007/s10620-009-0779-3

43. Food and Drug Administration, 2012. http://www.fda.gov

44. D. Tokuhara, K. Watanabe, Y. Okano, A. Tada, K. Yamato, T. Mochizuki, J. Takaya, T. Yamano, T. Arakawa, Wireless capsule endoscopy in pediatric patients: the first series from Japan. J. Gastroenterol. (Springer) **45**, 683–691 (2010)

45. T. Fawcett, An introduction to ROC analysis. Pattern Recognit. Lett. **27**, 861–874 (2006)

# 5

# A router for the containment of timing and value failures in CAN

Roland Kammerer[1][*], Roman Obermaisser[2] and Bernhard Frömel[1]

**Abstract**

The dependability deficiencies and bandwidth constraints of the controller area network (CAN) can prevent its use in safety-relevant and performance-demanding applications. This paper introduces mechanisms for fault detection and fault isolation based on an intelligent CAN router, which exploits a priori knowledge about the permitted behavior of attached electronic control units (ECUs) in order to detect and contain failures. Experiments using an FPGA-based implementation of the CAN router evaluate these mechanisms under different failure modes (e.g., timing failures, masquerading failures). Due to its compatibility to the CAN standard, the router can improve the dependability and performance of systems with existing ECUs. In addition, we extend the application areas of CAN to systems with higher performance and dependability requirements than can be supported with a conventional bus-based network.

**Keywords:** CAN, CAN router, Fault detection, Fault location, Fault isolation, MPSoC design, ACROSS MPSoC

## Introduction

The communication protocol controller area network (CAN) is used for asynchronous fieldbus networks in many application domains including the automotive industry, the avionic industry and factory automation. For example, cars typically contain several CAN buses for powertrain, infotainment and comfort functions.

The benefits of CAN include its simplicity, the decentral structure and the low cost for CAN controllers and wiring. However, severe limitations concerning reliability have been identified in literature such as the ability of a single faulty node to cause a global communication failure by monopolizing the bus [1], the susceptibility to bus short-circuits [2] or the absence of an atomic broadcast in case of asymmetric bit flips [3,4]. In addition, CAN exhibits diagnostic deficiencies such as the inability to trace back faulty message identifications to the sender nodes [5].

Therefore, a single CAN bus does not support the construction of embedded systems where the correct operation of the communication system is required to ensure safety. As a result, new communication protocols are introduced in different application domains to address the reliability issues such as FlexRay [6] in the automotive area.

This paper provides improvements of CAN w.r.t. fault-tolerance, which can provide an alternative to the replacement of CAN in many applications. Thereby, system developers can benefit from the low cost, the high numbers of existing CAN-based applications and the widespread expertise in CAN hardware and software.

We replace the CAN bus with a star topology based on an intelligent CAN router. *Fault isolation* is one of the primary objectives of the router and our main focus of this paper. The CAN router eliminates the hazard of medium failures of an individual CAN bus leading to a global communication failure. Furthermore, the router exploits a priori knowledge about the permitted behavior of CAN nodes in the time and value domains for the containment of node failures. In the time domain interarrival times are monitored and enforced. In the value domain, permitted message identifiers and constraints on the application data within a message are enforced.

As CAN is widely used in different domains, *legacy CAN-interface support* is of utmost importance. Modifying the legacy CAN-interface would result in tremendous cost for redeveloping existing systems. Therefore, the CAN router provides interfaces that are compatible to standard CAN. This includes electrical compatibility and standard-conforming services of the data link layer (e.g., arbitration mechanism, message ordering) [7].

*Correspondence: kammerer@vmars.tuwien.ac.at
[1]Vienna University of Technology, Vienna, Austria
Full list of author information is available at the end of the article

Further, the router overcomes limitations of existing CAN networks concerning overall cable length and overall bandwidth (40 m at 1 Mbit/s) by its star topology. Naming incoherences are solved by a CAN identifier translation. As today's breakdown logs do not assist the technician in a proper way [8,9], the router also provides new diagnostic services for the detection of timing failures (e.g., crash failure of a node, babbling idiot) and value failures (e.g., invalid CAN identifiers, implausible message contents).

Major contributions of the paper are the introduction of a system model of a fault-tolerant CAN-based system using the CAN router, as well as the explanation of the basic services of the CAN router for fault isolation. Furthermore, we provide an experimental evaluation of the effectiveness of the fault isolation mechanisms.

The paper is organized as follows: Section Controller area network provides an overview about CAN and its limitations. In Section CAN router we define the system model of the CAN router, present failure modes of CAN, and state the basic services of the router. In Section Fault detection and isolation we describe how the router detects and isolates previous mentioned failure modes. In Section Implementation of fault detection and isolation we concentrate on the implementation of the router and describe how the means of fault detection and isolation are realized. Section Test framework gives an overview about the test framework we used for our evaluations of the CAN router, where Section Experiments presents the experiments we conducted and their results. Section Discussion discusses the gathered results, and finally Section Conclusion concludes the paper.

## Controller area network

CAN belongs to the class of event-triggered communication protocols. It uses a broadcast bus with "carrier sense, multiple access with collision avoidance" (CSMA/CA) for medium access control [7]. The bit transmission takes two possible representations. The recessive state appears only on the bus when all nodes send recessive bits. The dominant state occurs, if at least one node sends a dominant bit. A given bit-stream is transmitted using the "Non-Return-to-Zero" (NRZ) code. Bit stuffing prevents that more than five consecutive bits of identical polarity are transmitted. A node delays its transmission if the bus-line is busy. If the bus is idle the node can start sending. Bus access conflicts are resolved by observing the message identifier bits on the bus-line. While transmitting a communication message identifier, each node monitors the serial bus-line. If the transmitted bit is recessive and a dominant bit is monitored, the node gives up transmitting and starts to receive incoming data. The node sending the object with the highest priority will succeed and acquire bus access. The information exchange occurs using four types of protocol data frames:

1. *Data frames* are used for the transmission of CAN message objects. A data frame contains a unique identifier, which identifies the message object and denotes the message priority.
2. By transmitting a *remote frame* the dissemination of a communication object is explicitly requested. For the same identifier, the data frame takes precedence over the remote transmission request.
3. An *error frame* is used for error signaling. It contains an error flag.
4. The *overload frame* serves the purpose of extending the interframe space to handle overload conditions.

After a loss in the arbitration process or the reception of an error frame, the sender automatically performs a retransmission of the corresponding communication object. The integrity of data and remote frames are checked by a 15-bit cyclic redundancy code (CRC).

CAN was originally developed for non safety-critical applications and exhibits the following limitations w.r.t. predictability, dependability and performance:

- A CAN communication system possesses a large variability in the transmission latency. A message's transmission latency depends on the network load. This latency jitter causes an error in the temporal domain and introduces an additional measurement error if there is no global notion of time.
- The arbitration logic of CAN limits the throughput, because the propagation delay of the channel must be smaller than the length of a bitcell. A CAN network of 40 m results in a maximum bandwidth of 1 Mbit/s.
- CAN does not prevent babbling idiot failures. A node can continuously send highest priority messages and thereby prevent communication of other nodes.
- The CAN protocol does not include a clock synchronization service. If a global notion of time is required, it must be implemented at the host level.
- Communication errors are handled with immediate message retries. Errors cause increased latencies.
- Handling of station failures is performed with error counters by recording the receive and transmit errors. A threshold is defined for entering the error passive mode. In this mode, a node must wait for a minimum idle time on the bus before starting a transmission. If bus contention is low, this results in interleaving of correct and invalid messages. Exceeding of another error counter threshold results in entering the bus-off state. Under the assumption that failed nodes reach the bus off state, the worst-case inaccessibility time at 1 Mbit/s is bounded by 2.5 ms [10-12].

- Since the temporal properties of a CAN system are changed during the integration of the system, CAN does not support temporal composability [13]. The transmission of a message is triggered explicitly by a transmission request from the host. The temporal coordination of the communication activities is a global issue and depends on the host software in all nodes.
- CAN error recovery mechanisms are unable to ensure a consistent state, if an error is detected in the last but one bit of a frame. Possible consequences are an inconsistent message duplication or an inconsistent message ordering. Establishing consistency requires modifications to the host software [4,14] or a dedicated hardware component [3].

## CAN router

This section describes the system model and states the terminology that is used in the rest of the paper. Figure 1 depicts a CAN system using the CAN router.

CAN segments, consisting of a CAN bus with at least one node are connected to the router via a CAN port. The router is implemented as a multi-processor-system-on-a-chip (MPSoC), where every CAN port is served by its own CAN interface subsystem (CIS). Each CIS consists of a CPU, local memory, and a CAN controller. The CPU executes software used for message processing. Every CIS contains a routing configuration that allows the router to forward messages from a source CAN segment to one or more destination segment(s). We use a time-triggered network-on-chip (TTNoC) [15] for the message transport between CISes. All processing in the router is time-triggered. Additionally, the router possesses a management port, served by the the management unit (MU), which is used for diagnosis and configuration (e.g., update of the routing configuration).

### Fault hypothesis

In this section we define the fault containment regions of the CAN router and describe the failure modes we expect to occur.

A *FCR* is a region of the system that operates correctly regardless of faults outside of this region [16]. In our case this includes arbitrary logical or electrical faults. We distinguish two types of fault containment regions: The CAN router itself and the individual CAN segments. We assume the router to be free of faults. In case compatibility to standard CAN is not a strict requirement, a setup with two redundant CAN routers can be used to tolerate a single failure in one FCR.

A definition of *failure modes* is fundamental for the design of the CAN router as well as for error handling and containment of these failures. The following failure modes, which are subcategories of the arbitrary failure mode, are assumed for the CAN segments:

### Stuck at dominant/recessive failures

If a node or the bus is affected by a stuck at dominant failure, the state of the bus becomes dominant (e.g., a node constantly sends '0'). In the bus-based CAN segment this means that no further communication is possible. In case of a stuck at recessive failure we have to distinguish between the node and the bus. If a node is affected by this kind of failure this node is not able to participate in the communication on the bus. If the bus itself is affected by a stuck at recessive failure, no nodes can communicate.

### Crash/omission failures

Crash/omission failures are one of the most frequent failure types in CAN. The CAN standard also defines mechanisms (e.g., error counters) for mapping different types of faults into crash/omission failures ([7], p. 42). FCRs affected by this kind of failure either provide the specified

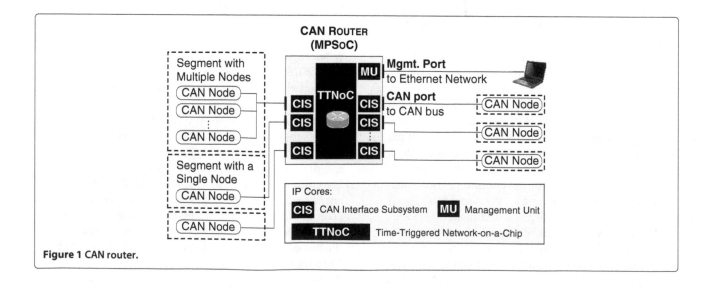

**Figure 1** CAN router.

service (i.e., sending CAN messages), or they do not provide the service at all. Crash/omission failures are extreme scenarios of late message failures.

### Asymmetric bit-flip failures

Even though in literature it is sometimes assumed that CAN provides an atomic broadcast, this is not the case. If the last but one bit of the end of frame (EOF) delimiter is affected by an asymmetric bit flip, the nodes on the bus can be split in two sets, one accepting the message, and one not. In this case the sender retransmits the message, which leads to a duplication of that message in the set of nodes that previously accepted the message [4,14]. A subsequent crash failure can lead to an inconsistent message omission.

### Babbling idiot failures

As the former mentioned crash/omission failures, babbling idiot failures are in the category of message timing failures [17]. A babbling idiot failure is an extreme case of an early timing failure. Since conventional CAN does not provide effective mechanisms for handling babbling idiot failures [1], a node that sends high priority messages can disrupt the communication of all other nodes which share the same bus.

### Masquerading failures

Masquerading failures, which are part of the value domain, occur, if one node impersonates the identity of another node. In case of CAN, one node could send its messages with the CAN identifier reserved for another node, which might lead to severe consequences. For example consider an environment where node $A$ sends a temperature value, node $B$ sends a velocity value, and node $C$ opens a valve according to the temperature value from node $A$. If node $B$ sends velocity values with the identifier of node $A$, node $C$ misinterprets the velocity value as a temperature value. Masquerading failures in combination with diagnostic deficiencies of CAN are one of the reasons why today's automotive breakdown logs do not assist the technician adequately in the identification of faulty Electronic Control Units (ECUs) [9,18].

### Basic services of the CAN router

The CAN router provides basic services which will be explained in the rest of this section.

### Message rate control

In classic CAN a node $k$ sends messages with a specific identifier $i$ in the overall set of CAN identifiers $I \subset \{0, \ldots, 2^z-1\}$. A basic CAN identifier contains 11 bits (i.e., $z = 11$), whereas extended identifiers contain 29 bits (i.e., $z = 29$). As CAN is an event-triggered protocol, the interval between two messages with the same identifier is a stochastic variable. In order to provide fault isolation and

enhanced diagnosis, we constrain the rate of messages. The behavior of a CAN node $k$ is defined by the set $M_k$:

$$M_k = \{\langle i, d, e \rangle \mid \text{where } i \in I \text{ and } d, e \in \mathbb{Q}^+\}$$

where the positive rational numbers $d$ and $e$ are the *minimum* and *maximum interarrival times* associated with the identifier $i$. The router contains an entry that specifies these interarrival times for every CAN identifier that is valid on the corresponding CAN segment. In case of a violation, the message is discarded and the violation is reported to the MU. Blocking of untimely messages is one of the key aspects of fault isolation.

Properties for minimum and maximum interarrival times are often known and in the automotive domain they can be for example extracted from a fieldbus exchange format (FIBEX) [19] specification. Tools which generate a routing configuration from a FIBEX specification are described in [20].

### Message multicasting

In conventional CAN a message that is successfully sent on the bus gets broadcasted to all other nodes. In order to overcome the limitations of CAN, the router supports selective multicasting, which uses the existing bandwidth more efficiently. The router contains knowledge about the destination CAN segment(s) of a message and forwards the message exactly to these segment(s). Broadcasting, which is a special case of multicasting, is supported by the router (i.e., the router forwards a message to all other CAN segments).

### Message scheduling

On a CAN bus every transmitting node monitors the state of the bus. Whenever a node tries to send a recessive bit, and reads back a dominant bit, it backs off and retries to send the interrupted message at a later point in time. As high-priority message identifiers contain more leading dominant bits than low-priority identifiers, a message with a high priority is sent first (i.e., it wins the arbitration). In order to reproduce this behavior, the CAN router maintains a priority queue at every destination CIS and transmits the messages to the destination CAN bus according to their priority.

### Identifier validation and translation

In a classic CAN setup a faulty node $A$ could send messages with an identifier reserved for another node $B$. Therefore, the router contains knowledge about valid identifiers of a CAN segment in its routing configuration. If a node sends a message with an identifier not specified in the routing configuration, the router discards this message and sends a report to the MU. In addition to identifier validation, the router supports identifier translation. This is important in the case of legacy system integration, where two legacy systems use the same CAN identifiers. It is possible to specify a translation ID for every CAN identifier used in the system.

### Message checks

For every CAN identifier it is possible to specify a function that gets called with the content of the message. If, and only if, the message passes the check, the message gets forwarded to its destination. For example a message that contains an engine coolant temperature variable can be checked if the temperature is within a meaningful specified range.

### Message content translation

As legacy system integration is one of the goals of our approach, the router supports the translation of the content of CAN messages. It is possible to specify a *translation function* per valid CAN ID. One practical example is the conversion between different measurement units (e.g., converting between degrees Celsius and Fahrenheit).

### Diagnosis and management

The router contains a dedicated MU which is capable of collecting violations in the time and value domain. This includes violations of the minimum and maximum interarrival time, as well as invalid message identifiers. This information can then be used as input for further analysis. Additionally, the MU can be used to change the routing configuration at run-time. This includes the addition and removal of valid CAN identifiers, the modification of minimum and maximum interarrival times, as well as changing multicast patterns (i.e., the destination of CAN messages).

## Fault detection and isolation

The purpose of this section is to describe how the failure modes mentioned in Section Fault hypothesis are detected and contained by the CAN router.

### Asymmetric bit-flip failures

Based on the star topology, if the CAN router is correct, it is ensured that messages are consistently received by all correct CAN segments. If a node in a CAN segment transmits a message and the CIS does not accept this message, then the node has to retransmit the message. However, no destination CIS is influenced, therefore, the state is consistent over all CISes. If the source CIS accepts the message, it will forward the message to the destination CIS(es). The CAN router will subsequently send the messages on all correct destination CAN segments, thus ensuring a consistent overall state of all correct CISes. If a CAN segment exhibits a transient fault, the CAN controller at the destination segment will retransmit and try to eventually deliver the message.

### Stuck at dominant/recessive failures

By the use of a star topology, stuck at dominant and stuck at recessive failures are contained at their corresponding source CAN bus. Therefore, a faulty node can only disrupt the communication of all the other nodes that share the same CAN segment, but it is not possible to influence the communication of other, separated CAN segments.

### Crash/omission failures

As described in Section Basic services of the CAN router, the router contains knowledge about maximum interarrival times of messages for each valid CAN identifier. Further, the source CIS stores a timestamp of the last successful reception per CAN ID in its internal data structure. The router checks if the difference between the current time and the time of the last reception exceeds the maximum interarrival time. If this is the case, this temporal violation is reported to the MU. As the router cannot enforce messages from a potentially failed node, reporting the violation is the next best thing to do. On the MU this knowledge can be used to initiate a reconfiguration of the system. For example an $\alpha$-count can be increased every time the maximum interarrival time is violated in order to discriminate between transient and permanent faults as discussed in [21]. In case of a permanent fault, the MU could initiate a reconfiguration that uses a spare node instead of the apparently failed one.

### Babbling idiot failures

The router provides means for fault isolation when messages are sent too fast, e.g., in case of a babbling idiot failure. Whenever the difference between the current timestamp and the timestamp of the last reception is less than the specified minimum interarrival time, it is considered a temporal violation. In that case the router blocks this message and does not forward it to the destination CISes. Therefore, the fault is contained in the specific source CAN segment. In addition to that, the violation is reported to the MU, which then takes further actions (e.g., log the violation for later analysis conducted by a maintenance engineer).

### Masquerading failures

The CAN router isolates masquerading failures and contains them in their source CAN segment. The routing configuration contains entries for every valid CAN identifier. Whenever a faulty node tries to send a CAN message with an identifier that is not specified in the routing configuration, the source CIS blocks this message and sends a violation report to the MU. This prevents the propagation of messages with an identifier not specified for the given CAN segment. Nodes sharing the same CAN segment can sill masquerade IDs of nodes on the same segment. The router provides the best fault detection and isolation capability if CISes consist of a single CAN node.

## Implementation of fault detection and isolation

Figure 2 shows the internal structure of the CAN router. The router itself is realized as a MPSoC, where every CAN port is served by its own CIS based on a Nios II softcore CPU. We use the ACROSS MPSoC [22] as our underlying platform. Our design allows us to cleanly decouple the temporal behavior of each CIS. Additionally, higher scalability and fault isolation is achieved. From a scalability point of view it is much easier to add additional CISes, compared to software or single-core designs where the addition of every new message requires extra processing power at one processing core that is shared among all CAN segments. The presented MPSoC design also provides better fault isolation compared to single core solutions because the TTNoC [15] ensures that a transient or permanent fault of a core does not affect the operation of other cores.

The operation of the router is strictly time-triggered and divided into *rounds of activity*. The underlaying ACROSS MPSoC [22] provides a generic timer service which is used to synchronously trigger activity rounds in all CISes. The trigger-period ($2^{-15}$ s $\equiv 30.52\,\mu$s) is faster than the minimum interarrival time of CAN messages at 1 Mbps. Within one activity cycle each CIS checks if a newly arrived CAN message at the CAN port has to be processed, then it processes this message according to the associated routing configuration, and forwards

the message to the TTNoC. Additionally, the CIS checks if it received a message from the TTNoC (i.e., this message was originally sent in the last activity cycle), and if this is the case, it processes the message and finally sends the message with the highest priority to the destination CAN bus.

The router introduces a delay of one CAN message due to its store and forward behavior and a maximum of three activity cycles from the instant a message is successfully sent on the source CAN bus, until it is stored in the priority queue at the destination CIS. This includes finishing the current activity cycle (i.e., which started before the new message arrived), and one additional activity cycle for processing the message and forwarding it to the TTNoC. As the message transport of the TTNoC is triggered by the system frequency, it is guaranteed that the message is available at the destination CIS until the next activity cycle starts. The third and last activity cycle is consumed at the destination CIS for processing and storing the message to the priority queue. If the queue is empty or there are no other higher priority messages, the newly arrived message is sent to the CAN bus attached to the destination CIS in the same activity cycle.

As shown in Figure 2, every CIS contains a local *routing configuration*. This configuration contains an entry for every CAN identifier that is valid on the given CIS. We use the configuration to store properties important for routing messages to their destination as well as to specify temporal properties important for fault detection. A sample entry is shown in Listing 1.

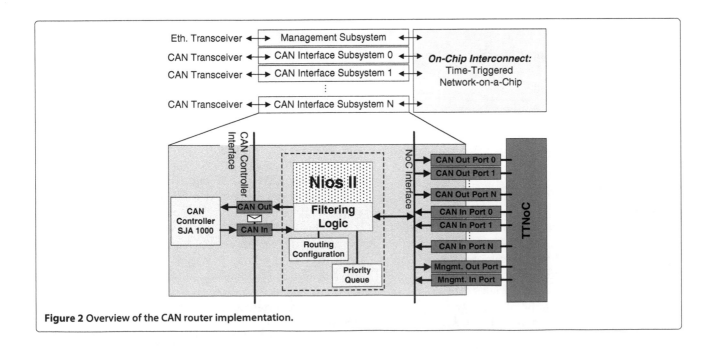

**Figure 2** Overview of the CAN router implementation.

**Listing 1** An example routing entry

```
typedef struct {
    time64 min;

    time64 max;

    time64 last_arrived_min;

    time64 last_arrived_max;

    uint16_t message_check;

    uint16_t message_translation;

    uint16_t forward_to;

} routing_entry;
```

The variables min and max contain the specified minimum and maximum interarrival time, forward_to is a bit array that specifies the destination CIS(es). Variables starting with last_arrived are used to store timestamps of the last successful message reception. The variables message_check and message_translation contain a position in an array of function pointers that can be used to validate the content of a message, respectively translate the content.

As a direct mapping from CAN ID to a position in the routing configuration is not feasible (i.e., this would require $2^{29}$ entries in the routing configuration), we look up the configuration with the help of a binary search. This has the advantage that the memory footprint can be kept small and that the lookup is bounded by $O(log(n))$. For the lookup we use a sorted array of CAN identifies, which is generated off-line by configuration tools and checked during start-up by the MU. The structure of a search entry is shown in Listing 2.

**Listing 2** Structure of an entry used for configuration lookup

```
typedef struct {
    uint32_t can_id;

    uint32_t pos; /* in the routing_config */

} searchstruct;
```

### Temporal domain

A CIS checks for violations of the minimum interarrival time whenever it receives a message from its CAN controller and has to forward the message to one or more destination CAN segments. In Figure 2, this is represented by a message flow from the left to the right. In order to get precise timestamps of message receptions, we store the timestamp as soon as the CAN message arrives (i.e., even between two activity cycles). As the activity cycles are shorter than the minimum interarrival times of CAN messages, we have to store at most one timestamp. In every activity cycle the CPU checks if a new message has to be processed. If this is the case, the CPU transfers the message over the CAN Controller Interface to its own memory and does further processing. In the first step the router has to look up the configuration that is associated with the CAN identifier of the newly arrived message. If the ID is found, the routing configuration associated with the CAN ID gets evaluated.

The router checks the properties that are important for fault isolation. For minimum interarrival time validation the router builds the difference between the timestamp of the current reception and the timestamp stored for the last successful reception (last_arrived_min). If the specified minimum is violated, the router sends a message to the MU. In case of a violation of the minimum interarrival time, the message gets blocked. If there was no violation we update last_arrived_min and send the message to the destination CIS(es). The timestamp for last_arrived_max is updated on every reception, whether it was a minimum interarrival time violation or not, which is the reason we have to store two timestamps (i.e., one for last_arrived_min and one for last_arrived_max).

As previously described, it is sufficient to check the minimum interarrival time on every reception of a CAN message. Checking the maximum interarrival time is different because it has to be done in every activity cycle. If we would check it on reception of a new message, we would potentially detect the violation later than specified, and crash failures would remain even undetected. If we detect a violation of the maximum interarrival time, we report it and update last_arrived_max. This variable contains either the timestamp of the last successful reception or the timestamp of the last reported violation.

### Value domain

As described in the previous section, whenever a new CAN message arrives from a CAN segment, the respective CIS tries to lookup the routing configuration associated with the CAN ID of the newly arrived message. If the search is not successful, a CAN node sent a message with an identifier which is not valid for the given CAN segment. In that case the router does not further process the message and sends an error report to the MU. If the lookup is successful, the specified check function for the message content is called. Whenever the message does not pass the check, the violation will be reported and the message is not further processed.

## Test framework

We developed a test framework to validate the fault detection and fault containment mechanisms of the CAN router. The framework consists of a 4-port router, 4 independent CAN buses, a MU and several CAN test nodes (CTNs) that generate CAN messages according to a predefined CAN traffic pattern. We designed the MU in a way that it not only takes care about configuration and collecting violations, but also initiates experiments, monitors all CAN buses individually, stores the test results and performs a preliminary analysis. Tools take the preliminary analysis results and visualize [23] the output data off-line.

### Test setup

We use an Altera Stratix III Devkit to host the complete test framework, i.e., the CAN router design, the CTN and CAN buses. Figure 3 gives an overview of the test framework.

- *CAN router design:* The CAN router design consists of four CISes and a MU which are connected by a TTNoC in a configuration that allows each CIS to send to and receive from all other CISes and the MU. The TTNoC communication schedule guarantees timely delivery of all CAN messages and minimum interarrival time and maximum interarrival time violation messages within the router, especially during maximum load. Additionally, each CIS is able to handle the maximum load arriving from either the TTNoC or the CAN bus. Specifically for the test framework, the MU contains four independent CAN controllers for monitoring all CAN buses within the design and a DDR2 controller which is attached to a 1 GB memory module for storing test results. All CISes and the MU are accessible over serial communication (UART), and the MU is also accessible by 100 Mbit/s Ethernet for high volume data up/download.

- *CTN:* A CTN emulates a CAN-based device. Each of the CTN is realized by a small Nios II softcore CPU system and a CAN controller to generate or consume CAN messages. The 8 byte payload of each generated CAN message contains a timestamp that is set shortly before the CAN message is transferred to the CAN controller. In case a CAN message transmit attempt fails (i.e., another CAN message with a higher priority is sent simultaneously), the CAN controller will retry sending indefinitely until it succeeds. Each CAN controller has a transmit FIFO buffer with a length of 30 messages. In case the FIFO buffer is overrun, new messages are lost. All CTNs are also connected to the TTNoC; specifically they can receive configuration messages from the MU.

- *CAN buses:* All CAN buses in the test framework operate independently from each other at a baud rate of 256 Kbit/s. While each node on a specific CAN bus can send and receive CAN messages, the MU is only allowed to receive them.

We use the TTNoC global time [24] as the time base for all timestamps. In our design the granularity of this time base is $2^{-21}$ s.

### Test application

The test application conducts experiments using the described setup. An experiment is defined by *experiment parameters* that consist of the router configuration (see Section Implementation of fault detection and isolation, Listing 1) for the CISes and CAN traffic patterns for each CTN. A CAN traffic pattern describes CAN message contents and message rates over the duration of an experiment (i.e., message rates may change during the progression of an experiment). A single execution of an

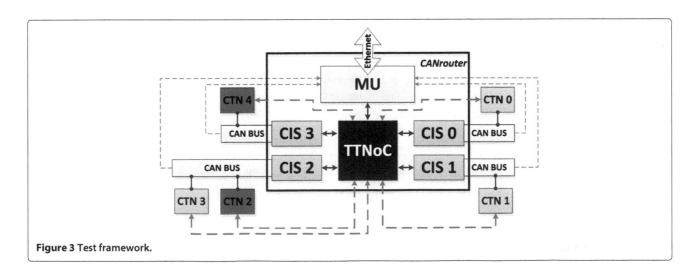

**Figure 3** Test framework.

experiment is called *experiment run*. By design, the MU controls the hardware reset of all CISes and takes care of (re)configuring them. After all components of the test framework are configured and operational, the MU logs minimum interarrival time and maximum interarrival time violations from the CISes. For the test framework, we realized the MU software to

- control experiments: The MU autonomously controls the execution of a large number (i.e., several thousands) of experiment runs.
- monitor all CAN buses: Any observed CAN message is timestamped and stored for analysis in the main memory.
- log all minimum interarrival time and maximum interarrival time violations: Any observed violation emitted from a CIS is timestamped and stored for analysis.
- perform preliminary analysis of collected data: The MU evaluates the collected data by periodically calculating message rates according to a specified observation time (e.g., each 0.25 s). Also the MU logs dropped CAN messages (i.e., messages that appear on the source CIS but do not appear on the destination CIS), for example, caused by the router's fault isolation with respect to minimum interarrival time violations or masquerading failures.

Those additions to the MU software are usually not present in the CAN router. However, they do not influence any of the router's characteristics that we want to evaluate: After the CISes are configured, the MU does not take part in the actual service of the router and only collects experiment relevant data.

We divide an experiment into several consecutive phases as depicted in Figure 4. In the *startup phase* all CISes and CTNs remain in the reset state until the MU is configured for the experiment. Configuration is done by commands issued over Ethernet to the MU. Following the configuration, the MU releases the reset of the CISes and CTNs. Then an experiment run starts at the *sign-on phase* where the CISes and CTNs boot and start to send periodically alive messages to the MU. The

MU realizes startup synchronization by waiting until all nodes have sent at least one alive message. Eventually all CISes and CTNs have indicated their readiness to the MU and the *configure phase* starts. There the MU sends routing and rate constraint information to all CISes. After all configuration messages are sent, the MU begins the *experiment phase* by sending a start message to all CISes and CTNs which immediately get operational at the same global time instant. During the experiment phase the MU

- collects minimum interarrival time and maximum interarrival time violations reported by the originating CISes.
- calculates CAN message end-to-end latencies. Latency measurements start when a CAN message is queued for transfer in a CTN (i.e., before bus arbitration on the source CAN bus) and stop when the MU observes the message on the destination CAN bus.
- counts dropped CAN messages.

Each CTN notifies the MU after it has finished its CAN traffic pattern. The MU waits until all CTNs have completed which also marks the end of an experiment run. In case the last experiment run is complete, the *analysis and presentation phase* concludes the evaluation of an experiment. Otherwise, the MU starts the next experiment run and issues a reset of the CISes and CTNs. Following to the reset, execution continues at the sign-on phase. The analysis and presentation phase is the last phase of an experiment, where statistical parameters (e.g., mean message throughput, mean end-to-end latencies, ...) are calculated from the individual experiment runs and presented to the user. All of the collected data can be downloaded over Ethernet or serial communication (UART) for further analysis.

## Experiments

For the evaluation of the CAN router and its proposed means for fault detection and isolation we conducted experiments. In the following we define the hypotheses for the router, define the individual experiments, and present the gathered results.

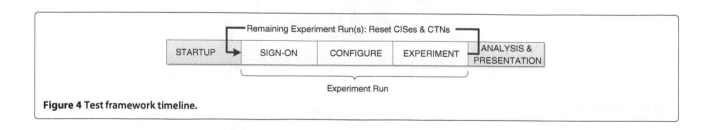

**Figure 4 Test framework timeline.**

## Hypotheses

The following hypotheses were evaluated by the experiments:

**Hypothesis 1.** *Fault Detection. The router detects the faults in the value and time domain that are specified in Section Fault hypothesis. These include stuck at dominant/recessive failures, asymmetric bit-flip failures, crash/omission failures, babbling idiot failures, and masquerading failures. Additionally, the router detects failures that that are covered by standard CAN controllers (e.g., cyclic redundancy check (CRC) failures, bit-stuffing failures). Detected faults are reported to the MU.*

**Hypothesis 2.** *Fault Containment. With the exception of late message failures the router contains detected faults in the value domain as well as in the temporal domain. A violation of the maximum interarrival time can only be detected and reported. Thus the late messages will be delivered, while all other messages violating their specified properties are discarded at their source CIS.*

**Hypothesis 3.** *Latencies. By means of the minimal interarrival time it is possible to specify upper bounds for message latencies. As the number of messages is constrained, there is a bounded influence a potentially faulty node can have on messages from nodes connected to a separated CIS.*

## Experiments

In order to evaluate the hypotheses, we conducted two experiments by using the previously described test framework. Each of the experiments is executed 10,000 times to minimize stochastic effects: Each experiment run (i.e., a single execution of an experiment) is carried out with the exact same experiment parameters. Even though CAN messages are event-triggered and occurrences are sporadic, we decided for our experiments to use periodic CAN messages only. By setting and controlling a specific CAN message rate, we are able to evaluate corner cases (i.e., right before and right after minimum interarrival time or maximum interarrival time violations occur) and investigate on interference effects among different prioritized CAN messages.

### Experiment I

The experiment lasts 12 s and uses the following routing configuration: CTN 1, 2, and 4 send CAN messages to CTN 0. Concerning the value domain, error-free CTNs send only CAN messages where the CAN ID matches the CTN node number: e.g., CTN 1 is only allowed to send messages with ID 1. CTN 0 is only an receiver and does not produce any CAN messages.

Regarding the temporal domain, messages originating from CAN buses on CIS 0, 1 and 3 are not constrained, while messages with CAN ID 2 originating from the CAN bus on CIS 2 have a minimum interarrival time of 125 Kbit/s and a maximum interarrival time of 15 Kbit/s specified: i.e., according to the router's configuration only rates between 15 Kbit/s and 125 Kbit/s are valid.

CTN 1 generates CAN messages at a constant rate of 37.5 Kbit/s during the whole experiment phase. CTN 4 also sends at a constant rate of 37.5 Kbit/s CAN messages, but with alternating CAN IDs 1 and 4. This results in two 18.75 Kbit/s CAN message streams where only the one with CAN ID 4 is valid according to the router's configuration. Further, CTN 2 sends at first at a constant rate of approximately 8 Kbit/s. Starting from second 2.25 the traffic pattern rate function passes over into a linear ramp where the message generation rate is gradually increased each 0.25 s until it reaches 220 Kbit/s at the end of an experiment run. The following function describes the CAN message rate of CTN 2:

$$r_{CTN=2,\ CAN\_ID=2}(t) = \begin{cases} \min_{\text{rate}} & t \leq a \\ k \cdot t + \min_{\text{rate}} & a < t < b \\ k \cdot b + \min_{\text{rate}} & t \geq b \end{cases}$$
$$t \in \{0, 0.25, 0.5, \ldots, 12\}$$

CTN 3 is unused in this experiment and does not generate any CAN messages. This experiment contains in total two erroneous CTNs: CTN 4 violates the value domain and CTN 2 violates the time domain. Those two nodes are also marked red in Figure 3.

### Experiment II

Experiment II is the same as Experiment I with the only difference that CTN 3 is active and generates CAN messages with CAN ID 3 at a constant rate of 37.5 Kbit/s. This additional node neither violates the time nor the value domain according to the router's configuration, but there is now a CAN segment with two senders CTN 2 and CTN 3) attached to CIS 2. There will be interference effects between CAN ID 2 and CAN ID 3 messages. This experiment compares classic CAN bus with segmented CAN bus behavior (as established by the CAN router) in terms of fault containment and end-to-end message latencies during temporal violations. Referring to CAN message interference effects, the two experiments are well comparable, because they only differ in a single experiment parameter.

### Results

Here we present the results we gathered from our experiments. A detailed interpretation and discussion of the results follows in Section Discussion. The following figures present the arithmetic mean of all experiment runs for a specific experiment.

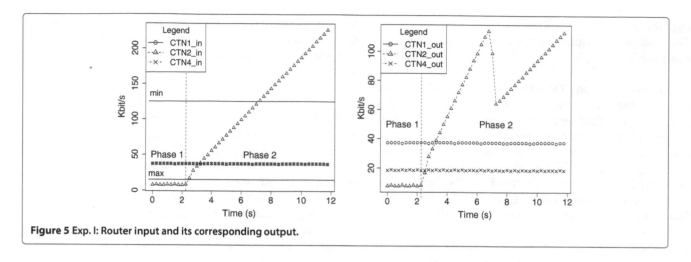

**Figure 5** Exp. I: Router input and its corresponding output.

## Experiment I

Figure 5a depicts the input traffic applied by the CTNs to their CAN buses. CTN 1 and 4 send at a constant rate, while the message generation of CTN 2 is divided into two phases. In the first phase, it sends too slow and violates the maximum interarrival time. In the second phase, it constantly increases its CAN message generation rate which leads to minimum interarrival time violations. Note that the traffic pattern of CTN 4 consists of messages with the CAN ID 1 and 4, though CAN ID 1 is not in the specified set of CAN IDs for the corresponding CIS.

Figure 5b shows the output on the CAN bus attached to CIS 0. The output of CTN 1 is constant and not influenced by any erroneous node. The router forwards only half of the total CAN messages generated by the erroneous node CTN 4 to the CAN bus on CIS 0: Every second message of CTN 4 has the valid CAN ID 4, while the other half has the invalid CAN ID 1 (i.e., only CTN 1 is allowed to send with CAN ID 1).

The send rate of CTN 2 at the source CIS 2 corresponds to the rate at the destination CIS 0 until CTN 2 starts to violate its specified minimum interarrival time. Starting from that instant a pattern occurs that oscillates to an upper bound.

Figure 6a shows CTN 2's number of messages violating the specified minimum interarrival time. In Experiment I the first violations start at the same instant where the input pattern (cf. Figure 5a) of CTN 2 crosses the horizontal line of the bandwidth limit defined by the minimum interarrival time. As there is no difference between the experiments concerning maximum interarrival time violations, they will be shown for Experiment II.

The oscillating output of CTN 2 can be explained as follows: In our test setup messages are sent periodically with different period lengths $l$. Figure 6b gives an illustrative example where period lengths of four, three, two, and one are examined. The interval in which messages are blocked due to violations of the minimum interarrival time are pictured as gray boxes. Successful send instants are denoted by arrows with an arrowhead, whereas blocked messages contain only an arrowtail.

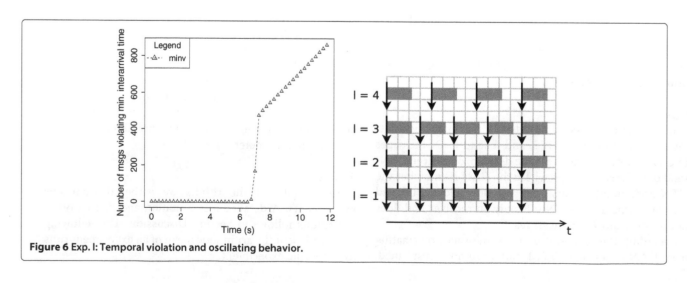

**Figure 6** Exp. I: Temporal violation and oscillating behavior.

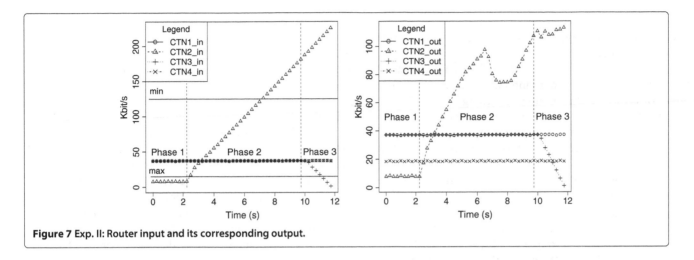

**Figure 7** Exp. II: Router input and its corresponding output.

In the period with the length 4, messages are sent too slow to achieve a decent throughput. If messages are sent faster in the period with length 3, a higher number of messages is successfully sent, because successfully sent messages get closer to the gray boxes. In the output (cf. Figure 5b) this can be seen as a rising edge. In the period with the length 2, messages are sent a bit too fast and every second message gets blocked. Although we are trying to send more messages in the period with the length 2 than in the period of the length 3, less messages pass the temporal validity check. This corresponds to the falling edges of the oscillating output. If messages are sent even faster, 2 out of 3 messages get blocked in the period with the length 1, but as messages are sent that fast, a spot shortly after a gray box gets hit and therefore the throughput increases. This continues and we see again a rising edge until the message coming closer to the gray box gets blocked, which leads to a falling edge again. As the periods get shorter and shorter over time, the influence of blocked messages gets smaller and smaller.

*Experiment II*

The input pattern (cf. Figure 7a) of Experiment II is very similar to the previous experiment with the exception that CTN 3 also generates messages at a constant rate. The experiment is now divided into three phases. The first phase is equivalent to Experiment I. In the second phase CTN 2 increases its bus load and starts to violate its minimum interarrival time. In the third phase, CTN 2 keeps increasing the send rate and therefore starts to influence CTN 3 on the shared CAN bus.

Figure 7b shows the output on CIS 0. The output of CTN 1 is constant and not influenced by any erroneous node. The same applies for CTN 3 until its messages get blocked by the erroneous node CTN 2. Again, the router forwards only half of CTN 4's messages.

Figure 8a shows that, contrary to Experiment I, there are minimum interarrival time violations caused by messages from CTN 2 before the actual configured minimum interarrival time. Those violations increase slowly starting from approximately second 5 until they sharply

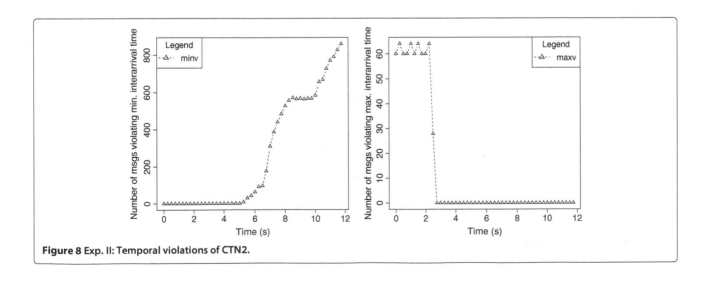

**Figure 8** Exp. II: Temporal violations of CTN2.

go up when the specified minimum interarrival time is undershot. This difference of the two experiments will be discussed in Section Discussion.

Figure 8b gives an overview about the number of messages violating the maximum interarrival time. In the first phase of Figure 7a the number of messages from CTN 2 is below the specified maximum interarrival time. Therefore, every missing message in that phase gets reported. In the second and third phase the erroneous node CTN 2 sends messages in the specified range, or even faster. Therefore, the number of violations of the maximum interarrival time drops to zero.

Figure 9 depicts the end-to-end latencies of CAN messages measured from the time the message was queued for transmission on the source CAN segment until it gets successfully received on the destination bus. As in phase 3 messages from CTN 3 get blocked by the erroneous node CTN 2 on the source bus, the latencies of messages with CAN ID 3 dramatically increase. At the same time the latencies of messages with a lower priority drop to the next lower level (i.e., CTN 4's latencies drop to the previous level of CTN 3).

In all our experiment runs we did not encounter a single experiment run where the router lost valid CAN messages.

## Discussion

Hypothesis 1 concerning fault detection was confirmed by the experiments. In the temporal domain, the router has detected violations of the maximum interarrival times (Phase 1 in Figure 7b) and violations of the minimum interarrival times (late Phase 2, and Phase 3 starting approx. at second 7 in Figure 7b).

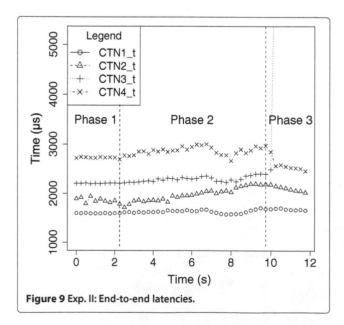

**Figure 9** Exp. II: End-to-end latencies.

In the value domain, the routing configuration permits the detection of invalid message identifiers, while the recognition of errors in the user data occurs using message checks. In addition, the CAN controllers [25] detect errors (e.g., stuffing error, CRC error, acknowledgment error) that are reported to the MU.

The experiments also provide evidence for hypothesis 2 and the fault containment of the CAN router. At each CAN port messages are blocked where value or timing failures are detected by the CAN controller or the CIS' CPU. In contrast to a bus-based system, no faulty messages or error frames are relayed by the CAN router. Thus, faulty messages do not cause inaccessibility times (e.g., due to bit errors, stuffing errors, CRC errors, form errors and acknowledgment errors) as described for bus-base systems in [26].

Besides eliminating these inaccessibility times, the fault containment coverage of the CAN router is significantly higher compared to bus-based systems. In a bus-based system, local error detection mechanisms are assumed to shutdown a CAN node that is affected by a fault. However, error detection mechanisms should be part of separate fault-containment regions in order to ensure that the error detection mechanisms are not impacted by the same fault that caused the message failure [27].

In addition to the containment of errors detected by the CAN controller at a CAN port, the CAN router blocks messages with invalid message identifiers and messages that violate the minimum interarrival time. The experiments show the impact of timing failures on messages on the same CAN segment and messages from other CAN segments. In the same CAN segment, message timing failures with a given priority affect all messages with lower priorities (cf. Figure 7). In contrast, the effect on messages from other CAN segments is bounded by the minimum interarrival times. The worst-case delay for a given message occurs when the bus of a CAN segment is not idle at the time of the transmission request and all higher priority messages are sent according to their minimum interarrival times. The experiments show that even lower priority CAN messages can introduce additional latencies for higher-priority ones (i.e., when a high priority message is queued for sending, but a lower priority message is currently being transmitted on the non-preemptive bus). The additional delay, regardless whether caused by a lower or higher priority message, can push two messages with the same CAN ID from a sender closer together. This behavior occurs when the last CAN message was delayed and the current one is not. In case those messages come too close, a minimum interarrival time violation occurs, even though the actual message rate (assuming a sufficiently large observation time) is not violated. For example, Figure 8a shows this behavior for messages sent by CTN 2, where violations of the minimum interarrival time occur before CTN 2 actually exceeds its allotted message rate. Consequently, the worst case delay (beside message size and CAN bus bitrate) must also be considered for the minimum interarrival time, if a maximum message rate should be guaranteed. This worst case delay can be computed using existing approaches for response time analysis in CAN [28].

For the given scenario of Experiment II, Figure 9 shows experimental results for these bounded effects of timing failures on the end-to-end latencies. Thus, hypothesis 3 was confirmed by the experimental results.

Due to its benefits concerning error detection and fault isolation, the CAN router can improve the reliability of existing CAN-based systems. Furthermore, for certain safety-relevant applications the CAN router can provide an alternative to more costly protocols (such as FlexRay in the automotive industry). If compatibility to existing CAN nodes is not required, two redundant CAN routers can be employed to tolerate an arbitrary single failure of a fault-containment region.

## Conclusion

In this paper we showed that standard CAN exhibits limitations with respect to reliability, diagnosis and scalability. We presented an intelligent CAN router based on a star topology that allows to overcome these existing limits. We experimentally validated the proposed capabilities and showed fault detection and isolation in the temporal as well as in the value domain. In the time domain this includes monitoring of minimum and maximum interarrival times and enforcing minimum interarrival times. In the value domain the router successfully enforced the permitted CAN identifiers of given CAN segments. We showed that the router enables the extension of application areas of CAN to systems with higher dependability and performance requirements, while still providing legacy CAN interface support.

### Competing interests

The authors declare that they have no competing interests.

### Acknowledgements

This work has been supported in part by the European research project INDEXYS under the Grant Agreement ARTEMIS-2008-1-100021 and in part by the European research project ACROSS under the funding ID ARTEMIS-2009-1-100208. The responsibility for the content rests with the authors.

### Author details

[1]Vienna University of Technology, Vienna, Austria. [2]University of Siegen, Siegen, Germany.

### References

1. K Tindell, H Hansson, in *Proceedings of the 1st International CAN Conference*, (Mainz, Germany, 1995), pp. 722–728
2. J Rufino, P Verissimo, G Arroz, in *Twenty-Ninth Annual International Symposium on Fault-Tolerant Computing*, (Madison, USA, 1999), pp. 286–293
3. M Livani, in *Proceedings of 6th International CAN Conference (ICC6)*, (Torino, Italy, 1999)
4. J Rufino, P Veríssimo, G Arroz, C Almeida, L Rodrigues, in *Proceedings of the 28th International Symposium on Fault-Tolerant Computing Systems*, (Munich, Germany, 1998), pp. 150–159
5. H Salmani, SG Miremadi, in *Proceedings of the 11th, Pacific Rim International Symposium on Dependable Computing* (IEEE Computer Society, Washington, DC, USA, 2005), pp. 310–316
6. FlexRay Consortium, BMW AG, DaimlerChrysler AG, General Motors Corporation, Freescale GmbH, Philips GmbH, Robert Bosch GmbH, Volkswagen AG, *FlexRay Communications System Protocol Specification Version 2.1*, (2005)
7. ISO11898 International Standardization Organisation, *Road vehicles—Interchange of Digital Information—Controller Area Network (CAN) for High-Speed Communication*, (1993)
8. M Mateos, P Robin, S Sauvage, V Joloboff, G Madhusudan, Y Bennani, in *Convergence International Congress & Exposition On Transportation Electronics*, (Detroit, USA, 2002)
9. J Barkai, in *Proceedings of Automotive & Transportation Technology (ATT) Congress & Exhibition*, vol. 5, (Barcelona, Spain, 2001)
10. P Veríssimo, J Rufino, L Rodrigues, in *Proceedings of the 10th IFAC Workshop on Distributed Computer Control Systems*, (Semmering, Austria, 1991)
11. P Verissimo, J Rufino, L Ming, in *Proceedings of Symposium on Fault-Tolerant Computing*, (Seattle, USA, 1997), pp. 112–121
12. J Rufino, *Dual-media redundancy mechanisms for CAN. Technical Report CSTC RT-97-01*. (Centro de Sistemas Telemáticos e Computacionais do Instituto Superior Técnico, Lisboa, Portugal, 1997)
13. H Kopetz, R Obermaisser. Computing and Control Engineering Journal. **13**, 156–162 (2002)
14. J Kaiser, M Livani, in *Dependable Computing – EDCC – 3*, (1999), pp. 351–363
15. R Obermaisser, H Kopetz, C Paukovits, in *IEEE Transactions on Industrial Informatics*, (2012), pp. 548–567
16. J Lala, R Harper, in *Proceedings of the IEEE*, vol. 82, issue 1, (1994), pp. 25–40
17. F Cristian. Commun. ACM Journal. **34**(2), 56–78 (1991)
18. J Suwatthikul, R McMurran, in *Proceedings of the International Symposium on Industrial Embedded Systems*, (Antibes, France, 2006), pp. 1–4
19. Association for Standardisation of Automation and Measuring Systems, *ASAM MCD-2 NET Data Model for ECU Network Systems (Field Bus Data Exchange Format) Version 3.1.0*, (2009)
20. R Obermaisser, R Kammerer, A Kasper, in *Proceedings of AmE 2011—Automotive meets Electronics*, (Dortmund, Germany, 2011)
21. A Bondavalli, S Chiaradonna, FD Giandomenico, F Grandoni. IEEE Tansactions on Computers Journal. **49**(3), 230–245
22. CE Salloum, M Elshuber, O Höftberger, H Isakovic, A Wasicek, in *15th Euromicro Symposium on Digital System Design (DSD)*, (Izmir, Turkey, 2012)
23. R Development Core Team, *R: A Language and Environment for Statistical Computing*. (R Foundation for Statistical Computing, Vienna, Austria, 2011). http://www.R-project.org/. ISBN 3-900051-07-0
24. C Paukovits, *The Time-Triggered System-on-Chip Architecture. Ph.D. thesis, TU Vienna*, (2008)
25. P Riekert, F Sprenger, *IFI NIOSII Advanced CAN module. Tech. rep., Ingenieurbüro für IC-Technologie*, (2010)
26. J Rufino, P Veríssimo, in *2nd International, CAN Conference*, (London, UK, 1995), pp. 7.12–7.21
27. H Kopetz, in *Proceedings of the International Symposium on Autonomous Decentralized Systems*, (Pisa, Italy, 2003), pp. 139–146
28. K Tindell, A Burns, A Wellings. Control Engineering Practice Journal. **3**, 1163–1169 (1995)

# 6

# Feasibility of backscatter RFID systems on the human body

Jasmin Grosinger

**Abstract**

In this contribution, the author examines the feasibility of on-body backscatter radio frequency identification (RFID) systems in the ultra high frequency range. Four different on-body RFID systems are investigated operating monopoles or patch antennas at 900 MHz or 2.45 GHz. The systems' feasibility is analyzed by means of on-body channel measurements in a realistic test environment. The measured channel transfer functions allow to evaluate if enough power is available for a reliable backscatter communication. This evaluation is done with the aid of outage probabilities in the forward link and the backward link of the systems. Using these probabilities, the on-body systems prove feasible when using state-of-the-art reader and transponder chips. In particular, the use of semi-passive RFID transponder chips leads to a reliable performance in the systems' forward links. The robust performance of the systems' backward links is clearly shown for the 900 MHz monopole antenna configuration, while the limitations in the backward links of the other systems have to be overcome by the use of a second reader unit on the person's back. The novel feasibility analysis presented here allows to examine each system parameter individually and thus leads to reliable and robust backscatter RFID systems.

**Keywords:** Wireless body area networks, Backscatter Radio Frequency Identification (RFID) systems, On-body RFID systems, RFID outage probabilities, On-body channel measurements, Feasibility analysis

## 1 Introduction

Wireless body area networks (WBANs) enable many new promising applications in the field of remote health monitoring, therapy support at home, wellness, and fitness. Therefore, the attention of the industry and the scientific community is highly drawn to WBANs [1,2]. WBANs connect sensor nodes situated in clothes, on the body, or under the skin of a person through a wireless communication channel.

A promising communication technology for WBANs is backscatter radio frequency identification (RFID) in the ultra high frequency (UHF) range. Backscatter RFID relies on the radio communication between an RFID reader, acting as a control unit, and a multitude of passive or semi-passive RFID transponders (tags), acting as sensor nodes. The principle of communication for transmitting information from the tag to the reader relies on a modulated backscatter signal. All power for the transmission

of the sensor data is drawn from the electromagnetic field radiated by the reader. Hence, their low-power consumption makes backscatter tags appropriate for WBANs that require small, light-weight, and low-maintenance sensor nodes. In addition, research efforts are ongoing to integrate sensing capabilities in backscatter tags without further enhancing their power consumption [3-5]. Such sensor tags can then be beneficially used to monitor the physiological parameters of a person (e.g., blood pressure, temperature, heartbeat, or body motion).

In backscatter RFID systems, it is vital to ensure a reliable power transmission to the backscatter tags and to realize a robust wireless communication between the reader and the tags [6]. To assure this, it is advisable to investigate the on-body radio propagation channel including the effects of the antennas and to study the wireless power transmission and communication in realistic operating environments. These characteristics are investigated in this contribution which studies the feasibility of four different backscatter RFID systems in a WBAN.

Correspondence: jasmin.grosinger@gmail.com
Vienna University of Technology, Institute of Telecommunications, Gusshausstrasse 25/389, 1040 Vienna, Austria

Previous studies on UHF RFID-based WBANs have focused on in-body [7-9] and off-body [10-12] communication systems. So far, the investigation of backscatter communication systems on the human body has received less attention in the literature. A first feasibility analysis of an on-body backscatter RFID system is presented in [13] and is based on indoor backscatter measurements at 870 MHz. The investigated RFID system consisted of an on-body reader with a patch antenna and five on-body tags composed of custom-built wearable felt antennas.

This contribution provides a feasibility analysis of four different on-body RFID systems. The feasibility analysis is based on outage probabilities derived from on-body channel measurements in a realistic test environment at 900 MHz and 2.45 GHz. In comparison to backscatter measurements, the analysis based on channel measurements allows to examine each system parameter individually and thus gives a deeper insight in the wireless power transmission and communication of backscatter RFID systems. The investigated RFID systems are composed of custom-built monopole or patch antennas operating at 900 MHz or 2.45 GHz. Each antenna acts as both reader and tag antennas.

The article is organized as follows. Section 2 describes the investigated on-body RFID systems and defines outage probabilities for a backscatter RFID system. The outage probabilities of the investigated RFID systems are then found by means of on-body channel measurements in Section 3. Section 4 analyzes the feasibility of the different on-body RFID systems based on these measurements.

## 2 On-body RFID systems

This contribution provides an investigation of four different on-body backscatter RFID systems. Figure 1 shows the arrangement of the on-body RFID reader and sensor tags situated on the body of an adult female. The RFID reader is situated on the stomach of the female, while four RFID tags are placed at various positions on the female's body: on the right chest, on the middle of the back, on the left side of the head, and on the right wrist. This arrangement leads to four typical on-body links which represent two trunk-to-trunk, a trunk-to-head, and a trunk-to-limb links following a classification of on-body links as introduced in [14].

The investigated RFID systems are composed of custom-built monopole or patch antennas operating at 900 MHz or 2.45 GHz (see Figure 2). Each antenna acts as both reader and tag antennas. For an adequate antenna design, a human body model has been created in Ansys' HFSS (high frequency structure simulator) [15]. The simplified model is an appropriate tool to design on-body antennas [16,17].

Practically, monopole antennas are not suitable for WBAN applications because they are not low profile.

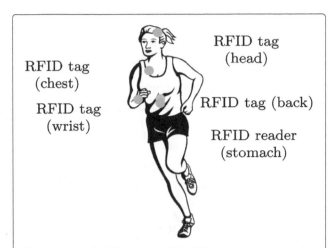

**Figure 1 On-body RFID systems.** The RFID reader is situated on the stomach of a female, while four RFID sensor tags are placed at various positions on the female's body—on the right chest, on the middle of the back, on the left side of the head, and on the right wrist. The sensor tag on the back is represented by an orange circle. The investigated RFID systems are composed of custom-built monopole or patch antennas operating at 900 MHz or 2.45 GHz. Each antenna acts as both reader and tag antennas (reprinted from [20], ©2012 IEEE).

However, monopoles show the best performance in on-body systems [18,19] and are used as a best-case reference in this study to define an upper bound for the performance of practical system implementations. Conversely, low profile patch antennas are especially suitable for on-body applications [18]. In this study, the less efficient patch antennas provide an insight in the performance of practical system implementations [20].

### 2.1 RFID outage probabilities

In backscatter RFID systems, a bidirectional radio link is established between the reader and the tag—the reader-tag-reader link—which can be subclassified into a forward link and a backward link. Figure 3 outlines the link budget of a backscatter radio system.

In the forward link, the reader transmits radio frequency (RF) power, $P_{\text{TX,Reader}}$, and data to the tag. The RFID tag consists of an antenna and a microchip. The power absorbed by the chip, $P_{\text{Chip}}$, is defined as

$$P_{\text{Chip}} = \tau P_{\text{Tag}} = \tau |S_{21}|^2 P_{\text{TX,Reader}}, \qquad (1)$$

where $\tau$ is the power transmission coefficient between the tag's antenna and chip [17] and $P_{\text{Tag}}$ is the power received by the tag's antenna. $S_{21}$ is the channel transfer function between the reader antenna and the tag antenna, $|S_{21}|^2$ defines the channel gain in the forward link of the system.

If $P_{\text{Chip}}$ is smaller than the minimum power which is required to activate the chip—which is denoted by the chip's sensitivity, $T_{\text{Chip}}$,—the backscatter communication

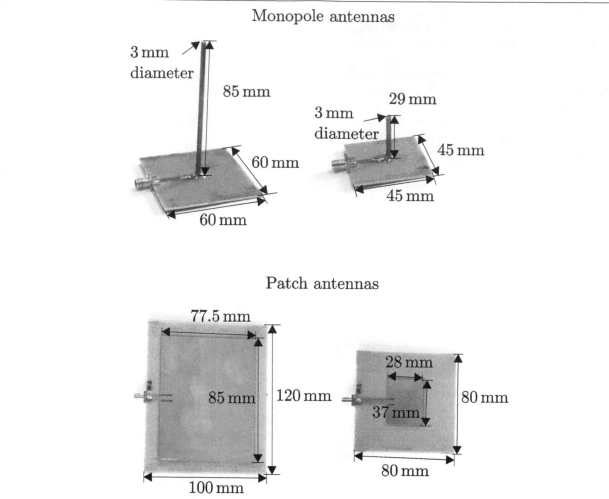

## Monopole antennas

3 mm diameter

85 mm

60 mm

60 mm

3 mm diameter

29 mm

45 mm

45 mm

## Patch antennas

77.5 mm

85 mm

120 mm

100 mm

28 mm

37 mm

80 mm

80 mm

**Figure 2 On-body antennas.** On-body monopole and patch antennas resonant at 900 MHz (left) and 2.45 GHz (right): The antennas were designed by means of a human body model and realized on FR-4 substrate with a thickness of 1.6 mm. The designs were optimized for an antenna-to-body separation distance of 5 mm. Details about the antenna properties can be found in [20] (reprinted from [20], ©2012 IEEE).

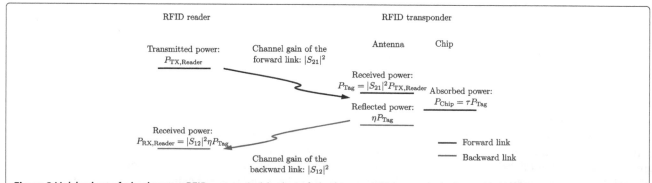

RFID reader

RFID transponder

Antenna      Chip

Transmitted power:
$P_{\text{TX,Reader}}$

Channel gain of the forward link: $|S_{21}|^2$

Received power:
$P_{\text{Tag}} = |S_{21}|^2 P_{\text{TX,Reader}}$

Absorbed power:
$P_{\text{Chip}} = \tau P_{\text{Tag}}$

Reflected power:
$\eta P_{\text{Tag}}$

Received power:
$P_{\text{RX,Reader}} = |S_{12}|^2 \eta P_{\text{Tag}}$

——— Forward link
——— Backward link

Channel gain of the backward link: $|S_{12}|^2$

**Figure 3 Link budget of a backscatter RFID system.** Link budget of a backscatter RFID system: In the forward link, the reader transmits RF power and data to the tag. The RFID tag consists of an antenna and a microchip. The power received by the tag antenna is $P_{\text{Tag}} = |S_{21}|^2 P_{\text{TX,Reader}}$. The power absorbed by the chip is $P_{\text{Chip}} = \tau P_{\text{Tag}}$, where $\tau$ is the power transmission coefficient of the tag. In the backward link, the tag responds to the reader by modulating the backscattered signal. The received power at the reader can be written as $P_{\text{RX,Reader}} = |S_{12}|^2 \eta P_{\text{Tag}}$, $\eta$ is the modulation efficiency of the tag.

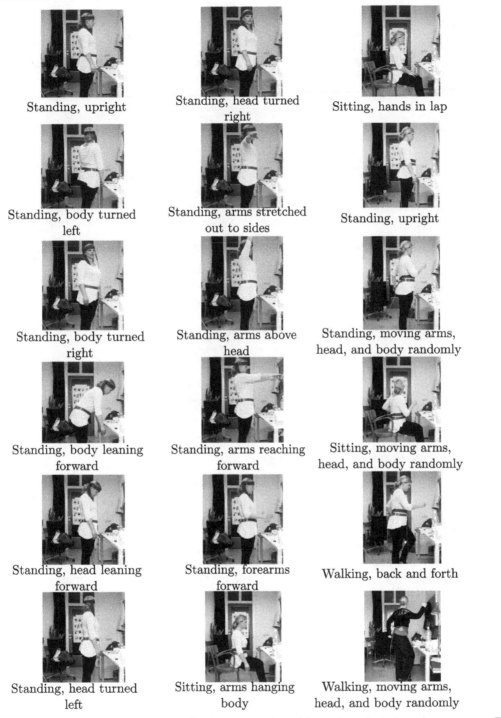

**Figure 4 Snapshot of different body postures.** Snapshots of body postures performed during the on-body channel measurements: The channel transfer functions, $S_{21}$ and $S_{12}$, of all four on-body RFID systems were measured versus 18 different stationary and moving body postures in an indoor multipath environment. The snapshots were taken during several measurement runs of the stomach-head and stomach-back links.

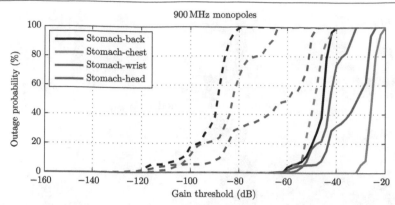

**Figure 5 Outage probabilities of 900 MHz monopoles.** Outage probabilities of the on-body RFID system operating the 900 MHz monopoles: The outage probabilities of the forward link and the backward link are plotted for all four on-body links versus their respective gain thresholds (solid lines: forward link, dashed lines: backward link). The outage probability of the forward link can be found by plotting the CDF of the measured channel gain of the forward link, $P_F = P\{|S_{21}|^2 \leq F_{Th}\}$. The gain threshold of the forward link, $F_{Th}$, is defined as the minimum channel gain that is necessary to initiate the chip's data transmission. The outage probability of the backward link can be found by plotting the CDF of the product of the measured channel gains in forward and backward links, $P_B = P\{|S_{21}|^2|S_{12}|^2 \leq B_{Th}\}$. The gain threshold of the backward link, $B_{Th}$, is defined as the minimum channel gain of the forward and backward links that is necessary to correctly receive the tag's data.

is limited in its forward link [6]. The minimum channel gain, $|S_{21}|^2$, that is necessary to avoid such a limitation, defines a gain threshold for the system's forward link (see Equation (1), $P_{Chip} = T_{Chip}$),

$$F_{Th} = \frac{T_{Chip}}{\tau P_{TX,Reader}}. \tag{2}$$

The probability that the channel gain is equal or smaller than this gain threshold is

$$P_F = P\left\{|S_{21}|^2 \leq F_{Th}\right\} \tag{3}$$

and defines the outage probability of the system's forward link, more precisely the probability that the backscatter system operates at its limit. This outage probability can be found by plotting the cumulative distribution function

(CDF) of the measured channel gain in the forward link, $|S_{21}|^2$ [21].

In the backward link, the tag responds to the reader by modulating the backscattered signal [22]. The power of the tag's signal at the receiver (RX) of the reader, $P_{RX,Reader}$, can be written as

$$P_{RX,Reader} = |S_{12}|^2\eta P_{Tag} = |S_{12}|^2\eta|S_{21}|^2 P_{TX,Reader}, \tag{4}$$

where $\eta$ is the modulation efficiency of the tag [17]. $S_{12}$ is the channel transfer function between the tag antenna and the reader antenna. $|S_{12}|^2$ defines the channel gain in the backward link.

$P_{RX,Reader}$ should be equal or bigger than the RX's sensitivity, $T_{RX,Reader}$, that is defined as the minimum input power at the reader to assure a successful reception of the tag's data. If $P_{RX,Reader}$ is smaller than $T_{RX,Reader}$, the

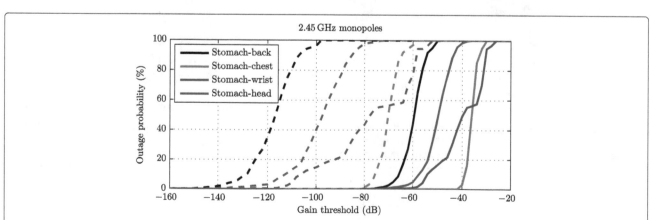

**Figure 6 Outage probabilities of 2.45 GHz monopoles.** Outage probabilities of the on-body RFID system operating the 2.45 GHz monopoles: The outage probabilities of the forward link and the backward link are plotted for all four on-body links versus their respective gain thresholds (solid lines: forward link, dashed lines: backward link).

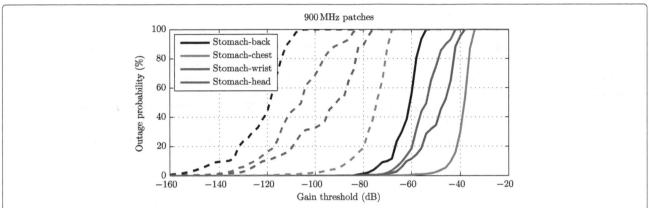

**Figure 7 Outage probabilities of 900 MHz patches.** Outage probabilities of the on-body RFID system operating the 900 MHz patches: The outage probabilities of the forward link and the backward link are plotted for all four on-body links versus their respective gain thresholds (solid lines: forward link, dashed lines: backward link).

communication system is limited in its backward link [6]. The total minimum channel gain, $|S_{21}|^2|S_{12}|^2$, that is necessary to realize $P_{RX,Reader} = T_{RX,Reader}$, characterizes a gain threshold for the backward link of the system (see Equation (4)),

$$B_{Th} = \frac{T_{RX,Reader}}{\eta P_{TX,Reader}}. \tag{5}$$

The outage probability of the system's backward link is defined as the probability that the total channel gain is equal or smaller than this gain threshold,

$$P_B = P\left\{|S_{21}|^2|S_{12}|^2 \leq B_{Th}\right\}. \tag{6}$$

This probability can be found by plotting the CDF of the product of the measured channel gain in the forward link and the backward link, $|S_{21}|^2|S_{12}|^2$.

## 3 On-body channel measurements

To examine the outage probabilities of the on-body backscatter systems, the channel transfer functions, $S_{21}$ and $S_{12}$, were measured for all four antenna configurations by means of a vector network analyzer [16,17]. The channel transfer functions depend on the antenna characteristics of the reader and the tag (e.g., antenna gain and polarization) and on the properties of the on-body radio links (e.g., path length and fading). The functions were measured in a realistic test scenario versus 18 different stationary and moving body postures in an indoor multipath environment. Figure 4 shows snapshots of the different postures that are based on a list of body postures published in [14]. Each posture was held 20 s, the repetition rate of the measurement was 5 s$^{-1}$. As a result, the channel transfer functions are composed of 1800 measurement points at the specific frequency.

The measurement results are plotted in Figures 5, 6, 7, and 8 for all four antenna configurations. Each figure plots

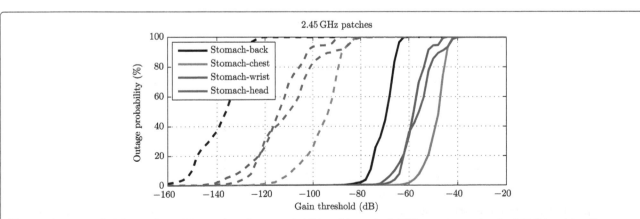

**Figure 8 Outage probabilities of 2.45 GHz patches.** Outage probabilities of the on-body RFID system operating the 2.45 GHz patches: The outage probabilities of the forward link and the backward link are plotted for all four on-body links versus their respective gain thresholds (solid lines: forward link, dashed lines: backward link).

the outage probabilities of the forward and backward links versus their respective gain thresholds. As introduced in the previous section, the outage probability of the forward link is found by plotting the CDF of the measured channel gain, $|S_{21}|^2$, according to Equation (3). The outage probability of the backward link is found by plotting the CDF of the product of the measured channel gains in the forward link and the backward link, $|S_{21}|^2|S_{12}|^2$, according to Equation (6). Figures 5 and 6 show the outage probabilities of the RFID systems operating the 900 MHz and 2.45 GHz monopole antennas, while Figures 7 and 8 plot the results for the 900 MHz and 2.45 GHz patch antenna configurations.

## 4 Feasibility analysis

In the following, the different on-body RFID systems are analyzed by means of the outage probabilities found in the previous section.

As expected from theory and from previous measurement campaigns at 2.45 GHz [14], Figure 5 shows that on-body links with longer path lengths have higher outage probabilities in comparison to links with shorter distances (compare, e.g., the stomach-back link with the stomach-chest link). In addition, the link geometry and thus the channel gain are influenced by the movements of the body.

The strength of this influence depends on the on-body link. An on-body link with a higher mobility experiences a wider range of outage probabilities than trunk-to-trunk links with lower mobility (compare, e.g., the stomach-wrist link with the stomach-chest link). These behaviors can be observed for all four antenna configurations in their forward and backward links (see Figures 6, 7 and 8).

In addition, the figures show that the outage probabilities of the 900 MHz antennas are lower than the probabilities of the 2.45 GHz antennas (compare, e.g., Figures 5 and 6). This difference is due to an increased energy absorption in human tissues at higher frequencies [23]. Again, this behavior can be observed for both antenna types, the monopoles and the patch antennas.

Furthermore, the probability curves of all four figures show that the monopoles act indeed as best-case references.

### 4.1 State-of-the-art example

Subsequently, the outage probabilities for all four antenna configurations are explored individually for each system parameter of a state-of-the-art system example, i.e., $P_{TX,Reader}$, $\tau$, $T_{Chip}$, $\eta$, and $T_{RX,Reader}$. In general, the maximum permitted outage probabilities are governed

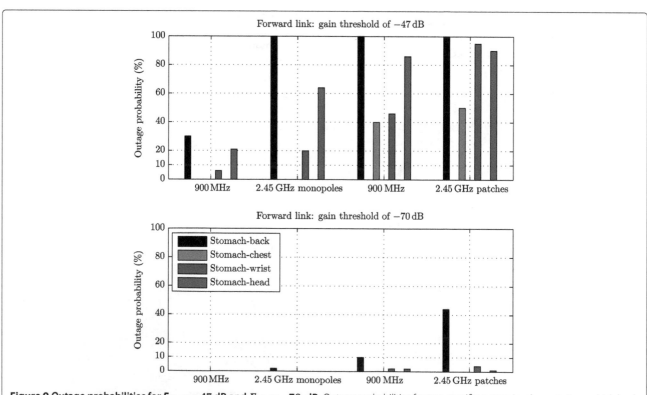

**Figure 9 Outage probabilities for $F_{Th} = -47$ dB and $F_{Th} = -70$ dB.** Outage probabilities for two specific system implementations which lead to gain thresholds of $F_{Th} = -47$ dB and $F_{Th} = -70$ dB (upper bar chart: −47 dB, lower bar chart: −70 dB): The outage probabilities of the forward link are plotted for all four on-body links and for all four antenna configurations (900 MHz and 2.45 GHz monopoles, 900 MHz and 2.45 GHz patches). The allowed outage probabilities are 10% for all on-body RFID system implementations.

by the application. The outage probabilities should be close to zero for a system that monitors life parameters of patients in clinical care, while systems used in sports analysis can deal with higher outage probabilities. In the following, the systems allow a maximum outage probability of 10%.

In the state-of-the-art system, the on-body reader consists of an Impinj Indy reader chip with an external power amplifier [24]. The reader provides a maximum transmit power of $P_{TX,Reader} = 30\,dBm$ and an RX sensitivity of $T_{RX,Reader} = -95\,dBm$. The on-body tags consist of passive Monza 5 tag chips [25]. The passive chips provide a sensitivity of $T_{Chip} = -17.8\,dBm$. The power transmission coefficient is assumed to be 100%, while the modulation efficiency is 20%. These system parameters lead to gain thresholds of $F_{Th} = -47\,dB$ and $B_{Th} = -118\,dB$ (see Equations (2) and (5)).

The upper bar chart of Figure 9 shows the outage probabilities of the forward link for the gain threshold of $F_{Th} = -47\,dB$. The figure plots the probabilities for each antenna configuration and for each on-body link. The probabilities are deduced from Figures 5, 6, 7, and 8. Figure 9 shows that the investigated RFID systems are considerably limited in their forward link, i.e. the outage

probabilities are above 10%. There are different strategies to overcome these limitations. An increase in the transmit power is not an option because of the safety regulations and power constraints in on-body systems [26,27]. Another strategy is to use semi-passive backscatter tags with chip sensitivities down to $-40\,dBm$. Such a sensitivity leads to a gain threshold in the forward link of $F_{Th} = -70\,dB$. The lower bar chart of Figure 9 shows that semi-passive tags lead to a good performance in the on-body systems' forward links, i.e., to outage probabilities lower than 10%. However, there is still a rather large limitation in the stomach-back link of the 2.45 GHz patch antenna system. This constraint can be resolved by the use of more efficient patch antennas realized on a low-loss substrate or by the use of higher mode patches which benefit surface waves along the human body like monopole antennas. Another solution would be the use of a second RFID reader on the female's back to reduce the path lengths.

The upper bar chart of Figure 10 shows the outage probabilities in the systems' backward links for a gain threshold of $B_{Th} = -118\,dB$. Limitations can be observed in the on-body systems operating the 2.45 GHz monopoles, the 900 MHz and 2.45 GHz

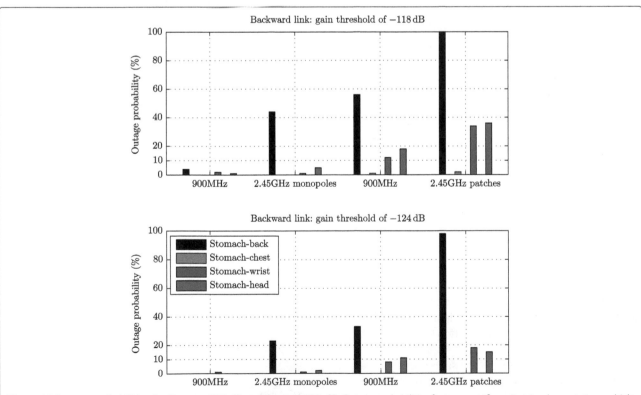

**Figure 10 Outage probabilities for $B_{Th} = -118$ dB and $B_{Th} = -124$ dB.** Outage probabilities for two specific system implementations which lead to gain thresholds of $B_{Th} = -118\,dB$ and $B_{Th} = -124\,dB$ (upper bar chart: $-118\,dB$, lower bar chart: $-124\,dB$): The outage probabilities of the backward link are plotted for all four on-body links and for all four antenna configurations (900 MHz and 2.45 GHz monopoles, 900 MHz and 2.45 GHz patches). The allowed outage probabilities are 10% for all on-body RFID system implementations.

patches. To overcome these limitations, a phase-modulated backscatter signal can be used [17]. This modulation scheme provides a maximum modulation efficiency of $\eta = 81\%$ and leads to gain threshold of about $-124\,\text{dB}$. However, if a phase-modulated backscatter signal is applied, there should be no substantial limitations in the system's forward link [17]. The lower bar chart of Figure 10 shows the outage probabilities in the backward link for the $-124\,\text{dB}$ threshold. The 6 dB difference in the threshold only slightly improves the performance of the systems. Further strategies have to be applied to overcome all limitations in the backward links, in particular in the stomach-back links. A promising strategy is to use a second reader unit on the female's back, other strategies are e.g., the realization of more sophisticated antennas or the use of a reader RX with a lower sensitivity.

## 5  Conclusions

In conclusion, the author demonstrated the feasibility of backscatter UHF RFID systems on the human body at 900 MHz and 2.45 GHz. Until now, the investigation of on-body backscatter RFID systems has received less attention in the literature. A first feasibility analysis of an on-body backscatter RFID system was based on indoor backscatter measurements at 870 MHz, where the investigated RFID system consisted of an on-body reader with a patch antenna and on-body tags composed of custom-built wearable felt antennas. In this contribution, four different on-body RFID systems are investigated operating two different types of on-body antennas. Monopole antennas act as best-case references, while the less efficient patch antennas are used to give an insight into practical RFID system implementations.

In this article, the author presents a novel feasibility analysis based on on-body channel measurements in a realistic test environment. In particular, the channel transfer functions of the systems were measured versus different stationary and moving body postures and led to outage probabilities of the systems' forward and backward links. These outage probabilities helped to easily identify limitations in the backscatter systems and to evaluate strategies to overcome these barriers for the realization of reliable on-body RFID systems. In comparison to backscatter measurements, the analysis based on channel measurements allows to examine each system parameter individually and thus gives a deeper insight in the wireless power transmission and communication of backscatter RFID systems.

It is worth pointing out that the presented analysis can be performed for any kind of backscatter RFID system. The analysis provides an initial overview of a backscatter system and ultimately allows to realize a reliable power transmission to the chips and a robust wireless communication between the reader and the tags.

**Competing interests**
The author declares that she has no competing interests.

**Acknowledgements**
This study was performed as part of the project "MAS—Nanoelectronics for Mobile Ambient Assisted Living-Systems" which is funded by "ENIAC Joint Undertaking" and Austria's "Österreichische Forschungsförderungsgesellschaft".

**References**
1. Y Hao, R Foster, Wireless body sensor networks for health-monitoring applications. Physiol. Meas. **29**(11), R27–R56 (2008)
2. S Patel, H Park, P Bonato, L Chan, M Rodgers, A review of wearable sensors and systems with application in rehabilitation. J. NeuroEng. Rehab. **9**(21), 1–17 (2012)
3. A Sample, D Yaeger, P Powledge, A Mamishev, J Smith, Design of an RFID-based battery-free programmable sensing platform. IEEE Trans. Instrum. Meas. **57**(11), 2608–2615 (2008)
4. G Marrocco, Multiport sensor RFIDs for wireless passive sensing of objects—basic theory and early results. IEEE Trans. Antennas Propag. **56**(8), 2691–2702 (2008)
5. J Grosinger, J Griffin, in *Proc. IEEE Antennas and Propagation Society International Symposium.* A bend transducer for backscatter RFID sensors, (2012), doi:10.1109/APS.2012.6349258
6. P Nikitin, K Rao, in *Proc IEEE Antennas and Propagation Society International Symposium.* Performance limitations of passive UHF RFID systems, (2006), pp. 1011–1014, doi:10.1109/APS.2006.1710704
7. A Sani, M Rajab, R Foster, Y Hao, Antennas and propagation of implanted RFIDs for pervasive healthcare applications. Proc. IEEE. **98**(9), 1648–1655 (2010)
8. C Schmidt, D Valderas, J Garcia, I Ortego, X Chen, in *Proc. European Conference on Antennas and Propagation.* Passive UHF RFID near field link budget for implanted sensors, (2011), pp. 3479–3483
9. C Occhiuzzi, G Contri, G Marrocco, Design of implanted RFID tags for passive sensing of human body: the STENTag. IEEE Trans. Antennas Propag. **60**(7), 3146–3154 (2012)
10. M Polivka, M Svanda, P Hudec, S Zvanovec, UHF RF identification of people in indoor and open areas. IEEE Trans. Microw. Theory Tech. **57**(5), 1341–1347 (2009)
11. C Occhiuzzi, S Cippitelli, G Marrocco, Modeling, design and experimentation of wearable RFID sensor tag. IEEE Trans. Antennas Propag. **58**(8), 2490–2498 (2010)
12. S Cotton, W Cully, W Scanlon, J McQuiston, in *Proc. Loughborough Antennas and Propagation Conference.* Channel characterisation for indoor wearable active RFID at 868 MHz, (2011), pp. 1–4, doi:10.1109/LAPC.2011.6114085
13. S Manzari, C Occhiuzzi, G Marrocco, Feasibility of body-centric systems using passive textile RFID Tags. IEEE Antennas Propag. Mag. **54**(4), 49–62 (2012)
14. P Hall, Y Hao, *Antennas and Propagation for Body-Centric Wireless Communications.* (Artech House Inc., USA, 2006)
15. ANSYS Inc ANSYS HFSS (2012). [http://www.ansys.com/Products/Simulation+Technology/Electromagnetics/High-Performance+Electronic+Design/ANSYS+HFSS]
16. J Grosinger, M Fischer, in *Proc. IEEE-APS Topical Conference on Antennas and Propagation in Wireless Communications.* Indoor on-body channel measurements at 900 MHz, (2011), pp. 1037–1040, doi:10.1109/APWC.2011.6046824
17. J Grosinger, Backscatter radio frequency systems and devices for novel wireless sensing applications (2012). *Ph.d. thesis,* Vienna University of Technology
18. G Conway, W Scalon, Antennas for over-body-surface communication at 2.45 GHz. IEEE Trans. Antennas Propag. **57**(4), 844–855 (2009)
19. P Hall, Y Hao, Y Nechayev, A Alomainy, C Constantinou, C Parini, M Kamarudin, T Salim, D Hee, R Dubrovka, A Owadally, W Song, A Serra, P Nepa, M Gallo, M Bozzetti, Antennas and propagation for on-body communication systems. IEEE Antennas Propag. Mag. **49**(3), 41–58 (2007)

20. J Grosinger, M Fischer, in *Proc. International EURASIP Workshop on RFID Technology*. Evaluating on-body RFID systems at 900 MHz and 2.45 GHz, (2012), pp. 52–58, doi:10.1109/RFID.2012.14

21. G Lasser, R Langwieser, F Xaver, C Mecklenbräuker, in *Proc. IEEE International Conference on RFID*. Dual-band channel gain statistics for dual-antenna tyre pressure monitoring RFID Tags, (2011), pp. 57–61, doi:10.1109/RFID.2011.5764637

22. JP Curty, M Declercq, C Dehollain, N Joehl, *Design and, Optimization of Passive UHF RFID Systems*. (Springer Science+Business Media, LLC, New York, 2007)

23. S Gabriel, R Lau, C Gabriel, The dielectric properties of biological tissue: III. parametric models for the dielectric spectrum of tissues. Phys. Med. Biol. **41**(11), 2271–2293 (1996)

24. Impinj, Inc, Indy R1000 Reader Chip (IPJ-P1000) (2012). [http://www.impinj.com]

25. Impinj, Inc, Monza 5 Tag Chip Datasheet (IPJ-W1600) (2012). [http://www.impinj.com]

26. A Ahlbom, U Bergqvist, J Bernhardt, J Cesarini, L Court, M Grandolfo, M Hietanen, A Mckinlay, M Repacholi, D Sliney, J Stolwijk, M Swicord, L Szabo, M Taki, T Tenforde, H Jammet, R Matthes, Guidelines for limiting exposure to time-varying electric, magnetic, and electromagnetic fields (Up to 300 GHz). Health Phys. **74**(4), 494–522 (1998)

27. IEEE standard for safety levels with respect to human exposure to radio frequency electromagnetic fields, 3 kHz to 300 GHz. IEEE Std C95.1-1991 (1992)

# 7

# Hybrid WSN and RFID indoor positioning and tracking system

Zhoubing Xiong[1]*, Zhenyu Song[1], Andrea Scalera[2]*, Enrico Ferrera[2], Francesco Sottile[2], Paolo Brizzi[2], Riccardo Tomasi[2] and Maurizio A Spirito[2]

## Abstract

Wireless sensor networks (WSNs), consisting of a large number of nodes to detect ambient environment, are widely deployed in a predefined area to provide more sophisticated sensing, communication, and processing capabilities, especially concerning the maintenance when hundreds or thousands of nodes are required to be deployed over wide areas at the same time. Radio frequency identification (RFID) technology, by reading the low-cost passive tags installed on objects or people, has been widely adopted in the tracing and tracking industry and can support an accurate positioning within a limited distance. Joint utilization of WSN and RFID technologies is attracting increasing attention within the Internet of Things (IoT) community, due to the potential of providing pervasive context-aware applications with advantages from both fields. WSN-RFID convergence is considered especially promising in context-aware systems with indoor positioning capabilities, where data from deployed WSN and RFID systems can be opportunistically exploited to refine and enhance the collected data with position information. In this paper[a], we design and evaluate a hybrid system which combines WSN and RFID technologies to provide an indoor positioning service with the capability of feeding position information into a general-purpose IoT environment. Performance of the proposed system is evaluated by means of simulations and a small-scale experimental set-up. The performed analysis demonstrates that the joint use of heterogeneous technologies can increase the robustness and the accuracy of the indoor positioning systems.

## 1 Introduction

Recent technological developments in the miniaturization of electronics and wireless communication technology have motivated the development of small-sized, low-power, and inexpensive sensing and radio-equipped devices, and dramatically reduce the cost of deploying pervasive monitoring and tracking applications in large-scale scenarios where various data are collected from hundreds of different locations. Since it has been practical in the last few years to collect, process, and exploit massive data from millions or even billions of devices, new paradigms are emerging based on the global Internet of Things (IoT) to extend the border of the current Internet to the physical world. The IoT makes every physical object become a potential part of a distributed network in which heterogeneous devices autonomously and spontaneously abstract and share context information from the real world [1].

Unlike the traditional pervasive systems, which are specifically designed to monitor a predefined set of interested physical phenomena, e.g., vibration for structural health monitoring systems and temperature for energy optimization systems, the IoT conceives a single pervasive network to support seamless, interoperable, cross-application data collection from any kind of device for any type of information. In addition to the data collection procedures, establishment of the relationship among the collected samples is commonly recognized as another significant issue in such a scenario, i.e., constructing the 'context' information [2]. In IoT environments, position information covers a primal role because it provides useful context knowledge to be associated with other monitored parameters. For example, the meaning of a temperature reading could vary significantly in case it is close to a window, or on top of an heater, etc.

*Correspondence: zhoubing.xiong@polito.it; scalera@ismb.it
[1] Department of Electronics and Telecommunications, Politecnico di Torino, Torino, Italy
[2] Pervasive Technologies, Istituto Superiore Mario Boella, Torino, Italy

Wireless sensor networks (WSNs) represent a key technology for IoT scenarios (such as environmental monitoring, e-health, surveillance, and manufacturing [3]). A WSN is a community of objects, where those objects are usually small-embedded devices with capability of sensing physical phenomena in the environment and are equipped with radio components to communicate with each other wirelessly. Through their on-board radio interfaces, these devices can collect or disseminate data and collaboratively form a cooperative network either *ad hoc* or with a cluster-based architecture to perform some specific actions in large-scale static or mobile environments [4]. WSN nodes leverage on a common set of protocols and algorithms to set-up an *ad hoc* network to transport data in multi-hop fashion to one or more central nodes namely 'sink nodes' or gateways, which in turn provide connectivity towards the Internet. As an innovative and powerful solution for various kinds of applications, WSN is especially suitable to be adopted when the range of the monitored area exceeds a single device's radio range, when cost-effective monitoring is required and/or simple in-network processing of physical parameter is needed.

By associating a unique digital identifier with each physical item, radio frequency identification (RFID) technology becomes a fundamental technique in the IoT scenario [5]. The confluence of the absence of batteries, the low cost, and the rapid proliferation of passive RFID tags in the past decade have made the RFID technology revolutionize the tracing and tracking industry and become a *de facto* reference technology [6].

Although WSN and RFID can be considered as substitutive technologies in some use cases, they are historically born to cover different needs. Recently, a number of researchers are endeavoring to jointly utilize these technologies to exploit the advantages of both systems [7-9].

This work evaluates how the joint use of RFID and WSN technologies can be effectively exploited within IoT positioning and tracking systems. The motivating goal of this research is to provide a whole range of location-based service with more precise and more reliable results according to various needs. To achieve this goal, the diverse data collected by WSN nodes are associated with a wider set of position information which are allowed to be further exploited by context-aware systems.

According to the work in [10], the locating systems can be preliminarily grouped into two major categories: *receptive* locating systems and *transmissive* locating systems. In the *receptive* locating systems, the position information is distributed ubiquitously, and the mobile device can derive its own location from this information [the global positioning system (GPS) is the most representative example]. The mobile device can independently locate the derived position in a map, so a local service (without revealing its position to a third party) can be easily provided on top of this locating information, or some value-added services can be obtained by sharing this locating information with others. Conversely, in the *transmissive* locating systems, the position is derived by a fixed station which either sees the mobile device or receives a beacon from it. The station can transmit the derived locating result back to the device or use it to generate other value-added services. Sub-cell global system for mobile communications or GSM positioning is a prime example employs this approach, which leverages the mobile communication channel beacon. Also *hybrid* techniques combining these principles are possible, and this paper will actually underline this possibility.

Despite years of research and experimentation, very few positioning technologies, apart the GPS, have nowadays a significant economical impact. Only a few sets of technology are available for indoor locating, usually designed for niche or legacy markets. The reasons of this poor diffusion include high costs compared to the added value achieved, technology constraints (regarding precision, reliability, and performances), and, generally speaking, the lack of killer applications.

Starting from previous works where the feasibility of the joint use of WSN and RFID in indoor positioning applications was assessed through simulations [11,12], this paper outlines the reference design of a hybrid indoor positioning system leveraging both WSN radio information and RFID detection events. Parts of this paper was presented in our previous work in [13], which provided the initial glance of the hybrid WSN-RFID localization system. First, this paper goes into more details of the proposed hybrid reference architecture. Second, it details the formulation of the designed hybrid positioning algorithm and provides an analysis of the related computational complexity. Third, it compares the performance of different variants of the same hybrid approach. Forth, it calibrates the received signal strength indicator (RSSI) model on the basis of real experimental measurements. Finally, it improves the performance of the localization algorithm by introducing some new robustness conditions based on the WSN and RFID ranging models. In particular, the performance is evaluated by means of both computer simulations and through a small-scale experimental set-up.

The remainder of the paper is organized as follows: Section 2 provides a brief overview of the state of the art of indoor positioning systems. Then the reference architecture and structural components (namely the WSN and the RFID segment) of the proposed solution are elaborated together with the field trial scenario in Section 3. The positioning algorithm employed by the system is deeply analyzed and illustrated in Section 4. Furthermore, the system is validated in the controlled conditions, and the simulation and experimental results are presented in the Section 5. In Section 6 we draw the conclusions.

## 2   Related work

Positioning systems generate a lot of interest and effort both in academic and industrial research and nowadays, a lot of technologies can be used and mixed (e.g., ultrasound, laser scanner, infrared, camera vision, radio frequencies, and custom sensors). Each system has addressed the aggregation of sensor data into location estimations via most suitable methods.

Positioning and tracking are crucial features in many ubiquitous computing and robotics applications where knowledge about the location of the entities (i.e., people and objects) is required [14,15].

Nowadays, most widely advanced positioning services have been thought for outdoor scenarios. Indeed, radar locating systems for ships and aircrafts are used for the longest time for historical reasons. Global navigation satellite systems (GNSS) - such as GPS and Galileo - are mature technologies for vehicle navigation and are widely adopted in everyday life. Unfortunately, both these technologies are not suitable for indoor environments, the first because of the severity of multipath noise from which it is afflicted and the difficulties of multi-object localization, the second because of the buildings obstructiveness on GNSS signals.

In order to achieve people and object localizations in indoor environments by overcoming such disadvantages, significant research has been conducted over the years in different indoor positioning systems (IPSs) [16-18].

Dempsey [19] defines an IPS as a system which can infer the position of a target inside the physical space where the detection system is installed, within a maximum time delay or in real time. In the second case, it is usual to speak of real-time locating system (RTLS), which, standing to an ISO definition [20], *is the ability to locate the position of an item anywhere in a defined space at a point in time that is, or is close to, real time.* Generally speaking, the RTLS definition is used when discussing about asset locating and about products or goods tracking and traceability.

IPSs are based on some prior knowledge about position of special nodes, namely the *anchor* nodes, and aim at estimating position of one or more *mobile* nodes, whose positions are unknown, by processing ranging data collected and exchanged by both mobile and anchor nodes.

According to Liu [21], there are four different system topologies for IPSs: (1) remote positioning system, (2) self-positioning systems, (3) indirect remote positioning systems, and (4) indirect self-positioning systems. In remote positioning system, a mobile node acts as main signal transmitter and several anchor measuring units receive and measure its broadcasted signal. The results from all measuring units are collected, and the location of the transmitter is computed in a central master station. In self-positioning systems, the mobile acts instead as measuring unit. This unit receives the signals of several transmitters in known locations and computes its location locally based on the measured signals. Two middle-way approaches are also possible: in indirect remote positioning systems, measurements collected by the mobile node are transmitted via a wireless data link for remote position computation; in indirect self-positioning systems, measurements collected locally by fixed stations are transmitted to the mobile through a wireless data link.

IPSs can also be classified according to the employed position estimation technique. Different positioning techniques can be combined to compensate the limitations of a single method.

Angle of arrival or AoA method is based on the receiver antenna amplitude or phase response. The accuracy of this method depends on the antenna directivity, multipath reflection, and signal shadowing; overall they can achieve 2 to 4 m accuracy [22]. It presents two main problems: nodes require a directional antenna with beam forming and line of sight propagation path is needed between the transmitter and the receiver.

Time of arrival (ToA) and time difference of arrival or TDoA methods are both based on measurement of the propagation time. These methods are hard to implement in radio frequency IPSs because very accurate timers are needed to reach an acceptable accuracy. Furthermore, within environments affected by multipath, the detection of time of arrival is accurate only for very large signal bandwidths. For this reason, some systems use ultra-wide band (UWB) technology for an accurate ToA estimation. The proximity method, also known as cell of origin (CoO), consists in detecting an entity presence inside a limited area, or cell, in which coordinates are known.

RSSI method is instead based on the measurement of radio power at the receiver. Despite the fact that RSSI measurement is time varying and unstable under most circumstances, RSSI-based solutions are widely used as localization technique in WSN systems. RSSI measurements are in fact adopted in many wireless sensor network (WSN) communication standards and are thus made available at no cost by normal radio transceivers installed on-board WSN nodes, without need for additional hardware affecting power consumption and size or cost of WSN nodes.

Two common techniques to exploit RSSI for localization are based on fingerprinting signal strengths and conversion of signal strength to distance. In fingerprinting techniques, a map of the signal strength behavior in the coverage area is constructed. In a first phase, a set of offline measurements is performed to build a database; then, during the real-time location phase, the algorithm searches for the best matches between the RSSI samples and the stored values. Precision of such methods is normally limited: MoteTrack [23] can achieve an 80% location-tracking accuracy of 1.6 m and Ekahau positioning engine [24] achieves an accuracy of 1 to 2 m. The disadvantage of this method is the tiresome calibration phase, during which large amounts of measurements are collected to construct the database. Furthermore, if prior measurements are used when an environmental change occurs, a new calibration phase is needed.

Another family of techniques involves conversion of RSSI to distance using Friis equation [25]. This equation establishes the strength of a signal sent by a radio transmitter in free space at one particular distance, following an exponential relation. In this kind of algorithms, transmitting nodes (either anchors or mobiles) broadcast their last known position along with any RSSI information previously collected from other nodes. Using the exponential relation, the receiver can convert the RSSI measurements into distances and, using triangulation, estimate its location in relation to the anchors. Locating errors using these methods are in average slightly higher than in fingerprinting due to two main reasons: the way that the empirical RSSI-distance relation differs from the theoretical model assumed in the algorithm and the environmental changes affecting RSSI stability. Although this kind of algorithms provide lower accuracy than other techniques, their simplicity makes them more suitable to be employed in low-power systems.

Finally, IPSs can be classified on the different underlying technologies adopted for ranging. In the field of those working at radio frequency, each adopted technology brings unique advantages and disadvantages in the indoor position inference. Wireless local area network (WLAN) technology [17,26] is widespread; and all types of mobile device, from laptop to smartphone and tablet, are nowadays able to communicate with this standard. WLAN can be used to estimate the location of a mobile device within the local network without line-of-sight necessity. Most positioning methods in WLAN locating systems are based on RSSI. The accuracy obtained using this technology ranges from meters to tens of meters. Room-level accuracy can be reached using Bluetooth [27-30]. The major issue using this technology is the unsuitability in RTLS applications because of the delay caused by the inquiry scan process that is performed by a device to detect other devices. UWB is a short-range and high-bandwidth communication technology, with strong multipath resistance and building penetrability. UWB has recently gained a lot of interest in indoor positioning researches thanks to its theoretical accuracy that is in the order of few centimeters [31-34]. An issue of UWB regards the expensive cost of a single node which makes the technology unsuitable for extensive deployments.

In the following subsections, two technologies will be introduced which have been used for the implementation of the hybrid positioning system explained in this paper: WSN based on IEEE 802.15.4 standard and RFID.

## 2.1 IEEE 802.15.4-based WSN positioning systems

IEEE 802.15.4 is a standard which specifies the physical and media access control layers for a low-power and low-rate wireless personal area networks (PANs). It is the basis for a number of specifications, such as ZigBee, which further extend the standard by developing the upper layers which are not defined in IEEE 802.15.4.

ZigBee nodes can communicate each other within a range of nearly 100 m outdoors, in free space, but indoors it is usually 5 to 20 m. To determine the distance between two nodes, RSSI technique is typically adopted. ZigBee is particularly affected by service interruptions which is also due to the band frequency in which it communicates, and its band is also occupied by noisy communication protocols such as WiFi and Bluetooth. ZigBee is particularly affected by service interruptions which are due to the overlapping of its operating frequency band with noisy communications protocols such as WiFi and Bluetooth.

Tadakamadla [35] deployed ZigBee network for monitoring the presence and movements of vehicles and humans into an indoor environment. It uses the RSSI to determine the position of tagged entities; the randomness of RSSI and the dependency on the user's body and orientation cause the main error contribution. In this work an accuracy of 3 m and 35% precision were obtained.

Larranaga et al. [36] used ZigBee network to monitor an area of 432 $m^2$. The network consists of eight reference nodes, and RSSI is used to locate mobile nodes. In this work an average localization accuracy of 3 m was obtained.

My Bodyguard [37] is a commercial system that tracks objects and people. It is based on the ZigBee for indoor environments and on GNSS and cellular networks for outdoor environments. With this device a room-level accuracy is obtained.

Alternatively, IEEE 802.15.4 can also be used with 6LoWPAN and standard Internet protocols to build a wireless embedded Internet. The WSN used for the IPS developed for this work is based on 6LoWPAN.

## 2.2 RFID positioning systems

RFID is a technology that allows to identify an object, called tag, and reading the unique code stored within tag itself. A typical RFID system is made by at least three components: the radio frequency transponder, the reader (a transceiver controlled by a microprocessor used to inquiry a tag), a client software (communicate with a reader through a reader protocol, collecting, storing, and/or processing codes retrieved from the tags). In RFID-based positioning systems, CoO positioning method is principally used. Using these positioning methods, the accuracy is highly dependent on the number of tags involved and on the maximal reading range. RSSI is used for applying multilateration positioning method. Povalac and Sandebesta

[38], Nikitin et al. [39], and Arnitz et al. [40] analyzed both phases of arrival positioning methods for RFID-based locating systems.

Because of the characteristics of electromagnetic waves to penetrate solids, RFID-based locating systems have the ability to detect a tag even without direct line of sight (without metal or water). Thanks to this characteristics, it is possible to embed tags into the wall, ceiling, or pavement of a building, providing almost completely unobtrusive systems. Some scalability issues can rise when a large number of tags and readers are used: a complex system configuration and management is required. In active RFID system, the readers communicate with active tags equipped with internal batteries. Active tags are more expensive than passive tags but allow a longer communication range (tens of meters). Passive RFID tags have the advantage of the small size, high level of ruggedness, relatively inexpensive installation, and low maintenance needs; the theoretical detection range is within 10 m but the reflections can cause false readings which heavily affect the effectiveness of the localization. IPSs based on RFID systems have been widely explored and discussed in scientific literature [41-46]. While in WSN-based IPSs, anchor and mobile nodes are normally realized using the same hardware and exchange ranging information in a peer-to-peer fashion; in RFID-based IPSs, two distinct schemes are instead generally possible [44]: (1) in the 'active' scheme, the mobile node is implemented by a portable RFID reader, while tags are used as anchors; (2) in the 'passive' scheme, RFID tags are instead objects to be located while RFID readers are in known position. While the choice of the scheme to be applied depends on application requirements (e.g., the number of objects to locate, etc.), both schemes can be used with different types of tags (e.g., HF/UHF tags, active/passive tags, etc.), providing different performance in terms of maximum range (from a few centimeters to 10 m), propagation model, and costs [45]. Seco et al. [47] deployed a system that use nearly 70 active tags scattered into 55 rooms and covering 1,600 m$^2$ area. Using RSSI method in this work. a 1.5-m accuracy is obtained. Kimaldi [48] provides commercial systems for hospitals in locating application deployment. Personnel monitoring and access control have been obtained using wristbands and keyring tags. Daly et al. [49] deployed a passive RFID-based positioning system which has been embedded with passive RFID tags in pavement for navigation purpose. Kiers et al. [50] deployed a navigation system using arrays of passive RFID tags which have been installed under a carpet to provide path indication to blind people. Peng et al. [51] deployed an hybrid system composed by active RFID system and GNSS in order to make a positioning system that works seamlessly outdoor and indoor. By using Kalman filters in this work, a meter accuracy is obtained.

**Table 1 Typical accuracy and positioning methods of radio frequency positioning technologies**

| Technology | Accuracy | Positioning methods |
| --- | --- | --- |
| WLAN | Meters | Fingerprinting and CoO |
| Bluetooth | Decimeters to meters | Fingerprinting and CoO |
| ZigBee | Meters | RSSI |
| RFID | Decimeters to meters | Fingerprinting and CoO |
| UWB | Centimeters to decimeters | ToA |

Table 1 shows the typical values of accuracy and positioning methods used in radio frequency IPSs.

IPSs can use single location technology or the combination of multiple technologies together in hybrid systems to increase both positioning accuracy and system robustness.

## 3   Reference architecture and design

The proposed positioning system combines WSN and RFID in order to compensate the limitations of each technology. On one hand, the WSN provides a good radio coverage but with a low positioning accuracy due to the high noise on RSSI measurements. On the other hand, the RFID technology provides the following: (1) in the case of high-frequency (HF), very precise positioning information but limited coverage and temporal discontinuity; (2) in the case of ultra-high frequency (UHF), good coverage and reliability but high granularity of the location. The appropriate combinations of the two technologies could be a good strategy in building indoor positioning and tracking system with increased positioning accuracy and availability.

Figure 1 presents the hybrid architecture of the hybrid positioning system, and the field data are collected by two different systems, WSN segment and RFID segment.

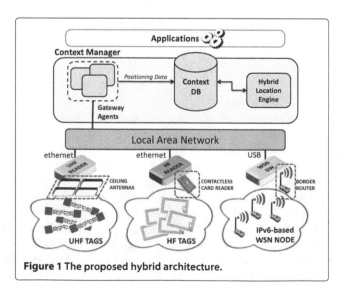

**Figure 1 The proposed hybrid architecture.**

## 3.1 WSN segment

The WSN segment is a self-configuring, IPv6-based sensor network which have been implemented and tested on Telos rev.B [52] and STM32W [53] nodes as shown in Figure 2. On the software side, each node runs a Contiki operating system [54]; on the hardware side, each node is equipped with a radio transceiver, a microcontroller (TI MSP430 for Telos rev.B and ARM Cortex-M3 for STM32W; Moteiv Corporation, El Cerrito, CA, USA) and some on-board sensors (e.g., button sensors, temperature sensors and light sensors).

In the network level, out-of-band control messages are exchanged among the nodes to help each node to build its neighbor list and autonomously form the network. Each node periodically updates its neighbor list and dynamically builds an optimal route to every potential destination.

Within the WSN segment, the positioning data are collected in the following process:

1. The distances between the mobile node (node to be located) and other nodes (two anchor nodes and/or any other possible mobile nodes) are measured in terms of the RSSI.
2. The measured RSSI values by the mobile node (node to be located) are directly sent to a fixed infrastructure, or forwarded by the router nodes (could be an anchor node or a mobile node), to a fixed infrastructure when a multi-hop transmission is required.
3. After being processed by the positioning algorithm that is running on the fixed infrastructure, the locating result is sent back to the requester (the mobile to be located).

In terms of communication, a WSN segment is divided into three levels:

- The main gateway, also called the concentrator
- The fixed gateway
- The network nodes

In order to obtain the RSSI information, each mobile node periodically broadcasts a user datagram protocol or UDP ranging request, which is used by neighbor nodes to measure uplink RSSI. Anchor nodes reply in turn with a ranging response, including the measured uplink RSSI. Finally, the mobile node measures all downlink RSSI, aggregates all ranging responses, and forwards all the uplink-downlink tuples (one for each neighbor) to the WSN gateway. The WSN gateway is a simple commercial off-the-shelf (COTS) low-power PC running Linux (Vancouver, Canada).

## 3.2 RFID segment

The RFID segment is composed of two systems, a UHF-RFID system and an HF RFID system. They are independent from each other and provide separate detection for the RFID tags.

In the HF RFID system, some contactless badge readers are placed at the room entrances, and they produce positioning information while the user register (or request access) his passage through a door. This information is extremely accurate, but could instantly lose value even over a short period of time - when the user enters or exits a room - if not fused with other information. The UHF system is composed of a set of RFID reader plus four compliant antennas deployed on the ceiling. When a UHF tag is under, Figure 3 depicts the test-bed scenario while Figure 4 provides a snapshot of the actual deployment (within ISMB labs). The typical 4-antennas/reader combination has been used, in order to simplify the field trial; however, a more complex antennas multiplexing should be used in an hypothetical wider deployment (at least

**Figure 2** Multi-technology node used for tests.

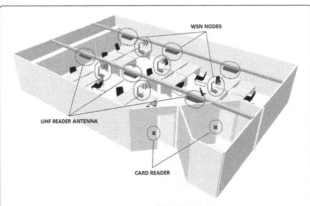

**Figure 3** RFID-enhanced WSN positioning system schema.

**Figure 4** RFID antennas on the ceiling.

32 antennas/reader). The physical attributes, the relative position, and the power irradiation level of each antennas has been chosen to optimize the coverage area, trying to avoid the overlap of each antenna coverage range. Of course it is impossible to avoid reading the same tag by different antennas: for this reason, it has been used as a simple algorithm based on the number of readings of a single antenna, in order to univocally associate a position (as a 'zone').

The RFID segment is based on a set of HF COTS and UHF-RFID readers which irradiate periodically and issue an event when a new tag is detected.

Data collected by the two segments are preprocessed by technology-specific gateways and then transferred through local area network to a central entity named *context manager*, which is a virtually distributed entity capable of handling generalized context information extracted from different platform-specific components. Within the context manager, a virtual delegate named *gateway agent* is configured to filter all the data from the specific gateway and feed them into any subscribing entity, e.g., a system which is interested in receiving these specific data. Based on such data and configuration data hosted inside the context manager, the location engine (described in Section 3.3) is able to extract the physical location of objects (RFID tags and WSN nodes) associated with the sources of the physical-world events.

Since different types of technology are adopted, the proposed system is classified as a hybrid scheme exploiting both indirect remote positioning systems and indirect self-positioning. Hence, the location engine is named as hybrid location engine.

### 3.3  Hybrid location engine

The hybrid location engine is the core of the positioning and tracking system. As it can be seen from Figure 1, it is a centralized location engine where a hybrid positioning algorithm is implemented to periodically estimate the positions of all the unknown mobile nodes. As shown in Figure 2, a typical mobile node is equipped with three radio frequency (RF) devices: a WSN node, a UHF-RFID

tag, and an HF badge. Moreover, the system allows the existence of other combination of RF devices: two of the three different elements (e.g., a WSN node and an HF badge) or just with single device (e.g., a WSN node or a UHF-RFID tag).

As indicated in Figure 1, three different observations (RSSI measurements derived from WSN nodes, detection of events from UHF-RFID tags, and HF badges) are sent to a context data base (DB). Since the UHF-RFID and HF-RFID detection events are available at the corresponding readers, these data are not forwarded to the corresponding unknown mobile nodes, for instance, through the WSN technologies, to implement a distributed positioning algorithm. On the contrary, in order to reduce communication latency and network traffic, all data, including also RSSI measurements from WSN devices, are collected in the DB, then the hybrid location engine estimates the position of the mobile nodes in a centralized way.

The main task of the hybrid location engine is to estimate the positions of mobiles. But some other tasks, for instance, reading location information of anchors and measurements for mobile nodes, are done to accomplish this task. In every $\Delta T_p$ seconds, it completes the following processes:

1. **Location information reading**. At the beginning of each time step $\Delta T_p$, the hybrid location engine queries the DB about the location information for all the devices. In more detail, the location information includes the unique device ID and the corresponding device category (e.g., WSN, UHF RFID, or HF RFID). For simplicity, the device ID is a five-digit number and is general for all the device. For each device there is a flag which indicates if it is *fixed* or *mobile*. A fixed device may be either a WSN anchor, a UHF-RFID antenna, or an HF badge reader whose positions are perfectly known and are stored in the DB; while a mobile device is a movable node whose position is not known. In addition, the device association information is read. As mentioned above, a mobile node may be equipped with different RF devices and the association information specifies how different RF devices are bound with together. The association information is useful, since in the DB an observation (a RSSI measurement and a detection of UHF tag or HF badge) is only related to a single RF device. Please note that this information reading step is performed at each $\Delta T_p$, because the network topology may change with time, for example, node changing (e.g., a new node joins the network, a node leaves, or the known position changes), association changing (e.g., new devices are bound together or the old association changes), or role changing (e.g., a mobile node becomes an anchor node or an anchor

node becomes a mobile node). By doing this, the location engine is able to follow the latest change of network topology and to have the capability of good position estimates.

2. **Measurements reading**. During this step, the hybrid location engine reads all the available observations from the DB. These observations could be RSSI, UHF-RFID tag, and HF badge detection events, and the time interval is chosen from some previous time to current time $t_k$, that is, $[t_k - \Delta T_{DB}, t_k]$, where $\Delta T_{DB}$ is the width of the temporal window. In general, $\Delta T_{DB}$ is set equal to position update time step $\Delta T_p$, so that all the observations are used only once. It is worth mentioning that $\Delta T_{DB}$ could be larger or smaller than $\Delta T_p$. Sometimes, there may be not enough RSSI observations for an unknown node in low dynamic scenario, and $\Delta T_{DB}$ is set larger than $\Delta T_p$ in order to use the previously collected measurements. On the contrary, there may be too many RSSI observations for a mobile node in high dynamic scenario, and $\Delta T_{DB}$ is set smaller than $\Delta T_p$ in order to use the freshest measurements. In principle, $\Delta T_{DB}$ is chosen, depending on the prior knowledge of mobility degree of the unknown nodes. In practice, it may happen that more than one measurement is available between two WSN nodes at certain times. In this case, a weighted average scheme is applied, and the weight associated to a measurement is calculated according to an exponential function which takes as input the time difference between the current time $t_k$ and the time stamp attached to this measurement. In other words, much lower weight is assigned to the old measurement while much higher weight is assigned to the new one. For the multiple detections of RFID devices, however, weighted average is not necessary because only the freshest one is used. It is supposed that the RFID detection is exceedingly reliable and the old detection event can be neglected.

3. **Position estimation**. In this step the hybrid location engine estimates the positions of mobile nodes by using location information and measurements which are provided by the previous two steps. Moreover, a cooperation scheme is applied where the location engine, apart from RSSI measurements from anchors, uses also RSSI measurements performed between mobile nodes, since two mobile WSN nodes are able to communicate with each other and to perform corresponding RSSI observations. The adoption of cooperation improves not only the positioning accuracy but also system robustness (i.e., position estimation availability), as more measurements are available to localize the mobile nodes. Nevertheless, the cooperation can be merely applicable to mobile nodes equipped with WSN devices, because both UHF-RFID tag and HF badge are passive devices and cannot communicate with other passive devices for range or range-related observations. Since the HF badge can be detected by the reader in a very short distance (e.g., a few centimeters), this badge detection event can be seen as quite accurate localization information. In principle, whenever an HF badge is detected, the estimated position of the associated mobile node is set to the HF reader's position, and other observations (e.g., RSSI or UHF-RFID detections) are ignored. Since the HF badge readers are only installed at the door, mainly for the purpose of access control, they provide only sporadic detection events. In most of the time, the hybrid location engine relies on RSSI measurements from WSN devices and UHF-RFID events for localization. In order to have a good estimate of a mobile's position, the location engine adopts a hybrid cooperative tracking algorithm, namely hybrid cooperative extended Kalman filter (hcEKF), which takes into account all the available observations, that is, RSSI measurements performed between WSN nodes (i.e., WSN mobiles to WSN anchors or WSN mobiles to WSN mobiles) and UHF-RFID tag detection events. More details of the adopted hcEKF is presented in Section 4. At the end of the estimation process, all the estimated positions are displayed on the map and are uploaded to the DB with a time stamp.

The periodic repetitions of these three steps form the whole procedure of the hybrid location engine, which can be summarized as pseudo code as Algorithm 1.

## 4 Hybrid cooperative positioning algorithm

The implemented hybrid cooperative positioning algorithm is based on Kalman filter (KF), which is an efficient and recursive estimator for discrete time linear filtering problem [55]. There are many extensions and generations of KF, and here the standard extended KF (EKF) is adopted due to its simplicity. Here the formulation of EKF is simply introduced in order to have a better understanding of the proposed positioning system.

### 4.1 EKF introduction

EKF is a simple extension of KF for nonlinear problems [55] and is widely applied in navigation and tracking systems. In principle, EKF includes two phases: prediction phase, during which the system state is estimated based on system behaviors, and update phase, during which the system state is corrected by using the available observations.

---

**Algorithm 1** Hybrid location engine procedure

**repeat**{every $\Delta T_p$}
    Read location information from DB
    Extract all the measurements from DB within the interval $[t_k - \Delta T_{DB}, \ t_k]$
    **for** $m = 1$ **to** $M$ **do** {mobile index}
        **if** there are HF-badge events for $m$ **then**
            Set estimated position of $m$ to the location of the HF badge reader according to the latest detection event
        **else**
            Select measurements related to mobile $m$
            Select reference location information according to the selected measurements
            **if** there are measurements for $m$ **then**
                estimate the mobile's position using hcEKF
            **else**
                position estimation is not available and do not do any estimate
            **end if**
        **end if**
        Display the estimated position on the map
        Upload the estimated position to the DB
    **end for**
    Pause if $\Delta T_p$ is not fully consumed
**until** stop

---

### 4.1.1 Prediction

In prediction phase, the current *a priori* estimates of state $\hat{\mathbf{x}}_{k|k-1}$ and of error covariance $\mathbf{P}_{k|k-1}$ are drawn from the previous *a posteriori* ones of state $\hat{\mathbf{x}}_{k-1|k-1}$ and of error covariance $\mathbf{P}_{k-1|k-1}$ by using the following two equations:

$$\hat{\mathbf{x}}_{k|k-1} = f\left(\hat{\mathbf{x}}_{k-1|k-1}, \mathbf{w}_{k-1}\right), \tag{1}$$

$$\mathbf{P}_{k|k-1} = \mathbf{A}_k \mathbf{P}_{k-1|k-1} \mathbf{A}_k^T + \mathbf{Q}_{k-1}. \tag{2}$$

where $f$ is the state transition function and $\mathbf{A}_k = \left.\frac{\partial f}{\partial \mathbf{x}}\right|_{\hat{\mathbf{x}}_{k-1|k-1}}$ is the corresponding Jacobian matrix calculated at the previous *a posteriori* state estimate $\hat{\mathbf{x}}_{k-1|k-1}$. $\mathbf{w}_{k-1}$ is the process noise and is assumed as Gaussian distributed with covariance $\mathbf{Q}_k$, that is, $\mathbf{w}_{k-1} \sim \mathcal{N}(0, \mathbf{Q}_{k-1})$.

### 4.1.2 Update

In update phase, the *a priori* estimates ($\hat{\mathbf{x}}_{k|k-1}$ and $\mathbf{P}_{k|k-1}$) are corrected the *a posteriori* estimates ($\hat{\mathbf{x}}_{k|k}$ and $\mathbf{P}_{k|k}$) by using the available measurements $\mathbf{z}_k$. In more detail, innovation vector $\tilde{\mathbf{y}}_k$ and optimal Kalman gain $\mathbf{K}_k$ are computed as (3) and (4), respectively, as follows:

$$\tilde{\mathbf{y}}_k = \mathbf{z}_k - h\left(\hat{\mathbf{x}}_{k|k-1}, \mathbf{v}_k\right), \tag{3}$$

$$\mathbf{K}_k = \mathbf{P}_{k|k-1} \mathbf{H}_k^T \left(\mathbf{H}_k \mathbf{P}_{k|k-1} \mathbf{H}_k^T + \mathbf{R}_k\right)^{-1}, \tag{4}$$

where $h$ is the observation function and $\mathbf{H}_k = \left.\frac{\partial h}{\partial \mathbf{x}}\right|_{\hat{\mathbf{x}}_{k|k-1}}$ is the corresponding Jacobian matrix evaluated around the *a priori* state estimate $\hat{\mathbf{x}}_{k|k-1}$. $\mathbf{v}_k$ is the measurement noise and is also assumed as Gaussian distributed with covariance $\mathbf{R}_k$, that is, $\mathbf{v}_k \sim \mathcal{N}(0, \mathbf{R}_k)$.

After that, the *a posteriori* estimates are obtained as follows:

$$\hat{\mathbf{x}}_{k|k} = \hat{\mathbf{x}}_{k|k-1} + \mathbf{K}_k \tilde{\mathbf{y}}_k, \tag{5}$$

$$\mathbf{P}_{k|k} = (\mathbf{I}_n - \mathbf{K}_k \mathbf{H}_k) \mathbf{P}_{k|k-1}. \tag{6}$$

The recursive computation of Equations 1 to 6 makes up the EKF solutions of a dynamic system.

## 4.2 Measurement modeling

The available measurements are related to the distance between two RF devices using different models, which are adopted in hcEKF.

### 4.2.1 WSN measurement model

The RSSI measurements performed among WSN nodes are linked to the distance observation by adopting the *log-normal shadowing path loss model* [56], where the received power $\tilde{P}$ (expressed in dBm) is seen as a logarithmic function of the distance ($d$ in meters) between the transmitter and the receiver:

$$\tilde{P}(d) = P_0 - 10\alpha \log_{10}(d/d_0) + X_\sigma, \tag{7}$$

where $P_0$ (expressed in dBm) is the mean power received at the reference distance $d_0$ (typically 1 m), $\alpha$ is the path loss exponent, and $X_\sigma$ is an additive measurement noise. For simplicity, $X_\sigma$ is assumed to be Gaussian distributed with zero mean and variance $\sigma_{dB}^2$, that is, $X_\sigma \sim \mathcal{N}(0, \sigma_{dB}^2)$. This model only considers the path loss of RF signal and does not takes into account multipath or any other effects. It is worth reminding that these parameters depend greatly on the environment and the operating frequency. Calibrations are required before applying this model.

### 4.2.2 UHF-RFID measurement model

Concerning the UHF-RFID measurements, as in [11], each detection event is translated to a distance measurement equal to half of the reader interrogation range, $r$. In other words, the UHF-RFID detection is seen as constant distance measurement,

$$\tilde{d} = r/2 + n, \tag{8}$$

where $n$ is the measurement noise, and it is hard to know the exact distribution of this noise. Here we assume it satisfies Gaussian distribution with zero mean and a variance depending on the radio coverage $r$. This assumption may be not true but it is suitable for EKF to use the UHF-RFID observations. It is worth reminding that the RFID detection is treated as distance measurement equal to $r/2$, and this measurement is always positive.

### 4.3 Hybrid cooperative EKF

The adopted hybrid cooperative EKF (hcEKF) is first proposed in [12], and it adds hybrid and cooperative features onto the standard EKF. In principle, the hcEKF algorithm is divided into three parts: state modeling, hybridization, and cooperation, which are introduced in the following.

### 4.3.1 State modeling

The positioning complexity strongly depends on the modeling of the system dynamics, and in this algorithm we choose the system state which is the position of unknown mobiles, that is, $\hat{\mathbf{x}}_k = [\hat{x}_k, \hat{y}_k]$. Here only 2D localization is considered but the extension to 3D case is straightforward.

According to the this model, the state transition function $f$ is a linear function of the state:

$$\hat{\mathbf{x}}_{k|k-1} = f\left(\hat{\mathbf{x}}_{k-1|k-1}, \mathbf{w}_{k-1}\right) = \hat{\mathbf{x}}_{k-1|k-1} + \mathbf{w}_{k-1}. \tag{9}$$

In this case, the process noise $\mathbf{w}_{k-1}$ models the unknown movements along $x$ and $y$ axes. We let $\triangle t_k$ denote the time difference between $\hat{\mathbf{x}}_{k|k-1}$ and $\hat{\mathbf{x}}_{k-1|k-1}$, and the covariance matrix $\mathbf{Q}_{k-1}$ can be expressed as:

$$\mathbf{Q}_{k-1} = [\triangle t_k \mathbf{I}_2] \operatorname{diag}\left(\sigma_{\dot{x}}^2, \sigma_{\dot{y}}^2\right) [\triangle t_k \mathbf{I}_2]^T. \tag{10}$$

where $\mathbf{I}_2$ is a 2×2 identity matrix and $\operatorname{diag}(\sigma_{\dot{x}}^2, \sigma_{\dot{y}}^2)$ is a 2×2 diagonal matrix whose diagonal elements are corresponding to the moving speed, which are the differentials of system state.

### 4.3.2 Hybridization

The art of hybridization is to fuse heterogeneous measurements together and to build the corresponding observation functions. Let $\mathcal{A} = \{1, 2, ...A\}$, $\mathcal{M} = \{1, 2, ...M\}$, in which $\mathcal{R} = \{1, 2, ...R\}$ denote the sets of fixed WSN anchors, WSN mobiles, and fixed RFID readers, respectively. For a generic mobile node $m$ at time $k$, $\mathcal{A}_k \subseteq \mathcal{A}$,

$\mathcal{M}_k \subseteq \mathcal{M}$, and $\mathcal{R}_k \subseteq \mathcal{R}$ denote the subsets of connected devices (WSN anchors, WSN mobiles, and RFID readers). Note that here $m$ is abbreviated for simplicity of denotation.

Therefore, the generic observation vector can be written as

$$\mathbf{z}_k = \left[\tilde{\mathbf{P}}_{\mathcal{A}_k} \ \tilde{\mathbf{P}}_{\mathcal{M}_k} \ \tilde{\mathbf{d}}_{\mathcal{R}_k}\right]^T, \tag{11}$$

where $\tilde{\mathbf{P}}_{\mathcal{A}_k}$ and $\tilde{\mathbf{P}}_{\mathcal{M}_k}$ denote the sets of RSSI measures from WSNs, while $\tilde{\mathbf{d}}_{\mathcal{R}_k}$ denotes the set of RFID-based distance measurements. Note that the RSSI is not transformed into distance measurement and is directly used to feed the positioning algorithm, because the assumption of Gaussian measurement errors does not hold for RSS-based distance measurements [57].

For the *a priori* estimate $\hat{\mathbf{x}}_{k|k-1}$, the corresponding observation function could be one of the three forms

$$h\left(\hat{\mathbf{x}}_{k|k-1}\right) \in \left[\ h_{\mathcal{A}_k}\left(\hat{\mathbf{x}}_{k|k-1}\right) \ h_{\mathcal{M}_k}\left(\hat{\mathbf{x}}_{k|k-1}\right) \ h_{\mathcal{R}_k}\left(\hat{\mathbf{x}}_{k|k-1}\right)\right],\tag{12}$$

where $h_{\mathcal{A}_k}(\hat{\mathbf{x}}_{k|k-1})$, $h_{\mathcal{M}_k}(\hat{\mathbf{x}}_{k|k-1})$, and $h_{\mathcal{R}_k}(\hat{\mathbf{x}}_{k|k-1})$ are the relative observation functions, referring to the subsets of connected WSN anchors, WSN mobiles, and RFID readers, respectively. More specifically, $h_{\mathcal{A}_k}(\hat{\mathbf{x}}_{k|k-1})$ is calculated by using Equation 7,

$$h_{\mathcal{A}_k}(\hat{\mathbf{x}}_{k|k-1}) = P_0 - 10\alpha \log_{10}\left(\operatorname{dist}\left(\hat{\mathbf{x}}_{k|k-1}, \boldsymbol{p}_k^i\right)/d_0\right),\tag{13}$$

where $\boldsymbol{p}_k^i$ ($i \in \mathcal{A}_k$) is the position of $i$th WSN anchor at time k and $\operatorname{dist}(\cdot)$ is the operator of the Euclidean distance computation, e.g., $\operatorname{dist}(\mathbf{x}_1, \mathbf{x}_2) = \sqrt{(x_1 - x_2)^2 + (y_1 - y_2)^2}$.

In Equation 13, $h_{\mathcal{M}_k}(\hat{\mathbf{x}}_{k|k-1})$ is calculated similarly, but the positions of mobile are used instead of those of anchors. Note that the uncertainty of mobile's position is considered on the measurement noise and it is found in Section 4.3.3. In addition, $h_{\mathcal{R}_k}(\hat{\mathbf{x}}_{k|k-1})$ can be computed by using (8)

$$h_{\mathcal{R}_k}(\hat{\mathbf{x}}_{k|k-1}) = \operatorname{dist}\left(\hat{\mathbf{x}}_{k|k-1}, \boldsymbol{p}_k^l\right),\tag{14}$$

where $\boldsymbol{p}_k^l$ ($l \in \mathcal{R}_k$) is the position of $l$th RFID reader at time $k$. More details about how to set the observation function can be found in [12].

### 4.3.3 Cooperation

Cooperations among mobile nodes increase the signal of opportunities for more range or range-related measurements. Uncertainty about mobile's position, however, should be taken into appropriate considerations. Otherwise, cooperation might do harm to the position estimation, that is, the estimated positions could even diverge further away from the real ones than the noncooperative case. Usually, the uncertainty of mobile's position is evaluated as the trace of its error covariance matrix.

In hcEKF this uncertainty is mapped on the RSSI measurement and is modeled as additional additive noise on the RSS measurements. In other words, the measurement noise variance from mobile nodes is as the sum of the intrinsic measurement variance plus a contribution from the neighboring mobile position's uncertainty, i.e.,

$$\sigma^2_{\mathcal{M}^j_k} = \sigma^2_{\text{dB}} + \sigma^2_{\mathcal{X}^j_k}, \tag{15}$$

where $j \in \mathcal{M}_k$ is the $j$th connected mobile nodes and $\sigma^2_{\text{dB}}$ is the intrinsic noise variance. Moreover, $\sigma^2_{\mathcal{X}^j_k}$ is the additional noise variance and is a function of the trace of error covariance matrix ($\text{trace}(\mathbf{P}^j_k)$), which is indicated in more details in [12].

Supposing that all the available measurements are independent with each other, the measurement error covariance matrix $\mathbf{R}_k$ is a diagonal matrix given by:

$$\mathbf{R}_k = \text{diag}(\underbrace{\dots \sigma^2_{\mathcal{A}^i_k} \dots}_{i \in \mathcal{A}_k} \underbrace{\dots \sigma^2_{\mathcal{M}^j_k} \dots}_{j \in \mathcal{M}_k} \underbrace{\dots \sigma^2_{\mathcal{R}^l_k} \dots}_{l \in \mathcal{R}_k}). \tag{16}$$

In distributed localization systems, cooperations among mobile nodes increase network traffic to transmit the cooperation packets. In this case, however, cooperations are done in the centralized location engine and no network traffic is generated. The whole hcEKF procedure is presented as pseudo code as Algorithm 2.

### 4.4 Complexity analysis

The computational complexity of EKF is mainly upon the matrix inversion and matrix multiplication. For each state estimate, in (4), matrix inversion is computed with asymptotic complexity $\mathcal{O}(\mathbb{R}^3)$ [58], where $\mathbb{R}$ is the dimension of measurement noise covariance $\mathbf{R}$ or the number of available measurements; in (6), matrix multiplication is computed with asymptotic complexity $\mathcal{O}(\mathbb{P}^3)$ [58], where $\mathbb{P}$ is the dimension of error covariance or the dimension of the state vector. In the positioning applications, the number of measurements is usually larger than the dimension of state in order to solve the ambiguity of position estimate. Hence, the complexity of EKF is the computation of inverting matrices in our application. Let $|\mathcal{A}_k|$, $|\mathcal{M}_k|$, and $|\mathcal{R}_k|$ denote the cardinality of the corresponding sets $\mathcal{A}_k$, $\mathcal{M}_k$, and $\mathcal{R}_k$. The complexity of adopted hcEKF is asymptotically $\mathcal{O}((|\mathcal{A}_k| + |\mathcal{M}_k| + |\mathcal{R}_k|)^3)$. For the standard EKF algorithm, the used measurements are only in set $\mathcal{A}_k$, and the complexity is asymptotically $\mathcal{O}(|\mathcal{A}_k|^3)$. Therefore, the complexity of hcEKF is increased $(1 + \frac{|\mathcal{M}_k| + |\mathcal{R}_k|}{|\mathcal{A}_k|})^3$ times with respect to standard EKF. For example, suppose that at a specific time, there are two RSSI measures from anchors $|\mathcal{A}_k| = 2$, one RSSI measure from mobile node $|\mathcal{M}_k| = 1$, and one RFID observation $|\mathcal{R}_k| = 1$, the computational complexity of hcEKF is increased about eight times. It is worth reminding that the hcEKF can still localize the mobile node in this case by using the observations from RFID technology.

## 5 Simulation and experimental results

The performance of the proposed tracking system is first evaluated through simulations and then by means of real experiment deployment.

The selected validation scenario is based on the Pervasive Radio Technologies Laboratory at Istituto Superiore Mario Boella (ISMB) and is composed of two adjacent rooms, namely, room 1 and room 2, which are connected by a corridor (see in Figure 5). This scenario is office environment with building structure mainly composed of metal and the size of it is about $25 \times 12$ m. In Figure 5, the blue and the red rectangles inside room 1 and room 2 represent the tables and those at the edges represent the walls, and their material properties are not considered

---

**Algorithm 2** Hybrid cooperative EKF (hcEKF)

---

**Input:** hybrid measurements vector $\mathbf{z}_k = \begin{bmatrix} \tilde{\mathbf{P}}_{\mathcal{A}_k} & \tilde{\mathbf{P}}_{\mathcal{M}_k} & \tilde{\mathbf{d}}_{\mathcal{R}_k} \end{bmatrix}^T$, the previous *a posteriori* estimates $\hat{\mathbf{x}}_{k-1|k-1}$ and covariance $\mathbf{P}_{k-1|k-1}$, positioning information $\mathbf{x}^j_k$ and $\text{trace}(\mathbf{P}^j_k)$, $\forall j \in \mathcal{M}_k$

**Output:** update the *a posteriori* estimates $\hat{\mathbf{x}}_{k|k}$ and covariance $\mathbf{P}_{k|k}$

1: calculate noise covariance for mobile $\sigma^2_{\mathcal{M}^j_k}$ as (15), $\forall j \in \mathcal{M}_k$
2: update noise covariance $\mathbf{R}_k$ using (16)
3: predict state $\hat{\mathbf{x}}_{k|k-1}$ as (1)
4: predict error covariance matrix $\mathbf{P}_{k|k-1}$ as (2)
5: compute innovation $\tilde{\mathbf{y}}_k$ as (3)
6: compute Kalman gain $\mathbf{K}_k$ as (4)
7: update state $\hat{\mathbf{x}}_{k|k}$ using (5)
8: update error covariance matrix $\mathbf{P}_{k|k}$ using (6)
9: broadcast $\hat{\mathbf{x}}_{k|k}$ and $\text{trace}(\mathbf{P}_{k|k})$ to neighbors

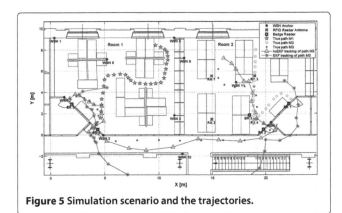

**Figure 5** Simulation scenario and the trajectories.

yet, since it is not an easy task. Our work is concentrated on the realization of the hybrid WSN-RFID localization system. These tables and walls are plotted to provide apparent references to the estimated positions.

## 5.1 Simulation results

In the simulation scenario, the following deployment of RF devices is adopted. Eleven WSN anchor nodes (WSN 1 to 11 in Figure 5) are placed around the rooms to optimize the geometry distribution for positioning; four UHF-RFID antennas (RA 1 to 4 in Figure 5) are deployed only in room 2; five badge readers (BA 1 to 5 in Figure 5) are installed at the doors to provide access control; three hybrid mobile nodes are considered; and all of them are equipped with a WSN device, a UHF-RFID tag, and an HF badge.

Three different trajectories are considered, and the three mobile nodes move along them respectively. Figure 5 shows the exact positions of three paths: the first one is in room 1 and is represented by red pentagrams and mobile; the second one is in room 2 and is represented by green circles; the third one connects from room 1 to room 2 through the corridor and is represented by blue dots.

RSSI measurements are generated by using the lognormal model reported in (7). The model parameters are from an experiment carried out in 2009 [59]; in more details, $P_0 = -49$, $\alpha = 3.3$, and $\sigma_{dB} = 5.5$. The sensitivity of the WSN receiver is set to $-90$ dBm, which determines the connectivity of two WSN nodes. A badge event is generated by the badge reader when a badge passes through the doors. A tag detection event is provided by the UHF-RFID antenna when a passive UHF-RFID tag is within the coverage area, which is modeled as a circle with radius $r = 2$ m.

One hundred Monte Carlo (MC) simulations are performed to provide steady statistics. The tracking performance is evaluated as root mean square of positioning errors (RMSE) given by:

$$\text{RMSE} = \sqrt{\frac{1}{N \cdot K} \sum_{i=1}^{N} \sum_{k=1}^{K} \left\| \hat{\mathbf{p}}_k^i - \mathbf{p}_k^i \right\|^2}, \quad (17)$$

where $N$ is the number of MC runs and $K$ is the number of positions in each trajectory. In addition, $\hat{\mathbf{p}}_k^i$ and $\mathbf{p}_k^i$ denote the corresponding estimated and exact positions of mobile node at $i$th run and $k$th position. The distance of two positions, $\left\| \hat{\mathbf{p}}_k^i - \mathbf{p}_k^i \right\|$, is also known as the positioning error.

Moreover, four different tracking algorithms are tested for comparison: the hcEKF which uses all the available measurements, the hEKF which uses RSSI from WSN anchors and detection events from RFID, the cEKF which uses only RSSI measures from WSN nodes, and the EKF (noncooperative and nonhybrid) which uses only RSSI measurements from WSN anchors.

Figure 5 shows the tracking result of one realization, where only the estimated positions of hcEKF and EKF related to mobile node M3 are plotted to avoid an overcrowded figure. Thanks to the HF badge detection, the hcEKF is accurately initialized, while the EKF has to be initialized to the coordinates of the scenario's center because it can only use RSSI measures. When M3 is in the corridor, the EKF diverges due to the bad geometry of the WSN anchor deployment while the hcEKF is able to follow the real trajectory thanks to hybridization of RFID detection and the cooperation with the other mobile nodes. When M3 approaches room 2, the standard EKF diverges again while the hcEKF is still able to track the mobile by fusing measurements from HF badge reader and UHF-RFID tag reader.

Figure 6 shows the simulated tracking performance in terms of cumulative distribution function (CDF) and RMSE of the positioning errors. It can be observed that the hcEKF, which fuses hybrid measurements of RSSI

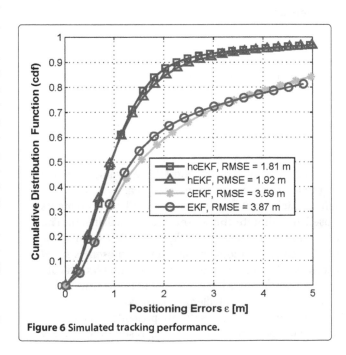

**Figure 6** Simulated tracking performance.

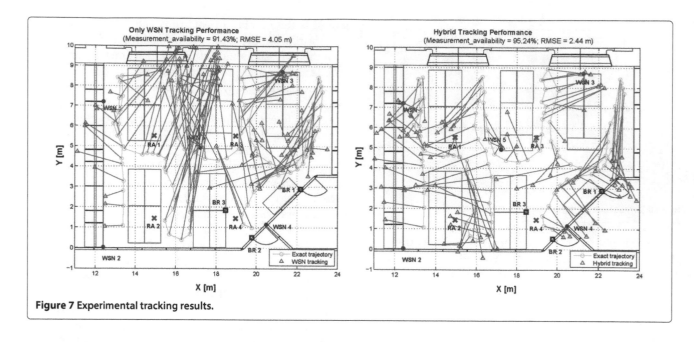

**Figure 7** Experimental tracking results.

from WSN and detection events from RFID readers and adopts cooperation among mobile nodes, shows the best tracking performance, i.e., best CDF curve and smallest RMSE. The hEKF outperforms cEKF, which indicates that the integration of RFID technology can overcome the inherent disadvantages of WSN RSSI localization. The cEKF and standard EKF provide similar performance, because there are lots of anchors nodes that provide enough RSSI observations and the gain of cooperation is not obvious. The gain of the adoption RFID is showed by the simulation, and it is difficult to define the numerical gain on the positioning lower bound since heterogeneous measurements are used.

### 5.2 Experimental results
Due to the lack of devices, the availability of WSN devices was not sufficient to allow a full deployment as the simulation. The experiment was carried out only in room 2, and the RF devices were only deployed in room 2 as Figure 7. In total, five WSN nodes (WSN 1 to 5), four UHF-RFID antennas (RA 1 to 4), and three HF badge readers (BA 1 to 3) were deployed. A mobile equipped with the previously mentioned RF devices did a pedestrian movement along a zigzag trajectory in the experimental area.

Before tracking the mobile, some RSSI measurements are used to calibrate the log-normal model in (7). The relative results are shown in Figure 8. Based on these measurements, the model parameters is chosen as $P_0 = -50.8$, $\alpha = 1.3$, and $\sigma_{dB} = 6.1$. These parameters indicate that the environment is harsh and the RSSI measurements is quite noisy, posing a challenge for tracking.

The final experimental results are presented in Figure 7, where the left part shows the tracking result of only WSN

measurements and the right part shows that of hybrid tracking. Since the RSSI measurements contained large noise, we adopt an optimization method that corrects the bad position estimate to the position of RFID reader when RFID detection is available. Moreover, the measurement availability and RMSE are reported in the upper part.

Due to the large noise on the RSSI measurements, the tracking trajectory has large errors and the performance is worse than the simulation. By fusing the measurements from RFID technology, the hybrid tracking algorithm is able to track better the maneuvers of mobile, which is consistent with the simulation result. Due to the high packet loss rate, sometimes there is no RSSI measurement to

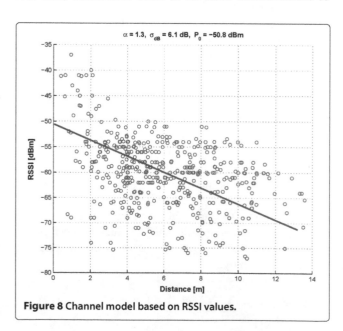

**Figure 8** Channel model based on RSSI values.

be used to track the mobile, and the observation from RFID can improve system availability. The adoption of hybridization provides improvement of 1.6 m in RMSE and of 4% in availability.

## 6 Conclusions

This work presented a hybrid WSN-RFID system for tracking people and objects in indoor scenarios. The joint use of heterogeneous technologies can overcome the limitations of each other: WSN system provides adequate RSSI observations but with large errors, and RFID system provides accurate detections but with sparse observations. Thanks to the hybridization of RFID measurements and cooperation among mobile nodes, the proposed positioning solution based on EKF is able to increase the robustness and accuracy of indoor positioning systems in harsh propagation conditions. Simulation and experimental results showed that the hybrid WSN-RFID configuration outperformed the set-ups employing single technology. Therefore, we can conclude that indoor positioning systems can effectively benefit from hybrid WSN and RFID technologies. Furthermore, the proposed configuration is cost-effective in situations where WSN and RFID devices are already deployed for other purposes such as environment monitoring or access control.

## Endnote

[a]This article is an extended version of a conference paper [13] published at 'The fourth International EURASIP Workshop on RFID Technology.'

### Competing interests
The authors declare that they have no competing interests.

### Acknowledgements
This paper has been partially supported by regional project 'GA-RF-WSN' and by the European FP7 project BUTLER, under contract no. 287901.

## References

1. O Vermesan, P Friess, P Guillemin, S Gusmeroli, H Sundmaeker, A Bassi, IS Jubert, M Mazura, M Harrison, M Eisenhauer, P Doody, Internet of Things strategic research roadmap. Technical report, The IoT European Research Cluster - European Research Cluster on the Internet of Things - IERC (2009)
2. G Chen, D Kotz, A survey of context-aware mobile computing research. Dartmouth Computer Science Technical Report TR2000-381, Darmouth College (2000)
3. IF Akyildiz, W Su, Y Sankarasubramaniam, E Cayirci, Wireless sensor networks: a survey. Comput. Netw. **38**(4), 393–422 (2002)
4. SA Munir, B Ren, W Jiao, B Wang, D Xie, J Ma, in *Proceedings of the 21st International Conference on Advanced Information Networking and Applications Workshops, Washington, DC, May 2007*, vol. 2. Mobile wireless sensor network: architecture and enabling technologies for ubiquitous computing (IEEE Computer Society, Washington, 2007), pp. 113–120
5. B Nath, F Reynolds, R Want, RFID technology and applications. Pervasive Comput. IEEE. **5**(1), 22–24 (2006)
6. E Welbourne, L Battle, G Cole, K Gould, K Rector, S Raymer, M Balazinska, G Borriello, Building the Internet of Things using RFID: the RFID ecosystem experience. Internet Computing, IEEE. **13**(3), 48–55 (2009)
7. J Sung, T Sanchez Lopez, D Kim, in *Fifth Annual IEEE International Conference on Pervasive Computing and Communications Workshops*. The EPC sensor network for RFID and WSN integration infrastructure. White Plains, 19-23 March 2007, pp. 618–621
8. C Ma, Y Wang, G Ying, in *2011 Fourth International Conference on Information and Computing*. The pig breeding management system based on RFID and WSN. Shanghai, 25-27 April 2011, pp.30–33
9. L Guo, W Fang, G Wang, L Zheng, in *2010 International Conference on Computer and Communication Technologies in Agriculture Engineering*. Intelligent traffic management system base on WSN and RFID. Chengdu, 12-13 June 2010, pp. 227–230
10. S Long, R Kooper, GD Abowd, CG Atkeson, in *Proceedings of the 2nd Annual International Conference on Mobile Computing and Networking, MobiCom96*. Rapid prototyping of mobile context-aware applications : the cyberguide case study 2 scenarios for a mobile context-aware application. White Plains, NY, 11-12 November 1996 (ACM Press, New York, 1996), pp. 97–107
11. Z Xiong, F Sottile, MA Spirito, R Garello, in *2011 4th IFIP International Conference on New Technologies Mobility and Security*. Hybrid indoor positioning approaches based on WSN and RFID. Paris, 7–10 February 2011, pp. 1–5.
12. Z Xiong, F Sottile, MA Caceres, MA Spirito, R Garello, in *in 2011 IEEE-APS Topical Conference on Antennas and Propagation in Wireless Communications (APWC)*. Hybrid WSN-RFID cooperative positioning based on extended Kalman filter (IEEE Conference Publications, Piscataway, 2011), pp. 990–993
13. X Zhoubing, S Zhen Yu, A Scalera, F Sottile, R Tomasi, MA Spirito, in *2012 Fourth International EURASIP Workshop on RFID Technology (EURASIP RFID)*. Enhancing WSN-based indoor positioning and tracking through RFID technology. Torino, 27–28 September 2012, pp. 107–114
14. J Hightower, G Borriello, A survey and taxonomy of location systems for ubiquitous computing. Technical Report UW-CSE 01-08-03, University of Washington, Computer Science and Engineering (2001)
15. J Hightower, G Borriello, Location systems for ubiquitous computing. Computer. **34**(8), 57–66 (2001)
16. R Want, A Hopper, V Falcão, J Gibbons, The active badge location system. ACM Trans. Inf. Syst. **10**(1), 91–102 (1992)
17. P Bahl, VN Padmanabhan, Radar: an in-building RF-based user location and tracking system (2000), in Proceedings of INFOCOM 2010. Nineteenth Annual Joint Conference of the IEEE Computer and Communications Societies, Victoria Conference Centre, March 2010, vol. 2 (IEEE Conference Publications, Piscataway, 2010), pp. 775 –784
18. LM Ni, Y Liu, Y Cho Lau, AP Patil, LANDMARC: indoor location sensing using active RFID Wireless Netw. **10**, 701–710 (2004). doi:10.1023/B:WINE.0000044029.06344.dd
19. M Vossiek, L Wiebking, P Gulden, J Wiehardt, C Hoffmann, P Heide, Wireless local positioning. IEEE Microwave Mag. **4**(4), 77–86 (2003)
20. Iso/IEC 24730–1:2006. (ISO, 2006). http://www.iso.org. Accessed 15 Feb 2006
21. H Liu, H Darabi, P Banerjee, J Liu, Survey of wireless indoor positioning techniques and systems. IEEE Trans. Syst. Man Cyber. **37**(6), 1067–1080 (2007)
22. D Niculescu, B Nath, in *Proceedings of the 10th annual international conference on Mobile computing and networking, MobiCom 2004*. VOR base stations for indoor 802.11 positioning. Taormina, 26 September to 1 October 2004, (ACM, New York, 2004), pp. 58–69
23. K Lorincz, M Welsh, *MoteTrack : A robust, decentralized approach to RF-based location tracking. Location-and Context-Awareness*. (Springer, Berlin Heidelberg, 2005), pp. 63–82
24. B Eissfeller, D Gänsch, S Müller, A Teuber, in *Proceedings of the 17th International Technical Meeting of the Satellite Division of The Institute of Navigation (ION GNSS 2004)*. Indoor positioning using wireless LAN radio signals. Long Beach Convention Center, Long Beach, 21–24 September 2004
25. W Tranter, K Shanmugan, T Rappaport, K Kosbar, *Principles of Communication Systems Simulation with Wireless Applications*, 1st edn. (Prentice Hall Press, Upper Saddle River, 2003)

26. Skyhook location technology(Skyhook, 2012). (Skyhook, 2012), http://www.skyhookwireless.com. Accessed 2012

27. KC Cheung, SS Intille, K Larson, An inexpensive Bluetooth-based indoor positioning hack. http://architecture.mit.edu/house_n/documents/CheungIntilleLarson2006.pdf. Accessed 2006

28. L Aalto, N Göthlin, J Korhonen, T Ojala, in *Proceedings of the 2nd International Conference on Mobile Systems, Applications, and Services, MobiSys 2004*. Bluetooth and WAP push based location-aware mobile advertising system, ACM, New York, 2004), pp. 49–58

29. MS Bargh, R de Groote, in *Proceedings of the First ACM international Workshop on Mobile Entity Localization and Tracking in GPS-less Environments MELT '08*. Indoor localization based on response rate of Bluetooth inquiries (ACM, New York, 2008), pp. 49–54

30. ZONITH Indoor Positioning System (ZONITH, 2012). http://www.zonith.com/products/ips. Accessed 2012

31. H Kroandll, C Steiner, in *2010 International Conference on Indoor Positioning and Indoor Navigation (IPIN)*. Indoor ultra-wideband location fingerprinting. ETH Zurich, Zurich, 15–17 September 2010, pp. 1–5

32. S Wang, A Waadt, A Burnic, D Xu, C Kocks, GH Bruck, P Jung, in *7th International Symposium on Wireless Communication Systems (ISWCS), 2010*. System implementation study on RSSI based positioning in UWB networks. The University of York, 19–22 September 2010, pp. 36–40

33. Zebra enterprise solutions (Zebra, 2012). http://zes.zebra.com/. Accessed 2012

34. Ubisense Real-time Location Systems Ubisense, 2012. http://www.ubisense.net. Accessed 2012

35. S Tadakamadla, Indoor local positioning system for ZigBee based on RSSI , Thesis. Mid Sweden University, 50 (2006)

36. JM Lopez Garde, J Larranaga, L Muguira, JI Vazquez, in *Proceedings of the 2010 International Conference on Indoor Positioning and Indoor Navigation (IPIN)*. An environment adaptive ZigBee-based indoor positioning algorithm. ETH Zurich, Zurich, 15–17 September 2010

37. My-bodyguard (smartTracker, 2012). http://smarttracker.tellu.no/?portfolio-item=my-bodyguard. Accessed 2012

38. A Povalac, J Sandebesta, in *2010 Conference Proceedings ICECom*. Phase of arrival ranging method for UHF RFID tags using instantaneous frequency measurement. Dubrovnik, Croatia, 2023 September 2010, (IEEE Press, Piscataway, 2010), pp. 1–4

39. PV Nikitin, R Martinez, S Ramamurthy, H Leland, G Spiess, KVS Rao, in *2010 IEEE International Conference on RFID*. Phase based spatial identification of UHF RFID tags. Orange County Convention Center, 14–16 April 2010, pp. 102–109

40. D Arnitz, K Witrisal, U Muehlmann, Multifrequency continuous-wave radar approach to ranging in passive UHF RFID. IEEE Trans. Microw. Theory Techno. **57**(5), 1398–1405 (2009)

41. H Don Chon, S Jun, H Jung, S Won, An Using RFID for accurate positioning. J. Global Pos. Syst. (2004). **3**(1), 32–39 (2005)

42. SL Ting, SK Kwok, AHC Tsang, GTS Ho, The study on using passive RFID tags for indoor positioning. Int. J. Eng. Bus. Manage. **3**(1), 9–15 (2011)

43. M Bouet, AL dos Santos, RFID tags: positioning principles and localization techniques, in *1st IFIP Wireless Days, 2008*. Dubai, 24–27 November 2008, pp. 1–5

44. C Wang, H Wu, N-F Tzeng, in *26th IEEE International Conference on Computer Communications, INFOCOM 2007*. RFID-based 3-D positioning schemes. Anchorage, 6–12 May 2007, 1235–1243

45. M Zhu, G Retscher, K Zhang, Integrated algorithms for RFID-based multi-sensor indoor/outdoor positioning solutions. Geospatial Sci. **22**, 451–465 (2011)

46. G Retscher, Q Fu, Integration of RFID, GNSS and DR for ubiquitous positioning in pedestrian navigation. **6**(1), 56–64 (2007)

47. F Seco, C Plagemann, AR Jimee, W Burgard, in *2010 International Conference on Indoor Positioning and Indoor Navigation (IPIN)*. Improving RFID-based indoor positioning accuracy using Gaussian processes. ETH Zurich, Zurich, 15–17 September 2010, pp. 1–8

48. Kimaldi (Kimaldi, 2012). http://www.kimaldi.com/. Accessed 2012

49. D Daly, T Melia, G Baldwin, in *2010 International Conference on Indoor Positioning and Indoor Navigation (IPIN)*. Concrete embedded RFID for way-point positioning' andnez. ETH Zurich, Zurich, 15–17 September 2010, pp. 1–10

50. M Kiers, E Krajnc, M Dornhofer, W Bischof, Evaluation and improvements of an RFID based indoor navigation system for visually impaired and blind people. (IPIN, 2011), http://ipin2011.dsi.uminho.pt/PDFs/Shortpaper/44_Short_Paper.pdf. Accessed 2011

51. J Peng, M Zhu, K Zhang, in *2011 International Conference on Indoor Positioning and Indoor Navigation (IPIN)*. New algorithms based on sigma point Kalman filter technique for multi-sensor integrated RFID indoor/outdoor positioning. Guimaraes, Portugal, 21-23 September 2011, 21–23

52. *Telos rev.B datasheet* (Crossbow Technology, 2012). http://bullseye.xbow.com:81/Products/Product_pdf_files/Wireless_pdf/TelosB_Datasheet.pdf. Accessed July 2012

53. *STM32W datasheet* (ST Microelectronics, 2012). http://www.st.com/internet/mcu/subclass/1377.jsp. Accessed July 2012

54. A Dunkels, B Gronvall, T Voigt, in *29th Annual IEEE International Conference on Local Computer Networks, 2004*. Contiki - a lightweight and flexible operating system for tiny networked sensors. Tampa, 16–18 November 2004 (IEEE Computer Society Press, Los Alamitos, 2004), pp. 455–462

55. G Welch, G Bishop, An introduction to the Kalman filter. Technical Report Chapel Hill, NC 27599–3175. University of North Carolina at Chapel Hill (2006)

56. S Rao, Estimating the ZigBee transmission-range ISM band. EDN. **52**(11), 67–74 (2007)

57. N Patwari, A Hero, M Perkins, N Correal, RO'Dea, Relative location estimation in wireless sensor networks. Signal Process. Mag. **8**(51), 2137–2148 (2003)

58. Computational complexity of mathematical operations (Wikipedia, 2012). http://en.wikipedia.org/wiki/Computational_complexity_of_mathematical_operations. Accessed 2012

59. D Dardari, F Sottile, WPR.B database: annex of progress report II on advanced localization and positioning techniques: data fusion and applications. Technical Report Deliverable DB.3 Annex 216715, Newcom++ NoE, WPR.B (2009)

# 8

# A methodology for hand and finger motion analysis using adaptive probabilistic models

Chutisant Kerdvibulvech

## Abstract

A methodology for motion analysis and hand tracking based on adaptive probabilistic models is presented. This is done by integrating a deterministic clustering framework and a particle filter together in real time. The skin color of a human hand is firstly segmented. A Bayesian classifier and an adaptive process are utilized for determining skin color probabilities. The methodology enables us to deal with luminance changes. After that, we determine the probabilities of the fingertips by using semicircle models for fitting curves to fingertips. Following this, the deterministic clustering algorithm is utilized to search for regions of interest, and then the Sequential Monte Carlo is also performed to track the fingertips efficiently. Representative experimental results are also included to ensure workability of the proposed framework. Several issues about using the presented method in embedded systems are discussed. The method presented can be used to further develop the associated applications of embedded robotic and virtual reality.

**Keywords:** Motion analysis; Hand tracking; Extended sequential Monte Carlo; Finger tracking; Color segmentation; Bayesian classifier; Embedded system; Adaptive learning; Clustering algorithm

## 1 Introduction

Recently, embedded systems are beneficially applied to many autonomous and intelligent robotic fields. One of the possible keys is to make the embedded robot see and understand automatically. In many embedded systems, vision-based methods are used interestingly. Their algorithms are embedded in robots in both hardware and software, including a method about hand motion analysis. This is because if embedded robotic systems are able to recognize human organs automatically, they can apply to various related real-life applications practically. An example includes embedded robots used and researched after 9/11 which are designed to automatically operate and rescue humans within a challenging environment by recognizing human organs without using human eyes. Thus, it is very important to design the embedded robots that can recognize and analyze the motion of human organs in recent years. For this reason, researches about hand motion recognition based on digital image processing technology are becoming popular for embedded

systems. This is because computer vision has been applied to many kinds of recent application to assist human motion tracking, especially fingertip tracking methodologies. Previous fingertip tracking methods were presented. For example, a correlation with pre-defined templates was presented in [1]. A chromatic distance was discussed in [2]. Mackie and McCane [3] also proposed image-division-based decision tree recognition. However, these aforementioned methods are not directly applicable to the self-occlusion fingertip tracking. Moreover, the background they used is usually uniform. As a result, it is more complicated to locate the fingertip positions correctly for self-occlusion and in non-uniform background. The proposed methodology for tracking the hand and fingertips solves these aforementioned issues.

To begin with, the hand is segmented in each frame from the background using an adaptive color detection algorithm. A Bayesian classifier is utilized during off-line phase [4]. An adaptive algorithm for determining skin probability is then applied to refine the classifier to train the system robustly [5]. Following this, we determine probabilities for fingertips by cropping the models of semicircle shape for a fit to the fingertip [6]. After superimposing the models on every candidate in the test

Correspondence: chutisant.k@rsu.ac.th
Department of Information and Communication Technology, Rangsit University, 52/347 Muang-Ake, Paholyothin Road, Lak-Hok, Patum Thani 12000, Thailand

image, we normalize the results which will be used as the fingertip probability map for tracking. Next, a clustering approach [7] is used to determine for regions of interest (ROIs) and sequential Monte Carlo [8] method is used for tracking by distributing the particles inside the corresponding ROIs. This vision-based methodology enables us to track the fingertips even when some fingers are not fully stretched out or when the luminance changes.

This paper is structured as follows. Literature on previous and conventional works is reviewed in Section 2. Next, the series of steps presented for hand and finger motion analysis using adaptive probabilistic models is described in Section 3. After that, Section 4 provides the experimental setup, including the results and discussion. Ultimately, Section 5 gives a summary of the paper and discusses possible associated embedded robotic applications using the proposed vision-based method.

## 2 Related work

Previous works about gesture recognition have been shown useful for various applications. Martínez et al. [9] developed a system for sign language to recognize motion primitives and full sentences. They assume that the same sign has different meanings depending on context. Matilainen et al. [10] presented a finger tracking system using template matching for gesture recognition, focusing on mobile devices. Krejov and Bowden [11] presented a system using a weighted graph and depth information of the hand for determining the geodesic maxima of the surface. In [12], Kereliuk et al. detected the positions of fingertips. The circular Hough transform is used for determining the tips of the fingers.

Nevertheless, these aforementioned gesture recognition methods are not suitably applicable to the fingertip tracking when self-occlusion occurs. Also in [11], the hand and wrist localization works not so smoothly and robustly, while from our experiments, utilizing the Hough transform to detect the fingertips in [12] is not robust enough. This is because fingertip edges cannot be easily detected due to the noise around the fingertips. Also, they did not aim to deal with luminance changes in online process.

We overcome these problems by attempting to segment the skin color of hand robustly. To solve this issue, it is important to understandably address a problem to control the lighting [13]. The levels of light between off-line and online phases are important for getting the correct registration. A major decision has to be made when deriving a model of color. By simply setting the threshold in color model, the accurate and robust results are rarely obtained. Another method [14] is to use histogram models. Still, it cannot perform adaptively when the levels of light between off-line and online phases are totally different.

To solve this issue, a Bayesian classifier is utilized. Applying this method, the first advantage is that the system can automatically and adaptively learn the probabilities by itself during online phase. From a small amount of training data, the probability is adapted during online phase and converges automatically to a proper value. Thus, it allows us to segment the regions we need robustly even though changing of luminance happens.

## 3 Methods

The schematic of the implementation will be explained in this section. After capturing the images, a Bayesian classifier is utilized adaptively to segment the human hand. As the next step, we apply a matching algorithm to determine the probabilities of the fingertips (i.e., fingertip probability map). Then, we extend the standard particle filter by utilizing the clustering algorithm to create ROIs for tracking. In this way, the positions of human hand and fingertips can be visually tracked.

### 3.1 Hand region segmentation

If the projection matrix is known, we can calculate the homography for warping a pre-captured known background. However, the background we used is sometimes dynamic and the background for that area cannot be easily synthesized. The luminance changing also causes a problem for using pre-captured known background image. The pixel color of pre-captured known background and the one from current input would be very different.

In our approach, we want to segment a hand from the input image. We built a color model of the hand image. During learning phase, the color model is also adapted according to changing luminance. In other words, we assume that the hand is a known foreground color model.

To begin with, we calculated the color probabilities being skin color by applying [4] which is composed of two main phases: off-line phase and online phase. First, we selected some images to train the system manually. Second, the probability is updated automatically and adaptively from the new input images [5]. In our implementation, we set that the adapting process is automatically disabled as soon as the probabilities are stable. Hence, when we start to learn the online skin color adaptation, we assume that there is enough skin in the image. As soon as the online adapting process is enough as we prefer (i.e., the skin color probability converges to a proper value), we manually stop the adapting process. In this way, after finishing the online learning process, though the skin area disappears from the scene, it does not affect the skin color probability.

### 3.1.1 Off-line phase

Wei et al. [15] suggested that skin color model based on this space for object segmentation and classification using 3D range camera can provide interesting coverage of human in many races. Similarly, we use their assumption for a 3D color representation (YUV). Nevertheless, we use only UV as it demands less memory storage. This disregard of the luminance value has also been shown to be useful in detection and tracking of color night vision [16]. During an off-line phase, Bayes' rule is used for estimating the probability $P(s|c)$ of a color, with $c$ being a skin color using

$$P(s|c) = \frac{P(c|s)P(s)}{P(c)} \tag{1}$$

where $P(s)$ is the proportion of the trained skin-colored pixels during off-line phase to the total number of pixels of whole images, $P(c)$ is the proportion of the number of occurrences of each color $c$ to the total number of image points during training, and $P(c|s)$ is the proportion of the number of occurrences of a color $c$ within the skin-colored regions to the number of skin-colored image points during training. After that, we use depth-first search method (DFS) to assign non-similar labels to the image pixels of non-similar regions. Filtering based on size of found regions is used to remove noise. Hence, connected components that consist of less than the threshold size are assumed to be noise and then rejected from further consideration. The threshold size for size filtering we used is 500 pixels. It is important to note that we do not need the intrinsic and extrinsic parameters in this step, since we assume that if the noise is smaller than the value we set, we simply eliminate it.

### 3.1.2 Online phase
This phase is similar to the off-line phase. We recalculate the probabilities again, but we use the values from the new input images. During an online phase, we update the adapted probabilities according to

$$P_A(s|c) = \gamma P(s|c) + (1-\gamma)P_W(s|c) \tag{2}$$

where $P_A(s|c)$ is the probability adapted of a color $c$ being a skin color, $\gamma$ is a sensitivity parameter, and $W$ is the number of history frames. If $W$ value is too high, the length of history frames will be too long; if $W$ value is set too low, the history for adaptation will be too short. Figure 1 shows an example of skin segmentation by adaptive learning robustly. Using this adaptive framework, it is able to deal well with obvious luminance changes.

### 3.2 Determining the probabilities of tips
After segmenting the hand region, we use the semicircle models for a fit to the curved fingertip [6]. Six models are utilized to deal with different sizes and orientations of the tips of the fingers. We match semicircle templates against the results of hand segmentation by using

$$R(x,y) = \frac{\sum_{x',y'}[T(x',y')-H(x+x',y+y')]^2}{\sqrt{\left[\sum_{x',y'}\left(T(x',y')^2\right)\sum_{x',y'}H(x+x',y+y')^2\right]}} \tag{3}$$

where $T(x,y)$ is a searched template at coordinates $(x,y)$, and $H(x,y)$ is a hand segmentation result when the search is running. Following this, we summarize the results of the fingertip models using $R_{sum}(x,y) = \sum_{i=1}^{N_0} R_i(x,y)$ where $N_0$ is a number of fingertip models.

Our experimental results have revealed that using the sum of the matches of all fingertip models gives the better result than other combinations (such as using maximum of the matches). A possible reason is that every model is weighted so that the information of all matches is used. In the case that if any matches of all fingertip models are not close to the answer (but the mean of the matches is close to the answer), this can still produce the promising result. However, using the maximum of the matches would give the good result if the results of the matches are very scattered, but from our experiments, this case rarely happens when matching the models for tracking the fingertips.

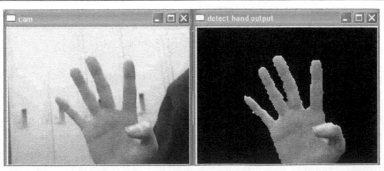

**Figure 1 Skin segmentation by adaptive learning.**

The models are then superimposed on every candidate during testing. Next, we normalize results of each model by using

$$R_{\text{normalized}}(x, y) = \frac{R_{\text{sum}}(x, y)}{R_{\text{sum}}(x_{\text{max}}, , y_{\text{max}})} \tag{4}$$

where $\forall_{(x,y)}\{R_{\text{sum}}(x_{\text{max}}, y_{\text{max}}) \geq R_{\text{sum}}(x, y)\}$. As a result, the probabilities to the fingertips of each pixel can be obtained.

### 3.3 Multiple fingertip tracking

Our method takes the advantages of sequential Monte Carlo [8] about automatic track initialization and recovering whenever the tracking fails. When the fingertips disappear from the scene and then appear back, we can still track the fingertips correctly due to the advantage of utilizing particle filter. However, direct application of sequential Monte Carlo method on multiple object tracking is not feasible because it does not define an obvious way to identify individual hypotheses.

In our previous work [17], we used different colored fingertip markers for tracking. Using colored markers, it is easy to use the standard particle filter to track each marker separately (because of the different colors). However, in the case of markerless tracking, particles are not distributed to each fingertip consistently since each fingertip represents the same hypothesis. To solve this problem, we extend the standard particle filter by applying a deterministic clustering approach as proposed in [7]. We create rectangular ROIs in each fingertip, and then we distribute the particles only inside the corresponding ROIs (while the standard particle filer will distribute particles all over the image).

### 3.3.1 Clustering algorithm

As explained in [8], the idea of clustering is to create rectangular ROIs by determining if the contours found in the fingertip probability map, i.e., $R_{\text{normalized}}(x, y)$ are consistent enough using a buffer. The intensity in the gray scale image illustrates the probabilities of the fingertips (higher brightness means higher probability). In this way, after we compute the gray scale image of the fingertip probability map, contours are extracted from the *FindContours* function implemented in the Intel OpenCV library. In other words, contours meant the area of high probability of the fingertips. Every contour found is stored in the following vector: $Y_t = \left\{y_{1,t}^T, ..., y_{m_t,t}^T, ..., y_{M_t,t}^T\right\}^T$. We called this $Y_t = \left\{y_{1,t}^T, ..., y_{m_t,t}^T, ..., y_{M_t,t}^T\right\}^T$ a contour vector. At any particular time, there are a total of $M_t$ contours found from the fingertip probability map image. The system receives a

contour vector $Y_t = \left\{y_{1,t}^T, ..., y_{m_t,t}^T, ..., y_{M_t,t}^T\right\}^T$ from the fingertip probability map (because the received contours may be noise also).

Denote a set of selected ROIs by $Z_t = \{Z_t^{(j)}, j = 1, ..., J_t\}$, where $J_t$ is the number of regions we found at $t$ within $Y_t$. Every region $Z_t^{(j)}$ is built according to a cluster of measurements obtained in $Y_t$ and is stored in terms of a set of time and contour indices, i.e., pairs of indices $(t, m_t)$. The concept is to group a collection of contours $Y_t$ that are in the spatial vicinity of each other at various time steps. If the targets are divided obviously, the contours from their targets are clustered in the locations where the targets have been visited from $t - \tau$ to $t$. In this case, $\tau$ represents the buffer's width.

Given a set of independent contours $Y_t$, we need to find a set of selected regions. Denote a set of selected ROIs by $Z_t = \{Z_t^{(j)}, j = 1, ..., J_t\}$, where $J_t$ is the number of ROIs found at $t$ within $Y_t$. The $j$th region $Z_t^{(j)}$ comprises $P_t^{(j)}$ contours at successive scans in $Y_t$ that are possible to obtain from the true interesting targets. The concept is to put a collection of contours $Y_t$ together. Again, if the targets are divided clearly, the contours from their targets are clustered in places where the targets have been potentially visited from $t - \tau$ to $t$, where $\tau$ is the width of the buffer.

Next, we build each region $Z_t^{(j)}$ according to a cluster of contours received in $Y_t$. It is then stored in terms of a set of time and contour indices, i.e., pairs of indices $(t, m_t)$. We denote the $m$th contour of $y_{t'+1}$ and the $l$th contour of $y_{t'}$ by $y_{m,t'+1}$ and $y_{l,t'+1}$, respectively. The normalized distance $d_{m,l}(t'+1, t)$ between $y_{m,t'+1}$ and $y_{l,t'+1}$ can be calculated from the intersection area between two contours. Our assumption is if the intersection area of two contours is high enough, these two contours should be grouped into the same cluster $Z_t^{(j)}$ (so the normalized distance $d_{m,l}(t'+1, t)$ will be set low). The minimum distance between two contours is also determined to calculate the normalized distance $d_{m,l}(t'+1, t)$. For every contour of $y_{t'+1}$, a set of normalized distances $\left\{d_{m,l}(t'+1, t), t'\right\}_{m=1}^{M_{t'+1}}$ is obtained, where $m \in \{1, ..., M_{t'+1}\}$. It is important to note that $d_{m*,l}(t'+1, t)$, $m^* \in \{1, ..., M_{t'+1}\}$ is the set minimum. The contours $\{y_{m*,t'+1}, y_{l,t'+1}\}$ and contour indices $(t'+1, m^*_{t'+1})$ and $(t', l_{t'})$ are clustered together according to

$$0 \leq d_{m*,l}(t'+1, t') \leq \eta_0 \tag{5}$$

where $\eta_0$ represents a given threshold.

After we detect the ROIs, their classification is performed. We classify them differently if they are noise or ROIs. The ROIs we mentioned are possibly both active and inactive. Thus, we carefully determine this issue also. In order to decide this, we find a relationship between the active tracks and the regions that we are interested in. By continuously finding the association and determining the appearance and disappearance of the regions, the system can recognize the number of tracking targets (this case is tips of the fingers) for different stages. Figure 2 depicts an example of gesture hand and fingertip recognition using the deterministic clustering algorithm.

### 3.3.2 Sequential Monte Carlo

In fact, there are two possible ways to use skin color probability in the particle filter step. Firstly, we can use the skin color probability itself. Secondly, we do threshold before and then use the binarized image. However, in our implementation, we use the second way in this paper. Each sample is propagated from the set $s'_{t-1}$ according to

$$s_t^{(n)} = g\left(s_t'^{(n)}\right) + E \tag{6}$$

where $E$ is Gaussian noise and $g(s'^{(n)}_t)$ is a propagation function. We use the noise information as the propagation function, i.e., $g(x) = x$. Figure 3 presents an example of finger tracking using the extended particle filter. After that, weights are generated by using the probabilities of fingertips from Equation 4. $p(X_t)$ represents the probability density function. Then, the sample set representation $\{(s_t^{(n)}, \pi_t^{(n)})\}$ of the state density for time $t$ is calculated according to

$$\pi_t^{(n)} = p\left(X_t = s_t^{(n)}\right) = R_{\text{normalized}}(x, y) \tag{7}$$

where $p(X_t = s_t^{(n)})$ represents the probability that a fingertip is at position $s_t^{(n)}$. After that, just similarly as a normal particle filter process, the total weights are normalized. Moments of the pixel recognized are calculated at time-step $t$ according to

$$\varepsilon[f(X_t)] = \Sigma_{n=1}^{N} \pi_t^{(n)} s_t^{(n)} \tag{8}$$

where $N$ is sample that has been built and $\varepsilon[f(X_t)]$ is the tip of finger's centroid. Using the aforementioned framework, it enables us to track and achieve recognition.

## 4 Results

Figure 4 shows an example tracking of such online experimental results from the total 300 frames. The reported experimental result was run online using an Intel® Core™ i5-3317U Processor at 1.70 GHz. The top-left image represents the input images. This input image is captured from a camera. Note that the camera we used has $320 \times 240$ display resolution. We capture a scene where a user is showing his hand in front of the camera. The top-right image represents the hand segmentation adaptively. The bottom-left image shows the fingertip probability map. The intensity in this gray scale image represents the probabilities of the tips of the fingers. Higher brightness is higher probability, while lower brightness is lower probability. After performing the clustering algorithm and extended particle filter, the tracked results of fingertips are finally shown in the bottom-right images. The number of particles in the system is 300 particles. From our experimental results, this number of particles is suitable for the proposed methodology.

First, processing time is an important aspect of many embedded systems, especially if we would like to apply the vision-based method to use in embedded systems. However, the computation time for the sequence shown is real time (approximately 12 frames per second without optimization). From this processing time, it is quite convenient to implement the proposed method to use in the embedded systems architecture, especially embedded robotic systems. This is because robots using embedded systems usually need an image processing-based algorithm that can run in real time, or nearly real time. Thus, our experimental speed indicates that the proposed method can support embedded systems positively in this aspect.

The second issue about embedded systems is power. Any system that requires too much electric power is not feasible for embedded robotic systems. In our system, we test to run the system with a portable laptop using an Intel® Core™ i5-3317U processor. The system does not need any additional power. In fact, the system can

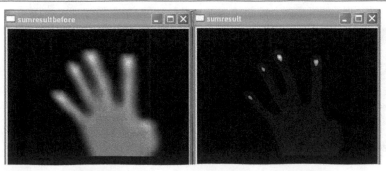

**Figure 2** The deterministic clustering algorithm is used for gesture hand and fingertips recognition.

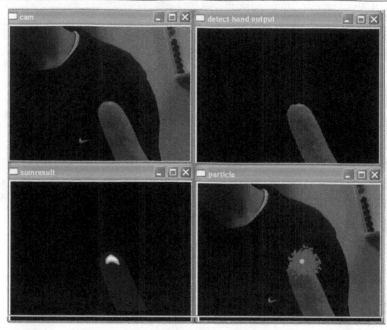

**Figure 3** An extended particle filter is utilized for fingering tracking and recognition.

be powered portably from a lightweight tablet requiring only small amount of power. The laptop battery we used is eight-cell, 14.8 V 47 Wh/3,060 mAh lithium ion battery. It lasts at least 3 h when fully running the proposed tracking algorithm. Note that when it is not running the process, the battery lasts for approximately 4 h. For recharging the battery, the battery we used takes only 2 h which is also obviously convenient for utilizing

in many smart embedded robots. Thus, from our experiments, the autonomy of the battery is practical for embedded applications even when it is fully running the tracking method. This means that the proposed vision-based method can easily apply to use in robots in terms of power for battery-powered embedded systems.

At the commencement of the experiment, a user enters the camera view field. Then he starts to change

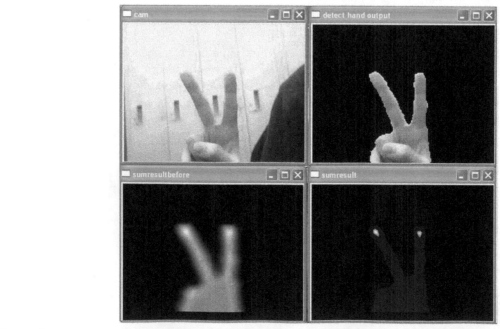

**Figure 4** Representative snapshot at the commencement of the experiment while a user is showing his two fingers.

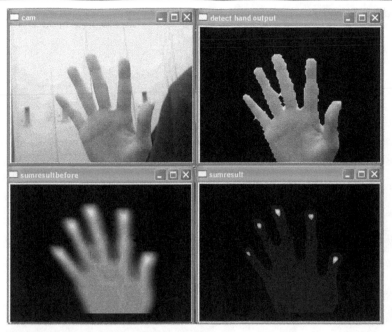

**Figure 5** A user starts to change his hand to show five fingers clearly.

his hand in different poses. In our method, the number of detected ROIs can be varied according to the number of fingertips appeared in the input images (the number of ROIs is automatically found by the algorithm described in the previous section). For example, there are five fingertips appearing in Figure 5, while there are three and four fingertips appearing in Figures 6 and 7, respectively. However, the system is able to automatically determine the accurate number of appeared fingertips. The experiments have revealed that the system can successfully track the fingertip positions even when the luminance markedly changes from the off-line phase.

In order to evaluate quantitatively the accuracy of this method presented, we select 50 frames from 300 consecutive frames for evaluation, as depicted in Table 1. The predicted trajectory positions found by using the

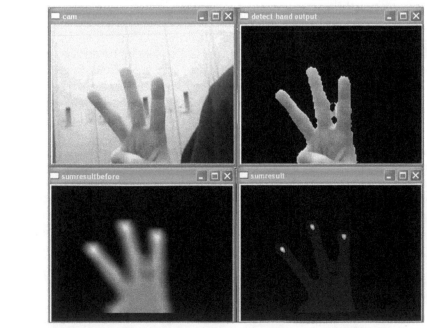

**Figure 6** The number of detected ROIs can be varied, as correctly as the number of appeared fingers.

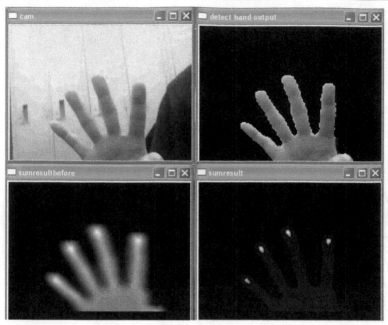

**Figure 7** The tracker can automatically determine the correct number of appeared fingertips.

proposed tracking method are compared to the manually measured ground truth positions (actual). Such ground truth measurements are obtained by manually selecting the positions of the fingertips by mouse clicks. The positions of the tracked tips of the fingers are received by our system. Then we determine the Euclidean distance errors from $320 \times 240$ total image size in pixels. After obtaining the distance errors in each image, the mean distance error is computed. The standard derivation error is also calculated. It can be seen that the forefinger introduced the maximum mean error at 11.23 pixels, if comparing to the other fingers (5.31 pixels for the little finger, 7.42 pixels for the ring finger, 9.71 pixels for the middle finger, and 8.65 pixels for the thumb). This is because the forefinger usually moves quite fast in this experiment, comparing relatively to the movements of other fingers. So, it gives that the sequential Monte Carlo we used may not perform perfectly when the tracking objects move too quickly.

In this experiment, we use a unique input which is different from other inputs of the previous methods. Thus, it is not easy to compare directly the experimental results exactly to the results obtained by other algorithms. However, even though we do not compare directly to the same sequence of experimental input with other conventional methods, it is obviously seen that our proposed method outperforms qualitatively the previous methods, such as the results obtained by [6]. Also, although we do not use the same measurement with [3], with the numbers in Table 1, it is clear that our algorithm outperforms quantitatively the method presented in [3]. We believe these errors presented in Table 1 are sufficiently accurate to make the proposed framework a suitable methodology for human hand motion recognition and fingertip tracking.

## 5 Conclusions

This paper has developed an algorithm that tracks the positions of the hand and fingertips accurately. The skin-colored region of a user is segmented by applying a Bayesian classifier adaptively and automatically. After that, a matching algorithm is used to determine the probabilities of the fingertips based on their primitives. Following this, we extend the particle filter by using a deterministic clustering algorithm for tracking fingertips. The experimental results have shown that the proposed methodology is effective even with non-uniform backgrounds. The substantial analysis of the proposed method applied in embedded context, such as power, processing time, and the autonomy of battery-operated equipment, has also been

**Table 1 Mean error and standard derivation in five fingertips**

|  | Little finger | Ring finger | Middle finger | Fore finger | Thumb |
|---|---|---|---|---|---|
| Mean error (pixels) | 5.31 | 7.42 | 9.71 | 11.23 | 8.65 |
| Standard deviation | 3.12 | 5.41 | 3.34 | 7.53 | 6.22 |

discussed. We believe that the proposed system can reach acceptably accurate results. However, we plan to solve the finger self-occlusion while using multi-cameras. This usually happens when using more than two cameras for stereo images. As part of our future work, we also intend to use this implementation to further develop the associated virtual-reality applications and related embedded robotic systems such as in [18] and [19].

**Competing interests**
The author declares that he has no competing interests.

**References**
1. K Oka, Y Sato, Real-time modeling of face deformation for 3D head pose estimation, in *Proceedings of the International Workshop on Analysis and Modelling of Faces and Gestures, AMFG '05, Beijing, China, 16 October 2005* (Springer, Berlin Heidelberg, 2005), pp. 308–320
2. J Letessier, F Bérard, Visual tracking of bare fingers for interactive surfaces, in *Proceedings of the ACM Symposium on User Interface Software and Technology, ACM/UIST '04, Santa Fe, NM*, 2004, pp. 119–122. ISBN 1-58113-957-8
3. J Mackie, B McCane, Finger detection with decision trees, in *Proceedings of the Image and Vision Computing New Zealand, IVCNZ '04, Akaroa, New Zealand*, 2004, pp. 399–403
4. C Kerdvibulvech, Real-time framework of hand tracking based on distance transform, in *Proceedings of the 11th International Conference on Pattern Recognition and Image Analysis, PRIA-11 '13, Samara, Russian Federation, 23–28 September 2013* (RAS and Springer, Pleiades, 2013), pp. 590–593
5. KE Papoutsakis, AA Argyros, Integrating tracking with fine object segmentation. Image. Vision Comput. **31**(10), 771–785 (2013)
6. CM Baris, N da Vitoria Lobo, Open hand detection in a cluttered single image using finger primitives, in *Proceedings of the IEEE International Conference on Computer Vision and Pattern Recognition Workshop, CVPR '06 Workshop, New York, NY*, 2006, p. 148. ISBN 0-7695-2646-2
7. TCT Chan, H-C So, KC Hom, Particle filtering based approach for landmine detection using ground penetrating radar. IEEE Trans. Geosci. Remote Sens. **46**(11), 3739–3755 (2008)
8. C Kerdvibulvech, H Saito, Model-based hand tracking by chamfer distance and adaptive color learning using particle filter. EURASIP J. Image Video Process (2009). (Springer, Hindawi, New York, 2009). Article ID 724947, 10 pages
9. AM Martínez, RB Wilbur, R Shay, AC Kak, Purdue RVL-SLLL ASL database for automatic recognition of American sign language, in *Proceedings of the IEEE International Conference on Multimodal Interfaces, Pittsburgh, PA*, 2002, pp. 167–172
10. M Matti, H Jari, F Li-Xin, Fan finger tracking for gestural interaction in mobile devices, in *18th Scandinavian Conference on Image Analysis, SCIA '13, Espoo, Finland, 17–20 June 2013*. Lecture Notes in Computer Science, vol. 7944 (Springer, Heidelberg, 2013), pp. 329–338
11. P Krejov, R Bowden, Multitouchless: real-time fingertip detection and tracking using geodesic maxima, in *Proceedings of the 10th IEEE International Conference on Automatic Face and Gesture Recognition, FG '13, Shanghai, China*, 2013, pp. 1–7
12. C Kereliuk, B Scherrer, V Verfaille, P Depalle, MM Wanderley, Indirect acquisition of fingerings of harmonic notes on the flute, in *Proceedings of the International Computer Music Conference, ICMC '07, Copenhagen, Denmark*, vol. I, 2007, pp. 263–266
13. C Kerdvibulvech, H Saito, Markerless guitarist fingertip detection using a Bayesian classifier and a template matching for supporting guitarists, in *Proceedings of the 10th ACM/IEEE Virtual Reality International Conference, VRIC '08, Laval, France*, 2008, pp. 201–208
14. A Asthana, TK Marks, MJ Jones, KH Tieu, MV Rohith, Fully automatic pose-invariant face recognition via 3D pose normalization, in *Proceedings of the IEEE International Conference on Computer Vision, ICCV '11, Barcelona, Spain*, 2011, pp. 937–944
15. X Wei, SL Phung, A Bouzerdoum, Object segmentation and classification using 3-D range camera. J. Vis. Commun. Image Represent. **25**(1), 74–85 (2014)
16. S Shi, L Wang, J W-q, Y Zhao, Yuanmeng color night vision based on color transfer in YUV color space, in *Proceedings of the International Symposium on Photoelectronic Detection and Imaging, Beijing, China, 9 September 2007*, vol. 6623, 2007, p. 66230B. doi:10.1117/12.791275
17. C Kerdvibulvech, H Saito, Vision-based guitarist fingering tracking using a Bayesian classifier and particle filters, in *IEEE Pacific-Rim Symposium on Image and Video Technology, PSIVT '07, Santiago, Chile, 17–19 December 2007*. Lecture Notes in Computer Science, vol. 4872 (Springer, Berlin Heidelberg, 2007), pp. 625–638. ISBN 978-3-540-77128-9
18. M Bianchi, P Salaris, A Bicchi, Synergy-based hand pose sensing: optimal glove design. Int. J. Robot. Res. **32**(4), 396–406 (2013)
19. J Huang, A Raabe, K Huang, C Buckl, A Knoll, *A framework for reliability-aware design exploration for MPSOC based systems*. Design Automation for Embedded Systems (DAEM), vol. 16, no. 4 (Springer Science+Business Media, New York, 2013), pp. 189–220. doi:10.1007/s10617-013-9105-6

# 9

# Automatic leaking carrier canceller adjustment techniques

Gregor Lasser[1]*, Robert Langwieser[2] and Christoph F Mecklenbräuker[2]

## Abstract

In this contribution, four automatic adjustment algorithms for leakage carrier cancellation in radio frequency identification (RFID) readers are compared: full search, gradient search, fast and direct I/Q algorithms. Further, we propose two enhanced adjustment procedures.

First, we analytically calculate the performance of the fast adjustment algorithm in the presence of noise and derive its theoretical bias. We compare the theoretical results with the numerical results from accompanying simulations. Further, we evaluate the performance of these algorithms based on real-world measurements acquired with our RFID testbed.

Finally, we propose and discuss the merits of two enhanced adjustment procedures based on the fast adjustment algorithm. The fast adjustment procedure with bipolar probing signals achieves the isolation gain of the (much slower) gradient search algorithm at the expense of a mean penalty of 0.48 dB. We observe that the fast adjustment aided gradient algorithm requires 72% less steps than the gradient search algorithm in our measurements.

## 1  Introduction

Radio frequency identification (RFID) is a technique to remotely identify and detect objects that are branded with a special transponder called RFID tag [1]. RFID systems operate at several frequency bands and use different methods to transfer data and energy between an RFID reader and the tags. In this work, we will focus on RFID systems that use electromagnetic waves for communications, especially ultrahigh frequency (UHF) RFID systems.

An RFID tag consists of an antenna that is connected to an electronic circuit, which in most cases is built on an integrated circuit. Many RFID systems use the so-called passive or semi-passive tags that do not use an internal power source to communicate with the RFID reader. They instead use backscattering, a technique which is based on the fact that the amplitude and phase of the waves scattered from an antenna depend on the antenna termination impedance. Thus, the tag sends data to the reader by modulating the impedance that the tag chip presents to the antenna terminals [2,3]. While this backscattering technique, seen from the tag, enables remotely powered

communication, it necessitates a constant carrier signal to be transmitted from the RFID reader during the tag to reader data transfer [4-6]. Therefore, the RFID reader has to transmit a carrier signal while it simultaneously receives a weak backscattered signal from the tag. To separate transmit an receive paths, readers either use separate transmit and receive antennas or use circulators or directional couplers. In analogy to radar systems, the first case is called bistatic, while the second one is called monostatic. Still, both system concepts struggle with low transmitter to receiver isolations [7]. This demands for receivers with very large dynamic ranges, which enhance costs, both on the analog front end as well as on the analog to digital converters. To reduce these demands, many authors [6,8-17] as well as commercial monolithic RFID reader chip manufacturers [18,19] propose or use active leakage cancellation techniques. These techniques, which originate in radar [20,21], extract a part of the transmit signal, adjust it in amplitude and phase and inject it at the receiver. When the amplitude is adjusted to be equal and the phase to be opposite of the leakage signal, the deliberately added signal and the leakage signal cancel. While there exist many publications on hardware implementations of these leaking carrier cancellers (LCCs), few exist

*Correspondence: gregor.lasser@nt.tuwien.ac.at
[1] Institute of Telecommunication, Vienna University of Technology, 1040, Vienna, Austria
Full list of author information is available at the end of the article

on adjustment algorithms to adapt them. However, adaption is critical [22,23] because typical RFID scenarios like warehouses and conveyor belts change permanently and therefore cannot be adjusted statically.

In this paper, we will accomplish the following:

- Present a comparison of four adjustment algorithms regarding their demands on hardware linearity, detector type and LCC calibration, and their setting speed,
- Analytically and numerically analyse the noise performance of the fast algorithm including a bias derivation,
- Practically compare the fast algorithm with the gradient search algorithm using our RFID testbed,
- Present an enhancement to the fast algorithm, which both gives better results under nonlinear detector conditions as well as a better noise performance,
- Report on observed step number reductions using the result of the fast algorithm for initialising the gradient algorithm: 72% reduction on average in our experiment.

The paper is structured as follows: In Section 2, we will describe the principals of leakage cancellation based on a generic RFID reader model. We will then present four automatic LCC adjustment routines and compare them regarding hardware demands and speed. This will be discussed in the context of detector types and positions with regard to our generic reader. In Section 3, we will provide a noise analysis for the fast algorithm which includes analytic and numeric results. Measurements on our RFID testbed will be described in Section 4. Finally, we will present two enhanced adjustment procedures based on the practical findings of the measurements, and we will compare them with the algorithms described before.

## 2  LCC adjustment principles

In this section, we explain the principal possibilities of active leakage cancellation adjustment techniques. Figure 1 illustrates a simplified block diagram of a bistatic RFID reader. The upper part of the figure shows the transmitter, which is composed of a signal generator, a modulator to send data to the tag, a power amplifier to create the necessary output power and a directional coupler. This coupler is used to extract a small part of the transmit signal and feed it into the LCC. Most of the transmit power is fed to the transmit antenna, where it is radiated. The lower part of Figure 1 illustrates the reader's receiver part. The receive antenna picks up the tag's response and an unwelcome leakage signal from the transmitter. Both signals path a band pass filter and directional couplers. The first coupler enables injection of the cancellation signal from the LCC. The second coupler feeds detector

(Det.) A. The coupler is followed by a low-noise amplifier (LNA) and a mixer stage. The received signal is filtered and amplified by a variable gain amplifier. Here, again a directional coupler is present to feed Det. B. The coupler is followed by an analog to digital converter (ADC), which converts the received signal into a data stream. Detector C is implemented in the digital domain.

The LCC consists of a vector modulator and an amplifier. The vector modulator is controlled by the reader control block and enables to adjust the amplitude and phase of the transmit signal sample to cancel the leakage signal in the receiver's directional coupler. The amplifier compensates for the coupling losses and enables cancellation of strong leakage signals.

Conventional RFID readers rarely have that many detectors as were described before. However, at least one is necessary to implement any LCC adjustment routine, but not every detector position or type supports every algorithm. We use the very general set-up described in Figure 1 to exemplify RFID reader implementations with focus on possible LCC control implementations. Besides the location, we distinguish between scalar power detectors and vector detectors which also capture the phase of the incoming signal. The second type requires a reference signal that is either supplied from the reader's transmitter part or from the ADC sampling clock. We use this generic RFID reader model through the next sections where we describe different automatic LCC adaption techniques, which aim to find the optimum inphase ($I$) and quadrature ($Q$) component settings for the LCC.

Our generic model is applicable to stationary RFID readers as well as to handheld devices. The latter usually employ integrated antennas which enable a better control of the typical expected leakage values and potentially a simpler LCC design. To save space and costs, the LCC may also be included in the antenna which was presented in [16]. Besides these differences, all LCC circuits need to be adjusted. While it might be desirable for mobile devices to reduce hardware complexity for smaller packages and lower costs, we will see that there is a trade-off between adjustment speed and necessary hardware complexity for the different adjustment algorithms. Since handheld readers most likely are moved all the time during their use, permanent and fast adjustment routines are beneficial.

### 2.1  Full search algorithm

The most primitive way to find the optimum setting for an LCC is by trying all possible LCC settings and picking the one which proved to have the best result. If inphase and quadrature components both have $N$ settings, $N^2$ measurements have to be performed. Thus, one obvious drawback of this technique is the large amount of measurements and adjustment steps which need to be

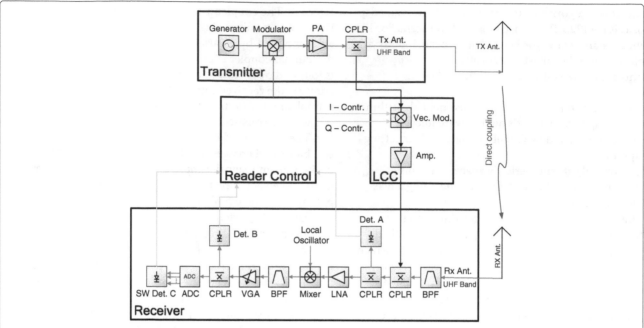

**Figure 1 Block diagram of an RFID reader.** Block diagram of a simplified RFID reader showing possible detector positions for LCC adjustment routines. PA, power amplifier; CPLR, coupler; I, inphase; Q, quadrature; Det., detector; ADC, analog to digital converter; VGA, variable gain amplifier; BPF, band pass filter; LNA, low-noise amplifier; TX Ant., transmit antenna; RX Ant., receive antenna; UHF, ultrahigh frequency; Vec. Mod, vector modulator; SW, software.

performend before the final result is gained. Depending on the speed of the given detector hardware, this corresponds to a large overall scanning time of the LCC which might be inadequate even for moderately changing environments. In these cases, this algorithm may completely fail to find an LCC setting because the slowly moving optimum LCC setting might never be hit during the scanning process. Besides these obvious disadvantages, the full search algorithm has the benefit of accepting any type of power detector as long as it shows a monotone, but not necessary linear input-output relation. Here, we mean monotone if the output of the detector is increasing (or remains constant) when the input power is increasing. Even if the receiver is completely overloaded by the leakage signal for most LCC settings, the power detector will provide the lowest output signal at the appropriate LCC setting. Therefore, this algorithm may be used in receiver structures, which do not employ a special power detector for LCC adjustment, and it has very limited demands on receiver linearity. For these reasons, some commercial reader chips use this algorithm [18]. An improvement to reduce the scanning time, which is also implemented in [18], is to divide the algorithm into two steps and to scan only a fraction of all $N^2$ setting in the first step. When this subgrid is properly chosen, at least one of the scanned subgrid points is close to the appropriate LCC setting, and therefore, the receiver operates in the linear regime and gives useful power detector readings. In the second step,

only the vicinity of the point with the lowest measured remaining LCC power is scanned.

## 2.2 Gradient search algorithm

The gradient search algorithm, which is also called method of the steepest descent ([24], Sec. 5.3), is an iterative approach to find the optimum LCC setting. For every step $n$, the algorithm finds the local gradient $\nabla_n$ of the power distribution versus the LCC setting. This is done by performing three measurements: First, the power at the actual LCC setting $c_n$ is recorded. Then, the LCC setting is changed for some small value $\delta$ in the inphase component only, and again, the resulting power is recorded. The last measurement records the power after applying a small change in the LCC's quadrature component only. Based on these three power values, the local gradient to the power distribution $\nabla_n$ is calculated, and a new LCC setting is found by the following:

$$c_{n+1} = c_n - \mu \nabla_n, \tag{1}$$

where $\mu$ is a positive, real-valued constant called the step-size parameter. Beginning from a starting point that is usually set to zero, $c_0 = 0$, the gradient search algorithm step by step tries to approach the optimum LCC setting. Setting the step-size parameter $\mu$ is critical for this algorithm to work: If it is too small, many steps are necessary to obtain the final value. Setting it too high results in oscillations, and the algorithm will not converge. A similar problem exists for the deviation value $\delta$ that is used to measure the gradient. Choosing $\delta$ too large will possibly lead to false gradient measurements when it is applied at close proximity to the optimum value. A small $\delta$ implies a small change in power and in the presence of noise an unreliable gradient measure.

Since it is an iterative technique, the gradient search algorithm is well suited for changing environments. Another benefit of this technique are the moderate linearity constraints which it imposes on the reader. As long as the power detector is strictly monotone and the step width is chosen small enough to ensure stability, the algorithm will converge to the optimum LCC setting point. Few authors explicitly state adjustment algorithms, but the authors in [16] are using a gradient-based approach as well as in [12], who describe a similar approach and use a variable step width.

### 2.3 Fast algorithm

The fast algorithm is a new technique which was first published in [25]. In this section, we will give a short description of the principle operation, while in later sections, a noise analysis, numerical simulations and measurement results are presented.

The algorithm gains the optimum LCC setting by obtaining three amplitude measurements. These measurements are very similar to the ones performed to gain the gradient in the gradient algorithm, but in contrast to the gradient algorithm, they do not provide an enhancement in information for the next iteration but immediately provide the correct LCC setting.

In the first step, the plain leakage amplitude without any LCC signal is measured by setting the complex LCC output $c_0 = 0$ and measuring the input amplitude:

$$r_0 = \sqrt{x^2 + y^2},$$
(2)

where $x$ and $y$ are the unknown $I$ and $Q$ components of the leakage signal.

In the second step, we apply a signal of amplitude $r_0$ with the $I$ channel of the LCC. Thus, the complex output signal of the LCC is $c_1 = r_0 + j0$. The amplitude measurement in this step equals

$$r_1 = \sqrt{(x + r_0)^2 + y^2}.$$
(3)

In the third step, we now probe the quadrature component of the leakage by setting the LCC to $c_2 = jr_0$ and receive

$$r_2 = \sqrt{x^2 + (y + r_0)^2}.$$
(4)

With these measurements, we find the components of the leaking signal by calculating the following:

$$\hat{x} = \frac{\frac{1}{2}r_1^2 - r_0^2}{r_0} = x,$$

$$\hat{y} = \frac{\frac{1}{2}r_2^2 - r_0^2}{r_0} = y.$$
(5)

Thus, the optimum LCC setting is found to be $c_{opt} = -x - jy$.

In contrast to the techniques described before, the detector has to be linear in amplitude for this algorithm to perform satisfactorily. The benefit of this approach is that it is very fast and may be used for changing environments as long as the leakage channel remains constant during the three measurement steps, which is the same condition as for the gradient algorithm. However, the fast algorithm requires calibration of the LCC settings, which means that for a pure LCC signal the relation between detector readings and LCC setting has to be known. A practical implementation of this calibration is explained in Section 4.1. Based on the calibration, it is possible to generate the appropriate probing signal amplitudes and finally the compensation signal $c_{opt}$ based on Equation 5.

### 2.4 Direct I/Q algorithm

This is a straightforward technique which requires a receiver equipped with a vector signal detector. Additionally, the LCC settings have to be calibrated with respect to this detector. Once a leakage signal is received, the inphase and quadrature components of this leakage signal are detected in the vector detector. The only necessary step is to set the LCC $I$ and $Q$ values opposite to the leakage signal. The benefit of this approach is extreme speed, when compared to all other techniques. However, it is the technique with the highest hardware demands, both for the detector type and the necessary LCC calibration.

The vector detector may either be implemented in the digital domain as detector C in Figure 1 or as a separate hardware vector detector in positions A or B. The authors of [10] present a receiver structure which employs a dedicated hardware receiver in position A which is suitable for a direct $I/Q$ detection algorithm.

### 2.5 Comparison of adjustment principles

Before we start our description of detector positions and their influence on detector performance, we summarise the descriptions of the described algorithms in Table 1. The algorithm name is given in the first column; the second column states the detector type which is employed. While the full search and gradient search algorithms only require power values, the fast algorithm commands for amplitude values, and the direct $I/Q$ algorithm even

**Table 1 Comparison of LCC adjustment techniques**

| Algorithm | Detector type | Linearity constraint | Number of steps | LCC calibration |
|---|---|---|---|---|
| Full search | Power | None | $N^2$ | No |
| Gradient search | Power | Low | 3 to $\frac{3N}{2}$ | Minimal |
| Fast algorithm | Amplitude | High | 3 | Yes |
| Direct $I/Q$ | $I/Q$ amplitude | High | 1 | Yes |

This table compares four LCC adjustment algorithms with respect to hardware demands and number of steps, where every setting of the LCC counts as one step. The number of LCC settings in $I$ and $Q$ domains is assumed to be identical and equal to $N$.

demands for a vector amplitude, i.e. an $I/Q$ detector. The third column lists the linearity constraints of the algorithms, and the fourth column states the number of steps which every algorithm requires to find $c_{\text{opt}}$. Here, we define the step as the process of setting the LCC to a certain value and taking a measurement. The full search algorithm scans the complete $I/Q$ plane of the LCC, so it takes $N^2$ steps when $N$ is the number of $I$ and $Q$ settings. As the gradient algorithm is iterative, the necessary number of iterations is unknown. Every iteration requires three measurements; therefore, the minimum number of steps is equal to three. When the algorithm converges without oscillations, the maximum number of iterations is half of the $I$ and $Q$ plane width, corresponding to $\frac{3N}{2}$ steps. The fast algorithm takes three measurements which corresponds to three steps in Table 1. As was described before, the full search and the gradient search do not require any LCC calibration, while the fast algorithm and the direct $I/Q$ method do. However, for picking the proper step width $\mu$, the maximum change per LCC step needs to be known which corresponds to the 'minimal' entry in Table 1.

### 2.6 Detector positions

We now discuss the possible detector positions with respect to our principal RFID reader described in Figure 1. Detector A is positioned right at the beginning of the receiver. No active components precede this detector, so only the detector itself is defining its output linearity. Therefore, this position is well suited for algorithms which require a linear detector behaviour like the fast algorithm or the direct $I/Q$ method. However, for the second, a more complex vector detector needs to be implemented. The other two algorithms will also operate properly with this detector.

Detector position B is positioned at the end of the analog receiver chain either at a low intermediate frequency or at the baseband. When compared to detector A, higher signal levels and lower frequencies are present at position B, and therefore, the implementation of the detector itself is less demanding. However, the receiver chain which precedes the detector might degrade the linearity of the detector. Therefore this position is well suited

for techniques with low linearity constraint, like the full search algorithm or the gradient search approach.

Detector C in general does not require any additional hardware because it is implemented in a software. It is relatively easily implemented as a vector power detector. The drawback of this detector is the fact that the complete receiver chain including amplifiers, mixers and ADCs is passed before the detector. For linear functionality, this complete chain has to operate in the linear domain as well. This increases the requirements on the whole receiver and at the end makes the use of an LCC questionable - if the receiver operates in a linear fashion under leakage carrier conditions, why bother to implement an LCC? It still makes sense to compensate the leakage in this case because the requirements on dynamic range regarding detecting the weak received tag response under the presence of leakage are very demanding, especially when we concern the necessary ADC resolution.

### 3  Noise analysis

In this section, we will present a detailed noise analysis for the fast algorithm. We will derive the estimator's bias and error variance as a function of the carrier to noise ratio (CNR). For the other algorithms, a short description follows.

As the full search algorithm searches the lattice of $N^2$ LCC setting points and picks the best one, the final setting error is not only constraint on the CNR at the detector but also on the quantisation error due to the finite number of setting points. For high CNR values, the correct point will be picked with high probability, and the setting error is dominated by the quantisation error which is proportional to $\frac{1}{N^2}$ ([26], Chap. 5.6). For the low CNR regime or when $N$ is very large, noise limits the detection of the minimum power at the optimum LCC setting point when scanning the complete $I/Q$ plane. Since this null is rather distinct [15,17], the noise influence is low.

For the gradient search algorithm, the noise influence is uncritical due to its iterative nature. This is of course only true if the step size is chosen small enough to guarantee convergence under noise influence.

The noise analysis for the direct $I/Q$ algorithm is straightforward and we will use it as a reference for the fast algorithm. Since the $I$ and $Q$ components of the leakage signal are directly measured by an appropriate detector, the detector noise variance and bias are equal to the algorithm's error noise variance and bias.

### 3.1 Analytic analysis

In this section, we expand the noise free description of the fast algorithm given in Section 2.3 for the case which includes noisy $I$ and $Q$ components. In an actual RFID reader implementation, many parts in the transmitter, channel, receiver, detector and possibly an ADC following the detector contribute to noise which degrades the measurements described in Equations 2 to 4. Depending on the underlying physics of these noise sources and their position in the TX-RX chain, their noise has to be modelled in different ways. In the following section, we will focus on strictly white, statistically independent noise that adds to the $I$ and $Q$ components. Further, we focus on the estimation of the inphase component $\hat{x}$, as these results later may easily be adapted to $\hat{y}$.

To include the noise, we replace the noise-free leakage components $x$ and $y$ with the following:

$$x_i = x + u_i, \quad y_i = y + v_i, \tag{6}$$

where $u_i$ and $v_i$ are the realisations of the statistically independent noise processes $U$ and $V$, respectively. We expand Equation 2 and get the following:

$$r_0 = \sqrt{x_0^2 + y_0^2} = \sqrt{(x + u_0)^2 + (y + v_0)^2}, \tag{7}$$

which includes the noise realisations $u_0$ and $v_0$ of the first step. We apply noise to the second measurement as well and receive

$$r_1 = \sqrt{(x_1 + r_0)^2 + y_1^2} = \sqrt{(x + u_1 + r_0)^2 + (y + v_1)^2}. \tag{8}$$

We proceed to calculate the expectation of the estimated $I$ component $\hat{x}$:

$$E\{\hat{x}\} = E\left\{\frac{\frac{1}{2}r_1^2 - r_0^2}{r_0}\right\} = E\{x\} + E\{u_1\}$$

$$+ E\left\{\underbrace{\frac{xu_1 + yv_1 + \frac{u_1^2 + v_1^2}{2}}{r_0}}_{E_1}\right\} \tag{9}$$

$$- E\left\{\underbrace{\frac{xu_0 + yv_0 + \frac{u_0^2 + v_0^2}{2}}{r_0}}_{E_2}\right\}$$

$$= x + \mu_u + E\{E_1\} - E\{E_2\}.$$

This expectation includes $x$ and an additive bias term. To treat the bias, we specialise our noise model: The noise of both signal components $U$ and $V$ is white and Gaussian and has zero mean $\mu_u = \mu_v = 0$. The noise variances are $\sigma_u^2$ and $\sigma_v^2$. As stated before, we presume statistical independence of the $I$ and $Q$ noise components.

The first bias term $E_1$ can be divided in the expectations of the numerator and $1/r_0$ since the numerator and denominator are statistically independent. Therefore, we compute the expectation of $E_1$ as follows:

$$E\{E_1\} = E\left\{xu_1 + yv_1 + \frac{u_1^2 + v_1^2}{2}\right\} E\left\{\frac{1}{r_0}\right\} = \frac{\sigma_u^2 + \sigma_v^2}{2}$$

$$\times E\left\{\frac{1}{\sqrt{x^2 + y^2 + 2xu_0 + 2yv_0 + u_0^2 + v_0^2}}\right\}$$

$$= \frac{\sigma_u^2 + \sigma_v^2}{2r} E\left\{\frac{1}{\sqrt{1 + \frac{2xu_0 + 2yv_0}{r^2} + \frac{u_0^2 + v_0^2}{r^2}}}\right\}$$

$$= \frac{\sigma_u^2 + \sigma_v^2}{2r} E\left\{\frac{1}{\sqrt{1 + \varepsilon}}\right\}, \tag{10}$$

where $r = \sqrt{x^2 + y^2}$ is the noise-free amplitude of the leakage signal. To compute the result of the remaining expectation operator, which acts as a weighting factor for the preceding term including the noise variances, we approximate the root expression by a first-order Taylor expansion for $\varepsilon$. This approximation holds when the noise components are small when compared to the carrier power $r^2$, i.e. the CNR is high.

$$E\{E_1\} \approx \frac{\sigma_u^2 + \sigma_v^2}{2r} E\left\{1 - \frac{\varepsilon}{2}\right\} = \frac{\sigma_u^2 + \sigma_v^2}{2r}$$

$$\times E\left\{1 - \frac{xu_0 + yv_0}{r^2} - \frac{u_0^2 + v_0^2}{2r^2}\right\} \tag{11}$$

$$= \frac{\sigma_u^2 + \sigma_v^2}{2r} - \frac{\sigma_u^4 + 2\sigma_u^2\sigma_v^2 + \sigma_v^4}{4r^3}.$$

We treat the second bias term $E_2$ in a different way, since here the separation of numerator and denominator is not possible. Instead, we reformulate the following problem:

$$E_2 = \frac{xu_0 + yv_0 + \frac{u_0^2 + v_0^2}{2}}{r\sqrt{1 + \frac{2xu_0 + 2yv_0}{r^2} + \frac{u_0^2 + v_0^2}{r^2}}}$$

$$= \frac{r\left(-1 + 1 + \frac{2xu_0 + 2yv_0}{r^2} + \frac{u_0^2 + v_0^2}{r^2}\right)}{2\sqrt{1 + \underbrace{\frac{2xu_0 + 2yv_0}{r^2} + \frac{u_0^2 + v_0^2}{r^2}}_{\varepsilon}}} \quad (12)$$

$$= \frac{r}{2}\left(\sqrt{1 + \varepsilon} - \frac{1}{\sqrt{1 + \varepsilon}}\right).$$

Similar to the step we used before, we approximate the expression in the brackets using a second-order Taylor expansion. We compute the expectation as follows:

$$E\{E_2\} \approx E\left\{\frac{r}{2}\left(\varepsilon - \frac{\varepsilon^2}{2}\right)\right\}$$

$$= r\left(\frac{\sigma_u^2 + \sigma_v^2}{2r^2} - \frac{x^2\sigma_u^2 + y^2\sigma_v^2}{r^4} - \frac{3\sigma_u^4 + 2\sigma_u^2\sigma_v^2 + 3\sigma_v^4}{4r^4}\right), \quad (13)$$

using the fact that $E\{u_0^4\} = 3\sigma_u^2$ and $E\{v_0^4\} = 3\sigma_v^2$, since $U$ and $V$ are Gaussian variables. Finally, we compute $E\{\hat{x}\}$ as follows:

$$E\{\hat{x}\} = x + E\{E_1\} - E\{E_2\}$$

$$\approx x + r\left(\frac{x^2\sigma_u^2 + y^2\sigma_v^2}{r^4} + \frac{\sigma_u^4 + \sigma_v^4}{2r^4}\right). \quad (14)$$

For the case of equal noise variances of the $I$ and $Q$ components, we further simplify this expression using $\sigma_u^2 = \sigma_v^2 = \sigma^2/2$, where $\sigma^2$ denotes the variance of the circularly symmetrical complex Gaussian variable composed of $U + jV$. Using this variance, the CNR is defined as the ratio of the leaking carrier power and the complex noise variance:

$$E\{\hat{x}\} \approx x + r\left(\frac{\sigma^2}{2r^2} + \frac{\sigma^4}{4r^4}\right) = x + r\left(\frac{1}{2\text{CNR}} + \frac{1}{4\text{CNR}^2}\right),$$

$$\text{with} \quad \text{CNR} = \frac{r^2}{\sigma^2}. \quad (15)$$

We see that the proposed fast algorithm acts as a biased estimator. Since the bias is approximately known, it can be compensated if the CNR is known as well. In most RFID applications, leakage carrier compensation is performed to reduce a large leakage signal, so high CNRs are expected. In this case, the bias may be neglected.

## 3.2 Monte Carlo simulations

We performed a Monte Carlo simulation of the fast algorithm using the same circularly symmetric complex Gaussian noise model as described before. For every CNR value, $4 \times 10^6$ simulations were performed. Figure 2 shows a comparison between the simulated average bias and the analytic approximate bias of Equation 15 derived before. We see that for CNRs larger than 3 dB, both curves match very closely, and the bias of the estimator is well described in Equation 15. For lower CNR values, the approximations made in Equations 11 and 13 do not hold any more, and the curves start to diverge. This means that the bias of the estimator can be removed if the CNR is known. However, we will see that there is a good reason not to aim for an unbiased estimator for this particular problem.

Figure 3 shows the standard deviation of the standardised error $\frac{\hat{x} - x}{r}$ of the estimation of the $I$ component $x$. This is compared to the standard deviation of the standardised noise on the $I$ component, which is computed to $\frac{\sigma_u}{r} = \sqrt{\frac{1}{2\text{CNR}}}$. For low CNRs, the error variance is severely increased when compared to the noise variance. However, in the higher CNR regime, the difference is not so large, and both curves tend to zero. This comparison may also be interpreted as performance comparison between the fast algorithm and the direct $I/Q$ algorithm, since the latter algorithm's noise performance is directly given by the noise on each component. Thus, it is evident that the direct vector measurement of the leakage employed by the direct $I/Q$ algorithm does not show the noise enhancement and is superior for low CNRs. The third curve of the enhanced fast algorithm is discussed in Section 5.1.

Up to now, we just discussed the moments of the estimator based on the fast algorithm. Based on the Monte Carlo simulations, we now discuss scatter plots and histograms

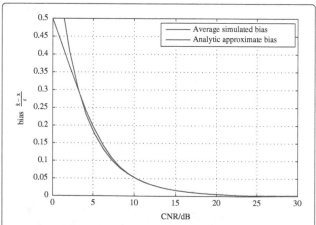

**Figure 2 Relative bias of the $I$ component estimate.** Comparison of the relative bias of the $I$ component estimate for the averaged Monte Carlo simulation results and the approximate analytic results plotted over the CNR.

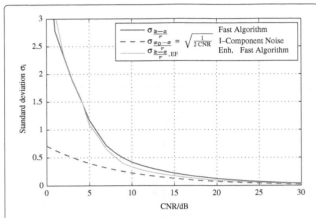

**Figure 3 Comparison of standard deviation $\sigma_i$ of relative $I$ component errors plotted vs. CNR.** Comparison of the standard deviation of the fast algorithm, the $I$ component's noise, i.e. the standard deviation of the direct $I/Q$ algorithm, and the standard deviation of the enhanced fast algorithm discussed in Section 5.1.

to analyse the statistical distribution of the estimation error. Figure 4a illustrates the error distribution for a very low CNR of CNR $= -5$ dB by showing 8,000 error points from the Monte Carlo simulations. We see that the noise is centered around the origin but, additionally, is quite spread in the sector of positive $I$ and $Q$ components. The diagram also shows the mean of the error, which was obtained by $4 \times 10^5$ simulations and which is at $0.87 + 0.87j$. Applying a bias correction following Equation 15 leads to catastrophic overcompensation since the bias is not well captured at low CNRs as we discussed before. Further, from Figure 4a, we see that there are good reasons not even to try to compensate for the bias and use the

slightly biased estimator as it is: The mode of the error, which is the peak of the histogram of the error, is slightly negative ($-0.5 + -0.4j$), and therefore, most of the estimates of $x$ and $y$ will be slightly negatively biased. This is also clear from the histogram shown in Figure 4b. The distribution has a long tail towards positive values which shifts the mean to this side. The unbiased estimator is found by shifting this distribution to negative values, but this of course will shift the negative mode even further. Therefore, we suggest not to apply any bias correction.

The situation gets less distinct for a CNR of 0 dB as it is used in Figure 5. Here, the bias compensation still leads to overcompensation, but at least, the magnitude of the remaining bias is smaller. Since the mode of the error is still slightly negative for both components, the bias compensation can be omitted in favor of the closer error mode.

We see from the histogram in Figure 6b that for medium to high CNRs, the error distribution becomes not only more compact, but also the long tail towards positive values is shortening. The same is observed from the scatter plot (Figure 6b), and both mean error and error mode tend to the origin. Since the whole issue of carrier cancellation is tackled to combat strong leakage signals, we expect that most RFID readers will operate in high CNR regimes so that the skewness of the fast algorithm's error distribution is not an issue, and bias compensation is superfluous.

## 4 Measurements

We performed measurements to compare the fast algorithm with the gradient algorithm. These measurements were based on our RFID testbed described in [27], which

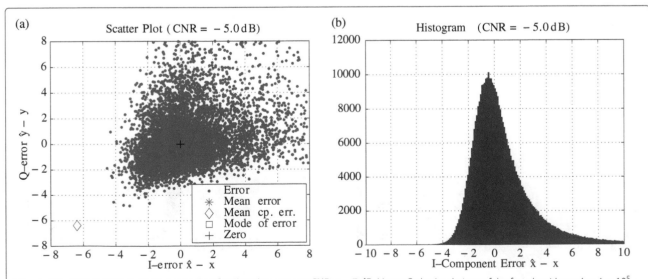

**Figure 4 Scatter plot (a) and histogram (b) of estimation error at CNR $= -5$ dB.** Monte Carlo simulations of the fast algorithm using $4 \times 10^5$ realisations. (a) A scatter plot of 8,000 error points and additionally the mean and mode of the error as well as the mean of the error with compensated bias (Mean cp. err.) based on Equation 15. (b) Histogram showing the distribution of the relative error of the $I$ component.

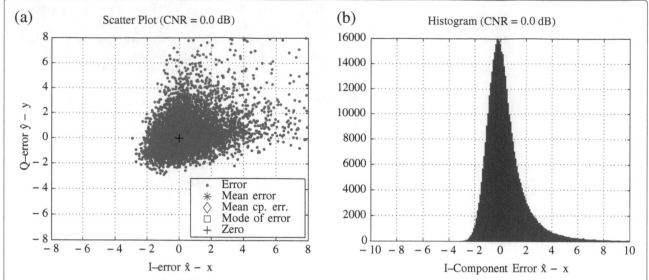

**Figure 5 Scatter plot (a) and histogram (b) of estimation error at CNR = 0 dB.** Monte Carlo simulations of the fast algorithm using $4 \times 10^5$ realisations. (a) A scatter plot of 8,000 error points and additionally the mean and mode of the error as well as the mean of the error with compensated bias (Mean cp. err.) based on Equation 15. (b) Histogram showing the distribution of the relative error of the *I* component.

was controlled via a standard PC. The detailed measurement set-up is described in the next section. Further, we will present the results of the pure gradient algorithm, the fast algorithm and two enhanced algorithms based on these two.

### 4.1 Set-up

Figure 7 illustrates the measurement set-up used throughout the measurements. A photograph of the measurement set-up is shown in Figure 8. The algorithms were evaluated for a pure sine wave carrier signal, which was created in the generator shown in the upper left corner. Its output signal is split up into the upper leakage generating path, and the lower cancellation path, which consists of an LCC module called carrier cancellation unit 1 (CCU1), which is described in detail in [13]. It consists of a vector modulator and an amplifier, which raises the level of the compensation signal to compensate for the coupling losses in

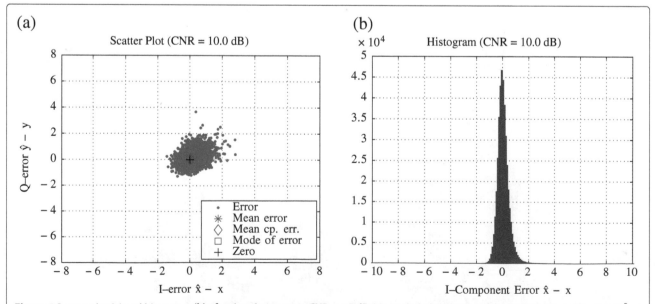

**Figure 6 Scatter plot (a) and histogram (b) of estimation error at CNR = 10 dB.** Monte Carlo Simulations of the fast algorithm using $4 \times 10^5$ realisations. (a) A scatter plot of 8,000 error points and additionally the mean and mode of the error as well as the mean of the error with compensated bias (Mean cp. err.) based on Equation 15. (b) Histogram showing the distribution of the relative error of the *I* component.

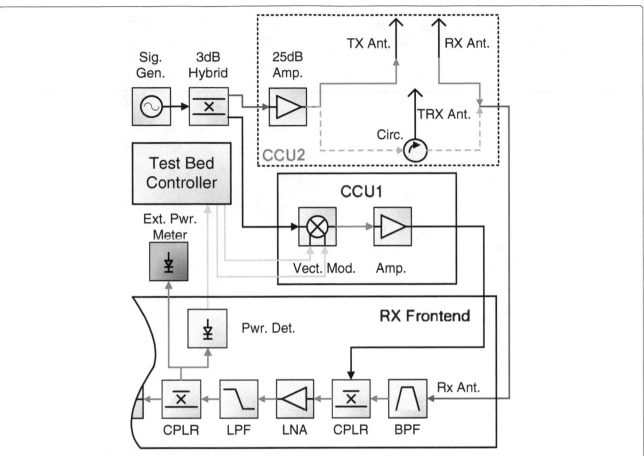

**Figure 7 Measurement set-up.** This is a block diagram of the measurement set-up that was used to compare the fast algorithm with the gradient algorithm. The lower part of the picture shows the front end of our testbed's RFID receiver, where the first power detector output is fed into the testbed controller (TBC), which commands all hardware necessary for LCC adaption. The LCC consists of a module called carrier cancellation unit 1 (CCU1), which is controlled from the testbed controller. The leakage signal is either generated by one of two antenna configurations or by replacing this complete block with another CCU2 for artificial leakage generation.

the receiver. The upper leakage generating part either consists of one of two antenna scenarios or is replaced by a second CCU to artificially generate a well-defined leakage signal. When using the antennas, we first amplify the signal using an amplifier with a gain of 25 dB and then either feed a transmit (TX) antenna and pick up the signal with a receive (RX) antenna to mimic a bistatic RFID scenario, or we use a monostatic scenario with a single transceive (TRX) antenna and a circulator. The antennas had a gain of 8 dBi, and in the bistatic scenario, they were placed side by side facing the same direction for reasonable TX-RX decoupling.

Both leakage and compensation signals were routed to the front end of our RFID receiver [27] where they combine in the first directional coupler. This summed signal is then fed through a LNA and a LPF and finally reaches the second directional coupler. Here, a part of the received signal is extracted and fed to the internal power detector and an external power metre. The internal logarithmic

power detector output is routed to the testbed controller (TBC) where it is used as a source signal for the tested LCC adjustment routines. Except for the LNA chosen for its highly linear operation, it is not affected by nonlinearity of any receiver hardware component and, therefore, is comparable to detector A discussed in Section 2.6. The external power metre was used to obtain measurement data only, but not for use in the adjustment algorithms. The TBC provides 16-bit ADCs to capture the power metre output signals and 12-bit DACs to control the $I/Q$ channels of CCU1 and CCU2, corresponding to 4,096 possible settings for each channel.

The receiver's power detector provides a voltage which is logarithmically dependent on the power detector's input power. Since the fast algorithm demands for a linear amplitude detector, we used a function to convert every voltage measurement from the TBC corresponding to a power measurement from the power detector into a number. This linearising function consists of an exponential

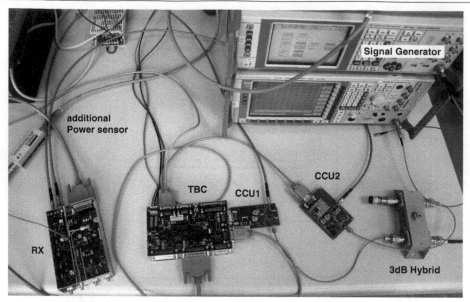

**Figure 8 Measurement set-up.** This picture shows the measurement set-up that was used for all measurements presented in this paper. Reprinted from Fig. three in [25], with permission from the IEEE.

function and additionally a multiplicative constant. This constant was chosen to result in most linear amplitude readings with respect to the output of the function. The LCC composed of CCU1 was calibrated with respect to these amplitude measurements by disconnecting the red antenna input signal in Figure 7 and by performing separate sweeps in the $I$ and $Q$ domains, always setting the unswept channel to zero. These sweeps were performed with a step size of 10 corresponding to 410 recorded amplitude measurements per channel. The values obtained in these measurements were stored in a lookup table and aided by interpolation enabled to set the LCC to the correct probing values $c_1$ and $c_2$ necessary for steps two and three of the fast algorithm and finally to $c_{opt}$ found by Equation 5.

### 4.2 Measurement results

For a first feasibility test of the hardware and the fast algorithm in a realistic RFID scenario, we conducted measurements using the monostatic and bistatic set-ups. For different orientations of the antennas in the laboratory room, isolation gains of the fast algorithm ranging from 8.1 to 27.9 dB were reached. Here, we define the TX to RX isolation gain $G_I$ as the ratio of uncancelled leakage power $P_L$ divided by the remaining power of the cancelled leakage signal $P_{CL}$:

$$G_I = \frac{P_L}{P_{CL}} = \frac{r^2}{|\hat{x} - x|^2 + |\hat{y} - y|^2}. \qquad (16)$$

According to this definition, the isolation gain directly reveals the improvement of the used cancellation

algorithm in comparison to a system without LCC usage. When expressed in decibels, the isolation gain ranges from small negative values for badly misadjusted LCCs to large positive values for properly adjusted LCCs.

For comparison, we also implemented a gradient search algorithm according to Section 2.2, where we chose the gradient finding step size to be $\delta = 10$ in general and $\delta = 2$ for LCC settings close to the optimum LCC setting point. We used a variable step size $\mu$ which was adapted proportional to $\sqrt{\nabla_n}$ according to an empirically chosen factor. Both adaption schemes aided to securely find the optimum LCC setting by reducing the step sizes close to the optimum point. The gradient search algorithm reached isolation gains ranging from 14.7 to 24.7 dB.

For a more systematic analysis, we replaced the RFID antenna scenario with a second CCU module to retrieve systematic leakage cancellation measurements. CCU2 was swept over the $I/Q$ space in 65 steps per channel producing 4,225 points in total. Figure 9 shows the resulting isolation gain $G_{I,F}$ of the fast algorithm in a pseudo-colour plot. The figure is plotted with respect to the $I/Q$ leakage plane, i.e. the CCU2 DAC control plane. Since 12-bit DACs are used for both the $I$ and $Q$ channels, this plane ranges from $-2,048$ to $2,047$. In the centre, no isolation gain is obtainable since the input power $P_L = 0$. For increasing input powers, the isolation gain of the fast algorithm increases as well. Here, the presented gain is also limited by the low end of the power metre's dynamic range, since the absolute power levels at the power metre after the coupler and splitting losses are rather low. We note a decrease in isolation gain in three of the four

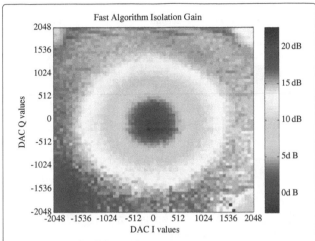

**Figure 9 Fast algorithm isolation gain.** Isolation gain $G_{I,F}$ plotted on the $I/Q$ plane spanned by the leakage-generating CCU2. The plot is compensated for the power metre temperature drift using the power metre reading of the gradient algorithm's final result as reference.

corners for high input leakage powers. This effect is also visible in Figure 10. Here, the ratio of the isolation gains of the gradient algorithm and the fast algorithm is plotted. Since we believe the gradient algorithm converges to the optimum LCC setting point under the given hardware constraints, we may interpret Figure 10 as the fast algorithm's isolation gain deviation from the optimum value. For large areas, the performance of the fast algorithm is very good; in 95% of the measured points, the error is below 3 dB. We again see the degradation at the same three corners.

For further analysis of this behaviour, we discuss the relative error vector magnitude of the fast algorithm when compared to the gradient algorithm

$\sqrt{|\hat{x} - \hat{x}_G|^2 + |\hat{y} - \hat{y}_G|^2}/N$, which is shown in Figure 11. In contrast to the plots discussed before, we now have drawn the plot with respect to the LCC's $I/Q$ plane, i.e. the CCU1 DAC values. Each plotted point corresponds to the estimated $I$ and $Q$ values $\hat{x}_G$ and $\hat{y}_G$ of the gradient algorithm for this leakage signal. We see that the resulting diagram is a square which is slightly smaller than the LCC's $I/Q$ space and rotated counterclockwise. The good agreement of the shape of the diagram to a perfect square is a sign that the gradient algorithm captures the true leakage values very closely. The rotation is due to the phase shift between leakage and compensation paths, which is mainly caused by the cabling of the measurement set-up. The maximum leakage power was chosen to be slightly smaller than the maximum cancellation power so that all leakage settings can be compensated. The majority of the measured points, 68%, exhibit an error smaller than 3%.

We see that the lower left quadrant exhibits very low error magnitudes, typically below 2%. For all other quadrants, we notice a behaviour which is primarily dependent on the leakage amplitude which results in concentric circles of higher and lower estimation errors of the fast algorithm. For large amplitudes in these quadrants, relative error magnitudes larger than 5% are observed - which corresponds to the degraded performance in the three corners that we noted before. This behaviour is explained by the imperfect amplitude detector. Although the detector is situated almost directly at the receiver input, which is a prerequisite for linear operation under the constraints of reasonable receiver hardware demands (see Section 2.6), we see that the estimation error grows for larger amplitudes. This is due to the fact that we are

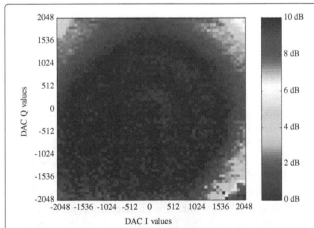

**Figure 10 Isolation gain ratio.** Isolation gain ratio $\frac{G_{I,G}}{G_{I,F}}$ of the gradient algorithm and the fast algorithm plotted on the $I/Q$ plane spanned by the leakage-generating CCU2 (compare with Fig. seven in [25], with permission from the IEEE).

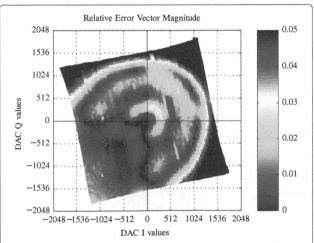

**Figure 11 Relative error vector magnitude.** Relative magnitude of the setting error of the fast algorithm when compared to the gradient search algorithm $\sqrt{|\hat{x} - \hat{x}_G|^2 + |\hat{y} - \hat{y}_G|^2}/N$, plotted on the $I/Q$ space of CCU1 on the estimated leakage values $\hat{x}_G$ and $\hat{y}_G$ (compare with Fig. six in [25], with permission from the IEEE).

using a logarithmical power detector which decreases the sensitivity for high input amplitudes, and the conversion to linear values is not perfect. In the lower left quadrant, this effect is not observed, since here the probing signals of the fast algorithm have opposite polarity to the leakage signals and therefore result in small signal amplitudes for steps two and three of the fast algorithm according to Equations 3 and 4. This theory is fortified when we inspect Figures 12 and 13, which separately show the relative estimation errors of the $I$ and $Q$ components with respect to the gradient algorithm estimate. Figure 12 represents the error of the inphase component, which is very small for leakage signals with a negative $I$ component, and fluctuates for leakage signals with a positive $I$ component until it rapidly rises for large leakage amplitudes. In this domain, the estimator overestimates the $I$ component. The critical step in the fast algorithm is the second measurement where the probing signal is applied and the resulting sum amplitude is measured. In the left quadrants of Figure 12, this sum amplitude is ranging from 0 to $\sqrt{2}r$, where $r$ is the amplitude of the leakage signal. In the right quadrants, the sum amplitude ranges from $\sqrt{2}r$ to $2r$. The relatively high sum amplitude with a small relative change and the use of the logarithmic detector lead to the worse performance of these right quadrants. The same is true for the upper quadrants of the $Q$ error shown in Figure 13. Combining these two error patterns finally leads to the estimation error we see in Figure 11.

## 5 Enhanced procedures

Based on the practical and theoretical findings, we present two enhancements to the set of algorithms described in Section 2.

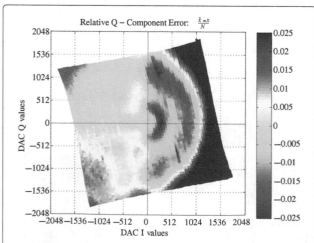

**Figure 12 $I$ component error.** Relative $I$ component setting error of the fast algorithm $\frac{\hat{x} - \hat{x}_G}{N}$, plotted on the $I/Q$ space of CCU1 on the estimated leakage values $\hat{x}_G$ and $\hat{y}_G$.

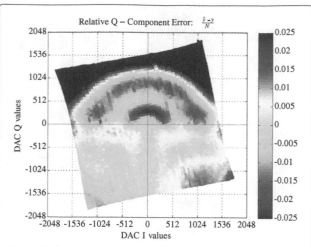

**Figure 13 $Q$ component error.** Relative $Q$ component setting error of the fast algorithm $\frac{\hat{y} - \hat{y}_G}{N}$, plotted on the $I/Q$ space of CCU1 on the estimated leakage values $\hat{x}_G$ and $\hat{y}_G$.

### 5.1 Fast algorithm with bipolar probing signals

We have seen from the measurement results that for our practical system, the fast algorithm is limited by the non-linear behaviour of the logarithmical power detector. The quadrant which lies in the negative $I$ and $Q$ sectors of the leakage signal is only slightly affected, since here the probing signal and the leakage signal partially cancel each other and result in a low amplitude signal which is measured in the second and third steps of the fast algorithm. We extend this beneficial behaviour to all four $I/Q$ quadrants using positive and negative probing signals for $I$ and $Q$ components. For the negative probing signals, Equation 5 becomes

$$
\hat{x} = \frac{r_0^2 - \frac{1}{2}r_1^2}{r_0} = x,
$$

$$
\hat{y} = \frac{r_0^2 - \frac{1}{2}r_2^2}{r_0} = y.
$$

(17)

Since the fast algorithm in the first step measures the leakage amplitude $r$, it is immediately clear after the second step if this step should be repeated with a negative probing signal, because the resulting measured amplitude in the second step is smaller than $\sqrt{2}r$ when the $I$ component lies in the beneficial region. Using this conditional re-measurement technique, the fast algorithm's step count stated in Table 1 is increased from three to three to five, which has an average number of four steps. Of course, it is also possible to always perform all five measurements; then, even averaging of the two estimates of the same $I/Q$ component is possible. This possibly makes sense for leakage signals whose signal power is concentrated in the other $I/Q$ component so that the leakage signal and probing signal are almost orthogonal to each other.

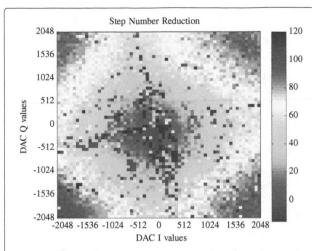

**Figure 14 Step reduction.** Reduction in number of steps required to converge to final value when comparing the pure gradient search algorithm with a gradient search algorithm aided by a fast algorithm starting point.

When using this technique of bipolar probing signals, the bias derived in Section 3.1 does not change as long as the statistical properties of the noise components $U$ and $V$ are the same; since then, Equation 15 does not depend on $x$ or $y$. The variance of the standardised estimation error for medium to high CNR values for this algorithm is smaller than the standard deviation of the regular fast algorithm, as we see from our Monte Carlo simulations in Figure 3. Therefore, this improvement which we had considered to overcome limitations due to the linearity of the amplitude detector also improves the estimation in the case of noise-limited operation.

Based on the measurements presented in Figure 10, we calculate the average isolation gain ratio of the beneficial quadrant shown as the lower left quadrant in Figure 11 and get 0.48 dB. Thus, we conclude that using the bipolar probing method for the fast algorithm, we reach the isolation gain of the gradient algorithm with a mean penalty of only 0.48 dB.

### 5.2 Fast algorithm-aided gradient algorithm

In practical RFID scenarios, many factors limit the performance of the fast algorithm, which are mainly based on nonlinear detector behaviour and imperfect LCC calibration. However, the fast algorithm may be used to aid the gradient algorithm by setting the starting point of the iterative search to the values found by the fast algorithm. We compare this fast algorithm-aided gradient algorithm with our standard gradient algorithm using the same measurement set-up as described in Section 4.1. Using the monostatic and bistatic antenna scenarios, we compare the necessary number of steps for the algorithms to converge. If we stick to our step definition as stated in

Section 2.6, the pure gradient algorithm required 39 to 135 steps, while the aided algorithm for the same scenarios was content with 21 to 60 steps.

We repeated the measurements with the systematic leakage sweep generated by CCU2 to compare the two algorithms on the complete $I/Q$ plane. A graphical representation of the results is given in Figure 14, which shows the reduction in number of steps when compared to the gradient algorithm starting at zero. We see that close to zero, no improvement is possible since the starting point of the pure gradient search algorithm is zero anyway. For larger leakage amplitudes, which are practically more relevant, the fast algorithm provides a better starting point, and reductions up to 120 steps are possible. On average, the pure gradient algorithm requires 75 steps while the aided algorithm only demands 21 steps, which is a decrease by 72%.

### 6 Conclusions

This contribution discussed the performance of well-known algorithms and novel enhanced procedures for the automatic adjustment of leakage carrier cancellers in RFID readers. We briefly described three well-known algorithms and the fast algorithm published in [25] and discussed their requirements on receiver hardware and performance in terms of their step count. Further, we carried out an analytical noise analysis for the fast adjustment algorithm and derived its bias behaviour. The presented analytic approximation of the estimator bias holds for the high CNR regime where the bias is very small and can be safely ignored. The analytical results were compared to numerical simulation studies which were used to show the estimator's error distribution for varying CNR levels. We found that the bias at low CNR values is negligible in favour of a mode of the error which is close to zero. Thus, it was shown that for both high and low CNR regions, bias compensation of the fast algorithm is not an issue.

We demonstrated the practical performance of the fast adjustment algorithm using our unmodified RFID reader hardware platform. Although this hardware only implements a logarithmic power detector, a systematic scan of the leakage $I/Q$ plane demonstrated that 95% of the measurements show a maximum penalty in isolation gain of 3 dB when compared to the much slower gradient search algorithm. We further proposed and discussed two enhanced procedures based on the fast algorithm. The first procedure is an extension and uses bipolar probing signals, which enables accurate LCC setting with a mean error of 0.48 dB, while the average step count is only increased to four. The second procedure is an enhancement to the gradient search algorithm by setting an improved starting point. This reduces the average step count by 72%.

**Competing interests**
The authors declare that they have no competing interests.

**Acknowledgements**
This work has been funded by the Christian Doppler Laboratory for Wireless Technologies for Sustainable Mobility. The financial support by the Federal Ministry of Economy, Family and Youth and the National Foundation for Research, Technology and Development is gratefully acknowledged. We would further like to thank our colleague Robert Dallinger for the many inspiring and valuable discussions.

**Author details**
[1]Institute of Telecommunication, Vienna University of Technology, 1040,Vienna, Austria. [2]Christian Doppler Laboratory for Wireless Technologies for Sustainable Mobility, Vienna University of Technology, 1040, Vienna, Austria.

**References**
1.  R Want, An introduction to RFID technology. IEEE Pervasive Comput. **5**, 25–33 (2006)
2.  H Stockman, Communication by means of reflected power. Proc. IRE. **36**(10), 1196–1204 (1948)
3.  PV Nikitin, KVS Rao, R Martinez, Differential RCS of RFID tag. Electron. Lett. **43**(8), 431–432 (2007)
4.  PV Nikitin, KVS Rao, Theory and measurement of backscattering from RFID tags. IEEE Antennas Propag. Mag. **48**(6), 212–218 (2006)
5.  DM Dokin, *The RF in RFID*, 1st edn. (Newnes/Elsevier, Burlington, 2008)
6.  JP Curty, M Declercq, C Dehollain, N Joehl, *Design and Optimization of Passive UHF RFID Systems*, 1st edn. (Springer, New York, 2007)
7.  K Penttilä, L Sydänheimo, M Kivikoski, Implementation of Tx/Rx isolation in an RFID reader. Int. J. Radio Freq Identification Technol Appl. **1**, 74–89 (2006)
8.  Y Liu, Q Zhang, M Zheng. Signal analysis and design criteria for UHF RFID reader. ITS Telecommunications Proceedings, Chengdu, June 2006 (IEEE, Piscataway, 2006), pp. 233–236
9.  TI Al-Mahdawi, Adaptive coherent RFID reader carrier cancellation, U.S. patent US. 2006/183454. 17 Aug 2006
10. DP Villame, JS Marciano Jr. Carrier suppression locked loop mechanism for UHF RFID readers. IEEE International Conference on RFID, Orlando, April 2010 (IEEE, Piscataway, 2010), pp. 141–145
11. R Langwieser, G Lasser, C Angerer, M Fischer, AL Scholtz. Active carrier compensation for a multi-antenna RFID reader frontend. 2010 IEEE MTT-S International Microwave Symposium Digest, Anaheim, May 2010, (IEEE, Piscataway, 2010), pp. 1532–1535
12. I Mayordomo, J Bernhard. Implementation of an adaptive leakage cancellation control for passive UHF RFID readers. IEEE International Conference on RFID, Orlando, April 2011 (IEEE, Piscataway, 2011), pp. 121–127
13. G Lasser, R Langwieser, AL Scholtz. Broadband suppression properties of active leaking carrier cancellers. IEEE International Conference on RFID, Orlando, April 2009 (IEEE, Piscataway, 2009)
14. P Pursula, M Kiviranta, H Seppä, UHF RFID reader with reflected power canceller. IEEE Microw. Wireless Compon, Lett. **19**, 48–50 (2009)
15. T Xiong, X Tan, J Xi, X Min, High TX-to-RX isolation in UHF RFID using narrowband leaking carrier canceller. IEEE Microw. Wireless Compon, Lett. **20**(2), 124–126 (2010)
16. LW Mayer, AL Scholtz. Circularly polarized patch antenna with high Tx / Rx-separation. IEEE International Conference on RFID, Orlando, April 2009 (IEEE, Piscataway, 2009), pp. 213–216
17. JY Wang, B Lv, WZ Cui, W Ma, JT Huangfu, LX Ran, in *Progress in Electromagnetics Research Symposium*. Isolation enhancement based on adaptive leakage cancellation, pp. 1059–1063. Xi'an, 22–26 March 2010
18. Inc. Impinj. Indy® R2000 Reader Chip (IPJ-R2000). REV, 1.3 2012, Impinj, Inc., Seattle
19. J Lee, j Choi, KH Lee, B Kim, M Jeong, Y Cho, H Yoo, K Yang, S Kim, SM Moon, JY Lee, S Park, W Kong, J Kim, TJ Lee, BE Kim, BK Ko. A UHF mobile RFID reader IC with self-leakage canceller. IEEE Radio Frequency Integrated Circuits RFIC Symposium, Honolulu, June 2007 (IEEE, Piscataway, 2007), pp. 273–276
20. P Beasley, A Stove, B Reits, B As. Solving the problems of a single antenna frequency modulated CW radar. Record of the IEEE 1990 International Radar Conference, Arlington, May 1990 (IEEE, Piscataway, 1990), pp. 391–395
21. K Lin, YE Wang, CK Pao, YC Shih, A Ka-Band FMCW radar front-end with adaptive leakage cancellation. IEEE Trans. Microw. Theory Tech. **54**(12), 4041–4048 (2006)
22. R Langwieser, G Lasser. Measurement and simulation of crosstalk and crosstalk compensation in UHF RFID. Fourth International EURASIP Workshop on RFID Technology, Torino, September 2012 (IEEE, Piscataway, 2012)
23. G Lasser, R Langwieser, R Dallinger, CF Mecklenbräuker. Broadband leaking carrier cancellation for RFID systems. IEEE MTT-S International Microwave Symposium, Montreal, June 2012 (IEEE, Piscataway, 2012)
24. S Haykin, *Adaptive Filter Theory*, 1st edn. (Prentice-Hall, Upper Saddle River, 1986)
25. G Lasser, W Gartner, R Langwieser, CF Mecklenbräuker, in *Fourth International EURASIP Workshop on RFID Technology*. Fast algorithm for leaking carrier canceller adjustment. Torino, 27-28 September 2012
26. IA Glover, PM Grant, *Digital Communications*, 2nd edn. (Pearson, Edinburgh, 2004)
27. R Langwieser, G Lasser, C Angerer, M Rupp, AL Scholtz, in *The 2nd International EURASIP Workshop on RFID Technology*. A modular UHF reader frontend for a flexible RFID testbed. Budapest, 7–8 July 2008

# 10

# Using field strength scaling to save energy in mobile HF-band RFID-systems

Manuel Menghin[1*], Norbert Druml[1], Christian Steger[1], Reinhold Weiss[1], Holger Bock[2] and Josef Haid[2]

**Abstract**

Radio frequency identification (RFID) is a technology enabling a contactless exchange of data. This technology features the possibility to wirelessly transfer power to the transponder (opponent). HF-RFID is used in mobile devices like smart phones and shows potential for applications like payment, identification, etc. Unfortunately, the needed functionality increases the battery drain of the device. As a countermeasure, power-management techniques are implemented. However, these techniques commonly do not consider the whole system, which also consists of the communication to the transponder, to prevent wasting energy. One cross-system technique of reducing the wasted energy is magnetic field strength scaling, which regulates the power transfer to the transponder. This article shows three investigations made, regarding field strength scaling to prevent this wastage of energy. The results of one investigation, how to use field strength scaling at card detection phase in form of the PTF-Determinator method, is described in detail. This method determines the Power Transfer Function (PTF) during run-time and scales the provided power accordingly to save energy. As a case study the PTF-Determinator is integrated in an application to read digital business cards. The resulting power consumption and timing has been evaluated by simulation and measurement of a development platform for mobile phones. Furthermore, the impact of field strength scaling to the energy consumption of a state of the art NFC-enhanced smart phone has been analyzed. The results of the case study shows that up to 26% less transmission energy (energy drain of NFC) is needed, if field strength scaling is applied (proofen by measurement). According to this result a smart phone's battery drain (energy drain of the whole system) can be decreased by up to 13% by using field strength scaling for this case study.

**Keywords:** RFID, NFC, Power consumption, Magnetic field strength scaling, Power transfer, Power-management

## 1 Introduction

HF-band radio frequency identification (RFID) is a wireless form of communication. One feature of this wireless communication form is the possibility to transfer power from the reader (sender) to the transponder (receiver). There are many standards using this communication form. One of them is near field communication (NFC). An exemplary application of NFC is using it in mobile devices like smart phones, which opens a wide set of applications like payment, identification, and ticketing. Unfortunately, NFC increases the battery drain, because of the additional power-consumption needed by the reader during communication. Minimizing this consumption is the goal of the power-management algorithms implemented in software

and hardware. These algorithms commonly focus on one component and do not consider the whole system.

The considered target system consists of multiple components as shown in Figure 1. The mobile RFID-Reader includes a battery, which can only provide a limited amount of energy. The reader also has to power the Reader-IC needed for the RFID communication. The transponder has no own power source and is powered over RF. This wireless power transfer includes losses (more power has to be provided by the reader to satisfy the power requirements of the transponder). This discussed RFID communication (HF-Band) is based on inductive coupling where an alternating magnetic field is used to transfer the data and the power to the transponder.

The reader is able to control this transferred power by scaling the strength of the magnetic field. In most cases, the provided power by the reader is set to a maximum value to ensure the transponder's proper supply at an

*Correspondence: manuel.menghin@tugraz.at
[1] Graz University of Technology, Graz, Austria
Full list of author information is available at the end of the article

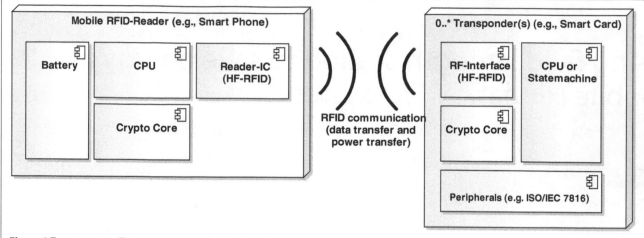

**Figure 1 Target system.** This component model describes the target system considered in this article. Basically, it consists of the battery-powered HF-RFID reader and zero to multiple transponder(s). The case study of this article considers the case of one reader connected to one transponder.

expected transmission distance (about 5–10 cm) regardless of the transponder-type. This provided power output is in most cases (e.g., closer distance) too high and leads to an oversupply of the transponder. To give an example, the power consumption of a state-of-the-art smart phone with NFC has been measured, which is shown in Section 5.4 in detail. The result shows that the smart phone needs 50% more power when NFC is activated but no transponder is in range compared to the consumption without NFC. However, if a transponder is read over NFC, then the device consumes up to 107% more power. This shows that reducing the power consumption of NFC plays a relevant role in decreasing the battery drain of the RFID-Reader (e.g., smart phone). One way to achieve that is the dynamic configuration of the magnetic field strength by the reader during run-time. To perform this dynamic configuration, the reader has to know, which field strength is currently needed to supply the transponder properly. The investigations made to realize this dynamic configuration can be divided into three parts:

- The first investigation regards dynamic field strength scaling during card detection phase. The challenge lies in gathering the needed parameters (e.g., distance between reader and transponder) to evaluate the power transfer function (PTF) after a transponder has been detected. Based on the PTF knowledge, the reader is able to properly scale the magnetic field strength. Additional methods to prevent a wastage of energy can be implemented based on the knowledge of the PTF, which will be discussed later on [1].
- During the phase of RFID communication, the distance between reader and transponder can change (user typically moves the transponder in the direction to the reader), which results in a changing PTF. Furthermore, different operations, like reading data

from the transponder or performing an encryption, lead to a change of the transponder's power requirements. The adaption of the magnetic field strength during communication is important, to preserve a proper supply for the transponder at all time [2].
- The RFID technology is able to read multiple transponders in range. Multiple transponders in the magnetic field influence the PTF, which also depends on the states of these transponders (e.g., selected and active or deselected). These dependencies occur because different transponder states provoke different power consumption requirements. With this knowledge, the PTF can be redetermined and the consumed energy can be reduced by a proper field strength scaling algorithm.

The contribution of this article consists of three parts:

- Three investigations of magnetic field strength scaling in HF-Band RFID-Systems to create a power-aware system are presented.
- The investigation how to use field strength scaling during card detection phase in form of the novel PTF-Determinator method is described in detail in [1] (see Figure 2).
- A case study using the PTF-Determinator in an application of reading digital business cards (including a feature to restrict the maximum transmission distance) is shown [1].

The remainder of this article is split into five main parts. The first part can be found in Section 2, which shows the related work and highlights the contribution. The second part shows the three investigations to realize magnetic field strength scaling. As third part, which can be found in Section 4, the PTF-Determinator and its integration into

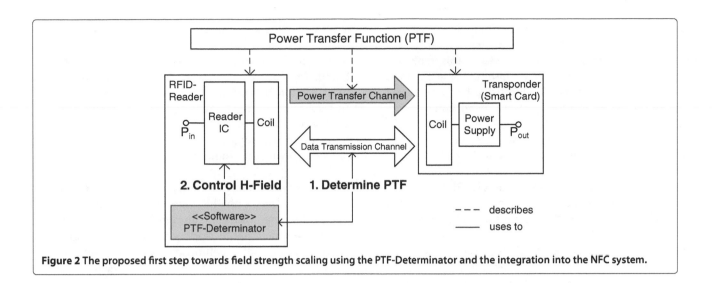

**Figure 2** The proposed first step towards field strength scaling using the PTF-Determinator and the integration into the NFC system.

the RFID-System is shown in detail. The case study is presented in the fourth part in Section 5. The fifth part in Section 6 finally concludes this article.

## 2 Related work

This section is split into four parts. The first part deals with the state-of-the-art possibilities to acquire the physical relation factor (simplified the distance between reader and transponder). The second part shows investigations regarding the influence of the transponder's operation to it's power requirements. In addition, the related work regarding multiple transponders is shown in part three. In the fourth part, known system-based power-management concepts including reader and transponder are shown.

### 2.1 Acquisition of the physical relation factor

One consideration regards acquiring the physical relation, like the distance between the reader and the transponder coil, and other dynamic parameters, during run-time. An approach is to find a known parameter that describes this physical relation. Cheng et al. [3] show that there is a relation between the provided power of the reader and the distance to the transponder. The analysis has been concluded by altering the signal strength of the reader and checking if the transponder has enough power to be active. Another approach is distance bounding, which uses the delay between the request and the response as known parameter to calculate the physical distance between reader and transponder to detect relaying attacks [4]. To use this information to determine the PTF, the parameter has to be measured during run-time. Furthermore, transmission characteristics (e.g., coil dimensions) have to be included into the determination. These characteristics depend on the system's setup (e.g., different types of transponders). Xu et al. [5] use power stepping to detect different positioned transponders (distance to the

reader). This consideration does not include the physical principles of the power transfer but leads to a evaluation of a parameter, which is similar to a distance value, during run-time. Another method measures the voltage on transponder side and to use it for the PTF determination [6].

### 2.2 Power requirements of the passive transponder

Another fact to consider is that the transponder is only passively powered by the reader [7]. This means that the transponder cannot respond, if the provided power drops under a certain threshold. Furthermore, the power consumption of the transponder itself depends on the currently executed operation, which influences the level of needed power [8]. Power-consuming operations are especially encryptions/decryptions [9]. Mercier et al. [10] show the relation between the provided power and the consumption of the circuit. To consider this in the determination of the PTF, the transponder has to be in a state that is aware of its power consumption. The last point of consideration is the transmission of the data (response), which is realized through load modulation on transponder side. The influence on the modulation is similar to the power consumption of the transponder [11]. One possibility to acquire the power consumption of the transponder during run-time is using the principle of using power estimation units directly on the transponder. This information can be transferred to the reader afterwards [12].

### 2.3 Influence of multiple transponders on the PTF

Multiple transponders in RF field influence the power consumption of the RFID-System, and a PTF used for one transponder is not enough to describe this environment. Collisions for example influence the power consumption of the total system. The reader sends a request and gets the response from the transponders. These messages can collide and have to be detected. There is a protocol included in the detection algorithm to deal with this challenge. Most of the publications made in this topic are dealing with the question, how to optimize or avoid these collisions. Kamineni et al. [13] are using the power level information on transponder side to avoid collisions by defined delays according this power level. Other published approaches deal with the avoidance of collisions to increase the performance of the system [14,15].

### 2.4  System-based power-management for RFID

Liu and Tong [16] describe energy provisioning services. They show that knowing the system can lead to optimization possibilities. Their concept focuses on a multi-tag multi-reader application but it can be adapted to the challenge of field strength scaling. This knowledge can be used to optimize the system in terms of power consumption and stability. This should especially be considered in combination with mobile readers [17]. The challenge is to manage the distributed information and the calculation among the system for power-optimization. The Cinder operating system is an example how such optimizations can be done. This approach is designed for smart phones but the model can be extended to include externally powered devices as well [18].

## 3  Investigations made for field strength scaling

This section describes the three investigations made to use magnetic field strength scaling in RFID-Systems as mentioned in Section 1. These investigations are separated according to the overview of the RFID communication flow and the dependencies to the PTF as shown in Figure 3. The reader should know the PTF at each point in time to react on changes. The first investigation regards the determination of the PTF during card detection phase. The second investigation deals with the dependencies to the currently executed operation invoked by the reader and sent to the transponder (e.g., read block), and the changing physical relation factor (distance) of the transponder. The third investigation regards the influence of the multiple transponders in range to the PTF.

### 3.1  Field strength scaling during card detection phase

If a transponder gets in range, the reader is able to establish the communication by sending the request (e.g., REQA) and an anti-collision command (needed for multi-transponder communications). The transponder answers to this anti-collision command with its unique identification number (UID). This procedure is followed by a selection command, which elevates the transponder to the ready state. During this card detection phase, data are already exchanged between the reader and the transponder. If this phase is modified to determine the PTF, the reader would be able to scale the magnetic field

strength accordingly before the communication process begins (e.g., reading a digital business card). The challenge of this approach is getting the information needed for the determination during this phase (a detailed description is given in Section 4) [1]. One issue, which is not covered by this approach, is the changing physical relation factor during communication. An initial magnetic field scale can lead to an oversupply or to an undersupply of the transponder during the communication process.

### 3.2  Dynamic field strength scaling during communication

This approach deals with the issue of dynamically scaling the field strength during communication. A scenario can scaling the field while reading the data of a digital business card. Thus, this method avoids an oversupply or undersupply by inappropriate scaling. The challenge of this approach can be split into two parts. The first part is detecting changes of the physical relation factor (distance) during communication. These changes occur by pulling the transponder from or pushing it towards the reader, which can be a scenario (e.g., access card is held by the user against the reader). Redetermining the PTF using the same method as in the card detection would result in a considerable communication overhead. This redetermination has to be made fast enough to react on the change of the physical relation factor. Thus, another way has to be found to detect the changes like finding an easy to acquire equivalent parameter to the physical relation factor on reader side. The second part concerns the fact that different transponder commands demand different transponder power requirements, e.g., reading a memory-block versus performing cryptographic operations. This also has to lead to a redetermination of the PTF and to a proper scaling [2].

### 3.3  Field strength scaling for multiple transponders

The two described ways of accomplishment do not consider multiple transponders in range. The usage of multiple transponders with one reader is not restricted to logistic applications, like reading tagged packets. An example of other applications is a briefcase, with multiple access cards. These transponders influence the PTF in two ways. First, each transponder has a different physical relation factor (distance to the reader). The transponders cannot be on the same position. The PTF depends on the currently selected transponder. Second, the instantaneous power consumption of a transponder influences the PTF of all other transponders. Therefore, the reader has to be aware of the presence of all transponders and their states to properly scale the magnetic field to avoid an oversupply or undersupply. Furthermore, a policy has to be defined how to interact with the transponders. The transponders, which are not selected, can either get a proper supply to remain in their states, or the policy allows the undersupply

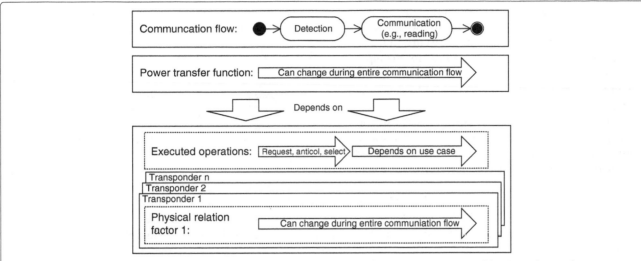

**Figure 3 Overview of the dependencies of the PTF during communication.** This figure gives an overview of the dependencies during communication regarding the PTF. The upper part visualizes the communication flow. The lower two parts are the dependencies of the PTF during the communication.

of those deselected transponders to save energy with the disadvantage of a loss of connection to them.

## 4 Method - Field strength scaling during card detection in detail

In this Section, the investigation of field strength scaling during card detection phase and the used method called PTF-Determinator is shown. The challenge to determine the PTF in the card detection phase is to collect the needed information during this phase and to pass this information to the reader side. With the determined PTF, the field strength can dynamically be scaled. To realize the above described steps, the RFID-System has to be defined and examined. For examination, the target system is reduced to one reader and one transponder. The RFID communication channel between them is split into two main parts. The first part is the power transmission path. It describes how the provided power, which can be altered by the reader, is transferred to the transponder. The second part is the communication channel used to exchange data between reader and transponder. The solution how to integrate the PTF-Determinator method into an existing RFID-System is shown in Figure 2.

At first, the needed electrical characteristics for the realization of the method are shown. The realization itself is split into four considerations. The first one deals with gathering the needed parameters from the reader and transponder. The second relates to the evaluation of the physical relation factor, which cannot be acquired directly. The third consideration deals with the integration of the method into the RFID-System's existing communication flow. The fourth consideration describes a library providing an interface to access the determined PTF. This library can be used for power-management methods.

### 4.1 Electrical characteristics

This section explains the used replacement circuit and equations for the method to calculate the PTF. The equations describe how the power is transferred from the Reader-IC to the supply of the transponder. The replacement circuit describes the connection between them, as shown in Figure 4. The calculation is split into four parts.

The first part describes the power control of the Reader-IC, which can be configured by a resistance ($R_{rel}$) serial to a constant voltage-source ($U_1$) as shown in Equation (1).

$$i_r = \frac{U_1}{Z_c + R_{rel}} \tag{1}$$

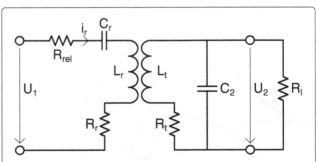

**Figure 4 Replacement circuit of the power transfer over RFID.** This replacement circuit describes the power transfer from the reader to the transponder without the voltage regulation on transponder-side, adapted from [19]. In this case, the input current $i_r$ is scaled by the resistance $R_{rel}$. $U_2$ represents the supply voltage of the transponder.

Increasing the resistance causes a reduction of the overall power (decrease of $i_r$) consumption with the disadvantage of loosing transmission range [20]. The current $i_r$ also depends on the configurable resistance $R_{\text{rel}}$ and the input resistance $Z_c$ of the circuit beyond. $Z_c$ alters according to the inductive coupling between reader and transponder and is therefore not static.

The second part consists of the equation used to calculate the provided magnetic field H of the reader, which is provoked by the electrical current $i_r$. The considered orientation of the sender and receiver coil is shown in Figure 5.

Equation (2) can be used for rectangular-shaped sender coils and is based on the law of Biot-Savart. It is based on the physical principle of loose inductive coupling. The needed parameters are the dimensions $a_r$ and $b_r$ of the reader coil and the number of windings $N_r$. The distance to the coil can only be used if the coils are coaxial oriented [19].

$$H = \frac{i_r \cdot N_r \cdot a_r \cdot b_r}{4 \cdot \pi \cdot \sqrt{(\frac{a_r}{2})^2 + (\frac{b_r}{2})^2 + d^2}}$$

$$\cdot \left( \frac{1}{(\frac{a_r}{2})^2 + d^2} + \frac{1}{(\frac{b_r}{2})^2 + d^2} \right) \tag{2}$$

The third part deals with the transformation of the magnetic field strength back to a voltage on transponder side (see Figure 4). A resonance circuit, consisting of a parallel capacitance and the coil's inductance, is used to amplify the received voltage. First of all the coupling coefficient $k$ is calculated with Equations (3) and (4). The coefficient represents an abstract relation between reader and transponder and requires the magnetic field strength as input. Equation (5) calculates the resulting voltage on transponder-side. This is only valid for rectangular receiver coils. The needed input parameters are the

dimensions $a_t$ and $b_t$, the number of windings $N_t$, and the coil's inductance $L_t$ [19].

$$M_{12} = \frac{\mu_0 \cdot H \cdot N_t \cdot a_t \cdot b_t}{i_r} \tag{3}$$

$$k = \frac{M_{12}}{\sqrt{L_r \cdot L_t}} \tag{4}$$

$$u_2 = \frac{w \cdot k \cdot \sqrt{L_r \cdot L_t} \cdot i_r}{\sqrt{(\frac{(w \cdot L_t)}{R_l} + w \cdot R_t \cdot C_2)^2 + (1 - w^2 \cdot L_t \cdot C_2 + \frac{R_t}{R_l})^2}} \tag{5}$$

The fourth part describes that the output voltage is limited by a Zener-diode to prevent the smart card's electronics from power surges. It is also necessary to provide a minimum voltage. If the supply drops below the minimum threshold voltage, the circuit is set to power down. Figure 6 shows an example of the relation between reader/transponder distance, and the supply voltage of the transponder (the power consumption of the transponder is considered static) for several reader power output levels.

## 4.2  Gathering needed parameters

As first consideration, the needed parameters have to be collected from the RFID-System. They are distributed between reader and transponder. Some of them are physical values, which have to be stored in digitalized form. Because of the system's variability during run-time (e.g., different transponders), the storage of all parameters in a single location is inappropriate. Table 1 depicts the number of parameters, their location, and their required space.

These parameters shall be provided on the described location shown in Figure 7. One approach is to store this data into a memory during the device's production phase

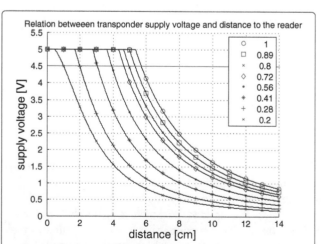

**Figure 6 Relation to the supply voltage of the transponder.** Plot of the relation between the supply voltage of the transponder to the distance between the reader and the transponder. The relation is shown using different input power levels as described in the legend. The two coils are oriented coaxial.

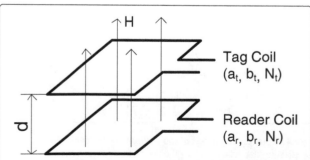

**Figure 5 Considered coaxial orientation of coils.** This figure visualizes the considered coaxial orientation of the reader to the transponder by using rectangular shaped sender and receiver coils.

**Table 1 Number of parameters needed for the PTF-Determinator including their location and needed space in bytes**

| Location | Number of parameters | Accuracy [b] | Space [B] |
|---|---|---|---|
| Mobile RFID-Reader | 5 | 32 | 20 |
| | | 8 | 5 |
| Transponder | 8 | 32 | 32 |
| | | 8 | 8 |

The space is shown with different accuracies of the parameters.

**Table 2 Comparison of the saved energy for the RFID-transmission in percent between the method with and without an improved version of the PTF-Determinator from [1] in the simulation**

| Simulated distance (cm) | Energy with PTF (Norm.) | Energy no PTF (Norm.) | Energy saved (%) |
|---|---|---|---|
| 0–1 | 0.202 | 1.000 | 79.78 |
| 1–2 | 0.263 | 1.000 | 73.75 |
| 2–3 | 0.391 | 1.000 | 60.92 |
| 3–4 | 0.674 | 1.000 | 32.59 |
| 4–5 $x > x_{max}$ | 0,072 | 1.000 | 92.78 |
| 5–6 $x > x_{-max}$ | 0,067 | 1.000 | 93.33 |

(reader and transponder). The needed storage space is 32 byte on transponder-side if an accuracy of 32 bit is used. In practice, the needed storage can be decreased by adapting the resolution of the values according to the needed PTF accuracy requirements. An example is shown in Table 2 where the needed space is reduced to 8 bytes. These values have to be transferred to a central computation unit. This can either be the reader or the transponder. In this study, the reader has been chosen because of its advanced computational resources and a direct control of the needed input parameters for the PTF (parameter of provided power). This also means that the parameter-values from the transponder have to be transferred to the reader which can costly be in terms of time and power. For comparison, sending a ping request to the transponder requires 7-bit and results in a 2-byte response [19]. The request could be the same size but the response would be 16 times greater. If the bit length of the send values is reduced to 8 bits, which should be enough in practice, the bytes to sent can be four times greater.

### 4.3 Evaluation of the physical relation factor

The second consideration regards the physical relation factor, which is independent from the type of reader and transponder used. Furthermore, its value is unknown and has to be evaluated during run-time. It cannot directly be measured because of the lack of sensing mechanisms on both sides.

To solve this problem, the PTF described in Section 4.1 is used. The equations of the PTF described in Section 4.1 have to be transformed to determine the physical relation using the provided power by the reader and the corresponding supply voltage of the transponder as input parameters. The supply voltage is also unknown because of the lack of an integrated sensor at transponder side. To approximate this value the current power state of the transponder can be used. This means if the transponder is not responding, the supply voltage is too low for operation ($< U_t$). Otherwise, the transponder responds that the operation voltage is above the needed one ($> U_t$) as shown in Figure 6 ($U_t$ is marked as red line). If the reader's provided power is altered until the transition from power down to idle state is reached, the value of the supply voltage from the transponder is slightly above $U_t$ (see Figure 8).

The execution time needed for the approximation depends on the selected resolution of the power steps on reader-side. To use this method in practice, a balance between the power step resolution and the execution time needed for the algorithm has to be found. In case of ten steps this would also mean that four iterations have to be made with a successive approximation approach ($2^n$). This

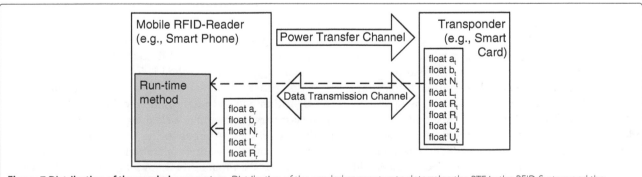

**Figure 7 Distribution of the needed parameters.** Distribution of the needed parameters to determine the PTF in the RFID-System and the possible paths to transfer them to a central location.

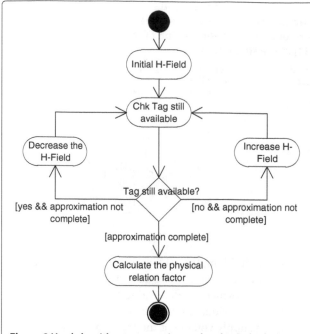

**Figure 8** Used algorithm to approximate the physical relation factor between the reader and transponder needed for the determination of the PTF based on the ability to scale the magnetic field strength on reader side.

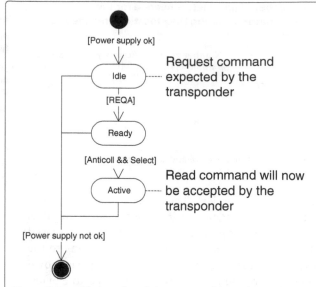

**Figure 9** Simplified version of the state machine, adapted from [21], used to establish a connection between the reader and the transponder invoked by the reader (reader talks first).

leads to a longer time needed for the whole execution and an increase of needed energy compared to a simple card detection phase. To keep this overhead as small as possible the operation to proof if the transponder is responding (state "Chk Tag still available" as shown in Figure 8) should only invoke a small response and computation-effort for the transponder, which would otherwise lower the benefit of field strength scaling to save energy. In this approach, the request command (REQA) to the transponder can be used.

### 4.4 PTF-Determinator flow integration

The third consideration deals with the inclusion of the PTF-Determinator into the existing communication flow of reader and transponder. The transponder supports different states, which influence the accepted commands from the transponder (see Figure 9).

When the transponder receives enough power it switches to idle state. In this state, a request from the reader is expected. After the request is issued it is possible to select the card by sending an anti-collision command followed by a select command with the appropriate UID. After this procedure, the transponder enables extended commands like reading values from the memory. This read command is needed by the PTF-Determinator. If the power supply drops below a certain threshold (e.g., by exceeding the maximum transmission distance between reader and transponder) the state is set back to

power down. To return to the active state the navigation through the state-machine of the transponder by sending a request (e.g., REQA) and select command has to be redone.

The integration of the PTF-Determinator method into the existing flow is split into three parts. The first part is executing the approximation algorithm as shown in Figure 8, but without calculating the physical relation factor. This approximation does not need any parameter information of the transponder, only a specified command to call. This can be REQA, which leads to a response which can be used to find out if the transponder is available or not. The second part is gathering the needed parameters from the transponder as shown in Figure 7, which needs to select the card to enable the command for reading. The third part is responsible for calculating the physical relation factor based on the gathered information from the other two parts. All needed information is now available to determine the PTF.

As last step of integration, it has to be defined, in which communication phase the PTF-Determinator is executed. As a first approach the method is included into the card detection phase. If a new transponder has been detected, the algorithm begins to determine the PTF, as described in the last paragraph, and is locked for operation until the method is finished. After that, the transponder is set to ready state and the wanted operations can be executed. Thanks to this approach, the knowledge of the PTF can be used after the card detection phase. Unfortunately, the time needed for this card detection phase increases.

Furthermore, changes to the PTF after this phase cannot be detected.

### 4.5 PTF library integration

The last consideration is to provide the determined PTF in form of a library, which can be used for power-management methods. This library is integrated on reader-side. It provides an application interface, which can be used to build a control loop to regulate the provided power of the reader according to the calculation result of the PTF. Furthermore, additional functions are provided by the interface to increase the optimization-possibilities (e.g., getting the current value of the physical relation factor to prevent long and power consuming transmission ranges). This design also makes it possible to integrate this as a hardware component to decrease the calculation time and to be more power efficient.

### 5 Case study

This section describes how the contributed method is implemented and tested. The overview is split into four parts. The first part describes the case study. In the second part, the simulation of the case study and the results are shown. In the third part, the implementation is deployed on real hardware and the measurement results are depicted. The fourth part consists of a measurement of a state-of-the-art mobile NFC-device (smart phone) and the comparison to the results of part two and three to evaluate the benefit to a mobile system.

### 5.1 Description of the case study

In this case study, the PTF-Determinator is implemented in an RFID-System. Furthermore, a feature to restrict the maximum transmission distance $x_{\max}$ between reader and transponder is implemented. When the limit is reached, the system automatically cuts off the power transfer to the transponder to save energy. As a use case the process of reading digital business cards is used. The flow diagram of the use case is shown in Figure 10.

### 5.2 Simulation results

In the first phase, the PTF-Determinator is designed, implemented, and tested using a simulation model for an NFC-System consisting of reader and transponder. The program is an Android application running on an emulator and includes the functionality described in Section 5.1. The SystemC simulation model is based on the target NFC-System but the possible values for $R_{\mathrm{rel}}$ have been modified to show the potential of the method to approximate the physical relation factor over the whole transmission range. The original target hardware has limited possibilities to alter the value $R_{\mathrm{rel}}$. The used simulation model features the possibility to provide the current

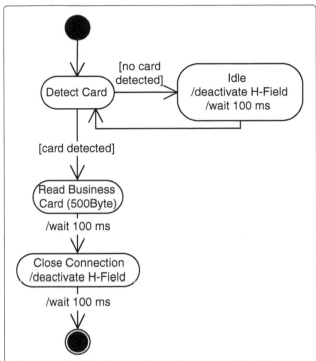

**Figure 10** This flow diagram shows the use case of reading a digital business card using NFC. This use case is needed for the case study.

power consumption of its components and the whole system. The model is implemented on transaction layer and is therefore not cycle accurate. The power values are based on the measurement results of the target NFC-Reader and transponder.

The simulation procedure is configured to step through different distances between reader and transponder. The simulator assumes that the two coils are oriented coaxial. The procedure is designed to wait until the execution of the PTF-Determinator with the described use case is finished before the next simulation with another distance is invoked. To deliver realistic results, the use case for reading digital business cards is used.

Figure 11 shows the comparison of the physical and the approximated relation factor of the method between the reader and the transponder. The steps of the approximation depend on the resolution of the $R_{\mathrm{rel}}$ (see Section 4.1). With the modified hardware (more possible values for $R_{\mathrm{rel}}$), the physical relation factor can be approximated over the whole transmission range.

In Figure 12, the power consumption is shown when detecting a transponder with and without the PTF-Determinator. The case of $x > x_{\max}$ is shown in Figure 13. The power increase of the central processing unit is simulated using a simple power state machine on reader side. The result shows that the effectiveness of the PTF-evaluation depends on the time relation between

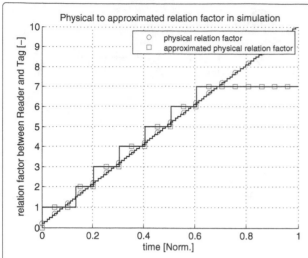

**Figure 11 Result of simulation physical relation factor.** This plot is generated by simulation, which shows the comparison of the physical relation factor and the approximated distance of the PTF-Determinator between reader and transponder.

the execution of PTF-Determinator and the use case. Figure 13 shows the result of the simulation in case of the physical relation factor $x > x_{max}$. If this case occurs, the PTF-Determinator invokes a forced cut-off in the power transfer on reader side to the transponder. With this method an energy wastage is prohibited. A comparison of the saved energy in relation to the simulated distance $d$ between reader and transponder is shown in Table 2.

The saved transmission energy (energy needed by the Reader-IC for the power transfer to the transponder) is as high as 80% in close distance. Thus, this approach offers a lot of potential in saving energy. This result depends on the use case and can only be achieved by adapting the hardware and no further influence is given by the environment. The benefit of saving energy decreases if the physical relation increases because the transmission power has to be increased to provide enough power for the transponder. If the physical relation factor $x$ is higher than $x_{max}$, then the power supply is cut off as described.

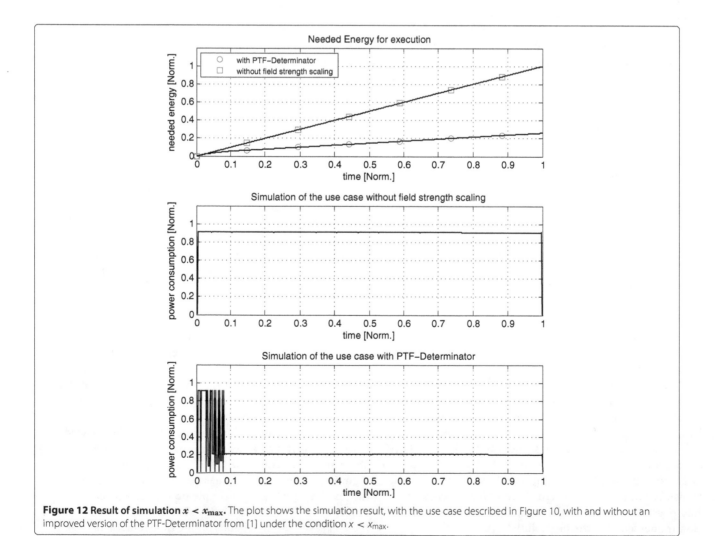

**Figure 12 Result of simulation $x < x_{max}$.** The plot shows the simulation result, with the use case described in Figure 10, with and without an improved version of the PTF-Determinator from [1] under the condition $x < x_{max}$.

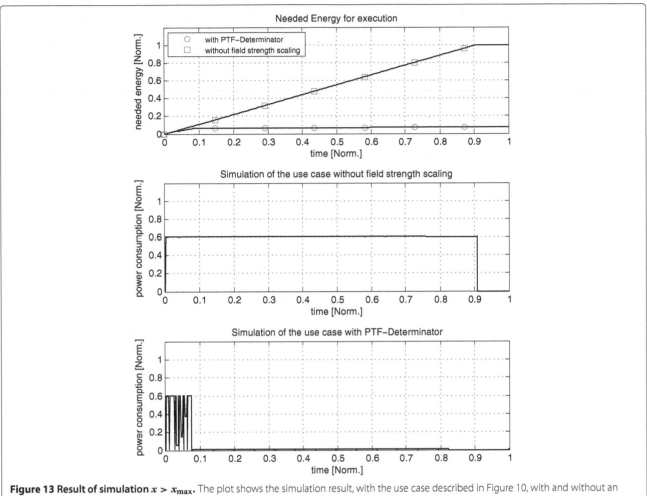

**Figure 13 Result of simulation $x > x_{\mathrm{max}}$.** The plot shows the simulation result, with the use case described in Figure 10, with and without an improved version of the PTF-Determinator from [1] under the condition $x > x_{\mathrm{max}}$.

This leads to a power saving of 93% with the disadvantage of loosing connectivity to the transponder. To reestablish a communication, the transponder's current physical relation factor has to be below the maximum allowed physical relation factor.

### 5.3 Measurement results

In the second phase, the PTF-Determinator is implemented and tested on real hardware. Power consumption measurements are conducted for verification purposes. The program is the same used during the simulation and includes the functionality described in Section 5.1. The used set-up is shown in Figure 14 and described in Table 3. To verify the method and compare the resulting power consumption of the simulation and a real environment behavior, the method is deployed and tested on a target NFC-System. To get the needed measurement data, the hardware is placed into a hardware-in-the-loop measurement suite. The suite is configured to acquire the power consumption of the whole system while the program under test is executed. For comparison, the use case of reading a digital business card without the PTF-Determinator is also measured. The physical relation between reader and transponder is altered to validate the functionality of the program and to evaluate its influence on its power consumption.

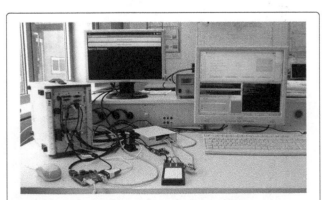

**Figure 14 Setup used for the measurement of the use case.** It consists of the development board, the RFID-Reader, the measurement device from National Instruments and an evaluation software in Matlab.

**Table 3 The setup used for the power measurement needed for the case study**

| | |
|---|---|
| Program language | Java |
| Development board | Beagleboard |
| Operating system | Android 2.3.4 |
| NFC-Reader | USB-Reader connected to the development board |
| Measurement device | Hardware-in-the-loop Measurement-suite |

Figure 15 shows the power consumption of the NFC-System with and without the PTF-Determinator. In Figure 16, the power consumption of the NFC-System is shown when physical relation factor $x > x_{max}$. This leads to cutting off the power supply of the transponder. This cut-off prevents the energy waste invoked by the power loss in the reader circuit and the loosely coupled power transfer to the transponder. The measurement results also show that the influence of the physical relation factor on the consumed energy, invoked by the influence of the reader and transponder coil, has to be considered. The execution of the PTF-Determinator results in a small overhead as shown in Figures 15 and 16.

In Table 4, a comparison between the simple card detection and the usage of the PTF-Determinator is made. It includes the needed energy of the whole procedure. The needed energy is compared and the saved energy can be evaluated when using the PTF-Determinator instead of the simple card detection. The approximation of the physical relationship is limited on the real hardware, because only few steps to scale the magnetic field are supported. However, it can be shown that the needed energy for the power transmission is 26% lower when considering the execution of the PTF-Determinator in case of $x <= x_{max}$. The needed energy in case of $x > x_{max}$ for the power transmission is about 75% lower compared to the use case without PTF-Determinator.

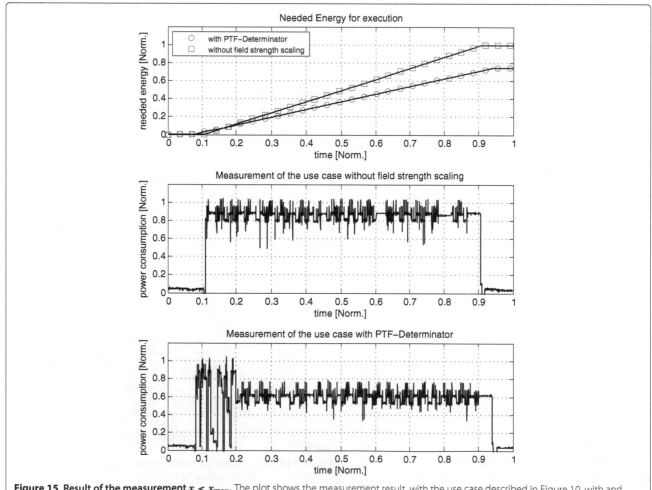

**Figure 15 Result of the measurement $x < x_{max}$.** The plot shows the measurement result, with the use case described in Figure 10, with and without an improved version of the PTF-Determinator from [1] under the condition $x < x_{max}$.

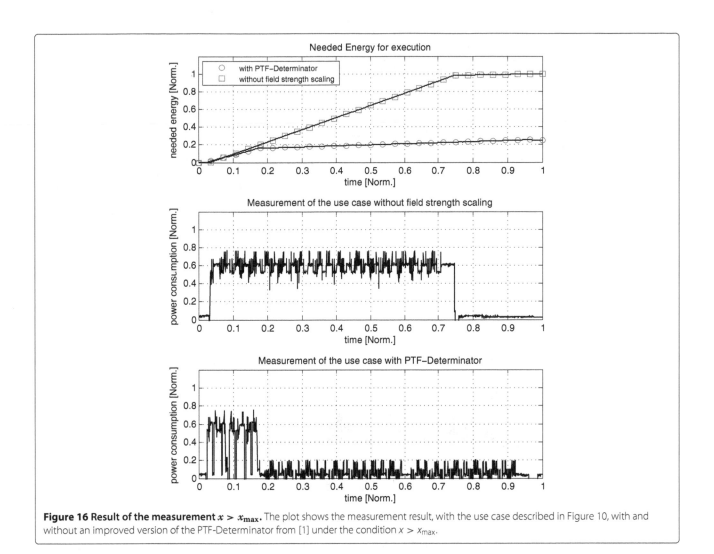

**Figure 16** Result of the measurement $x > x_{max}$. The plot shows the measurement result, with the use case described in Figure 10, with and without an improved version of the PTF-Determinator from [1] under the condition $x > x_{max}$.

## 5.4 Comparison to an NFC-enhanced smart phone

In this section, a power measurement of a state-of-the-art smart phone is done. The idea is to get results, how field strength scaling is influencing the power consumption of such a device. The power consumption is measured directly at the battery source and therefore includes all components (e.g., display and processor). The measurement setup is listed in Table 5. The results of the simulation in Section 5.2 and the measurement in Section 5.3 can then be combined with this measurement to one result to get an approximation of the possible power reduction using field strength scaling on a state-of-the-art smart phone.

To achieve the evaluation goal, the power consumptions of the different smart phone states concerning the Reader-IC (RFID) (e.g., "reading the tag" or "RFID is powering the transponder") are extracted from the power measurement. The power consumption of the smart phone during the state idle and reading the transponder (tag) is shown in Figure 17. It can be seen that there is a significant

**Table 4** Comparison of the saved energy for the RFID-Transmission in percent between the method with and without an improved version of the PTF-Determinator from [1] in the measurement

| Physical | Energy with PTF (Norm.) | Energy without PTF (Norm.) | Energy saved (%) |
|---|---|---|---|
| $x <= x_{max}$ | 0.745 | 1.000 | 25.51 |
| $x > x_{max}$ | 0.251 | 1.000 | 74.88 |

**Table 5** The measurement setup for the acquisition of the smart phone's power consumption including the devices used for the measurement

| | |
|---|---|
| Smart phone | Samsung Nexus S |
| Operating system | Android 2.3.4 |
| Application | NFC TagInfo from |
| | NFC Research Hagenberg |
| Measurement device | PXI NI 6221 using DAQ SignalExpress |
| Transponder | Infineon Tag Type 2 (2kB) |

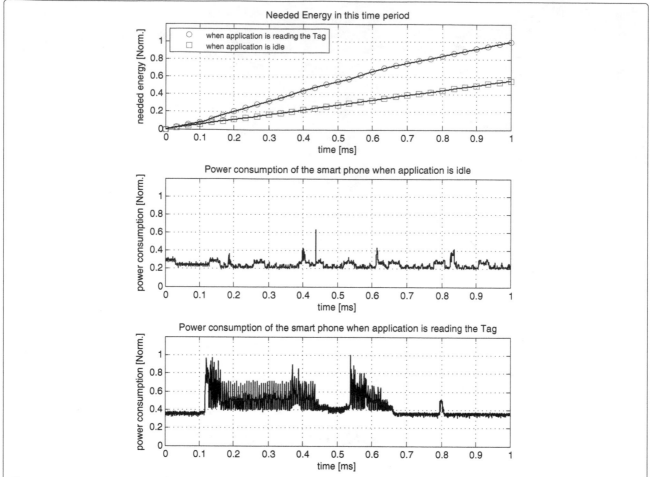

**Figure 17 Power consumption of the state-of-the-art smart phone with NFC.** This figure shows the power consumption during the execution of the application described in the measurement setup (see Table 3). The figure is divided into three plots, showing the energy consumption as well as the power consumptions in idle state and during the smart phone's reading process of the transponder.

smart phone power consumption rise during the process of reading the transponder. Table 6 shows this different power consumptions of the smart phone.

The extraction shows that during the reading process of the transponder the power consumption increases up to 107% compared to the idle state power consumption. Furthermore, the state while the transponder is powered by the Reader-IC without executing any operation consumes 50% more power. The presented numbers show

that reducing this power consumption has potential of saving energy in the whole system (smart phone).

These results of a state-of-the-art smart phone are now used to scale the results ($E_{unscaled}$) of Sections 5.2 and 5.3 to get an approximation of the expectable results ($E_{scaled}$) of field strength scaling on a state-of-the-art smart phone using Equation 6.

$$E_{scaled} = 100 - \frac{(100 - E_{unscaled}) \cdot 1,07 + 100}{207} \cdot 100 \quad (6)$$

Theses combined results (transmission power saving and the power states of the art smart phone) show that approximately 41% of the energy can be saved compared to simulation with a modified hardware and 13% can be expected in a real environment without changing the hardware. In case of $x > x_{max}$ the approximated saved energy is as high as 48% in simulation and 39% in a real environment.

**Table 6 Results of the state-of-the-art smart phone's measurement are presented in form of its power consumptions during different states**

| State | Consumed power [%] |
|---|---|
| NFC is on but no transponder in range | 100 |
| Transponder is powered over NFC | 150 |
| Transponder is powered over NFC and reading operations are performed | 207 |

## 6 Conclusion

The additional energy consumption by using RFID in mobile system is a challenging task. This article shows that magnetic field strength scaling in HF-Band RFID-Systems is a good way to reduce this energy wastage. The three investigations made are a way to deal with the challenges of the dynamic behavior during communication like the changing physical relation factor (e.g., the user is moving the transponder towards the reader). This study has also shown that the integration of the run-time method to determine the PTF on reader side is feasible. The energy saving potential of the presented PTF-Determinator, using the PTF to scale down the magnetic field strength, is shown by simulation and is verified through measurement. In simulation using a improved hardware model (more suitable steps to scale the magnetic field strength are included) up to 80% less transmission energy is needed. In the measurement, using existing hardware, the energy needed by the transmission is reduced by 26% compared to a simple card-detection method. Thus, a state-of-the-art NFC smart phone featuring our proposed method would reduce the battery drain by up to 13%. The implemented feature to set a maximum physical relation factor, by cutting off the power supply to avoid energy-consuming transactions, has been proven by measurement to reduce the transmission energy by up to 75%. This results into a reduction of 39% less battery drain of a state-of-the-art smart phone.

The combination of simulation and verification through measurement in one tool chain has proven to be a good way for developing power-aware systems. The simulation gives the opportunity of reconfiguring the hardware (design hardware and software together) to evaluate the potential of ideas like magnetic field strength scaling.

In future work, the proposed PTF-Determinator method shall be improved, focusing on optimizing the approximation of the physical relation factor. Furthermore, the other investigations made regarding the dynamic field strength scaling during communication and the usage in an environment with multiple transponders will be verified by simulation and measurement.

**Competing interests**
The authors declare that they have no competing interests.

**Acknowledgements**
We would like to thank our industrial partners Infineon Technologies Austria AG as well as Enso Detego GmbH for their support. Furthermore, we would like to thank the Austrian Federal Ministry for Transport, Innovation, and Technology, which funded the project META[:SEC:] under the FIT-IT contract FFG 829586.

**Author details**
[1]Graz University of Technology, Graz, Austria. [2]Infineon Technologies Austria AG, Graz, Austria.

**References**
1. M Menghin, N Druml, C Steger, R Weiss, J Haid, H Bock, in *Fourth International EURASIP Workshop on RFID Technology (EURASIP RFID) 2012*. The PTF-Determinator: a run-time method used to save energy in NFC-Systems (Turin, 2012), pp. 92–98
2. M Menghin, N Druml, C Steger, R Weiss, J Haid, H Bock, in *5th International Workshop on Near Field Communication (NFC 2013)*. NFC-DynFS: a way to realize dynamic field strength scaling during communication (Zurich, 2013), pp. 1–6
3. D Cheng, Z Wang, Q Zhou, in *4th International Conference on Wireless Communications, Networking and Mobile Computing (WiCOM'08)*. Analysis of distance of RFID systems working under 13.56 MHz (Dalian, 2008), pp. 1–3
4. J Clulow, GP Hancke, MG Kuhn, T Moore, in *Third European conference on Security and Privacy in Ad-Hoc and Sensor Networks (ESAS'06)*. So, near and yet so far: distance-bounding attacks in wireless networks (Springer, New York, 2006), pp. 83–97
5. X Xu, L Gu, J Wang, G Xing, in *IEEE International Conference on Pervasive Computing and Communications (PerCom 2010)*. Negotiate power and performance in the reality of RFID systems (Mannheim, 2010), pp. 88–97
6. Wireless Power Consortium. System Description Wireless Power Transfer, Vol. I, Part 1, (2011), p. 32. http://www.wirelesspowerconsortium.com/downloads/wireless-power-specification-part-1.html. Accessed 11 April 2013
7. M Wendt, M Grumer, C Steger, R Weiss, U Neffe, A Muehlberger, in *Proceedings of the 2008 ACM Symposium on Applied Computing (SAC'08)*. System level power profile analysis and optimization for smart cards and mobile devices (ACM, New York, 2008), pp. 1884–1888. doi:10.1145/1363686.1364144
8. A Genser, C Bachmann, C Steger, R Weiss, J Haid, in *IEEE Asia Pacific Conference on Circuits and Systems (APCCAS 2010)*. Estimation-based run-time power profile flattening for RF-powered smart card systems, (Kuala Lumpur, 2010), pp. 1187–1190
9. T Lohmann, M Schneider, C Ruland, in *Smart Card Research and Advanced Applications, vol. 3928 of Lecture Notes in Computer Science*, ed. by J Domingo-Ferrer, J Posegga, and D Schreckling. Analysis of power constraints for cryptographic algorithms in mid-cost RFID tags (Springer, Berlin, 2006), pp. 278–288. doi:10.1007/1173344720
10. J Mercier, C Dufaza, M Lisart, in *Proceedings of the 2007 International Symposium on Low Power Electronics and Design (ISLPED'07)*. Signoff power methodology for contactless smartcards (ACM, New York, 2007), pp. 407–410. doi:10.1145/100000
11. E Rolf, V Nilsson. Near field communication (NFC) for mobile phones (Master's Thesis, Lund University, 2006), p. 25. http://www.es.lth.se/teorel/Publications/TEAT-5000-series/TEAT-5082.pdf. Accessed 11 April 2013
12. N Druml, M Menghin, C Steger, R Weiss, A Genser, J Haid, in *15th Euromicro Conference on Digital System Design (DSD 2012)*. Adaptive field strength scaling—a power optimization technique for contactless reader/ smart card systems (Izmir, 2012), pp. 616–623
13. N Kamineni, X Li, in *International Conference on Computing Communication and Networking Technologies (ICCCNT 2010)*. Analysis of anti-collision multi-tag identification algorithms in passive RFID systems (Karur, 2010), pp. 1–8
14. DF Tseng, ZC Lin, Anti-collision algorithm with the aid of interference cancellation and tag set partitioning in radio-frequency identification systems. IET Commun. **3**, 143–150 (2009)
15. K Wu, Y Liu, in *Second International Conference on Future Networks (ICFN'10)*. A new energy-aware scheme for RFID system based on ALOHA (Sanya, Hainan, 2010), pp. 149–152
16. J Liu, W Tong, in *IEEE International Conference on Cloud Computing and Intelligence Systems (CCIS 2011)*. Dynamic share energy provisioning service for one-hop multiple RFID tags identification system, (Beijing, 2011), pp. 342–347
17. J Haid, W Kargl, T Leutgeb, D Scheiblhofer, in *Proceedings of Tele-communications and Mobile Computing Graz Series (TCMC 2005)*. Power management for RF-powered vs. battery-powered devices, (Graz, 2005)

18. A Roy, SM Rumble, R Stutsman, P Levis, D Mazières, N Zeldovich, in *Proceedings of the sixth conference on Computer systems, (EuroSys'11)*. Energy management in mobile devices with the cinder operating system (ACM, New York, 2011), pp. 139–152. doi:10.1145/1966445.1966459
19. K Finkenzeller, *RFID Handbook: Fundamentals and Applications in Contactless Smart Cards and Identification*, 2nd edn. (Wiley, New York, 2003)
20. X Xu, L Gu, J Wang, G Xing, SC Cheung, Read more with less: an adaptive approach to energy-efficient RFID systems. IEEE J. Sel. Areas Commun. **29**(8), 1684–1697 (2011)
21. W Rankl, W Effing, *Smart Card Handbook: Physical and Electrical Properties*, 3rd edn. (Wiley, New York, 2003)

# 11

# Performance analysis of optimal schedulers in single channel dense radio frequency identification environments

Javier Vales-Alonso[*], Francisco Javier Parrado-García and Juan J Alcaraz

## Abstract

Schedulers in radio frequency identification dense environments aim at distributing optimally a set of $t$ slots between a group of $m$ readers. In single-channel environments, the readers within mutual interference range must transmit at different times; otherwise, interferences prevent identification of the tags. The goal is to maximize the expected number of tags successfully identified within the $t$ slots. This problem may be formulated as a mixed integer non-linear mathematical program, which may effectively exploit available knowledge about the number of competing tags in the reading zone of each reader. In this paper, we present this optimization problem and analyze the impact of tag estimation in the performance achieved by the scheduler. The results demonstrate that optimal solutions outperform a reference scheduler based on dividing the available slots proportionally to the number of tags in each reader. In addition, depending on the scenario load, the results reveal that there exist an optimum number of readers for the topology considered, since the total average number of identifications depend non-linearly on the load. Finally, we study the effect of imperfect tag population knowledge on the performance achieved by the readers.

## 1 Introduction

Passive radio frequency identification (RFID) is increasingly being used to identify and trace objects in supply chains, in manufacturing process, and so forth. These environments are characterized by a large number of items with attached tags which flow on conveyor belts, inside pallets or boxes, and the like, entering and leaving facilities. In large realistic installations, several readers are commonly deployed; these are the so-called *dense reader environments*, comprising multiple readers within a mutual range.

In these scenarios, the rate of tags identified per reader is limited by the reader collision problems, namely:

- Reader-to-tag interferences (RTI) occur when two or more readers, irrespectively of the working frequency, transmit at the same time, overlapping their read ranges (reader-to-tag range) and powering the same tags. For instance, in Figure 1, if readers $R$ and $R'$ are

feeding tag $A$ simultaneously, tag is not able to produce a correct response to any of the readers.

- Reader-to-reader interferences (RRI) occur when two or more readers working at the same frequency are in mutual range, that is, one reader that powers a tag within its reader-to-tag range can receive stronger signals from other readers, ruining the weaker signal from the tag. For example, in Figure 1, tag $B$ cannot be read by $R$ if at the same time $R'$ tries to read the tag $C$.

Another kind of interference is tag-to-tag interference which is internal to the reader's cell and is produced among tags competing to be identified by the reader. This latter type occurs even with a single reader, whereas the former ones (external) are only present with more than one reader. Indeed, the way of addressing internal and external interferences is completely different and independent. External ones are addressed by reserving (in real-time or with a preconfigured scheduling) resources to particular readers. Then, the reader uses these resources (time, frequency, power, etc.) to execute some algorithm to solve the tag-to-tag interference problem, as the static frame slotted ALOHA (static-FSA). Later in Section 2.1, we analyze the way how static-FSA and its derivate

*Correspondence: javier.vales@upct.es
Department of Information Technologies and Communications, Technical University of Cartagena, Cartagena, Spain

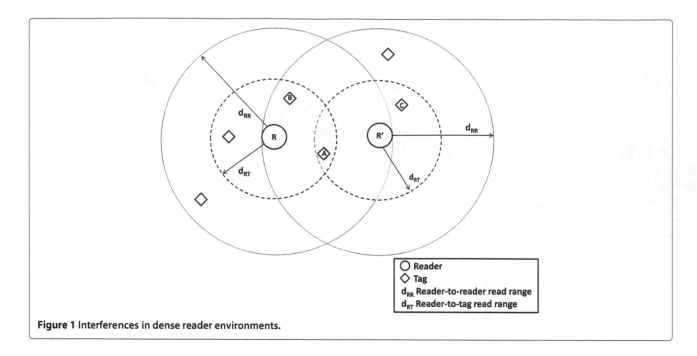

**Figure 1** Interferences in dense reader environments.

dynamic-FSA work, since their operation is relevant to decide the readers' scheduling.

External interferences are directly related to the readers' output power, which delimit the interference range. For example, in Europe, output power may reach up to 2 W and guarantees a reader-to-tag range up to 10 m, while this may cause interferences with readers up to some hundreds of meters typically, determining interference ranges:

- If two or more readers are within two times the reader-to-tag range ($d_{RT}$), either part or the whole reading area overlaps, preventing tag operation. Hence, both RTI and RRI interferences are present. In this case, reader operation should be allocated at different working times.
- If the distance among the readers is between $d_{RT}$ and the maximum distance determined by the RRI ($d_{RR}$), only RRI appears. The reader operation can be multiplexed either in frequency or in time.
- If the distance among the readers is larger than the maximum RRI distance, they do not suffer interferences.

Table 1 summarizes the restrictions applying to reader operation for dense reader environments.

**Table 1 Reader operation restrictions versus $d$**

|         | = Freq       | ≠ Freq       |
| ------- | ------------ | ------------ |
| = Time  | $d > d_{RR}$ | $d > d_{RT}$ |
| ≠ Time  | $d > 0$      | $d > 0$      |

Therefore, in dense reader environments, the problem is how to distribute the reading resources available among the readers to perform optimally. The main parameters involved in this problem are the following:

- The number of readers, $m$.
- The number of available frequency channels, $F$.
- The number of time-slots available in each frequency, $t$.
- The topology of the readers.
- The implemented identification procedure in each reader (e.g., static-FSA, dynamic-FSA, Query-Tree protocols, etc.).
- The characteristics of the traffic of tags (e.g., static tags vs. tag flow, random vs. deterministic number of tags, etc.).

Current standards (see Section 2) propose some solutions to reduce collision issues but exclusively focused on minimizing RRI. On the other hand, a number of papers (see also Section 2) deal with minimization of the RTI but without considering reader-to-reader interferences.

In a previous paper [1], a particular simplified problem with two readers $m = 2$ in reader-to-reader range (*dual reader environment*) is addressed. Besides, in our previous paper [2], the scheduling problem for single-channel environments is firstly introduced, that is, we consider the case of any arbitrary number of readers ($m$) and for any particular network topology. Attending to the restrictions given above, in this case, the readers cannot transmit simultaneously if the reader-to-reader interferences are present, that is, if the distance between them is less than $d_{RR}$ (note that this case also comprises reader-to-tag interferences).

In addition to [2], in this work, we provide insight on the impact of the schedulers derived from the knowledge of the tag population associated to each reader. To the best of our knowledge, all previous optimization models (see Section 2) have largely ignored the availability of this information. This information can be effectively exploited to construct a scheduler with the goal of maximizing the number of identifications in the whole interrogation period. In this work, we assume that this information is known and show how it can be used to develop an optimal scheduler. Moreover, we analyze the improvement obtained when this information is available and the effect on the expected performance when errors occur in tag estimation.

This resource allocation problem is addressed both for static and dynamic frame length identification procedures (which are described later in Section 2.1) and that the tags remain in coverage of their corresponding reader at least during the whole period of identification ($t$ time-slots). The goal is to maximize the expected number of identified tags in the whole network.

The rest of the paper is organized as follows: In Section 2, the most relevant research proposals are shown. Section 2.1 describes the identification procedures commonly used in RFID readers. Section 3 describes the optimization model. Section 4 shows the performance results achieved by the optimal algorithm. Section 5 deals with the analysis of the impact of tag population estimation in the scheduler. Finally, Section 6 concludes and describes future works.

## 2 Related work

A number of proposal for coordinating dense reader environments have been presented in the literature; most of them are based on heuristic approaches and are, thus, suboptimal by nature. A summary of these works is contained in [3]. Besides, a number of papers [4-10] propose different system models and schedulers based on the optimization of some metric, defined upon the corresponding model.

Choi and Lee [4] propose a mixed integer linear program to minimize the reader interference problem as well as other performance metrics by selecting channel, timeslots, and output power for each reader. Their strategy is based on achieving a minimal signal-to-interference-plus-noise ratio for the signal received from tags, as well as on maximizing network utilization and minimizing power consumption. However, they neglect the availability of information about the number of tags present in the reading area of each reader and the operation of the underlying reading protocols, which are major factors determining the performance of the reading process.

Kim et al. [5] propose the TPC-CA algorithm based on a power control approach. It consists of controlling the reader output power optimally to reduce reader-to-reader collisions. Optimality criterion is related to minimize the area where interferences among readers occur.

Chui-Yu et al. introduces GA-BPSO in [6] a scheduler based on genetic algorithm and swarm intelligence meta-heuristics for single-channel environments. These schedulers aim at minimizing the overall sum of transaction times. However, these times are provided as parameters for the scheduler and are not based on the impact of resource allocation on the reading protocols.

Deolalikar et al. derive in [7] optimal scheduling schemes for readers in RFID networks for four basic configurations. As in our work, the authors aim at maximizing the number of identification within the scheduling period($t$), but they model the performance of the reading process with an approximation: the number of tags identified increases linearly up to a saturation point. From that point on, the number of identifications remains constant. As we demonstrate in Section 2.1, this approach is not realistic for different tag-to-tag anti-collision protocol configurations (e.g., in static-FSA, there is a drop on the throughput). As in our work, only reader-to-reader interference (and thus single-channel) environments are considered.

The study of Mohsenian-Rad et al. [8] is the work more closely related to ours. The authors design two optimization-based distributed channel selection and randomized interrogation algorithms for dense RFID systems: FDFA (which is fully distributed and achieves a local optimum) and SDFA (semi-distributed and reach to the global optimum). In addition, the authors realistically assume that the reader may operate asynchronously. Similarly to our work, they consider a FDMA/TDMA scheduler, where the medium access control layer of the readers complies with EPCglobal Class-1 Gen-2 standard (therefore, a reader may allocate a number of interrogation frames within its allocated time). In this work, the authors focus on the probability that a reader starts an interrogation interval without experiencing either reader-to-reader or reader-to-tag collisions. The goal is to achieve max-min fairness in the network; as a result, the processing load is evenly distributed among all readers. However, this paper does not consider the knowledge about the number of contending tags in range of each reader. This information allows us to formulate the optimization problem in terms of reading efficiency (maximizing the number of tags identified in the overall time period). An additional contribution of [8] is to develop a protocol to construct the topology (i.e., reader-to-reader and reader-to-tag constraints) by exchanging some messages in three control channels.

This protocol may be implemented in other schedulers (like ours) to determine the network topology in real time.

Tanaka and Sasase [9] also determine an interference model which they apply later to formulate constraints in a binary integer linear program aimed at maximizing the ratio of total time where readers can successfully communicate with the tags and total interrogation time of the readers. As in our model, the goal is selecting suitable timeslot and channels for each reader. They also propose two heuristics (one distributed and one centralized) to solve the allocation problem efficiently.

Seo and Lee [10] propose a FDM/TDM scheduler (RA-GA) based on a reader-to-reader interference model, which seeks to maximize a utility function depending upon the operating time slots. This problem is solved using a genetic algorithm meta-heuristic.

As many of the previous works, neither in [9] nor in [10] the reading protocol or the current load (unidentified tags) of each cell is considered. Summarizing, to the best of our knowledge, all previous optimization models ignore the availability of information about the number of tags within the range of each reader. This information can be very effectively exploited to construct a scheduler with the goal of maximizing the number of identifications in the interrogation period. Besides, most previous works assume a model view from the physical layer perspective and are usually aimed at minimizing interference. This view has notable limitations since tag identification performance, and thus scheduling, heavily depends on the underlying tag-to-tag anti-collision protocol, as discussed in the next Section.

## 2.1 Tag identification procedure

The identification process involves communications between the reader and the tags and takes place in a shared wireless channel. Basically, the reader *interrogates* tags nearby by sending a *Query* packet (the exact format of this packet depends on the particular standard). The tags are energized by the reader's signal and respond to this request with their identification. When several tags answer simultaneously, a tag-to-tag collision occurs, and the information cannot be retrieved. Therefore, a tag-to-tag anti-collision mechanism is required when multiple tags are in range. ALOHA-based protocols, also called probabilistic or random access protocols, are the most prevalent in the UHF band. They are designed for situations in which the reader does not know exactly how many tags will cross its checking area. The most common ALOHA RFID protocol is FSA, a variation of slotted ALOHA. As in slotted ALOHA, time is divided into time units called *slots*. However, in FSA, the slots are subject to a super-structure called a 'frame'.

Two options of the FSA are commonly used in the RFID technology:

1. *static frame length FSA (static-FSA)*. The reader starts the identification process with an identification frame by sending a Query packet with information about the frame length ($k$ slots) to the tags. The frame length is kept unchanged during the whole identification process. At each frame, each unidentified tag selects a slot at random from among the $k$ slots to send its identifier to the reader. FSA achieves reasonably good performance at the cost of requiring a central node (the reader) to manage slot and frame synchronization. FSA has been implemented in many commercial products and has been standardized in the ISO/IEC 18000-6C [11], ISO/IEC 18000-7 [12], and EPCGlobal Class-1 Gen-2 (EPC-C1G2) standards [13].

2. *dynamic frame length FSA (dynamic-FSA)*. When the tags outnumber the available slots, the identification time increases considerably due to frequent tag-to-tag collisions. On the other hand, if the slots outnumber the tags, many slots will be empty in the frame, which also leads to long identification times. Dynamic-FSA protocols were conceived to address this problem. They are similar to static-FSA, but the number of slots per frame is variable. In other words, parameter $k$ may change from frame to frame in the Query packet to adjust the frame length. Dynamic-FSA operation is optimal in terms of reading throughput (rate of identified tags per slot) when the frame length equals the number of contenders [14]. Therefore, to maximize throughput, the reader should ideally know the actual number of competing tags and allocate that number of slots to the next frame. Different dynamic-FSA algorithms have been proposed to estimate the number of competing nodes based on the collected statistical information. The most relevant ones have been studied in depth in our previous papers [15,16].

In the next Section, both algorithms (static-FSA and dynamic-FSA) are considered in order to propose an optimal slot distribution for the single channel environment. In the case of static-FSA, the frame length is $k$ for all readers; in the case of dynamic-FSA, we are assuming that each reader $j$ actually knows the number of competing nodes at frame $i$ ($n_{j,i}$) and that the reader is adjusting $k_{j,i} = n_{j,i}$ if the number of the remaining available slots is greater than $n_{j,i}$.

## 3 Optimal time distribution

Recall from the introduction that a dense-reader environment with the limitation of a single frequency channel

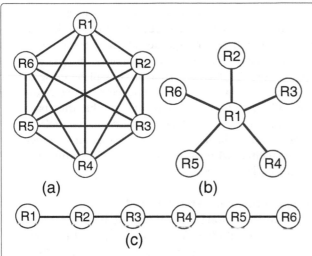

**Figure 2 Example scenarios for $m = 6$. (a)** Full-mesh topology. **(b)** Star topology. **(c)** Line topology.

$F=1$, $m$ readers, and $t$ slots available in the channel is assumed. In addition, for each reader $j = 1, \ldots, m$, let us denote

- $n_j$, the tags unidentified in the range of the reader $j$
- $t_j$, the number of slots assigned to reader $j$.

Let us remark that the methods used in dynamic-FSA tag-to-tag anti-collision protocols to determine the number of contenders can be directly applied in our case to estimate $n_j$ in real-time (see [15] and [16] for details). Besides, topological dependencies among readers are defined by an $m \times m$ matrix $A = (a_{jj'})$, the elements of which are 1 if reader $j$ and $j'$ cannot operate at the same time, and 0 otherwise.

Let $\varphi(n, t)$ denote the expected number of identified tags when $n$ tags contend in $t$ slots, and let us define $\Phi$

**Table 3 Star scenario**

| Number of tags | $\Phi$ | R1 | R2 | R3 | R4 |
|---|---|---|---|---|---|
| 10 | 40.000 | 78 | 74 | 76 | 77 |
| 20 | 80.000 | 126 | 115 | 155 | 116 |
| 30 | 119.999 | 128 | 128 | 128 | 128 |
| 40 | 159.427 | 128 | 128 | 128 | 128 |
| 50 | 186.355 | 128 | 128 | 128 | 128 |
| 60 | 189.195 | 94 | 140 | 139 | 139 |
| 70 | 210.000 | 0 | 512 | 512 | 512 |
| 80 | 240.000 | 0 | 512 | 512 | 512 |
| 90 | 270.000 | 0 | 512 | 512 | 512 |
| 100 | 300.000 | 0 | 512 | 512 | 512 |

Optimal assignment of slots for the dynamic-FSA protocol.

as the whole expected number of identified tags in the network, that is,

$$\Phi = \sum_{j=1}^{m} \varphi(n_j, t_j). \tag{1}$$

Then, the optimization problem can be stated as solving

$$\max_{\substack{t_j \\ j=1,\ldots,m}} \Phi. \tag{2}$$

Subject to

$$t_j \geq 0 \tag{3}$$

and

$$t_j + I_{t_j} \sum_{j'=1, j' \neq j}^{m} t_{j'} a_{j'j}, \leq t \text{ for all } j = 1, \ldots, m, \tag{4}$$

where $I_{t_j}$ is 1 if $t_j$ is greater than 0, and 0 otherwise.

Constraint (3) expresses a basic limiting condition on the values assigned to the number of assigned slots. The key in our problem formulation is constraint (4) which

**Table 2 Full-mesh scenario**

| Number of tags | $\Phi$ | R1 | R2 | R3 | R4 |
|---|---|---|---|---|---|
| 10 | 40.000 | 128 | 128 | 128 | 128 |
| 20 | 80.000 | 126 | 115 | 155 | 116 |
| 30 | 119.999 | 128 | 128 | 128 | 128 |
| 40 | 159.427 | 128 | 128 | 128 | 128 |
| 50 | 186.355 | 128 | 128 | 128 | 128 |
| 60 | 189.195 | 94 | 140 | 139 | 139 |
| 70 | 189.113 | 110 | 70 | 166 | 166 |
| 80 | 188.949 | 80 | 162 | 190 | 80 |
| 90 | 188.992 | 0 | 212 | 89 | 211 |
| 100 | 188.905 | 157 | 157 | 99 | 99 |

Optimal assignment of slots for the dynamic-FSA protocol.

**Table 4 Line scenario**

| Number of tags | $\Phi$ | R1 | R2 | R3 | R4 |
|---|---|---|---|---|---|
| 10 | 40.000 | 85 | 86 | 165 | 221 |
| 20 | 80.000 | 118 | 118 | 124 | 248 |
| 30 | 120.000 | 153 | 153 | 171 | 171 |
| 40 | 160.000 | 173 | 170 | 169 | 173 |
| 50 | 199.913 | 174 | 169 | 169 | 174 |
| 60 | 236.153 | 176 | 168 | 168 | 176 |
| 70 | 254.481 | 188 | 162 | 162 | 188 |
| 80 | 263.693 | 215 | 172 | 125 | 215 |
| 90 | 273.451 | 242 | 180 | 90 | 242 |
| 100 | 287.462 | 256 | 256 | 0 | 453 |

Optimal assignment of slots for the dynamic-FSA protocol.

establishes local conditions to regulate the spatial reuse of the resources in our network. This condition states that the number of slots assigned to a reader $j$ plus those assigned to its neighbors can not surpass the number of available slots. $I_{t_j}$ is included since readers without slots assigned should be considered as disconnected, and no constraints have to be applied to that particular readers.

The former constraint guarantees that enough slots are available for each node in each neighborhood (set of nodes bonded with topological constraints, i.e., $a_{j'j} = 1$) to obey with the limit of $t$ slots among all neighbors. Note that it does not guarantee that these slots can be allocated consecutively. However, this is not an issue since tags do not proceed with the next slot until a *QueryRep* packet arrives from the reader. Hence, even if the slots are not consecutively allocated, the tags perceive continuity and the identification can be performed seamlessly.

We must remark that this set of constraints produces feasible solutions regardless of the considered topology. However, in some cases (as we will show in the next section), the constraint is too strict and may lead to suboptimal solutions since space reutilization is limited. If the network graph has a large density (i.e., the number of edges is close to the maximal number of edges), the results provided by solving problem (1) will be close to the optimal solution with maximal space resource reutilization. Whereas, for sparse network graphs, the space reutilization will be small. The first kind of scenario will likely occur (due to the large reader-to-reader interference range) in facilities with non-screened readers; thus, the solutions found will be realistic.

### 3.1 $\varphi(n_j, t_j)$ computation for static-FSA

Finally, in order to solve the optimization problem, the expected number of identifications $\varphi(n, t)$ must be computed. The next sections deal with its computation both for static-FSA and for dynamic-FSA.

In this case, the reading process for each reader $j$ consists of several consecutive reading frames of length $k$ until all the $t_j$ reading slots are eventually exhausted. It

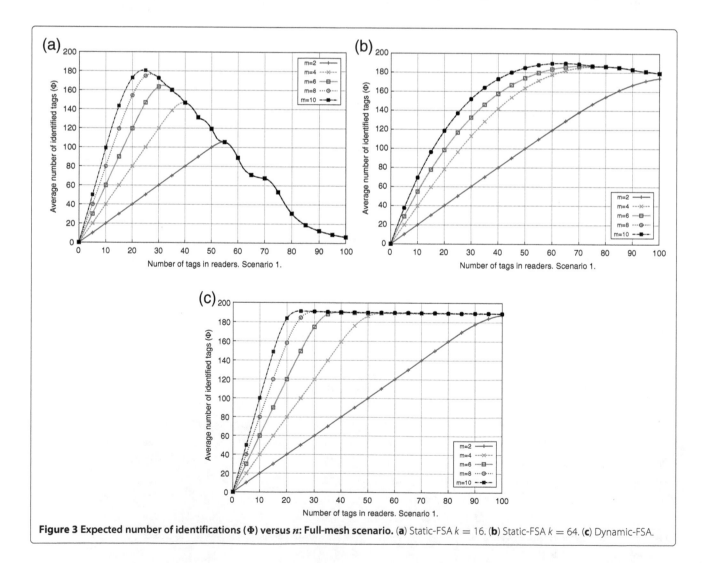

**Figure 3 Expected number of identifications ($\Phi$) versus $n$: Full-mesh scenario. (a)** Static-FSA $k = 16$. **(b)** Static-FSA $k = 64$. **(c)** Dynamic-FSA.

is assumed that $t_j = ka$, being $a$ a positive integer or zero. Given the last condition, and since expectation is a linear operator, $\varphi(n_j, t_j)$ can be computed as the sum of the average number of tags identified in the first frame ($\varphi(n_j, k)$) plus those identified in the remainder process ($\varphi(n_j - \eta, t_j - k)$), where $\eta$ denotes the random number of tags identified in the first frame.

The former part can be computed if the distribution of the random variable $\eta$ is known; so, let us denote $P(a|n_j, k)$ as the probability that $a$ tags are identified if $n_j$ tags contend in $k$ slots. Then

$$\varphi(n_j, k) = \sum_{u=0}^{n_j} a P(a|n_j, k). \tag{5}$$

The second part, can be computed given the joint probability of identifying $a$ tags in the first frame and $a'$ in the remainder process if $n_j$ tags contend in $t_j$ slots, which we will denote as $P(a, a'|n_j, t_j)$. We obtain

$$\varphi(n_j - \eta, t_j - k) = \sum_{a=0}^{n_j} \sum_{a'=0}^{n_j} a' P(a, a'|n_j, t_j). \tag{6}$$

But, clearly $P(a, a'|n_j, t_j) = P(a|n_j, k)P(a'|n_j - a, t_j - k)$, and this leads to

$$\varphi(n_j - \eta, t_j - k) = \sum_{a=0}^{n_j} \varphi(n_j - a, t_j - k)P(a|n_j, k) \tag{7}$$

Appendix 1 demonstrates that the value of $P(a|n_j, t_j)$ is given by (where the technique in [17] was used to compute the probability $P(a|n, t)$)

$$P(a|n_j, t_j) = \frac{n_j!}{t_j^{n_j}} \binom{t_j}{a} \sum_{c=0}^{n_j-a} (-1)^c \binom{t-a}{c} \frac{(t_j - a - c)^{n_j-a-c}}{(n_j - a - c)!}. \tag{8}$$

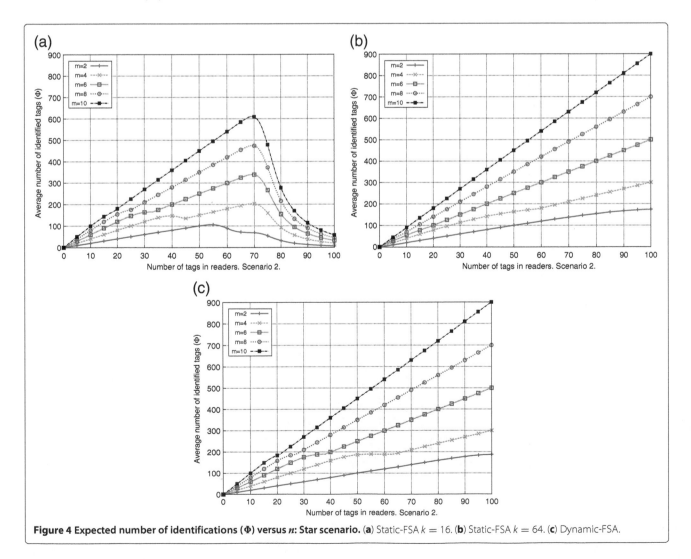

**Figure 4 Expected number of identifications ($\Phi$) versus $n$: Star scenario. (a)** Static-FSA $k = 16$. **(b)** Static-FSA $k = 64$. **(c)** Dynamic-FSA.

Thus, the following recursive equation results:

$$\varphi(n_j, t_j) = \begin{cases} \sum_{a=0}^{n_j}(a + \varphi(n_j - a, t_j - k))P(a|n_j, k), \text{if } t_j \geq k \\ 0, \text{otherwise} \end{cases}$$

$$(9)$$

### 3.2  $\varphi(n_j, t_j)$ computation for dynamic-FSA

In this second case, the reading process for each reader $j$ also consists of several reading frames but of variable length $k_{j,1}, k_{j,2}, \ldots$, until all the $t_j$ reading slots are exhausted. Besides, denote the number of contenders in each frame as $n_{j,1}, n_{j,2}, \ldots$. Since the dynamic-FSA operation is used (see Section 2.1), the reader seeks to maximize reading throughput and allocates the optimal number of slots in each frame. That is, as much slots as the number of contending tags ($k_{j,i} = n_{j,i}$). This is possible while $n_{j,i} < t_j - \sum_{c=1}^{i-1} k_{j,c}$, that is, if the remainder number of slots is greater that the number of contenders. Otherwise, we assume that a last frame is allocated with all the remaining slots ($k_{j,i} = t_j - \sum_{c=1}^{i-1} k_{j,i}$).

Like in the previous case $\varphi(n_j, t_j)$ can be described through a recursive equation:

$$\varphi(n_j, t_j) = \begin{cases} \varphi(n_j, n_j) + \sum_{a=0}^{n_j} \varphi(n_j - a, t_j - n_j)P(a|n_j, n_j), \text{if } n_j < t_j \\ \varphi(n_j, t_j) \text{ if } n_j \geq t_j. \end{cases}$$

From Equation (5),

$$\varphi(n_j, n_j) = \sum_{a=0}^{n_j} aP(a|n_j, n_j),$$

and

$$\varphi(n_j, t_j) = \sum_{a=0}^{n_j} aP(a|n_j, t_j), \text{if } n_j \geq t_j.$$

Hence,

$$\varphi(n_j, t_j) = \begin{cases} \sum_{a=0}^{n_j}(a + \varphi(n_j - a, t_j - n_j))P(a|n_j, n_j) \text{ if } n_j < t_j \\ \sum_{a=0}^{n_j} aP(a|n_j, t_j) \text{ if } n_j \geq t_j. \end{cases}$$

$$(10)$$

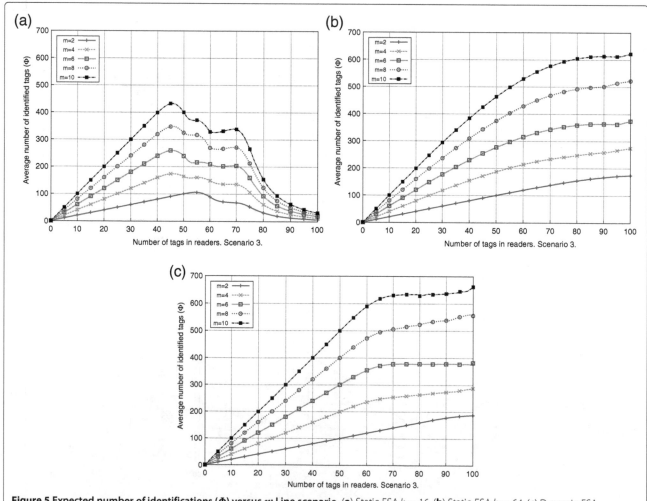

**Figure 5 Expected number of identifications ($\Phi$) versus $n$: Line scenario. (a)** Static-FSA $k = 16$. **(b)** Static-FSA $k = 64$. **(c)** Dynamic-FSA.

## 4   Results

The optimal assignment has been computed in static-FSA and dynamic-FSA cases using the recursive formulas described in the previous section. Three representative scenarios (see Figure 2) have been selected. The edges (i.e., connecting lines) represent the existence of interference between two vertices (readers). On the first scenario, a full-mesh topology of $m$ readers has been selected. It is a typical configuration in facilities, since the RRI distance is large (in the order of hundreds of meters) as discussed in the introduction. On the other hand, the star topology of $m$ readers selected for scenario two represents another practical case, where readers are confined to some areas (e.g., by screening the reading area), and interferences are restricted to some particular pairs, exclusively between R1 and the other readers in this example. Finally, the line scenario is representative of an assembly line, where neighbor readers are in range.

Besides, the following parameters have been considered:

- $t = 512$,

- $n$ tags to be identified at each reader, from 1 to 100 tags,
- $m = 2, 4, 6, 8,$ and 10,
- and for static-FSA $k = 16$ and 64.

Our optimization algorithm has been implemented using the *General Algebraic Modeling System*, a high-level modeling system for mathematical programming and optimization, and AlphaECP, a MINLP (Mixed-Integer Non-Linear Programming) solver based on the extended cutting plane method. It allowed us to define our optimization problem directly from the mathematical description provided in Section 3.

Tables 2, 3, and 4 show the optimal configurations (slots assigned to each reader) for the dynamic-FSA protocol in all scenarios with $m = 4$. Let us remark that the optimal solutions are non-trivial, that is, can be obtained through an educated guess. Clearly, this solution is not unique: a circular permutation of the optimal solution, replacing the slots from R$j$ to R$(j + 1)$ if $j < m$, and from R$m$ to R1 is also an optimal solution for the full-mesh scenario. The

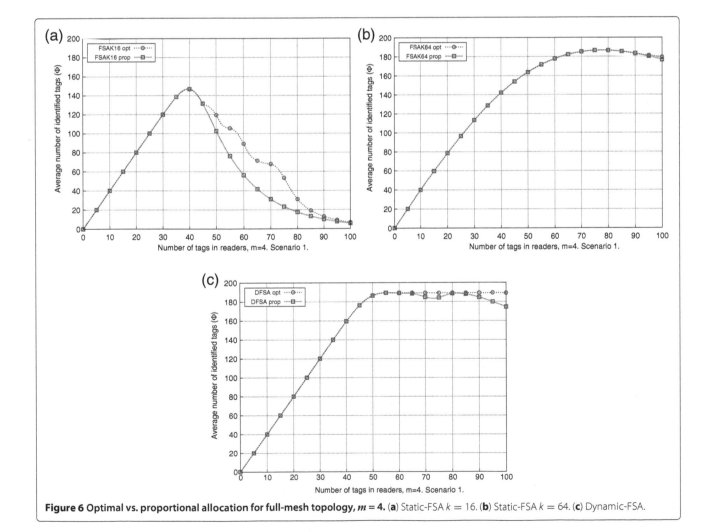

**Figure 6** Optimal vs. proportional allocation for full-mesh topology, $m = 4$. (**a**) Static-FSA $k = 16$. (**b**) Static-FSA $k = 64$. (**c**) Dynamic-FSA.

same applies to the star scenario if the slots in R1 are kept constant while any permutation is applied to the rest of the readers and to the line scenario replacing the slots from R$j$ to R$(m − j)$.

In addition, note that the results obtained for the star scenario (Table 3) can be improved. For example, for $n = 30$, after assigning 128 slots to R1, it would be possible to assign 384 to all remainder readers, which will provide a solution better than that obtained by solving problem (1). As discussed in Section 3, this is caused by the strict resource reutilization obtained by applying the set of constraints given by Equation (4). This problem does not appear for networks characterized by a dense graph, as the full-mesh scenario.

Besides, Figures 3, 4, and 5 show the expected number of tags identified ($\Phi$) for all the possible values of $m$ using the optimal assignments. Note that the resources available ($t = 512$) are the same for all the configurations; however, the performance clearly varies. This illustrates how the underlying reading protocol determines the final system

performance. Dynamic-FSA performs better than static-FSA assignment for both configurations of $k$ (16, 64), as can be expected. This is reasonable since dynamic-FSA achieves an optimal reading throughput frame-by-frame while the number of available slots is at least equal to the number of contenders.

Another important result shown in these figures is the existence of saturation points in the system. That is, in some cases, the throughput does not increase when the load is increased. For dynamic-FSA, in all cases, the throughput never decreases; this is caused by the flexibility of dynamic-FSA to adapt to different loads. For static-FSA $k = 64$, the effect is almost similar to the dynamic-FSA case, except in the full-mesh scenario where the throughput slightly decreases when the tag is beyond $n = 60$. However, for all static-FSA $k = 16$ cases, the effect of the load in the throughput is dramatic, with a throughput minima and a step decreasing performance. This is of considerable importance, since static-FSA $k = 16$ is the default configuration of many readers in the

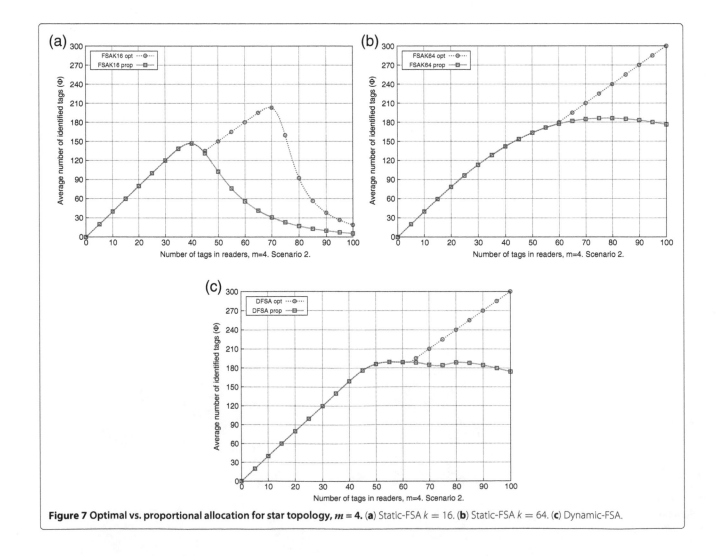

**Figure 7** Optimal vs. proportional allocation for star topology, $m = 4$. (**a**) Static-FSA $k = 16$. (**b**) Static-FSA $k = 64$. (**c**) Dynamic-FSA.

market, and this configuration leads to poor collective performance.

In addition Figures 6, 7, and 8 show, for $m = 4$, the performance of the optimal allocation versus a non-optimal allocation scheme selected for comparison, namely, using $\frac{1}{m}$ of time allocated to each reader ('proportional' resource sharing), that is, $t_1 = \ldots = t_4 = 128$. This heuristic is a natural choice, since the number of tags in the range of each reader is the same; therefore a good performance could be expected. In fact, the proportional scheme achieves in a range of $n$ a performance nearly equal to the optimal one, as can intuitively be expected, in some cases (e.g., static-FSA $k = 64$ and dynamic-FSA in the full-mesh topology). However, for some cases, the allocation is clearly suboptimal (e.g., star and line scenarios for $n > 60$). Noteworthy, in the star scenario, there is a point ($n \geq 70$) where the best option is directly to disconnect the central reader. In this case, without restrictions in the network, the remainder readers can be allocated each all the 512 slots. A similar behavior

occurs for the line scenario, disconnecting some readers when there is a high load (e.g., see Table 4; if $n = 100$ the third reader is disconnected).

## 5 Tag estimation impact on scheduler performance

The aim of this section is twofold:

(1) Quantify the improvement achieved in the scheduler when tag instant population estimation is available.
(2) Quantify the impact of tag population estimation errors on the performance achieved by the scheduler.

As stated in Section 2, previous works do not assume knowledge about the tag population and are mostly based on minimizing interferences. To establish a comparison between our model and a reference model that do not use population information, at least, we must focus on the same performance metric, i.e., the expected number of identifications (which can also be viewed as throughput).

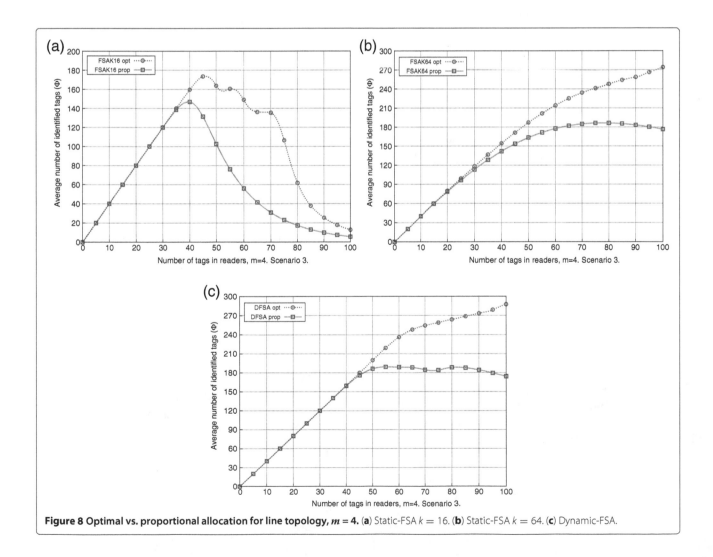

**Figure 8** Optimal vs. proportional allocation for line topology, $m = 4$. (a) Static-FSA $k = 16$. (b) Static-FSA $k = 64$. (c) Dynamic-FSA.

Although our reference model does not use information about the instant population, it is rational to assume at least a coarse knowledge of the environment, typically the average number of competing tags. This allows the designer to configure the system for a standard case. Note that if this information is unavailable, the designer should guess somehow a configuration, and the performance would be lower than in the reference model.

Henceforth, let us assume that our reference model is based on the availability of information about the average tag population and that the designer is able to select the optimal scheduler configuration for this case (e.g., by solving problem (1)).

For simplicity, let us denote by $\vec{n}$ the $m$-dimensional vector $(n_1, \ldots, n_m)$, and by $\Phi_{\vec{n}}(\vec{n}')$ the expected number of identifications when the optimal solution to problem (1) with tag estimation parameter $\vec{n}$ is applied to the actual population $\vec{n}'$. Besides, let $\vec{n}^*$ denote the $m$-dimensional vector, where the $j$th component is the average number of tags in reader $j$.

Thus, if the probability distribution of tag population, i.e., $P(\vec{n})$ is known, the improvement ($\Delta$) achieved by our scheduler over the reference scheduler is

$$\Delta = \sum_{\forall \vec{n}} (\Phi_{\vec{n}}(\vec{n}) - \Phi_{\vec{n}^*}(\vec{n})) P(\vec{n}). \quad (11)$$

By solving problem (1), both optimal slot assignments can be computed. Let us denote $\widehat{t}$ and $\widehat{t}^*$ to the optimal assignments for tag populations $\vec{n}$ and $\vec{n}^*$, respectively, and $\widehat{t}_j$ and $\widehat{t}^*_j$ the slots assigned to particular reader $j$th.

Then, $\Delta$ can be rewritten as

$$\Delta = \sum_{\forall \vec{n}} \left( \sum_{j=1}^{m} \varphi(n_j, \widehat{t}_j) - \sum_{j=1}^{m} \varphi(n_j, \widehat{t}^*_j) \right) P(\vec{n}), \quad (12)$$

where $\varphi(n, t)$ is computed directly with formulas (9) and (10) for static-FSA and dynamic-FSA, respectively.

In addition, it could be argued that instant tag population estimation may be subject to errors. This can be included in our computations through an error vector $\vec{\epsilon}$, where the $j$th component is $\epsilon_j = \check{n}_j - n_j$, $n_j$ the estimation, and $\check{n}_j$ is the actual number of tags. Therefore, the real tag distribution is $\vec{n} + \vec{\epsilon}$, and $\Delta$ should be modified as

$$\Delta = E_{\vec{\epsilon}} \left\{ \sum_{\forall \vec{n}} \left( \sum_{j=1}^{m} \varphi(n_j y + \epsilon_j, \widehat{t}_j) - \sum_{j=1}^{m} \varphi(n_j + \epsilon_j, \widehat{t}^*_j) \right) P(\vec{n}) \right\}. \quad (13)$$

**Table 5 Full-mesh scenario**

| Number of readers | Dynamic-FSA | Static-FSA, $k = 64$ | Static-FSA, $k = 16$ |
|---|---|---|---|
| 2 | 0.0273 | 0 | 0.0889 |
| 4 | 0.0120 | 0.0008 | 0.2891 |
| 6 | 0.0423 | 0.0050 | 0.4831 |
| 8 | 0.0791 | 0.0086 | 0.6024 |
| 10 | 0.0947 | 0.0086 | 0.6731 |

Ratio of improvement using tag estimation. $\epsilon = 0$.

Note that in this last case, $\widehat{t}_j$, is still computed with the estimation vector $\vec{n}$. So, if $\vec{n}$ and $\vec{\epsilon}$ are independent, we finally reach to

$$\Delta = \sum_{\forall \vec{\epsilon}} \left[ \sum_{\forall \vec{n}} \left( \sum_{j=1}^{m} \varphi(n_j + \epsilon_j, \widehat{t}_j) - \sum_{j=1}^{m} \varphi(n_j + \epsilon_j, \widehat{t}^*_j) \right) P(\vec{n}) \right] P(\vec{\epsilon}). \quad (14)$$

Note that we use a perfect knowledge of the average number of tags; therefore, we are assuming the least-favorable comparison case for our scheduler versus the reference model.

### 5.1 Numerical examples

For the sake of example, let us assume that for each reader, the number of tags is given by a uniformly distributed random variable $\mathbf{n}$ in the range $[0, 100]$. That is, $n_j = \mathbf{n}$ for all $j = 1, \ldots, m$. Hence, $\vec{n}^* = (50, \ldots, 50)$. Tables 5, 6, and 7 show the average performance improvement achieved for the examples described in the previous section and for the dynamic-FSA and static-FSA tag-to-tag anti-collision protocols. The results are shown as the ratio of improvement ($\Delta$) to the expected readings without using tag estimation.

The results clearly depend on the scenario and on the tag-to-tag anti-collision protocols. Improvement ranges from nearly 0% in many static-FSA $k = 64$ cases, while it may reach up to 67% for static-FSA, $k = 16$ in the full-mesh scenario. For dynamic-FSA, the improvement

**Table 6 Star scenario**

| Number of readers | Dynamic-FSA | Static-FSA, $k = 64$ | Static-FSA, $k = 16$ |
|---|---|---|---|
| 2 | 0.0273 | 0 | 0.0889 |
| 4 | 0.1592 | 0.1702 | 0.2636 |
| 6 | 0.0509 | 0.0023 | 0.1940 |
| 8 | 0.0417 | 0.0005 | 0.1756 |
| 10 | 0.0333 | 0.0000 | 0.1683 |

Ratio of improvement using tag estimation. $\epsilon = 0$.

**Table 7 Line scenario**

| Number of readers | Dynamic-FSA | Static-FSA, $k = 64$ | Static-FSA, $k = 16$ |
|:---:|:---:|:---:|:---:|
| 2 | 0.0266 | 0 | 0.0817 |
| 4 | 0.0331 | 0.0144 | 0.2114 |
| 6 | 0.0049 | 0.0018 | 0.2105 |
| 8 | 0.0298 | 0.0050 | 0.2073 |
| 10 | 0.0101 | 0.0013 | 0.2056 |

Ratio of improvement using tag estimation. $\epsilon = 0$.

**Table 9 Star scenario**

| Number of readers | Dynamic-FSA | Static-FSA, $k = 64$ | Static-FSA, $k = 16$ |
|:---:|:---:|:---:|:---:|
| 2 | 0.0275 | 0 | 0.0704 |
| 4 | 0.1541 | 0.1750 | 0.2087 |
| 6 | 0.0543 | 0.0017 | 0.2123 |
| 8 | 0.0406 | -0.0002 | 0.1878 |
| 10 | 0.0302 | 0.0000 | 0.1925 |

Ratio of improvement using tag estimation. $\epsilon \sim U[-10, 10]$.

is between 2.7% and 21.14%, depending on the particular scenario. Let us remark again that this comparison is performed against the average tags identified when the optimal configuration is computed using as information the mean number of competing tags. Therefore, this is the *minimum* improvement ratio: non-optimal schedulers (as the reference heuristic used in Section 4) will obtain worse results.

Besides, we can consider the estimation error. In our test we have assumed for each reader an error distributed uniformly $\epsilon \sim U[-10, 10]$. Results are shown in Tables 8, 9, and 10.

Again, the results heavily depend on the configuration, but in most cases, even assuming an error in the tag number estimation, they show a positive feedback using the estimation. In some cases, in the full-mesh and line scenarios, there is a negative impact, but almost negligible. Therefore, we can conclude that even assuming errors, the utilization of tag estimators is worth to be considered.

## 6  Conclusions

This work introduced a novel optimal scheduler for a particular dense reader environment composed by $m$ readers which must share a single frequency channel. The scheduler proposed exceeds in performance to heuristic algorithms, improving the average number of tags identified in an RFID facility. Besides, the effect of the reading protocols has also been studied in depth, concluding that a dynamic FSA algorithm excels static frame length ones.

Indeed, the impact of using knowledge about tag population in the scheduler has been analyzed. It has been concluded that even assuming errors in the estimation, our scheduler is able to obtain a higher performance than a reference model, where the average population is perfectly known.

As future works, we aim at extending our model to multi-channel scenarios, developing a model that allow full resource reutilization and further analyze RFID realistic scenarios to propose optimal configuration strategies.

## Appendix
### Computation of $P(a|n, t)$

To compute the probability $P(a|n, t)$, we apply the technique in [17], where the authors formulate probabilistic transforms for urn models that convert the dependent random variables describing urn occupancies (slot occupancies in our case) into independent random variables. Due to the independence of random variables in the transform domain, it is simpler to compute the statistics of interest, and afterwards the transform is inverted to get the desired result.

Let us denote $P(a|n, t)$ as the probability of interest and $P(\lambda, t, i)$ its transformation, with $\lambda$ as parameter meaningful in the transform domain only. Indeed, there is no dependence on the number of balls (tags), $n$, in the transform domain.

The procedure is as follows: first, the appropriate transform for a particular urn model is selected. In our case,

**Table 8 Full-mesh scenario**

| Number of readers | Dynamic-FSA | Static-FSA, $k = 64$ | Static-FSA, $k = 16$ |
|:---:|:---:|:---:|:---:|
| 2 | 0.0284 | 0 | 0.0527 |
| 4 | 0.0064 | 0.0007 | 0.2334 |
| 6 | 0.0361 | 0.0040 | 0.4107 |
| 8 | 0.0580 | 0.0101 | 0.5515 |
| 10 | 0.0747 | 0.0070 | 0.5712 |

Ratio of improvement using tag estimation. $\epsilon \sim U[-10, 10]$.

**Table 10 Line scenario**

| Number of readers | Dynamic-FSA | Static-FSA, $k = 64$ | Static-FSA, $k = 16$ |
|:---:|:---:|:---:|:---:|
| 2 | 0.0442 | -0.0006 | 0.0023 |
| 4 | 0.0324 | 0.0212 | 0.0991 |
| 6 | 0.0003 | 0.0019 | 0.1169 |
| 8 | 0.0279 | 0.0071 | 0.0815 |
| 10 | 0.0118 | 0.0012 | 0.0942 |

Ratio of improvement using tag estimation. $\epsilon \sim U[-10, 10]$.

both the $t$ urns (slots) and the $n$ balls (tags) are distinguishable. In this case, the independent random variables $Z_1, \ldots, Z_t$ describing the occupancy of an urn in the transform domain are Poisson distributed with mean $\lambda$ [17]. That is, $P(Z_i = j) = e^{-\lambda} \frac{\lambda^{(j)}}{j!}$. Second, the probability of interest, $\boldsymbol{P}(\lambda, t)$, is computed in the transformed domain. In our case, given a frame of length $t$ and taking into account the independence of $Z_i$, the probability of having $i$ urns (slots) with one ball (tag) is

$$
\begin{aligned}
\boldsymbol{P}(\lambda, t) &= \binom{t}{i} P(Z = 1)^i (1 - P(Z = 1))^{t-i} \\
&= \binom{t}{i} (e^{-\lambda} \lambda)^i (1 - e^{-\lambda} \lambda)^{t-i}.
\end{aligned} \tag{15}
$$

Finally, the inverse transform is computed as

$$
P(a|n, t) = \frac{n!}{t^n} [\lambda^n] \{ e^{\lambda t} \boldsymbol{P}(\lambda, t) \}, \tag{16}
$$

with $[\lambda^n]\{h(\lambda)\}$ denoting the coefficient of $\lambda^n$ in the power series $\{h(\lambda)\}$. So, we have to rewrite Equation (15) as a power series in $\lambda$ and extract the appropriate coefficient. We use first the binomial expansion $(a + b)^c = \sum_{k=0}^{h} \binom{h}{k} a^k b^{h-k}$:

$$
P(a|n, t) = \frac{n!}{t^n} [\lambda^n] \left\{ \binom{t}{i} \sum_{c=0}^{t-i} \binom{t-i}{c} (-1)^c e^{\lambda(t-i-c)} \lambda^{c+i} \right\}, \tag{17}
$$

and using the expansion of the exponential function as a power series, the sum in Equation (17) can be rewritten as

$$
\begin{aligned}
& \sum_{c=0}^{t-i} \binom{t-i}{c} (-1)^c \sum_{j=0}^{\infty} \frac{(t-i-c)^j}{j!} \lambda^j \lambda^{c+i} = \\
& = \sum_{j=0}^{\infty} \lambda^{j+i} \left( \sum_{c=0}^{j} (-1)^c \binom{t-i}{c} \frac{(t-i-c)^{j-c}}{(j-c)!} \right),
\end{aligned} \tag{18}
$$

and extracting the coefficient of $\lambda^n$ for the appropriate $n$ value, $n = j + i$, we obtain the result in Equation (8).

**Competing interests**

The authors declare that they have no competing interests.

**Acknowledgements**

This work has been supported by project CALM TEC2010-21405-C02 which is funded by the Spanish Ministerio de Innovación y Ciencia. It has been developed within the framework of 'Programa de Ayudas a Grupos de Excelencia de la Región de Murcia', funded by Fundación Seneca, Agencia de Ciencia y Tecnología de la Región de Murcia (Plan Regional de Ciencia y Tecnología 2007/2010). We are also indebted to Javier Fernández-Nogueira for his help in MINLP optimization.

**References**

1.  J Vales-Alonso, MV Bueno-Delgado, JJ Alcaraz, in *Paper presented in 2011 IEEE international conference on RFID-technologies and applications (RFID-TA)*. Optimal scheduling in dual reader RFID environments (Sitges Spain, 15–16 September 2011)
2.  J Vales-Alonso, FJ Parrado-Garcia, JJ Alcaraz, E Egea-Lopez, in *Paper presented in 2012 fourth international EURASIP workshop on RFID technology (EURASIP RFID)*. Optimal scheduling in single channel dense reader RFID environments (Torino, Italy, 27–28 September 2012)
3.  MV Bueno-Delgado, J Vales-Alonso, C Angerer, M Rupp, in *Paper presented in IEEE international conference on industrial technology*. A comparative study of RFID schedulers in dense reader environments (Viña del Mar, Chile, 14–17 March 2010)
4.  J Choi, C Lee, An MILP-based cross-layer optimization for a multi-reader arbitration in the UHF RFID system. Sensors **11**(3), 2347–2368 (2011)
5.  J Kim, W Lee, E Kim, D Kim, K Suh, Optimized transmission power control of interrogators for collision arbitration in UHF RFID systems. IEEE Commun. Lett. **11**(1), 22–24 (2007)
6.  C Chui-Yu, K Cheng-Hsin, KY Chen, in *Paper presented in IEEE international conference on systems, man and cybernetics*, Optimal RFID networks scheduling using genetic algorithm and swarm intelligence (San Antonio, USA, 11–14 October 2009)
7.  V Deolalikar, J Recker, M Mesarina, S Pradhan, *Optimal scheduling for networks of RFID readers Paper presented at the first international workshop on RFID and ubiquitous sensor networks*. (EUC Workshops LNCS 3823), Nagasaki,Japan, 6–9 December 2005)
8.  AH Mohsenian-Rad, V Shah-Mansouri, VWS Wong, R Schober, Distributed channel selection and randomized interrogation algorithms for large-scale and dense RFID systems. IEEE Trans. on Wireless Commun. **9**(4), 1402–1413 (2010)
9.  Y Tanaka, I Sasase, Interference avoidance algorithms for passive RFID systems using contention-based transmit abortion. IEICE Trans. Commun. **E90-B**(11), 3170–3180 (2007)
10. H Seo, C Lee, in *Paper presented in 2010 IEEE international conference on communications (ICC)*. A New GA-Based Resource Allocation Scheme for a Reader-to-Reader Interference Problem in RFID Systems. (Cape Town, South Africa, 23–27 May 2010)
11. International Organization for Standardization, *ISO/IEC 18000-6C:2004: information technology – radio frequency identification for item management-Part 6: parameters for air interface communications at 860 MHz to 960 MHz*. (International Organization for Standardization, Geneva, Switzerland, 2010)
12. International Organization for Standardization, *ISO/IEC 18000-7:2008: information technology – radio frequency identification for item management – Part 7: parameters for active air interface communications at 433 MHz*. (International Organization for Standardization, Geneva, Switzerland, 2010)
13. EPC Global Inc., *EPC Radio-Frequency Identity Protocols Class-1 Generation-2 UHF RFID Protocol for Communications at 860 MHz–960 MHz Version 1.2.0*. (EPC Global Inc., Brussels Belgium, 2008)
14. N Abramson, in *Proc. National Computer Conference*. Packet switching with satellites (ACM Press, New York, 1973), pp. 695–702
15. MV Bueno-Delgado, J Vales-Alonso, FJ González-Castaño, in *Paper presented in proceedings of the 35th international conference of the IEEE Industrial Electronics Society*. Analysis of DFSA anti-collision protocols in passive RFID environments (Porto,Portugal, 3–5November 2009)
16. J Vales-Alonso, MV Bueno-Delgado, E Egea-López, J Alcaraz, FJ González-Castaño, Multi frame maximum likelihood tag estimation for RFID anti-collision protocols. IEEE Trans. on Industrial Informatics. **7**(3), 487–496 (2011)
17. O Milenkovic, KJ Compton, Probabilistic transforms for combinatorial urn models. Comb. Probab.Comput. **13**(4-5), 645–675 (2004)

# Agile methods for embedded systems development - a literature review and a mapping study

Matti Kaisti[1*], Ville Rantala[1], Tapio Mujunen[1,2], Sami Hyrynsalmi[3], Kaisa Könnölä[1], Tuomas Mäkilä[1] and Teijo Lehtonen[1]

## Abstract

There is a wide area of applications that use embedded systems, and the number of such systems keeps growing. The required functionality and complexity of embedded systems are also constantly increasing, and development of such products is becoming increasingly harder. This requires new thinking on the product development processes, and one such emerging philosophy is the agile methods. These methods were created by the software engineering community where they are commonly used. Since then, they have been adopted in embedded systems development; however, whether they can improve the embedded systems product development processes remains an open question. This study aims to bring forth what is known about agile methods in embedded systems development and to find out if agile practices are suitable in this domain and what evidence is there to support the findings. We conducted a literature review and a mapping study to answer these questions. The scope of this study is not only limited to embedded software development, but also to embedded hardware and integrated circuits. We have found that agile methods can be used in the embedded domain, but the methods and practices need to be adapted to suit the more constrained field of embedded product development. Furthermore, the field of embedded product development has wide diversity of products with different needs and domain-specific problems so that no single method is applicable, but rather many methods and practices are needed for different situations.

**Keywords:** Agile; Lean; Method; Embedded software; Embedded systems; Hardware; Integrated circuits

## 1 Review

### 1.1 Introduction

An embedded system is a specialized computer system designed for a dedicated task or a purpose which is embedded as component to a larger system usually including hardware and mechanics. There is a wide area of applications that use embedded systems from cell phones, navigation tools, video cameras, cars to appliances to name a few. The amount of functionality and complexity of embedded systems has increased substantially, making it increasingly harder to efficiently develop embedded systems products. A similar trend has been seen in software engineering where the traditional plan-based methodologies have not been able to answer to this increasing complexity and unpredictability, and as reaction to this, lightweight agile methods have gained wide popularity in the software product development. Even though embedded systems differ from the conventional software application development in many ways, there is increasing awareness in the embedded field about agile methods. However, this information is somewhat scattered on various forums, and it is additionally fairly incoherent. Development of embedded systems consists of development of software and hardware that is commonly part of a larger system or device. The purpose of this study is to bring forth the current state of agile development in the embedded systems domain and classify current academic papers to acquire the needed cohesion of the literature in a way that it is useful for both the practitioners and academics as well. The scope of the review is in the context of embedded systems where the components of

*Correspondence: mkaist@utu.fi
[1] Business and Innovation Development (BID), University of Turku, Turku 20520, Finland
Full list of author information is available at the end of the article

such systems are explicitly included in our search strategy rather than only concentrating on embedded software. As it was found in our trial searches that substantial amount of information can be found as non-academic material, we included an independent search to address this issue.

Earlier reviews [P1,P22] have found out that agile methods could be used in an embedded domain, but their use is not yet widespread. Furthermore, these studies focused on embedded software development, whereas our focus is broader. In this study, a number of studies were found that were not included in the previous reviews. In this review, also non-academic material is included. These sources generally have practical ideas on how to actually apply agile methods in the embedded domain.

This paper in organized as follows: in Section 1.2, we discuss about agile methodologies and give an overview of previous literature reviews and state the objectives of this study. In Section 1.3, we describe the research method. In Section 1.4, the results are discussed. We show what kind of studies have been done and briefly summarize the main points of the studies and discuss what is known about agile methods in the embedded world in general. Section 1.5 is a discussion about non-academic articles found by the Google search engine. The findings of this study are discussed in Section 1.6, and the paper is concluded and future directions are presented in Section 2.

## 1.2 Background

In this section, we start with a brief introduction to agile methods - the main idea of agile and how it relates to embedded systems development. This is followed by a summary of previous reviews in agile development, emphasizing surveys on the embedded domain after which the research questions are stated.

### 1.2.1 Agile methods

Plan-driven development methods were practically the only alternative for organizations until the 1990s. Royce [1] introduced a model that became known as the waterfall model in the 1970s. It has commonly been considered that the presented single-pass waterfall cycle is an exemplary development model when, in fact, Royce used it as a simplified example before proceeding to iterative models that he actually preferred.

The foundation of agile methods is in the iterative and incremental development. Agile methods have gained increasing popularity since the 1990s when the agile movement begun and several software production processes evolved such as the well-known Extreme Programming (XP) and Scrum methods. The teams are commonly small, self-organizing and co-located, working closely together that helps in producing a high-quality software. Frequent feedback from closely collaborating customers is also promoted as a means of fulfilling customer needs [2].

The agile methods are a set of practices created by experienced software developers. The agile methods can be seen as a response to plan-driven processes that emphasize extensive planning and documentation with strict processes, and have a view that specifiable and predictable solutions to problems exist [3]. In contrast to plan-driven methods, Agile Manifesto [4] highlights the following: individuals and interactions over processes and tools, working software over comprehensive documentation, customer collaboration over contract negotiation and responding to a change over following a plan. Even though the manifesto highlights the values of the items on the left more than the ones on the right, it does not abandon the ones on the right either. The main differences between the plan-driven and the agile development paradigms are illustrated in Figure 1. In plan-driven development, there are consequent phases which are usually handled by phase-specific teams. Information between the phases is transferred using extensive documentation. In agile methodologies, the development is done in incremental iterations in integrated teams. Requirements for the developed system are stored in the product backlog.

Besides the manifesto, there is no single and exact definition of agile, but rather there are various methods that share the same philosophy which call themselves agile. Most methods have iterations with continuous refinement of plans and goals. However, each method has its own practices and terminology, putting emphasis on different issues in software development, and hence can be adopted to suite for different situations.

For example, XP is a set of pragmatic practices that emphasize extensive testing, code revise and pair programming [5], whereas Scrum is a development framework that focuses on management issues in projects where planning is difficult. The core of Scrum is in frequent feedback loops and Sprints that take place in daily stand-up meetings and with monthly (or more frequent) planning meetings [6]. Another popularity-gaining methodology, Kanban, differs from the previous as only having few practices and promoting gradual change and a constant flow over timeboxed iterations [7].

In this paper, the methodological analysis is based on the division between the plan-driven and the agile paradigms. It has been argued that other methodological paradigms also exist. For example, open source development has been seen as a distinguished development approach. On the other hand, the open source development can be seen as one of the many development domains where agile methods can be successfully applied [8].

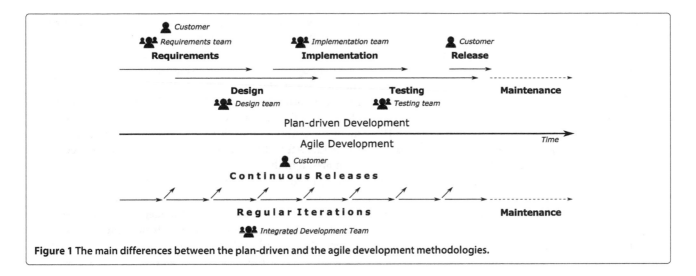

**Figure 1** The main differences between the plan-driven and the agile development methodologies.

### 1.2.2   Review questions

In this review, the main objective was to find out the current state of agile methods in the field of embedded systems development. We made a clear distinction between *embedded software* and *embedded systems* development. In our discussion, the former is software development which is constrained by the used hardware, whereas the latter is not only constrained by hardware but also includes hardware development.

As the purpose of this study was to find out what is currently known about agile methods in embedded systems development and if these methods are suitable in this domain, we focused on the following questions:

RQ1   What is currently known about agile methods in embedded systems and embedded software development?

RQ2   Are agile methods suitable for embedded systems and embedded software development?

RQ3   What kind of evidence is there to support these findings?

### 1.2.3   Summary of previous reviews

The first found review about agile methods in general was published by Abrahamsson et al. [9] in 2002, reviewing the existing agile methods and practices. Dybå and Dingsøur have written a review on the existing empirical studies in agile software development [3].

There have also been systematic literature reviews on agile methods in embedded systems development prior to this study [P1,P22] which are analyzed in more detail in Section 1.4.1. Albuquerque et al. [P1,P22] present a systematic literature review, which is similar to our survey, on agile methods in embedded systems development. In the review, the current state of agile methods is examined; the most often used agile method is found, and the challenges in adopting these methods in embedded systems

are discussed. The authors point out that the suitable agile methods for embedded systems development should be surveyed in more detail.

Even though the starting point of Albuquerque et al. [P1] is close to our survey, the results, to some extent, differ. Our approach is more hardware development oriented, and we have emphasized embedded hardware and integrated circuit development in our review. Albuquerque et al. have included a total of 23 articles from which 12 articles are also selected to this study. The difference in the found articles is due to slightly different viewpoints in the article selection process and in the inclusion and exclusion criteria. Albuquerque et al. emphasize agile methods, such as Scrum or XP, while our study concentrates on agile and lean methods putting more emphasis in the actual agile hardware development including integrated circuits.

The literature study by Shen et al. [P22] concentrates on studies about the usage of agile methods in embedded software development. The emphasis in the selected articles is in the application of agile principles. The survey includes 40 articles. Regardless of the slightly different approach, there are 12 same articles in these surveys where the difference is mostly due to different search strategies. The observation made by Albuquerque et al. is shared in that a more rigorous research is needed.

In our study, we did not limit the review to any particular agile method and we also included lean methods as an important part of the review. We also decided to include several search strings that emphasize hardware and not just embedded systems to make the search more comprehensive. The development of embedded hardware and integrated circuits is included because of their essential role in the development of embedded systems. This study also includes non-scientific forums which were found to be a relevant source of information on agile methods.

## 1.3  Research process

A systematic literature study is a systematic and repeatable approach to identify and study all relevant evidences, i.e. primary studies, on a specific research question or phenomenon [10]. The method consists of literature search, study selection, data extraction and synthesis. Systematic literature studies can be roughly divided in two categories [10]: systematic literature review (SLR) focuses on finding existing evidence on a specific question, while systematic mapping study (SMS) categorizes existing studies on the topic in order to show the gaps of knowledge.

In this paper, we performed a study that incorporates features on both SMS and SLR on the use of agile software development methodologies in the context of embedded software and embedded systems development. We decided to map the existing evidence and, thus, to identify gaps in current research in addition to synthesizing the found primary papers.

We use major publication databases and search engines available at our university. We started the search process by conducting several pilot searches using different search terms and search options and decided to concentrate on the terms 'agile' and 'lean' from the process method viewpoint and to the terms 'embedded software', 'embedded system', 'hardware' and 'integrated circuit' from the viewpoint of domain knowledge. Thus, we used the following search string: [agile AND ('embedded software' OR 'embedded system' OR 'embedded systems' OR hardware OR 'integrated circuit' OR 'integrated circuits')] OR [lean AND ('embedded software' OR 'embedded system' OR 'embedded systems' OR 'integrated circuit' OR 'integrated circuits')]. The search was performed using full text option, when it was available in the search engine. The searches were done in December 2012.

A study was selected if it was from the field of agile development of embedded systems, embedded software, electronics hardware or integrated circuits. We included expert opinions, lessons learned papers and articles presenting empirical results from students, professional software developers and academics. We did not include editorials, book reviews, or interviews. Papers documenting the same original work were considered as duplicates, and therefore, only one of them was included. Only articles written in English were included.

The article search was divided into three stages as shown in Figure 2. In the first stage, the search engines were divided between three authors and the studies were included based on the title of an article. An article was selected if the article was from the field of agile development of embedded systems, embedded software, electronics hardware or integrated circuits. From 20,430 hits, only 379 were selected (most of the duplicates removed) for the second stage.

In the second stage, the abstract of each selected paper was read by two authors. By using the same criteria as in the first stage, the two authors voted on each article to include it or not for the third stage. The authors agreed in about 80% of cases. In a case where one author suggested inclusion and the other did not, a third opinion was used to decide. After the second stage, 58 articles remained to be analysed in the third stage.

In the third stage, the articles were randomly distributed to three authors so that each article was skimmed through by at least two authors. In this stage, the papers were checked in detail in terms of the inclusion and exclusion criteria. In the end of the third stage, a total of 28 articles were selected for the final review where the articles were read carefully and data was extracted from them.

In the data extraction, the articles were categorized in terms of their content and type. The categories were pre-defined, and each article was classified by at least two authors. From the content, we divided the studies to be either embedded systems or embedded software related. In our analysis, a 'systems article' is defined to have some content on hardware or mechanical development, and a 'software article' is about embedded software development possibly with embedded systems-related constraints. In addition, articles were categorized being qualitative, quantitative or neither. Also, the used agile method from each article was mapped. The results from the first extraction phase are collected in Table 1.

After the categorization, the selected studies were read carefully and they were summarized. We used descriptive synthesis to analyse the findings. We identified three themes - method development, adoption of agile methods and experience reports - that recurred in different papers, and we classified the articles based on these categories.

## 1.4  Results

The 28 chosen articles were classified in terms of their content and type as described. The selected articles have been published quite recently. The first published paper was in 2003. The amount of published studies per year has remained fairly stable as shown in Figure 3.

The selected articles have several different approaches in studying agile methods. Some of them focus on previously known methodologies, such as Scrum or XP, while others concentrate on the agile practices and the original Agile Manifesto [4] without utilizing any certain methodology. There are also papers focusing on development of new agile methods. The distribution of different agile methods appearing in the selected papers is illustrated in Figure 4. The figure shows that XP is the most frequently mentioned method. From the more detailed information,

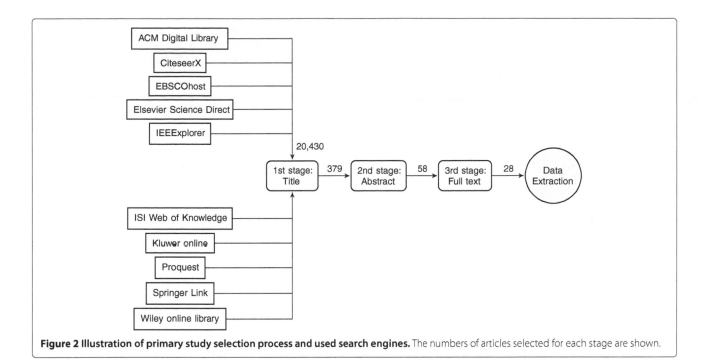

**Figure 2 Illustration of primary study selection process and used search engines.** The numbers of articles selected for each stage are shown.

presented in Table 1, one can notice that in many studies, XP and Scrum methodologies are used together. The *Applied agile* category includes studies where the used method is unique and typically based or modified from previously known methods such as Scrum or XP. The category *other* includes methodologies such as test-driven development (TDD) and agile manufacturing. All of the different methods appearing in the other category are named in Table 1. The final method category is for studies which include *multiple* agile methods. These articles are typically reviews which survey the previous works on the field.

From the selected articles, 18 included a case study or an experiment report. Project-specific characteristics are presented in Table 2. The projects and teams were quite often small, but the specific team size was left unmentioned in half of them. Few of the articles concentrated on large organization-related challenges. Quite many projects had changing requirements, which had led to selection of agile methods. Project areas were quite wide in embedded system and software development, e.g. satellites, telecommunication and processor firmwares. In the majority of the articles, the success of a project was based on the impression of the authors. In six cases, there were also some measurements based on which success was defined: effective code lines per hour [P3,P26], defect rates monitored [P26,P27], time used [P2,P26], failures in field and upload success rate [P13], performance measurements compared to previous similar products [P20] or test coverage [P3]. One case [P3] used a survey to get insight about how people felt.

### 1.4.1 Review articles

Among the selected articles, there are three studies which are considered as surveys. These articles include two systematic literature reviews [P1,P22], and they were briefly presented in Section 1.2.3. Albuquerque et al. [P1] present a systematic literature review on the agile methods in embedded systems development. The authors in [P1] have found out that agile methods have had a positive impact on embedded systems development while their use is still not widespread. They present potential research lines which should be investigated in more detail. Research should be conducted on suitability of different agile methods to the development of embedded systems and how these methods affect the product quality as well as to the development cost and effort. They also point out a need for investigation on how to adopt agile methods when safety intensive requirements have to be taken into account. Albuquerque et al. have made a conclusion that the suitable methods for embedded systems development should be surveyed in more detail.

The other extensive SLR among the selected studies is authored by Shen et al. [P22]. It surveys the studies on agile methods of embedded software development. The selected articles are surveyed especially in terms of the application of the agile principles. Shen et al. share the observation of Albuquerque et al. that more rigorous research of the field is needed. They have noted that XP and Scrum are the two most used agile methods in the field of embedded software and see that the characteristics of embedded software development bring new challenges into applying these methods. The authors see that the

**Table 1 Article content**

| Number | Embedded | | Analysis | | Agile Method | | | | Number |
|---|---|---|---|---|---|---|---|---|---|
| | Software | Systems | Qualitative | Quantitative | Scrum | XP | Applied | Other | |
| P1 | | x | x | x | | | | | P1 |
| P2 | x | | x | | x | x | | Plaform-based design | P2 |
| P3 | x | | x | x | | x | | | P3 |
| P4 | x | | x | | | x | | TDD | P4 |
| P5 | x | | x | | x | x | | | P5 |
| P6 | x | | x | | | x | | | P6 |
| P7 | x | | x | | x | | | | P7 |
| P8 | | x | x | | | | x | | P8 |
| P9 | x | | x | | | | | Agile manufacturing | P9 |
| P10 | x | | x | | | | | | P10 |
| P11 | x | | x | | | | | | P11 |
| P12 | x | | | | | | | DDD | P12 |
| P13 | x | | x | x | | | x | | P13 |
| P14 | x | | x | | | x | | | P14 |
| P15 | | x | x | | | x | x | | P15 |
| P16 | x | | x | | | | x | | P16 |
| P17 | x | | x | x | x | x | | | P17 |
| P18 | x | | x | | | | x | | P18 |
| P19 | x | | x | | x | x | | | P19 |
| P20 | | x | x | | | | | HW/SW co-design | P20 |
| P21 | | x | x | | x | | | | P21 |
| P22 | x | | | x | | | | | P22 |
| P23 | x | x | x | | | | | TDD | P23 |
| P24 | x | | | | | x | | TDD | P24 |
| P25 | | x | x | | | | x | | P25 |
| P26 | x | | x | | | x | | | P26 |
| P27 | | x | x | | | x | | | P27 |
| P28 | | x | x | | | | x | | P28 |
| Total | 20 | 9 | 25 | 5 | 6 | 11 | 7 | | |

DDD, document-driven development; TDD, test-driven development.

investigation should be extended to a wider scope outside the well-known XP and Scrum methods. They also conclude that active collaboration with embedded industry is essential in the research of agile methods for embedded software development.

While surveying the used agile methods for embedded systems development, Srinivasan et al. [P25] have noted that there are both technical and organizational issues in adoption of the agile practices. They noticed that the main gap in the literature is the absence of reports on failures in the agile adoption in embedded systems development. Based on the published literature, the authors made recommendations on how the focal principles, such as test-driven development or requirements

management, should be utilized to evade the issues. They, for instance, recommend to tailor the agile practices into larger organizational context and harmonize the requirement management to support modifiability, maintainability and dependability. They conclude that adoption of agile methods needs organizational support. Willingness for organizational culture change is required especially because of the soft factors present in the agile practices.

### 1.4.2 Method development
The selected articles include three studies that propose a new development method for embedded software [P2,P24] and systems development [P12]. Smith et al. [P24] propose a method that emphasizes test-driven

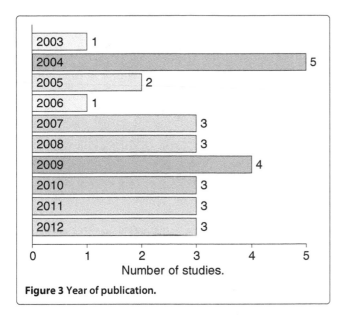

**Figure 3** Year of publication.

approach that could be considered most suitable for embedded software development. Cordeiro and Barreto [P2], in turn, propose a platform-based design method where a platform consisting of frequently used functionality can easily be extended and modified for different projects. The method proposed in [P12] might be better suited for embedded systems design as it is based on an appropriate documentation system that simplifies information sharing between stakeholders. Four other studies can be considered as method development, which do not propose a new method, but rather extensions to existing ones. In [P11], various pragmatic suggestions are proposed on how large-scale organizations can better utilize agile methods. Articles [P9] and [P10] compare agile methods to other methods, and in [P28], agile methods are introduced into requirements engineering, and it is tested by a case study.

Smith et al. [P24] propose a development process where the authors try to find the most suitable practices from test-oriented processes that can be adapted to the embedded software development. The proposed

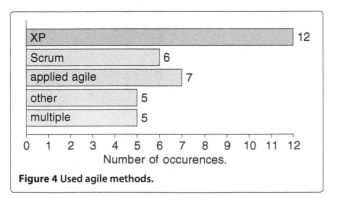

**Figure 4** Used agile methods.

development method, to some extent, lies on the findings of an experience report by Smith et al. [P23] where undergraduate students experimented with test-driven development in embedded domain. The core of this new embedded test-driven development approach is a subset of practices from XP. The practices that were modified to the embedded domain include test-driven development, refactoring, simple design, pair programming and continuous integration. To implement test-driven development in the embedded domain successfully, some changes are required to the practices. For example, refactoring should be interpreted as making improvements in speed and in lower power consumption even if this might reduce the portability, clarity and modularity. The proposed method addresses the issue of different life cycles in embedded products compared with conventional software applications and proposes how this difference could be addressed in product development.

In [P28], Waldmann points out that in agile, requirements engineering process should be transparent to all stakeholders. In the presented case study, agile practices had been applied in requirements engineering of a new generation of platform components (generic components that can be used over different products) for hearing solutions. It was found that the same product should be customizable to answer the needs of different customers instead of developing different products for all the different customers. A similar view is found in [P2] where Cordeiro and Barreto propose a platform-based design development method where a microprocessor-based architecture can be rapidly extended, customized for a range of applications and quickly delivered to customers. Most of the used practices in the proposed method are adopted from XP and Scrum methods. Cordeiro and Barreto also briefly discuss the results of the proposed method, applying it in three small projects with one to four developers in a project with two to three sprints. It is argued that the proposed method showed a reduction of development time in the case studies, but it is acknowledged that development methods are difficult to compare.

In [P12], Luqi et al. introduce a new document-driven development (DDD) method. They point out the importance of documentation especially in complex real-time systems and emphasize the use of appropriate documentation. The core of the proposed method is in the document repository where all information concerning the development is stored. Information can be represented in different forms, depending on who needs the information and thus providing the means of communication between stakeholders, e.g. managers, developers, sponsors, maintainers and end-users. The aim is also to use the DDD to integrate all used methods and tools into this new system,

**Table 2 Case studies and experiment reports**

| Number | Method(practices) | Team size | Success | Discipline | Project characteristics |
|---|---|---|---|---|---|
| P2 | A new platform-based design method based on XP, Scrum and agile patterns (e.g. Sprint and Product backlogs) | 1-4 | The development platform reduced substantially development time of the product | Three embedded system projects: pulse oximeter, digital soft-starter and the induction motor simulator equipments | Team uses pre-designed and pre-characterized components instead of full custom design methods |
| P3 | XP (The planning game, short development cycles, pair programming, test first programming, collective code ownership, frequent integration, never solving a problem that has not occurred, refactoring, minimal documentation) | Total 29 people in 4 teams | XP can be used to develop complex mission-critical systems after the team starts to work | Software development of mission-critical two-way radio systems projects | There were four about 18-month projects, where requirements change |
| P4 | XP practices (unit test first with mock objects, automate building software and testing, write code in testable fashion) | N/A | Agile techniques can be used also in embedded development | Software for control boards of automated guided vehicles | The team had used agile in web and desktop applications previously |
| P5 | Selected practices from Scrum (Sprint, Sprint planning meeting, Daily scrum, Sprint review/ Retrospective) and XP (simple design, unit testing, refactoring, pair programming, collective code ownership, continuous integration, on-site customer, sustainable pace, coding standards) | 7 | Experiences are mostly positive, but full adoption is seen a slow process | Firmware for processors | The team members have specialized domain knowledge, the requirements change and hardware dependencies force change. Team is also distributed |
| P6 | XP (planning, small releases, metaphor, simplicity, test, refactoring, pair programming, common code ownership, continuous integration, 45-h week, on-site customer, coding standards) | N/A | In small teams, development cycles were shorter, but in the whole project, the results were not satisfactory | Telecommunication software development | The specifications and requirements are fuzzy in the beginning of project and change during the project |
| P7 | A new piloting method when introducing Scrum to the company | 20 and 15 | Team can be Agile, even though the company is not and piloting can reduce resistance to change | Software and hardware solutions for the wireless and automotive industries. | A large, distributed company |
| P8 | Agile manifesto-based method (individuals and interactions, emphasis on working system, collaborative interface with sponsor, responding to change) | N/A | Project was successfully finished within short schedule and limited time | Design and development of two small satellites | The project has high level requirements of uncertainty, cost and schedule |
| P12 | Document-driven development (DDD) | N/A | Improvement was seen in more effective design procedure and improved communication between all stakeholders | Software for a system to administer therapeutic intravenous fluids | The deployment is for long periods of time and used globally. There are mission-critical requirements; frequent changes and components are developed in different organizations with variety of stakeholders |

**Table 2 Case studies and experiment reports** (*Continued*)

| ID | Agile method/practices | Findings | Team size | Application domain | Context |
|---|---|---|---|---|---|
| P13 | Agile practices (unit test, test first) | Agile elements are serious options for development of embedded software | N/A | Embedded software for busses and coaches | High degree of customer-specific functionality to be implemented, e.g. within days |
| P15 | XP and Agile (user stories, start simple, user involvement, refactor) | Project was viewed successful both internally and externally | N/A | A system for scheduling satellite tracking stations | The developed system is large, and the organization complex. The development team is inexperienced, and there have been previous failures in the project using waterfall |
| P18 | Agile in general (e.g. Boehm's spiral model, common room, pair programming) | Successfully created first software versions in schedule despite some requirement changes | 4 | A control software for satellite camera equipment | The requirements change, and the schedule is tight. Engineers share time with hardware development |
| P19 | Scrum and XP (e.g. user stories) | In large organizations, agile development requires very skilled developers and has to be a combination of old and new practices | N/A | Telecommunication | There are challenges in work allocation between teams in large organizations when using agile. Requirements engineering is also used in this project |
| P20 | HW-SW codesign (hardware simulation and code analysis tools) | Higher performance was seen relative to conventional HPC design | N/A | A high performance computing system | There are power and performance challenges |
| P21 | Scrum (sprints, daily stand-ups, sprint backlogs, sprint review and sprint retrospective and customer involvement) | Agility was applied only to software team, and to fully benefit from it, it should be broadened and deepened | 15 people in 4 teams | Advanced communication system project | The original waterfall project suffered from frequent requirement changes, lack of communication and expensive overheads |
| P23 | TDD-based tool and method | Current unit testing tools can be adapted to embedded environment | N/A | Experience on a tool in digital signal processing applications | Experience on embedded test-driven development tool usage in university laboratory course with undergraduate students |
| P26 | XP (e.g. collective code ownership, unit tests, always enabled tracing system) | Unexperienced team's productivity cannot be distinguished from best teams in industry, when the team uses Agile practices | 4-6 | Software for a grain monitor | The software developer team is unexperienced and small |
| P27 | XP testing techniques (always on trouble log, dual-targeting, unit tests, domain level tests) | Amazingly low bug rate and it was easy to distinguish whether the problem is in software or hardware | About 5 | Software for a mobile spectrometer | A new product is developed from a scratch with changing hardware |
| P28 | Agile requirements engineering | Flexible requirements engineering provides business value, even with severe resource constraints | Over 100 in the project | Hearing solutions based on platforms | The new platform project is large with inherited functionality and professional requirements engineers included for the first time |

but how this could be achieved remains an open question for the researchers.

Articles [P9] and [P10] compare agile to other methods. In [P9], Kettunen compares agile manufacturing and agile software development models and also finds out new manufacturing concepts that could potentially be adopted in software production. An example case of network element products also proves the similarities between these two methods. In [P10], Kettunen and Laanti compare eight different software process models from which three are agile methods, namely feature-driven development, adaptive software development and XP. The analysis results can be used for selection of a suitable model based on the anticipated project problems. The validation of the results is done through four examples based on certain past real-life projects. Kettunen and Laanti [P11] also have various pragmatic suggestions on how agile methods could be used in large-scale embedded software products based on industrial experience. It is noted that in a large-scale new product development organization, it is important to have a comprehensive view of the whole organization. One simple suggestion on creating a more efficient work-flow is to co-locate related hardware and software developers. It is pointed out that in a large company to work in an agile manner, it is not enough to concentrate only on teams and projects, as is usually done in agile methods. Furthermore, a company should understand what are the goals it tries to achieve with agile methods and, hence, what kind of methods or practices are needed. The answer is company dependent, and not all companies should adopt the same ways.

### 1.4.3 Adoption of agile development methods

Only four studies [P4,P5,P13,P14] have addressed the introduction of agile development methods in the embedded domain. However, all of them are expert reports from different projects in the industry; [P4,P5,P13] reported a case while [P14] compared experiences from previous projects to the XP's practices. All these studies focused mainly on the embedded software development. None of the articles included into this review addressed the question of introducing agile methods in embedded systems development.

The adoption of agile methods in a new domain has raised arguments. On one hand, Matthews [P14] argues that the XP's practices are not agile nor software development specific; instead, they are the baseline for every practical working method. Matthews acknowledged that agile methods will be adopted in the embedded world in the near future; however, he demands consideration on which practices should be adopted. Also, [P5,P13] noted that an agile method should not be followed dogmatically in the new domain. On the other hand, Fletcher et al. [P4] remark that there was nothing which would have

prevented them from using the same methods that were used in the conventional software development.

Only a few disadvantages were reported. In [P4], the authors raise the lack of support of the software tools to utilize agile practices as one of the challenges. Mannhart and Schneider [P13] and Greene [P5] argued that the importance of domain knowledge in the embedded software development hinders the use of the principle of shared responsibilities.

Drivers for agile adoption varied: Constant changes required by the hardware team were mentioned as one of the main reasons in [P5]. In [P13], the main focus was to clarify the process on adding specialized functionalities and individualizations asked by the customers to the buses with embedded software. In [P4], the team decided to use the same methods that they had been using previously. All studies judged that adoptions were successful - although one engineer left the team arguing that they 'were not acting enough as a team' in the case of [P5].

Similarly, the ways of introducing agile differed. In the case of [P5], no formal education was reported before the adoption of Scrum and XP - the members of the team read through a book of XP beforehand. In [P4], a team that had a long experience on XP, in other domains, was hired to work with embedded software. However, their report focuses on introducing test-first practices to the embedded domain. In [P13], the agile methods were introduced to the process step by step: in the first phase, they presented only test-first and unit-testing practices to embedded software teams. They used also Goal-Question-Metrics approach (see e.g. [11]) to foster the adoption; however, no results were reported as the project was still ongoing.

### 1.4.4 Experience reports and case studies

Experience reports and case studies discuss either techniques used for improving quality and predictability early in the development process, or reasons and practices behind successful adoption of agile methods in embedded systems development.

In [P27], Van Schooenderwoert and Morsicato introduce how using domain-level simulations helped in isolating bugs easier while developing a mobile spectrometer, whereas in [P20], Shalf et al. present how performance and power consumption of a high-performance computation application could be estimated by simulating the system model in different abstraction levels. In both articles, it is also described how a simulation environment was developed to enable and support these approaches.

A few articles mentioned the importance of adaptation of agile. For example, when applying XP into telecommunication software development [P6] and mission-critical two-way radio systems [P3] development, some sort of top-level documentation is needed which is not pointed out in XP practices [P3,P6]. In [P6], Gul et al. also noted that applying XP in small teams resulted in shorter development cycles, but applying XP to the whole project did not give satisfactory results. In [P3], Drobka et al. suggest using strong outsider coach, training, periodic audits and code spot-checks.

Also, articles [P8,P15,P21] emphasize the importance of process tailoring to get the best out of agile practices in embedded systems development. In their experience report [P8], Huang et al. describe how the organisational structure and process for developing high technology satellites could be modified according to the agile principles to meet cost and schedule requirements. As Morgan [P15] points out, the process tailoring can also mean that the development team itself can operate in an agile manner, whereas it has to adapt working with non-agile teams. In a government-funded development project of a system for scheduling satellite tracking stations, the team had to create some design artefacts that were used only externally. Shatil et al. [P21] bring forth several topics that were considered important during the agile adoption process. Involving management in early stage of the adoption process enabled multidisciplinary teams to be familiarized with the software team's process and help other teams to be more synchronized with the software team. The project management also started to manage the project by taking into account the software team's iterations. As a means of getting members of the development team committed to the adoption process, it described how their feedback was used to find main concerns and solving these. Finally, agile practices taken in to use were tailored to find the best fit for the development environment.

Instead of adapting some specific agile method, [P18] and [P26] used some agile practices in development. In [P18], dos Santos Jr. et al. describe the usage of an iterative model with agile characteristics in a small team that developed a control software for a satellite camera equipment. Creation of useful and reliable software rapidly was achieved by reacting to changes, using pair programming especially in complex routines, strong communication and allowing developers to make most technical decisions.

In [P26], Van Schooenderwoert describes a novice development team challenging an experienced team where the performance of the teams was measured by several industry standards. The agile practices behind the success were collective code ownership and strong unit tests. The lack of experience of some team members was overcome by agile software development techniques and the presence of senior level developers that allowed knowledge transfer between teams.

Studies presented in [P7] and [P19] focus on agile methods in large organizations. In [P7], Heidenberg et al. suggest that piloting is a good way to overcome resistance to change and to convince management that a team can be agile even though the rest of the company is not. A three-step piloting method (marketing the pilot, preparing the pilot and executing the pilot) is introduced and validated as a case study in two pilots within the same company. In [P19], Savolainen et al. describe challenges of large organizations in embedded systems when transitioning into using agile process models. Using user stories may present a problem in large embedded systems, since user interaction might be far from the implemented framework. Use of Scrum with key requirements engineering practices is seen a good way to introduce agile methods to embedded systems. Savolainen et al. also conclude that it is a good idea to preserve some of the key practices instead of starting from scratch when introducing agile methods.

In [P16], Ronkainen and Abrahamsson analyse prospects of using agile methods in embedded software development under hardware constraints based on observations in signal processing application development. They point out that agile methods are not targeted for developing embedded software and that new methods for embedded software development need to solve many challenges: real-time constraints of the hardware, need to experiment the software on hardware and need for documentation so that all stakeholders stay informed and that the development is inherently test-driven with hardware-related constraints. The authors conclude that agile methods might offer solutions for embedded software development, but the methods need to concentrate on the embedded domain-specific requirements.

Salo et al. [P17] have arranged a questionnaire of the actual use and usefulness of XP and Scrum in organizations developing embedded software. The survey involved 35 individual software development projects and focused on observing the level of use as well as the experienced or expected usefulness of the agile methods. The questionnaire concentrated to XP and Scrum and the separate practices involved in these two methods. Authors have asked which methods have been utilized, if any. They also asked how frequently the separate practices of Scrum and XP were utilized and have they been found useful. The results show that at least two thirds of the respondents have utilized one or both of the methods. From these two methods, XP was used more in the investigated companies. Those familiar with the methods have found them mostly useful. However, the authors point out that no broad generalizations can be made from the results.

### 1.5 Non-academic material

In order to review non-academic material available, a Google search was conducted on January 16, 2013 using the same search terms as for the literature review. Since it was assumed that plural forms of search terms should be automatically included by the Google search engine, they were excluded from the search. This resulted in seven distinct search strings with 50 first results from each taken for further analysis. Following the procedure used in the literature review, search results were then split between two authors and non-relevant search results having little or no content discussing agile or lean were excluded. In the next step, two authors read through all 48 search results that passed the previous step and voted for inclusion or exclusion of each with a third opinion used when two authors did not agree. After this step, 21 search results were left for deeper analysis. Search results were excluded if there was no agile or lean content, they were already covered by the SLR, or they were duplicates pointing to a same web page. It is notable that searches done using search term 'lean' resulted only in three results passing through all phases. Even though the 14 of the selected search results were from the recent 3 years (2010, 2011, 2012), also some older ones were found starting from 2004. We have included the most relevant sources concerning our study in the references.

The results can be categorized into two groups by the author type: one group was those whose work was included in the literature review (e.g. Michael Karlesky, Pekka Abrahamsson, Petri Kettunen and Nancy Van Schooenderwoert), while the other group consists of people contributing to agile embedded HW/SW development mainly by maintaining blogs, writing articles to electronic newsletters, providing training and/or consulting and giving speeches in agile conferences (e.g. Zubin Irani, Neil Johnson and Timo Punkka).

Instead of bringing new and revolutionary ideas, search results had generally a practical approach in applying agile practices into embedded systems design. A couple of the search results provided information about where to find more information about agile in embedded software development, or whom to ask for more information [12,13]. Some considered the characteristics of embedded systems that should be taken into account when adopting agility, and others gave practical advice on useful agile practices in embedded systems design [14]. Applying agile methods to hardware development was also discussed in several sites [15-18].

It is also noted that even though hardware developers should look for the common practices in the software development domain when adopting agile practices, the characteristics of hardware development should be taken into account and practices adapted according to those [17,19-21]. For example, delivering a working prototype in the end of each iteration is not possible. The key for hardware developers is to resist getting caught up with the differences between software and hardware and to instead focus on the similarities [17,18].

Common themes found involve use of test-driven development, continuous integration, dual targeting, iterative development and customer collaboration [16,17,22,23].

Dual targeting answers to the lack of prototypes in the end of every iteration, but it also brings carefully thought design to the software-hardware interface [17,21]. Continuous integration including automatic testing will help to identify failures in the early stage [16,17,23]. There are several ways to improve customer collaboration, e.g. user stories can be used, but the term user can also refer to nearer customers, not necessarily to the end user [21].

## 1.6  Discussion

In this paper, we studied what is currently known about using agile methods in the development of embedded systems and embedded software (RQ1). The results showed that the research is rather scattered and mainly driven by industry reports. It was found that there is no one method for the diverse world of embedded systems development, but many emphasize different viewpoints. There were multiple new development methods proposed that would better suit the needs and constraints of the embedded domain in addition to ideas on how to scale agile methods in large organizations and in ways agile methods have been adapted to suit various needs of different companies.

Our second research question was whether the agile methods are suitable for the development of embedded systems and embedded software. For example, Ronkainen and Abrahamsson [P16] lay out requirements for agile methods that need to be addressed when used in embedded product development. The characteristics of embedded product substantially differ from what agile was originally targeted for. Meeting real-time requirements of embedded systems is pointed out to be the most important difference that new agile methods should be able to support. In embedded systems, the role of architecture and up-front designing cannot be avoided. This requirement also leads to a need to find techniques that take into account the suitable amount of documentation and specification. Furthermore, it is pointed out by Ronkainen and Abrahamsson that top level documentation is important due to many different stakeholders involved in the project, and for this problem, it is pointed out that coordination and communication methods are required. The view that system-level documentation is required in embedded product development is also supported by [P3,P6,P12]. In [P12], a document-driven development approach is proposed where the importance of documentation is believed to be prominent especially in complex real-time systems. The main idea is in a coherent and appropriate documentation system that can be used to effectively share information between project stakeholders through a document repository.

Ronkainen and Abrahamsson [P16] also observe that experimenting cannot be avoided as the hardware constraints affect the code in an unpredictable way and that the amount of the embedded software generated with experimenting is significant. In addition, it is pointed out that as the development progresses and more teams are getting involved (as the product gets more and more integrated), the embedded software has to become more rigid as all the changes made in the later stages of development ripple further and further to other teams and developers. This requires changing practices during the project, which is not supported at the moment. This discussion was on constrained embedded software development, but in this study, we also looked for ways to develop embedded products including hardware. This idea is suited well to the embedded product development where later stage changes have a huge impact on the project. One of the ways in reducing the impact is proposed by Punkka [24] where SW and HW co-design is emphasized. The point is in starting early with what you can and using, e.g., bread boards and evaluation boards and rapidly build a demo or a prototype of the product by experimenting. This should help the problem with later stage changes as the development needs to become more rigid only after demo and prototype rounds. At this point, most of the uncertainty and the whole product-related changes should have been done, and required changes would not ripple down too far.

Ronkainen and Abrahamsson also discuss the problems in test-driven approach. Testing is the cornerstone of embedded systems as most of the generated code needs to be tested against hardware and the code can be hardware dependent. It is pointed out that test-driven approach is problematic because the test environment is different in the embedded domain, e.g. it has more severe memory and performance constraints. A need for an appropriate test suite is pointed out, a view shared in [P4]. Work from [P23,P24] advances test-driven approach where the most suitable testing practices from XP are adapted into the embedded systems development. Smith et al. [P24] also point out that practices should take into account the constraints of embedded systems, e.g. refactoring should emphasize making improvements in speed and in lowering the power consumption rather than making the code modular or readable.

Another view was in an experience report from Waldmann [P28]. It was found that with many different customers requiring slight modifications to a product, the product should be customizable instead of developing a whole new product for all the different customers. A similar problem is addressed in [P2] where Cordeiro and Barreto discuss a customizable platform-based design method. The platform contains a customizable processor that can be modified and extended on different products (a platform is not suitable to be used in [P28], but the same need is observed in both). This method can be used when a similar product is modified slightly to different customers or with completely new products that share the same basic functionality. The key is to determine the functionality that is shared over projects.

We also studied what kind of evidences there are to support the suitability of using agile methods in embedded software or embedded systems development (RQ3). The results showed that most of the studied academic and non-academic articles were experience reports from the industry and expert opinions. We did not find any rigorous controlled experiments. Therefore, it seems that the evidences in the suitability of agile methods and pros and cons of the methods need more research.

Some articles discuss about new product development in large-scale organizations, where embedded systems development requires hardware and mechanics in addition to software. Kettunen and Laanti [P11] suggest that a large company should understand what it tries to achieve with agile methods, instead of focusing only on team and project level. One way to introduce agile methods to a large company is piloting in several teams [P7]. A good idea is to preserve some of the key practices, like requirements engineering practices, instead of starting from a scratch.

There were many experience reports which stated that agile methods could be used in the embedded domain. In most of these cases, the chosen agile method was adjusted to fit the business model by choosing agile practices that could be implemented easily and would support the development work. It seems that practices that were felt to bring the best return on investment to the development process were implemented first. Depending on the case, these prioritized practices vary a lot due to the different nature of the business cases and, possibly, due to different customer interface, technical maturity, or adopted working methods and competences of development teams. Generally, there were no opposing views that agile methods could not be used in the embedded domain. However, evidence about the suitability is mostly based on opinions and uncontrolled case studies with inadequate description of research methods that strict conclusion could be made. There was only one questionnaire on the usefulness of XP and Scrum in embedded development. It was found that to some extent agile practices were used by at least two thirds of the respondents and that those who were familiar with them found them useful. It is also noteworthy to point out that failures or bad experiences from adopting agile were not reported in any of the studies. All studies state that agile methods could be beneficial in embedded domain and that most experience reports are in favour of agile methods.

Our survey included not only the development of embedded software, but also embedded hardware and integrated circuits development, and we found out that very little has been done from the hardware development point of view. However, in the study concerning non-academic papers, more discussions about agile methods for hardware development were found than in peer-reviewed academic articles. The studies close to hardware development typically concentrate on more abstract issues such as communication or requirement management. Therefore, there is a need for more rigorous research on utilization of agile methods in the actual development work of hardware and integrated circuit designers.

## 2  Conclusions

It was found that there are embedded domain-specific problems about agile methods that need to be solved before agile methods can be successfully applied to the embedded domain. To some extent, there are studies that address these issues, but the amount of evidence still remains scarce. Most of the studies address the issues of embedded software development. Some studies concerning embedded systems development were also found, but the amount of hardware-related agile studies remains low. Some discussions, however, were found among the non-academic articles concerning agile methods in embedded systems and hardware development.

Most of the found experience reports and case studies find no reason why agile methods could not - at least to some extent - be used for the embedded domain, but the lack of rigorous empirical research is a clear gap on the evidence of the actual benefits of agile methods in the embedded domain.

### Selected academic articles

P1.  C.O. Albuquerque, P.O. Antonino and E.Y. Nakagawa. An Investigation into Agile Methods in Embedded Systems Development. *Computational Science and Its Applications — ICCSA 2012*, Salvador de Bahia, Brazil, pages 576–591, June 2012.

P2.  L. Cordeiro, R. Barreto and M. Oliveira. Towards a Semiformal Development Methodology for Embed ded Systems. *International Conference on Evaluation of Novel Approaches to Software Engineering*, Funchal, Madeira, Portugal, pages 5–12, May 2008.

P3.  J. Drobka, D. Noftz and R. Raghu. Piloting XP on Four Mission-Critical Projects. *IEEE Software*, 23(6), pages 70–75, November–December 2004.

P4.  M. Fletcher, W. Bereza, M. Karlesky and G. Williams. Evolving into Embedded Development. *Agile Conference*, Washington, DC, USA, pages 150–155, August 2007.

P5.  B. Greene. Agile Methods Applied to Embedded Firmware Development. *Agile Development Conference*, Salt Lake City, Utah, USA, pages 71–77, June 2004.

P6.  E. Gul, T. Sekerci, A.C. Yücetürk and Ü. Yildirim. Using XP in Telecommunication Software

Development. *The Third International Conference on Software Engineering Advances*, Sliema, Malta, pages 258–263, October 2008.

P7.  J. Heidenberg, M. Matinlassi, M. Pikkarainen, P. Hirkman and J. Partanen. Systematic Piloting of Agile Methods in the Large: Two Cases in Embedded Systems Development. *11th international conference on Product-Focused Software Process Improvement*, Limerick, Ireland, pages 47–61, 2010.

P8.  P.M. Huang, A.G. Darrin and A.A. Knuth. Agile Hardware and Software System Engineering for Innovation. *IEEE Aerospace Conference*, Montana, USA, March 2012.

P9.  P. Kettunen. Adopting key lessons from agile manufacturing to agile software product development – A comparative study. *Technovation*, 29(6–7), pages 408–422, July 2009.

P10. P. Kettunen and M. Laanti. How to Steer an Embedded Software Project: Tactics for Selecting the Software Process Model. *Information and Software Technology*, 47(9), pages 587–608, June 2005.

P11. P. Kettunen and M. Laanti. Combining Agile Software Projects and Large-scale Organizational Agility. *Software Process Improvement and Practice*, 13(2), pages 183–193, July 2007.

P12. Luqi, L. Zhang, V. Berzins and Y. Qiao. Documentation Driven Development for Complex Real-Time Systems. *IEEE Transactions on Software Engineering*, 30(12), pages 936–952, December 2004.

P13. P. Manhart and K. Schneider. Breaking the Ice for Agile Development of Embedded Software: an Industry Experience Report. *26th International Conference on Software Engineering*, Edinburgh, Scotland, pages 378–386, May 2004.

P14. C.E. Matthews. Agile Practices in Embedded Systems. *SPLASH'11 Workshops*, New York, USA, pages 249–250, October 2011.

P15. D. Morgan. Covert Agile: Development at the Speed of Government? *Agile Conference*, pages 79–83, Chicago, USA, August 2009.

P16. J. Ronkainen and P. Abrahamsson. Software Development Under Stringent Hardware Constraints: Do Agile Methods Have a Chance? *4th International Conference on Extreme Programming and Agile Processes in Software Engineering*, Genova, Italy, pages 73–79, May 2003.

P17. O. Salo, P. Abrahamsson. Agile Methods in European Embedded Software Development Organisations: a Survey on the Actual Use and Usefulness of Extreme Programming and Scrum. *IET Software*, 2(1), pages 58–64, February 2008.

P18. D. dos Santos Jr., I.N. da Silva, R. Modugno, H. Pazelli and A. Castellar. Software Development Using an Agile Approach for Satellite Camera Ground

Support Equipment. *Advances and Innovations in Systems, Computing Sciences and Software Engineering*, pages 71–76, 2007.

P19. J. Savolainen, J. Kuusela and A. Vilavaara. Transition to Agile Development – Rediscovery of Important Requirements Engineering Practices. *18th IEEE International Requirements Engineering Conference*, Sydney, Australia, pages 289–294, September–October 2010.

P20. J. Shalf, D. Quinlan and C. Janssen. Rethinking Hardware-Software Codesign for Exascale Systems. *IEEE Computer*, 44(11), pages 22–30, November 2011.

P21. A. Shatil, O. Hazzan and Y. Dubinsky. Agility in a Large-Scale System Engineering Project: A Case-Study of an Advanced Communication System Project. *IEEE International Conference on Software Science, Technology and Engineering*, Herzlia, Israel, pages 47–54, June 2010.

P22. M. Shen, W. Yang, G. Rong and D. Shao. Applying Agile Methods to Embedded Software Development: A Systematic Review. *2nd International Workshop on Software Engineering for Embedded Systems*, Zurich, Switzerland, pages 30–36, June 2012.

P23. M. Smith, A. Kwan, A. Martin and J. Miller. E-TDD – Embedded Test Driven Development a Tool for Hardware-software Co-design Projects. *6th International Conference on Extreme Programming and Agile Processes in Software Engineering*, Sheffield, UK, pages 145–153, June 2005.

P24. M. Smith, J. Miller and S. Daeninck. A Test-oriented Embedded System Production Methodology. *Journal of Signal Processing Systems*, 56(1), pages 69–89, July 2009.

P25. J. Srinivasan, R. Dobrin and K. Lundqvist. 'State of the Art' in Using Agile Methods for Embedded Systems Development. *33rd Annual IEEE International Computer Software and Applications Conference*, Seattle, Washington, USA, pages 522–527, July 2009.

P26. N. Van Schooenderwoert. Embedded Agile Project by the Numbers with Newbies. *Agile Conference*, Minneapolis, Minnesota, USA, July 2006.

P27. N. Van Schooenderwoert and R. Morsicato. Taming the Embedded Tiger – Agile Test Techniques for Embedded Software. *Agile Development Conference*, Salt Lake City, Utah, USA, pages 120–126, June 2004.

P28. B. Waldmann. There's Never Enough Time – Doing Requirements Under Resource Constraints, and What Requirements Engineering Can Learn from Agile Development. *19th IEEE International Requirements Engineering Conference*, Trento, Italy, pages 301–305, August–September 2011.

**Competing interests**
The authors declare that they have no competing interests.

**Acknowledgements**
The research reported in this article has been conducted as a part of AgiES (Agile and Lean Product Development Methods for Embedded ICT Systems) project. The project is carried out in collaboration with Finnish Institute of Occupational Health and industry partners BA Group, FiSMA, Lindorff Finland, LM Ericsson, Neoxen Systems, Nextfour Group and Nordic ID. The project is mainly funded by Tekes - the Finnish Funding Agency for Technology and Innovation.

**Author details**
[1] Business and Innovation Development (BID), University of Turku, Turku 20520, Finland. [2] Oy LM Ericsson Ab, Jorvas 02420, Finland. [3] Turku School of Economics, Department of Management and Entrepreneurship, University of Turku, Turku 20014, Finland.

**References**
1. W Royce, Managing the development of large software systems: concepts and techniques, in *Proceedings of the IEEE WESTCON*, (Los Angeles, USA, August 1970)
2. C Larman, *Agile & Iterative Development: A Manager's Guide* (Addison-Wesley, Boston, 2003)
3. T Dybå, T Dingsøyr, Empirical studies of agile software development: a systematic review. Inf. Softw. Technol. **50**(9–10), 833–859 (2008)
4. Agile Manifesto. http://www.agilemanifesto.org
5. K Beck, *Extreme Programming Explained: Embrace Change* (Addison Wesley Professional, Boston, 1999)
6. K Schwaber, SCRUM development process, in *Proceedings of the 10th Annual ACM Conference on Object Oriented Programming Systems, Languages, and Applications (OOPSLA)*, (Austin, Texas, USA, October 1995), pp. 117–134
7. DJ Anderson, *Kanban: Successful Evolutionary Change for Your Technology Business* (Blue Hole Press, Washington, 2010)
8. J Warsta, P Abrahamsson, Is open source software development essentially and agile method?, in *3rd Workshop on Open Source Software Engineering*, (Portland, Oregon, USA, May 2003)
9. P Abrahamsson, O Salo, J Ronkainen, J Warsta, Agile software development methods: review and analysis. VTT Technical Report (2002)
10. BA Kitchenham, S Charters, Guidelines for performing systematic literature reviews in software engineering. version 2.3. *EBSE Technical Report*, EBSE-2007-01, Keele University, Keele, Staffs, UK, (2007)
11. VR Basili, G Caldiera, HD Rombach, The goal question metric approach, in *Encyclopedia of Software Engineering* (Wiley, Hoboken, 2002)
12. N Johnson, Top 8 people and resources for agile hardware development. http://www.axcon.dk/blog/process/top-8-best-people-and-resources-for-agile-hardware-development.htm. Accessed 16 January 2013
13. M Levison, Agile for hardware and embedded systems. http://agilepainrelief.com/notesfromatooluser/2008/12/agile-for-hardware-and-embedded-systems.html. Accessed 16 January 2013
14. T Punkka, Taming the big animal – agile intervention in a large organization. http://citeseerx.ist.psu.edu/viewdoc/download?doi=10.1.1.105.3719&rep=rep1&type=pdf. Accessed 16 January 2013
15. M Bartley, Agile development in hardware. http://testandverification.com/articles/agile-development-in-hardware/. Accessed 16 January 2013
16. J Grenning, Deep agile embedded panel questions – hardware. http://www.renaissancesoftware.net/blog/archives/42. Accessed 16 January 2013
17. N Johnson, Agile hardware development – nonsense or necessity? http://www.eetimes.com/design/eda-design/4229357/Agile-hardware-development-nonsense-or-necessity-. Accessed 16 January 2013
18. L Maccherone, Top 10 questions when using agile in hardware projects. http://maccherone.com/larry/2010/02/23/top-10-questions-when-using-agile-on-hardware-projects/. Accessed 16 January 2013
19. D Dahlby, Applying agile methods to embedded systems development. http://www.embuild.org/dahlby/agileEm/agileEm.pdf. Accessed 16 January 2013

20.  Z Irani, Challenges of adopting agile in combined hardware and software
     environments. http://www.cprime.com/blog/2012/08/01/challenges-of-
     adopting-agile-in-combined-hardware-and-software-environments/.
     Accessed 16 January 2013
21.  N Van Schooenderwoert, Embedded agile is different from vanilla agile.
     http://leanagilepartners.com/blog/blog/2011/10/10/embedded-agile-is-
     different-from-vanilla-agile/. Accessed 16 January 2013
22.  MR Bakal, J Althouse, P Verma, Continuous integration in agile
     development. http://www.ibm.com/developerworks/rational/library/
     continuous-integration-agile-development/continuous-integration-
     agile-development-pdf.pdf. Accessed 16 January 2013
23.  M Karlesky, G Williams, W Bereza, M Fletcher, Mocking the embedded
     world: test-driven development, continuous integration, and design
     patterns. http://www.methodsandtools.com/archive/archive.php?id=59.
     Accessed 16 January 2013
24.  T Punkka, Agile hardware and co-design. http://www.ngware.eu/blog/
     papers/Agile2011_agile%20hardware%20and%20co-design_Punkka.pdf
     Accessed 16 January 2013

# 13

# Embedded reconfigurable synchronization & acquisition ASIP for a multi-standard OFDM receiver

Mahmoud A Said[*], Omar A Nasr and Ahmed F Shalash

**Abstract**

Embedded reconfigurable architectures are currently attracting increasing attention in the wireless communications industry due to the escalating number of wireless standards in today's market. Application specific instruction-set processors (ASIPs) present a reconfigurable solution that offers a compromise between programmability and low power consumption. In this article, the design and implementation of an embedded synchronization and acquisition ASIP for OFDM based systems is proposed. The engine architecture is presented and the programming model is explained in details. The proposed engine is scalable and it can be configured to support a multitude of synchronization algorithms and OFDM standards. While applicable to many OFDM systems, the proposed architecture was successfully verified on long term evolution (LTE Rel. 8) and WiMAX 802.16e systems. A partial list of synchronization and acquisition algorithms are tested on the engine for the two standards, and the results highlight the capabilities of the engine. The processor has been synthesized with 0.18$\mu$m standard cell CMOS library. It is estimated to occupy 1.1 mm$^2$ and the projected power consumption is 7.9mW at 120 MHz, which meets the speed requirements of the tested standards. More results are included within the article.

**Keywords:** reconfigurable ASIP, embedded processors, baseband processors, low-power design, OFDM synchronization

## 1 Introduction

Contemporary wireless standards allow for the radio to have connectivity with more than one technology at the same time. For example, the radio can be connected to a Wi-Fi hotspot when a signal exists, or to a WiMAX base station if the Wi-Fi signal is weak or does not exist. The ability to connect to more than one technology increases the reliability and the use of the radio's connectivity. It also enables applications that require constant connectivity, such as remote health care and remote industrial automation, which cannot tolerate any loss of connectivity at any time. Moreover, there are still competition, enhancements, regional variants, and new versions of the wireless standards that emerge with time. For example, in the field of 4G and beyond, the marginal competing standards and the need to have an easy migration path between different systems increases

the need for configurability without sacrificing throughput, area or power consumption. This line of thinking gave a boost to the concept of the software defined radio (SDR) [1]. SDR, in general, is based on general purpose digital signal processors (DSPs). Thus, it suffers from limitations in throughput and power consumption. However, the need for programmability and configurability is unabated due to the proliferation of wireless standards. Another approach to achieve configurability without sacrificing power consumption is to use application specific instruction-set processors (ASIP) [2-4]. In ASIP technology, a core unit is programmed using a specific instruction set that configures the core unit to perform multiple functionalities.

For most of today's and emerging standards, orthogonal frequency division multiplexing (OFDM) was the modulation scheme of choice in systems such as high performance LAN type 2 (HIPERLAN/2) [5], IEEE 802.11a [6], IEEE 802.16 family [7] and 3GPP long term evolution (LTE). OFDM's main advantage is its ability

* Correspondence: mahmoudabdelall2005@yahoo.com
Center for Wireless Studies, Faculty of Engineering, Cairo University, Cairo, Egypt

to alleviate the inter-symbol interference (ISI) caused by multi-path fading channels, even for large

channel delay spreads. Hence, at the receiver, there is no need to design complex channel equalizers, which reduces the complexity and the power consumption of the receiver. On the other hand, OFDM systems are very sensitive to synchronization errors [8]. Therefore, there is a need to design, and efficiently implement high accuracy synchronization algorithms using embedded reconfigurable engines that can support the increasing number of OFDM-based standards. The concept of reconfigurable engines for wireless applications has been previously explored in the literature. Configurable radio architectures that can support multiple standards were proposed in [9,10], where the engine core consists of an array of reconfigurable units. Poon [11] uses five different configurable units to perform all tasks for the digital part of the radio. Application specific processor architecture was proposed in [4] for OFDM channel estimation. In our previous study [3], an ASIP architecture is proposed to support synchronization tasks in OFDM systems. In [3], we proposed only the architecture of reconfigurable engine architecture to achieve a compromise between powerful dedicated hardware implementations and very flexible general DSP processors, but with limited programming capabilities.

Expanding on [3], an embedded reconfigurable ASIP-based engine that can efficiently carry out OFDM synchronization and acquisition tasks is presented. The main building block of the engine is a core unit that was designed to efficiently carry out synchronization tasks. The core unit can be programmed with a special instruction set to optimize the usage of the hardware resources. Memories for data and instructions, registers for intermediate data storage, and an instruction decoder are all parts of the the engine. The engine and the instruction set are optimized for vector instructions, which are frequently used in synchronization and acquisition algorithms. The results show that the hardware multiplexing in this ASIP solution reaches a smaller implementation area than the solution of multiple dedicated implementations. In addition, it allows a higher degree of hardware reuse between different algorithms in different standards.

The organization of the article is as follows: Section 2 introduces the OFDM system model. The detailed engine architecture is proposed in Section 3. Section 4 discusses the algorithm selection and analysis of the processing tasks, while the programming model is discussed in Section 5. Results of the proposed engine are presented in Section 6. Section 7 concludes the article.

## 2 OFDM system model

A typical OFDM receiver is shown in Figure 1 The used transmission model is described in detail in [8]. The resulting time domain signal $s(t)$ is composed of successive symbols where Symbol $l$ is formed from $N$ subcarriers, $a_{l,k}$ (transmitted data), where $l$ denotes the symbol index and $k$ is the subcarrier index. The subcarrier spacing $\Delta = F_s N$ where $F_s$ is the sampling frequency. The sampling time of the OFDM signal is $T_s = \dfrac{1}{F_s}$ The $N$ subcarriers are divided between data, pilots and guard bands according to the used OFDM standard. Pilots are reference signals known at the receiver which are used in data-aided estimations for synchronization or channel estimation purposes. Guard bands are used in order to limit the bandwidth of the transmitted signal to be less than $\dfrac{1}{T_s}$ A guard interval of length $N_g$ samples is added before each OFDM symbol to combat the multi path fading channel effects. The total number of time samples in one OFDM symbol is $N_s = N + N_g$.

The received signal, when the transmitted signal passes through a channel with an impulse response $h(t)$ is

$$r(t) = \sum_i h_i(t)s(t - \tau_i) + n(t) \tag{1}$$

where delays $\tau_i$ are channel tap delays and $n(t)$ is the complex-valued additive white Gaussian noise (AWGN). Sampling the signal at time instants $nt_s$, and removing the guard interval yielding

$$r_{l,n} = r((lN_s + n)t_s) \tag{2}$$

Demodulation of the subcarriers via a Fast Fourier Transform (FFT) yields the received data symbols:

$$X_{l,k} = \sum_{n=0}^{N-1} r_{l,n} e^{-j2\pi nk/N} \tag{3}$$

This is equivalent to

$$X_{l,k} = a_{l,k}.H_{l,k} + n_{l,k} \tag{4}$$

where $H_{l,k}$ is the channel frequency response at subcarrier $k$ in symbol $l$ and $n_{l,k}$ is the additive noise samples at subcarrier $k$ in symbol $l$.

Three major synchronization problems result in increasing the error rates at OFDM receivers:
- Inaccurate frame beginning detection.
- Carrier frequency offset (CFO) [8].
- Sampling clock frequency offset (SCFO) [8].

Figure 2 summarizes the synchronization processes in a typical OFDM receiver. First, the incoming signal passes through a packet detection block that will, besides detection of packet existence, give a rough estimate of the symbol beginning. Once a signal is detected, exact frame boundary detection and compensation for

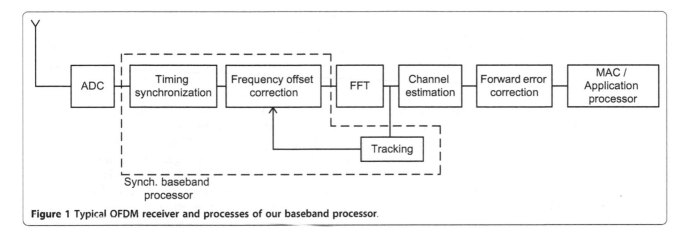

**Figure 1** Typical OFDM receiver and processes of our baseband processor.

timing offset are performed. To maintain subcarrier orthogonality, CFO is estimated, refined and corrected after determination of frame boundaries. The signal then passes through the FFT block to estimate the transmitted symbols.

Tracking the variations of the CFO and SCFO is critical in OFDM systems due to their sensitivity to frequency offsets. SCFO and the residual part of the CFO (RCFO) are estimated and corrected in a tracking phase.

The synchronization functions are divided into two main phases:

1. Acquisition phase. Four processes are performed in this phase: symbol timing (frame boundary detection), initial fractional CFO (FCFO) estimation, cell-search (CS) and ICFO estimation. Correction of the estimated errors is shown in Figure 2

2. Tracking phase. In this phase RCFO and SCFO are estimated and corrected.

From the implementation point of view, a significant amount of baseband processing takes place in the synchronization sub-system. Optimized architectures that fulfill the needs of the synchronization sub-system with

a high degree of configurability will have the advantage in terms of area and power.

## 3 Design of the proposed engine
### 3.1 Engine architecture
The proposed application specific instruction set (ASIP) synchronization engine achieves a compromise between powerful dedicated hardware implementations and very flexible general DSP processors. All of the used units are grouped together in one pipelined configurable unit (CU). This core unit is optimized for synchronization purposes as well as many other algorithms and allows the execution of many complex operations. We enabled a high degree of hardware reuse, and this resulted in less area and removed many control overheads while a lower degree of parallelism was attained. The choice of a single unit without external accelerators is based on a careful study of synchronization tasks involved within OFDM systems and throughput requirement in the supported standards. Most of the commonly used accelerators like COordinate Rotation DIgital Computer (CORDIC) [12], maximum likelihood (ML) [11] and

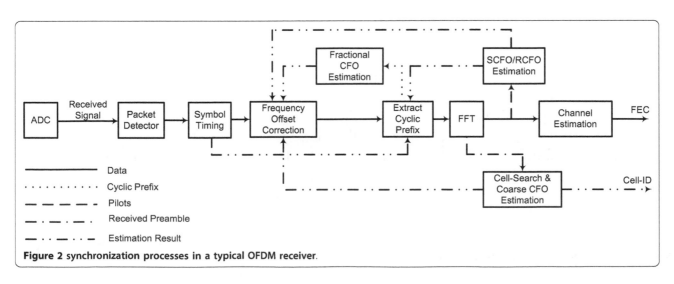

**Figure 2** synchronization processes in a typical OFDM receiver.

other accelerators are included with the ordinary complex multiply-accumulate (C-MAC) unit to be executed on CU. This will keep power and area levels as low as possible. The general architecture of the proposed engine is shown in 3 It consists of the main CU, two dual-port memory banks, embedded ROM for any used reference sequences, an output updater (bank of registers) with a simple controller, two register files and the control part (instruction decoder (ID), program memory (PM), specialized control registers).

### 3.1.1 Configurable unit (CU)

The CU is connected to the output of a CU input generator and controlled directly by the instruction decoder (ID) with a 26-bit control vector, which identifies the working operation and the used elements inside the CU. Figure 4 shows the internal design of CU. Many operations are executed on the same CU. CU configuration for major CU supported operations and the resulting operation are listed in Table 1 Even though the inputs to the CU are complex most of the time, the engine uses real data buses. This design was chosen to remove the limitations imposed by complex data buses on real data operations, especially on phase calculations.

The main operation of the CU is the Complex Multiply ACcumulate (C-MAC). Mathematically, it can be implemented in two ways, using either three or four real multipliers. To limit the number of multipliers, three multipliers are used, although five adders are required as opposed to four adders in the four multipliers

scheme. An extra adder is added to allow the summation of eight different real inputs or four complex inputs. In addition to the two large accumulators, the CU uses internal multiplexers to configure the running operation according to the control vector (CV).

The CU consists of six 12-bit real adders, three 13-bit real multipliers followed by two 12-bit rounders, two 24-bit accumulators, two two's complement operations, ten 13-bit multiplexers (MUX) and two 24-bit shifters. The eight ports (I1 ... I8) in Figure 4 are intended for operations on real data while the six ports (I1 ... I6) can be used alone to implement the complex multiplication process. Real ADD/SUB operations are executed with two different precisions (12-bit and 24-bit).

The CU is optimized by pipelining into three pipeline stages. The first stage is an addition stage used for normal and vector complex multiplications. This adds the benefit of having a first stage capable of adding eight real numbers before passing its output to the next addition stage (stage 3). The second stage is the multiplication stage. It has only one multiplier between two registers to minimize the critical path of the overall unit. The third stage is the second addition stage like the first stage but it has only two adders instead of four.

One cycle of latency is achieved when pipelining the CU in normal instructions. Vector instructions are executed on a time multiplexing manner on the CU with a maximum vector length of 256 elements. Among different supported operations, the controlled accumulation

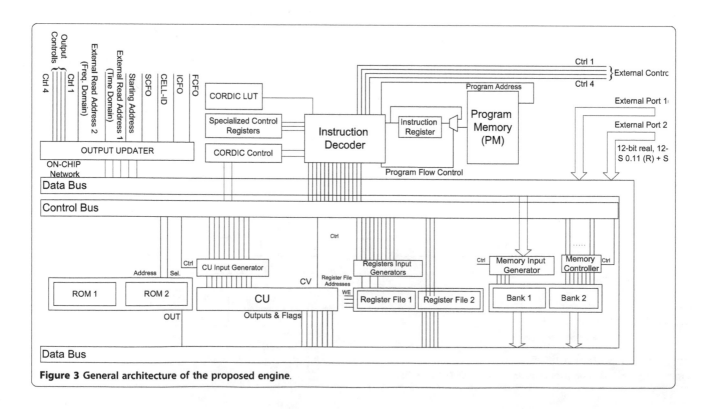

**Figure 3** General architecture of the proposed engine.

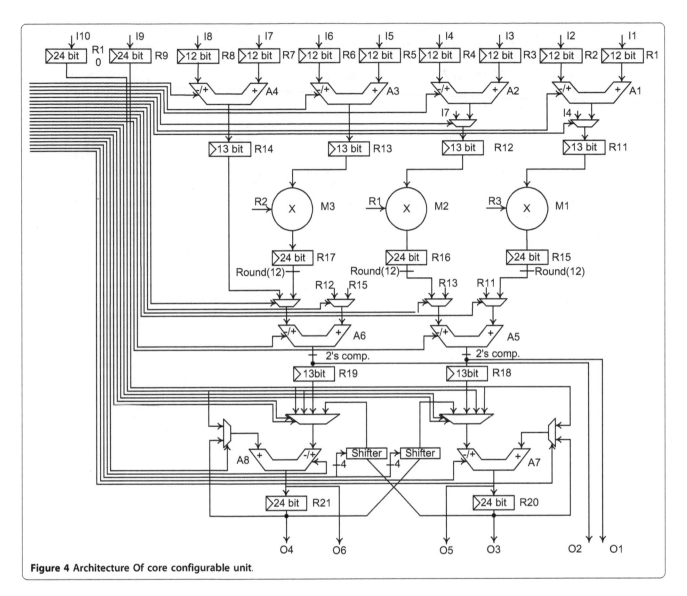

**Figure 4 Architecture Of core configurable unit.**

(CACC) operation needs the largest number of simultaneous complex input signals. CACC operation adds or subtracts four complex words every cycle. This puts a constraint on the memory system to supply the unit with a maximum of four words every cycle. However in this mode, no write operations can be executed. To work in CACC mode, hardware configuration of the CU with respect to the control vector is done. M1, M2, and M3 multipliers of Figure 4 are bypassed while a running configuration of the Add/Sub operations (A1 ... A8) are controlled via a stored control sequence.

Time multiplexing of operations running on the engine core limits its multi-process/cycle capabilities. A maximum of one operation/cycle can be executed on the engine core, no matter wither this operation is simple like addition or computationally complex like complex-multiplications. Although the architecture has one CU, the engine is scalable via adding multiple CU units connected with each other by the two ports I9 and I10 to support larger systems.

### 3.1.2 Memory system

Memory is divided into two 286 word dual-port banks (24-bit). Memory size is dominated by the maximum

**Table 1 Major CU supported operation**

| CU-configuration | Resulting operation |
| --- | --- |
| C-MAC | Auto-correlation |
| | Cross-correlation |
| | Euclidean distance calculation |
| | Vector complex multiplication |
| Real multiply-add | ab + cd |
| Controlled C-ACC | BPSK preamble correlation |
| CORDIC | Vectoring mode |
| | Rotation mode |
| Maximum likelihood | On-line comparison |

supported correlation length of 256 in addition to the free space needed to store any internal outputs. The choice of the maximum correlation length was based on the required performance in 802.16e and 3GPP-LTE release 8. Inputs to the memory system is connected to a Memory Input Generator in Figure 3, which is controlled by the instruction decoder. Memory could accept inputs from the external ports, Register File 2, main CU output or the memory itself in a MOV operation. Memory controller handles the write operations and prevent any racing conditions. The two banks are running on the same operating frequency of the core unit. No special addressing modes are required, and hence, address generators are basically counters. Time sharing between different tasks running on the processor allowed further optimization in the memory system by increasing the memory reuse option.

Two general purpose register files, Register File 1 and Register File 2, in Figure 3 are used with a register input generator controlled by the instruction decoder directly. Register File 1 is of size 12-bit and holds 8 general purpose registers to facilitate data flow operations, counting, set outputs and many other useful operations. Register File 2 is of size 24-bit but it consists of four general purpose registers only. The first advantage of them comes when dealing with movements of complex data inside the engine. These optimization methods beyond the traditional one fixed size register file allows faster execution of real and complex data operations. For example, moving a complex word from the memory system as two (real, imaginary) parts would take double latency beside the complexity in dealing with the two parts as a one word in the executed program.

Reference correlation sequences are stored in 3072 byte ROM for the both of 802.16e and LTE release 8. The ROM takes its address directly from the instruction decoder with an internal counter for its address only. All data can be transferred between different parts of the engine through a data bus of four complex words maximum.

### 3.1.3 Input/output interface

The engine interfaces with the outer world through a set of input control signals (*IC*) and output control signals (*OC*) beside two external ports for data transfers. Four *IC* signals are connected directly with the instruction decoder and used for acknowledgment about a certain event. Another four *OC* signals output from the controller of the output updater to identify the state of the engine at any stage. The two external data transfer ports are 24-bit wide each (12-bit real, 12-bit imaginary). One port is connected to the time domain side, while the other port is connected after the FFT operation. Any read operation is carried out through one of these two ports and with the two addresses external read address

1 and external read address 2. The accuracy of the chosen number of bits is verified in Section 6.

The output updater holds the same output value on the same port, until a control signal comes from the instruction decoder to its controller to update the output with a newer value in a certain register. The output registers are general registers used to set any value as an output. Here, we give output registers restricted names to clarify the engine operation. The five output registers holds the starting address, FCFO, CELL-ID, ICFO, and SCFO. All of the five registers are 12-bit each. Typically, Starting Address goes to the input buffer that holds the FFT window to identify the first sample in the incoming frame. The estimated FCFO is used by the CFO correction complex-multiplier to derotate the input samples. CELL-ID is transferred to higher layers. ICFO is added to the fractional part of the CFO to guarantee correct reception with time. Estimated value of SCFO is considered as the seed for the ROB/STUFF correction algorithm in [13].

While transferring data from any port to the internal memory banks, no execution of any other instruction is carried out. This control mechanism is achieved when the controller holds the instruction inside the instruction register by re-entering the same instruction to the instruction register till the end of the transfer process. The same mechanism works for vector instructions, where the controller re-enter the vector instruction to the instruction register till the end of the execution phase.

### 3.1.4 CORDIC algorithm

The CORDIC algorithm [12] can carry out many trigonometric operations and is used here only for angle measurements. The CORDIC stage is composed of adders and shifters, as shown in Figure 5 The precision of the output depends on the number of stages used. Each additional stage adds one bit of precision. There

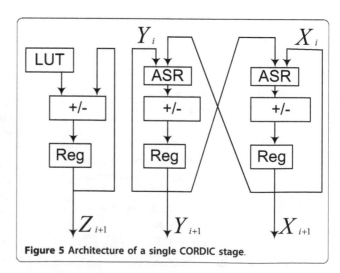

**Figure 5 Architecture of a single CORDIC stage**.

are three methods of implementation to the CORDIC algorithm [12]; spatial multiplexing, time multiplexing and joint spatial-temporal multiplexing. The time multiplexing method perfectly meets our engine design with the addition of the two shifters in Figure 4 to implement the CORDIC stage. The associated memory required with it is called CORDIC look up table (LUT) of size 14 byte. Another control register is required to control the sign of ADD/SUB module used in the next CORDIC stage. The output angle here has a precision of 12 bits and executes in 18 cycles.

### 3.2 Engine programming

Programming of the proposed embedded ASIP includes three types of instructions. The first type is the ordinary classes like program flow instructions (conditional and unconditional jumps), move instructions, real, and complex ADD/SUB instructions, interfacing control instructions (external reads, output set). The second type is optimized instructions to facilitate the implementation of synchronization subsystem tasks as well as other algorithms in different parts of the engine. The third type is vector instructions.

Ordinary instructions operate on single data points stored in registers (RF1 & RF2), and the result is automatically stored in another register. Most of instructions of this type take one cycle to complete. All control instructions belong to this simple class of instructions. Optimized instructions are special instructions for special purposes like the *ANGLE* instruction and the *BPCACC* (discussed later). This kind of instructions operates on single point or vector of complex numbers stored either in the memory like *BPCACC* or in registers like *ANGLE*, and the result stored also in either memory or registers. Execution of these instructions always consist of multiple execution stages. Vector instructions operate on vectors of complex numbers

stored in memories. The output is either stored in another memory if there is no accumulation associated with it, or in a register from register file 2 if there is an accumulation. The number of cycles needed for vector instructions depend on the vector length.

In normal operation, one instruction is fetched while another one is decoded and executed as shown in Figure 6a In the execution of special type instructions like the *ANGLE* instruction that measures the angle of a complex number, the pipeline is stalled till the end of the CORDIC subroutine. This operation is shown in Figure 6b When a vector instruction is fetched, a program flow control mechanism is activated and the pipeline initiates a counter with a control value and enter a stall state till the end of execution before fetching the next instruction as shown in Figure 6c

To illustrate the difference in execution of various types of instructions, Table 2 shows an example of the units used and units bypassed in the execution of an instruction of each type. Each instruction is 20-bit wide and the whole size of the required program memory is 512 instructions.

The CORDIC subroutine is executed when fetching the *ANGLE* instruction (special type) in 18 cycles for a precision of 12-bits (as stated before). Shifters included with the engine core are not general purpose shifters that accept arbitrary inputs; they are used only in the execution of the iterative CORDIC algorithm and are controlled by a counter attached with the instruction decoder.

Although most of the instructions are either control instructions or instructions that operate on single data (ADD, SUB,...), the processor operates most of the time on vector data. Hence, the processor is optimized for operations on vectors of complex data or specialized operations associated with many supported tasks. The assembly program becomes relatively long for control or single data instructions compared to what it fulfills.

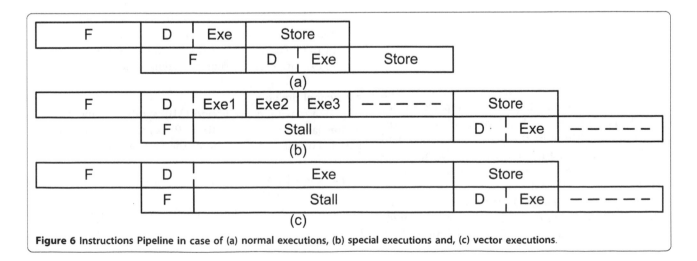

**Figure 6** Instructions Pipeline in case of (a) normal executions, (b) special executions and, (c) vector executions.

**Table 2 Execution of three operations of different types**

| Operation | Inputs source | DM1, DM2 | M1, M2, M3 | A1,..., A6 | A7, A8 | CORDIC control | CORDIC LUT | shifters | ROMS | output updater |
|-----------|---------------|----------|------------|------------|--------|----------------|------------|----------|------|----------------|
| CMAC | Data path (DM) | active | active | active | active | off | inactive | inactive | inactive | inactive |
| Angle | Register file 2 | inactive | bypassed | bypassed | active | on | active | active | inactive | inactive |
| Read | Data path (External) | active | inactive | inactive | inactive | off | inactive | inactive | inactive | inactive |

The engine is programmed via a script (contain the entire program) enters a primitive compiler. The compiler outputs a (.hex and.mif) memory initialization file for the program memory. The output file containing the binary vector is downloaded into the program memory to begin the program fetching.

## 4 Example algorithms analysis

In this section, we explain a set of typical synchronization tasks usually performed in OFDM receiver. Typically, the receiver perform the following tasks:

1. Obtain coarse frame boundaries with a packet detector.

2. Initiate a search over the samples selected from step (1) to obtain fine frame boundaries. This step with step (1) are called Frame boundary determination (FBD).

3. With the first sample in the frame known, estimate and correct fractional CFO.

4. After FFT, estimate the ICFO and update the value of the frequency of offset estimated in step (3).

5. For OFDM cellular standards, estimate the CELL-ID from the given reference sequence.

6. Track and update the residual CFO (RCFO) and SCFO with the non-preamble OFDM symbols.

For testing and evaluation purposes of the proposed architecture, high level Matlab floating/fixed point models of IEEE802.16e and LTE Rel. 8 have been created to apply the chosen algorithms in [8,13-15]. The proposed embedded ASIP can be configured to implement the chosen synchronization algorithms. It is capable of supporting not only the chosen algorithms but it can support other algorithms as well.

### 4.1 Packet detection

Detection of the correct boundaries of the incoming OFDM packets has a major impact on the performance of all post FFT sub-systems. Therefore, good timing synchronization algorithms in the acquisition stage will allow early locking on the incoming signal. Using correlation-based algorithms as a detection method directly as in [16] and [17] will cost more energy in the ideal state (no transmitted signals). On the other hand, using a simple, but not accurate detection method, like single or double sliding window (DSW) algorithms [18] to detect the packet and then refine the estimate using correlations will cost us lower energy.

In DSW algorithm, a decision variable is measured and compared with a chosen threshold which depends on the target probability of miss detection and the probability of false alarm. Assume that the decision variable is $m_n$ and the chosen threshold is $th$. A packet is detected if $m_n > th$ at any sample instant $n$

$$a_n = \sum_{m=0}^{M-1} |r_{n-m}|^2 = a_{n-1} + |r_n|^2 - |r_{n-M}|^2 \qquad (5)$$

$$b_n = \sum_{l=0}^{L-1} |r_{n+1}|^2 = b_{n-1} + |r_{n+L}|^2 - |r_n|^2 \qquad (6)$$

$$m_n = \frac{a_n}{b_n} \qquad (7)$$

where $a_n$, $b_n$, and $M$, $L$ are the energies and sizes of window $A$ and window $B$, respectively.

The energy contained in any sample $|r_n|^2$ can be measured with a complex multiplication unit in Figure 7a with a conjugate flag at the second port. The comparison process is executed with a simple subtraction flag check. The size of each window is chosen to be 64 samples, which gives a good performance at low signal to noise ratio (SNR). From the implementation point of view, a total of 384 bytes of memory are required here with ADC resolution of 12-bit (12-bit real, 12-bit imaginary); accuracy is verified by the engine results in Section 6. The packet detector should re-evaluate the decision parameter $m_n$ every new sample, so a decimation in the incoming signal is carried out to leave room for the execution of the required computations.

### 4.2 Symbol timing

In [14], a maximum likelihood (ML) symbol timing estimator based on cyclic prefix (CP) correlation was proposed. The estimated timing of the first sample, $\hat{t}$, is

$$\hat{t} = \arg \max_n \left[ 2 \left| \sum_{m=0}^{L-1} r_{n+m} * r_{n+m+N}^* \right| - \rho \sum_{k=0}^{L-1} |r_{n+m}|^2 + |r_{n+m+N}|^2 \right] \qquad (8)$$

where $\rho$ is the correlation coefficient between $r_k$ and $r_{k+N}$

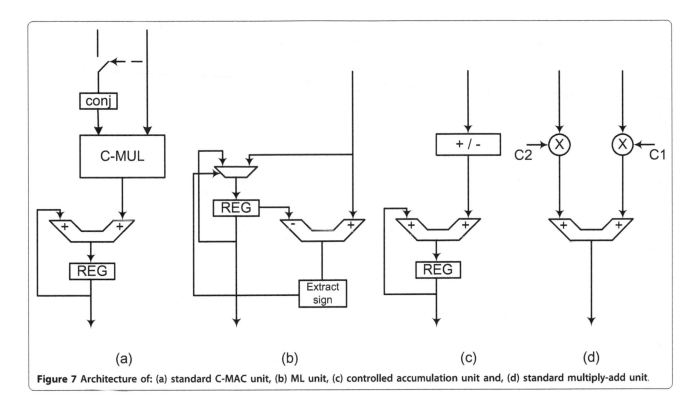

**Figure 7** Architecture of: (a) standard C-MAC unit, (b) ML unit, (c) controlled accumulation unit and, (d) standard multiply-add unit.

$$\rho = \left| \frac{E(r_n * r_{n+N}^*)}{\sqrt{E\left(|r_n|^2\right) E\left(|r_{n+N}|^2\right)}} \right| = \frac{\sigma_s^2}{\sigma_s^2 + \sigma_n^2} = \frac{SNR}{SNR + 1} \quad (9)$$

The boundaries of the search window come from the packet detector. To prevent inter-symbol interference, a reasonable shift inside the cyclic prefix is done. Hence, if the detector gives an estimate for the first sample in the symbol at $m$, the first correlation window begins at $m-s$, where $s$ denotes the safety shift back. The correlation window slides over time till a search size of $2s + 1$ are evaluated. This implies that the maximum absolute value between $2s + 1$ output correlation result corresponds to the maximum likelihood starting sample. This algorithm has proven its robustness against multi-path fading channels, besides the advantage of being unaffected by the received power level. Only the number of samples $L$ contributing in the cyclic prefix (CP) correlation is affecting the performance of the estimator.

The proposed embedded engine is capable of supporting a maximum correlation length of 256 samples. This maximum is chosen with respect to the required accuracy. This maximum is justified by the comparison between floating point results and the proposed engine results in Section 6. The maximum length of the contributing samples is 256 and can be scaled easily with respect to the required performance. The most complex operation here is the complex multiplication in Equation

(8). Auto-correlation and Euclidean distance (ED) calculation (energy) in Equation (8) can be realized by the standard complex multiply-accumulate (C-MAC) unit shown in Figure 7a Subtraction of the output of ED from the output of CP auto-correlation is performed on-line by controlling the accumulation sign. Adders in accumulators are two's complement Add/Sub modules controlled by the processor control unit. The last step is the maximum absolute search between the $2s + 1$ evaluated result with the ML unit shown in Figure 7b

### 4.3 Fractional CFO estimation

After determination of the FFT window boundaries, the CP is removed according to the indices given by FBD. Fast acquisition of the FCFO requires a pre-FFT algorithm that works without the need of training symbols. With the existence of a frequency offset ($\Delta f$) in the received signal $r_{l,n}$, it will take the form in equation (10)

$$r'_{l,n} = r_{l,n} e^{j2\pi \Delta f n t_s} \quad (10)$$

The task now is to derotate (multiply by exponential) the received symbols with the term $e^{-j2\pi \Delta f n t_s}$ to establish accurate subcarrier orthogonality quickly. Multi-stage synchronization strategy is used to achieve both fast and accurate acquisition. In particular, two acquisition stages (pre-FFT for FCFO and post-FFT for ICFO) are used in our system, and then come the tracking of any possible variations. The authors in [8] have proposed a non-data aided estimation algorithm of the FCFO based on the correlation result of the removed CP in Equation (11).

$$\Delta f = \frac{1}{2\pi N t_s} * \arg\left(\sum_{n=\theta}^{L-1} r_{T+n} r_{T+n+N}^*\right) \tag{11}$$

where $T$ is the estimated starting sample index from FBD, $\theta$ is the starting point of the correlation window and $L$ is the cyclic prefix length. The reason for not starting the correlation window from the beginning of the cyclic prefix is the multi-path fading channel delay spread $\tau$ effect on the estimation performance. The value of $\theta$ is chosen such that $\theta > \tau$, so that the channel effect is the same in the two parts of the correlation and the output is affected only by the added white noise.

Equation (11) can simply be executed on the same complex multiply-accumulate (CMAC) unit used for FBD in Figure 7a Memory requirements here depend on the selected correlation window length with a maximum of 256 samples as stated before. The only difference is the calculation of the correlation angle before multiplying it by a constant. Angle estimation is carried out using the iterative CORDIC algorithm [12]. More details about the implementation of this algorithm were described in Section 3.

### 4.4 Joint ICFO & CS estimation

In the literature, estimation of the ICFO usually depends on the reference preamble symbol like in 802.16e (WiMAX) or a special synchronization symbols like in LTE. These reference symbols carry also the CELL-ID information. Joint CELL-ID detection and ICFO estimation algorithms are proposed in [19,20]. The task of finding the CELL-ID is named Cell Search (CS). In standards like 802.16e and LTE release 8, reference signals that are used to carry such information are binary random sequences. This feature can make the implementation of this block easier. Assume that the received preamble is $Q$ $(k)$, where $k$ is the subcarrier index. $H(k)$ is the channel impulse response at subcarrier number $k$. Autocorrelation of the received reference symbol is evaluated as follows:

$$\begin{aligned}\Re\{Q(k)Q^*(k-1)\} &= \Re\{H(k)P_j(k+I)H^*(k-1)P_j^*(k+I-1)\} \\ &\approx |H(k)|^2 D_j(k+I)\end{aligned} \tag{12}$$

where
- $Q(k-1)$ : is the first non-zero subcarrier before $k$.
- $P_j(k)$ : is the stored reference sequence of index $(j)$.
- $D_j(k) = P_j(k).P_j^*(k-1)$: is the autocorrelation result of the stored sequences $P_j$.
- $I$ : is the integral frequency offset normalized to the subcarrier spacing.

For correlation purposes, shifted versions of $P_j$ must also be stored. For example, if we have a maximum

ICFO of $I_m$, $[-I_m, I_m]$, we must store $2I_m + 1$ version from each correlation sequence $P_j$.

The autocorrelation in Equation (5.4) is used to mitigate the effect of the multi-path fading channel $H(k)$ by multiplying each active subcarrier by the conjugate of its predecessor assuming the channel added phase is nearly equal on both of them. A correlation of the reference patterns shifted by the expected values of the ICFO is evaluated as follows:

$$M_i^{l,j} = \sum_{k=0}^{N_p-1} D_j(k+I)\Re\{Q(k)Q^*(k-1)\} \tag{13}$$

Where $\Re\{Q(k)Q^*(k-1)\}$ is called the differential signal and $N_p$ is the number of reference subcarriers contributing to the cross-correlation between the received reference sequence and the stored sequences. The estimated ICFO and CELL-ID is given by:

$$\left(\hat{I}, \hat{j}\right) = \arg\max_{I,j} M_I^{l,j} \tag{14}$$

The complexity of this method is acceptable and can be implemented easily on the proposed embedded ASIP, noting that $D_j(k+I)$ in Equation (13) does not have to be calculated on the fly, but can be calculated in advance and stored in the receiver memory. The calculation of $\Re\{Q(k). Q^*(k-1)\}$ for $k = 0, 1, ..., N_p - 1$ in Equation (13) requires an $N_p$ complex multiplications. The binary nature of $D_j(k+i)$ in Equation (13) makes the remaining computations needed to obtain $M_I^{l,j}$ Binary correlations can be performed using the controlled accumulation (C-ACC) unit shown in Figure 7c Accumulation sign is controlled via stored (shifted and normalized) reference sequence. The constraint on the defined maximum possible shift $I_m$ comes from the symbol duration and the available cycle budget. For example, in IEEE 802.16e, for a maximum ICFO of nine subcarriers (in the range [-9,9]) we need to evaluate 722 [20] different correlation outputs to choose the maximum absolute value as the correct estimate. Comparison between the evaluated correlation results is done on the fly after every new correlation output. Further optimizations of this processing type is done in the design of processor computational core. The engine is optimized not only for this algorithm, but for many other algorithms as well.

### 4.5 Joint RCFO & SCFO estimation

All previous tasks belong to the acquisition phase. After the acquisition phase, subcarrier orthogonality is loosely established. However, OFDM based systems are very sensitive to the variations of frequency offset. Hence, tracking of these variations with time is important to maintain the resulting signal to error ratio (SER). Another important issue is the SCFO between the transmitter and receiver. A joint data-aided estimation algorithms for RCFO and SCFO are proposed in [15,13], where reference pilot subcarriers are used. In [15], the joint effect of a RCFO $\delta f_r$ with the existence of a SCFO $\zeta$ on the received subcarrier phases after the FFT are shown in Figure 8 This effect is translated in Equation (15)

$$X'_{l,k} = e^{-j2\pi\delta f_r(l(N+N_g)-\frac{N}{2})t_s}\,e^{-j2\pi k\left(l\frac{N+N_g}{N}-0.5\right)\varsigma}X_{l,k} \qquad (15)$$

To obtain Equation (15), some terms were neglected. In reality these terms are not neglected and will cause ICI that is measured and stated in the engine results in Section 6.

In general, the symbol number $l$ will have a phase error line with bias $-2\pi\delta f_r(l(N + N_g))$ and slope $-2\pi\varsigma\left(\frac{l(N+N_g)}{N} - 0.5\right)$. In [13], pilot subcarriers are used to form a phase error line that has a bias $b$ and slope $a$. Let the differential angle at pilot subcarrier index $k$ in symbol number $l$ is $\varphi_{k,l}$, and $x_k$ is the pilot index. Estimation of the phase error line bias $b$ and slope $a$ is carried out as follows:

$$a\sum x_k^2 + b\sum x_k = \sum x_k\phi_{k,l}$$
$$a\sum x_k + bN_p i = \sum \phi_{k,l} \qquad (16)$$

The differential angle $\varphi_{k,l}$ is evaluated by multiplying the pilot $k$ at symbol $l$ with the conjugate of the similar pilot at the same index $k$ at symbol $l$ - 1 (the similar pilot could be in an earlier symbol) to mitigate the channel effect. The SCFO $\zeta$ is evaluated from the estimated line slope $a$ and the RCFO $\delta f_r$ could be found from the bias $b$.

$$\varsigma = \frac{aN}{2\pi(N + N_g)}$$
$$\delta f_r = \frac{b}{2\pi t_s(N + N_g)} \qquad (17)$$

The complexity of this algorithm on the proposed embedded engine is dominated by the vector complex conjugate multiplication of the received pilot pattern every symbol and the measurement of pilots angles in Equation (16) using the CORDIC Algorithm [12]. These measured angles are accumulated in two manners: normal accumulation, real multiply accumulate in Figure 7d The memory used to same successive pilot patterns plus the resulting vectors after the conjugate multiplication is relatively large and considered well in the design of the memory system.

## 5 Algorithm programming on the engine
### 5.1 Packet detection
The engine was programmed to run the packet detection algorithm, where a new sample read operation is issued every $t_s$ (one sample duration). In order to implement the packet detection algorithm with the time requirements of 802.16e and LTE release 8, a down sampling of the received signal by a factor of 5 is required. Simulation results showed that there is no significant performance loss due to the down sampling needed for the execution of this task on the engine core. The whole packet detection program executes in 31 cycles and repeated with the next new sample. Once a packet is detected a detection control signal will rise to begin the symbol timing procedure.

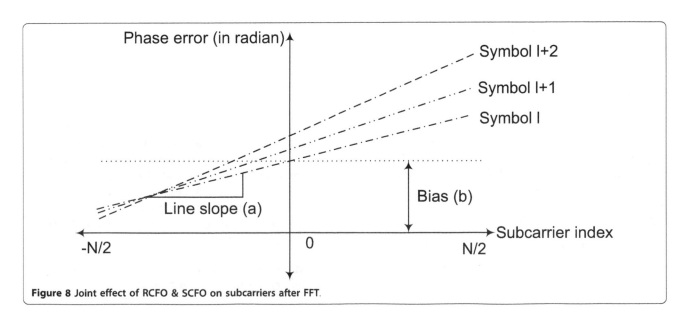

**Figure 8** Joint effect of RCFO & SCFO on subcarriers after FFT.

## 5.2 Symbol timing

The symbol timing algorithm begins with a read operation of the two parts of the cyclic prefix from External Port 1. In the read operation, we identify the destination memory bank and the length of the read vector (Ex: *READ P*1 : *DM*1,276). The core unit is configured to run the auto-correlation operation through a CMAC instruction with a conjugate flag set on the second input. The output is stored in a register from Register File 2 till the energy (Euclidean distance *EDACC*) contained in the first and the second part of the cyclic prefix are evaluated. A 24-bit subtraction operation (*LADD*) between the stored result and the resulting energy will give the first correlation output. Till now this is considered the only and the largest result, so its index is stored in a register from Register File 1.

Beginning the correlation in Equation 8 from scratch every time is not practical and consumes more energy. The next correlation output can be extracted directly from the estimated correlation output by setting the memory address step by 1 and repeat what is done for the evaluation of the first correlation output. The correlation length this time is not the whole cyclic prefix length but only a single data point. This iterative approach reduces the required execution energy as well as the program length. Once we get a new correlation result, comparison between the stored largest correlation result and the new result is executed. If the new result is larger, an update is done for both the stored value and the index of the largest. A time locking control signal is flagged from the engine when the whole $2 * s + 1$ results are evaluated. The stored index, which corresponds to the largest correlation result, is the correct start location. The output Starting Address is updated via the output updater by a *SET* instruction with the stored value in Register File 1.

To clarify how the assembly code looks like, a part of the used programming code for symbol timing is shown in Figure 9

```
MOV        Vector_Length,236;
VCMAC      DM1,R1,DM2,R2,LR1,LR2;
VEDAC      DM1,R1,LR2;
SUBL       LR1,LR2,LR1;
VEDAC      DM2,R1,LR2;
SUBL       LR1,LR2,LR1;
MOV        Vector_Length,1;
VCMAC      DM1,R1,DM2,R1,LR2,LR3;
SUBL       LR1,LR2,LR3;
VCMAC      DM1,R8,DM2,R8,LR2,LR3;
ADDL       LR3,LR2,LR3;
VEDAC      DM1,R1,LR2;
SUBL       LR3,LR2,LR3;
VEDAC      DM2,R1,LR2;
SUBL       LR3,LR2,LR3;
VEDAC      DM1,R8,LR2;
ADDL       LR3,LR2,LR3;
VEDAC      DM2,R8,LR2;
ADDL       LR3,LR2,LR3;
ADDI       R1,1,R1;
ADDI       R8,1,R8;
ADDI       R3,1,R3;
CMPL       LR3,LR1;
CJMP       011,36;
MOV        LR1,LR3;
ADDI       R7,1,R7;
CMPI       R3,21;
CJMP       '011',17;
SET        BEGINNING_ADDR,R7,R1;
SET        out_ctrl_1,1,R1;
```

**Figure 9** Part of the assembly code used for symbol timing.

## 5.3 Fractional carrier frequency offset estimation

At this stage, the cyclic prefix is still stored in DM1 and DM2. So, no read operation is issued and the correlation begins directly with the known estimated index from FBD. The correlation output then passes by the CORDIC algorithm using the *ANGLE* instruction to estimate the output phase. The output of the *ANGLE* instruction is stored in a register from Register File 1. According to Equation (11), FCFO is estimated from the output phase by a constant multiplication by $\frac{1}{2\pi Nt_s}$.

The update on the output FCFO register is carried out via the output updater with the same *SET* instruction.

## 5.4 Cell-search & integral carrier frequency offset

With the existence of an ICFO, the number of correlations needed to identify the transmitter (CELL-ID) in modern cellular networks can be very large due to the large number of reference sequences associated with each standard (114 for 802.16e, 504 for LTE release 8). A special instruction, called *BPCACC*, is used for the evaluation of a correlation with a binary sequence. The *BPCACC* instruction is capable of evaluating a binary correlation of length $N_c$ in $\frac{N_c}{4} + 1$ clock cycles. The core unit should have 4 new complex numbers every cycle in the execution of the *BPCACC* instruction.

The symbol number of the received reference symbol is known at the receiver. Separation of this symbol is done after the FFT, as well as the removal of the guard bands. A read operation from External Port 2 is issued to store the received reference symbol in DM1. To read four successive complex samples from the received reference symbol, a copy of the received reference symbol is stored in DM2. Memory step registers are set to four, so that each port from the four ports of the two memory banks will provide the engine by a different complex data sample every cycle. This allows the memory system to output four consecutive complex words each cycle. We use DM1 to get the differential signal in, which is of length $N_c$, and store it in DM2. Then, a copy of the contents of DM2 is moved again to DM1. The core unit is configured to perform the binary correlation by adding four complex numbers together with the ADD/SUB signals controlled by the correlation sequence. Every combination of 4-bits from the correlation sequence correspond to a combination of 8 ADD/SUB signals to control the operation of the adders $A1$ to $A8$.

Every new correlation result is compared with the maximum previous result and the index of the maximum correlation output is stored in a register from Register File 1. This index corresponds to the correct ICFO and the attached CELL-ID. The final step in the aquistion phase is updating the values of ICFO and CELL-ID output registers.

## 5.5 Joint RCFO & SCFO
For symbols that carry pilot subcarriers, an input control signal is activated and a read operation is issued from External Port 2. For example, in IEEE 802.16e and 3GPP LTE release 8, indices of pilots in a certain symbol are shifted from the indices of pilots in the previous symbol. Figure 10 shows the pilot pattern in IEEE 802.16e in case of DL-PUSC. Pilots are arranged in the data memory with the same order they are received. Pilot patterns are arranged as follows: The first received pilot pattern and the third pilot pattern are stored in $DM1$, while the second pattern and the fourth pattern are stored in $DM2$. This arrangement helps to make the cross-correlation in Equation (16) easier. The CU is configured to perform the cross-correlation between DM1 and DM2 initialized at the correlation starting point (number of the contributing pilots is scalable). The output of the cross-correlation between the first received pilots (P1) and previously received pilots that have the same indices (P3 in 802.16e and LTE release 8) is stored in DM2. Every output complex data word is passed through the CORDIC algorithm with the $ANGLE$ instruction to estimate its phase angle. Operations on the estimated angles are easier with the real data paths chosen for the implementation of the proposed engine. Estimated angles are multiplied with the corresponding known pilot indices and accumulated to get the term $\Sigma x_k \varphi_{k,l}$ in Equation (16). Then, the output phases are summed together to get the term $\Sigma \varphi_{k,l}$. Now, all terms of Equation (16) are known and stored in the internal registers or given as immediate values (like the number of pilots $N_p$). The estimated RCFO is added to the current total CFO and updated on the output ports. With another $SET$ instruction, SCFO is fed to the ROB/STUFF correction Algorithm [13] connected with the SCFO port.

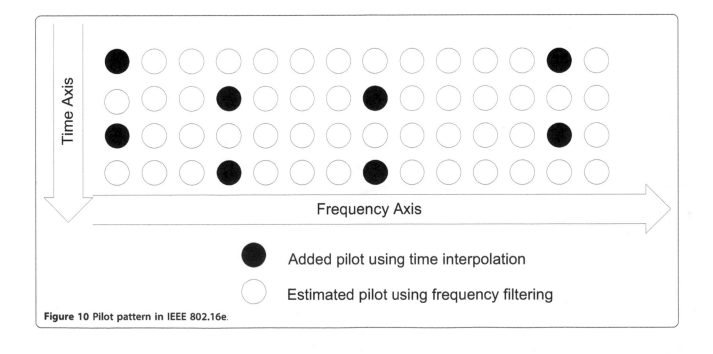

**Figure 10 Pilot pattern in IEEE 802.16e.**

● Added pilot using time interpolation

○ Estimated pilot using frequency filtering

## 6 Performance evaluation

The performance of the proposed engine is measured against floating point Matlab model to assess its accuracy and the effect of round-off errors. The implementation efficiency is projected for the resulting core area and power consumption to implement the supported operations.

Bit-accurate fixed point simulations are used for functional verification, the generation of test vectors and building verification suites. The word length chosen for the execution unit is determined by the maximum precision needed in any algorithm. FCFO estimation needs 24-bit word, which turned out to be the largest number needed. To verify the accuracy of the chosen number of bits, comparison between floating point (FP) results and engine results for FCFO estimation (normalized by subcarrier spacing) is shown in Figure 11 with a correlation length of 96 and 60 in WiMAX and LTE, respectively.

The processor uses one embedded configurable unit (CU) besides the controller core. A total of 47.4 Kbit of memory is distributed among the main data banks, the reference ROMS, CORDIC LUT and a 10 Kbit program memory.

The Altera Stratix III FPGA kit is used to functionally verify the proposed design while Synopsys Design Compiler is used to estimate the chip area and the design static power consumption (ASIC design). The engine is coded using Verilog HDL, which is compatible with Synopsys Design Compiler. Mentor-Graphics Modelsim was used for functional simulations.

First the design was synthesized with the Altera Quartus II and programmed on a Stratix III (Stratix III EP3SC150 FPGA kit) FPGA to verify the design functionality. Then, The processor was synthesized in a $0.18\mu$m CMOS process at a voltage of 1.8 V using Synopsys Design Compiler. The engine, without the memory, is estimated to occupy $1.1\text{mm}^2$ and is estimated to consume an average static power of 7.9 mW when running at a speed of 120 MHz.

The proposed engine's control overhead is less than 10% of the total processing cycles. Pipelined processing of data is interrupted mainly by CORDIC subroutine in an average of 4820 cycles/symbol. A total of 95 MIPS are supported @ 120 MHz.

Engine features that helped to get a low chip area and power consumption are:

1. The use of optimized instruction set. This removed many control overheads and allowed faster executions.

2. Memory architecture that reduces memory interactions, even with complex vector instructions.

3. The mechanism of data movement to/from the CU and the memories.

4. Grouping of all units and increasing the degree of hardware reuse.

5. No cache memory is used.

Comparison between the engine results and other dedicated and configurable architectures results in terms of power consumption, not accounting for memory in our engine, is shown in Table 3 The powers of the stated architectures are scaled (technology & frequency

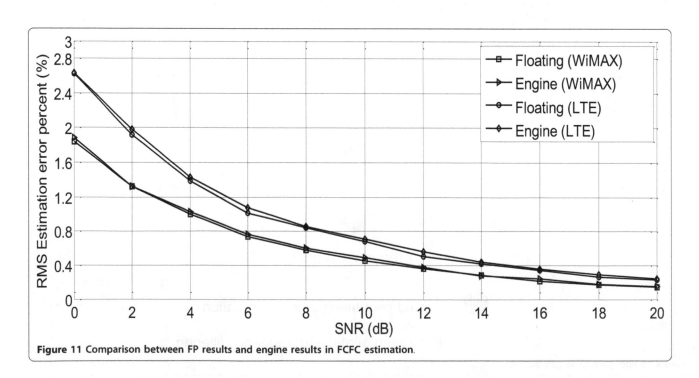

**Figure 11 Comparison between FP results and engine results in FCFC estimation.**

**Table 3 Power comparison between the proposed engine and other architectures**

| Method | Implementation type | Task | Scaled power (mW) |
|--------|---------------------|------|-------------------|
| [21] | Configurable | Symbol timing | 148.58 |
| [22] | Dedicated | Symbol timing | 22.5 |
| [23] | Dedicated | Symbol timing, FCFO | 5.13 (Conventional) |
|  |  |  | 0.3541 (sign ML) |
| Proposed ASIP | Configurable | All in Table 4 | 8 |

**Table 5 Parameters in IEEE 802.16e, LTE Rel. 8 (PSS, SSS are primary and secondary synchronizationsymbols)**

| parameter | IEEE 802.16e | LTE Rel. 8 |
|-----------|--------------|------------|
| Useful symbol time ($\mu s$) | 91.428 | 66.667 |
| Subcarrier spacing (KHz) | 10.9 | 15 |
| Max. CP length (samples) | 256 (22.85 $\mu s$) | 160 (10.41 $\mu s$) |
| Max. number of pilots | 240 | 200 |
| Max. preamble length | 2048 | 72 (PSS), 72 (SSS) |

scaling) to match the proposed engine. Based on the estimated power consumption of the proposed engine, the engine is more power. In [23], the proposed architecture supports only symbol timing and FCFO estimation. It is ten times power efficient as it uses only the signs of the data samples, but it causes large performance degradation.

Table 4 illustrates the cycle budget for various synchronization sub-tasks in IEEE802.16e and 3GPP LTE Rel. 8 for the most demanding parameters specified in Table 5

A comparison between FPGA dedicated hardware implementation results and engine results in WiMAX is shown in Table 6 for the parameters specified in Table 5 The area is reduced by a factor of three while the latency is slightly increased in some tasks but still meeting the standard requirements.

Syntheses results of the CU on a STRATIX III FPGA are tabulated in Table 7

We programmed the processor using one complete program that is executed at the beginning of every new frame. Otherwise, only the packet detection part of the code is executed till the beginning of an incoming frame. Tracking algorithms have proven to be the most power consuming as it is executed every symbol, unlike the acquisition algorithms that executes only at the beginning of reception.

To fully utilize the capabilities of the proposed engine, it is recommended to maximize the utilization of operations that have a fast execution phase in the instruction set. This requires understanding the proposed architecture with the attached instruction set when developing the algorithms. The assembly programmer should take

**Table 6 Comparison between dedicated implementations and engine results in WiMAX**

| Process | # Gates (k) | # Mul. | # Cycles | Max. Freq. (MHz) |
|---------|-------------|--------|----------|------------------|
| FBD | 49 | 1 | 21 | 147 |
| FCFO | 18 | 1 | 142 | 161 |
| CS # ICFO | 251 | 4 | 5112 | 107 |
| RCFO | 54 | 2 | 2644 | 145 |
| SCFO | 54 | 2 | 2640 | 145 |
| Proposed | 118 | 3 | Table 4 | 159 |

care of various parameters that make the execution faster. For example, if pilot subcarriers are arranged at the same indices over time, there is no need to use special arrangements like the one shown in Figure 10 Normal arrangement of pilots beside each other will reduce the complexity when executing the rest of RCFO & SCFO estimation algorithm.

The engine is verified by running all the synchronization subsystem tasks in 802.16e and LTE release 8. It meets the timing requirements @ 120 MHz, while the maximum operating frequency is 149 MHz. To support larger systems in a scalable way, more than one CU can be inserted and controlled with the same control vector. In this case, accumulation outputs O3, O4 in Figure 4

**Table 7 Synthesis results**

| FPGA type | Altera Stratix III EP3SC150 |
|-----------|------------------------------|
| Total ALUT | 752/113,600 (< 1%) |
| DSP blocks (18bit) | 3 |
| Dedicated logic registers | 262/113,600 (< 1%) |
| Block RAM | 54.4844/5499 Kbit (< 1%) |
| Max. clock frequency | 159MHz |

**Table 4 Resulting cycle budget for different tasks**

| Processing Task | # Cycles (WiMAX) | Latency @ 120 MHz ($\mu s$) | # Cycles (LTE) | Latency @ 120 MHz ($\mu s$) |
|-----------------|------------------|------------------------------|----------------|------------------------------|
| FBD | 894/frame | 7.45 | 606/frame | 5.05 |
| FCFO | 214/frame | 1.78 | 142/frame | 1.16 |
| CS # ICFO | 10830/frame | 90.25 | 3520/frame | 29.33 |
| RCFO | 5288/symbol | 44.117 | 4408/symbol | 36.73 |
| SCFO | 5284/symbol | 44.08 | 4404/symbol | 36.70 |

are fed directly to another unit through the two input ports I9, I10.

## 7 Conclusion

In this article, a scalable embedded reconfigurable baseband ASIP for OFDM synchronization sub-system has been proposed. The processor can support a multitude of OFDM-based standards. Although the engine is optimized for OFDM synchronization purposes through detailed analysis of synchronization tasks in the different OFDM-based standards, it also offers a high degree of flexibility to support other simple and vector operations. Area, power and hardware complexity are reduced through reconfiguration of a single unit to support multiple special operations optimized for synchronization sub-system. The processor was successfully tested on IEEE 802.16e and 3GPP LTE Rel. 8 standards. Synthesis results show that it is efficient in terms of throughput, area and power consumption.

**Acknowledgements**
The authors would like to thank H.A.H. Fahmy, K. Osama, and H. Hamed for their invaluable comments while preparing this article.

**Competing interests**
The authors declare that they have no competing interests.

## References

1. Glossner J, Iancu D, Jin L, Hokenek E, Moudgill M: **A software-defined communications baseband design.** *IEEE Commun Mag* 2003, **41**:120-128.
2. Vogt N, Wehn T: **A Reconfigurable ASIP for convolutional and turbo decoding in an SDR environment.** *IEEE Trans Very Large Scale Integrat (VLSI) Syst* 2008, **16**:1309-1320.
3. Abdelall M, Shalash AF, Fahmy HAH: **A reconfigurable baseband processor for wireless OFDM synchronization sub-system.** *IEEE Int Symp Circ Syst* 2011.
4. Azar C, Ojail M, Chevobbe S, David R: **CERA: a channel estimation reconfigurable architecture.** *IEEE Int Conf Telecom-mun ICT* 2010, **17**:957-964.
5. *ETSI Broadband radio access networks (BRAN), Hiperlan type2; physical (PHY) layer, ETSI BRAN, Technical Report* 2000, **101**:475.
6. *IEEE802.11, Wireless LAN Medium Access Control(MAC) and Physical Layer (PHY) specification: High-Speed Physical Layer in the 5GHz Band, IEEE Std 802.11a-1999, IEEE Computer Society* 2000.
7. *IEEE, (IEEE) Standard for Local and metropolitan area networks, Part 16: Air Interface for Fixed and Mobile Broadband Wireless Access Systems, IEEE 802.16e-2005 and IEEE 802.16-2004/Corl-2005* 2006.
8. Speth M, Fechtel SA, Fock G, Meyr H: **Optimum receiver design for wireless broad-band systems using OFDM: Part I.** *IEEE Trans Commun* 1999, **47**:1668-1677.
9. Mei B, Lambrechts A, Verkest D: **Architecture exploration for a reconfigurable architecture template.** *IEEE Des Test Comput* 2005, **22**:90-101.
10. Ebeling C, Fisher C, Xing G, Shen M, Liu H: **Implementing an OFDM receiver on the RaPiD reconfigurable architecture.** *IEEE Trans Signal Process* 2004, **53**:1436-1448.
11. Poon ASY: **An energy-efficient reconfigurable baseband processor for wireless communications.** *IEEE Trans VLSI* 2007, **15**:319-327.
12. Dawid H, Meyr H: **CORDIC algorithms and architectures.** *Digital Signal Process Multimedia Syst* 1999, **2**:623-655.
13. Wu J-M, Chou C-H: *Baseband Sampling Clock Frequency Synchronization for WiMAX Systems, Institute of Communications Engineering National Tsing Hua University Hsinchu* 2005.
14. van de Beek JJ, Sandell M, Borjesson PO: **ML Estimation of Time and Frequency Offset in OFDM Systems.** *IEEE Trans Signal Process* 1997, **45**:1800-1805.
15. Speth M, Fechtel SA, Fock G, Meyr H: **Optimum receiver design for OFDM-based broadband transmission.** *II A case study IEEE Trans Commun* 2001, **49**:571-578.
16. Bhatt T, Sundaramurthy V, Zhang JC, McCain D: *Initial Synchronization for 802.16e Downlink,Signals, Asilomar Conference on Systems and Computers ACSSC* 2006, **40**:701-707.
17. Tang H, Lau KY, Brodersen RW: **Synchronization Schemes for Packet OFDM System.** *IEEE Int Conf Commun ICC* 2003, **5**:3346-3350.
18. Heiskala H, Terry JT: **OFDM wireless LANs: A Theoretical and Practical Guide.** *Sams Publishing, Indianapolis* 2002.
19. Hung K-C, Lin DW: **Joint detection of integral carrier frequency offset and preamble index in OFDMA WiMAX downlink synchronization.** *IEEE Wireless Communications and Networking Conference (WCNC)* 2007, 1959-1964.
20. Lin Y-C, Su S-L, Wang H-C: **A low complexity cell search method for IEEE 802.16e OFDMA systems.** *International Conference on Advanced Communication Technology (ICACT)* 2009, **2**:980-984.
21. Harju L, Nurmi J: **A synchronization coprocessor architecture for WCDMA/ OFDM mobile terminal implementations.** *International Symposium on System-on-Chip* 2005, 141-145.
22. Troya A, Maharatna K, Krstic M, Grass E: **Low-power VLSI implementation of the inner receiver for OFDM-Based WLAN systems.** *IEEE Trans Circ Syst* 2008, **55**:672-686.
23. Li X, Zheng Y, Lai Z: **A low complexity sign ML detector for symbol and frequency synchronization of OFDM systems.** *IEEE Trans Consumer Electron* 2006, **52**:317-320.

# 14

# Dynamic voltage and frequency scaling over delay-constrained mobile multimedia service using approximated relative complexity estimation

Jihyeok Yun[*], Deepak Kumar Singh and Doug Young Suh

## Abstract

This paper deals with dynamic voltage and frequency scaling (DVFS) in mobile multimedia services. The multimedia services that consume a large amount of energy cannot be continuously used in mobile devices because of battery limitation. The DVFS has been applied to multimedia services in previous studies. However, they have only addressed the issue of power saving and overlooked the fact that mobile multimedia services are sensitive to delays. The proposed method is intended to apply DVFS to multimedia services considering potential delays. Another problem with previous studies is that either separate devices have been employed or appropriate frequency scaling values have been determined through complicated calculation processes to apply DVFS to multimedia services. On the contrary, the proposed method determines appropriate frequency scaling values using the characteristics of multimedia contents without employing any separate devices or undergoing complicated calculation processes. This has the advantage of allowing DVFS to be applied to real-time multimedia content. The present paper proposes a DVFS application method that divides multimedia services into video conferences, which are real-time services, and video streaming, which is a non-real-time service, and that reduces energy consumption in a simple manner while considering the constraints of service delays.

**Keywords:** Dynamic voltage and frequency scaling; Mobile; Multimedia; Real-time; Power saving

## Introduction

The quality requirements for handheld devices' video services have been continuously increasing. As a result, it has been challenging to maintain the high level of quality required to satisfy consumers. In this paper, we propose a dynamic voltage and frequency scaling (DVFS) complexity estimation algorithm that can produce power-saving effects close to those produced using previous DVFS with no additional devices or complexity. DVFS is a method of reducing a processor's power consumption by adjusting applied voltage to a processor dynamically.

According to [1-3], the power consumption of a processor is proportional to the square of its supply voltage, and supply voltage is proportional to frequency. Based on these relationships, power consumption can be reduced

by adjusting voltage and frequency appropriately. After estimating the complexity of a processor, which is required for decoding, voltage and frequency will be applied appropriately to the estimated complexity.

In the case of [1], although DVFS was adopted as a power-saving method for wireless mobile devices with limited power, video quality was allowed to deteriorate to reduce the complexity of the codec as with [4]. However, the methods proposed by [1,4] are not suitable for the recent trend of mobile video services in which high-resolution and high-definition video services are preferred.

Ma et al. [2] proposed modeling the complexity of video frames by analyzing the individual module units of video decoders using an appropriate complexity model proposed by [5,6], which adds a complexity profiler to video decoders. This model increases complexity due to the added extra profiler and does not consider the frame drop or buffering phenomenon, which is generated due

* Correspondence: jihyeok.yun@gmail.com
Department of Electronics and Information, Kyunghee University, Yongin 446-701, South Korea

to an estimation error that may occur because of the jittering.

Cho and Cho [3] proposed an algorithm to find the optimum combination of frequency and voltage in which the decoding slack time is 0 while decoding time information is stored because of the frequency and voltage applied to a processor. To this end, Cho and Cho [3] used complexity interpolation based on the frame information (e.g., frame size, frame type) under [7] and the feedback control proposed by [8]. However, since Cho and Cho [3] evaluated the performance of this complexity estimation conducted through interpolation based on super low-resolution images (e.g., 240 × 128, 192 × 144, 192 × 112) with small differences in complexity between frames, its applicability to the current trend of using high-resolution images is uncertain. High-resolution and high-definition images involve significant differences in complexity between frames, and thus, complexity estimation errors using linear interpolation are substantial. In addition, this algorithm has to store decoding information between certain periods and cannot prevent a frame drop or a buffering phenomenon since an estimation of the next frame is calculated after taking into account the overhead due to estimation errors.

In this paper, we propose an estimation method that requires simple profilers or calculations for complexity estimation as well as a DVFS method that prevents frame drop and buffering, which is in contrast with the methods proposed in [2,3]. Our proposed estimation method does complexity estimation with simple profilers or calculations by using the characteristic of multimedia content requiring the repeated processing of similar calculations.

For video content, as the coded frame type is the same and frames are temporally nearer, the similarity becomes higher. This principle is based on the most representative principle of video codec compression. As described in [9], the H.264/AVC standard, which is the most widely used reference codec, also increases the compressibility of the codec using the similarities between temporally close frames. Therefore, it is effective to perform voltage and frequency scaling by taking advantage of complexity information of frames that have been decoded most recently and the same coded frame types requiring no extra calculation processing. In addition, our proposed method sets the limited delay bound of the delays caused by estimation errors, and if the limited delay bound is exceeded, the corresponding frame is decoded with a processor's maximum frequency. As such, if one frame is decoded with maximum frequency, the delay problem is solved, but overhead still exists in terms of power. However, since the number of estimation errors is small due to the offset caused by adding and subtracting repeatedly, and decoding time is reduced significantly when decoded with the maximum frequency, the related overhead is minimal. With such a small amount of energy consumption, frame drop or buffering caused by estimation errors does not occur, and energy-saving effects can be obtained, unlike in existing methods.

## Complexity estimation with delay control

As shown in [9], the complexity estimation method proposed in this paper is performed with regard to frame types constituting videos used in H.264/AVC such as intra-frames (I-frame), unidirectionally predicted frames (P-frame), and bidirectionally predictive frames (B-frame), respectively, as shown in Figure 1. It refers the same type of complexity information that has been decoded most recently without extra modeling or estimation algorithms.

The equations for estimation are dependent on the structure of the group of pictures (GOP). The GOP structures usually used in H.264/AVC are shown in Figure 1a, b.

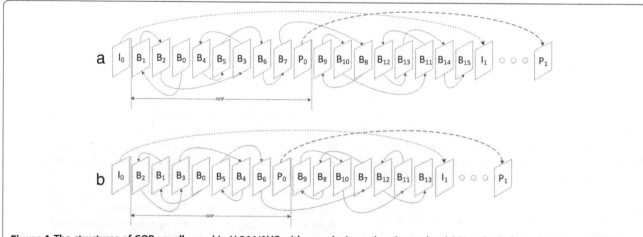

**Figure 1 The structures of GOP usually used in H.264/AVC with complexity estimation order.** (a) Non-dyadic hierarchical structure. **(b)** Dyadic hierarchical structure. The round dot dashed line shows the reference structure for the I frame, the long dashed line shows the reference structure for the P frame, and the solid dashed line shows the reference structure for the B frame.

Figure 1a is a non-dyadic hierarchical structure, and Figure 1b is dyadic hierarchical structure.

Since our proposed model targets video service, it takes advantage of one characteristic of videos: their similarity between temporally close frames. In our method, referenced frames for complexity can be searched using the GOP size and the intra-period, which are parameters of the video coder according to [9,10].

If the GOP size is $s$ and the intra-period is $p$, then the $n$th expected complexity of the I-frame $c_{exp\_i}[n]$ can be calculated using Equation 1. Similarly the $n$th expected complexity of the P-frame $c_{exp\_p}[n]$ can be calculated using Equation 2. The $n$th expected complexity of the B-frame $c_{exp\_b}[n]$ can be calculated using Equations 3 and 4. Equations 3 and 4 are the case of non-dyadic hierarchical structure and the case of dyadic hierarchical structure, respectively.

$$\text{I-frame}: c_{exp\_i}[n] = c[n-p] \quad \text{for} \quad (n\%p) = 0, \tag{1}$$

where $(n\%p)$ means ($n$ modulo $p$).

$$\text{P-frame}: c_{exp\_p}[n] = c[n-s] \text{ for } (n\%s) = 0, (n\%p) \neq 0 \tag{2}$$

B-frame (non Dyadic hierarchy with 4 temporal levels)

$$: c_{exp\_b}[n] = \begin{cases} c[n-4] & \text{for } (n\%3) = 0 \\ c[n+2] & \text{for } (n\%3) = 1 \\ c[n-1] & \text{for } (n\%3) = 2 \end{cases} \tag{3}$$

Equation 2 represents the non-dyadic hierarchical B-frame with four temporal levels.

B frame (Dyadic hierachy with 4 temporal levels) $: c_{exp\_b}[n]$

$$= \begin{cases} c\left[n-\left(\frac{s}{2^m}+1\right)\right] \text{ for } \left(n\%\frac{s}{2^m}\right) = 0, m = 1 \\ \begin{cases} c[n-\left(\frac{s}{2^m}+1\right) \text{ for } n > \frac{s}{2^{m-1}}, \left(n\%\frac{s}{2^m}\right) = 0, 2 \leq m < \log_2 s \\ c[n+\left(\frac{s}{2^m}\right) \text{ for } n < \frac{s}{2^{m-1}}, \left(n\%\frac{s}{2^m}\right) = 0, 2 \leq m < \log_2 s \\ \begin{cases} c[n-2] \text{ for } (n\%4) = 3, (n\%2) \neq 0 \\ c[n+1] \text{ for } (n\%4) = 1, (n\%2) \neq 0 \end{cases} \end{cases} \end{cases} \tag{4}$$

Equation 4 represents the dyadic hierarchical B-frame with four temporal levels.

$$\Delta = t[n-1] - \{t_{slack} \cdot (n-1)\}, \tag{5}$$

where $\Delta$ is the discrepancy between $t_{slack} \cdot (n-1)$, which is the time to be decoded, and $t[n-1]$, which is the time when decoding is finished. $|\Delta|$ will be controlled to converge to 0 and to be no larger than $J_{max}$, the jitter limit.

$$f_{exp}[n] = c_{exp}[n]/t_{slack}, \tag{6}$$

where $c_{exp}[n]$ and $f_{exp}[n]$ represented by Equation 6, $c[n]$ respectively, estimate the complexity of frame $n$ and

frequency, which enables a frame to be decoded for $t_{slack}$. In order to lower jitter, the expected frequency $f_{exp}[n]$ is modified according to $\Delta$.

$$f[n] = \begin{cases} f_{max} & \text{for } J_{max} < \Delta \\ f_{exp}[n] + \left(f_{max} - f_{exp}[n]\right)\frac{\Delta}{J_{max}} & \text{for } 0 < \Delta \leq J_{max} \\ c_{exp}[n]/(t_{slack} - \Delta) & \text{for otherwise} \end{cases} \tag{7}$$

If the process is significantly behind schedule, as in Figure 2a, then the highest frequency is used, as shown in Equation 7 for $J_{max} < \Delta$, while the process is accelerated, as in Figure 2b, in Equation 4 for $0 < \Delta \leq J_{max}$ and the process is decelerated, as shown in Figure 2c, in Equation 7 for *otherwise* to control delay variation.

Ma et al. [2] assumed that jitters would not occur, as shown Figure 2c, and thus, that spare time that could be utilized for frame decoding would always exist. However, in the present study, jitters that may occur when DVFS is utilized in the process of video decoding were considered in preparation for situations, as shown in Figure 2a, b.

In our proposed estimation method, when there is no anchor for estimation such as the start time for decoding or the changing of a channel, decoding is performed by applying maximum frequency to a processor. For each frame type, after one frame undergoes performance decoding, the previous frame can act as an anchor so that estimation can be done.

In the present study, approximated complexity is used as the reference complexity to estimate the next frame's decoding complexity. Whereas the reference complexity was determined using the number of bits applied to all compositors of the decoder in the case of [2], in the present study, the reference complexity is determined using main modules' major processing time compared to the decoding time. The approximated complexity can be relatively expressed, as shown in Figure 3, if the share of the main modules in the entire process is known. Therefore, the reference complexity can be drawn without decoding an entire video's data. As the main modules, the inverse transform, inverse quantization, interpolation, motion compensation, and loop filter can be selected, which are the decoder's most frequently used modules among the parameters in Tables two and three in [5].

On measuring the calculations of all modules of H.264/AVC using [11], it can be seen that the aforementioned main modules spend an average of 80% of the entire execution time. After getting the values of execution time of each module and the current frequency of the processor, we use them in Equation 6 to calculate the complexity of frame. This process is known as complexity profiling used in [2,10,12,13]. Since this value hardly changes with changes in diverse compression options supported by H.264/AVC, in the present study, an approximate value estimated based

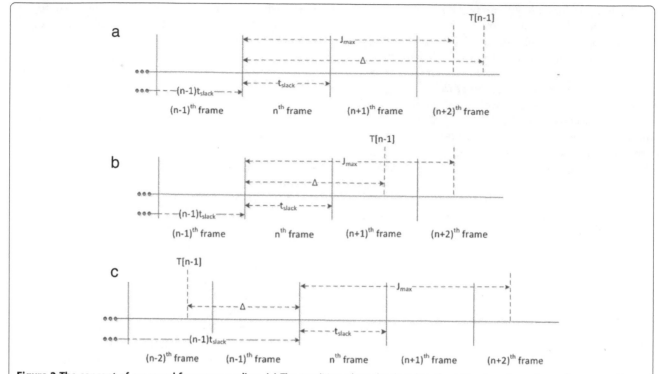

**Figure 2 The concept of proposed frequency scaling. (a)** The condition where the decoding should be done in maximum frequency without DVFS. **(b)** The condition where the decoding should be done in DVFS within the jitter limit. **(c)** The condition where the decoding should be done in DVFS within the slack time.

on the main modules' complexity, as shown in Figure 3, is used as the anchor complexity information.

By using the anchor complexity measured as such, the next frames can be estimated with approximated relative complexity, as shown in Figure 4, until the next scene-to-scene transition occurs and the similarity between frames disappears.

In Figure 5, the whole operating process of the proposed estimation algorithm, profiling algorithm, and frequency scaling algorithm while decoding is shown.

Below, Figure 6 shows a scatter graph of the actual complexity compared to the estimated complexity for all frames (167,857 frames) of [12], using our proposed method. Figure 6a shows a case composed of only I-frames

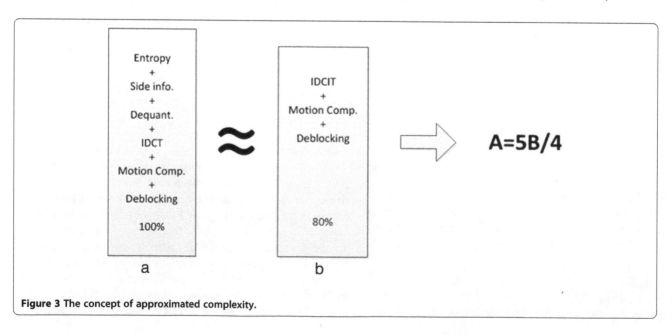

**Figure 3 The concept of approximated complexity.**

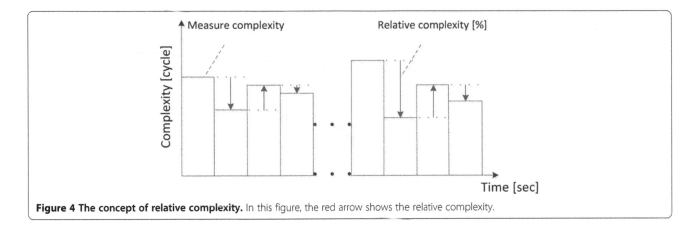

**Figure 4 The concept of relative complexity.** In this figure, the red arrow shows the relative complexity.

and P-frames, a combination of frame types used for general real-time video services (e.g., video conversations), and Figure 6b shows a case composed of I-frames, P-frames, and B-frames, a combination of frame types used for general non-real-time video services (e.g., videos on demand).

If many scene changes occur, the proposed complexity estimation method generates estimation errors as a result of reduced similarity between neighboring frames. If the estimation value is larger than the actual value, it generates energy wasting, and if the estimation value is smaller than the actual value, it generates delay. As shown in Figure 6, since the estimation error shows a symmetrical form between the right and left sides, the estimation error is offset. As a result, we can see that delay and power-saving efficiency have a tradeoff relationship with each other.

Figure 7 shows a logarithmic scaled negative cumulative density function (cdf) of estimation error. The cdf becomes almost 1 near the zero error value. This shows that the proposed estimation is valid, while large errors also

exist even at low probability. Large errors may be caused by scene changes. In the case of Figure 7a, b for real-time services, despite the numerous scene-to-scene transitions occurring in 167,857 frames, approximately 90% of the frames show estimation errors of approximately 10%, indicating a high level of similarity between adjacent frames.

Figure 7a illustrates a case where two types of frames - I-frames and P-frames - were used to compose image sequences, and Figure 7b depicts a case where three types of frames - I-frames, P-frames, and B-frames - were used to compose image sequences.

Figures 6 and 7 show the estimation accuracy of the proposed method. From these figures, we can see that the proposed method can show the unexpected large estimation errors that may occur. Usually, the frame correlation is high because of the same frame type and being adjacent to each other. However, during cases like scene change, the frame correlation becomes low. This is the case where there occur large estimation errors. In

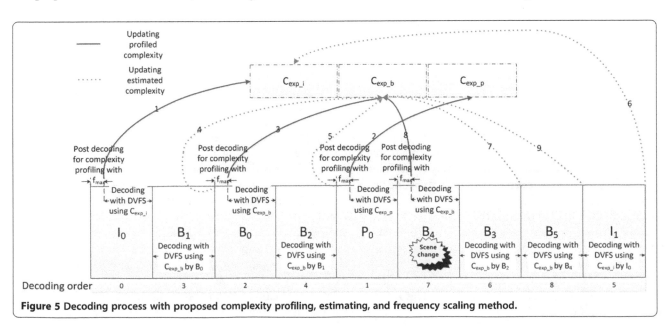

**Figure 5 Decoding process with proposed complexity profiling, estimating, and frequency scaling method.**

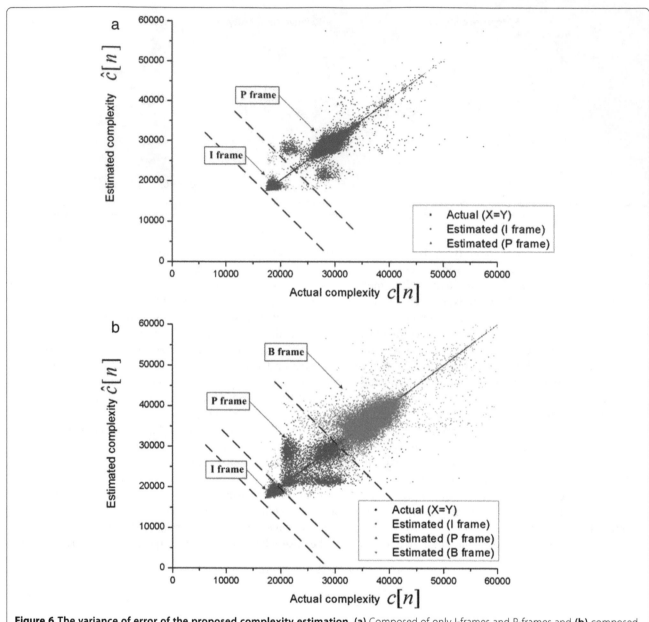

**Figure 6 The variance of error of the proposed complexity estimation. (a)** Composed of only I-frames and P-frames and **(b)** composed of I-frames, P-frames, and B-frames.

this case, complexity information for estimation for the next frame cannot be used, and we should update the complexity information. So, we use complexity profiling with max frequency of processor which is explained in Equation 7.

Regarding delay and power wasting, which are generated despite the offset between estimation errors while using our proposed method, we compare them by considering the accepted delay bound according to the characteristics of buffer and service [14,15]. Our proposed method for delay control, as shown in Figure 2, is performed using Equation 7.

The proposed complexity profiling is operated at the beginning of decoding or when there is scene change. The profiling is done for each frame type (i.e., I-, P- and B-frames). The proposed complexity profiler detects the execution time of modules of the decoder (i.e., inverse transform, inverse quantization, interpolation, motion compensation, and loop filter) same as that of [2,10,12]. When the correlation between the frames of the same type is high, we do not use the profiler and just estimate by execution time of the previous frame.

In [2], profiling is performed in all frames. Each module has the complexity coefficient where complexity coefficient

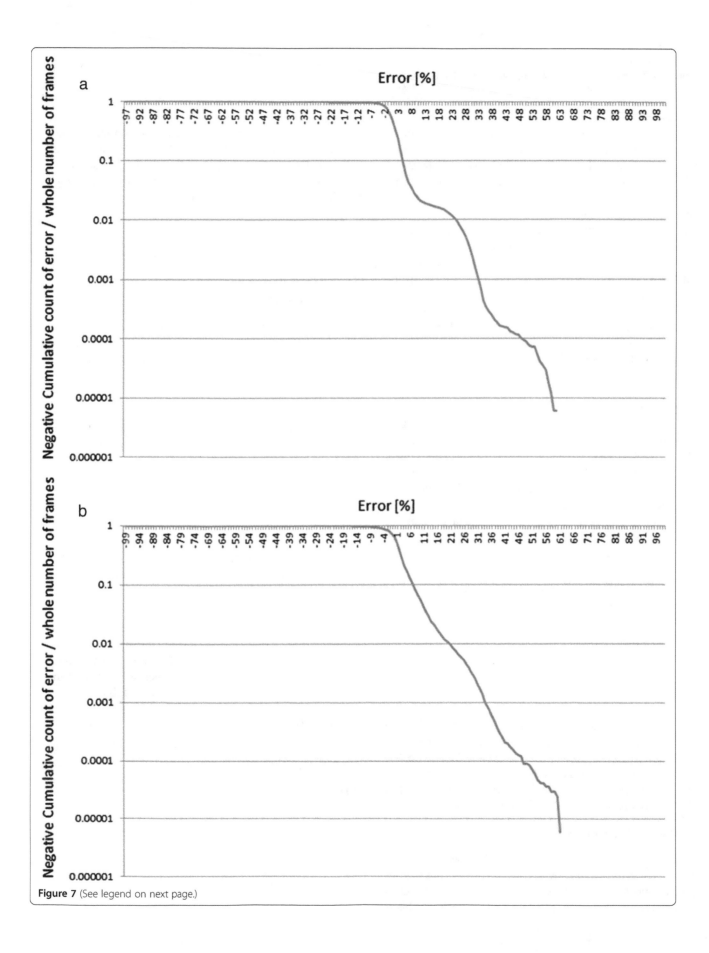

**Figure 7** (See legend on next page.)

(See figure on previous page.)
**Figure 7 Negative cumulative density function of complexity estimation error. (a)** Where I-frames and P-frames were used to compose image sequences and **(b)** where I-frames, P-frames, and B-frames were used to compose image sequences.

means complexity of the module operating in 1 bit. During decoding, the number of bits in each module is known; thus, we can determine the total complexity of the frame.

In [10], complexity profiling is done in every frame using the execution time like that mentioned in our proposed profiling method.

In [12], complexity profiling is done in every frame using the execution cycle of each module.

In [2,10,12], complexity is predicted using different algorithms, but all of them performed post-decoding for all of the frames. However, in our proposed method, we perform post-decoding when there is scene change and on the first frame of each frame type (i.e., I, P, B). Therefore, the proposed method reduces the post-decoding of all frames. This reduction of post-decoding may reduce the access to profiling memory.

## Energy consumption

DVFS is a method used to control a processor's calculation frequency to reduce the amount of energy used for calculations. Basically, when the number of calculations is large, the voltage is amplified to increase the processor's frequency. The correlation formula can be calculated using formulas 8 and 9 as with [2,16,17].

Frequency $f$ is determined using formula 8 below as with [2,16,17].

$$f = c/t \qquad (8)$$

As shown in the above formula, the frequency (Hz) of the processor is inversely proportional to calculation time $t$ (s) and proportional to the number of calculations $c$ (cycle). Supply voltage in complementary metal-oxide-semiconductor (CMOS) circuits can be expressed as shown in formula 9.

$$V_{dd} = \omega f^{\varphi} + \theta, \qquad (9)$$

where, $\omega$, $\varphi$, $\theta$ are coefficients determined by the underlying platform. As a representative example, Intel Pentium M1.6GHz (Intel Corporation, Santa Clara, CA, USA) of 90-nm processes has values $\theta = 0.61$, $\varphi = 1$, and $\omega = 5.6 \times 10^{-10}$, as shown in [18]. As mentioned in [16], the power (W) of CMOS circuits is expressed by formula 10 below.

$$P_{\text{total}} = P_{\text{dyn}} + P_{\text{DC}} + P_{\text{on}} \qquad (10)$$

According to [16], $P_{\text{dyn}}$ is the dynamic power consumption, which is determined by the supply voltage and the frequency, and $P_{\text{DC}}$ is the static power consumption, which is the leakage power consumption of CMOS devices. This is

determined by the supply voltage and the constant value. $P_{\text{on}}$ is the power that maintains the 'power on' state of the processor. This is assumed as 0.1 W in the present study.

Dynamic power consumption $P_{\text{dyn}}$ is calculated using the following formula in Watt units.

$$P_{\text{dyn}} = K_{\text{eff}} V_{dd}^2 f \qquad (11)$$

Formula 11 can be expressed as formula 12 using formula 9.

$$P_{\text{dyn}} = K_{\text{eff}} (\omega f^{\varphi} + \theta)^2 f, \qquad (12)$$

where $K_{\text{eff}}$ is the effective circuit capacitance.

Dynamic calculation energy (J) is calculated as dynamic power $P_{\text{dyn}}$ multiplied by time $t$, as shown in formula 13.

$$E_{\text{dyn}} = P_{\text{dyn}} t \qquad (13)$$

Formula 13 can be expressed as formula 14 using formula 12, and formula 14 can be re-expressed as formula 15 using formula 8 so that the proposed estimation method can be applied to obtain dynamic energy.

$$E_{\text{dyn}} = K_{\text{eff}} (\omega f^{\varphi} + \theta)^2 f t \qquad (14)$$

$$E_{\text{dyn}} = K_{\text{eff}} \left( \omega \left( \frac{c}{t} \right)^{\varphi} + \theta \right)^2 c \qquad (15)$$

Static power consumption $P_{\text{DC}}$ can be calculated in voltage units using formula 16 and Table 1 based on [17].

$$P_{\text{DC}} = V_{dd} I_{\text{subn}} + |V_{\text{bs}}| I_j \qquad (16)$$

In formula 16, $V_{\text{bs}}$ is the body bias voltage, and this is assumed to be −0.7 V in the present invention. $I_j$ is the reverse bias junction current, which is a constant value. $I_{\text{subn}}$ is the sub-threshold current, which is calculated in Ampere units using formula 17 below and Table 1.

$$I_{\text{subn}} = K_3 e^{K_4 V_{dd}} e^{K_5 V_{\text{bs}}} \qquad (17)$$

Leakage power consumption $P_{\text{DC}}$ and $P_{\text{on}}$ can be obtained using the above formulas, and leakage energy

**Table 1 Underlying coefficient of CMOS circuit**

| Constant | Value | Constant | Value |
|---|---|---|---|
| $K_1$ | 0.063 | $K_6$ | $5.26 \times 10^{-12}$ |
| $K_2$ | 0.153 | $K_7$ | −0.144 |
| $K_3$ | $5.38 \times 10^{-7}$ | $I_j$ | $4.8 \times 10^{-10}$ |
| $K_4$ | 1.83 | $V_{\text{bs}}$ | −0.7 |
| $K_5$ | 4.19 | | |

consumption $E_{DC}$ and $E_{on}$ can be obtained by multiplying calculation time $t$.

The total calculated energy is as shown in formula 18, and it can be calculated in Joule units using the above formulas in Joule units.

$$E_{total} = E_{dyn} + E_{DC} + E_{on} \qquad (18)$$

Figure 7 below shows the energy consumption experiment results when coefficients $\omega$, $\varphi$, and $\theta$ determined by the underlying platform were set to $5.6 \times 10^{-10}$, 1, and 0.61, respectively, and a certain complexity was decided at different frequencies. On reviewing Figure 8, it can be seen that when the same complexity is decoded, the energy decreases as the frequency is reduced, and the energy increases exponentially as the frequency is increased.

### Results of theoretical simulation

In this paper, we use underlying coefficients of the Intel Pentium mobile processor 1.6 GHz (Intel Corporation), and 167,857 frames of video [19] (DVD ver. 720 × 480 pixel quality) are decoded using the H.264/AVC reference software 18.3 version by [20]. Warner Bros. Entertainment's The Matrix [19] is the famous movie with intensive scene change subject to the worst scenario in our proposed method. A snapshot of [19] is shown in Figure 9.

To display raw files that are the decoder's outputs, the raw files should be transformed into RGB files. This work conducts float computations in pixel units. Therefore, no differences in the complexity between frames are caused by the transformation work in general cases where images of the same frame size are continued.

**Figure 9** Snapshot of motion-intensive video 'The Matrix'.

However, even if the complexity necessary for transformation work remains constant, since DVFS is conducted, the transformation work will be affected by frequency scaling, and thus, the energy consumption necessary will vary by frame.

### Complexity estimation

The first simulation compares the decoding of energy consumption of the processor between methods that use DVFS and the method that does not use DVFS [2], using complexity modeling and our proposed method. This simulation uses a science fiction, action movie [19] which is the worst simulation environment for our proposed method. We also assume that the estimation error of the comparison counterpart method [2] is 0%, which represents the best possible estimation.

As shown in Figure 10, the proposed method saves 73% more energy for decoding than the conventional non-DVFS method. This performance is almost the same as

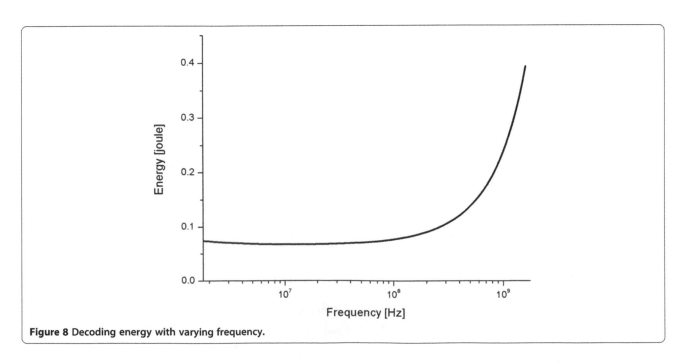

**Figure 8** Decoding energy with varying frequency.

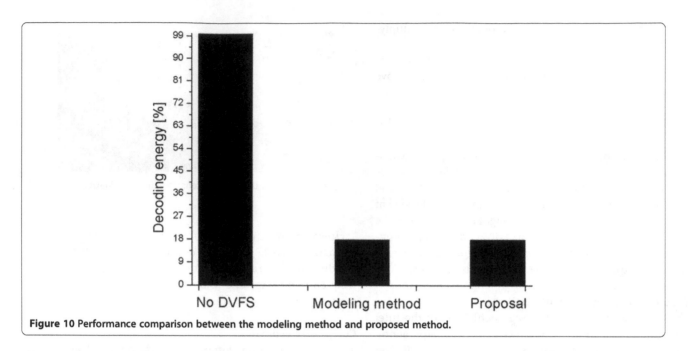

**Figure 10** Performance comparison between the modeling method and proposed method.

those of previous methods [2] in which the control algorithms used are much more sophisticated than ours.

### Delay control

The second simulation compares energy consumption while a method of frame drop prevention, which is generated by the estimation error of DVFS to support QoE, is used. Since Ma et al. [2] does not consider delay, in order to overcome an estimation error of 3%, DVFS shall be performed with a margin of 3% of complexity estimation. Our proposed method overcomes frame drop by setting a delay threshold as a buffer during DVFS operation to overcome the estimation error. The large buffer can overcome a large estimation error. This use of the buffer can make the proposed method adapted to real-time video service. When there is burst scene change, the total time required for post-decoding is large. So, the buffer can be used to overcome the delay caused by this time requirement.

Threshold values for delay, $D_{th}$, are set as three values such as 0.01 s (=10 ms), 0.1 s (=100 ms), and 1 s (=1,000 ms).

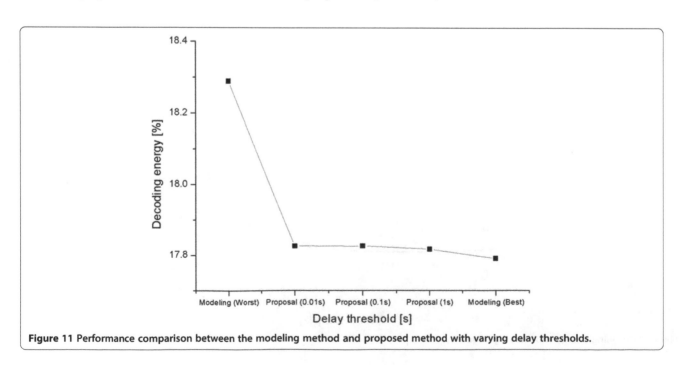

**Figure 11** Performance comparison between the modeling method and proposed method with varying delay thresholds.

The results of the second simulation show that energy efficiency improves 1.94% at a threshold of 0.01 s, 1.96% at 0.1 s, and 2% at 1 s, respectively, compared to the one using [2], as shown in Figure 11.

The third simulation compares reduction of post-decoding. We assume the scene change with a larger error rate than [2,10,12]. So, we perform the post-decoding to make the estimation error rate equal to the average estimation error of [2,10,12].

In case of [2], the average estimation error rate was 3%, so our assumed estimation error rate was higher than 3%. Similarly, for [10,12], the estimation rate was assumed based on their average estimation error rate.

Figure 12 shows reduction of post-decoding of the proposed method between the direct memory access (DMA) algorithm in [2]; RE-EST, Markov-1, and LMSE algorithm in [10]; and bitstream shaping algorithm in [12,13]. The result of Figure 12 shows that when compared with DMA performance for the same accuracy, the total number of post-decoding of the proposed method was more than that of the DMA algorithm. Though it is the bad result but when the target estimation error rate was increased to the average error rate of algorithms in [10,12], the proposed method shows better performance as the total number of post-decoding goes on decreasing. In this case, the threshold value for the optimal performance is 4%. So, if the achieved estimation error rate is more than 4%, then the proposed method can reduce the number of post-decoding. Therefore, the proposed method reduces the post-decoding and hence reduces the access to profiling memory.

**Table 2 Specific embedded testbed for experiment**

|  | Description |
| --- | --- |
| Processor | ARM Coretex™ - A9 dual core (2 GHz) |
| Memory | 1 GB LPDDR2 |
| LCD | 7" 800 × 400 resolution |
| System software | Linux Kernel 2.6.35.7, Android 2.3.5 (Gingerbread) |

**Results of experimental simulation**

On reviewing the results in theoretical simulation, it can be seen that quite excellent energy-saving effects can be obtained if the proposed method is used when the movie [19] is decoded using the H.264/AVC reference software 18.3 version. However, the results in the theoretical simulation only related to the energy consumed in the central processing unit (CPU) and did not consider the energy consumed in numerous background programs (e.g., display, system software, widget) as with cases where video services are used in actual mobile devices.

Energy-saving effects obtained when the method proposed in the theoretical simulation was applied to actual mobile devices were measured.

The system configuration of the embedded test board used in this experiment is shown in Table 2 below.

Linux Kernel-based android operating systems provide many forms of governors that support DVFS. The characteristics of representative governors are shown in Table 3.

Android-based mobile devices generally produced for commercial purposes use the on-demand governor that changes frequencies gradually depending on the load

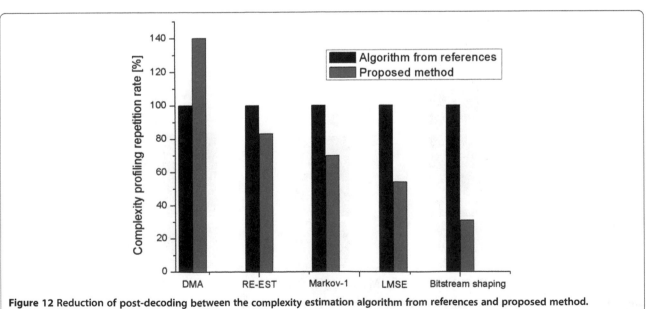

**Figure 12** Reduction of post-decoding between the complexity estimation algorithm from references and proposed method.

**Table 3 Characteristics of CPU governors on Linux-based operating system**

| Governor | Frequency scaling method |
| --- | --- |
| Performance | Uses only the maximum clock frequency that can be provided by the CPU |
| Powersave | Uses only the minimum clock frequency that can be provided by the CPU |
| Ondemand | Changes between the maximum/minimum frequencies depending on load conditions |
| Conservative | Gradually changes between the maximum ~ minimum frequencies depending on load conditions |
| Userspace | Uses the frequency designated by the user |

conditions of the CPU. However, since gradual frequency changes are not suitable for cases where loads vary according to the kind of frames that constitute videos, the userspace governor that changes frequencies as requested by the user was used in this experiment.

Please note that the frequencies that can be designated using the userspace governor in the aforementioned system configuration of the embedded testbed are limited to 2 GHz, 1.6 GHz, 1 GHz, and 400 MHz.

Figure 13 below shows the results of experiments using the proposed method in the aforementioned experimental environment.

As with the experiment in the theoretical simulation, this experiment compared decoding energy consumption among cases where DVFS was not used, cases where the method under [2] used complexity modeling, and cases where the proposed method was used. This experiment was conducted with [12], which is a science fiction, action movie with the lowest level of similarity among

frames; this experimental environment can show the worst performance of the proposed method, while the method under [2] with which the proposed method was compared was a case of best performance with an estimation error of 0%.

On reviewing Figure 13, it can be seen that the amount of energy corresponding to 91.08% of the energy consumed in cases where DVFS was not used was consumed in the case of best performance under [2], and 91.41% of the energy was consumed in the case where the proposed method was used despite the fact that no separate computation for estimation was conducted. Given these results, it can be seen that although the energy-saving efficiency was lower in this experiment than in the theoretical simulation where only the energy efficiency of the CPU was tested, since this experiment was conducted in an environment where numerous background programs operated together, as in actual use environments, when compared with [1], almost the same energy-saving effect could be identified despite the fact that the experimental environment was the worst for the proposed method similar to the results in the theoretical simulation.

## Conclusion

As discussed in the 'Introduction', conventional methods that apply DVFS to video decoding use extra estimation profilers or post-decoding (i.e., calculations). These methods generate additional complexity and estimation errors. This paper proposes an estimation method that takes advantage of the correlation between video frames of the same frame type, which is in contrast to other estimation methods that uses only post-decoding. This

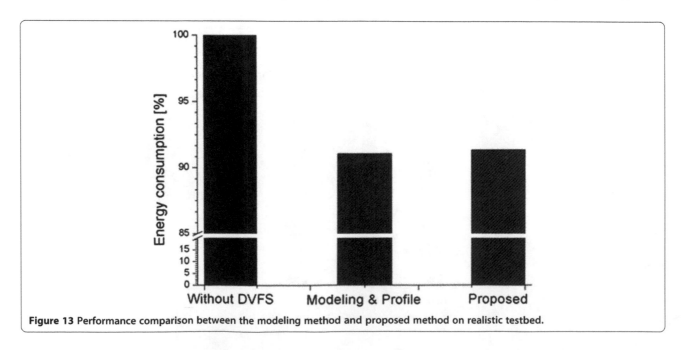

**Figure 13** Performance comparison between the modeling method and proposed method on realistic testbed.

proposed method shall have larger estimation errors compared to the conventional methods because it uses a less number of post-decoding than the conventional method.

When the estimation value is larger than the actual value, our proposed method controls decoding jitter from the estimation error if the range (i.e., $J_{max}$ in Figure 2) of estimation error is within the threshold value. On the other hand, since the conventional methods such as those of [2,3] do not consider delay, they can cause frame drop as a result of estimation errors. As shown in our simulation result, our proposed method, which uses fewer post-decoding, showed comparable performance with the performance of [2] that uses more post-decoding than the proposed method.

As a result of Figure 11, the proposed method, which sets the delay threshold (i.e., $J_{max}$ in Figure 2), is applied according to [14]. So, the proposed method can be used on different video types and services with delay acceptance (e.g., delay threshold for video conversation is 100 ms; delay threshold for video streaming is 1 s) and thus can be used to save energy.

Therefore, our proposed method reduces the number of post-decoding unlike the conventional algorithms where post-decoding is done to all frames. It may reduce the memory access of the profiler, but memory analysis was not performed to confirm it.

In this paper, we have discussed DVFS, which only considers video decoding. However, our future research can develop further energy-saving methods that can be used in the overall video service systems such as video data receiving, memory access, video decoding, and video display.

## Competing interests
The authors declare that they have no competing interests.

## Acknowledgments
This research was supported by the MKE (Ministry of Knowledge Economy), Korea under the ITRC (Information Technology Research Center) support program (NIPA-2012-H0301-12-1006) supervised by the NIPA (National IT Industry Promotion Agency). This research was funded by the MSIP (Ministry of Science, ICT & Future Planning), Korea in the ICT R&D Program 2013.

## References
1. Z He, Y Liang, Power-rate-distortion analysis for wireless video communication under energy constraints. IEEE Trans. Circuits Syst. Video Technol. 15(5), 645–658 (2005)
2. Z Ma, H Hu, Y Wang, On complexity modeling of H.264/AVC video decoding and its application for energy efficient decoding. IEEE Trans. Multimedia 13, 1240–1255 (2011)
3. J Cho, I Cho, A combined approach for QoS-guaranteed and low-power video decoding. IEEE Trans. Consumer Elec. 57, 651–657 (2011)
4. M van der Schaar, Y Andreopoulos, Rate-distortion-complexity modeling for network and receiver aware adaption. IEEE Trans. Multimedia 7(3), 471–479 (2005)
5. M Horowitz, A Joch, H.264AVC baseline profile decoder complexity analysis. IEEE Trans. Circuits Syst. Video Technol. 13(7), 704–716 (2003)
6. Z Ma, Z Zhang, Complexity modeling of H.264 entropy decoding, in *Proc. ICIP, San Diego, October 2008*
7. K Choi, W Cheng, Frame-based dynamic voltage and frequency scaling for an MPEG decoder, in *Proc. ICCAD, San Jose, November 2002*
8. Z Lu, J Lach, Reducing multimedia decode power using feedback control, in *Proceedings of International Conference on Computer Design, San Jose, October 2003*
9. T Wiegand, GJ Sulivan, Overview of the H.264/AVC video coding standard. IEEE Trans. Circuits Syst. Video Technol. 13(7), 560–576 (2003)
10. N Kontorinis, Y Andreopoulos, Statistical framework for video decoding complexity modeling and prediction. IEEE Trans. Circuits Syst. Video Technol. 19(7), 1000–1013 (2009)
11. Intel Parallel Studio, [Online], Available: software.intel.com/en-us/intel-parallel-studio-xe. Accessed 8 February 2012
12. E Akyol, M Scharr, Complexity model based proactive dynamic voltage scaling for video decoding systems. IEEE Trans. Multimedia 9(7), 1475–1492 (2007)
13. Y Andreopoulos, M van der Scharr, Complexity-constrained video bitstream shaping. IEEE Trans. Signal Process. 55(5), 1967–1974 (2007)
14. Nortel Networks, *QoS performance requirements for UMTS, 3GPP TSG SA S1* (Copenhagen, 1999)
15. S Wee, W Tan, Optimized video streaming for networks with varying delay, in *Proc. ICME, Lausanne, August 2002*
16. R Jejurikar, C Pereira, Leakage aware dynamic voltage scaling for real-time embedded systems, in *Proc. DAC, San Diego, July 2004*
17. S Martin, K Flautner, Combined dynamic voltage scaling and adaptive body biasing for optimal power consumption in microprocessors under dynamic workloads, in *Proc. ICCAD, San Jose, November 2002*
18. Intel Pentium Mobile Processor, [Online]. Available: http://www.intel.com/content/www/us/en/intelligent-systems/previous-generation/embedded-pentium-m.html. Accessed 15 January 2012
19. Warner Bros. Entertainment, *The Matrix* (United States, 1999)
20. Dolby Laboratories Inc., Fraunhofer-Institute HHI, Microsoft Corporation, *H.264/MPEG-4 AVC Reference Software Manual*. ISO/IEC JTC1/SC29/WG11 and ITU-T SG16 Q.6, JVT-X072, Geneva, 29 June–5 July 2007

# 15

# FPGA based wireless sensor node with customizable event-driven architecture

Junsong Liao, Brajendra K Singh, Mohammed AS Khalid and Kemal E Tepe[*]

**Abstract**

This article presents the design and implementation of modular customizable event-driven architecture with parallel execution capability for the first time with wireless sensor nodes using stand alone FPGA. This customizable event-driven architecture is based on modular generic event dispatchers and autonomous event handlers, which will help WSN application developers to quickly develop their applications by adding the required number of event dispatchers and event handlers as per the need of a WSN application. This architecture can handle multiple events in parallel, including high priority ones. Additionally, it provides non-preemptive operation which removes the timing uncertainty and overhead involved with interrupt-driven processor-based sensor node implementation, which is required in real-time wireless sensor networks (WSNs). Thus, higher computation power of FPGAs combined with the non-preemptive modular event-driven architecture with parallel execution capability enables a variety of new WSN applications and facilitates rapid prototyping of WSN applications. In this article, the performance of FPGA-based sensor device is compared with general purpose processor-based implementations of sensor devices. Results show that our FPGA-based implementation provides significant improvement in system efficiency measured in terms of clock cycle counts required for typical sensor network tasks such as packet transmission, relay and reception.

**Keywords:** Wireless sensor nodes, FPGA, ZigBee, Sensor networking

## Introduction

A wide variety of wireless sensor network (WSN) applications have been emerging that requires innovation in sensor devices. Most of the current sensor devices employ general purpose processor-based embedded system such as motes developed by the University California at Berkeley [1]. Those devices consist of a general purpose processor (also referred as commodity microcontroller), wireless transceiver and sensors subsystem. The general purpose processor needs event-based operating systems (OS) tailored for sensor network applications such as TinyOS [2] used in Berkeley motes. The available software tools and debugging platform offer easy development of WSN protocols and applications in these devices. That is why these motes are popular in academic research as well as in commercial applications.

General purpose processors are efficient in sequential execution of instructions and are not primarily designed

to exploit the inherent parallelism available in event-driven sensor applications. Furthermore, these processors requires a software based implementation of WSN protocol stack and application, which is always slower than their fully hardware based counterparts. Processor-based sensor nodes are interrupt-driven systems, which brings uncertainty about the processing time of an event as it can be interrupted by other events any time. Additionally, interrupt-driven system have overhead of storing all the states and variables of a running event in order to handle the other event that interrupted the processor. After processing the new event, the processor has to load the states and variables of the interrupted event [3]. Therefore, interrupt-driven systems are not suitable for real-time WSN applications, where strict deadlines and delay guarantees are necessary.

An alternative approach of WSN protocol and application development using the general purpose processor is to use virtual run-time environment instead of event-based OS such as TinyOS. The virtual run-time environment facilitates application development in higher level programming languages such as Java and C# as in IBM's

*Correspondence: ktepe@uwindsor.ca
Department of Electrical and Computer Engineering, University of Windsor, Windsor, Ontario, N9B 3P4, Canada

Moterunner [4]. Though virtual run-time environment offers rapid application development, it is slower and requires more hardware resources than the operating system based solutions such as TinyOS to accomplish the same amount of tasks.

In order to alleviate above mentioned problems with processor-based senor nodes and virtual run-time environments, a sensor device using a non-preemptive modular customizable event-driven processing architecture is proposed and described in this article. The design goal of the proposed sensor node is to provide real-time computation and communication capabilities to a wireless sensor node. Thus, the proposed architecture is implemented fully in hardware using a field programmable gate array (FPGA). In this architecture, an event dispatcher assigns an event to an event handler and allows it to complete the event. Removing preemption gives the ability to define the timeliness in our architecture and removes the need of storing states and variables of ongoing events and loading them back, which significantly reduces the memory usage and time needed for transitions. Apart from this, the proposed event-driven architecture is modular; therefore, a WSN application designer can take as many generic event dispatchers and autonomous event handlers as needed by a WSN application. This facilitates the rapid prototyping of WSN application. This type of modularization is not the inherent feature in interrupt-driven systems. The hardware implementation of the proposed design shows the significant improvement in the sensor device performance in terms of execution cycle count as compared to processor-based sensor nodes. The improvement in cycle count enables the FPGA based sensor device to run at slower system clock while maintaining the same performance as that of a processor-based system.

The proposed FPGA based implementation offers hardware flexibility and speed as compared to the software flexibility offered by the processor-based sensor node implementations. With this hardware flexibility, a WSN application developer can rapidly implement a sensor device for any complex WSN application for which commercial off-the-shelf sensor devices may not be an optimum choice. Additionally, if needed, then the FPGA based sensor device design can be used to develop economical system-on-chip (SOC) or application specific integrated circuit (ASIC) for large scale production.

The main contributions of this article are as follows.

1. A fully hardware based non-preemptive modular customizable event-driven architecture is proposed for a wireless sensor device. In this architecture, various autonomous functional modules such as event dispatchers and event handlers can be added or removed easily for rapid WSN application

development. This architecture can be particularly useful for real-time WSN applications.

2. The proposed architecture is implemented on an FPGA to utilize its speed, computation power, and hardware flexibility. Usage of FPGA further enables computationally extensive WSN applications related to multimedia, image processing, and security.

These benefits come at a cost. In order to utilize the proposed architecture, WSN developers have to design various types of autonomous event handlers for different subtasks of their specific WSN applications. They then can use as many copies of an event handler as needed. In the case of processor-based design, the developers are still required to write code for various subtasks, but they may not need to divide their tasks to various autonomous subtasks. Additionally, FPGA based sensor nodes seem to have higher energy consumption than processors based sensor node implementations. However, there are ways to mitigate the power consumption issue in FPGA based sensor nodes, which are discussed in Section Implementation details and test results.

The rest of the article is organized as follows: Section Related study presents a brief background of typical sensor node architectures and related research. Section System architecture and design describes the system architecture and design. Section System components describes the main components used in the implementation of the sensor node. Section Implementation details and test results presents implementation details and experimental results related to the performance of the sensor node. A discussion on the power consumption issue is also provided in this section. Finally, Section Conclusions concludes the article.

## Related study

WSNs have a range of applications with vastly varying requirements and characteristics [5]. For example, active sensors, such as sonar, require much more computational power for signal processing than passive sensors, such as smoke detector. Sensors for applications that support mobility need more processing power for complex network protocols and algorithms than their fixed relatives. That is why a single hardware platform is not sufficient to support such wide range of possible applications [6]. In order to cater this range of WSN applications, various sensor node implementations are available both in the academia and industry. Berkeley Mica [7], UCLA Medusa [8], and MIT $\mu$AMP [9] are some examples of dedicated embedded sensor device architecture. These embedded sensor devices have a general purpose processor on which the event-driven operating system, such as TinyOS [2] can be installed. The general purpose processor has to run the operating system (OS) routines and process interrupt handlers, which increase the execution cycles required per task. For example, a sequence of tasks of sampling sensor output, averaging the sampled data, and displaying the result in Berkeley's Mica Mote needs overhead of 781 cycles for interrupt handling and scheduling out of total 1118 execution cycles to complete the tasks, which translates into 70% overhead [10]. There have been efforts to design dedicated sensor network processors such as sensor network asynchronous processor (SNAP) [11] and second-generation sensor processor [12]. These processors have optimized instruction sets and improved architectures for better task scheduling for sensor network applications. However, OS related overhead still exists in these dedicated processors based sensor nodes. In addition to this, efforts have been made to put additional hardware modules along with processors to accommodate event-driven nature of WSN applications. For example, an event processor is proposed to work in conjunction with the general purpose processor in [13]. This event processor is designed to efficiently perform most of the basic functions of the processor in an efficient way. For example, it provides better repetitive interrupt handling and accelerates tasks such as message preparation and routing. As a result, this event processor-based sensor node is able to reduce 40% to 96% of execution cycle counts to process regular WSN application tasks [13] as compared to TinyOS based Mica2 sensor nodes. Though, the processor is proposed to be used minimally in this system, overhead and timing uncertainty related to interrupt handling still exists. Similar to this study, our sensor device implementation also tries to harness the event-driven nature of WSN applications. However, our implementation completely eliminates the need of a general purpose processor by directly implementing the proposed event-driven architecture into the dedicated hardware (an FPGA).

FPGAs are emerging as a viable option in implementation of WSN nodes. An extensive survey on the suitability and challenges of using FPGA for various WSN applications are provided in [14]. It is pointed out in this survey that FPGAs are particularly useful for computationally demanding WSN applications. For example, Xilinx Spartan-3 FPGA based WSN nodes are used to implement complex functions such as fuzzy logic based link cost calculation for routing decision, image compression, running Gaussian average for image background subtraction, and symmetric cryptography algorithm in [15-18], respectively. All above FPGA implementations are used to implement some specific type of WSN application to harness higher computational power capabilities of FPGAs. These tasks were either very time consuming or not possible due to limitation of resources in processor-based sensor nodes. The other category of WSN applications that use FPGA based sensor nodes are multimedia data transmission [19,20], sensor data security related to

encryption algorithms [21,22], environmental monitoring [23-25]. As a continuation of this effort, the proposed FPGA based sensor node can enable a new class of applications such as real-time WSN applications mentioned in [26-30]. In addition to this, our implementation will also enable WSN applications that need both higher computational power and real-time capability such as with smart grid gateway node [31].

In the literature, WSN nodes are implemented in four modes, (1) standalone FPGA based sensor nodes without processor core inside, (2) standalone FPGA based sensor nodes with processor core inside, (3) sensor nodes based on combination of onboard processor and FPGA, and (4) standalone processor-based sensor nodes. Each WSN application has its own requirements and one of the above sensor node implementation can offer a meaningful solution. It is up to the WSN developer to make this decision based on the application's requirement. For example, there are cases where sensor nodes with both onboard FPGA and processor, as in [32,33], have advantages such as utilizing high computational capability of FPGA combined with software programmability of processor. To get the advantage of both computational capability and software programmability while using only FPGA, there are various FPGA based wireless sensor device implementations proposed in the literature that use processor core inside the FPGA [34-37]. As mentioned earlier, standalone FPGA based sensor nodes without a processor core inside [15-18] are customized for various types of WSN applications, and these customized designs cannot be used for other WSN application. In this article, a generic modular event-driven architecture is implemented on standalone FPGA based sensor node without processor core which can be applied to any WSN application. As it avoids interrupt related overhead and timing uncertainties, it is particularly suitable to applications that require real-time processing and communication capabilities.

The following section, provides details of the proposed FPGA-based sensor node design.

## System architecture and design

The block diagram of the proposed hardware based sensor node implementation is shown in Figure 1. There are five main function units in this implementation and these are the event-driven systems, except the parsing and classification unit. Further details of these functional units are given in Section System components. The event-driven architecture of our sensor system is presented in the following three sections.

### Event-driven architecture

The general architecture of the event-driven system is shown in Figure 2. There are event handlers and event dispatchers in the architecture. The event dispatcher is

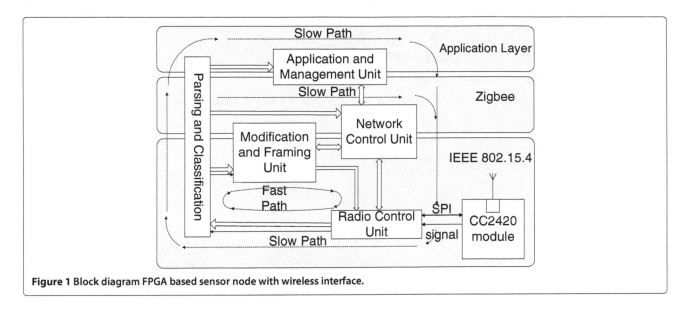

**Figure 1** Block diagram FPGA based sensor node with wireless interface.

used to detect the occurrence of an event and activate the corresponding event handler to perform the tasks related to this event. An event could be internal, such as a timeout, or external, such as detection of a packet in the radio module's buffer. Event handlers are specific processing hardware subsystems activated by an event dispatcher in response to a specific event or by an event handler in the case that a new event is triggered by that event handler. Event handlers consist of event processing unit, local registers and shared registers. The event processing unit contains customized state machine and data path for processing a particular event. Local registers are used for temporary storage of intermediate data during event processing. It could only be accessed by the event handler. The shared registers are used to store event information received from the event dispatcher. Both event handler and event dispatcher are able to access to the shared registers. A control signal is used to trigger the event handler to change its state from idle to active. The state signals indicate the state of event handlers to event dispatchers. The data bus is used to transfer event information from event dispatcher to event handler or from one event handler to another event handler. The output ports of the system are driven by the event handlers that are responsible for communication between functional units.

An event dispatcher is a state machine designed to monitor the input ports of hardware blocks, receive event information, decode event information and activate corresponding event handler. Figure 3 illustrates a simplified version of actual state machine of an event dispatcher. The event dispatcher stays in the idle state after resetting or power ON until an event happens. When an event happens, the event dispatcher receives preliminary event

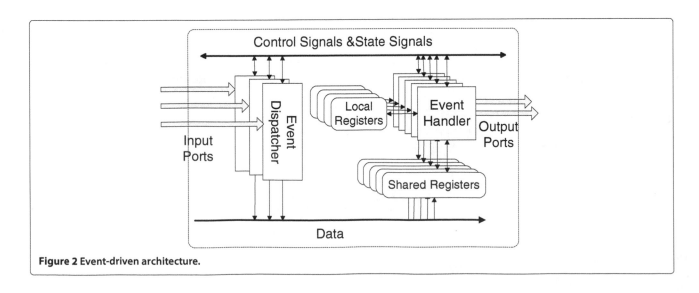

**Figure 2** Event-driven architecture.

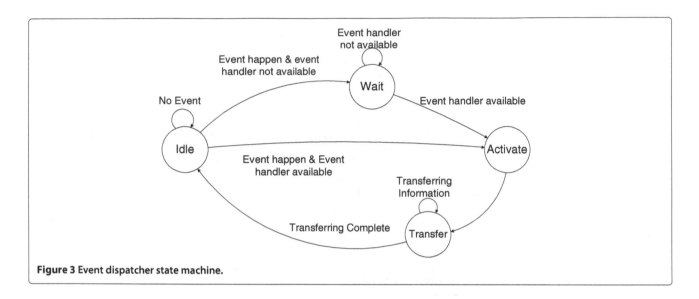

**Figure 3** Event dispatcher state machine.

information from the input port and determines the type of event to find out which event handler needs to be activated. If the corresponding event handler is idle, the event dispatcher activates the event handler by signaling the event handler and changing its state from idle to JobAdd state. Then the event dispatcher receives the complete information about the event from the input port and sends it to the shared registers of activated event handler. After the information transaction is complete, the event dispatcher signals the event handler to leave JobAdd state and begins processing the task. Finally, event dispatcher returns to idle state and continues to monitor the input interface. If the event handler is not in idle state when an event dispatcher detects an event, the event dispatcher will hold the communication on the input port and change its state to the wait state until the event handler is idle. When event handler is idle, the event dispatcher continues the activation procedure as mentioned above.

Each event handler is a small processing unit with customizable control logic and data path to perform a specific task. Figure 4 illustrates a simplified version of state machine of an actual event handler. There are three states in all event handlers' state machine: (1) Idle, (2) JobAdd, and (3) JobStart. All the event handlers have the same

functionality in any given state; and the change of state of a event handler from idle to JobAdd and from JobAdd to JobStart is solely controlled by the event dispatcher or another event handler. An event handler stays in Idle state after reset or power ON. In Idle state, the event handler is free and ready to accept a task. The event handler is signaled to change from Idle to JobAdd state after the event dispatcher detects an event. The JobAdd state shows that the event handler is engaged in receiving the event information. When in this state, the event handler waits for the completion of the transfer of necessary information for task processing from event dispatcher to its shared registers. When the information transfer is complete, the event dispatcher signals the event handler to change its state from JobAdd to JobStart. In that state, the event handler begins to process the specific task. After completing the task, the event handler will return to Idle state and wait for the next event to happen. The event handlers do not provide preemption operation and there is no priority to access a particular event handler. An event is processed on first-come-first-serve basis. When an event handler is busy, event dispatcher has to wait until it is free. The status bit of an event handler is used to ensure the non-preemptive operation of event handlers.

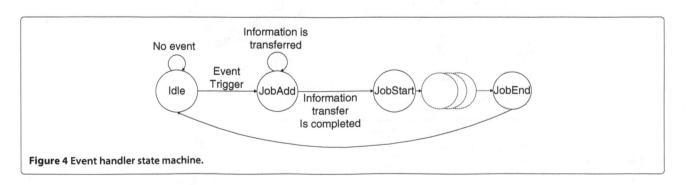

**Figure 4** Event handler state machine.

The status of an event handler is stored in a flip-flop. A '0' bit in the flip-flop indicates free status, whereas, '1' bit indicates busy status. Thus, when event dispatcher has input event, it checks the status of the event handler. If it is busy, then event dispatcher returns to wait state and does not assign any task until the event handler is free. Once event handler finishes its job, it switches its status to free; additionally, it informs the status change to event dispatcher as well so that the dispatcher can assign the next task to the event handler if it still has events in its queue to be processed. Not allowing preemption is not restricting the usability of the proposed architecture in event-driven WSN applications. For urgent or high priority events, some event dispatcher and event handler unit can be reserved, which will not be used for other normal events. Thus, a WSN application designer can choose the number of event dispatcher and event handler as per the WSN application demand and can reserve some of them for high priority applications. It is an alternate way of having the similar functionality as the preemption operation.

As described above, the event dispatcher is responsible for the event detection and the event handler is responsible for event processing. Therefore, the event detection and event processing phases could overlap. Also, because event handlers are able to work independently, the event processing phases of different events can overlap, which makes it possible to process the events in parallel. These are the key features that make our event-driven architecture as customizable and scalable. The proposed sensor node architecture locates all computation resources locally as needed by the event handler to process a particular event. Therefore, event handlers do not need to signal an interrupt to request the resources for task processing. As a result, there is no interrupt overhead in our architecture.

### Hardware acceleration

The most frequent activities of a sensor device are sending, receiving and relaying packets. These activities involve operations directly on packets, such as parsing, classification and framing. Those operations can be accelerated by hardware in network processor using parallel processing [38,39]. As illustrated in Figure 1, the proposed system adopts the architecture similar to network processor to accelerate packet operations. There are two information paths in the proposed system: (1) fast path and (2) slow path. The functional units connected with the fast processing path deal with operations that are directly performed on packets, such as header modification, parsing, classification, and packet framing. These fast processing paths are customized for handling IEEE 802.15.4 frames and ZigBee packets. The slow processing path deals with operations that relate to network management

and upper layer applications, such as network setup, route searching and routing table updates. Usually, these functions are implemented by the central processing units in a processor-based sensor node. However, in our system, a set of specific event handlers are used to perform these tasks.

### Parallel distributed computation

Each event handler and event dispatcher has its own data path and control hardware inside their respective functional units. As described earlier, the event handlers work in parallel. The parallel architecture in the proposed system increases the efficiency of message processing and the throughput of the system. The computation capability is distributed among event handlers enabling the designed system to respond to an event whenever it occurs. As shown by the test results in Section Implementation details and test results, the parallel distributed computation allows the system to respond faster to an application's needs.

### System components

As shown in Figure 1, the proposed system consists of five functional units. These are parsing and classification unit, framing unit, network control unit, application management unit, and radio control unit. These functional units are connected to each other through dedicated links. The functions of these units are described as follows.

### Parsing and classification unit

The parsing and classification unit parses the received packets into information fields. The parsed information is sent to a corresponding module for further processing based on the packet type. For example, the MAC command is sent to network control unit and the application data is sent to application and management unit.

### Framing unit

The framing unit is responsible for packing the data into a ZigBee frame before the packet is sent to other ZigBee nodes. It also requests the next-hop address from network control unit for relaying the packet received from parsing and classification unit. Some fields in these packets, such as MAC source address and MAC destination address need to be modified before being sent to ZigBee network.

### Network control unit

The network control unit is responsible for ZigBee network management. It provides network functions, such as network discovery, network start, network join, neighbor table maintenance, and routing. It also provides the operational parameters and commands to CC2420 transceiver.

### Application management unit

The application management unit is responsible for the application control and user interface. In order to test our system, we developed an application in this unit to read data from a counter, send the data over the network, and display the received data.

### Radio control unit

The radio control unit provides an interface with the CC2420 transceiver module. It performs three operations: get-packet, send-packet and transceiver-configuration. Get-packet operation gets packets from CC2420's buffer and sends the packets to parsing and classification unit. Send-packet operation receives packets from other module, transfer the packets to CC2420 TX buffer and issue send command. Transceiver-configuration operation is used to configure CC2420 module and control the operation of the transceiver.

### CC2420 unit

The low power, IEEE 802.15.4 [40] and ZigBee compatible, RF chip CC2420 [41] is used as a wireless transceiver. The chip provides features such as error detection and data buffering for the packets that need to be transmitted and received.

## Implementation details and test results

### Implementation details

Two sensor nodes were implemented using Celoxica's RC10 FPGA development boards [42] and CC2420 evaluation boards (CC2420EB) [41] from Chipcon. The FPGA on Celoxica's RC10 development boards is Xilinx Spartan3 XC3S1500-FG320-4, which contains 29,952 logic cells. Each logic cell has a 4 input look-up table (LUT) and a D flip-flop. The system capacity of the FPGA is equivalent to 1.5 million gates. The CC2420EB contains CC2420 chip and peripherals (i.e., antenna, receiver and transmitter filters) that support the normal operation of the chip. The integrated system is shown in Figure 5.

To compare the circuit sizes of hardware based implementation and the processor-based sensor node implementation, a Xilinx's soft core CPU, MicroBlaze, is also implemented in FPGA as a reference design of processor-based sensor node. MicroBlaze is a 32-bit soft processor with RISC architecture. The processor-based implementation includes a 32 Kbyte RAM, which is sufficient for both ZigBee protocol stack and the application program.

The hardware based sensor node implementation is developed in VHDL. This VHDL design and MicroBlaze CPU IP core are synthesized using Xilinx ISE7.0 [43] and simulated using Mentor's ModelSim simulator [44]. The synthesis details are given in Table 1. As illustrated in Table 1, the hardware based implementation of our event-driven architecture and a WSN packet generation and routing application uses 52% of the total FPGA logical capacity, and IP core of MicroBlaze processor uses 13%. Since the FPGA logic capacity usage is directly related to its circuit size, it is fair to say that the circuit size of the hardware-based sensor node implementation is about four times larger than that of the MicroBlaze processor-based software implementation. It is a trade-off between performance and circuit size. The proposed event-driven architecture is not loaded into the MicroBlaze processor as our event-driven architecture is not processor compatible. IP core of MicroBlaze processor is loaded in our FPGA just to know how much FPGA resources it takes as compared to our fully hardware based FPGA implementation of sensor nodes.

### Test results

In this article, a unique design of a non-preemptive modular customizable event-driven architecture is proposed for a standalone FPGA based sensor node. Therefore, the standard benchmark tests are not available to test our implementation. Thus, we tried to find standard application that can run on the proposed sensor node. As one of the prime objectives of WSN is to transmit and receive data packets, a standard ZigBee transceiver application is implemented to test the data packet processing and routing functionality of the proposed FPGA based sensor node. In general, every sensor node in a WSN has to have routing capability. Thus, implementing routing within the FPGA based sensor node is important. However, event handlers can be designed to provide any kind of sensor data processing and packet handling tasks in addition to routing functionality. Thus, the functional testing of routing capability of a sensor node is carried out. However, a full-fledged event-driven architecture for the FPGA based sensor node is designed and implemented using VHDL in this research rather than just FPGA based router. As transceiver application is implemented on a sensor node, measuring packet error rate (PER) and transmission range is the common practice to validate a transceiver. Thus, PER and transmission range are measured experimentally as part of functional verification of the HDL implementation. For performance analysis, the execution cycle count and the minimum clock frequency requirement to achieve the maximum possible throughput are recorded. Execution cycle count and minimum clock frequency requirement are measured using ModelSim simulator.

The transceiver test application mimics data monitoring scenario of a real-world sensor application, in which the system periodically collects sampled data and transmits packets to the destination node. The destination node receives packets, processes them and displays the sampled value. Functional test cases covered in this application include ZigBee network searching, network setup,

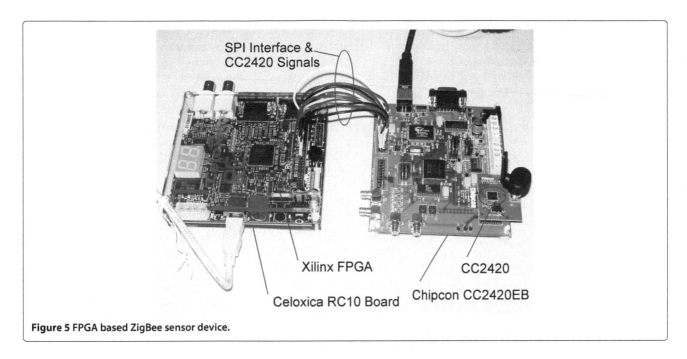

**Figure 5** FPGA based ZigBee sensor device.

network association, data sending, data receiving etc. The test results of transmission range and PER are shown in Figure 6. From the experiments, it is observed that our FPGA based sensor node is able to provide reliable communication up to 30 m at indoor environment and 55 m at outdoor environment with PER 2%. After these distances, the system still functions with higher PER (about 20%) up to 55 m at indoor environment and 85 m at outdoor environment, respectively. During these tests, FPGA board operated at 1.2 MHz clock frequency. Radio transmitter output power is 0 dBm and antenna gain is 4.4 dBi. Our PER results are consistent PER results obtained from the MicaZ motes based testbed developed for ZigBee performance measurement in our lab [45].

To evaluate the increase in speed provided by our hardware-based sensor device implementation, execution cycle counts are compared with the typical sensor devices found in the literature, namely general purpose processor-based solution [7], sensor processor-based solution [11], and event processor-based solution [13].

Execution cycle counts required for the regular sensor network tasks are used as a performance metric in order to identify the gain that is achieved with event-driven architecture based on FPGA design. The execution clock is used in the literature as one of the standard ways [11,13] to compare the efficiency of any implementation. From that, how fast a task can be executed can be derived by using the clock frequency. The need for fewer execution cycles means that system can either run for shorter time at the same clock frequency or run for longer time at lower clock frequency (while still ensuring the task completion on time).

**Table 1 Logic usage comparison between hardware based implementation and MicroBlaze CPU**

| Resource type | Resource available | Hardware based design | | MicroBlaze CPU based design | |
|---|---|---|---|---|---|
| | | Used | Percent | Used | Percent |
| Slices | 13312 | 6888 | 52% | 1665 | 13% |
| Slice flip flops | 26624 | 3549 | 13% | 1248 | 5% |
| 4 input LUTs | 26624 | 12967 | 49% | 2247 | 8% |
| bonded IOBs | 221 | 36 | 16% | 81 | 37% |
| GCLKs | 8 | 2 | 25% | 3 | 38% |
| BRAMs | 32 | 0 | 0% | 16 | 50% |
| DCM_ADVs | 4 | 1 | 25% | 2 | 50% |

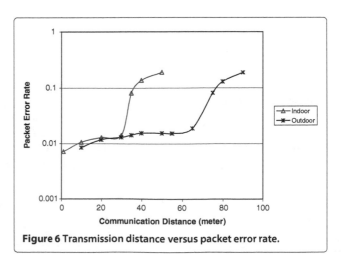

**Figure 6** Transmission distance versus packet error rate.

Completing a given task in shorter time or at lower clock frequency can reduce dynamic power consumption; however, the power consumption comparison is not made in this article. Here, it is worth mentioning that operating frequency of contemporary FPGAs for sensor nodes is 10 to 20 times more than the contemporary processor (i.e., microcontroller) for sensor nodes. Processors that are proposed for WSN operates at lower frequencies (such as ATMEL Atmega128 used in MICA2 motes operates at around maximum frequency of 16 MHz [43]), whereas the operating frequencies of Spartan-3 series FPGA can be from 20 to 200 MHz depending upon speed grade and the built-in functions of FPGA [43]. Newer generation FPGAs such as low power Artrix-7 series from Xilinx runs from 200 to 500 MHz; whereas the newer processors for sensor nodes such as Atmel's ATmega1281 microcontroller in IRIS motes still runs at 16 MHz [46]. Thus, because of disparity in maximum operating frequencies of contemporary FPGAs and microcontrollers for sensor nodes, the timing analysis based on clock frequency alone would make it difficult to identify the gain achieved with the proposed hardware implementation compared to processor-based software implementations for a given width of the datapath.

The regular sensor network tasks used to measure the cycle counts in the evaluation are described as follows.

1. Packet transmission: The application management unit periodically collects samples and sends these values to the network control unit, which decides the destination address for the packet and looks up next-hop address. All the packets are sent to framing unit to pack into a MAC frame. The frame is then transferred to radio control unit and transmitted.
2. Packet reception: The radio control unit fetches the MAC frame from CC2420 buffer when the packet is ready, and sends the frame to parsing and classification unit. If the destination of the packet is the current sensor node, then the content is parsed from the frame and sent to its network control unit or application management unit.
3. Packet relay: After reception of a packet, if the packet is not for the current sensor node, the system will modify the relevant fields of the frame, and send it to the next-hop device or to the destination node.

The execution cycle counts for the tasks explained above is provided in Table 2 for different sensor node implementations. From Table 2, our sensor node implementation is about 11 times faster than Mica2 nodes in packet transmission task and about 3 to 4 times faster in packet reception task and packet relay task. Our fully hardware based event-driven architecture has comparable cycle count performance in packet transmission and 30% less cycle count for packet reception as compared to the event processor-based architecture (implemented on general purpose processor). Thus, implementation of network tasks directly into hardware reduces the execution cycle count by 3 to 10 times as compared to a typical processor-based sensor device. Such improvements are possible due to the absence of an operating system and interrupt handling overhead as well as the utilization of parallel processing in our implementation. For example, in packet relay task, framing unit will start a route lookup event as soon as it receives the destination address of the relay packet. The framing event handler and route lookup event handler are able to run in parallel. The packet relay performance of our system is the best among all the systems evaluated in this article.

It is worth mentioning here that if we had operated Xilinx Spartan3 FPGA to its maximum possible operating frequency of 20 to 200 MHz, we would have got more increase in speed. Additionally, if we take high end FPGAs for sensor nodes such as low power Xilinx Artix-7 series, then certainly increase in speed would be better.

Figure 7 shows the minimum clock frequency requirement of our FPGA based implementation to maintain 250 kbit/s system throughput (the maximum possible data rate through CC2420 based wireless interface) for typical sensor node tasks described earlier in this section. The packet transmission graph shown in the figure includes the tasks of event sampling, packet generation and packet transmission, therefore, the minimum clock frequency requirement for transmission task is high as compared to relay and reception task. The performance of the proposed event-driven architecture is quite stable. Once the system clock frequency is increased to the level to achieve the maximum possible system throughput (250 kbit/s), the system throughput remains constant irrespective of increase in system clock frequency, frame size, or the incoming or outgoing packet load conditions.

**Table 2 The execution cycle counts for regular sensor network tasks for different sensor node implementations**

| Task | Mica2 node (8-bit) | SNAP node (16-bit) | Event processor-based node (8-bit) | FPGA based node (8-bit) |
|---|---|---|---|---|
| Packet transmission | 1532 | 331 | 127 | 137 |
| Packet reception | 234 | 258 | 136 | 71 |
| Packet relay | 429 | 418 | 165 | 115 |

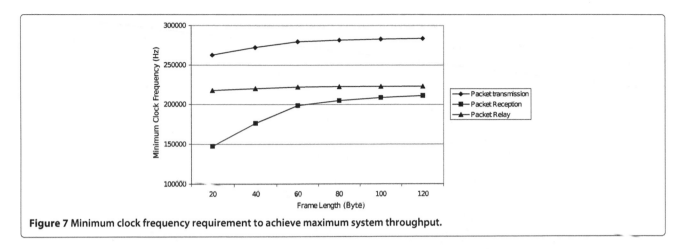

**Figure 7** Minimum clock frequency requirement to achieve maximum system throughput.

## Discussion on power consumption

In this research, the reason of using FPGAs for sensor nodes was not the minimization of energy consumption but improving timing efficiency to meet certain types of WSN application's demanding real-time operations and computation power. Some of these applications are multimedia data transmission and smart grid gateway nodes.

If low power consumption is required simultaneously with real-time and computational power, emerging low power FPGAs can be used to extend the lifetime of batteries on the WSN nodes. For example, IGLOO series from Actel consumes $2\,\mu W$ in ultra low-power mode. Thus, low power FPGAs based sensor nodes can compete with processor-based sensor nodes. Even our implementation with relatively older generation Xilinx Spartan3 XC3S1500-FG320-4 FPGA with its static power consumption of 41 mW provides comparable power consumption performance to that of commonly used processor-based implementations. For example, Mica2 mote with ATMega128 microcontroller operating at 7.4 MHz with CC1000 radio module consumes total active power of 89 mW, and similarly Telos-B mote with TiMSP430 microcontroller operating at 8 MHz with CC2420 radio module consumes total active power of 32 mW [14].

Another power mitigation technique is to implement the design in ASICs. The experimental study conducted in [47] with 90 nm CMOS FPGA and ASIC demonstrated that on average, an FPGA consumes 14 times more dynamic power than the ASIC implementation. Porting our implementation to both low power FPGAs and ASIC can be done with minimum effort as the code is written in VHDL.

We also would like to point out that high computational power provided by FGPA based sensor nodes allows better in-node data processing, which can minimize the amount of data that is to be forwarded/sent/received by a sensor node instead of forwarding/sending raw sensor data. Thus, FPGA's higher processing capability can be used to achieve higher level of data aggregation and compression, which can minimize the amount of transmission for a given amount of information.

## Conclusions

In this study, a fully hardware based sensor node is implemented using general purpose FPGA and ZigBee radio interface. This design eliminates timing problems associated with interrupt-driven processor-based WSN nodes and overhead associated with operating system's interrupt handling. The implementation can be tailored to meet strict deadlines, hence provide real-time operation. The hardware implementation can reduce the number of execution cycles required to complete a task by at least 30% when compared to processor-based implementations for the same datapath width. Although processor-based sensor node implementations offer flexible architecture for researchers, this study demonstrated that a hardware based sensor node implementation can provide performance improvement in terms of fewer execution cycle count for applications such as multi-media, data compression, and real-time transmission in WSNs. The proposed architecture provides an FPGA based viable WSN node architecture.

**Competing interests**
The authors declare that they have no competing interests.

**Acknowledgments**
This study was supported in part by the NSERC Discovery Grant program.

**References**
1.  J Hill, R Szewczyk, A Woo, S Hollar, D Culler, K Pister, in *ASPLOS-IX: Proceedings of the ninth international conference on Architectural support for programming languages and operating systems*. System architecture directions for networked sensors (ACM Press, New York, 2000), pp. 93–104
2.  TinyOS. http://www.tinyos.net
3.  J McGivern, *Interrupt Driven PC System Design*. (Annabooks, San Diego, 1998)
4.  IBM Moterunner. http://www.zurich.ibm.com/moterunner/
5.  F Zhao, L Guibas, *Wireless sensor networks: An information processing approach*. (Morgan Kaufmann Publishers Inc., San Francisco, 2004)

6.   K Romer, F Mattern, The design space of wireless sensor networks. IEEE Wirel. Commun. **11**(6), 54–61 (2004)

7.   JL Hill, DE Culler, Mica: a wireless platform for deeply embedded networks. IEEE Micro. **22**(6), 12–24 (2002)

8.   A Savvides, MB Srivastava, in *ICCD '02: Proceedings of the 2002 IEEE International Conference on Computer Design: VLSI in Computers and Processors (ICCD'02)*. A distributed computation platform for wireless embedded sensing (IEEE Computer Society, Washington, 2002), p. 220

9.   A Chandrakasan, R Min, M Bhardwaj, S Cho, A Wang, in *Proceedings of the 28th European Solid-State Circuits Conference (ESSCIRC)*. Power aware wireless microsensor systems (Florence, Italy, 2002), pp. 47–54

10.  L Nazhandali, B Zhai, J Olson, A Reeves, M Minuth, R Helfand, S Pant, T Austin, D Blaauw, in *ISCA '05: Proceedings of the 32nd annual international symposium on Computer Architecture*. Energy optimization of subthreshold-voltage sensor network processors (IEEE Computer Society, Washington, 2005), pp. 197–207

11.  V Ekanayake, I Clinton Kelly, R Manohar, in *ASPLOS-XI: Proceedings of the 11th international conference on Architectural support for programming languages and operating systems*. An ultra low-power processor for sensor networks (ACM Press, New York, 2004), pp. 27–36

12.  L Nazhandali, M Minuth, B Zhai, J Olson, T Austin, D Blaauw, in *CASES'05: Proceedings of the 2005 international conference on Compilers, architectures and synthesis for embedded systems*. A second-generation sensor network processor with application-driven memory optimizations and out-of-order execution (ACM Press, New York, 2005), pp. 249–256

13.  M Hempstead, N Tripathi, P Mauro, GY Wei, D Brooks, in *ISCA'05: Proceedings of the 32nd annual international symposium on Computer Architecture*. An ultra low power system architecture for sensor network applications (IEEE Computer Society, Madison, 2005), pp. 208–219

14.  A de la Piedra, A Braeken, A Touhafi, Sensor systems based on FPGAs and their applications: a survey. Sensors. **12**(9), 12235–12264 (2012)

15.  T Haider, M Yusuf, in *9th International Multitopic Conference, IEEE INMIC*. FPGA based fuzzy link cost processor for energy-aware routing in wireless sensor networks—design and implementation (IEEE Computer Society, Karachi, 2005), pp. 1–6

16.  Y Wang, A Bermak, F Boussaid, in *2010 2nd Asia Symposium on Quality Electronic Design (ASQED)*. FPGA implementation of compressive sampling for sensor network applications, Penang, Malaysia, 2010), pp. 5–8

17.  DM Pham, S Aziz, in *2011 Seventh International Conference on Intelligent Sensors, Sensor Networks and Information Processing (ISSNIP)*. FPGA architecture for object extraction in wireless multimedia sensor network (Adelaide, Australia, 2011), pp. 294–299

18.  E Eryilmaz, I Erturk, S Atmaca, in *International Conference on Application of Information and Communication Technologies*. Implementation of Skipjack cryptology algorithm for WSNs using FPGA (Baku, Azerbaijan, 2009), pp. 1–5

19.  M Kaddachi, A Soudani, I Nouira, V Lecuire, K Torki, in *2010 17th IEEE International Conference on Electronics, Circuits, and Systems (ICECS)*. Efficient hardware solution for low power and adaptive image-compression in WSN (Athens, Greece, 2010), pp. 583–586

20.  CH Zhiyong, LY Pan, Z Zeng, MH Meng, in *IEEE International Conference on Automation and Logistics*. A novel FPGA-based wireless vision sensor node (Shenyang, China, 2009), pp. 841–846

21.  P Hamalainen, M Hannikainen, T Hamalainen, in *48th Midwest Symposium on Circuits and Systems*. Efficient hardware implementation of security processing for IEEE 802.15.4 wireless networks. vol. 1 (Cincinnati, Ohio, USA, 2005), pp. 484–487

22.  O Song, J Kim, in *7th IEEE Consumer Communications and Networking Conference (CCNC)*. An efficient design of security accelerator for IEEE 802.15.4 wireless senor networks (Las Vegas, Nevada, USA, 2010), pp. 1–5

23.  R Garcia, A Gordon-Ross, A George, in *17th IEEE Symposium on Field Programmable Custom Computing Machines*. Exploiting partially reconfigurable FPGAs for situation-based reconfiguration in wireless sensor networks (Napa, California, USA, 2009), pp. 243–246

24.  H Liu, N Bergmann, in *2010 Conference on Design and Architectures for Signal and Image Processing (DASIP)*. An FPGA softcore based implementation of a bird call recognition system for sensor networks (Edinburgh, Scotland, UK, 2010), pp. 1–6

25.  P Muralidhar, C Rao, in *Fourth International Conference on Wireless Communication and Sensor Networks*. Reconfigurable wireless sensor network node based on Nios core (IIIT, Allahabad, 2008), pp. 67–72

26.  R Leon, V Vittal, G Manimaran, Application of sensor network for secure electric energy infrastructure. IEEE Trans. Power Delivery. **22**(2), 1021–1028 (2007)

27.  Y Yang, D Divan, R Harley, T Habetler, in *IEEE Power Engineering Society General Meeting*. Power line sensornet - a new concept for power grid monitoring (Montreal, Quebec, Canada, 2006), p. 8

28.  S Gumbo, H Muyingi, in *2008 Third International Conference on Broadband Communications, Information Technology Biomedical Applications*. Performance investigation of wireless sensor network for long distance overhead power lines; Mica2 motes, a case study, Pretoria, Gauteng, South Africa, 2008), pp. 443–450

29.  I Stoianov, L Nachman, S Madden, T Tokmouline, in *Proceedings of the 6th international conference on Information processing in sensor networks*. PIPENET: a wireless sensor network for pipeline monitoring (ACM, New York, 2007), pp. 264–273

30.  H Wang, Y Hou, Y Xin, in *International Conference on Measuring Technology and Mechatronics Automation*. Plant running management based on wireless sensor network. vol. 1 (Zhangjiajie, Hunan, China, 2009), pp. 138–141

31.  X Fang, S Misra, G Xue, D Yang, Smart grid—the new and improved power grid: a survey. IEEE Commun. Surv. Tutor. **14**(4), 944–980 (2012)

32.  O Berder, O Sentieys, in *Workshop on Ultra-Low Power Sensor Networks (WUPS), co-located with Int. Conf. on Architecture of Computing Systems (ARCS 2010)*. PowWow: power optimized hardware/software framework for wireless motes (Hannover, Allemagne, 2010), pp. 229–233

33.  X Zhang, H Heys, C Li, in *2011 6th International ICST Conference on Communications and Networking in China (CHINACOM)*. FPGA implementation of two involutional block ciphers targeted to wireless sensor networks (Harbin, China, 2011), pp. 232–236

34.  Y Sun, L Li, H Luo, in *2011 7th International Conference on Wireless Communications, Networking and Mobile Computing (WiCOM)*. Design of FPGA-based multimedia node for WSN (Wuhan, China, 2011), pp. 1–5

35.  G Chalivendra, R Srinivasan, N Murthy, in *International Conference on Electronic Design*. FPGA based re-configurable wireless sensor network protocol (Penang, Malaysia, 2008), pp. 1–4

36.  J Wei, L Wang, F Wu, Y Chen, L Ju, in *IEEE Youth Conference on Information, Computing and Telecommunication*. Design and implementation of wireless sensor node based on open core (Beijing, China, 2009), pp. 102–105

37.  S Lu, X Huang, L Cui, Z Zhao, D Li, Design and implementation of an ASIC-based sensor device for WSN applications. IEEE Trans. Consumer Electron. **55**(4), 1959–1967 (2009)

38.  P Crowley, *Network Processor Design: Issues and Practices*. (Academic Press Inc., Orlando, 2002)

39.  PC Lekkas, P Lekkas, *Network Processors: Architectures, Protocols and Platforms*. (McGraw-Hill Inc., New York, 2003)

40.  LAN/MAN Standards Committee of the IEEE Computer Society: IEEE Standard 802.15.4, *Wireless Medium Access Control (MAC) and Physical Layer (PHY) Specifications for Low-Rate Wireless Personal Area Networks (LR-WPANs) (2003). http://standards.ieee.org/getieee802/download/802.15.4-2006.pdf

41.  Texas Instruments: CC2420 Data Sheet. v1.4 (2006). http://www.ti.com/lprf

42.  Celoxica: RC10 Manual. http://www.celoxica.com

43.  Xilinx. http://www.xilinx.com

44.  Mentor Graphics Inc. http://www.model.com

45.  PR Casey, KE Tepe, N Kar, Design and implementation of a testbed for IEEE 802.15.4 (Zigbee) performance measurements. EURASIP J. Wirel. Commun. Netw. **2010**, 23:1–23:2 (2010)

46.  Atmel. http://www.atmel.com

47.  I Kuon, J Rose, Measuring the gap between FPGAs and ASICs. IEEE Trans. Computer-Aided Design Integrat. Circ. Syst. **26**(2), 203–215 (2007)

# 16

# An embedded multichannel telemetry unit for bone strain monitoring

Fahad Moiz[1], Sharika Kumar[1], Walter D Leon-Salas[2*] and Mark Johnson[3]

## Abstract

An embedded telemetry unit for bone strain monitoring is presented. The telemetry unit is designed using commercially available components to lower design time and manufacturing costs. The unit can read up to eight strain gauges and measures 2.4 cm × 1.3 cm × 0.7 cm. The unit is powered from a small Li-polymer battery that can be recharged wirelessly through tissue, making it suitable for implanted applications. The average current consumption of the telemetry unit is 1.9 mA while transmitting at a rate of 75 kps and at a sampling rate of 20 Hz. The telemetry unit also features a power-down mode to minimize its power consumption when it is not in use. The telemetry unit operates in the 915-MHz ISM radio band. The unit was tested in an *ex vivo* setting with an ulna bone from a mouse and in a simulated *in vivo* setting with a phantom tissue. Bone strain data collected *ex vivo* shows that the telemetry unit can measure strain with an accuracy comparable to a more expensive benchtop data acquisition system.

## 1   Introduction

Bones constantly adapt their mass and architecture in order to protect the internal soft tissue organs, provide structural support, and act as calcium reservoir. It is known that the mass and structural properties of bones adjust in proportion to changes in mechanical load, but the molecular basis of how this is accomplished is only partially understood [1]. In order to unravel the mechanisms of bone formation, scientists need to determine the mechanical load levels that trigger bone mass increase. To accomplish this task, localized bone strain levels need to be measured upon the application of a load to the bone. These types of bone biology studies can potentially lead to advances in musculoskeletal diagnostics and in the development of pharmaceutical targets enabling new paradigms and treatments for bone diseases such as osteoporosis.

In addition to its importance to bone biology studies, bone strain measurement is also of interest in orthopedic implant development and monitoring. The design of orthopedic implants requires information about the range of acting loads and resulting implant and bone deformations [2]. Knowledge of bone strain also facilitates rehabilitation monitoring and feedback as well as improved data collection in clinical studies [3]. In comparison to diagnosis using X-ray images, which only show bone callus growth, strain monitoring is more effective in guiding rehabilitation exercises, predicting implant malfunction, and allows continuous monitoring of the healing process [4].

Strain gauge sensors are typically employed to measure bone strain due to their small size, robustness, and good sensitivity of strain gauges [5]. Strain gauge sensors convert strain into electrical resistance. In a typical scenario, a strain gauge is attached to a bone [6], and an electronic sensing device is employed to read the strain gauge resistance and transmit it to a computer where it can be studied and stored. Ideally, the sensing device unit should be a small and wireless device because this would enable it to be implanted subcutaneously, thus improving its wearability, while a wireless link would allow unconstrained motion of its user.

Several efforts to develop wireless sensing or telemetric devices for bone strain monitoring have been reported [7-16]. These efforts include the design of application specific integrated circuits (ASICs) [7,8] as well as solutions using commercially available electronic components [9-16]. The small size of ASICs makes them an attractive solution for an implantable telemetry unit. The drawback

*Correspondence: wleonsal@purdue.edu
[2]Electrical and Computer Engineering Technology Department, Purdue University, West Lafayette, IN 47907, USA
Full list of author information is available at the end of the article

of an ASIC solution is its high design and fabrication costs, along with its long development time. In recent years, system-on-chip (SoC) solutions incorporating a radio transceiver, an analog-to-digital converter (ADC), and a central processing unit (CPU) in a single integrated circuit have become commercially available [17-20]. These SoC solutions provide a unique opportunity to develop low-cost and small telemetry units. In this work, we employ a SoC solution to develop an embedded telemetry unit for bone strain monitoring. The telemetry unit has a small size of 2.4 cm × 1.3 cm × 0.7 cm, which allows it to be implanted subcutaneously. Besides its basic function of strain sensing, the telemetry unit presented here includes a three-axis accelerometer, an inductively coupled battery charger, and a multichannel front-end. The telemetry unit also features a low-power mode to extend battery life and can be configured wirelessly. The telemetry unit has been tested in an *ex vivo* setting using mouse bones. The unit has also been tested in a simulated implanted scenario using a tissue phantom. Test results validate the design approach of the embedded telemetry unit.

The rest of this paper is organized as follows: Section 2 outlines the target application, the design requirements and the circuit design of the telemetry unit. Section 3 details the radio communication protocol. Section 4 describes the design and organization of the firmware. Section 5 presents the measurements results, and Section 6 concludes the paper.

## 2   Telemetry unit design

Understanding the target application requirements allows us to specify the design specifications more precisely. Hence, below, we describe the target application of the telemetry unit. With the target application in mind, a set of design requirements will be outlined. These design requirements have been used to guide us in designing the telemetry unit hardware.

### 2.1   Target application

The target application for the telemetry unit is bone biology studies in which localized bone strain needs to be monitored under different load conditions. Bone biology scientists use this information to understand the mechanisms that regulate bone formation. Currently, our collaborators use the setup depicted in Figure 1 to carry out bone strain measurements. The setup consists of a specialized benchtop data acquisition system for strain gauge measurements (Vishay Micro-Measurement System 7000, Vishay Micro-Measurement, Wendell, NC, USA) that is connected to a dedicated computer running specialized data acquisition software (WinTest* and StrainSmart*). In this setup, a mouse or other suitable small animal (the subject) is fully immobilized while a known force is applied to its ulna bone and strain readings are collected.

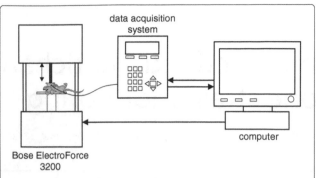

**Figure 1 Conceptual diagram of the current benchtop measurement setup.** The current setup consists of a Bose ElectroForce 3200 load test instrument and a Vishay Micro-Measurement 7000 data acquisition system. Both systems are controlled by a dedicated computer.

The force is applied with a Bose ElectroForce 3200 load instrument (Bose ElectroForce, Eden Prairie, MN, USA). This procedure is repeated for a period of several days after which the animal is sacrificed, and the ulna bone is studied for changes in the bone matrix and gene expression.

One important question that bone researchers would like to answer is to what degree exercise impacts bone formation. To this end, researchers would like to monitor bone strain as the subject performs a set of cage exercises. The current strain acquisition system is bulky and requires wires to be connected from the data acquisition unit to the bone. Hence, it is not suitable for use in animals that are moving during exercise. To provide a solution to this need, a wireless multichannel telemetry unit capable of reading strain is required. A conceptual diagram of the envisioned bone monitoring setup is shown in Figure 2. The telemetry unit is worn by the subject or implanted. The telemetry unit reads strain levels and transmits them to a nearby base station. The base station is connected via a cable to a computer where strain data can be plotted, analyzed, and stored.

### 2.2   Design requirements

Based on the target application, we consider the following design requirements:

- The telemetry unit should be small in size so that it can be either worn or be implanted subcutaneously in a small animal.
- The telemetry unit should have a wireless means of communication to allow unconstrained movement of the subject. Moreover, the communication range should be of 1 m or more to account for different cage sizes.
- The telemetry unit should have an adequate lifetime to allow researchers to take enough measurements

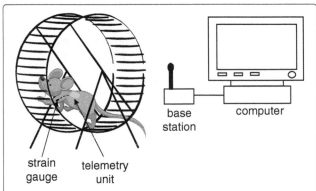

**Figure 2 Conceptual diagram of a real-time wireless bone strain monitoring system.** The subject is not constrained by the measurement equipment and is free to move and perform bone-growth stimulating exercises.

before replacing its batteries. It would be desirable to enable the battery to be recharged while measurements are not being taken.

- The telemetry unit should be able to read more than one strain gauge to allow strain readings to be taken at multiple bone locations.
- Since the user cannot interact directly with the telemetry unit once it is implanted, the user should be able to control the operation of the unit wirelessly. The user should be able to control parameters such as number of channels need to be read, sampling rate and duty cycle.
- A motion sensor would be desirable to have because it will allow researchers to establish the correlation between exercise and bone development.

To address the design requirements and to lower development cost and time, we decided to employ a commercially available SoC solution. Table 1 shows a comparison between several commercially available SoC platforms. All the selected platforms include in a single chip a microcontroller unit (MCU) and a radio transceiver. We decided to work with a radio band below 1 GHz to minimize the attenuation of electromagnetic waves due to tissue at higher frequencies [21]. The CC430F5137 microcontroller was selected because of its superior on-chip flash and RAM memory and peripheral resources. The CC430F5137 also features a 16-bit CPU with several low-power modes. The 915-MHz ISM radio band was selected to communicate with the base station because it is a license free band.

Some telemetry unit designs employ radio frequency identification technology (RFID) to transmit data wirelessly [15,16]. The advantage of the RFID-based designs is that power is supplied to the unit by a reader. Thus, there is no need to use a battery [22]. The drawback of RFID-based designs is that the communication range is limited

to few inches and because they have low data transmission rates, which limit the sampling rate of the sensor to only few samples per second. Due to these drawbacks, RFID technology was not employed for data communications in our design.

### 2.3  Strain sensing

Strain gauges are piezoresistive sensors, that is, their resistance changes when they are stretched or compressed. The most common type of strain gauge is the metallic strain gauge, which consists of a very fine wire arranged in a grid pattern. The wire is bonded to a thin and flexible substrate, which is then attached to the test specimen. As the test specimen is deformed, the thin wire in the gauge is stretched or compressed, thus changing its length and consequently its electrical resistance [23]. Other types of strain gauges are based on semiconductor materials, like silicon. Silicon-based strain gauges are usually more sensitive than metallic gauges. However, metallic gauges tend to have better linearity [24].

The change in resistance $\Delta R$ and the strain in a strain gauge are related by the following equation:

$$G = \frac{\Delta R}{R \times \varepsilon} \tag{1}$$

where $G$ is the gauge factor, $R$ is the nominal gauge resistance, and $\varepsilon$ is the strain experienced by the gauge commonly measured in units of micro-strain ($\mu\epsilon$).

We chose to work with the Vishay EA-06-015DJ-120 strain gauges due to their very small size and good linearity. The selected strain gauge has a nominal resistance of 120 $\Omega$ and a gauge factor of $G = 2.07$. The maximum bone strain that is expected in the experiments is about 3,000 $\mu\epsilon$. Therefore, the maximum expected change in resistance is 0.75 $\Omega$ or 0.625 % of its nominal resistance. The traditional approach to measure such small resistance changes is to use a Wheatstone bridge in combination with an amplifier as shown in Figure 3a. The output of the amplifier is then converted to digital using an analog-to-digital converter (ADC). In the figure, $R_S$ is the strain gauge resistance.

Letting $R_S = R + \Delta R$ and $R_1 = R_P = R_S = R$, the following expression for $V_{\mathrm{OUT}}$ can be obtained:

$$V_{\mathrm{OUT}} = A \cdot V_{\mathrm{EX}} \left( \frac{\alpha}{2(2 + \alpha)} \right) \tag{2}$$

where $\alpha = \Delta R/R$ and $A$ is the gain of the instrumentation amplifier, which is typically set by the external resistor $R_G$. Considering $V_{\mathrm{EX}} = 3.0\,\mathrm{V}$ and $\alpha = 0.00625$, yields $V_{\mathrm{OUT}} = 0.0047A$. The gain of the amplifier must be large enough to produce a voltage waveform with sufficient dynamic range so that it can be efficiently converted to digital format by

**Table 1 Comparison of several commercially available SoCs**

| | Microcontroller unit | | | Radio transceiver | | | |
| | CPU | Memory | Peripherals | Freq. band | Modulation | Current consumption | Data rate |
|---|---|---|---|---|---|---|---|
| CC430F5137 | 16-bit | 32kB flash | 12-bit ADC | 779 to | 2-FSK | Rx: 16 mA at | up to |
| | RISC | 4kB RAM | 30 GPIOs | 928 | 2-GSK | −100 dBm | 500 |
| | | (internal) | 2 16-bit timers | MHz | | Tx: 17 mA at | kbps |
| | | | 2 UARTs, 2 SPI | | | 0 dBm | |
| CC2510F32 | 8-bit | 32kB flash | 12-bit ADC | 2.4 | 2-FSK | Rx: 21 mA at | up to |
| | 8051 | 4kB RAM | 21 GPIOs | GHz | GFSK | −103 dBm | 500 |
| | | (internal) | 3 timers, 1 USB | | MSK | Tx: 26 mA at | kbps |
| | | | 2 UARTs | | | 0 dBm | |
| rfPIC12F675H | 8-bit | 2kB flash | 10-bit ADC | 850 to | FSK | Rx: N.A. | up to |
| | RISC | 64B RAM | 6 GPIOs | 930 | ASK | | 40 |
| | | (internal) | 2 timers | MHz | | Tx: 6.5mA at | kbps |
| | | | | | | 2 dBm | |
| nRF9E5 | 8-bit | 4kB RAM | 10-bit ADC | 868, | GFSK | Rx: 13 mA at | up to |
| | 8051 | (internal) | 8 GPIOs | 915 | | −100 dBm | 50 |
| | | EEPROM | 3 timers | MHz | | Tx: 14 mA at | kbps |
| | | (external) | 1 UART, 1 SPI | | | −2 dBm | |

the ADC. The dynamic range (DR) at the output of the amplifier can be expressed as:

$$DR = 20 \log \left( \frac{0.0047A}{V_{LSB}} \right) \; dB \qquad (3)$$

where $V_{LSB} = V_{DD}/2^n$, $V_{DD}$ is the power supply and the reference voltage of the ADC, and $n$ is the ADC's bit resolution. Considering $V_{DD} = 3.0$ V and $n = 12$ bits, to achieve a dynamic range of 60 dB or more, a gain of at least 155 is needed. In our design, we employed a gain of 330 yielding a DR of 66.5 dB.

A variable resistor $R_2$ is used in the Wheatstone bridge to calibrate the bridge such that $V_O = 0$ when no strain is applied. We ruled out the possibility of using a mechanical potentiometer to implement $R_2$ to avoid vibration-induced changes in its resistance. Moreover, a mechanical

potentiometer needs to be manually tuned complicating the calibration of the bridge once it is implanted. Another option is to use a digital potentiometer as digital potentiometers are not affected by vibrations. However, commercially available digital potentiometers do not have enough resolution to match the expected resistance change in $R_S$.

To address the calibration problem, we employed a calibration approach that is based on a high-resolution digital-to-analog converter (DAC) instead of a variable resistor. The branch of the Wheatstone bridge composed by $R_1$ and $R_2$ is replaced with a DAC controlled by the microcontroller as shown in Figure 3b. The calibration procedure is depicted in Figure 4. The basic idea of the calibration procedure is to generate a voltage ramp with the DAC and monitor the output of the instrumentation amplifier when no load is applied to the strain gauge. Calibration is achieved when the output of the amplifier,

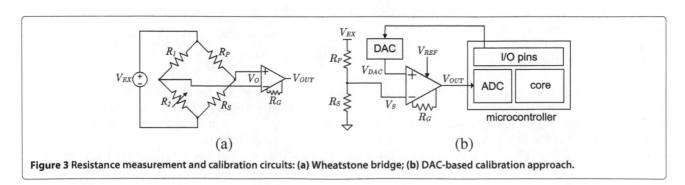

(a)                                      (b)

**Figure 3** Resistance measurement and calibration circuits: (a) Wheatstone bridge; (b) DAC-based calibration approach.

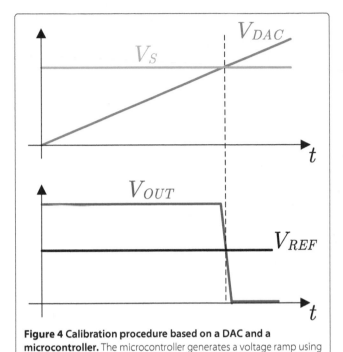

**Figure 4 Calibration procedure based on a DAC and a microcontroller.** The microcontroller generates a voltage ramp using a DAC until the amplifier's output equals the reference voltage $V_{REF}$.

$V_{OUT}$, equals the reference voltage $V_{REF}$. The digital input value of the DAC at the end of calibration is stored and applied in subsequent readings of the amplifier.

From Figure 3b, the output of the instrumentation amplifier is given by:

$$V_{OUT} = V_{REF} + A\left(V_{DAC} - V_S\right) \qquad (4)$$

Ideally, during calibration, we would like to set $V_{DAC} = V_S$ so that $V_{OUT} = V_{REF}$. In practice, the calibration procedure described above is limited by the resolution of the DAC. At the end of calibration, the maximum value of the difference $V_{DAC} - V_S$ is $V_{LSB}/2$, where $V_{LSB} = V_{DD}/2^n$ and $n$ is the DAC resolution. This input difference produces a maximum deviation of $A \cdot V_{DD}/2^{n+1}$ from the ideal value of $V_{REF}$ at the amplifier's output. Considering a target gain of $A = 330$, a supply voltage of 3.0 V and a 12-bit DAC resolution, the maximum output offset is 120 mV. This offset is much smaller than the supply voltage and will not constrain the voltage swing of the amplifier's output. Thus, a DAC resolution of 12 bits is sufficient for the target application. Moreover, since the offset due to finite DAC resolution remains constant throughout the measurement process, it is canceled out digitally.

### 2.4 Telemetry unit hardware

Figure 5 shows a simplified schematic diagram of the telemetry unit which is designed around the CC430 microcontroller. An eight-channel multiplexer (MUX) is employed to allow up to eight different strain gauges to be connected to the telemetry unit. The eight-channel multiplexer comprises two low-power low-on-resistance MUXs (ADG804). A precision instrumentation amplifier $A_1$ (INA333) is employed to amplify the voltage difference $V_{DAC} - V_S$. The gain of $A_1$ is set by the resistor $R_G$ according to:

$$A_1 = 1 + \frac{100\text{ k}\Omega}{R_G} \qquad (5)$$

A resistor $R_G$ of 300 Ω was employed yielding a gain of 334. The voltage $V_S$ is a function of the strain gauge resistance through the following voltage resistive divider relationship:

$$V_S = V_{DD}\frac{R_S}{R_S + R_P} \qquad (6)$$

The resistance $R_P$ is a precision resistor with a value matching the nominal resistance of the strain gauges. Using (5) and (6) yields the following expression for the output of the instrumentation amplifier:

$$V_{OUT} = V_{REF} + A\left(V_{DAC} - V_S\right)$$
$$= V_{REF} + \left(1 + \frac{100\text{ k}\Omega}{R_G}\right)\left(V_{DAC} - \frac{V_{DD}R_S}{R_S + R_P}\right) \qquad (7)$$

Thus, the amplifier's output is a function of the strain gauge resistance, $R_S$, which in turn is a function of strain applied to the gauge through (1). As a result, the strain experienced by the gauge can be calculated from the voltage output of the amplifier.

The current that flows through $R_S$ and $R_P$ is given by:

$$I_R = \frac{V_{DD}}{R_S + R_P}. \qquad (8)$$

Considering $R_S = R_P = 120$ Ω and $V_{DD} = 3$ V results in a current of 12.5 mA flowing through the strain gauge. This current is quite large for a low-power sensor that is expected to run for long periods of time from a small battery. To reduce the average current through $R_S$, the resistance $R_P$ could be increased. However, increasing $R_P$ results in a reduced voltage swing across the strain gauge. To reduce current consumption without sacrificing the signal swing, the MOSFET $M_1$ (PMV16) is added in series with $R_P$ and $R_S$. The MOSFET works as a switch allowing current to flow through resistors $R_P$ and $R_S$ only when an analog-to-digital conversion is taking place. Otherwise, the MOSFET is turned off. Using this approach, the average current through $R_S$ was reduced to approximately 1 mA.

A second DAC was added to provide a programmable voltage reference $V_{REF}$ to the instrumentation amplifier. A programmable reference level gives the flexibility of moving the amplifier's output baseline up or down to

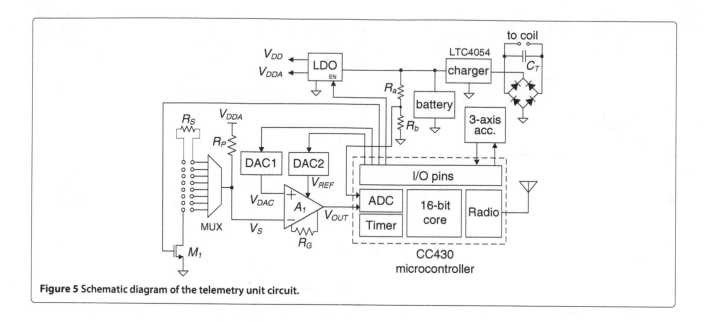

**Figure 5** Schematic diagram of the telemetry unit circuit.

match the range of certain test signals such as haversines which are unidirectional. A 12-bit DAC (DAC7311) with low-power consumption and small footprint was used to implement both DAC1 and DAC2.

A three-axis accelerometer was included in the telemetry unit to enable motion information capture. The MMA8453Q accelerometer was employed due to its small size (3 mm × 3 mm × 1 mm) and very low power consumption (0.54 mW). The accelerometer connects to the microcontroller via a two-wire I$^2$C bus. Motion information can be used at the sensor level to save power by triggering the transmission of strain data only when motion is detected. Furthermore, acceleration readings can be transmitted to the base station to allow researchers to establish correlations between physical exercise and bone growth. This paper focuses mainly on the acquisition and transmission of strain measurements. The transmission of acceleration readings can be accomplished with a small modification of the microcontroller's program (see Section 4).

A wireless inductive battery charger was also included on the design to enable full implantation of the unit. The charger is composed of a coil and a capacitor $C_T$ that form a resonant LC tank, a full-wave rectifier and the LTC4054 battery charger. A small and rechargeable lithium-polymer battery with a capacity of 45 mAh is used to power up the telemetry unit. The voltage level of the battery is monitored by the microcontroller using the $R_a - R_b$ resistive voltage divider. The battery voltage level is sent to the base station in every transmitted radio packet. Thus, the end user can be alerted when the battery is running low and can recharge it.

The inductive charger works at a frequency of 13.5 MHz. This frequency was chosen because it is low enough

to penetrate tissue [25] and it is an unlicensed band. The resonant tank is tuned to the right frequency by varying the value of capacitor $C_T$. A dual output low-dropout voltage regulator (LDO) was employed to provide a stable supply voltage to the analog and digital components of the telemetry unit. The dual output LDO allows portions of the telemetry unit hardware to be powered down to reduce power consumption when the unit is signaled to enter into the SLEEP power down-mode or when the battery voltage has dropped below 3.0 V.

In the SLEEP mode, the analog front-end (amplifier, DACs, and MUX) of the sensor as well as the accelerometer are turned off, the microcontroller is put into a low-power mode and the radio is turned off. In the SLEEP mode, the microcontroller wakes up every 3 min, turns its radio on, transmits a status packet, and listens for possible response from the base station. If no response is received, it goes back to the SLEEP mode. On the other hand, if a response from the base station is received, the unit exits the SLEEP mode and proceeds to read and transmit data from its input channels. The SLEEP mode is designed to minimize power consumption when the unit is not being used to collect strain or motion information.

## 2.5 Printed circuit board

A four-layer printed circuit board (PCB) to host all the electronic components was designed and fabricated. The PCB with mounted components is shown in Figure 6. Special effort was made in the PCB design to minimize noise coupling into the analog signal chain. Likewise, special efforts were made to minimize the size of the board. A PCB with a size of 2.4 cm × 1.3 cm was achieved. To reduce the number of discrete com-

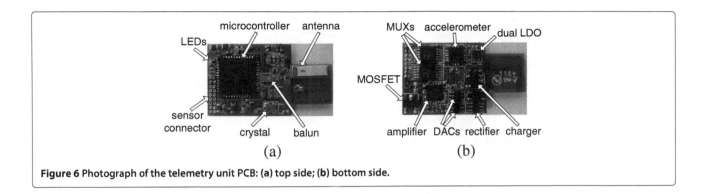

**Figure 6** Photograph of the telemetry unit PCB: **(a)** top side; **(b)** bottom side.

ponents needed by the radio, a balun from Johanson Technology (0896BM15A0001) was employed in the impedance matching network. A 915-MHz chip antenna from Johanson Technology (0915AT43A0026) and a small 26 MHz crystal oscillator were also employed to reduce board space.

Table 2 provides the cost of the electronic components in the telemetry unit. The total component cost of the telemetry unit is US$67.11. To this cost, we should add the engineering labor time required to design and assembly the telemetry unit. The engineering labor time is estimated to be approximately 320 h.

## 3  Radio communications

Communication between the telemetry unit and the base station is carried out using radio packets of fixed length. Each radio packet consists of a preamble, a sync word, a length field, an address field, a payload, and a 16-bit CRC. The payload has a fixed length of 60 bytes. The payload

**Table 2** Cost of the electronic components in the telemetry unit

| Component | Part number | Unit price (USD) |
|---|---|---|
| Microcontroller | CC430F5137 | 6.75 |
| Crystal | NX2016AB-26MHZ | 1.63 |
| Balun | 0896BM15A0001E | 1.09 |
| Antenna | 0915AT43A0026 | 0.38 |
| Accelerometer | MMA8453Q | 1.43 |
| LDO | TLV7113030 | 0.64 |
| Charger | LTC4054 | 3.49 |
| Rectifier | HSMS282P | 1.71 |
| DACs | DAC7311 | 2× 2.32 |
| Instrumentation amplifier | INA333 | 4.05 |
| Multiplexers | ADG804 | 2× 2.72 |
| Passive components | | 2.50 |
| Four-layer PCB | | 33.36 |
| Total | | 67.11 |

field contains the information that needs to be transmitted. Depending on the type of information, a packet could be of three types: (1) a CONTROL packet, (2) a STATUS packet, and (3) a DATA packet.

A CONTROL packet is transmitted by the base station to the telemetry unit and contains commands to set parameters such as the conversion rate, the active channel number, the transmission power and whether only strain or strain and motion information are to be transmitted by the unit. A CONTROL packet is also used to signal the unit to enter or exit the SLEEP mode.

STATUS packets are transmitted by the telemetry unit to the base station only when the unit is in SLEEP mode. In SLEEP mode the telemetry unit reduces its activity by turning off its analog front end and its radio transceiver. Every 3 min, the unit turns on its radio and transmits a STATUS packet and listens to the radio channel for 3 s. If the unit receives a 'wake up' CONTROL packet from the base station, it exits the SLEEP mode. To differentiate between a STATUS and a DATA packet, the first 3 bytes in the STATUS payload are set to 0xFF00FF.

DATA packets are transmitted by the telemetry unit to the base station. A DATA packet is used to send strain and motion information. A DATA packet also contains calibration and sampling rate data as well as channel number and battery voltage. The format of a DATA packet's payload is shown in Figure 7. The first 6 bytes of a DATA packet contain the values of both DACs (DAC1 and DAC2), Timer A period, the active channel number, and the battery voltage. The next 54 bytes contain sensor values. A strain value has a bit length of 12 bits. Thus, a single packet can transmit 36 strain samples. Motion information is conveyed as acceleration in the X, Y, and Z axes. A total of 3 bytes are needed to transmit an acceleration triplet. Thus, a single packet can transmit 12 samples of strain and acceleration.

The analog-to-digital conversion rate is set by an internal timer (Timer A), and it can be changed according to the application requirements by reprogramming the timer period. Every time the Timer A finishes one counting

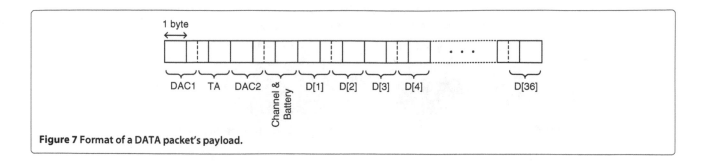

**Figure 7** Format of a DATA packet's payload.

period, the ADC output is read and a new conversion is started. Hence, the conversion rate is given by:

$$f_{\text{conv}} = \frac{f_{\text{clk}}}{\text{TA}}, \tag{9}$$

where $f_{\text{clk}}$ is the microcontroller's clock frequency which is set to 500 kHz and TA is the time period. Once enough samples have been collected to fill up a radio packet's payload, the packet is transmitted.

Given that it takes 36 strain samples to fill up a packet's payload, the inter-packet transmission period is equal to:

$$T_p = \frac{36}{f_{\text{conv}}} = \frac{36 \times \text{TA}}{f_{\text{clk}}}. \tag{10}$$

The total length of a radio packet is 576 bits including the other packet fields such as the preamble, synchronization, address, length, and CRC. Considering a radio transmission rate of 75 kbps, transmitting a radio packet takes 7.7 ms. After the transmission of every packet, the radio transceiver is switched to reception mode for 31.2 ms to listen for a possible transmissions from the base station. Therefore, the minimum inter-packet transmission period, $T_{p\text{min}}$, is 7.7 ms + 31.2 ms = 38.9 ms. Replacing $T_{p\text{min}}$ in (10), yields a maximum conversion rate of 925 Hz which divided among eight channels gives a maximum conversion rate of 115 Hz per channel. This sampling rate is enough for the target application. If higher sampling rates per channel are needed less number of channels would have to be scanned. The conducted *ex vivo* tests applied a 2-Hz haversine force to a mouse bone. Thus, by the Nyquist theorem, the sampling rate in the *ex vivo* tests can be as low as 4 Hz.

Radio transmissions are the most power-expensive operation performed by the telemetry unit. During transmission the radio transmitter consumes 17 mA for a power output of 0 dBm. In reception mode, the transceiver consumes 16 mA of current [17]. To reduce power consumption due to radio communications, the radio transceiver is turned off in between transmssions as illustrated in Figure 8. In the figure, $T_x$ is the time required to transmit a single packet while $T_{\text{rx}}$ is the listening time

that follows a packet transmission. $T_{\text{ff}}$ is the time during which the radio transceiver remains off. Thus, the average current consumption due to radio communications is given by:

$$I_{\text{avg}} = \frac{T_{\text{tx}}I_{\text{tx}} + T_{\text{rx}}I_{\text{rx}}}{T_{\text{tx}} + T_{\text{rx}} + T_{\text{off}}} \tag{11}$$

where, $T_{\text{off}}$ is the time the radio transceiver remains off, $T_{\text{tx}} = 7.7$ ms, $T_{\text{rx}} = 31.2$ ms, $I_{\text{tx}}$ is the current consumption during transmission and $I_{\text{rx}}$ is the current consumption during reception. Notice that $T_{\text{tx}} + T_{\text{rx}} + T_{\text{off}} = T_p$. Replacing this result in (10) yields the following relationship:

$$\begin{aligned} I_{\text{avg}} &= f_{\text{conv}}\left(\frac{T_{\text{tx}}I_{\text{tx}} + T_{\text{rx}}I_{\text{rx}}}{36}\right) \\ &= (Nf_s)\left(\frac{T_{\text{tx}}I_{\text{tx}} + T_{\text{rx}}I_{\text{rx}}}{36}\right), \end{aligned} \tag{12}$$

where $N$ is the number of active channels (channels being read) and $f_s$ is the sampling rate per channel.

Thus, the average power consumption due to radio communications is directly proportional to the sampling rate per channel and to the number of channels. Figure 9 shows the average current consumption predicted by the model in (12) for a data rate of 75 kbps and a transmission power of 0 dBm ($I_{\text{tx}} = 17$ mA and $I_{\text{rx}} = 16$ mA). An additional 1.5 mA has been added to $I_{\text{avg}}$ to account for the current consumption of the CPU, ADC, voltage regulation, and the analog signal chain (see Table 3).

From the battery's datasheet, we find that if 4.0 mA of current are continuously drawn from the battery, its voltage will drop to 3.0 V after approximately 12 h. Thus, from

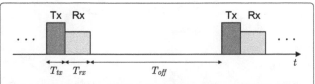

**Figure 8** Packet transmission (TX) and reception (RX) timing diagram.

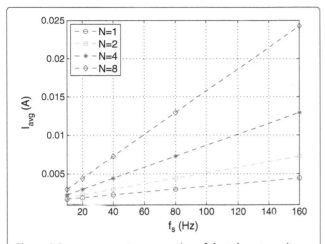

**Figure 9** Average current consumption of the telemetry unit. The current consumption is a function of the number of active channels (*N*) and the sampling rate per channel ($f_s$). The data rate is 75 kbps and a transmission output power is 0 dBm.

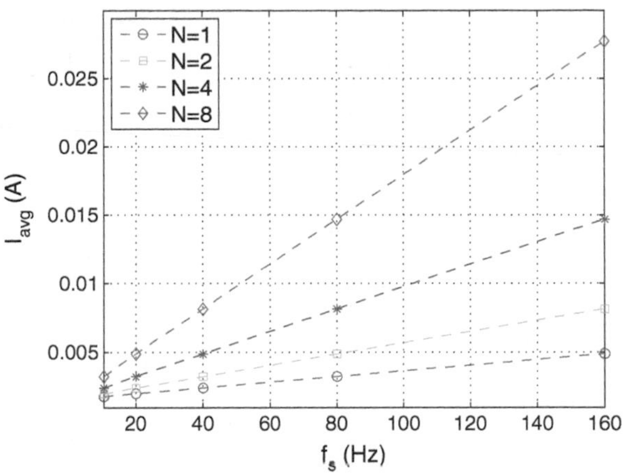

**Figure 10** Average current consumption of the telemetry unit. As a function of the number of active channels (*N*) and the sampling rate per channel ($f_s$). The data rate is 38 kbps and the transmission output power is 0 dBm.

Figure 9, we conclude that when transmitting at 75 kbps and 0 dBm, to collect 12 h of continuous data using all eight channels, the sampling rate needs to be about 18 Hz each. Alternatively, if only one channel is active, sampling at a rate of 33 Hz allows the battery to last 24 h before recharging. A typical sampling rate per channel is between 3 to 5 Hz. Hence, the telemetry unit can run for more than 24 h of continuous operation.

Figure 10 shows the average current consumption when the transmission data rate is decreased to 38 kbps. At 38 kbps, the packet transmission time $T_{tx}$ is 15.2 ms. Notably, the average current consumption increases due to the increase in $T_{rx}$. The advantage of using a lower transmission data rate is that the packet loss due to transmission errors decreases. Packet loss is analyzed in Section 5.3. To achieve a continuous operation of 12 h at 38 kbps, the sampling rate per channel should be 15 Hz when all eight

**Table 3 Current consumption of the MCU and analog signal chain in the telemetry unit**

| Component | Part Number | Current consumption (mA) |
|---|---|---|
| MCU | CC430F5137 | 0.080 |
| Accelerometer | MMA8453Q | 0.05 |
| LDO | TLV7113030 | 0.07 |
| Charger | LTC4054 | 0.025 |
| DACs | 2×DAC7311 | 2×0.11 |
| Instrumentation amplifier | INA333 | 0.05 |
| Multiplexers | 2×ADG804 | 2×0.004 |
| Strain gauge | EA-06-015DJ-120 | 1 |
| Total | | 1.5 |

channels are active. If only one channel is active, sampling it at 28 Hz will result in 24 h of continuous operation. Hence, packet loss can be traded off with battery lifetime by varying the transmission data rate.

## 4  Software design

The software design encompasses the development of three programs: one running on the telemetry unit, one running on the base station, and one running on the computer. The programs running on the telemetry unit and on the base station were written in C. The program running on the computer was written in Matlab. The program running on the telemetry unit has an interrupt-driven architecture. Interrupts are employed to process information only when an event occurs. Once an interrupt request has been serviced, the CPU enters into a low-power mode (LPM3) to reduce power consumption. Figure 11 shows the flow diagrams of the `main()` function (Figure 11a) and the Timer A interrupt service routine (ISR) (Figure 11b). The Timer A period changes depending on whether the unit is in SLEEP mode or not. In SLEEP mode, the timer period is 6 s. The default timer period when the unit is not in SLEEP mode is 2.5 ms. The timer period can be changed from the base station by transmitting a CONTROL package.

The main function of the Timer A ISR is to fill up a memory buffer (`packet[]`) with samples from the sensors. The variable `ptr` is employed to keep track of how many samples have been stored in the memory buffer so far. When the memory buffer is filled (`ptr = PACKET_LEN`), its contents are passed to the radio transceiver and a DATA packet is transmitted. Figure 11b shows the memory buffer being filled with

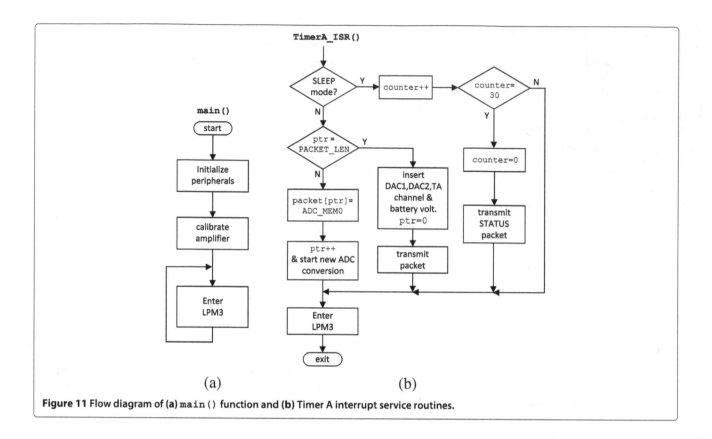

**Figure 11** Flow diagram of **(a)** `main()` function and **(b)** Timer A interrupt service routines.

readings from the ADC (strain data). To transmit acceleration data, the memory buffer should be filled with readings from the accelerometer.

Figure 12 shows the flow diagrams of the ADC ISR (Figure 12a) and the radio ISR (Figure 12b). In the radio ISR, incoming packets are checked for length and CRC. If an incoming packet has the correct length and no CRC errors, it is read into memory and decoded for possible commands from the base station.

The base station is equipped with a CC430F5137 microcontroller whose function is to receive radio packets from the telemetry unit and transmit the packets' payload contents to the computer via a FTDI serial-to-USB cable. The program in the base station also monitors how many packets are received without errors in a fixed period of time to calculate the packet loss.

Figure 13 shows a screenshot of the graphical user interface (GUI) of the program running on the computer. Using the GUI, the user can change the COM port, start and stop the display of incoming data, change the display length, save data and transmit a CONTROL packet to update the Timer A period, the DAC values, and the radio power level of the telemetry unit.

## 5   Results and measurements

The developed telemetry system was tested in an *ex vivo* setting and in a simulated implanted setting using a tissue

phantom. The measurement results from testing the unit in both settings are presented below.

### 5.1   *Ex vivo* test

To perform the *ex vivo* test, the ulna bone of a mouse was surgically removed. A small strain gauge (Vishay EA-06-015DJ-120) was glued to the bone using M-bond 2000 from Vishay Micro-Measurements. Figure 14 shows a photograph of the ulna bone and the attached strain gage. The bone was mounted on the Bose ElectroForce 3200 load test instrument, and the strain gauge was connected to the benchtop acquisition unit. An oscillating force with a haversine shape was applied to the bone by the ElectroForce 3200. The amplitude of the haversine was set to 3 N and its frequency to 2 Hz. Strain data was collected with the StrainSmart® software. The strain gauge mounted on the bone was then connected to the telemetry unit. A haversine force with the same parameters as before was applied to the bone. Strain data was collected by the telemetry unit. The sampling rate was set to 160 Hz.

Figure 15 shows strain measurements obtained from both the benchtop acquisition system and the telemetry unit. Notably, the telemetry unit is able to acquire strain measurements with a performance comparable to the more expensive and bulkier data acquisition system. The wireless transmission from the strain gauge implanted

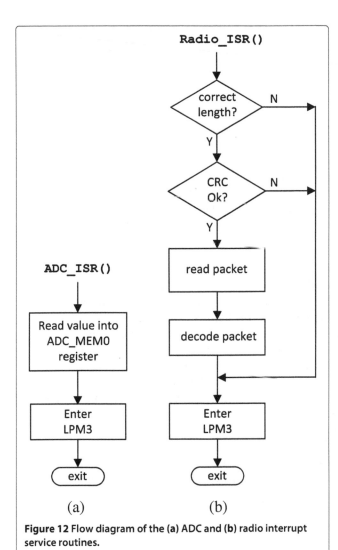

**Figure 12** Flow diagram of the **(a)** ADC and **(b)** radio interrupt service routines.

in an animal that is walking is expected to be a periodic pattern similar to the pattern shown in Figure 13 [26].

## 5.2 Current consumption

The current consumption of the telemetry unit was measured by placing a current-sense resistor of 1 Ω at the input of the LDO. The voltage across the current-sense resistor was amplified with an instrumentation amplifier and read with a data acquisition board. The current drawn by the telemetry unit was calculated from the voltage readings across the current-sense resistor. Figure 16 shows the measured current consumption of the telemetry unit for different values of the sampling frequency $f_s$ and for a single active channel. The transmission data rate was set to 75 kbps, and the transmission output power was set to 0 dBm. From the figure, it can be seen that at a sampling frequency of 10 Hz, the current consumed by the telemetry unit is only 1.75 mA. At a sampling frequency of 160 Hz, the current consumption increases to 4 mA which is in agreement with the current consumption predicted by Equation (12) (see Figure 9). During SLEEP mode, the unit consumes 0.4 mA.

## 5.3 Tissue phantom test

To assess the performance of the telemetry unit in an implanted scenario, a tissue phantom was created. Tissue phantoms are commonly employed to test the interaction of electromagnetic radiation and biological tissue [27]. Working with a tissue phantom has some advantages over working with cadaver animal tissue. One of the advantages is that a tissue phantom is more resistant to bacterial infection. Another advantage of a phantom

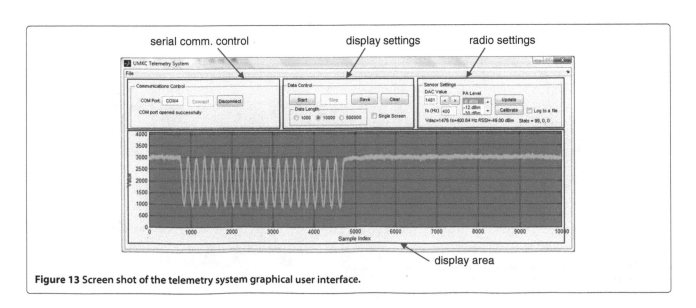

**Figure 13** Screen shot of the telemetry system graphical user interface.

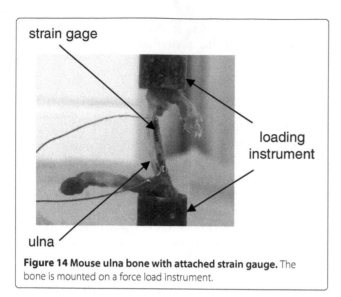

**Figure 14 Mouse ulna bone with attached strain gauge.** The bone is mounted on a force load instrument.

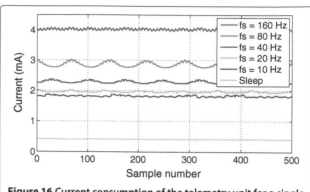

**Figure 16 Current consumption of the telemetry unit for a single active channel and different sampling frequencies.**

is that it does not decay and produces more consistent results than animal tissue [28].

We created a tissue phantom using gelatin and NaCl. In 500 ml of water, 15 g of gelatin was added and mixed with 1.2 g of NaCl and brought to boil [29]. The gelatin mixture was poured into a container and was allowed to solidify in a refrigerator. The telemetry unit was then placed on top of the solidified gelatin, and more gelatin mixture was then added to the container until it covered the telemetry unit by 1 cm. The telemetry unit was previously wrapped with polyimide film tape to electrically isolate the unit from the gelatin. Polyimide film was employed due to its demonstrated biocompatibility properties [30]. The container was placed back in the refrigerator to allow the mixture to solidify. Figure 17 shows the telemetry unit

encased in the tissue phantom. Two wires were left connected to the telemetry unit to allow us to measure the battery current as the battery is recharged.

In the first test, the wireless battery charging circuit was tested. A coil of diameter of 2 cm and 20 turns was connected to the voltage rectifier in the telemetry unit. An external transmitter with a 1-W power output at 13.5 MHz and a loop antenna were employed to generate an oscillating electromagnetic field. The loop antenna was placed on top of the phantom at a distance of 1 cm from the coil antenna attached to the telemetry unit. The telemetry unit was place in SLEEP mode by transmitting a CONTROL packet from the base station.

The current from the charger to the battery ($I_{batt}$) was measured using a current-sense resistor. Figure 18 shows the setup employed to measure the current $I_{batt}$. A 1-$\Omega$ resistor was placed between the charger and the battery. An external instrumentation amplifier (AD620) was employed to amplify the voltage across the 1-$\Omega$ resistor ($V_1 - V_2$). The gain of the instrumentation amplifier was

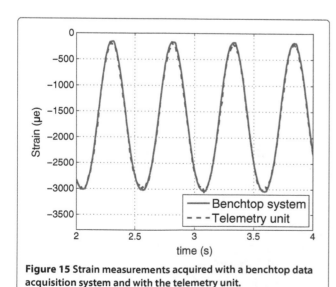

**Figure 15 Strain measurements acquired with a benchtop data acquisition system and with the telemetry unit.**

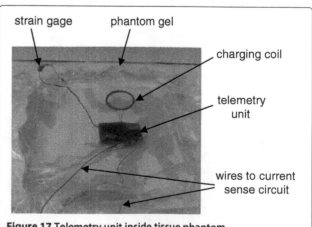

**Figure 17 Telemetry unit inside tissue phantom.**

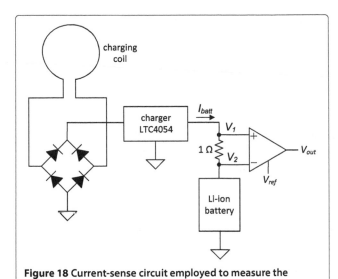

**Figure 18** Current-sense circuit employed to measure the current delivered from the wireless charger to battery.

set to 100 and its reference voltage $V_{ref}$ to 1 V. The output voltage of the instrumentation amplifier ($V_{out}$) was read with a data acquisition board. The battery current is calculated as follows:

$$I_{batt} = \frac{V_{out} - V_{ref}}{1\Omega \times 100} \tag{13}$$

Figure 19 shows the current delivered to the battery by the charger when the medium between the charging coil and the loop antenna is air and when it is the phantom. Figure 19 shows that the charger is able to deliver 3.4 and 1.3 mA to the battery when the medium air and the phantom, respectively. Hence, charging a 45-mA fully discharged battery through the phantom will take 34 h approximately. However, in most practical cases, the

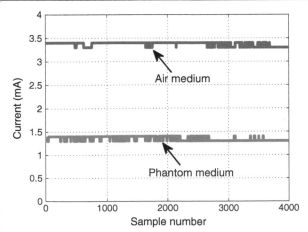

**Figure 19** Current delivered to telemetry unit during wireless charging for two different mediums: air and phantom.

**Table 4 Packet loss percentage for air medium and for different transmission data rates and distances**

| Tx power (dBm) | Data rate | | | | | |
| | 38 kbps | | | 75 kbps | | |
| | Distance | | | Distance | | |
| | 50 cm | 1 m | 2 m | 50 cm | 1 m | 2 m |
| --- | --- | --- | --- | --- | --- | --- |
| 0 | 0% | 0% | 0% | 5.46% | 7.08% | 7.72% |
| −12 | 0% | 0% | 1.14% | 7.82% | 9.32% | 9.8% |
| −30 | 0.34% | 0.76% | 1.4% | 30.84% | 31.36% | 42.78% |

battery is not fully discharged after one data collection session. Considering a sampling frequency of 20 Hz and one active channel, from Figure 16, we can see that the average current consumption is 2 mA. Under these conditions, in a 6-h data collection session, the battery capacity is drained by 12 mAh. Using the wireless charger, it will take 9.2 h to replenish the charge drained by a 6-h data collection session.

To achieve continuous operation spanning days or weeks, the current supplied by the charging coil should match or exceed the current consumption of the telemetry unit. Two strategies can be followed to achieve continuous operation. First, the current consumption of the telemetry unit can be lowered by reducing the sampling rate. However, the sampling rate cannot be made arbitrarily low to avoid introducing aliasing. Another approach to reduce current consumption is to transmit radio packets only when the accelerometer detects motion. The second strategy involves increasing the diameter and the number of turns of the charging coil so that a larger electromagnetic flux crosses the coil and induces a larger current. Alternatively, the power output of the external transmitter can be increased.

In a second test, the radio packet loss was measured. To measure packet loss, the base station counted the number of error-free packets that were received in a given amount of time. An error-free packet is a packet with the correct length and with the correct CRC. Given that the base station knows the sampling rate of the telemetry unit,

**Table 5 Packet loss percentage for phantom medium and for different transmission data rates and distances**

| Tx power (dBm) | Data rate | | | | | |
| | 38 kbps | | | 75 kbps | | |
| | Distance | | | Distance | | |
| | 50 cm | 1 m | 2 m | 50 cm | 1 m | 2 m |
| --- | --- | --- | --- | --- | --- | --- |
| 0 | 0% | 0% | 0% | 7.4% | 9.06% | 14.56% |
| −12 | 0% | 0% | 1.4% | 36.04% | 39.1% | 51.66% |
| −30 | 1.04% | 3.96% | 15.50% | 45.96% | 75.34% | 89.1% |

the base station is able to calculate how many packets from the telemetry unit are expected in a given amount of time. The difference between the number of expected packets and the number of received error-free packets is the packet loss. The packet loss was measured for air and for the phantom mediums at different data rates and different distances between the telemetry unit and the base station. Tables 4 and 5 show the packet loss in percentage for these different conditions. Notably, a 0% packet loss can be achieved for a transmission data rate of 38 kbps.

If a small percentage of packet loss can be tolerated, the transmission power can be lowered to −12 or −30 dBm while keeping a data rate of 38 kbps.

Table 6 presents a comparison between the telemetry unit presented in this work and other embedded telemetry units for biomedical applications reported in the literature. Although it is difficult to make a one-to-one comparison since each unit was designed for a specific application, our telemetry unit compares favorably in terms of size and sensing capabilities.

**Table 6 Comparison with other embedded telemetry units for biomedical applications**

|  | Sensor type | Size | Battery | Operation time | Radio band | Rechargeable | Sampling rate |
|---|---|---|---|---|---|---|---|
| This work | Strain gage (8 channels) three-axis accel. temperature | 1.3 cm ×2.4 cm ×0.7 cm | Li-Po 45 mAh | 24 h | 915 MHz | Yes (wireless) | 33 Hz |
| [9] | Strain gage (3 channels) | 9.0 cm ×9.0 cm ×1.8 cm | Li-ion | 33 h | 2.4 GHz | No | 617 Hz |
| [10] | Pressure (resistive) | 2.5 cm ×5 cm ×0.7 cm[a] | Li-Po 850 mAh | > 4 days | 433 MHz | No | 1 Hz |
| [11] | ECG (3 channels) three-axis accel. temp., light | 2.6 cm ×1.5 cm ×0.7 cm | Li-Po 40 mAh | > 12 h (20 % duty cycle) | 2.4 GHz | Yes (wired) | 1 kHz |
| [12] | ECG (3 channels) three-axis accel. | 5.7 cm ×3.6 cm ×1.6 cm | Li-Po 120 mAh | 5 h (100 % duty cycle) | 2.4 GHz | Yes (wired) | 1 KHz |
| [13] | Pressure & volume | 1.3 cm ×1.3 cm ×1.3 cm | Li-Po | N. A. | 433 MHz | Yes (wireless) | N. A. |
| [14] | Pressure | 2.7 cm ×1.9 cm ×1.9 cm | Li coin 30 mAh | 56 h | 433 MHz | No | 25 Hz |
| [15] | Pressure | 3.4 cm ×1.8 cm ×0.7 cm | Batteryless | Limited by external reader | 132 kHz | Externally powered | 10 Hz |
| [16] | Strain gage | 4.2 cm × 0.4 cm × 0.7 cm[a] | Batteryless | Limited by external reader | 125 kHz | Externally powered | 10 Hz |
| [31] | Strain gage | 3.4 cm Diameter[a] | Batteryless | Limited by external reader | 2.4 GHz | Externally powered | 87 Hz |

[a] Estimated from published work.

## 5.4 Discussion

Implanted strain gauges are typically waterproofed with different coatings to electrically isolate the gauge-wire contacts from bodily fluids and to improve the biocompatibility of the gauge. A common waterproofing technique involves coating the gauge surface with medical grade polysulfone dissolved in 1-1-2-2 tetra-chloroethane [32]. The gauge-wire junction can also be waterproofed using polymethyl-methacrylate (PMMA) followed by layers of M Coat B, M Coat D, and M Coat A from Measurements Group Inc [26]. Insulated wires need to be employed to avoid contact between the metallic conductors and the bodily fluids.

To prevent infections, the strain gauge, wires, and the telemetry unit need to be sterilized before implantation, and surgery should be performed using full sterile procedures. If the telemetry unit is placed outside the body, the incision that brings the wires from the implanted strain gauge to the telemetry unit should be sealed with a tissue glue (Henry Schein, Nexaband, Melville, NY, USA) [33]. Sealing the incision prevents pathogens from entering the body and causing infection. *In vivo* experiments will be performed in the future with the help of a surgeon to attach the strain gauge to the ulna bone of a mouse. This type of surgery requires particular skills and equipment to ensure survival of the mouse subject.

## 6 Conclusions

An embedded multichannel strain gauge telemetry unit has been presented. The telemetry unit was designed using a commercially available SoC platform. The SoC platform employed included a CPU, memory, ADC, and a radio transceiver. The integration of all these components in a single chip allowed us to design a small telemetry unit. Furthermore, the SoC allowed us to reduce the development time and the cost. The telemetry unit operates in 915-MHz ISM radio band and measures 2.4 cm × 1.3 cm × 0.7 cm. The unit is powered from a small 45-mA Li-polymer battery that can be recharged wirelessly through tissue making it suitable for implanted applications. The unit was tested in an *ex vivo* setting with an ulna bone from a mouse and in a simulated *in vivo* setting with a tissue phantom made in-house. Bone strain data collected by the telemetry unit were found to be in very good agreement with strain data collected by a benchtop data acquisition unit.

**Competing interests**
The authors declare that they have no competing interests.

**Acknowledgements**
The authors would like to thank the UMKC Center of Excellence for the Study of Mineralized Tissue for their support.

**Author details**
[1]Computer Science Electrical Engineering Department, University of Missouri-Kansas City, Kansas City, MO 64110, USA. [2]Electrical and Computer Engineering Technology Department, Purdue University, West Lafayette, IN 47907, USA. [3]Oral and Craniofacial Sciences Department, University of Missouri-Kansas City, Kansas City, MO 64108, USA.

**References**
1. F Di Palma, M Douet, C Boachon, A Guignandon, S Peyroche, B Forest, C Alexandre, A Chamson, A Rattner, Physiological strains induce differentiation in human osteoblasts cultured on orthopaedic biomaterial. Biomaterials **24**(18), 3139–3151 (2003)
2. F Burny, M Donkerwolcke, F Moulart, R Bourgois, R Puers, K Van Schuylenbergh, M Barbosa, O Paiva, F Rodes, J Béguerét, et al., Concept, design and fabrication of smart orthopedic implants. Med. Eng. Phys. **22**(7), 469–479 (2000)
3. LCY Wong, WK Chiu, M Russ, S Liew, Review of techniques for monitoring the healing fracture of bones for implementation in an internally fixated pelvis. Med. Eng. Phys. **34**(2), 140–152 (2012)
4. L Claes, J Cunningham, et al., Monitoring the mechanical properties of healing bone. Clin Orthop. Relat. Res. **467**(8), 1964 (2009)
5. GY Yang, G Johnson, WC Tang, JH Keyak, Parylene-based strain sensors for bone. IEEE Sensors J. **7**(12), 1693–1697 (2007)
6. J Cordey, E Gautier, Strain gauges used in the mechanical testing of bones Part II *in vitro* and *in vivo* technique. Injury **30**, SA14–SA20 (1999)
7. Q Huang, M Oberle, A 0.5-mW passive telemetry IC for biomedical applications. IEEE J. Solid-State Circuits **33**(7), 937–946 (1998)
8. F Graichen, R Arnold, A Rohlmann, G Bergmann, Implantable 9-channel telemetry system for in-vivo load measurements with orthopedic implants. IEEE Trans. Biomed. Eng. **54**(2), 253–261 (2007)
9. W De Jong, J Koolstra, J Van Ruijven, J Korfage, G Langenbach, A fully implantable telemetry system for the long-term measurement of habitual bone strain. J. Biomech. **43**(3), 587–591 (2010)
10. R Tan, T McClure, C Lin, D Jea, F Dabiri, T Massey, M Sarrafzadeh, M Srivastava, C Montemagno, P Schulam, et al., Development of a fully implantable wireless pressure monitoring system. Biomed. Microdevices **11**, 259–264 (2009)
11. C Park, Y Chou, PH Bai, R Matthews, A Hibbs, An ultra-wearable, wireless, low power ECG monitoring system, in *IEEE Biomedical Circuits and Systems Conference* (London, 29 Nov 2006–01 Dec 2006), pp. 241–244
12. V Shnayder, B Chen, K Lorincz, TRF Jones, M Welsh, Sensor networks for medical care, in *International Conference On Embedded Networked Sensor Systems*, vol. 2. (San Diego, 02–04 Nov 2005), pp. 314–314
13. R Sobot, Implantable RF telemetry for cardiac monitoring in the murine heart: a tutorial review. EURASIP J. Embedded Syst. **2013**, 1 (2013)
14. P Valdastri, A Menciassi, A Arena, C Caccamo, P Dario, An implantable telemetry platform system for in-vivo monitoring of physiological parameters. IEEE Trans. Inf. Technol. Biomed. **8**(3), 271–278 (2004)
15. J Coosemans, R Puers, An autonomous bladder pressure monitoring system. Sensors Actuators A Phys. **123**, 155–161 (2005)
16. C Moss, N Weinrich, W Sass, J Mueller, Integration of a telemetric system within an intramedullary nail for monitoring of the fracture healing progress, in *International Symposium on Applied Sciences in Biomedical and Communication Technologies (ISABEL)* (Rome, 07–10 Nov. 2010), pp. 1–5
17. CC430F613x, CC430F612x, CC430F513x MSP430 SoC With RF Core. http://www.ti.com/lit/ds/symlink/cc430f5137.pdf. Accessed Sept. 2013
18. Low-power SoC with MCU, memory, 2.4 GHz RF transceiver and USB controller. http://www.ti.com/lit/ds/swrs055g/swrs055g.pdf. Accessed Sept. 2013
19. Flash-based microcontroller with ASK/FSK transmitter. http://ww1.microchip.com/downloads/en/DeviceDoc/70091B.pdf. Accessed Sept. 2013
20. 433/868/915 MHz RF transceiver with embedded 8051 compatible microcontroller and 4 input, 10 bit ADC. http://www.nordicsemi.com/eng/products/sub-1-Ghz-RF/nRF9E5. Accessed Sept. 2013
21. E Grant, Interaction of radiowaves and microwaves with biological material. Br. J. Cancer **5**, 1 (1982)

22. K Finkenzeller, *RFID Handbook: Fundamentals and Applications in Contactless Smart Cards, Radio Frequency Identification and Near-Field Communication* (Wiley, Chichester, West Sussex, 2010)
23. Measuring Strain with Strain Gauges. http://www.ni.com/white-paper/3642/en/. Accessed Sept. 2013
24. C Johnson, *Process Control Instrumentation Technology* (Prentice Hall, Upper Saddle River, NJ, 2006)
25. AW Astrin, L Huan-Bang, R Kohno, Standardization for body area networks. IEICE Trans. Commun. **92**(2), 366–372 (2009)
26. B Rabkin, J Szivek, J Schonfeld, B Halloran, Long-term measurement of bone strain *in vivo*: the rat tibia. J. Biomed. Mater. Res. **58**(3), 277–281 (2001)
27. TL Wonnell, PR Stauffer, JJ Langberg, Evaluation of microwave and radio frequency catheter ablation in a myocardium-equivalent phantom model. IEEE Trans. Biomed. Eng. **39**(10), 1086–1095 (1992)
28. MK Chmarra, R Hansen, R Mårvik, T Langø, Multimodal phantom of liver tissue. PloS One **8**(5), e64180 (2013)
29. C Marchal, M Nadi, A Tosser, C Roussey, ML Gaulard, Dielectric properties of gelatine phantoms used for simulations of biological tissues between 10 and 50 MHz. Int. J. Hyperthermia **5**(6), 725–732 (1989)
30. PJ Rousche, DS Pellinen, DPJr Pivi, JC Williams, RJ Vetter, DR kirke, Flexible polyimide-based intracortical electrode arrays with bioactive capability. IEEE Trans. Biomed. Eng. **48**(3), 361–371 (2001)
31. JL Ouellette, An updated telemetry system for reliable powering *in vivo* coupled to a tablet computer. *PhD thesis*, University of Arizona, Graduate Interdisciplinary Program in Biomedical Engineering, 2013
32. J Szivek, R Roberto, D Margolis, *In vivo* strain measurements from hardware and lamina during spine fusion. J. Biomed. Mater. Res. B Appl. Biomater. **75**(2), 243–250
33. M Park, A Belhaj-Saif, P Cheney, Chronic recording of EMG activity from large numbers of forelimb muscles in awake macaque monkeys. J. Neurosci. Methods **96**(2), 153–160 (2000)

# Implantable RF telemetry for cardiac monitoring in the murine heart: a tutorial review

Robert Sobot

## Abstract

Research and development of implantable RF telemetry systems intended specifically to enable and support cardiac monitoring of genetically engineered small animal subjects, rats and mice in particular, has already gained significant momentum. This article presents the state of the art review of experimental cardiac monitoring telemetry systems, with strong accent on the systems designed to work with a dual pressure–volume conductance-based catheter sensor. These commercially available devices are already small enough to fit inside a left-ventricle of a mouse heart. However, if the complete system is to be fully implanted and the subject allowed to freely move inside a cage, the mouse's small body size sets harsh constrains on the size and power consumption of the required electronics. Consequently, significant portion of the research efforts is directed towards the development of low-volume and -power electronics, as well as RF energy harvesting systems that are required to serve as the energy source to the implanted telemetry instead of the relatively very bulky batteries.

## Introduction

Congestive heart failure (CHF), a condition in which the heart fails to pump efficiently, is identified as one of the major cardiovascular diseases; e.g. in 2008 cardiovascular diseases accounted for 29% of *all* deaths in Canada [1]. In order to evaluate a heart's functionality, cardiovascular researchers rely mostly on the shape and position of the heart's pressure–volume (PV) loops [2], with genetically engineered small animal subjects, such as mice, rats, and rabbits being the most important models used for researching diseases. Similarly to piston in a car engine, a heart is described by PV loops, where a heart of a healthy person is capable of closing a PV loop with large surface, i.e. it is capable of generating a large stroke volume (SV); versus a failing heart that is capable of generating much smaller SV (Figure 1). Therefore, it is essential to collect simultaneous data related to both blood pressure ($P$) and volume ($V$) of a heart on a beat-to-beat basis. To that end, one of the first micromachined (MEMS) type of $P$ sensors suitable for blood pressure monitoring was reported in [3], and soon after Baan et al. [4,5] followed by reporting the development of a catheter with the embedded conductance-based $V$ sensor. Today, these two types of sensors are commercially available as a single-package *dual-sensor* device that is small enough to be implanted into a mouse heart [6,7]. However, the small size of a mouse body still presents great challenge if the supporting electronics and antenna are to be encompassed as well.

Consequently, today's biomedical researchers still rely on small, heavily distorted samples of PV data collected by the external data-collection unit during an open heart operation while the subject is fully anesthetized. Thus, the lack of micro-sized implantable telemetry systems for cardiac monitoring remains an important problem. Therefore, it is extremely important to develop a fully implantable cardiac telemetry microsystem that can safely fit into small mouse's body and, eventually, be permanently implanted into a human heart [8]. Then, the researchers will be able to continuously monitor the subject's heart condition by collecting real-time data over longer periods of time while, in the case of the small animal subjects, the subject is fully conscious and freely moving inside a cage specifically designed for that purpose, i.e. inside a cage with the embedded communication antennas and RF energy harvesting infrastructure.

Correspondence: rsobot@uwo.ca
Western University, Electrical and Computer Engineering, London, Ontario, N6A 5B9, Canada

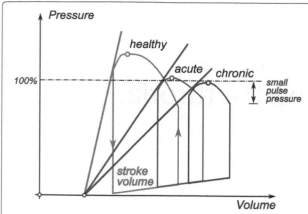

**Figure 1** Left ventricular (LV) PV loops in a healthy person (grey PV area) and for persons with acute (blue PV area) or chronic, congestive (red PV area) cardiac failure.

## Review

RF telemetry has already become an indispensable tool in clinical applications. A "radio pill" first reported in [9], over the time, has evolved into a fully functional "video pill" [10] that is now almost routinely used to monitor pH, temperature, and the human digestive system from the inside. The contemporary research on cardiac RF telemetry systems for a murine heart monitoring, however, may be broadly grouped under the following four themes:

### Conductance catheter model

Accurate modelling of the relationship between the blood conductance and the beating heart's volume is a very complex problem, which forces the researchers to rely on onerous use of numerical tools to develop practical working models [11]. Today, Baan's linear equation [12] and Wei's nonlinear equation [13] form the core of the conductance volumetric catheter model that is currently accepted by the researchers.

However, first apparent limitation of the conductance catheter based methodology is due to the random finite resistance of a heart's muscle, which causes dynamic fluctuations and the current leakage through the heart walls [14-16]. Second drawback of this volumetric method is its relativity, thus the need for the calibration methodology [15,17].

At the same time, the alternative noninvasive reported methods for the volumetric measurements are mostly based on ultrasound scanning [18], and three-dimensional (3D) microcomputed tomography (CT) imaging techniques [19]. However, these methods require a full size scanning equipment located in the laboratory, and numerically intensive post-processing of the data. In this article, we focus specifically on conductance catheter based invasive cardiac monitoring methods, while the detailed

review of the noninvasive methods is beyond the scope of this article and will be addressed in another publication.

### Wireless energy transfer

Although the reported energy harvesting techniques exploit various physical principles [20], due to the power consumption level and system size constrains specific to the mouse cardiac implant application, choice of the applicable power sources is drastically limited. Hence, the inductive resonance-based coupling techniques are emerging as the leading method [21], with various optimization proposals recently reported in [22-24]. In this article we focus specifically on inductive resonance-based coupling technique for RF energy harvesting.

### RF telemetry

A typical RF telemetry system consists of four main modules: (a) the sensor interface; (b) RF transceiver; (c) control; and (d) energy source and the voltage regulator (Figure 2). For instance, recently reported state-of-the-art experimental RF telemetry system [24] supports a single pressure sensor for a real-time blood pressure monitoring in a mouse. There, both the capacitive MEMS sensor and the accompanying RF transmitter are implanted in abdomen of a large mouse, i.e. outside of the heart. Similarly, while using their own capacitive MEMS pressure sensor, Chow et al. [25] reported different cardiac pressure monitoring system that has been approved for clinical use. Being work in progress, contemporary research is focused on further optimization of the RF telemetry subcircuits for their power consumption and size within other biomedical and robotic applications [26,27]. In this article we review typical telemetry designs and the future trend.

### Biocompatible package

Design of a biocompatible package and antenna intended for RF telemetry systems is, by all measures, very involved phase of the overall design process. Occasionally, design details of implantable micro-telemetry package itself are

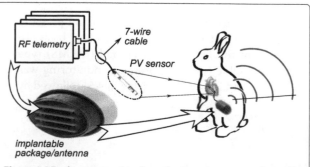

**Figure 2** RF telemetry system based on conductance catheter PV sensor for murine heart monitoring.

reported within the context of the overall system [24-26], while most of the published studies related to design of a package intended for various implantable systems focus only on the specific technological steps [28]. It is interesting, however, to observe that most current implantable designs, for instance a commercially available Cochlear implant, RF telemetry system in [24], and an active RFID micro tag [29], follow the same traditional system-level design approach. That is, the system package and the antenna are usually designed and manufactured as the two separate entities. Recently, the researchers are reporting more creative approach to the antenna/package assembly design, as is partially reported in [25], which resulted in the novel use of a well established medical stent device as structural support of the implant as well as an antenna for simultaneous wireless telemetry and powering. Thus, the electro-mechanical design process of a biocompatible package and the accompanying antenna for RF power and data transfer is still as much an art as it is engineering.

## Conductance based catheter

Basic heart volumetric method proposed by Baan et al. [4,5,12] is based on obtaining SV and cardiac output by the means of an intra-cardiac measurement of the electrical impedance of the time-varying conductance of blood contained within the left LV cavity. Custom designed conductance based catheter with several pairs of ring electrodes, whose geometry is the known variable, is inserted directly into the subject's LV cavity (Figure 3). Assuming constant AC current flow through the outmost pair of the ring electrodes (here, the rings $a$ and $d$), and constant value of the blood conductance, the heart volume is then estimated by measuring conductance between the two inner electrodes (i.e. the rings $b$ and $c$). Due to the size of a mouse heart, the catheter size is drastically limited and it allows only for two pairs of the ring electrodes, where the two inner electrodes (i.e. $b$ and $c$) define one cylindrical segment (whose height is $L$) of the heart volume. That is, a larger heart volume would allow for multiple pairs of ring electrodes and, therefore, it would be electrically divided into several smaller volume segments stacked on top of each other. In the case of larger animal subjects, it is not only possible to use a catheter with more than one inner pair of electrodes, but also it is possible to implant two catheters—one in each ventricle [30]. If the two-catheter measurement is to be used in a mouse heart then, in order to be able to fit inside of the RV, a new significantly smaller PV catheter must be developed first (Figure 3).

## Baan's linear model

As a material, blood has both conductive and dielectric properties, hence, each inner segment of the heart volume is considered as the equivalent resistor in parallel with a capacitor, whose height is determined by the

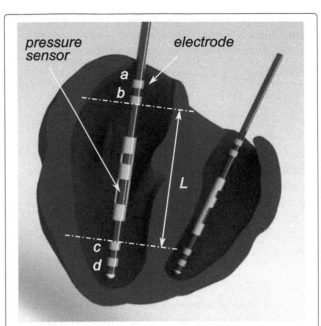

**Figure 3** Two tetra-polar PV conductance based catheters implanted into both left and right ventricles of a heart. The four ring electrodes are labeled $a$ to $d$. (The right ventricle is visibly smaller, which requires development of a new smaller catheter).

inter-electrode pair distance $L$ and time-varying median cross-sectional area $A(t)$ (Figure 3).

In deriving his linear model Baan et al. [12] makes the following four crude assumptions: (a) the intracardiac electric field distribution is uniform; (b) the ventricular wall is perfectly insulated from the cavity blood, i.e. the total measured conductivity is strictly due to the blood and not to the heart's muscle; (c) a heart cavity has a cylindrical shape; and (d) the catheter is stationary and always perfectly centred along the cylinder's axis.

Hence, straightforward calculation shows that the time-varying admittance (i.e. current/voltage ratio) of a segment between two adjacent electrodes, consists of an in-phase component:

$$g(t)' = \frac{1}{R(t)} = \frac{\sigma}{L}A(t) + \frac{\epsilon}{L}\frac{dA(t)}{dt} \tag{1}$$

and an out-of-phase component

$$g(t)'' = \omega\frac{\epsilon}{L}A(t), \tag{2}$$

where, $R(t)$ is blood resistance, $\sigma \approx 0.7\ \Omega^{-1}m^{-1}$ is conductivity and $\epsilon \approx 7 \times 10^{-10}\ Fm^{-1}$) dielectric constant of blood [31]. Therefore, the second term in (1) may be neglected, because the change of cross-sectional area $A(t)$ in time is tied to the heart pulse (a mouse heart beets up to 700 bpm), hence in the first approximation the second term is consider not large enough to relative to the first term. Linear approximation of the measured segment volume $\Delta V$ is simply volume of the cylindrical shape:

$$\Delta V(t) \approx A(t) \times L \tag{3}$$

after substituting (3) into (1), we write:

$$g(t)' = \frac{1}{R(t)} = \frac{\sigma}{L^2} V(t). \tag{4}$$

Therefore, volume of the segment is calculated by measuring conductance that corresponds to the resistance across the catheter length $L$, which is expressed as the difference of conductances between the first two electrodes ($ab$) and electrodes ($ac$), i.e.

$$\Delta V(t) \approx \frac{L^2}{\sigma}\left(\frac{1}{R_{ab}} - \frac{1}{R_{ac}}\right) = \frac{L^2}{\sigma} g_b(t) = \rho L^2 g_b(t) \tag{5}$$

where, $g_b(t)$ is the instantaneous blood conductance, and $\rho = 1\sigma$ is the blood resistivity in ($\Omega m$). By visual inspection of Figure 3 it should be obvious that this linear approximation is very crude for the case of a heart that is small relative to the catheter's size, as is the case of a small mouse. However, if the heart is large and if the catheter is manufactured with several inner electrode ring pairs, then the total instantaneous volume $V(t)$ is measured more accurately as the sum of the individual volume sections $\Delta V_n(t)$, as

$$V(t) = \sum_{n=1}^{n \to \infty} \Delta V_n(t) \tag{6}$$

where, each volume section $\Delta V_n(t)$ is calculated as in (5). Additionally, this method produces relative measurement that is function of the blood conductance $\sigma$, therefore the absolute value of the conductance must be determined beforehand by using an independent measurement methods.

Simplest way to increase accuracy of (5) is to add experimentally determined linear correction factors

$$V(t) = k \rho L^2 g_b(t) + V_c \tag{7}$$

where, $k$ is an empirical slope correction factor, and $V_c$ is the linear offset empirical correction factor. The two empirical linear correction factors are determined by comparing values for the volume $V(t)$ as calculated from the analytical expression (7) with the experimentally determined value after using an electromagnetic flow probe or Doppler ultrasound volume measurement method. Nevertheless, we conclude that the first order linear approximation model is overly simplified.

### Wei's nonlinear model

In order to compensate for the intrinsic error caused by the nonuniform internal electric field, while still keeping the other assumptions used in the linear model, Wei et al. [13] suggested the following nonlinear model.

Blood conductance $g_b$ can be found by definition

$$g_b = \frac{I}{V} = \frac{\oint_a \vec{J}\, d\vec{a}}{-\int_l \vec{E}\, d\vec{l}} = \frac{\oint_a \sigma \vec{E}\, d\vec{a}}{-\int_l \vec{E}\, d\vec{l}}, \tag{8}$$

where $I$ is current (A), $V$ is voltage (V), $\vec{E}$ is electric field intensity ($Vm$), $\vec{J}$ is current density ($Am^2$), $a$ is a surface enclosing the source electrode, $l$ is the path length for potential calculation, and $\sigma$ is the blood conductivity (the reciprocal of blood resistivity $\rho$).

Straightforward application of Laplace's equations $\nabla^2 V = 0$ and $\vec{E} = -\nabla V$ for the case of cylindrical coordinate system $(r, \theta, \varphi)$ yields

$$\frac{1}{r^2}\frac{\partial}{\partial r}\left(r^2 \frac{\partial V}{\partial r}\right) + \frac{1}{r^2 \sin\theta}\frac{\partial}{\partial \theta}\left(\sin\theta \frac{\partial V}{\partial \theta}\right)$$
$$+ \frac{1}{r^2 \sin^2\theta}\left(\frac{\partial^2 V}{\partial \varphi^2}\right) = 0 \tag{9}$$

The additional assumption that must be made is that the source electrodes are spheres with radius placed in an infinite homogeneous medium, which makes potential $V$ independent of $\varphi$. It can be shown [13,14] that the total blood admittance $Y$ is

$$Y = \frac{\pi d\left(d^2 - L^2\right)\left(\sigma_b + j\omega\varepsilon_b\right)}{4L}$$
$$\times \left(\frac{1}{\sqrt{a_0^2 + d^2/4}} - \frac{1}{\sqrt{R^2 + d^2/4}}\right) \tag{10}$$

where, $\sigma_b$ and $\varepsilon_b$ are the electrical conductivity and permittivity, respectively, of the fluid, $\omega$ is frequency of the AC current, $d$ is distance between two source ring electrodes ($a$ and $d$), $L$ is the distance between the two receiving inner ring electrodes ($b$ and $c$), and $a_0$ is radii of the spherical electrodes; and that the nonlinear analytical function for volume $V$ vs. blood conductance $g_b$ looks as

$$V = \frac{\beta}{\left(g_{\inf} - g_b\right)^2} - \frac{\beta}{g_{\inf}^2} \tag{11}$$

where,

$$\beta = f(SV, g_{\inf}, g_{bmax}, g_{bmin}) \tag{12}$$

is the empirical calibration factor and, $SV$ is the real SV as measured by using an independent method, $g_{\inf}$ is conductance of an infinite thick medium (i.e. assuming that the radius of the sensing electrodes is small enough so that their influences on the electric field distribution are negligible), $g_{bmax}$ is the maximum blood conductance, and $g_{bmin}$ is the minimum blood conductance. The blood conductance changes during the stroke cycle, with minimum

$g_{bmin}$ at the maximum contraction point (i.e. when blood is squeezed from the heart) and maximum $g_{bmax}$ at the maximum expansion point (i.e. when heart is filled in with the blood). The nonlinearity of the model is clearly demonstrated in Figure 4, and we note that $\beta = f(SV)$, as well as being function of all the other parameters through its dependance upon $g_{inf}$, which is to say that $\beta$ is also experimentally determined correction factor.

Consequently, the performance of the analytic approximation (11) is not fully satisfying either, since the analytic approximation was derived under the assumption that the electrodes are placed in a large medium. Further experimental empirical corrections should be applied again [13].

## Dubois model

The issue of parasitic conductance of the heart muscle, which from electrical perspective is parallel to the blood conductance, is addressed in [14,32,33]. Due to this parasitic conductance, the traditional conductance based volume measurement method fails to accurately correct for the parallel conductance contributed by the myocardium, resulting in overestimation of blood volumes.

While still relying on the cylindrical geometry of the ventricle, however with the addition of infinitely thick surrounding layer of the heart muscle, Figure 5, Dubois model builds upon the existing knowledge by specifically addressing the issue of the parallel admittance. Instead of accounting only for the blood properties, as in (10), Dubois also applies the same expression to the surrounding heart muscle tissue. Hence, the total measured admittance ($Y$) becomes the sum of blood ($Y_b$) and muscle ($Y_m$) admittances, i.e.

$$Y = Y_b + Y_m \tag{13}$$

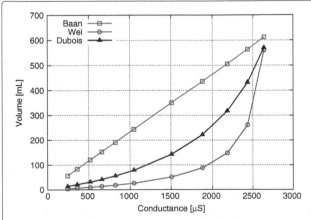

**Figure 4** The conductance-volume plot of MATLAB simulation of the three models, Baan's linear, Wei's nonlinear, and Dubois model.

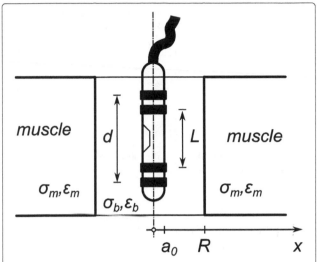

**Figure 5** Geometry of catheter placed in a cylindrical ventricle with a conducting fluid surrounded with infinitely thick muscle that is used in Dubois model.

where, expressions for both blood admittance $Y_b$ is as per (10) with the appropriate indexes and the boundary conditions of ($a_0 \leq x \leq R$). The muscle admittance follows the same equation (10), however, the boundary conditions must be set as ($a_0 \leq R \leq \infty$) (Figure 5). It can be shown [14] that analytical expression for blood volume can be expressed as

$$V = -\pi L \left[ \frac{d^2}{4} - \frac{\beta \pi^2 d^2 \left(d^2 - L^2\right) \left(\Delta\sigma + j\omega\Delta\varepsilon\right)^2}{16L^2 \left(Y - Y_{inf}\right)^2} \right] \tag{14}$$

where,

$$Y_{inf} = \frac{\pi d \left(d^2 - L^2\right) \left(\sigma_b + j\omega\varepsilon_b\right)}{4L\sqrt{a_0^2 + d^2/4}} \tag{15}$$

and, $\Delta\sigma = (\sigma_m - \sigma_b)$, $\Delta\varepsilon = (\varepsilon_m - \varepsilon_b)$, and $\beta = f(SV, Y)$ is an empirical calibration factor that is meant to compensate for the error due to the use of cylindrical model. Muscle admittance ($Y_m$) with boundary condition at $R = \infty$ is $Y_{inf}$.

## The calibration issue

Development of the analytical models for volumetric catheter is based on fundamental electromagnetic field theory applied to a simple cylindrical geometry. However, as it has been shown above, the set of crude simplifications has to be introduced in order to manage the mathematical complexity of the analytical model. Consequently, all analytical models developed so far rely on an independent evaluation of the SV, which is needed to experimentally

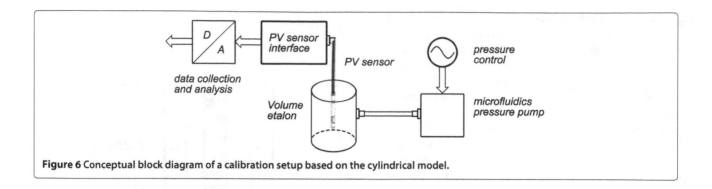

**Figure 6** Conceptual block diagram of a calibration setup based on the cylindrical model.

determine value of the correction factor $\beta$. This correction factor is determined by using calibration setup based on known cylindrical etalons (Figure 6). Recently, in an attempt to reach more accurate models the researchers are introducing various numerical methodologies [15,34], which include detailed 3D models of a complete heart, Figure 7 [11]. Hence, this particular issue is one of the main topics of the current research.

## Wireless energy transfer

Commonly, mobile devices depend on a battery as the energy source. However, a battery's energy density does

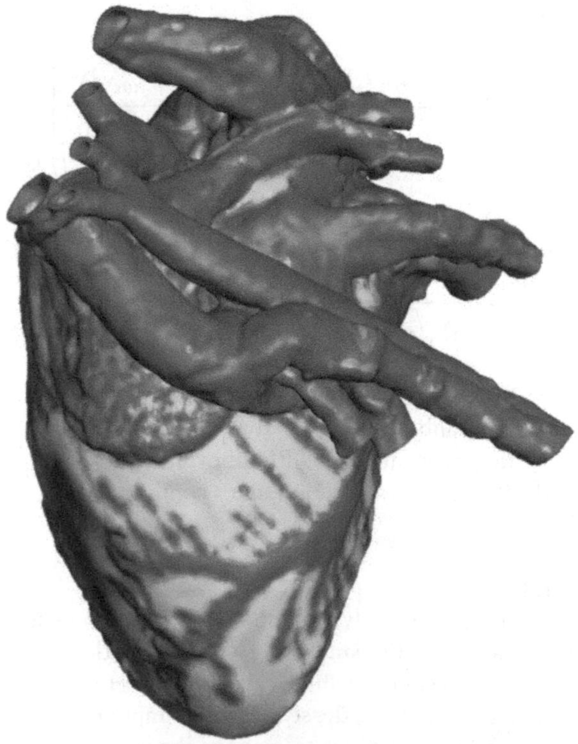

**Figure 7** Full 3D model of a mouse heart with exterior surface of tissue material coloured by feature size [11] (Courtesy of Dr. James P. Carson).

not scale at the same rate as an IC's physical size. Consequently, the battery size has become major bottleneck on the path to further miniaturization of mobile systems, which is especially important parameter for the implantable telemetry.

Overcoming this issue requires adaptation of alternative energy sources. For instance, recently, new developments and fabrication technologies have resulted in micro fuel cells [35] that are becoming competitive with the state of the art batteries. However, a holy grail of bioelectronics is to engineer biologically implantable systems that can be embedded without disturbing their local environments while harvesting from their surroundings all of the power they require. In particular, most important question is whether the implantable electronics can be powered by drawing the required energy from their surrounding tissues [36].

Various solutions to the problem of providing power to biologically implanted devices have been proposed, prototyped, or implemented [37]. Two principal solutions are currently in widespread use: single-use batteries, such as those used in implantable pulse generators for cardiac pacing, defibrillation, and deep brain stimulation, which are designed to have finite lifetimes and to be replaced surgically at intervals of several years; and inductive power transfer [38], typically accomplished transcutaneously at radio frequencies, as in cochlear implants. Inductive schemes can be used either to supply power continuously or to recharge an implanted power source [36]. A brief overview of some other physical principles that can be exploited for energy harvesting is shown in Table 1 [20]. Not all of the possible physical principles for energy harvesting are suitable for powering up micro-sized implantable electronics for cardiac monitoring in a mouse, which have very harsh size requirement.

Therefore, in this article we focus on the inductive power transfer techniques (Figure 8). A typical system topology includes inductive coupled RF power transfer system, RF data link, implanted AC/DC regulator, micro controller $\mu C$, RF transmitter, sensor interface, and the sensor itself (Figure 9).

**Table 1 Energy-harvesting sources**

| Energy source | Performance | Note |
|---|---|---|
| Ambient RF | $< 1 \, \mu W/cm^2$ | A few mW with a short distance inductive coupled systems [21] |
| Ambient light | 100 mW/cm$^2$ (direct sunlight) | Assuming common polycrystalline solar cells at 16–17% |
| | 100 $\mu W/cm^2$ (office light) | efficiency, while standard monocrystalline cells approach 20% at $\Delta T = 5°C$; typical thermoelectric generators $\leq$ 1% efficient for $\Delta T < 40°C$ |
| Thermoelectric | 60 $\mu W/cm^2$ | at $\Delta T = 5°C$; typical thermoelectric generators $\leq$ 1% efficient for $\Delta T < 40°C$. |
| Vibrational | 4 $\mu W/cm^3$ (human) | Predictions for 1 cm$^3$ generators |
| | 800 $\mu W/cm^3$ (machine) | |
| Ambient airflow | 1 mW/cm$^2$ | Demonstrated in microelectromechanical turbine at 30 liters/min |
| Push buttons | 50 $\mu J/N$ | MIT Media Lab Device |
| Hand generator | 30 W/kg | Nissho Engineering's Tug Power |
| Heel strike | 10–800 $\mu W$ | 7 W potentially available (1 cm deflection at 70 kg per 1 Hz walk) |

The basic idea of wireless energy transfer based on Tesla's coils, that is currently being exploited in many forms and modifications, is now a century old [39]. In the first approximation, the power density at the receiving RF antenna is produced through $E/Z_0$ relation, where $Z_0 = 377 \, \Omega$ is the radiation resistance of free space, and $E$ is the local electric field strength. An electric field of $E = 1 \, Vm$ thus yields about $0.26 \, \mu W/cm^2$. This crude analysis illustrates that the freely available RF energy is very limited, unless the radiation levels are set to dangerously high level, or the receiving antenna is very close to the transmitter. Which further imposes the upper limit of the total power that can be safely transmitted through a living tissue. Currently, as a "rule of a thumb", most researchers arbitrary set the upper total power budget for the implantable telemetry to a few hundred $\mu W$, i.e. less than approximately $300–500 \, \mu W$.

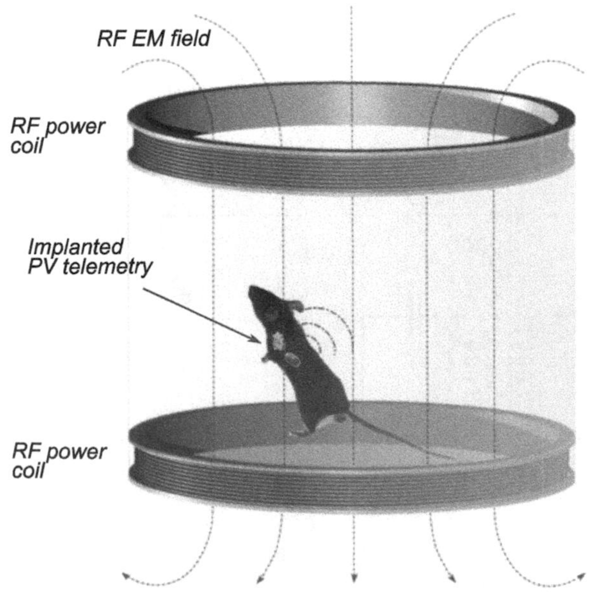

Thus, being able to control intensity and direction of the electro-magnetic filed vector is very important, because if energy being transmitted through a living tissue has too high radiation density level, then it can permanently damage the cells it passes through. In other words, the design of a mouse cage with the embedded RF energy harvesting system, Figure 8, is not much different from a microwave oven design.

The reason for ambiguity related to the accepted power levels is that, despite a large body of publicly available literature related to the topic of mobile phone radiation and health, there is no consensus on what energy level *exactly* is considered to be dangerous for the living tissue. Discussion on that topic is beyond the scope of this article, hence, in our research we take conservative approach and keep the transmitted energy levels significantly below those generated by modern cellphones.

**Figure 8** Conceptual diagram of a mouse cage with the embedded RF power generating coils.

### Inductive-coupling resonance

Considering that the RF energy transmission efficiency is the main design parameter, the bottleneck of the remote powering link is generally at the inductive link because the coupling factor between the coils of the inductive link is usually very small. Therefore, these coils should be designed properly to achieve high power transfer efficiency [21,22].

Inductive-coupling-based power transfer requires two coils (primary and secondary coils), and the efficiency of power transfer between the coils is a strong function of the coil dimensions and distance between them. Therefore, the recent alternative method of resonance-based power delivery [21,40] is explained through the coupled-mode theory [41], which is less sensitive to changes of the coil distance and typically employs two pairs of coils: one in

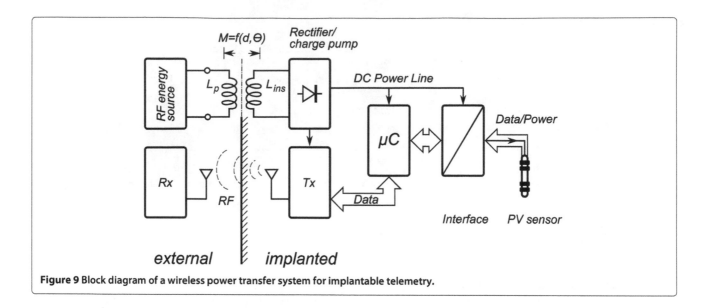

**Figure 9** Block diagram of a wireless power transfer system for implantable telemetry.

the external circuit called driver and primary coils, and the other in the implant itself called secondary and load coils (Figure 10). Most of the work in this area revolves around static large radii coils for relatively high power transfer applications [40].

However, for low-power applications when the subject carrying the implant moves freely inside the controlled space, the two inductors continuously change their relative position in space. Hence, the inductive coupling coefficient is function of both linear and angular displacements between the two coils, i.e. $M = f(d, \Theta)$, whose geometry is depicted in Figure 11. Therefore, the received energy levels vary over a wide range. This situation poses a problem for normal operation of the implanted signal processing and communication electronics. Consequently, it is important to design an efficient implantable voltage regulator that also consumes a minimal amount of energy for its own operation while providing continuous power to the load.

### Inductance coupling background

Since the maximum power transfer can only be achieved when the external and implanted inductors are perfectly aligned, the challenge is to design a powering system that would have low sensitivity to the coil orientation and distance [21,42]. Such designs, which are mainly focused on the generation of constant minimum power level inside the subject's cage, have been investigated in [43].

When $L_1$ and $L_2$ are the self-inductance of the two coils, $M$ and $k$ are related by

$$M = k\sqrt{L_1 L_2} \tag{16}$$

For two non-coaxial and non-parallel filamentary coils, the mutual inductance defined in [44] is

$$M = \frac{\mu_0}{\pi}\sqrt{R_P R_S} \int_0^\pi \frac{(\cos\theta - \frac{d}{R_S}\cos\phi)\Psi(k)}{\sqrt{V^3}}d\phi. \tag{17}$$

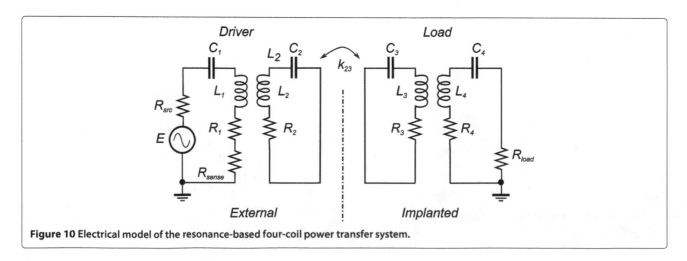

**Figure 10** Electrical model of the resonance-based four-coil power transfer system.

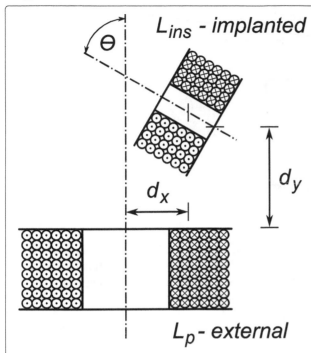

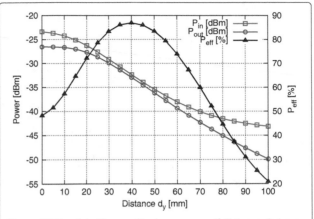

**Figure 12** Simulated transmitted power vs coil distance $d_y$ (case of perfectly aligned coils, i.e. $d_x = 0$ and $\Theta = 0$). Generated voltage is $V_{\text{ins}} \leq 1.5\,\text{V}$.

**Figure 11 Diagram of two non-coaxial and non-parallel circular coils cross-section.** Relative location, and therefore the coupling coefficient $M$, of the two power transfer coils (external and implanted) is defined by horizontal ($d_x$), vertical ($d_y$), and angular ($\theta$) misalignments. (The plot is not to scale).

For our case of multilayer helical coils with axial and angular misalignment, we apply the filament method [45] to (17) and calculate the mutual inductance, which produces the following equation:

$$M = \frac{N_1 N_2 \sum\limits_{g=-K}^{g=K} \sum\limits_{h=-N}^{h=N} \sum\limits_{l=-n}^{l=n} \sum\limits_{p=-m}^{p=m} M(g,h,l,p)}{(2S+1)(2N+1)(2m+1)(2n+1)} \quad (18)$$

where

$$M(g,h,l,p) = \frac{\mu_0}{\pi} \sqrt{R_P(h) R_S(l)} \\ \times \int\limits_{0}^{\pi} \frac{\left[\cos\theta - \frac{y(p)}{R_S(l)}\cos\phi\right] \Psi(k)}{\sqrt{V^3}} d\phi \quad (19)$$

while denotation of all variables in (17) to (19) follows [46].

Based on numerical analysis, the resonant based power transfer methods are expected to achieve maximum power at power efficiency of approximately 85%, while the maximum power efficiency is designed for a specific distance in between the two coils, for example $d_y = 40\,\text{mm}$ as in Figure 12.

## Rectifier

Most modern IC rectifier/charge-pump topologies are derived from the conventional multistage Dickson circuit [47], with modern variants based on self-$V_{\text{th}}$-cancellation (SVC) methodology published [48], where each two-diodes–two-capacitors stage acts as a voltage doubler, therefore contributing the $2(\hat{V}_{\text{in}} - V_D)$ voltage overdrive to the output, where $\hat{V}_{\text{in}}$ is the peak input voltage while $V_D$ is the diode turn-on voltage, and the diodes are implemented by MOS devices in CMOS technology. Hence, $V_D$ is equivalent to a MOS threshold voltage, $|V_{\text{th}}|$.

Our version of a three stage SVC type rectifier/charge-pump, Figure 13, also uses the conventional NMOS as the base reference, and it was optimized for medical RF wireless band. Depending upon the load presented to the rectifier, the time required by the output node to reach the constant voltage level may vary between 100ns and tens of microseconds (for low input voltage levels) (Figure 14).

Therefore, an important overall design compromise is the power efficiency of the rectifier circuit by itself, which is (for the given distance between the external and implanted coil) characterized as the function of the input RF signal frequency and the voltage $V_{\text{ins}}$ generated across the implanted coil, Figure 15. Our design is, currently, optimized for frequency range between 400 MHz and 1.2 GHz, and the input voltage levels in between 600 to 800 $\text{mV}_{\text{pp}}$. Under these conditions the simulated power efficiency is more than 80%. Lower input voltage levels result in apparent higher efficiency (i.e. close to 100%), however the transistors are operating in sub-threshold region and, therefore, the total useful power drops by orders of magnitude, which creates the additional design constrain. For future implantable circuits that can operate in deeper sub 1mW power region this mode of operation may be more suitable.

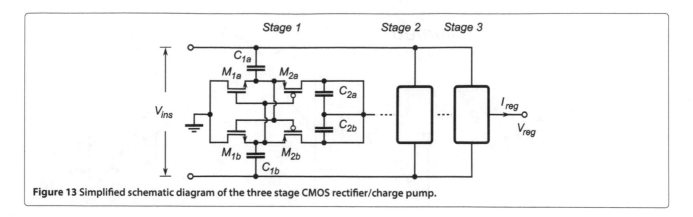

**Figure 13** Simplified schematic diagram of the three stage CMOS rectifier/charge pump.

### Voltage regulator

Utilizing energy collected at the receiver coil requires some sort of feedback control circuit that includes a rectifier, regulator and a bandgap voltage reference to deliver a stable, load-independent voltage to the circuit [49].

The widely fluctuating voltage generated by the charge-pump is regulated by a series regulator, which by itself has to work with very low power and low-voltage [50], if it is to be useful for implantable medical telemetry systems. Schematic block diagram of our regulator architecture, Figure 15, shows that a compromise between the voltage drop across $M_{00}$ and overall PSRR is made based on the specific application conditions.

The regulation feedback loop is formed by the amplifier OP, the PMOS driver $M_0$ and the voltage divider $R_1$ and $R_2$ network, which sets the ratio between $V_{PWR}$ and $V_{ref}$ voltages as

$$V_{PWR} = \left(1 + \frac{R_1}{R_2}\right) V_{ref} \qquad (20)$$

The voltage reference $V_{ref}$ is then routed back to the input of the loop. The loop is designed to be stable with wide range of load impedances, with full load set up to

$R_L = 250\,\Omega$ and $C_L = 50\,pF$. The maximum load corresponds to the maximum current drawn from $V_{PWR}$, which is designed to be $I_{PWR}(max) = 4\,mA$, which is far above the needs of our implantable telemetry electronics. By powering the reference circuit (BG) from $V_{PWR}$, the overall PSRR of the $V_{ref}$ is further improved. In this design, the regulated supply voltage is set to $V_{PWR} = 0.985\,V$ while the complete regulator consumes less than $11.6\,\mu A$ current (typically). The reference voltage also serves as a load to the regulator loop, which helps to keep the loop stable when its load is at the minimum.

### Power supply rejection ratio (PSRR)

By using simulations we compared the regulator performance versus two different structures of operational amplifier. In terms of PSRR, the regulator based on folded-cascode amplifier with the $M_{00}$ relative to the 2-stage amplifier exhibits approximately 6 dB better PSRR in the LF range (i.e. $-45\,dB$ vs. $-51\,dB$), which increases to 15 dB in the mid-band, and becomes similar in the HF band. In both cases, the PSRR is dominated by $M_{00}$ which improves the PSRR. At the same time, the bandgap voltage reference by itself exhibits $-68\,dB$ PSRR at LF and over $-80\,dB$ at HF (Figure 16).

The complete regulator circuit is also simulated with range of loading impedances, and the simulation confirmed that in the worst case scenario, the fully-loaded regulated supply with folded-cascode amplifier, the reference voltage $V_{ref}$ is stable for voltage supply in the range of $1.3$–$1.9\,V$ with a power supply sensitivity of $2.97\,ppm/V$. For moderate to low impedance loads, the reference operates with supply voltages as low as $0.9\,V$, while the regulated power supply voltage may be as low as $1\,V$ (Figure 17).

### RF telemetry system

In the previous sections we have seen that a batteryless low-power implant electronic system is critical for realizing the RF implantable wireless telemetry [51,52]. Once

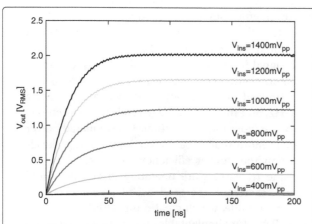

**Figure 14** Simulated time-domain response of the rectifier/charge pump circuit without $M_{00}$ transistor.

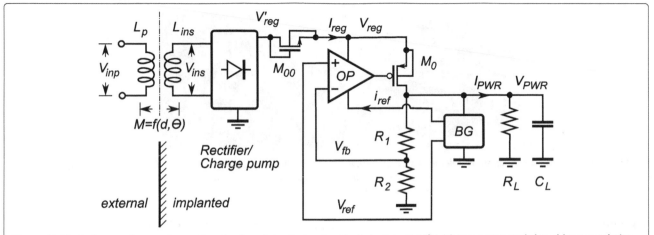

**Figure 15** Block digram of energy harvesting front-end circuit showing the inductors, rectifier/charge pump and closed-loop regulation with amplifier and bandgap (BG) voltage/current reference, (the compensation $R_C C_C$ network not shown). We characterized the circuit operation both with $M_{00}$ included, i.e. when $V'_{reg} \neq V_{reg}$, and without it, i.e. when $V'_{reg} = V_{reg}$.

the harvesting energy system designed, the remaining part of the implantable telemetry consists of the sensor interface, RF transmitter, and the controlling logic (Figure 9).

Our discrete version of a complete implantable RF telemetry system for cardiac monitoring using PV sensor, Figure 18 (shown with a LiPo micro-battery), is integrated into a cube shaped volume of about 13.5 mm a side, which amounts to 2.475 cm$^3$ and it weights 2.67 g without the battery. The top two PCB modules in the stack are used for PV sensor interface circuit, which are followed down by RF transceiver, microprocessor, and power supply/regulator PCB modules.

## PV sensor interface

A single-unit dual-sensor for conductance based PV measurements consists of two sensors in encapsulated a catheter. While the pressure sensor is based on a MEMS Wheatstone bridge structure ($R_1, R_2, P_1, P_2$) and is stimulated by a DC current reference DC$_{ref}$, the volume sensor (the four rings $(a, b, c, d)$) is stimulated by voltage reference AC$_{vref}$ that is converted into current reference AC$_{iref}$. Two operational amplifiers OP and the signal processing unit deliver the pressure $P_{out}$ and volume $V_{out}$ analogue levels (Figure 19). Complexity and power consumption of this interface is dominant relative to the overall size and the power consumption of the complete telemetry system. Further effort is needed to further reduce power consumption of both the PV sensor itself, as well as the required interfacing electronics [52].

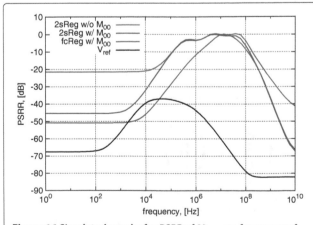

**Figure 16** Simulated graphs for PSRR of $V_{PWR}$ vs. frequency of the closed loop regulator driving a load ($R_L = 250\,\Omega$): using a two-stage classical amplifier without $M_{00}$ transistor (2sReg w/o $M_{00}$); using a two-stage classical amplifier with $M_{00}$ transistor (2sReg w/ $M_{00}$); using folded-cascoded amplifier with $M_{00}$ transistor (fcReg w/ $M_{00}$); and PSRR of the voltage reference itself ($V_{ref}$), (Typical process, $T = 37°C$, $V_{PWR} = 1.0\,V$).

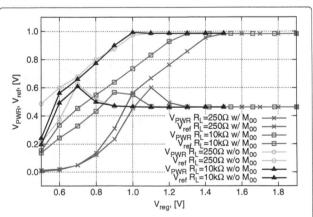

**Figure 17** Simulated output of the reference and regulator (using folded-cascode amplifier) voltages versus variation of the supply voltage (full load).

**Figure 18** 3D rendering of our complete RF telemetry system (left), and the manufactured unit compared to a Canadian penny (right).
The complete system occupies a volume of 2.475 cm³, and it weights 2.67 g without or 4.01 g with a micro LiPo battery.

### RF transmitter

A conventional low-power oscillator-based transmitter, Figure 20, is a good choice for transmitting the digitized blood volume–pressure information to an external receiver by using the traditional frequency-shift keying (FSK) modulation. This kind of transmitter has reduced sensitivity to distance and orientation between the transmitter antenna and external receiving antenna, which is suitable for wireless animal monitoring. A carrier frequency choice of 433 MHz from an Industrial, Scientific, and Medical (ISM) radio band provides good compromise due to the availability of commercial receivers in this band. Additionally, the 433 MHz frequency is also good compromise in respect to the excessive transmission loss through live tissues. At the same time, it is high enough to allow that a small coil-based antenna can be employed [24,53], or even to work with a non-standard shaped antenna [25].

### Biocompatible package and antenna

A living organism presents an extremely hostile environment for electronic circuits, which puts very harsh requirements on the overall system design, including constrains on specifications of the implantable package. For instance, while the specific shape and size of an eye predetermine possible options in terms of the system packaging and the antenna design [54,55], the overall eye volume provides relatively comfortable volume for implanting the modern HF antennas [26]. In addition, the design methodologies of implantable flexible antennas suitable for biomedical research remain vigorously pursued topic [56].

Moreover, even a casual review of contemporary experimental works specifically in the area of implantable RF telemetry for cardiac monitoring may lead to the conclusion that the currently used design methodology does

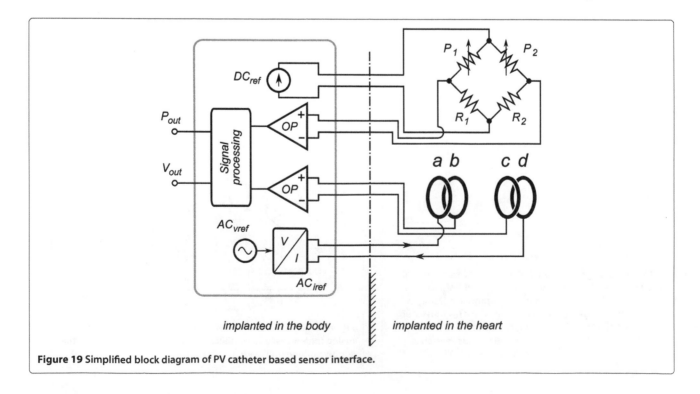

**Figure 19** Simplified block diagram of PV catheter based sensor interface.

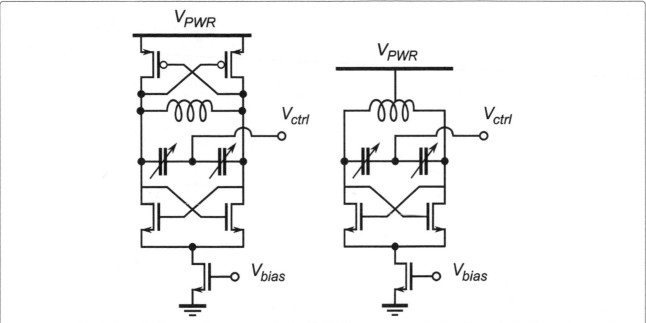

**Figure 20** Simplified schematic diagram of a conventional VCO with NMOS current source (left), and its equivalent low-voltage version (right).

not result in the systems that occupy the minimum volume allowed by the current technology. Thus, the current package designs may not be fully optimized mostly due to the constrains and technology limitations related to the geometry of the package/antenna/system assembly (Figure 21).

For instance, a typical system level assembly includes an active integrated circuit connected to the external RF coil, and then the assembly is sealed with a biocompatible material [24]. Consequently, each section of the system appears to be designed separately using different design tools, which are then integrated at the system's top level.

On the other hand, when a larger volume is available inside the patient to place the complete telemetry/antenna assembly, then there is also a room for a more creative approach and more integrated overall package design. As an example, Chow et al. [25] presented their package/antenna analysis within the content of the medical stent application. In our design, we aim to derive the minimum volume system that includes the electronics, the package, and the antenna.

## Conclusion

A number of research groups around the world have already focused their respective efforts on development of implantable telemetry technologies. Thus, when the core of an RF telemetry system for cardiac monitoring is reduced to $(2 \times 2 \times 2)\,\mathrm{mm}^3$ volume or less and, more importantly, when it is interfaced with various sensors it will drastically expand the list of potential industrial and scientific applications. Eventually, a wireless sensor network will be embedded, for instance, into crop fields, various constructions, and into a human body. That will enable real-time monitoring of growing crops, bridge integrity, or human health. This will then open up a wide range of other possible new applications for this potentially disruptive technology.

**Figure 21** 3D rendering of our current implantable package, which is designed to encompass the complete telemetry system, Figure 18. The PV catheter is connected to the telemetry using a 7-wire bundle (on the front side of the package), while the antenna is made of a single thin wire (on the right side of the package).

**Competing interests**
The authors declare that they have no competing interests.

## Acknowledgements

The author would like to express sincere gratitude to Scisense Inc, OCE, NSERC, CFI, and CMC Microsystems for providing support for our research. Additionally, I acknowledge contribution of Mr. Sorin Popa who created some of the plots and verified data used in this article. Also, I acknowledge cited contributions from the referenced sources used in this review.

## References

1. Statistics Canada. Mortality, Summary List of Causes. Catalogue no. 84F0209X, Table 1–1: 14, 2008

2. DA Kass, T Yamazaki, D Burkhoff, WL Maughan, K Sagawa, Determination of left ventricular end-systolic pressure–volume relationships by the conductance (volume) catheter technique. Circulation. **73**, 586–595 (1986)

3. CS Sander, JW Knutti, JD Meindl, A monolithic capacitive pressure sensor with pulse-period output. IEEE Trans. Electr. Dev. **27**(5), 927–930 (1980)

4. J Baan, T Jong, P Kerkhof, R Moene, A van Dijk, E van der Velde, A Koops, Continuous stroke volume and cardiac output from intra-ventricular dimensions obtained with impedance catheter. Cardiovasc. Res. **15**, 328–334 (1981)

5. J Baan, ET van der Velde, HG de Bruin, GJ Smeenk, J Koops, AD van Dijk, D Temmerman, J Senden, B Buis, Continuous measurement of left ventricular volume in animals and humans by conductance catheter. Circulation. **70**, 812–823 (1984)

6. Scisense Inc. http://www.scisense.com/. Accessed 2012/11/02

7. Millar Inc. http://www.millar.com/. Accessed 2012/11/02

8. MC Herrera, JM Olivera, MdIA Gómez López, in *IEEE 32nd International Conference EMBC*. Implantable hemodynamic monitors: can be conductance catheter system successfully implemented? (Buenos Aires, Argentina, 2010), pp. 3549–3552

9. VK Zworykin, JT Farrar, A 'radio pill'. Nature. **179**, 898 (1957). [A note]

10. MRaDT Yuce, telemetry Easy-to-swallow wireless. IEEE Microwav. Mag. **9**, 90–101 (2012)

11. JP Carson, AP Kuprat, X Jiao, F del Pin, DR Einstein, An anisotropic fluid–solid model of the mouse heart. Comput. Cardiol. **36**, 377–380 (2009)

12. G Mur, J Baan, Computation of the input impedances of a catheter for cardiac volumetry. IEEE Trans. Biomed. Eng. **BME-31**(6), 448–453 (1984)

13. CL Wei, JW Valvano, MD Feldman, JA Pearce, Nonlinear conductance-volume relationship for murine conductance catheter measurement system. IEEE Trans. Biomed. Eng. **52**(10), 1654–1661 (2005)

14. A Kottam, J Dubois, A McElligott, HK Henderson, in *IEEE 33rd International Conference EMBS1*. Novel approach to admittance to volume conversion for ventricular volume measurement (Boston MA, USA, 2011), pp. 2514–2517

15. CL Wei, MH Shih, Calibration capacity of the conductance-to-volume conversion equations for the mouse conductance catheter measurement system. IEEE Trans. Biomed. Eng. **56**(6), 1627–1634 (2009)

16. B Gopakumaran, JH Petre, B Sturm, RD White, PA Murray, Estimation of current leakage in left and right ventricular conductance volumetry using a dynamic finite element model. IEEE Trans. Biomed. Eng. **47**(11), 1476–1486 (2000)

17. C Jacoby, A Molojavyi, U Flögel, MW Merx, Z Ding, J Schrader, Direct comparison of magnetic resonance imaging and conductance microcatheter in the evaluation of left ventricular function in mice. Basic Res. Cardiol. **101**, 87–95 (2006)

18. CD Garson, Y Li, JA Hossack, Free-hand ultrasound scanning approaches for volume quantification of the mouse heart left ventricle. IEEE Trans. Ultrason. Ferroelectr. Freq. Control. **5**, 966–977 (2007)

19. SA Detombe, FL Xiang, J Dunmore-Buyze, JA White, Q Feng, D Drangova, Rapid microcomputed tomography suggests cardiac enlargement occurs during conductance catheter measurements in mice. J. Appl. Physiol. **113**, 142–148 (2012)

20. JA Paradiso, T Starner, Energy scavenging for mobile and wireless electronics. IEEE Pervasive Comput. **1**, 18–27 (2005)

21. AK RamRakhyani, S Mirabbasi, M Chiao, Design and optimization of resonance-based efficient wireless power delivery systems for biomedical implants. IEEE Trans. Biomed. Circ. Syst. **5**, 48–63 (2011)

22. KM Silay, C DM Dehollain, Inductive power link for a wireless cortical implant with two-body packaging. IEEE Sensors J. **11**(11), 2825–2833 (2011)

23. S Kim, JS Ho, Y PAS, Wireless power transfer to miniature implants: transmitter optimization. IEEE Trans. Antennas Propag. **10**, 4838–4845 (2012)

24. P Cong, N Chaimanonart, WH Ko, JD Young, A wireless and batteryless 10-bit implantable blood pressure sensing microsystem with adaptive RF powering for real-time laboratory mice monitoring. IEEE J. Solid-State Circ. **44**(12), 3631–3644 (2009)

25. EY Chow, AL Chlebowski, S Chakraborty, WJ Chappell, PP Irazoqui, Fully wireless implantable cardiovascular pressure monitor integrated with a medical stent. IEEE Trans. Biomed. Eng. **57**(6), 1487–1496 (2010)

26. YC Shih, T Shen, BP Otis, A 2.3 $\mu$W wireless intraocular pressure/temperature monitor. IEEE J. Solid-State Circ. **46**(11), 2592–2601 (2011)

27. R Njuguna, V Gruev, Low power programmable current mode computational imaging sensor. IEEE Sensors J. **12**(4), 727–736 (2012)

28. M Schuettler, M Huegle, JS Ordonez, J Wilde, F Stieglitz, in *IEEE 32nd International Conference EMBC*. A device for vacuum drying, inert gas backfilling and solder sealing of hermetic implant packages (Buenos Aires, Argentina, 2010), pp. 1577–1580

29. TY Lin, D Ha, WN de Vries, B Kim, A Chlebowski, SWM John, PP Irazoqui, WJ Chappell, in *IEEE MTT-S International Microwave Symposium Digest (MTT)*. Ultra-thin tag fabrication and sensing technique using third harmonic for implantable wireless sensors (Baltimore, MD USA, 2011), pp. 1–4

30. AL Dekker, GG Geskes, AA Cramers, WR Dassen, JG Maessen, KB Prenger, FH van der Veen, Right ventricular support for off-pump coronary artery bypass grafting studied with bi-ventricular pressure-volume loops in sheep. Eur. J. Cardio-thoracic Surg. **19**, 179–184 (2001)

31. C Gabriel, S Gabriel, RW Lau, E Corthout, The dielectric properties of biological tissues: literature survey. Phys. Med. Biol. **41**, 2231–2269 (1996). [These are two papers combined]

32. CC Wu, TC Skalak, TR Schwenk, CM Mahler, A Anne, PW Finnerty, HL Haber, RMI Weikle, MD Feldman, Accuracy of the conductance catheter for measurement of ventricular volumes seen clinically: effects of electric field homogeneity and parallel conductance. IEEE Trans. Biomed. Eng. **44**(4), 266–277 (1997)

33. JE Porterfield, ATG Kottam, K Raghavan, D Escobedo, JT Jenkins, ER Larson, RJ Treviño, JW Valvano, JA Pearce, MD Feldman, Dynamic correction for parallel conductance, $G_P$, and gain factor, $\alpha$, in invasive murine left ventricular volume measurements. J. Appl. Physiol. **107**, 1693–1703 (2009)

34. S Popa, K Fricke, R Sobot, in *IEEE International Conference for Upcoming Engineers, ICUE*, vol. 2012. Calibration and finite element numerical analysis of an admittance based volume sensor for the murine heart (Toronto ON, Canada, 2012), pp. 12–13

35. A Kamitani, S Morishita, H Kotaki, S Arscott, Miniaturized microDMFC using silicon microsystems techniques: performances at low fuel flow rates. J. Micromech. Microeng. **18**(12), 1–9 (2008). [125019]

36. BI Rapoport, JTSR Kedzierski, A glucose fuel cell for implantable brain-machine interfaces. PLoS ONE. **7**(6) (2012). doi:10.1371/journal.pone.0038436

37. J Olivo, S Carrara, G De Micheli, Energy harvesting and remote powering for implantable biosensors. IEEE Sensors J. **11**(7), 1573–1586 (2011)

38. F Mounaim, M Sawan, Toward a fully integrated neurostimulator with inductive power recovery front-end. IEEE Trans. Biomed. Circ. Syst. **6**(4), 309–318 (2012)

39. N Tesla, Apparatus for transmitting electrical energy. Patent number:1,119,732, Filing date: 18 Jan, 1902,Issue date: 1 Dec, 1914

40. A Kurs, A Karalis, R Moffatt, JD Joannopoulos, P Fisher, M Soljačić, Wireless power transfer via strongly coupled magnetic resonances. Science. **317**(5834), 83–86 (2007)

41. HA Haus, W Huang, Coupled-mode theory. IEEE Proc. **79**(10), 1505–1518 (1991)

42. L Luo, K De Gannes, K Fricke, S Senjuti, R Sobot, in *The 4th International EURASIP Workshop on RFID Technology, RFID 2012*. Low-power CMOS

voltage regulator architecture for implantable RF circuits (Torino, Italy, 2012)

43. D Russell, D McCormick, A Taberner, P Nielsen, P Hu, D Budgett, M Lim, S Malpas, in *IEEE Biomedical Circuits and Systems Conference, BioCAS 2009*. Wireless power delivery system for mouse telemeter (Beijing, China, 2009), pp. 273–276

44. S Senjuti, K Fricke, A Dounavis, R Sobot, in *IEEE Canadian Conference on Electrical and Computer Engineering, CCECE2012*. Misalignment analysis for resonance-based wireless power transfer to biomedical implants (Montreal QC, Canada, 2012), pp. 1–5

45. K Bong, E Levi, Z Zabar, L Birenbaum, Mutual inductance of noncoaxial circular coils with constant current density. IEEE Trans. Mag. **33**(5), 4303–4309 (1997)

46. S Babic, C Akyel, Calculating mutual inductance between circular coils with inclined axes in air. IEEE Trans. Magnet. **44**(7), 1743–1750 (2008)

47. J Dickson, On-chip high-voltage generation in MNOS integrated circuits using an improved voltage multiplier technique. IEEE J. Solid-State Circ. **11**(3), 374–378 (1976)

48. K Kotani, A Sasaki, T Ito, High-efficiency differential-drive CMOS rectifier for UHF RFIDs. IEEE J. Solid-State Circ. **44**(11), 3011–3018 (2009)

49. M Zargham, P Gulak, in *IEEE International Symposium on Circuits and Systems (ISCAS)*. High-efficiency CMOS rectifier for fully integrated mW wireless power transfer (Zarg12, Seoul, Korea, 2012), pp. 2869–2872

50. D Yeager, F Zhang, A Zarrasvand, N George, T Daniel, B Otis, $9\,\mu A$ addressable Gen2 sensor tag for biosignal acquisition. IEEE J. Solid-State Circ. **45**(10), 2198–2209 (2010)

51. P Cong, W Ko, D Young, Wireless batteryless implantable blood pressure monitoring microsystem for small laboratory animals. IEEE Sensors J. **10**(2), 243–254 (2010)

52. K Fricke, Wireless telemetry system for implantable sensors. Master's thesis, Western University, Canada, 2012

53. NJ Cleven, JA Muntjes, H Fassbender, U Urban, M Gortz, H Vogt, M Grafe, T Gottsche, T Penzkofer, T Schmitz-Rode, W Mokwa, A novel fully implantable wireless sensor system for monitoring hypertension patients. IEEE Trans. Biomed. Eng. **59**(11), 3124–3130 (2012)

54. EY Chow, AL Chlebowski, PP Irazoqui, A miniature–implantable RF—wireless active glaucoma intraocular pressure monitor. IEEE Trans. Biomed. Circ. Syst. **4**(6), 340–349 (2010)

55. C Varel, YC Shih, B Otis, T Shen, K Bohringer, in *IEEE 25th International Conference on Micro Electro Mechanical Systems (MEMS)*. Packaging for a wireless intraocular pressure sensor with a solder-filled microchannel antenna (Paris, France, 2012), pp. 981–984

56. M Scarpello, D Kurup, H Rogier, D Vande Ginste, F Axisa, J Vanfleteren, W Joseph, L Martens, G Vermeeren, Design of an implantable slot dipole conformal flexible antenna for biomedical applications. IEEE Trans. Antennas Propag. **59**(10), 3556–3564 (2011)

# 18

# A UHF/UWB hybrid silicon RFID tag with on–chip antennas

Philipp K Gentner[1*], Robert Langwieser[1], Arpad L Scholtz[1], Günter Hofer[2] and Christoph F Mecklenbräuker[1]

## Abstract

In this contribution, we describe and analyse a miniature wireless radio frequency identification (RFID) chip with on-chip antennas (OCA) and ultra wideband (UWB) signalling by real-world measurements. With the on-chip antenna approach, no external antennas are required, and the size of the overall tag is identical to the size of the chip alone (3.5 mm × 1 mm). The chip is powered through inductive coupling and controlled by an RFID signal at 866 MHz in the downlink, while the uplink transmits a quaternary pulse-position-modulated (4-PPM) UWB signal at 5.64 GHz with pulses having a duration in the order of nanoseconds. In this contribution, the hybrid or asymmetric communication scheme between prototype chip and reader, the embedded OCA, and the measurement setup are described. The prototype achieves 4-PPM bit rate of 126 Mbit/s based on a pulse-train transmission with a duration of 10 μs. The small size, high data rate, and fine time resolution of the UWB impulse radio offer new features and sensing capabilities for future RFID-like applications.

## Introduction

Tiny systems on chip (SoC) with on-chip antennas (OCAs) are useful if a transmission of data is necessary over a short distance. Especially for radio frequency identification (RFID) systems, the limited communication range increases security and protects privacy.

Small tags combined with sensing capabilities, such as temperature or shock sensors, allow the tracking of individual items for example frozen goods in a cold chain. Due to their small size, the systems on chip can be placed on or in objects while reducing the cost by avoiding bulky antennas.

In this contribution, a fully integrated system on chip is presented, which features on-chip antennas for a hybrid or in other words asymmetric communication scheme. It gives insight into our past achievements and current studies in the field of short range connectivity devices for RFID applications or for wireless sensors. At first, the scheme is explained in detail in section "Asymmetric communication scheme" with a survey of impulse transmitters and related achievements in research. Then our manufactured ultra-high frequency/ultra-wideband (UHF/UWB) hybrid

system on chip is introduced, with all its components and a focus on the on-chip antennas used, a dual antenna concept with an electric and a magnetic antenna.

After the description of the device under test, the development of the measurement setup is explained in detail, and also, results are presented in the time and the frequency domains. The decoding of the received wideband data signal from the hybrid UHF/UWB tag is shown. Before the conclusion, the transmission loss between the impulse-transmitting OCA and the according uplink reader antenna is calculated from measurements.

## Asymmetric communication scheme

The most famous example of an asymmetric communication scheme is used everyday all over the world through browsing of the web. In the downlink from the provider to the user, a much higher amount of data is needed by pictures, movies, or text. In the uplink, mostly control or request data are sent from a personal computer to the provider. This idea is also used in long-term evolution (LTE), where the downlink peak rates are higher as those in the uplink.

In the case of RFID or sensor applications, the high data rate is shifted to the uplink. Since the tags or sensors are very small and the available power has to be used as efficiently as possible, it is advantageous to have a fast

*Correspondence: philipp.gentner@nt.tuwien.ac.at
[1]Institute of Telecommunications, Vienna University of Technology, Gusshausstrasse 25/E389, Vienna 1040, Austria
Full list of author information is available at the end of the article

transmission in the uplink. The downlink, from a reader station to a sensor or tag, provides the energy, control commands, and clock for synchronisation in a UHF band, with the data rate being usually lower. A concept of an asymmetric communication scheme for RFID scenarios was introduced by Zheng et al. in [1] and has been manufactured and characterised in the works of Baghaei-Nejad and Radiom et al. in [2] and [3].

In the papers mentioned above, impulse radio UWB is considered as the appropriate scheme for the uplink, being able to provide a fast data rate and also being more power efficient. This has been shown by Calhoun et. al in [4], who summarise the necessary energy per pulse for UWB transmitters of recent research. The authors found that the energy per pulse is lower than 10nJ/bit and constant over a data rate from 1 Mbit/s to 10 Gbit/s, and compares it with the energy per bit for a bluetooth transmitter being typically 25 nJ/bit.

In our opinion, transmitting pulses in the baseband is not a good choice and should not be considered for the application in mind. The reasons are the following:

- The powering UHF field interferes with the spectrum of pulses transmitted in the baseband, which leads to an increased reader complexity.
- Reading multiple tags at the same time leads to collisions. Using modulated pulses, the probability of collisions can be reduced by changing the modulation frequency.
- A small size reader antenna is important for many applications.
- Using on-chip antennas with their small aperture, uplink frequencies in the C- or X-band are preferred.

Non-baseband impulse radio UWB transmitters can be realised in two ways [5]: firstly, baseband pulses can be upconverted with the aid of a local oscillator. Secondly, pulse creation, e.g. with delay lines following pulse shaping filter can be employed. In terms of reduced transmitter power consumption, a pulse-position modulation scheme is very promising because it allows to transmit multiple bits per pulse.

Impulse radio as an additional asset of a tag introduces a multitude of new possibilities and applications for RFID scenarios [6]. In recent UWB research, indoor localisation is studied extensively for example by Meissner et al. in [7]. Concerning localisation, the IEEE standard 802.15.4a provides a good basis for commercial applications. Zheng et al. describe in [8] a transceiver achieving a ranging accuracy of 3 cm. Readers for localisation will very likely use an array antenna to track the small device. In [9] and [10], UWB antenna arrays are introduced and analysed concerning their ability to operate in a wideband spectrum and are consecutively used to operate with the wideband tags.

Two inductively coupled magnetic loop antennas offer a wireless power transfer technique, which is used successfully for medical implants [11], such as pacemakers and biosensors, or for charging electric vehicles [12]. An RFID tag with an asymmetric communication scheme favourably should store energy from an energy source to be able to transmit pulses. Here, power-scavenging units harvest energy from the narrowband UHF downlink signal. Figures of merits are the efficiency of the rectifier and the value of the capacitor, where the harvested energy is stored. The downlink antenna will usually be an inductive antenna with high Q-factor, whereas a wideband antenna with low Q-factor is required in the uplink.

## Hybrid UHF/UWB system on chip

In our approach towards a short-range connectivity device, we started with externally powered complementary metal oxide semiconductor substrate (CMOS) structures (see Figure 1). These CMOS prototypes with OCAs were controlled and powered through bondwires. In order to compare the radiation of different types of OCAs, a voltage-controlled oscillator (VCO) was swept over a huge frequency range of several octaves [13]. Furthermore, nanosecond pulses were transmitted with a simple on-off keying pulse transmitter - created by a glitch generator, whose output was multiplied with the VCO frequency. A proof of concept concerning the energy transfer was done, with inductive coupling using a magnetic OCA [14]. With a modulated backscatter technique, the voltage induced into the miniaturised loop antenna was analysed over area and over distance. The power harvesting concept was studied and characterised with a small 3 mm × 1 mm system, where two different OCAs were used for receiving energy and for transmitting data [15]. The power-harvesting concept must be able to collect power of some $\mu$W in the long term. This energy, stored in an efficient way with on-chip batteries or capacitors, is used for driving the UWB front end, which requires some mW within a short period of time. The asymmetric scheme allows to replace the used harvesting concept, if clock and data for configuring the chip is provided through another communication channel. Also, this scheme allows to investigate the performance of on-chip antennas without having a galvanic connection. In the course of these investigations, we observed that bondwires used in earlier work have a huge influence due to coupling. Bondwires, typically the same size and in close vicinity of the chip, act as a high Q-factor antenna, and support either the transmitted pulses or the energy-harvesting path. In the downlink path, a coupling into the chips' $V_{SS}$ is established, which yields to a better efficiency of the rectifier. Using plane OCAs, the energy received by the reader (uplink path) was much lower than in the early experiments employing bondwires.

**Figure 1 Microscopic images of on-chip antennas (OCAs).** From left to right: external powered PPM UWB modulator front end with a meandered dipole on-chip antenna [13]; loop antenna on chip for inductive coupling [14]; prototype of a passive tag with two OCAs [15].

## Functionality of the system on chip

The device under test shown in detail in this contribution is a full system on chip. A transmitter, a receiver, a power harvester, and antennas are integrated within one host platform, which is placed on one piece of silicon. The device used for short-range connectivity were manufactured with a standard 130 nm CMOS technology. A loop structure and an electric monopole were integrated on the chip as can be seen in the chip photograph and antenna schematic in Figure 2. The loop structure is connected to a harvester and extracts the necessary energy to drive the circuit from a UHF signal by inductive coupling. The monopole, placed inside the loop antenna, is a meandered line which transmits the UWB pulses. With respect to the overall size of the SoC (3.5 mm × 1 mm), the antenna part is small (1 mm$^2$). The circuit on chip is programmable via the UHF link, and the signal sent on the uplink can be selected to be a continuous wave, a data sequence of pulses, or a continuous pulse stream. For characterising the device under test, the flexibility to be able to select different waveforms is helpful to detect the low-power transmitted signal. Compared to other work with OCAs and UWB transmitters [16] in the field, this SoC harvests and stores energy as a system and is operated and controlled without any wired contact [2].

## On-chip antennas

In the early research of on-chip antennas, these antennas were considered as replacements of wired clock distribution [17] or as wireless interconnects on chip [18,19]. OCAs are very common in the millimeter-wave region [20] because this is their native environment.

In the chip presented, a meandered monopole is placed inside a loop antenna, and both are located within the chip area. The antennas are placed on the chip in a way that no electrical circuits are below the antenna. The structure is shown in top of Figure 2. To support the monopole, the remaining part of the silicon is covered with metal and connected to the chips' $V_{SS}$, which acts as the ground plane. A single-ended antenna is used to avoid

a differential power amplification in the front end. This reduces the overall power consumption.

The silicon substrate thickness is 220 μm, with the conductivity being larger than 50 S/m. In [21], where exemplary dipoles have been simulated on a CMOS layer stack, it has been shown that the lossy substrate reduces the Q-factor of the antenna and therefore supports a wideband communication scheme, even when the aperture of the antenna is very small.

All antennas are placed in a so-called inductive layer in which metal filling structures between the turns are avoided. The width of the conductor used to form the monopole is 15 μm with a total unwrapped length of 4.85 mm which is approximately λ/10. The distance between each turn is 90 μm. With increasing distance to the excitation port, the width of the meandered monopole increases from 90 to 800 μm in eight steps. For the uplink and the downlink antenna, three metal layers each are connected in parallel by vias to increase the thickness of the conductor. The magnetic loop antenna with four turns and chamfered edges is square with a width of 989 μm. The conductor used for the loop has a width of 15 μm and a spacing of 2.6 μm. With a method of moments (MOM) simulator (Sonnet Software, North Syracuse, NY, USA) the inductance of the loop was calculated to be 50.2 nH, and the impedance of the meandered monopole was determined as $Z_{\text{uplinkMOM}} = (11.6 - 6.6j)$ Ω. The accurateness of the simulation result is dependent on the physical size of the antenna and the simulation method itself, especially for small wires such as the conductors for the OCAs [22]. Therefore, and for further investigations, the meandered monopole was simulated with a finite element method (FEM) solver (HFSS - Ansoft, Ansys, Inc., Canonsburg, PA, USA). The impedance thus obtained is $Z_{\text{uplinkFEM}} = (23.4 + 3.66j)$ Ω. The real part of the numerically calculated impedance from the FEM simulation is larger because the metallic antenna parts must be modelled as solid aluminium. This is in contrast to the MOM simulation, where all thin metal layers are accurately modelled as a combination of copper and aluminium. Therefore, the impedance's real part is lower in

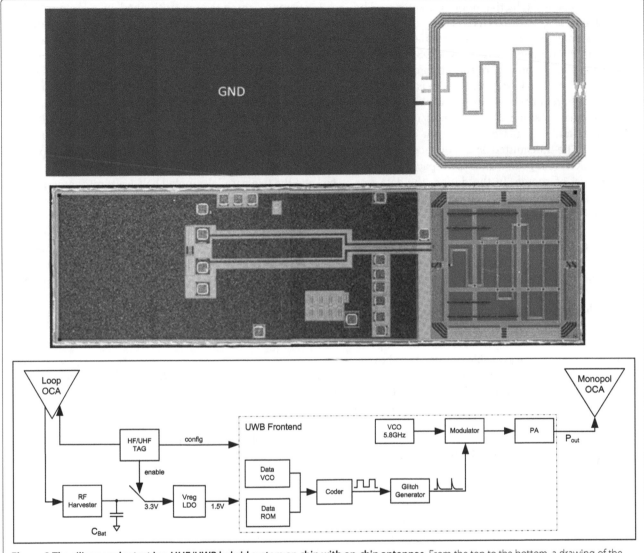

**Figure 2 The silicon under test is a UHF/UWB hybrid system on chip with on-chip antennas.** From the top to the bottom, a drawing of the antennas, a microscope picture of the system on chip, and a functional schematic of the integrated circuit.

the MOM simulation. In comparison to theoretical predictions for electrically small antennas, the real part is very much dominated by the losses due to the conductive silicon substrate underneath.

The far field gain of the monopole is determined to be $-41.5$ dBi with an efficiency of $-43.56$ dB at the targeted centre frequency of 5.8 GHz. The gain flatness is 0.9 dB from 5 to 6.2 GHz which is important for pulse transmission.

## Integrated circuit

In the downlink from the reader to the miniature device, a standard UHF RFID EPC protocol is used. The communication frequency is $f_c = 866$ MHz. A power harvester [23] stores the energy in a buffer capacitor with a capacitance of $C_{Bat} = 3.9$ nF. The HF rectifier of [23] is replaced by a

standard UHF rectifier. For the functionality of this component, it is not important if the tag is placed in the near or far field of a reader antenna. Moreover the used electric or magnetic antenna connected to rectifier is important, so that the tag can be operated either in the near or far field of a reader. The harvester needs a minimum input of $P_{min} = -15$ dBm for operation. The DC current consumption of the tag is 8.5 µA. Simulations show that a power of $P = -10$ dBm, not needed by the transponder circuitry, is redirected into the charge pump, placed before the buffer capacitor. A schematic of the tag is shown in the bottom of Figure 2.

Once the capacitor is fully charged and the command to transmit the hardwired sequence is triggered by the RFID reader, pulses with a nominal width of either $w_{low} = 0.78$ ns or $w_{high} = 1.3$ ns are created by the glitch generator and transmitted by the monopole antenna. The uplink frequency is $f_c = 5.8\,\text{GHz}$. The motivation of this uplink frequency is not triggered by standardisation; furthermore, it is a trade-off between CMOS transit frequency and hence a low power consumption of the active front end. Since a carrier-based pulse radio is considered in the tag, a centre frequency within an available ISM band is feasible. A pulse-position modulation is used, where four sub frames and one guard frame form one symbol frame (4-PPM). The transmitted data sequence consists of 16 symbols, which are repeated until the capacitor reaches a minimum level of charge. In the design, the data rate was calculated to be $117\,\text{Mbit/s}$ and the nominal symbol rate is $58\,\text{Msym/s}$. The supply voltage of the UWB front end is $1.5\,\text{V}$, controlled by a low-dropout (LDO) regulator placed before the UWB front end. The available power $P_{\text{out}}$ provided by the single-ended amplifier to the OCA monopole was simulated using Cadence software to be $-1.3\,\text{dBm}$. The simulated antenna impedance is connected in Cadence to the front end, and the peak output power of a continuous wave delivered by the front end is determined. In the following measurements, the pulse mode is analysed, hence the available power has to be corrected with the duty cycle of the pulse signal. Therefore, in pulse mode, with a pulse width of $w_{\text{low}} = 0.78\,\text{ns}$ and a duty cycle of $D = 4.5\%$, the available power fed to the OCA is $P_{\text{out}} = -28.2\,\text{dBm}$.

## Measurements with a hybrid UHF/UWB reader setup

A photograph of the measurement setup is shown in Figure 3. A UHF RFID reader (RFID ME™ USB Dongle, MTI, Inc., Hsinchu, Taiwan) acts as the signal source for the downlink path. The USB reader was programmed to be able to send control commands and select the different operating modes of the silicon under test.

Since the pulse burst transmitted by the silicon is as short as $10\,\mu\text{s}$, a triggering event is required. Therefore, the initial rising edge of the UHF signal is sampled by a coupler and consequently used as trigger source for the oscilloscope. Following the coupler two lowpass filters in series suppress the spurious harmonics produced by the UHF reader.

The scenario is shown in the subfigure in Figure 3: The downlink excitation coil is printed on a standard FR4 substrate and is matched to the downlink path (centre frequency $866\,\text{MHz}$). This external loop antenna replaces the internal antenna of the UHF reader. In this way, we have more degrees of freedom for characterising the device under test. The UWB silicon chip is fixed with adhesive tape in close vicinity to the excitation coil. We wish to point out, however, that the chip has not a single conductive connection to any part of the measurement equipment.

A reference antenna was positioned in a distance of $d_{\text{uplink}} \approx 5\,\text{mm}$ above the silicon, capturing the silicon's uplink. This reference antenna is also a loop structure with one turn of copper wire; designed to be resonant at the uplink frequency of $5.8\,\text{GHz}$. The SoC, the UHF excitation coil, and the reference antenna were located inside a brass box to suppress the local WLAN and other interferers.

As shown in schematic view of the measurement setup (Figure 3), a chain of bandpass filters and amplifiers is used before the signal is fed to a digital sampling oscilloscope.

The components of the uplink, such as the reference coil and the two parallel coupled half-wave resonators, are measured and the results presented in Figure 4. All passive components have been simulated and measured with respect to a reference of $50\,\Omega$. The transmission coefficients of the bandpass filters are $G_{\text{BP1}} = -1.3\,\text{dB}$ and $G_{\text{BP2}} = -1.4\,\text{dB}$. The influence of the splitter and the cables is summarised in $G_{\text{sc}} = -7.5\,\text{dB}$. The two amplifiers have a gain of $G_{\text{ZX60}} = 12.3\,\text{dB}$ and $G_{\text{ZVA183+}} = 27.2\,\text{dB}$. The amplification of the total uplink path is

$$G_{\text{meas}} = G_{\text{ZX60}} + G_{\text{ZVA183+}} + G_{\text{BP1}} + G_{\text{BP2}} + G_{\text{sc}} \tag{1}$$

which results in $G_{\text{meas}} = 29.3\,\text{dB}$. The power at the oscilloscope or spectrum analyser can be written as

$$P_{\text{meas}} = G_{\text{meas}} + L_{\text{uplink}} + P_{\text{out}}. \tag{2}$$

$L_{\text{uplink}}$ describes the transmission between the monopole and the reader antenna, including the gain and possible mismatch of both antennas.

### Frequency domain measurement

A spectrum analyser was used to characterise the uplink in the frequency domain. A resolution bandwidth of $10\,\text{MHz}$ and a video bandwidth of $50\,\text{kHz}$ were set. Since the impulse radio event of the tag is short in time and the sweep time of the analyser is too long to capture a transmission precisely, the max hold functionality was set and 32,500 sweeps were captured. The result of this measurement is shown in Figure 5. We observe that the harmonics of the $866\,\text{MHz}$ downlink signal are present at $5,196\,\text{MHz}$ and $6,062\,\text{MHz}$, indicating that more suppression in the downlink path of the measurement setup is necessary. The tag is set to transmit continuous pulses (constant pulse repetition rate), hence a comb line spectrum is expected. This spectrum is visible at a centre frequency of $f_c = 5.64\,\text{GHz}$, which differs only slightly from the targeted design frequency due to CMOS process variation. The spectral line at this centre frequency is $13\,\text{dB}$ above the noise floor. The $10\,\text{dB}$ bandwidth of the pulsed signal is $230\,\text{MHz}$. The coil antenna used for receiving the pulse signal is narrowing the observed frequency band. This can be seen in Figure 4 with the plotted reflection coefficients of the reference coil.

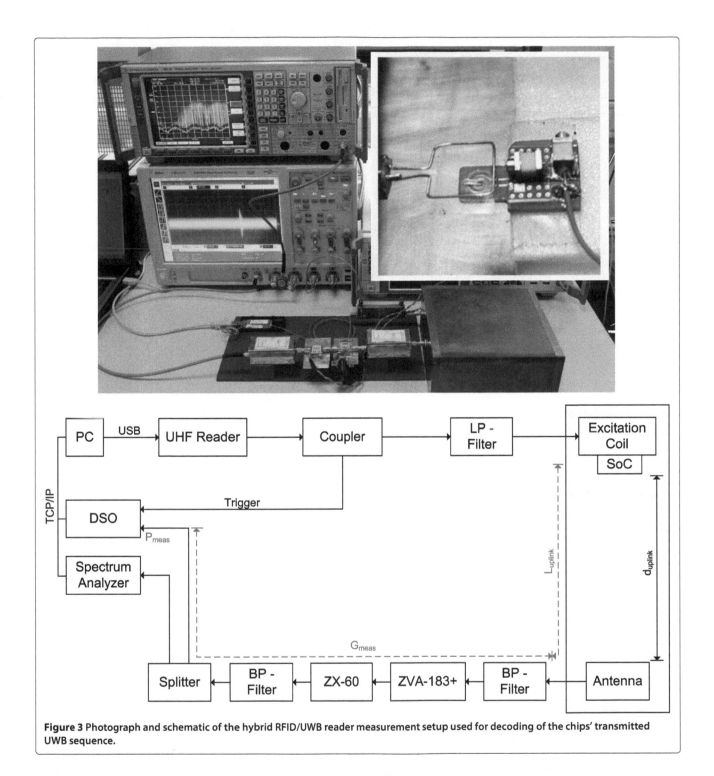

**Figure 3** Photograph and schematic of the hybrid RFID/UWB reader measurement setup used for decoding of the chips' transmitted UWB sequence.

## Time domain measurement

Two captures with a digital storage oscilloscope (40 GSa/s) as shown in Figure 6 were taken. In part (a) of Figure 6, a continuous stream of fixed 4-PPM symbols is presented. A 16-symbol data like sequence is shown in part (b). For both, the complete burst is shown on the left side. The right side is a window zoomed into the respective waveforms. The continuous pulse stream has an average frame length of 15.8 ns, which yields to a data rate of 63.3 MSym/s. Comparing the envelope of the burst amplitude of the continuous signal and the data sequence, one can observe that the latter is almost constant in time between 0 and 8 μs, whereas the amplitude of the continuous signal is initially higher and decreases with time.

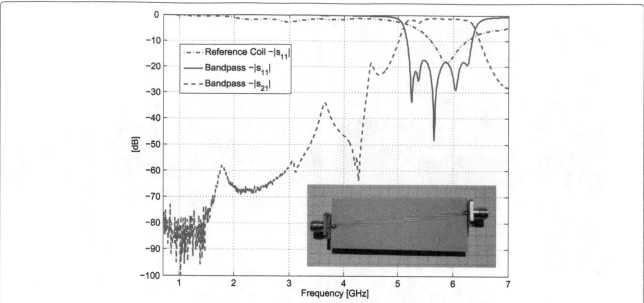

**Figure 4** Logarithmic transmission and reflection coefficients of reference coil and bandpass filters. These were used in the uplink path of the measurement setup.

From transient simulations, it is known that at $\approx 8\,\mu s$, the initial voltage of 3.3 V stored in the buffer capacitor discharges below the minimal supply voltage of 1.5 V, required by the UWB front end. The average amplitude of the continuous pulsed signal is higher than that of the waveform with the data sequence. The amplitude of the preamble, which is based on five continuous pulses, is higher than the amplitude of the following data sequence.

### Decoding of the UWB uplink 4-PPM signal

In this section, the 4-PPM signal is decoded step by step in a Matlab post processing step. The oscilloscope captured the waveform of the transmitted pulses, with the pulse width set to $w_{\text{low}}$ in the data sequence mode. Not to waste processing time, from the received signal $r(t) = s(t) + n(t)$ the pulse burst is extracted. This burst is squared and filtered with a Matlab FIR equiripple bandpass filter. The

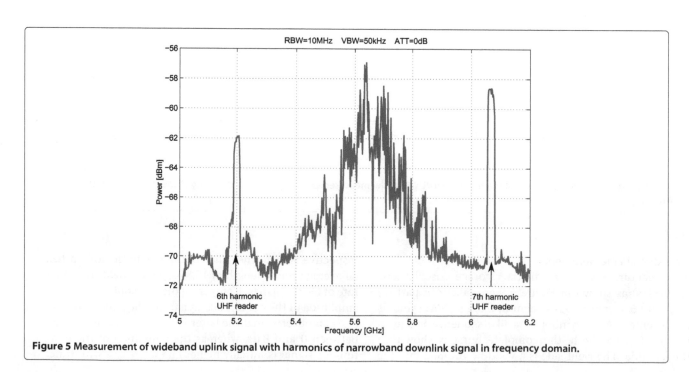

**Figure 5** Measurement of wideband uplink signal with harmonics of narrowband downlink signal in frequency domain.

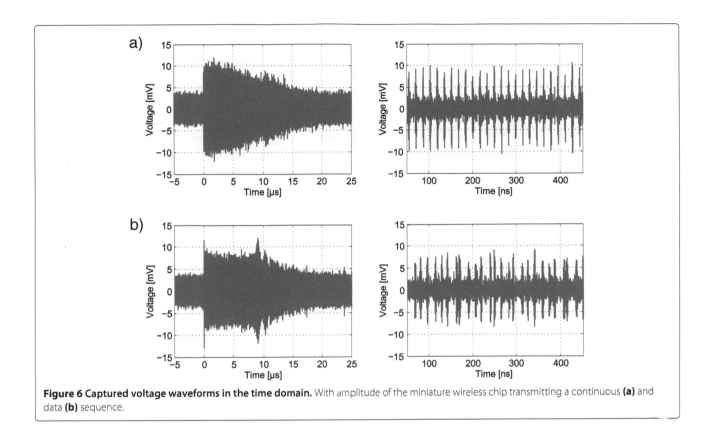

**Figure 6 Captured voltage waveforms in the time domain.** With amplitude of the miniature wireless chip transmitting a continuous **(a)** and data **(b)** sequence.

filter has a centre frequency of 5.6 GHz and a 60 dB bandwidth of 1.6 GHz. Now, the signal is squared again and subsequently normalised to the maximum peak.

$$r'(t) = \left(r(t)^2 * h_{\mathrm{BPF}}\right)^2 \qquad (3)$$

$$x(t) = \frac{1}{\max\left(r'(t)\right)} \times r'(t) \qquad (4)$$

The normalised signal $x(t)$ is shown in Figure 7a. In this representation, one can observe a deep fade in the amplitude at around 10 µs. At this instant, the voltage supplied by the on-chip capacitor becomes too weak for the UWB front end to operate.

The decoder itself is based on determining the time between the current pulse and the following pulse, taking into account the estimated symbol corresponding to the current pulse. Since a preamble of five symbols is transmitted at the beginning of the pulse burst, an initial state for decoding is given. In general, the amount of possible pulse distances $n_\Delta$ in an M-ary pulse position modulation scheme is given by

$$n_\Delta = 2M - 1. \qquad (5)$$

The pulse distances are calculated after a threshold comparator. In Figure 7b the pulse distances $t_\Delta$ of the first 600 symbols ($\approx$ 10 µs) are shown as a histogram. It shows the occurrence of pulse distances within the captured pulse burst. The amount of pulses having a pulse distance of 15.8 ns is maximum across all pulse distances. It represents consecutive equal symbols in the modulation scheme and being the frame length of the 4-PPM transmission. Only $n_\Delta = 6$ distances can be found in the burst. The reason is that one out of seven possible transitions is not present in the hardwired 4-PPM transmitted data. Clear peaks can be observed in this representation. We conclude that no significant timing drift is caused by a decreasing supply voltage to the UWB front end.

All occurring pulse distances $t_\Delta$ in the data sequence of the burst are plotted versus symbols together with the average $t_\Delta$ in Figure 7c. In this graph, one can observe that not only the frame rate ($t_\Delta = 15.8$ ns) but all other pulse distances are constant until 620 symbols. The pulse distances of all following symbols drift away and a successful decoding is not possible any more.

In the following, the transmitted symbols are estimated, with estimation borders positioned between the average pulse distances. The symbol error rate is calculated for pulse burst transmissions of several consecutive measurements. The result is shown in Figure 8 as symbol error versus decoded symbols. In most cases, a transmission

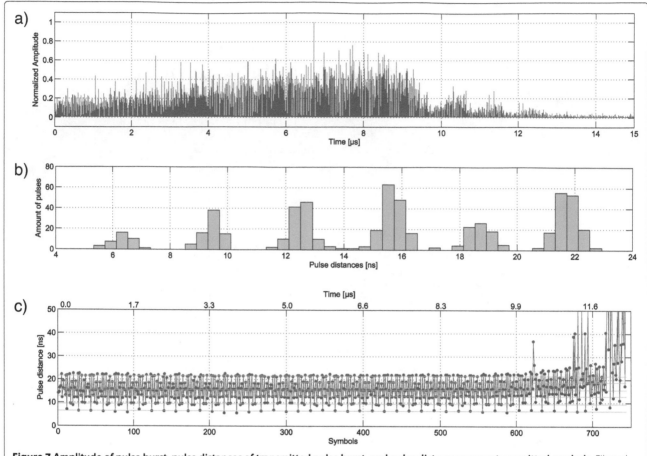

**Figure 7 Amplitude of pulse burst, pulse distances of transmitted pulse burst, and pulse distances versus transmitted symbols.** Filtered and normalised amplitude of the pulse burst **(a)**, histogram of pulse distances $t_\Delta$ of a transmitted pulse burst **(b)**, and the pulse distances versus transmitted symbols **(c)**.

without errors is possible until 600 symbols (equal to 1,200 bits). The theoretical and experimental limitation to decode up to the given number of symbols is given through the finite size of the buffer capacitor of the SoC, and the power efficiency of the TX-UWB front end, being the only consumer.

### UWB OCA transmission loss

The received power $P_{\mathrm{meas}}$ can be calculated with the root mean square voltage of the signal and the duty cycle of the impulse signal [24]:

$$U_{\mathrm{RMS}} = \frac{U_P}{\sqrt{2}} \times D \tag{6}$$

$$P_{\mathrm{meas}} = \frac{U_{\mathrm{RMS}}^2}{R} = \frac{1}{2R} \times \left( \frac{U_P \times T}{\tau} \right)^2. \tag{7}$$

With an average pulse amplitude of $U_p = 8\,\mathrm{mV}$ and a duty cycle of $D = T/\tau = 2.6\,\mathrm{ns}/15.8\,\mathrm{ns} = 0.16$ it is $P_{\mathrm{meas}} = -47.6\,\mathrm{dBm}$. The transmission coefficient between the monopole and the readers' loop antenna according to this measurement is $L_{\mathrm{uplink}} = -48.7\,\mathrm{dB}$.

### Comparison with related work

The figures of merit of the presented device using a UHF/UWB asymmetric communication scheme are compared to similar devices in Table 1. It has to be mentioned that the device from [16] is powered externally, and the devices in [25] and [6] use external antennas. In this table, the required power $P_{\mathrm{downlink}}$ necessary to establish a wideband connectivity over the distance $d_{\mathrm{downlink}}$ is used as a basis of comparison.

### Conclusions

In this contribution, the potential use of on-chip antennas for RFID tags with ultra-wideband signalling is investigated by a prototypical implementation. The SoC is described in detail featuring two on-chip antennas and an asymmetric wireless communication scheme.

The measurement setup is presented which comprises a commercially available UHF RFID dongle and a spectrum analyzer as well as a digital storage oscilloscope. An optimisation is carried out in the uplink path for increasing the signal-to-noise ratio of the received signal using

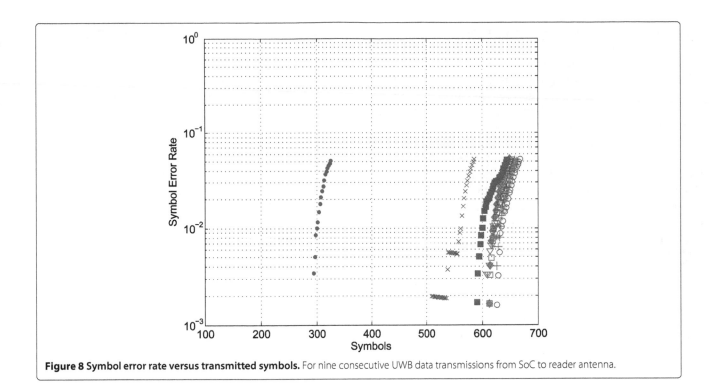

**Figure 8 Symbol error rate versus transmitted symbols.** For nine consecutive UWB data transmissions from SoC to reader antenna.

**Table 1 Important figures of merit for RFID tag with hybrid communication scheme in comparison to similar research**

| Path | Parameter | This work | Radiom [3] | Kulkarni [16] | Pelissier [25] | Vauche [6] |
|---|---|---|---|---|---|---|
| | Technology | 130 nm | 180 nm | 180 nm | 130 nm | 130 nm |
| | Die - Size | 3.5 mm² | 4.5 mm² | > 5.4 mm² | 4 mm² | 0.8 mm² |
| Downlink | OCA | Yes | Yes | - | Ext. antenna | Ext. antenna |
| | $f_{downlink}$ | 866 MHz | 5.8 GHz | - | 900 MHz | 900 MHz |
| | Receiver | Yes | Yes | - | Yes | UHF and UWB |
| | Antenna gain | - | −29.5 dBi ([2]) | - | - | 0 dBi |
| | $P_{downlink}$ | 13 dBm | 36 dBm | - | 14 dBm | 36 dBm |
| | $d_{downlink}$ | 0 mm | 75 mm | - | 100 mm | 10 m |
| Harvester | Capacitor | 3.9 nF | 6 nF | - | - | 56 pF |
| Uplink | OCA | Yes | Yes | Yes | Ext. antenna | Ext. antenna |
| | $f_{uplink}$ | 5.64 GHz | 5.8 GHz | 8 GHz | 7.9 GHz | 7.25 GHz (sim) |
| | Antenna gain | −41.5 dBi | - | −27.4 dBi | - | - (sim) |
| | IR-scheme | 4 PPM | OOK / BPSK | BPM | OOK | Localisation (sim) |
| | Data rate | 126.6 MBit/s | 1 MBit/s | 750 MBit/s | 112.5 Mbit/s | 200 Mbit/s (sim) |
| | Pulse width | 2.6 ns | 1 ns | 0.5 ns | 2.9 ns | 0.45 ns (sim) |
| | $P_{uplink}$ | −28.2 dBm | - | −42 dBm | −16.6 dBm | - |
| | $d_{uplink}$ | 5 mm | 75 mm | - | 100 mm | - |
| | Bits per burst | 1,248 | - | - | - | 1 (sim) |

bandpass filters and amplifiers. Further, interferers in the downlink path (e.g. local WLAN and harmonics of the powering UHF signal) had to be suppressed.

Bursts of nanosecond pulses from the UHF/UWB hybrid silicon RFID tag were captured and analysed with the optimised measurement setup. The time domain and frequency domain measurements were subsequently analysed by post processing. Due to the short transmission time, the low duty cycle and the low transmit power of the signal, we found that it is easier to detect the radiated signal in the time domain. The ability to switch the SoC between different operating modes for data transmission enhances the initial signal detection.

The transmitted ultra-wideband data sequence from the tiny SoC is decoded correctly up to sequence lengths of 1,248 bits. The embedded monopole OCA broaden the pulse width from 0.7 to 2.6 ns. A data transmission with simulated pulse width of 1.3 ns is therefore not successful.

The transmission loss from a CMOS OCA to a reader antenna is estimated to be $L_{uplink} = -48.7\,dB$ from transient simulations and measurements.

In comparison to related work in the field [3], the downlink distance is reduced which is reflected in a much lower power requirement for inductive coupling by 20 dB. We conclude that Impulse Radio is a promising low-power communication scheme for a fast, secure, and power-efficient data transfer for future RFID enhancements.

### Competing interests
The authors declare that they have no competing interests.

### Acknowledgements
This work was performed as part of the project 'ConSens' (Contactless Sensing) within the funding programme 'Forschung, Innovation, Technologie - Informationstechnologie' (FIT-IT) of the 'Bundesministerium für Verkehr, Innovation und Technologie' (BMVIT). The authors wish to thank the members of the COST action IC 1004, "Cooperative Radio Communications for Green Smart Environments," for countless fruitful discussions.

### Author details
[1]Institute of Telecommunications, Vienna University of Technology, Gusshausstrasse 25/E389, Vienna 1040, Austria. [2]Infineon Technologies Austria AG, Contactless and RF Exploration, Babenberger Strasse 10, Graz 8020, Austria.

### References
1. LR Zheng, MB Nejad, Z Zou, X DS Zou, Z Zhang, H Tenhunen, Future RFID and wireless sensors for ubiquitous intelligence, in *Proc NORCHIP* (Tallinn, 16-17 Nov. 2008), pp. 142–149
2. M Baghaei-Nejad, S Radiom, G Vandenbosch, LR Zheng, G Gielen, Fully integrated 1.2 pJ/p UWB transmitter with on-chip antenna for wireless identification, in *IEEE International Conference on Ultra-Wideband* (Nanjing, 20-23 Sept. 2010), pp. 1–4
3. S Radiom, M Baghaei-Nejad, K Aghdam, G Vandenbosch, L Zheng, G Gielen, Far-field on-chip antennas monolithically integrated in a wireless-powered 5.8-GHz downlink/UWB uplink RFID tag in 0.18 μm standard CMOS. IEEE J. Solid-State Circ. **45**(9), 1746–1758 (2010)
4. BH Calhoun, J Lach, J Stankovic, DD Wentzloff, K Whitehouse, AT Barth, JK Brown, Q Li, S Oh, NE Roberts, Y Zhang, Body sensor networks: a holistic approach from silicon to users. In Proceedings of the *IEEE*. **100**, 91–106 (2012)
5. D Wentzloff, A Chandrakasan, Gaussian pulse generators for subbanded ultra-wideband transmitters. IEEE Trans. Microwave Theory and Tech. **54**(4), 1647–1655 (2006)
6. R Vauche, E Bergeret, J Gaubert, S Bourdel, O Fourquin, N Dehaese, A remotely UHF powered UWB transmitter for high precision localization of RFID tag, in *IEEE International Conference on Ultra-Wideband*, (Bologna, 14–16 Sept 2011), pp. 494–498
7. P Meissner, D Arnitz, T Gigl, K Witrisal, Analysis of an indoor UWB channel for multipath-aided localization, in *IEEE International Conference on Ultra-Wideband*, (Bologna, 14–16 Sept. 2011), pp. 565–569
8. Y Zheng, MA Arasu, KW Wong, YJ The, AHS Poh, DD Tran, WG Yeoh, DL Kwong, A 0.18μm CMOS 802.15.4a UWB Transceiver for Communication and Localization, in *Solid-State Circuits Conference*, (San Francisco, 3–7 Feb 2008), pp. 118–120
9. PK Gentner, GS Hilton, MA Beach, CF Mecklenbräuker, Characterisation of ultra-wideband antenna arrays with spacings following a geometric progression. IET Commun. **6**(10), 1179–1186 (2012)
10. NM Gvozdenovic, PK Gentner, CF Mecklenbräuker, Antenna array for the reader of an ultra-wideband identification tag with on-chip antenna, in *Loughborough Antennas & Propagation Conference*, (Loughborough, 14–15 Nov. 2011), pp. 1–4
11. M Mahfouz, G To, M Kuhn, No strings attached. IEEE Microwave Mag., **12**(7), S34–S48 (2011)
12. N Shinohara, Power without wires. IEEE Microwave Mag., **12**(7), S64–S73 (2011)
13. PK Gentner, M Wiessflecker, H Arthaber, AL Scholtz, CF Mecklenbräuker, Measured wideband near-field characteristics of an UWB RFID tag with on-chip antenna, in *International Conference on Ultra-Wideband*, (Bologna, 14–16 Sept. 2011), pp. 479–483
14. PK Gentner, G Hofer, AL Scholtz, CF Mecklenbräuker, Accurate measurement of power transfer to an RFID tag with on-chip antenna, in *Progress In Electromagnetics Research Symp*, (Moscow, 18–21 Aug. 2012), pp. 227–230
15. PK Gentner, P Amreich, H Reinisch, G Hofer, A passive ultra wideband tag for radio frequency identification or wireless sensor networks, in *International Conference on Ultra-Wideband*, (Syracuse, 17–20 Sept. 2012), pp. 2–5
16. V Kulkarni, M Muqsith, A 750 Mb/s, 12 pJ/b, 6-to-10 GHz CMOS IR-UWB transmitter with embedded on-chip antenna. IEEE J. Solid-State Circ., **44**(2), 394–403 (2009)
17. K Kim, H Yoon, KK O, On-chip wireless interconnection with integrated antennas, in *Electron Devices Meeting*, (San Francisco, 10–13 Dec. 2000), pp. 485–488
18. Y Wang, D Makadia, M Margala, On-chip integrated antennas - the first challenge for reliable on-chip wireless interconnects, in *Canadian Conference on Electrical and Computer Engineering*, (Ottawa, 7–10 May 2006), pp. 2322–2325
19. T Kikkawa, PK Saha, N Sasaki, K Kimoto, Gaussian monocycle pulse transmitter using 0.18 μm CMOS technology with on-chip integrated antennas for inter-chip UWB communication. IEEE J. Solid-State Circ., **43**(5), 1303–1312 (2008)
20. T Yao, L Tchoketch-Kebir, O Yuryevich, Gordon M, SP Voinigescu, 65GHz Doppler Sensor with On-Chip Antenna in 0.18μm SiGe BiCMOS, in *MTT-S International Microwave Symposium Digest (2006)*, (San Francisco, 11–16 June 2006), pp. 1493–1496
21. PK Gentner, A Adalan, AL Scholtz, CF Mecklenbräuker, Impact analysis of silicon and bondwires on an on-chip antenna, in *European Conference on Antennas and Propagation*, (Prague, 26–30 March 2012), pp. 3168–3172
22. MD Estarki, Y Xing, XU H, RG Vaughan, The effect of gap size on dipole impedance using the induced EMF method, in *URSI International Symposium on Electromagnetic Theory (EMTS)*, Berlin, 16–19 Aug., (IEEE, Piscataway, 2010), pp. 373–376
23. H Reinisch, S Gruber, M Wiessflecker, H Unterassinger, G Hofer, W Pribyl, G Holweg, An electro-magnetic energy harvester with 190nW idle mode power consumption for wireless sensor nodes, in *European Solid-State Circ. Conference*, (Seville, 14–16 Sept. 2010), pp. 234–237

24. I Oppermann, M Hämäläinen, J Iinatti (eds.), *UWB: Theory and Applications* (Wiley, West Sussex, 2004)

25. M Pelissier, J Jantunen, B Gomez, J Arponen, G Masson, S Dia, J Varteva, M Gary, A 112 Mb/s full duplex remotely-powered impulse-UWB RFID transceiver for wireless NV-memory applications. IEEE J. Solid-State Circuits. **46**(4), 916–927 (2011)

# 19

# Implementation of a reconfigurable ASIP for high throughput low power DFT/DCT/FIR engine

Hanan M Hassan[*], Karim Mohammed and Ahmed F Shalash

## Abstract

In this article we present an ASIP design for a discrete fourier transform (DFT)/discrete cosine transform (DCT)/finite impulse response filters (FIR) engine. The engine is intended for use in an accelerator-chain implementation of wireless communication systems. The engine offers a very high degree of flexibility, accepting and accelerating performance approaches that of any-number DFT and inverse discrete fourier transform, one and two dimension DCT, and even general implementations of FIR equations. Performance approaches that of dedicated implementations of such algorithms. A customized yet flexible redundant memory map allows processor-like access while maintaining the pipeline full in a dedicated architecture-like manner. The engine is supported by a proprietary software tool that automatically sets the rounding pattern for the accelerator rounder to maintain a required signal to quantization noise or output RMS for any given algorithm. Programming of the processor is done through a mid-level language that combines register-specific instructions with DFT/DCT/FIR specific-instructions. Overall the engine allows users to program a very wide range of applications with software-like ease, while delivering performance very close to hardware. This puts the engine in an excellent spot in the current wireless communications environment with its profusion of multi-mode and emerging standards.

**Keywords:** DFT, DCT, FIR, ASIP, reconfigurable hardware

## 1 Introduction

The rapid increase in the performance demand of wireless communication systems combined with the proliferation of standards both finalized and unfinalized has increased the need for a paradigm shift in the design of communication system blocks. Recent trends favor Software Defined Radio (SDR) systems due to their scalability and the ability to support multiple standards on the same platform. However, keeping performance within acceptable levels while doing this is a challenging research question.

Different approaches have been taken to address this question. Authors of [1-3] used Digital Signal Processors (DSPs) owing to their high configurability and adaptive capabilities. Although DSP performance is improving, it is still impractical due to its high power consumption and low throughput. On the other hand [4,5] used configurable HW systems due to the high performance afforded by such platforms. However, these designs fail to catch up with the rapid growth in communication

standards; they only support a limited class of algorithms for which they are specifically designed. Application specific instruction processors (ASIPs) offer an interesting position between the two approaches, allowing programming-like flexibility for a certain class of applications under speed and power constraints.

Different approaches to ASIPs offer different levels of flexibility. For example: [6-8] proposed an ASIP design which has the reconfigurability to support all/some functions of the physical layer Orthogonal Frequency Division (OFDM) receiver chain including OFDM Modulation/Demodulation, channel estimation, turbo decoder, etc. This reconfigurability between non-similar functions has a severe effect on performance, lowering throughput, raising power, or both. Realizing that these blocks operate simultaneously in a pipeline in an OFDM receiver, a different approach to partitioning the problem can be taken.

The work presented provides a limited class of MICRO-CODED programmable solutions to support a large class of OFDM wireless applications. The receiver chain is divided to four main ASIP processors seen in Figure 1.

---

* Correspondence: sep_cameo@yahoo.com
Center for Wireless Studies, Faculty of Engineering, Cairo University, Giza, Egypt

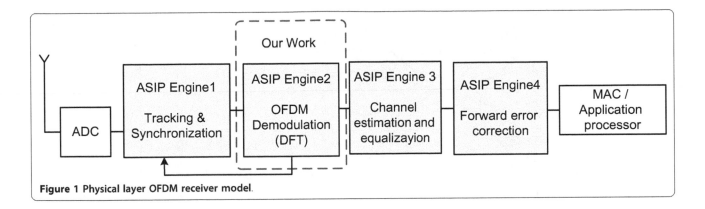

**Figure 1 Physical layer OFDM receiver model.**

Each block has enough flexibility to support an extensive set of applications and configurations within its class while at the same time preserving hardwired-like performance.

This chapter proposes the OFDM Modulation/Demodulation block which is basically based on Discrete Fourier Transform (DFT) and extended to support similar transformations like Discrete Cosine Transform (DCT) and finite impulse response filters (FIR). DFTs, DCTs, and FIRs are used in innumerable communication and signal processing applications. For example: the DFT is commonly used in high data rate Orthogonal Frequency Division Multiplexing (OFDM) systems such as Long Term Evolution (LTE), WiMax, WiLAN, DVB-T, etc; one of the main reasons is to increase robustness against frequency selective fading and narrow-band interference. One and two dimensional DCT are often used in audio and image processing systems such as interactive multimedia, digital TV-NTSC, low bit rate video conferencing, etc; owing to its compaction of energy into the lower frequencies. Finally FIR, is commonly used in digital signal processing applications that have a frequency spectrum with a wide range of frequency to filter frequency components by isolation, rejection or attenuation depending on system implementation.

### 1.1 Paper overview

We build on previous studies in [9,10] where we presented a memory based architecture controlled by an instruction set processor. In this study we combine all elements of the design: performing further optimization on the processing elements (PE) to increase their flexibility and performance; as well as presenting a complete implementation including the full memory map and the programming front-end.

The supported mathematical algorithms are discussed in Section 2, This is followed by the system architecture and embedded processor in Section 3. The hardware (HW) accelerators in Section 4, and engine programing with coding example in Section 5. Section 6 details ASIC results and comparison among previously published designs. Section 7 concludes the article.

## 2 Supported algorithms

The engine can support multiple algorithms some of these algorithms are listed below.

### 2.1 DFT

$N$-point Discrete Fourier Transform is defined as:

$$\text{DFT}(x_n) = \sum_{n=0}^{N-1} x(n) W_N^{kn} \tag{1}$$

where: $\begin{cases} k = 0, \ldots N - 1 \\ W_N = e^{-2\pi i/N} \end{cases}$

The direct implementation of Equation (1) is $O(N^2)$ which makes it difficult to meet typical throughput requirements. Common DFT symbol length in different communication and signal processing standard is in form $2^x$ except LTE down link which supports length $1536 = 2^9 \times 3$. Thus optimizing the throughput of a $2^x \times 3^y$-point DFT is our main concern.

Cooley-Tukey [11] proposed radix-$r$ algorithms, which reduce the $N$-point DFT computational complexity to $O(N \log_r N)$. The main principle of these algorithms is decomposing the computation of the discrete fourier transform of a sequence of length $N$ into smaller discrete fourier transforms see Figure 2.

For lower computation cycle counts, Higher radix algorithm should be used. In practice, the radix-2 algorithm throughput requires four times the number of cycles than the radix-4 algorithm and radix-4 algorithm requires four times the number of cycles of the radix-8 algorithm. On the other hand, higher radix implementations have big butterflies thus they consume higher power and need more complex address generators to handle data flow.

From this trade of between the radix-$r$ algorithm throughput and used butterfly size. We defined the

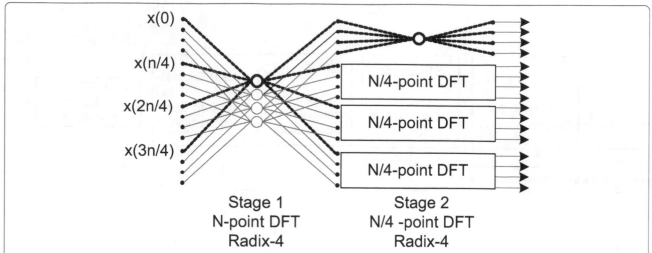

**Figure 2** Flow graph of the decimation-in-frequency decomposition of an *N*-point DFT computation into four (N/4)-point DFT computations (*N* = 16).

parameter power efficiency which introduces how much power is taken to have certain throughput. Table 1 shows a comparison between the three radix butterflies. For fair comparison we toke the following assumptions:

- Fix the address generators complexity, by assuming the data are read from memory 4 samples by 4 samples.
- Normalize butterfly power by number of complex multipliers on it, which is the the dominant power consumer in the butterfly.

$$\text{Power efficiency} = \frac{\text{Power}}{\text{Throughput}} \approx \frac{\text{No of multipliers}}{1/\text{No of cycles to end}} \quad (2)$$

From Table 1 The Radix-4 algorithm have a lowest power consumption in addition to its regularity, it more interested specially in memory based architectures. Radix-4 algorithm supports only $4^z$-point DFTs, So radix-2 and radix-3 algorithms are required to support all symbol lengths in the form of $2^x \times 3^y$. Radix-4, 2 and 3 butterflies are shown in Figures 3 and 4.

### 2.2 Inverse DFT

Swapping the real and imaginary parts of input and output data of DFT, we can get the *N*-point Inverse Discrete Fourier Transform (IDFT) (Equation 3) of a sequence $X(K)$ scaled by $N$ (Equation 4).

$$\text{IDFT}(X_k) = \frac{1}{N} \sum_{n=0}^{N-1} X(k) W_N^{-kn}, \quad k = 0, \dots, N-1 \quad (3)$$

$$\text{IDFT}(X_k) * N = \sum_{n=0}^{N-1} X(k) W_N^{-kn} = \left( \sum_{k=0}^{N-1} X^{*T}(k) W_N^{kn} \right)^{*T}$$

$$\text{IDFT}(X_k)^{*T} \underbrace{N}_{\text{scale factor}} = \underbrace{\sum_{k=0}^{N-1} X^{*T}(k) W_N^{kn}}_{\text{DFT of x*T}} \quad (4)$$

**Table 1 Energy consumed for *N*-point FFT vs.**

| Algorithm | Radix-2 | Radix-4 | Radix-8 |
|---|---|---|---|
| Number of butterflies | 2 | 1 | 1 |
| Number of stages | $\log_2(N)$ | $\log_4(N)$ | $\log_8(N)$ |
| Number of butterflies operations/stage | $\dfrac{N}{2}$ | $\dfrac{N}{4}$ | $\dfrac{N}{8}$ |
| Number of clock cycles/butterflies | 1 | 1 | 2 |
| Total number of clock cycles for *N*-point FFT | $\dfrac{N}{4}\log_2(N)\left(\dfrac{N}{4}\right)(x)$ | $\dfrac{N}{4}\log_4(N)\left(\dfrac{N}{4}\right)\left(\dfrac{x}{2}\right)$ | $\dfrac{N}{4}\log_8(N) \times 2\left(\dfrac{N}{4}\right)\left(\dfrac{x}{3}\right)$ |
| Normalized power | 2 | 3 | 7 |
| Power efficiency | $0.5 \times N \times x$ | $0.375 \times N \times x$ | $0.43 \times N \times x$ |
| As $N = 2^x$ | | | |

Radix-*r* algorithms

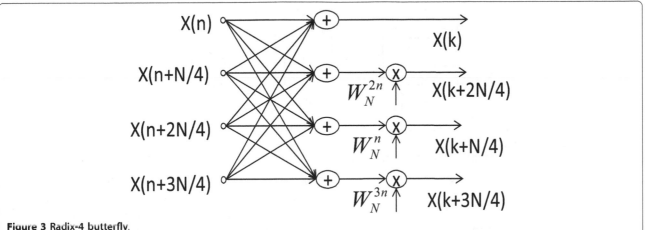

**Figure 3** Radix-4 butterfly.

## 2.3 DCT

Several types of the DCT of a sequence $x(n)$ are defined in [12]. The most popular being type II which is defined as:

$$\text{DCT}(x_n) = \omega(k) \sum_{n=0}^{N-1} x(n) \cos\left(\frac{(2n+1)\pi k}{2N}\right), \quad \omega(k) = \begin{cases} \sqrt{1/N} & k \neq 0 \\ \sqrt{2/N} & k = 0 \end{cases} \quad (5)$$

Braganza and Leeser [13] proposed an implemention to get a real DCT from the DFT by constructing a sequence $v(n)$ from real input data $x(n)$ as follows:

$$v(n) = \begin{cases} x(n) & n = 0 \ldots N - 1 \\ x(2N - n - 1) & n = N \ldots 2N - 1 \end{cases} \quad (6)$$

Then the output of $\text{DFT}(v_n)$ is multiplied by

$$2\omega(k)e^{\frac{-i2\pi k}{2N}}.$$

## 2.4 Inverse DCT

The inverse DCT of type II is type III which is defined as:

$$\text{IDCT}(x_k) = \sum_{k=0}^{N-1} \omega(k) X_k \cos\left(\frac{(2n+1)\pi k}{2N}\right), \quad \omega(k) = \sqrt{2/N} \quad (7)$$

For the IDCT, we reverse the above steps. First, $X(k)$ is rearranged to form a complex hermitian symmetric sequence $V(k)$:

$$V(k) = \frac{1}{2} e^{\frac{j\pi k}{2N}} [x(k) - jx(N - k)], \quad k = 0, 1, 2 \ldots N - 1 \quad (8)$$

Then construct $v(n)$ by getting the IDFT of $V(k)$, finally rearrange $v(n)$ to get $x(n)$.

### 2-Dimension modes

For 2D modes, the 1D mode is performed two times: one time in all rows of input frame then another time on the columns of the result Figure 5.

### 2.5 FIR

The FIR filter Equation (9) is handled using multiply accumulate (MAC) operations and accelerated by using Multiple computing units.

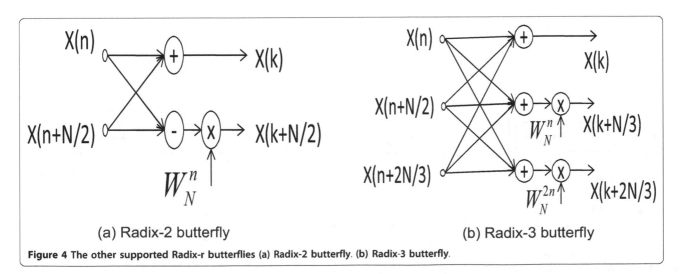

(a) Radix-2 butterfly

(b) Radix-3 butterfly

**Figure 4** The other supported Radix-r butterflies (a) Radix-2 butterfly. (b) Radix-3 butterfly.

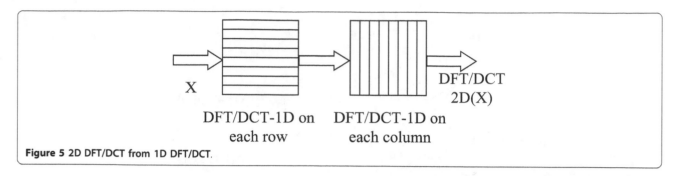

**Figure 5** 2D DFT/DCT from 1D DFT/DCT.

$$\gamma_t = \sum_{k=0}^{N-1} x(k)a_{t-k} \qquad (9)$$

where a's are the filter coefficients.

### 2.6 Other transformations

Other transformations like any-point DFT can also be handled using basic operations like MAC, accumulator and vector operations.

### 3 ASIP processor

Embedded architectures are divided to pipelined [14] and memory based architectures (iterative designs) [5,15]. The pipelined architectures are constructed from long chain from butterflies connected to individual memories. For example to support 4K-DFT by pipelined architecture like Radix-4 Singlepath Delay Feedback (R4SDF) [16] (seen in Figure 6). It needs six pipeline radix-4 butterflies (three complex multipliers) connected to six dual port memories. The memories have a read and write operation in each clock cycle. While The memory based architectures usually consist of one butterfly with only two dual port memories. The memories in the based architectures have also a read and write operation in each clock cycle which is approximately similar to the memory transactions in the pipelined architectures. From this discussion we prefer to use memory-based architecture and we prove our selection in Section 6 by comparing our results versus anther publish pipeline architecture.

The first step in the design of a flexible and efficient ASIP is to identify the common set of operations in the class of operations which must be supported. The computationally intensive operations are defined as coefficient-generation, address-generation, and PE. These operations are supported by HW acceleration.

To meet the high throughput demand, data operations are handled through vector instructions. Synchronization in the processing pipeline is handled through handshakes between the system blocks. This greatly reduces the load on decoders, allowing continuous flow in the pipeline and providing dedicated design-like throughput.

The critical path in the PE is relatively short. This simplicity combined with the high throughput of the pipeline allows the user to greatly under clock the circuit, thus allowing significant power scaling with application.

When a valid configuration radix-r stage is received, the HW accelerators are configured to operate on a user selected DFT/IDFT size. The read address generator is responsible for generating data addresses with their memory enables and giving its state to the coefficient generator to maintain synchronization between data and coefficients. The data and coefficients are handed to the PE which is configured to apply radix-$r$ calculations. Upon finishing, the PE enables the write address generator and finally the processed data is saved in the 2nd memory Figure 7.

To allow instantaneous reading and writing and to keep the pipeline full, two $N$-word memories are used

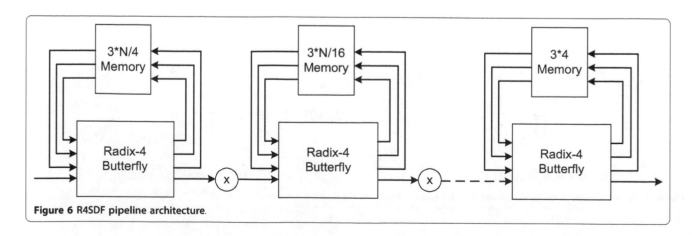

**Figure 6** R4SDF pipeline architecture.

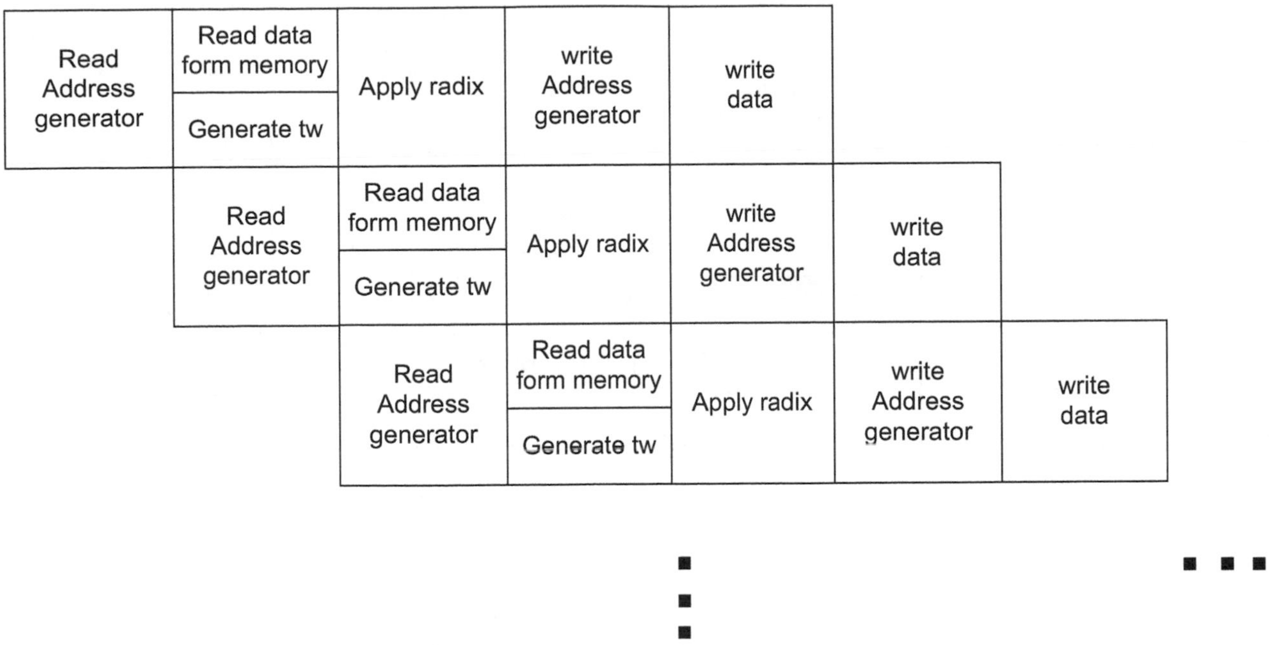

**Figure 7** Pipeline process.

one for reading data and another for writing results. The source and destination memories are exchanged each stage. Each memory contains four dual port banks and has four input and output complex data buses to match the configurable memory requirements. The memory bus controller is responsible for applying the input and output data to the corresponding memory banks depending on its bank number and the memory state (read or write). Memory architecture is shown in Figure 8.

In the embedded processor architecture seen in Figure 9, input/output signals handle the interface between the decoder and the external environment. Depending on the external environment state, the decoder enables data transmission, importing, exporting or both. The I/O data bus contains four complex word buses, two for importing data and the other for exporting.

The boot-loading memory consists of a non-volatile bank responsible for initializing the processor RAMs with the required micro-code. The engine is controlled by a non-pipelined decoder with 16 registers in the register file and a 26-bit instruction set with 66 instructions.

(1) The register file is divided into even and odd sets, the real parts of complex words are saved in the even registers and the imaginary parts in following odd registers. Complex words are called by their real register number while a real word may be saved in any register and called by its index.

(2) The instruction set is divided into five classes:

- Radix instructions like: Radix-2/3/4, Inverse Radix-2/3/4 used for DFT.
- MAC instructions for FIR: multiply two data vectors and accumulate, multiply data vector by coefficient and accumulate.
- Vector Multiplications instructions For DCT/IDCT: multiply by coefficient,
- Vector instructions like: accumulate, power, energy, addition, subtraction, multiplication, multiply by coefficient used to perform general vector arithmetic.
- Word instructions like: shift, set, load, store, complex or word addition, subtraction, multiplication used mostly for control.
- Data transmission instructions like: data arrangement, data importing and exporting.
- Control instructions like: compare, conditional/unconditional branches, disable/enable dealing with imaginary part.

All vector instructions are applicable on complex words and have the ability to define the order in which data is read or written. MAC instructions are used for general implementations of FIR equations. MAC allows multiplication of data by data or data by stored or generated coefficients. MAC and Vector multiplication instructions allow multiplication by coefficients or their inverse for general transformations purpose.

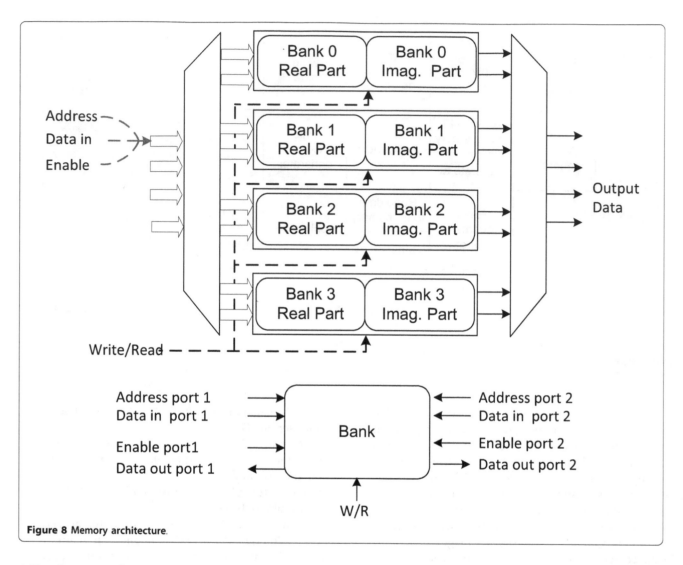

**Figure 8** Memory architecture.

## 4 Hardware accelerators

### 4.1 Processing element

The PE is the primary computational unit of the engine see Figure 10. The PE can be set to perform two radix-2 butterflies, one radix-3/4 butterfly For DFT implementations, multiply For DCT/IDCT multiplication stage, multiply accumulate for general FIR implementations in addition to other operations like accumulate, addition and subtraction. It is divided into four units: Constant multiplier unit, Addition unit, Multiplication unit, and finally Rounder unit. To increase utilization we time-share the complex multiplier to perform constant multiplication functions, that is to say constant multiplier CM and multiplier 1 $M1$ in Figure 10 use the same multipliers. Data width naturally grows with processing, this is a major question in fixed-point ASIP applications. A rounder unit is placed at the final stage to re-fit data in a constant number of bits (word length). Stage scale factors can be set by the programmer and a proprietary software

tool automatically generates the necessary scale factors for a given application. Complex multipliers are configured to multiply input 1 by input 2 or input 2 conjugate. Adder 3 is responsible for accumulate operations, so it is provided by a scalable truncator to prevent overflow. Multiplexers at the input and output data pins are used to swap their real and imaginary parts for inverse operations. The additional multiplexers configure the butterfly and bypass some stages like the multiplication stage.

### 4.2 Coefficient generator

The coefficient generator generates needed coefficients in two modes.

*Mode one:* Generates twiddle factors needed for Radix-$r$ and DCT/IDCT Multiplication stage calculations. The first N/4 coefficients are stored in RAM and the remaining coefficients are generated by using the even and odd symmetry properties in the phase and amplitude of twiddle factor (Equations 10 and 11).

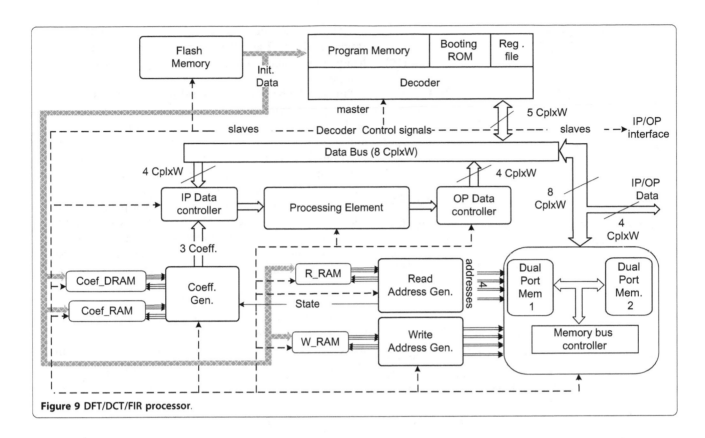

**Figure 9** DFT/DCT/FIR processor.

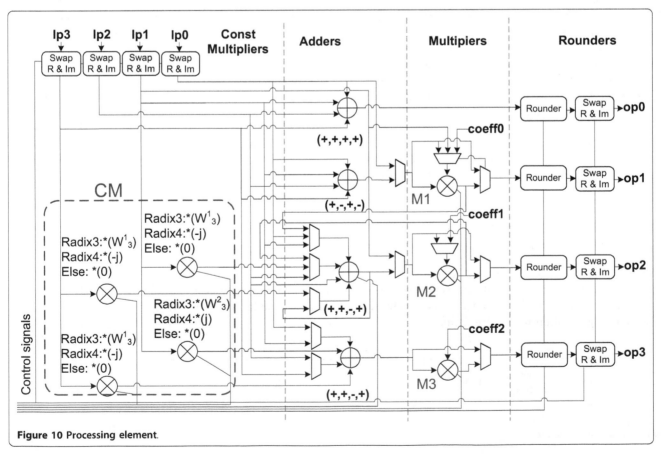

**Figure 10** Processing element.

$$e^{j2\pi \frac{n}{N}} = e^{j2\pi \frac{n'}{N}} e^{j2\pi \frac{x \times N/4}{N}} \tag{10}$$

$$= e^{j2\pi \frac{n'}{N}} \times E(x), \qquad n' = 0, \ldots, N/4$$

$$E(x) = e^{j2\pi \frac{x}{4}}, \quad x = 0, 1, 2, 3 \tag{11}$$

$$= 1, j, -1, -j$$

For $e^{-j2\pi \frac{n}{N}}$ we invert the imaginary part's sign. For radix-4 computations we need to generate three twiddle factors at a time, so we use two memories, the first memory is a dual-port RAM and is used to generate $e^{-j2\pi \frac{n}{N}}$ and $e^{-j2\pi \frac{3n}{N}}$. The second memory is a single-port RAM which is used to generate $e^{-j2\pi \frac{2n}{N}}$. For frame lengths with $x > 2$, the 2nd memory addresses are always even. So we remove all odd entries. This reduction adds a negligible noise in $x = 2$ case. For frame lengths with $x = 1$ we replace $N$ by $N'(N' = 4 \times 3^y)$. Consequently we save the first $N'/4 = 3^y$ coefficients in RAM. To save power the 2nd memory is enabled only in radix-4 stage.

This method reduces coefficient memory size to 18% of a direct LUT implementation.

*Mode two:* Read stored coefficients from the first RAM starting from selected address and going in ascending or descending order depending on selected mode. This is more suitable for FIR transformation and direct implementations of general filters.

### 4.3 Read and write address generators

Generate continuous write and read addresses depending on their modes. The address bus is divided into four partitions: real part enable, imaginary part enable, bank number and bank index see Figure 11.

Each generator is connected to a single port RAM to get off-line generated addresses. Read and write address memories hold two addresses in each entry. To enable reading four sequential addresses in one clock cycle, write address memory is divided into two single port RAMs, one for odd entries and another for even entries.

The address generation modes are defined as:

*Mode one:* Generate addresses for different radix-$r$ stages. Radix-4, 2 and 3 need to read 4, 4 (two radix-2 handled in parallel), 3 data samples respectively for their computations.

This can be handled in several ways: Read data from memory 2 samples by 2 samples with 2 clock latency for each radix operation, double memory clock frequency and read 2 samples by 2 samples with 1 clock latency for each radix operation at the expense of double memory power, or use 4-port memories. Each of the above techniques have drawbacks to different degrees like lower throughput, power or both. In [10] we proposed an address scheme to solve the above problem with conflict-free memory access. The scheme is contingent on partitioning the memory to 4 dual-port memory banks as well as the specific way data is distributed between the banks. This guarantees that at any stage we have at most two accesses to the same memory bank.

Initially data is saved and distributed between memory banks to be ready for the first radix stage (radix-4 or 3). As $N = 2^x \times 3^y$, $(x \neq 1)$, if $x$ is even (integer stages from radix-4) the butterfly performs radix-4 computations till the end then switches to perform radix-3 stages. Else (if $x$ odd) the butterfly performs $(\frac{x-1}{2})$ radix-4 stages followed by radix-2 then switches to perform radix-3 stages. Switching to radix-3 stages consumes a one-time additional stage to rearrange data in memory banks. At last radix-$r$ stage, radix output is saved in the same locations of radix inputs.

Samples at any stage are saved in memory depending on the current radix stage ($r$), current DFT frame length ($N$), DFT frame number ($f$), and sample index inside the DFT frame ($n$) see Figure 12. The bank number results from accessing the bank Look Up Table (LUT) (Table 1) by signal bank$_t$, and the data index in the bank (Equation 12).

$$\text{bank}_t = \text{floor}\left(\frac{n}{N/r}\right) \tag{12}$$

$$\text{Bank index} = n \times \text{mod}_{N/r} + f \times \frac{N}{r}$$

*Mode two:* Generate addresses for DCT/IDCT modes to arrange data in $v_n$ and $V_k$ order.

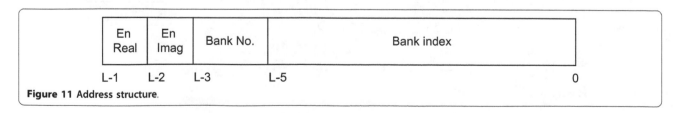

Figure 11 Address structure.

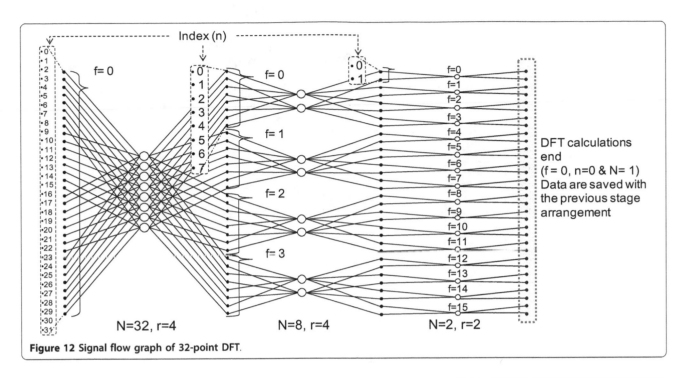

**Figure 12** Signal flow graph of 32-point DFT.

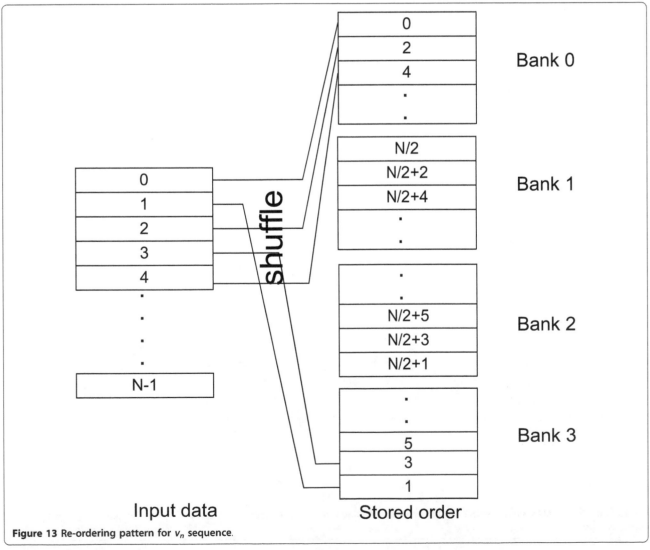

**Figure 13** Re-ordering pattern for $v_n$ sequence.

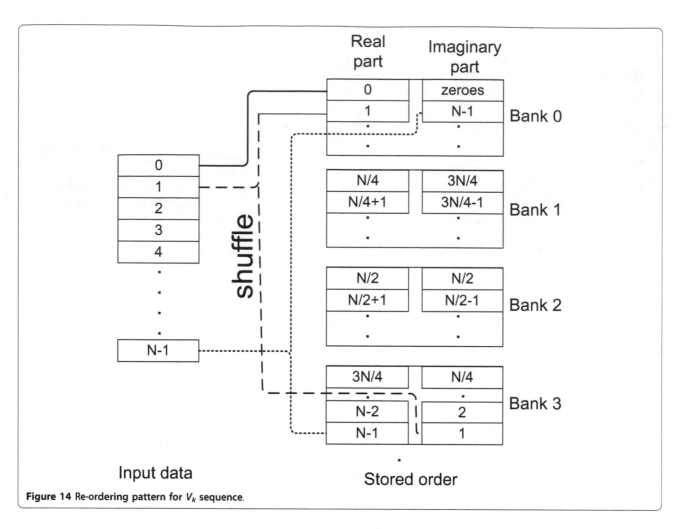

**Figure 14** Re-ordering pattern for $V_k$ sequence.

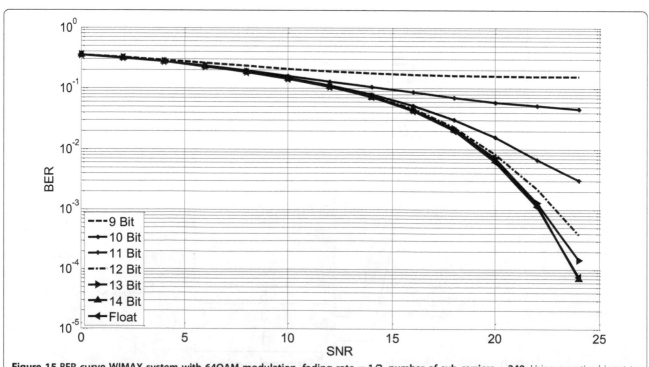

**Figure 15 BER curve WIMAX system with 64QAM modulation, fading rate = 1/2, number of sub carriers = 240.** Using quantized input to quantized DFT module.

For DCT inputs are saved in the shuffled order shown in Figure 13. Data is distributed in the memory banks to allow direct starting for the next radix stage.

In IDCT computation sequence data is ordered in $V_k$ order then multiplied by coefficients in the next stage. In order to save data arrangement time, data is saved in shuffle order shown in Figure 14 then at multiplication stage the multiplier is configured to multiply the coefficients by data conjugate to construct true $V_k$ sequence.

Each input sample is saved in two locations in memory and the data is imported 2 samples by 2 samples in order to reduce data transmission time. So, data is distributed in memory banks to prevent memory conflict.

*Mode three:* Generate addresses for other vector instructions like MAC. It generates two addresses for two data vectors or one data vector (two samples at time) in-order sequence or get them form memory. With start addresses and data length as an input parameters.

## 5 Engine programming

The embedded processor programming passes through three phases: Simulation, testing, and verification. We will discuss 1024-point DFT, 8 × 8 DCT and 64 tap FIR as case studies.

### 5.1 Simulation

The goal of these simulations is to find best values of our design which are: the scale factor which we divide on each radix-$r$ stage, word length and coefficient factors length.

#### 5.1.1 Scale factor

Due to the nature of DFT operation the output data range is growth with the radix stages. So, the data must be scaled after each radix-r stage to refit in fixed number of bits. If this scale is large the data will be lost, on the other hand if it is small many overflows will occur, so stage scale must be well chosen. We considerate this point and designed an optimum scales generator tool to select the best scale on each stage with two modes:

(1) Select the Highest SQNR.

(2) Guaranteed output RMS, to keep signal peaks which are needed in same applications.

The tool are designed by Matlab software, it generate all possible scale factors with corresponding signal to quantization noise (SQNR) and the RMS of the output then select the best scale vector Depending on the input mode. Using the first mode for our example reveals scale factors of (4 4 2 2 2) for 1024 point five stages, giving the highest SQNR with a Gaussian input.

```
% reset all registers
    set  0,r0
    set  0,r1
    set  0,r2
    set  0,r3
    set  0,r4
    set  0,r5
    set  0,r6
    set  0,r7
    set  0,r8
    set  0,r9
    set  0,r10
    set  0,r11
    set  0,r12
    set  0,r13
    set  0,r14
    set  0,r15

% Data length = 1024
    set  1024,r0
% load instructions to program memory
%start address of  Instructions  in flash = 0
    bootload   pm,0
% Load instructions to read address RAM
    bootload   r_mem,1024
    bootload   w_mem,2048
    bootload   ws_mem1,3072
    bootload   ws_mem2,4096
    set  2 ,r0
    bootload   s_reg,5120
    set  0,r0
% jumb to program memory
    jumb  pm
```

**Figure 16** Boot loading initialization instructions.

```
% Set parameters                          shiftr   r4,2,r4
% Input Data length = N/2 = 512           shiftr   r5,2,r5
    set 512,r0   % r0 = 512               shiftr   r0,2,r0
    set 256,r2                            shiftl   r1,2,r1    % r1 = r1 << 2
    set 256,r3                            addimm   r6,1,r6 % counter += 1
% Import new symbol in radix 4 order    % Compare counter,End
  in  (ordr_rdx4)                          comp   r6,r7
% Swap 2 memories                       % Branch if less than
    swap                                     bl      l2
    l1:                                      nop     % no operation after loop
% Radix parameters                      % Last stage radix-4, scale = 2^2
    set 256,r2    % N/4                     l_radx4 (Scape_multi,2)
    set 256,r3    % n/4                     swap
    set 64,r4     % n/16                    set   256,r3
    set 1024,r5   % n                       set   1024,r4
    set 192,r0    % 3n/16                   set   0,r5
    set 4,r1      % N'/N                    set   512,r0
                                           set   0,r1
    set 0,r6      % Counter = 0          % I/O Data
    set 4,r7      % 4 iterations         % Get addresses from memory for exporting data
l2:                                     % Import new symbol in radix 4 order
% Radix 4, scale = 2^2                    io  (mem0, ordr_rdx4)
    n_radx4 (2)                            swap
    swap                                 % Process new symbol
    shiftr   r3,2,r3   % r3 = r3 >> 2      jumb l1
```

**Figure 17** Implementation code example for 1024-point DFT.

```
  set 32,r2                             % disable writing imaginary part
% insert data and distributed it in vn order   % write real part only
  in  vn                                  dis_img write
  l1                                        set  162,r1
  set 0,r6                                  set  16,r2
  set 1,r7                                  set  2,r3
  l2                                        set  64,r4
  swap                                      set  8,r5
  set 648,r1                            % multiply data by coefficients
  set 16,r2                             % read data in order and write result using addresses in memory
  set 2,r3                                vmulti_coef0 (order, memory)
  set 1,r4                              % enale writing imaginary part
  set 8,r5                                en_img write
% radix 4 in all rows                       addimm r6,1,r6 % counter += 1
  n_radx4 (nlst,2)      Radix 4 not last    Compare counter,End
  swap                                      comp r6,r7
  shiftr r3,2,r3    n                      % Branch if less than
  shiftr r4,2,r4    n                      bl l2
  shiftr r5,2,r5    n                      nop % no operation after loop
  shiftl r1,2,r1    n                      set 6,r0
% radix 2 in all rows                       set 0,r1
  radx2 (lst,2)      Radix 4 not last    % out processed data and enter new one
  swap                                      io  (mem, vn)
                                         % repeat again
                                           jumb l1
                                           nop
```

**Figure 18** Implementation code example for 8 × 8 DCT.

```
% 64 tap filter                        | % Mac,Get coef in descending order
    set  64,r0                         | % get coefficint from start address= t
    set 64, r4                         |    mov  r1, r6
% coefficient start address in memory = 0 |    mac_coef2 (ordr,ordr,2) r3,r6
    set 0, r1                          | % next output
% data start address = 0               |    addimm r6,1,r6
    set  0,r3                          |    Compare counter,End
% insert data in order                 |    comp r6,r4
    in  order                          | % branch if less than
    I1:                                |    bl I2
    set 0,r6  % t                      |    nop
    I2:                                | % out processed data and inset new on in oder
                                       |    io (ordr,ordr)
                                       |    jumb I1
                                       |    nop
```

**Figure 19** Implementation code example for 64 tap FIR.

### 5.1.2 Word and coefficient lengths

Then, Fixed-point simulations of a 1024 point DFT in WiMAX see Figure 15 reveal that a 26 bit (13 real and 13 imaginary) complex word length and 20 bit complex twiddle factors are sufficient to keep quantization noise power under system noise by 15 dB at $10^{-3}$ Bit Error Rate (BER).

### 5.2 Testing

Code for the application is written using custom mnemonics that combine HW-specific instructions with application-specific instructions. This then passes through a assembly compiler (designed by Matlab software) which generates the boot-loading and program object files.

When processing begins, the decoder accesses address zero in the boot loading ROM and reads initialization instructions. These instructions are mainly used for loading data and instructions from flash memory to the corresponding RAM memory in the system. Upon finishing, the decoder jumps to program memory and starts processing.

Figure 16 shows boot loading ROM initialization instructions. The initialization process may include pre-loading some or all of: program memory instructions (pm), coefficients memory (ws_mem1, ws_mem2), coefficients memory length (s_reg), read address memory (r_mem) and write addresses ram (w_mem). Boot-loading is necessary if the engine is to switch modes or standards on-the-fly. Otherwise program RAMs can be replaced by ROMs carrying the required instructions.

### 5.2.1 1024-point DFT

Figure 17 shows code example for 1024-point DFT. In/Out operations read two words at a time, therefore for N words it takes only N/2 clock cycles. To save on processing overhead special control signals like r2 = N/radix (used by address generator) are inserted directly to reduce computational load (by adding this instruction we save the power and area of a full divider). After each stage these parameters are modified, and loop for the

### Table 2 Synthesis results (with memories)

| Up to 8K point-DFT 1D symbol 26 complex word length | |
| --- | --- |
| Technology | IBM 130 nm CMOS technology (6 layers) |
| Volt | 1.08 V |
| Libraries | Gates libraries: Typical (55°c) |
| | Fast library(125°c) used for worst case conditions |
| | Memories library: (125°c) |
| Number of Cells | 57,906 cell |
| Area | 0.612 × 0.6 (0.36) mm$^2$ |
| Power | 56 mw at 100 MHz |
| Max frequency | 700 MHz |

### Table 3 Number of clock cycles and SQNR for 1D-DFT including data transfer times between the embedded engine and the host

| N -point DFT | Cycles per | Latency @ 100 MHz | SQNR Scale factor | Scale factor | | | | | | |
| --- | --- | --- | --- | --- | --- | --- | --- | --- | --- | --- |
| DFT | DFT | (dB) | (µs) | s1 | s2 | s3 | s4 | s5 | s6 | s7 |
| 64 | 146 | 1.46 | 83.67 | 4 | 2 | 2 | | | | |
| 128 | 278 | 2.78 | 86.16 | 4 | 2 | 2 | 2 | | | |
| 256 | 470 | 4.7 | 96.839 | 4 | 4 | 2 | 2 | | | |
| 512 | 1002 | 10.02 | 96.37 | 4 | 4 | 2 | 2 | 2 | | |
| 1024 | 1898 | 18.98 | 99.1 | 4 | 4 | 2 | 2 | 2 | | |
| 2048 | 4222 | 42.22 | 98.97 | 4 | 4 | 2 | 2 | 2 | 2 | |
| 4096 | 8318 | 83.18 | 97.84 | 4 | 4 | 4 | 2 | 2 | 2 | |
| 8192 | 18578 | 185.78 | 95.25 | 4 | 4 | 4 | 2 | 2 | 2 | 2 |

**Table 4 Number of clock cycles for 1D-DCT including data transfer times between the embedded engine and the host**

| N -point DCT | Cyles per DCT | Latency @ 100 MHz (μs) |
| --- | --- | --- |
| 64 | 177 | 1.77 |
| 256 | 592 | 5.92 |
| 512 | 1247 | 12.47 |
| 1024 | 2399 | 23.99 |

next radix stage. The twiddle factors in the last stage in DFT calculations are ones so we add choice (Scape multi, multi) to disable the twiddle factors generator and bypass multiplication stage. Thus the last radix instruction is separated from the loop. Then apply *io* instruction to export the processed symbol and import a new one. finally, jump to the first radix stage and so on.

### 8 × 8 DCT

Figure 18 shows code example for 8 × 8 DCT. Data is read, row by row, saving each row in $v_n$ order discussed in Section 2. Then radix stages are applied until DFT calculations on all rows are completed. The data is multiplied by the twiddle factors, by getting addresses from read address memory (to arrange data after DFT operation and exchange row by column). Writing the result is in $v_n$ order (construct $v_n$ for new DCT-1D operation). The imaginary parts of result are set to zero by disabling writing of imaginary results. Then, the radix and multiplication stages are applied once more. Finally, the result is output in order and the new data is simultaneously loaded.

### 5.2.2 FIR filter

Figure 19 shows code example for a 64 tap FIR. Data is read in order. Multiply accumulate operation are applied on the data to generate first output $y(0)$. increment output index and apply MAC for next output and so on. Till the last output $(N - 1)$ is generated. Finally, the result is output in order and the new data is simultaneously loaded.

### 5.3 Verification

Verification of these and other examples is through bit-matching the results of random input patterns with fixed-point results from fixed point golden files. The golden files are verified and tested against a floating

**Table 5 Number of clock cycles for 2D-DCT including data transfer times between the embedded engine and the host**

| N × N-point DCT | Cycles per DCT | Latency @ 100 MHz (μs) |
| --- | --- | --- |
| 8 × 8 | 186 | 1.86 |
| 16 × 16 | 390 | 3.9 |
| 32 × 32 | 1724 | 17.24 |
| 64 × 64 | 6380 | 63.8 |

point model to make sure they perform the needed tasks. The golden files are used to verify the RTL design by generating test cases, both directed and random.

## 6 Implementation results and performance evaluation

### 6.1 Implementation

The engine is fully designed by the authors, using Verilog Hardware Description language and tested by applying various programming codes. Synthesis has been carried out using Cadence first encounter using IBM 130 nm CMOS technology. The post layout synthesis results report of the entire design with 26 bit complex word length, 20 bit complex twiddle factors and support for up to 8K-point DFT include system memories has been summarized in Table 2. The table also maintain all synthesis constraints. The engine parameters like the number of bits, memories size and types are parametrized to meet different requirements.

### 6.2 Performance evaluation

Tables 3, 4, and 5 show a summary of features of our proposed embedded processor.

Table 6 has a list of power consumption values for previously published articles. To eliminate the process factor to make the comparisons as fair as possible, the power consumption of each design has been normalized to 130 nm technology, 1.08 V and engine throughput by Equation (13) [17]. We define the parameter power efficiency which introduces how much power is taken to have certain throughput to make fair comparisons between the engines power in the case of they have same throughput. This shows, at the very least, that the proposed engine has a significant advantage in power consumption.

$$\text{Normalized power} = \text{Power} \times \left(\frac{130}{\text{Technology}}\right) \times \left(\frac{1.08}{\text{Volt}}\right)^2$$
$$\text{Power efficiency} = \frac{\text{Normalized power}}{\text{Throughput}} = \frac{\text{Normalized power}}{1/\text{Time to end}} \quad (13)$$

### 6.3 Discussion

Weidong and Wanhammar [14] proposed an pipeline ASIC for pipeline FFT processor. Here we prove our discussion in Section 3, the pipeline architecture have a higher throughput but loss on power efficiency.

The authors of [5,18,19] proposed memory based Application-Specific Integrated Circuit (ASIC) for scalable DFT engine. The proposed engine in [5] enables runtime configuration of the DFT length, where the supported lengths vary only from 16-points to 4096. while the proposed engine in [18] enables reconfigurable FFT Processor, the FFT lengths vary only from 128-points to 8192. and [19] can perform 64 2048-point FFT. This engines have high throughput rates. But, they only

**Table 6 Number of clock cycles and SQNR for 1D-DFT including data transfer times between the embedded engine and the host**

| Reference | Implementation | Technology (nm) | Parameters | | | | | | | |
|---|---|---|---|---|---|---|---|---|---|---|
| | | | volt (V) | Frequency (MHz) | Max-point DFT | Time to end (μs) | Power (mW) | Normalized power | Power efficiency | SQNR (dB) |
| [14] | Pipeline HW | 350 | 1.5 | 25 | 1K | 40.96 | 200 | 35.6 | 1.4 | N/A |
| [25] | Configurable HW | 180 | 1.8 | 86 | 8K | 805 | 75.51 | 19.6 | 15.8 | N/A |
| [18] | Configurable HW | 180 | 1.8 | 200 | 8K | 395 | 117 | 84.2 | 33 | N/A |
| [5] | Configurable HW | 65 | 1.3 | 866 | 4K | 7.1 | 35 | 48.3 | 0.3 | 71.90 |
| [26] | Configurable HW | 180 | 1.8 | 150 | 8K | 138 | 350 | 91 | 12.5 | N/A |
| [19] | Configurable HW | 180 | 1.8 | 70 | 2K | 224 | 140 | 36.4 | 8.15 | N/A |
| [2] | DSP | - | - | 100 | 1K | 403.3 | N/A | N/A | N/A | N/A |
| [20] | ASIP | 250 | 2.5 | 100 | 4K | 52.80 | 275 | 26.6 | 1.4 | 61.23 |
| [21] | ASIP | 180 | 1.8 | 300 | 1K | 13.8 | N/A | N/A | N/A | N/A |
| | | | | | 1K | 18.98 | 19 | 19 | 0.3 | 99.1 |
| Proposed | ASIP | 130 | 1.08 | 100 | 4K | 42.2 | 25 | 25 | 1.05 | 97.84 |
| | | | | | 8K | 185.7 | 56 | 56 | 10.3 | 95.25 |

[21]: Present the power consumption of functional unit and data address generator only

support certain kinds of algorithms for which they are designed.

In contrast, [2] used digital signal processors owing to their high reconfigurability and adaptive capabilities. Although DSP performance is improving, it is still unsuitable due to its high power consumption and low throughput. Hsu and Lin [2] proposed an approach for DFT implementation on DSP with low-memory reference and high flexibility, however it is optimized for $2^x$-point DFT, It needs 40,338 cycles to complete one 1024-point DFT.

The third solution, [20,21] is the ASIP which compromises between the above solutions. Zhong et al. [20] proposed an DFT/IDFT processor based on multi-processor rings. This engine presents four processor rings (8, 16-Point FFT) and supports DFT lengths from 16-points to 4096. Guan et al. [21] proposed an ASIP scalable

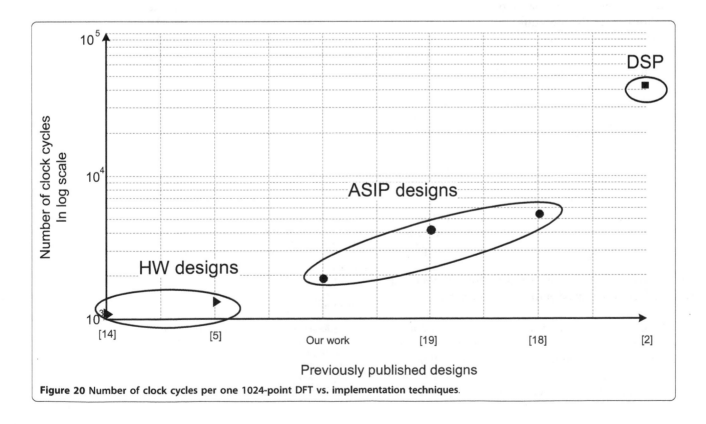

**Figure 20** Number of clock cycles per one 1024-point DFT vs. implementation techniques.

**Table 7 Applications that can be supported and the corresponding estimated clock frequency**

| DFT-1D applications | 90 MHz | LTE, WI-MAX, WLAN, DVB-T, DVB-T, DVB-H, DAB, ADSLs and VDSL |
|---|---|---|
| DCT-2D applications | 60 MHz | Low bit rate video conferencing, basic video telephony, interactive multimedia and digital TV-NTSC |

architecture of any-point DFT at the expense of a large PE (contains an 8-point butterfly). the authors present only the power consumption of functional unit and data address generator so we did not include it in the table.

From our investigation, Figure 20 shows comparison between implementation techniques throughput.

Shah et al. [22] presents a pipelined scalable any-point DFT 1D/2D engine which requires 256 clock cycles for (16 × 16)-DFT 2D, while [23] and this design require 512 cycles. Nevertheless, Sohil Shah's proposal has higher area.

For DCT-1D, we use the mathematical algorithm in [12] which implements ASIC DCT-1D bulting blocks common with DFT. The engine has a throughput of one 512-point DCT per 1,771 cycles, and one 1024-point DFT per 3435 cycles.

For DCT-2D existence designs, the engine in [24] has been tailored to a particular application needing 80 cycle for (8 × 8)-DCT 2D, and programmable DSP [1] supports scalable ($N \times N$)-DCT 2D as N = 4-64. needs 2,538 cycles for (16 × 16)-DCT 2D,

The proposed engines are more power efficient than most of other proposed architectures in the literature. Engine features:

- More power efficient than most of other proposed architectures in the literature.
- Could be support many OFDM Systems with relatively low power.
- High reconfigurability which allows users to program a very wide range of applications with software-like ease.
- Support peripheral operations beside the main processes like CP remover which was need in the proposed WiMAX demo.
- Simple interfaces (FIFO interface) which handle data transfer between the engine and asynchronous blocks with different clock domains.
- The engine parameters like the number of bits, memories size and types are parameterized to meet different requirements and higher symbol lengths

The features that helped to get a high throughput which helped to get good power efficiency are:

- A new address generation scheme allows reading and writing the butterfly data in one clock cycle which allow performing 1 butterfly operation each clock. This reduce processing time by 50% without doubling the clock frequency no loss on power.

- The selection of radix-4 algorithm which have best power efficiency.
- Using HW accelerators accelerate the processing and reduce the complicity of the decoder.
- Using pipeline processing of the vector instructions is also accelerate the processing.
- Using simultaneously input and output data transformations with four data buses which reduce data transformations time by 75%.
- Reduce time to market by supporting a compiler tool for the engine with a simple instruction set
- The use of classified engines allows high degree of optimization.

## 7 Conclusion

In this article, we propose an ASIP design for low-power configurable embedded processor capable supporting DFT, DCT, FIR among other things. The defining feature of our processor is its reconfigurability supporting multiple transformations for many communication and signal processing standards with simple SW instructions, high SQNR, and relatively high throughput. The engine overall performance allows users to program a very wide range of applications with software-like ease, while delivering performance very close to HW. This puts the engine in an excellent spot in the current wireless communications environment with its profusion of multi-mode and emerging standards. The proposed embedded processor is synthesized in IBM 130 nm CMOS technology. The 8k-point DFT can 56 mW with a 1.08 V supply voltage to end in 13 $\mu$s with SQNR of 95.25 dB. Table 7 shows some applications which can be supported.

**Acknowledgements**
This study was part of a project supported by a grant from STDF, Egypt (Science and Technology Development Fund).

**Competing interests**
The authors declare that they have no competing interests.

**References**
1. Liu X, Wang Y: **Memory Access Reduction Method for efficient implementation of Vector-Radix 2D fast cosine transform pruning on DSP.** *Proceedings of the IEEE SoutheastCon* 2010, 68-72.
2. Hsu YP, Lin SY: **Implementation of Low-Memory Reference FFT on Digital Signal Processor.** *Journal of Computer Science* 2008, 7:545-549.
3. Frigo M, Johnson SG: **The Design and Implementation of FFTW3.** *Proceedings of the IEEE* 2005, **93**:216-231.

4. Jo BG, Sunwoo MH: **New continuous-flow mixed-radix (CFMR) FFT processor using novel in-place strategy.** *IEEE Transactions on Circuits and Systems* 2005, **52(5)**:911-919.

5. Jacobson AT, Truong DN, Baas BM: **The Design of a Reconfigurable Continuous-Flow Mixed-Radix FFT Processor.** *IEEE International Symposium on Circuits and Systems ISCAS* 2009, 1133-1136.

6. Hangpei T, Deyuan G, Yian Z: **Gaining Flexibility and Performance of Computing Using Application-Specific Instructions and Reconfigurable Architecture.** *International Journal of Hybrid Information Technology* 2009, **2**:324-329.

7. Poon ASY: **An Energy-Efficient Reconfigurable Baseband Processor for Wireless Communications.** *(IEEE) Trans VLSI* 2007, **15(3)**:319-327.

8. Iacono DL, Zory J, Messina E, Piazzese N, Saia G, Bettinelli A: **ASIP Architecture for Multi-Standard Wireless Terminals.** *Design, Automation and Test in Europe (DATE '06)* 2006, **2**:1-6.

9. Hassan HM, Shalash AF, Hamed HM: **Design architecture of generic DFT/DCT 1D and 2D engine controlled by SW instructions.** *Asia Pacific Conference on Circuits and Systems APCCAS 2010* 2010, 84-87.

10. Hassan HM, Shalash AF, Mohamed K: **FPGA Implementation of an ASIP for high throughput DFT/DCT 1D/2D engine.** *IEEE International Symposium on Circuits and Systems (ISCAS) 2011* 2011, 1255-1258.

11. Cooley JW, Tukey JW: **An Algorithm for Machine Computation of Complex Fourier Series.** *Mathematics of Computation* 1965, **19**:297-301.

12. Nguyen T, Koilpillai RD: **The theory and Design of Aribitrary-length cosine-modulated filter Banks and wavelets, satisfying perfect reconstruction.** *IEEE Transaction on signal processing* 1996, **44(3)**:473-483.

13. Braganza S, Leeser M: **The 1D Discrete Cosine Transform for Large Point Sizes Implemented on Reconfigurable Hardware.** *IEEE International Conference on Application-specific Systems, Architectures and Processors ASAP* 2007, 101-106.

14. Weidong Li, Wanhammar L: **A PIPELINE FFT PROCESSOR.** *IEEE Workshop on Signal Processing Systems, 1999. SiPS 99* 1999, **19**:654-662.

15. Chidambaram R, Leuken RV, Quax M, Held I, Huisken J: **A multistandard FFT processor for wireless system-on-chip implementations.** *Proc International Symposium on Circuits and Systems* 2006, 47.

16. He S, Torkelson M: **Design and Implementation of a 1024-point Pipeline FFT Processor.** *Proceedings of the IEEE 1998 Custom Integrated Circuits Conference* 1998, 131-134.

17. Lin JM, Yu HY, Wu YJ, Ma HP: **A Power Efficient Baseband Engine for Multiuser Mobile MIMOOFDMA Communications.** *IEEE TRANSACTIONS ON CIRCUITS AND SYSTEMSI* 2010, **57**:1779-1792.

18. Sung TY, Hsin HC, Ko LT: **Reconfigurable VLSI Architecture for FFT Processor.** *WSEAS TRANSACTIONS on CIRCUITS and SYSTEMS* 2009, **8**.

19. Lee YH, Yu TH, Huang KK, Wu AY: **Rapid IP Design of Variable-length Cached-FFT Processor for OFDM-based Communication Systems.** *IEEE Workshop on Signal Processing Systems Design and Implementation, 2006. SIPS '06* 2006, 62-65.

20. Zhong G, Xu F, Willson AN Jr: **A power-scalable reconfigurable FFT/IFFT IC based on a multi-processorring.** *IEEE Journal of Solid-State Circuits (JSSC)* 2006, **41**:483-495.

21. Guan X, Lin H, Fei Y: **Design of an Application-specific Instruction Set Processor for High-throughput and Scalable FFT.** *IEEE International Symposium on Circuits and Systems ISCAS* 2009, 2513-2516.

22. Shah S, Venkatesan P, Sundar D, Kannan M: **Low Latency, High Throughput, and Less Complex VLSI Architecture for 2D-DFT.** *International Conference on Signal Processing, Communications and Networking ICSCN* 2008, 349-353.

23. Shah S, Venkatesan P, Sundar D, Kannan M: **A Fingerprint Recognition Algorithm Using Phase-BasedImage Matching for Low-Quality Fingerprints.** *IEEE International Conference on the Image Processing* 2005, 33-36.

24. Tumeo A, Monchiero M, Palermo G, Ferrandi F, Sciuto D: **A Pipelined Fast 2D-DCT Accelerator for FPGA-based SoCs.** *IEEE Computer Society Annual Symposium on VLSI* 2007, 331-336.

25. Cho YJ, Yu CL, Yu TH, Zhan CZ, Wu AYA: **Efficient Fast Fourier Transform Processor Design for DVB-H System.** *proc VLSI/CAD symposium* 2007.

26. sung TY: **Memory-efficient and high-speed split-radix FFT/IFFT processor based on pipeline CORDIC rotations.** *IEEE proceedings, Image Signal Process* 2006, **153**:405-410.

# Permissions

All chapters in this book were first published in JES, by Springer; hereby published with permission under the Creative Commons Attribution License or equivalent. Every chapter published in this book has been scrutinized by our experts. Their significance has been extensively debated. The topics covered herein carry significant findings which will fuel the growth of the discipline. They may even be implemented as practical applications or may be referred to as a beginning point for another development.

The contributors of this book come from diverse backgrounds, making this book a truly international effort. This book will bring forth new frontiers with its revolutionizing research information and detailed analysis of the nascent developments around the world.

We would like to thank all the contributing authors for lending their expertise to make the book truly unique. They have played a crucial role in the development of this book. Without their invaluable contributions this book wouldn't have been possible. They have made vital efforts to compile up to date information on the varied aspects of this subject to make this book a valuable addition to the collection of many professionals and students.

This book was conceptualized with the vision of imparting up-to-date information and advanced data in this field. To ensure the same, a matchless editorial board was set up. Every individual on the board went through rigorous rounds of assessment to prove their worth. After which they invested a large part of their time researching and compiling the most relevant data for our readers.

The editorial board has been involved in producing this book since its inception. They have spent rigorous hours researching and exploring the diverse topics which have resulted in the successful publishing of this book. They have passed on their knowledge of decades through this book. To expedite this challenging task, the publisher supported the team at every step. A small team of assistant editors was also appointed to further simplify the editing procedure and attain best results for the readers.

Apart from the editorial board, the designing team has also invested a significant amount of their time in understanding the subject and creating the most relevant covers. They scrutinized every image to scout for the most suitable representation of the subject and create an appropriate cover for the book.

The publishing team has been an ardent support to the editorial, designing and production team. Their endless efforts to recruit the best for this project, has resulted in the accomplishment of this book. They are a veteran in the field of academics and their pool of knowledge is as vast as their experience in printing. Their expertise and guidance has proved useful at every step. Their uncompromising quality standards have made this book an exceptional effort. Their encouragement from time to time has been an inspiration for everyone.

The publisher and the editorial board hope that this book will prove to be a valuable piece of knowledge for researchers, students, practitioners and scholars across the globe.

# List of Contributors

**Laszlo Hars**
CPU Technology, Pleasanton, CA 94588, USA

**Gyorgy Petruska**
Purdue University, Fort Wayne, IN, USA

**Bastien Vincke**
Univ Paris-Sud, CNRS, Institut d'Electronique Fondamentale, F-91405 Orsay, France

**Abdelhafid Elouardi**
Univ Paris-Sud, CNRS, Institut d'Electronique Fondamentale, F-91405 Orsay, France

**Alain Lambert**
IFSTTAR, IM, LIVIC, F-78000 Versailles, France

**Feng Zheng**
Institute of Digital Signal Processing, University of Duisburg-Essen, 47057 Duisburg, Germany

**Thomas Kaiser**
Institute of Digital Signal Processing, University of Duisburg-Essen, 47057 Duisburg, Germany

**Tareq Hasan Khan**
Department of Electrical and Computer Engineering, University of Saskatchewan, Saskatoon, SK S7N5A9, Canada

**Khan A Wahid**
Department of Electrical and Computer Engineering, University of Saskatchewan, Saskatoon, SK S7N5A9, Canada

**Roland Kammerer**
Vienna University of Technology, Vienna, Austria

**Roman Obermaisser**
University of Siegen, Siegen, Germany

**Bernhard Fröme**
Vienna University of Technology, Vienna, Austria

**Jasmin Grosinger**
Vienna University of Technology, Institute of Telecommunications, Gusshausstrasse 25/389, 1040 Vienna, Austria

**Zhoubing Xiong**
Department of Electronics and Telecommunications, Politecnico di Torino, Torino, Italy

**Zhenyu Song**
Department of Electronics and Telecommunications, Politecnico di Torino, Torino, Italy

**Andrea Scalera**
Pervasive Technologies, Istituto Superiore Mario Boella, Torino, Italy

**Enrico Ferrera**
Pervasive Technologies, Istituto Superiore Mario Boella, Torino, Italy

**Francesco Sottile**
Pervasive Technologies, Istituto Superiore Mario Boella, Torino, Italy

**Paolo Brizzi**
Pervasive Technologies, Istituto Superiore Mario Boella, Torino, Italy

**Riccardo Tomasi**
Pervasive Technologies, Istituto Superiore Mario Boella, Torino, Italy

**Maurizio A Spirito**
Pervasive Technologies, Istituto Superiore Mario Boella, Torino, Italy

**Chutisant Kerdvibulvech**
Department of Information and Communication Technology, Rangsit University, 52/347 Muang-Ake, Paholyothin Road, Lak-Hok, Patum Thani 12000, Thailand

**Gregor Lasser**
Institute of Telecommunication, Vienna University of Technology, 1040, Vienna, Austria

**Robert Langwieser**
Christian Doppler Laboratory for Wireless Technologies for Sustainable Mobility, Vienna University of Technology, 1040, Vienna, Austria

**Christoph F Mecklenbräuker**
Christian Doppler Laboratory for Wireless Technologies for Sustainable Mobility, Vienna University of Technology, 1040, Vienna, Austria

**Manuel Menghin**
Graz University of Technology, Graz, Austria

**Norbert Druml**
Graz University of Technology, Graz, Austria

**Christian Steger**
Graz University of Technology, Graz, Austria

**Reinhold Weiss**
Graz University of Technology, Graz, Austria

**Holger Bock**
Infineon Technologies Austria AG, Graz, Austria.

**Josef Haid**
Infineon Technologies Austria AG, Graz, Austria.

**Javier Vales-Alonso**
Department of Information Technologies and Communications, Technical University of Cartagena, Cartagena,Spain

**Francisco Javier Parrado-Garcí**
Department of Information Technologies and Communications, Technical University of Cartagena, Cartagena,Spain

**Juan J Alcaraz**
Department of Information Technologies and Communications, Technical University of Cartagena, Cartagena,Spain

**Matti Kaisti**
Business and Innovation Development (BID), University of Turku, Turku 20520, Finland

**Ville Rantala**
Business and Innovation Development (BID), University of Turku, Turku 20520, Finland

**Tapio Mujunen**
Business and Innovation Development (BID), University of Turku, Turku 20520, Finland
Oy LM Ericsson Ab, Jorvas 02420, Finland

**Sami Hyrynsalmi**
Turku School of Economics, Department of Management and Entrepreneurship, University of Turku, Turku 20014, Finland

**Kaisa Könnölä**
Business and Innovation Development (BID), University of Turku, Turku 20520, Finland

**Tuomas Mäkilä**
Business and Innovation Development (BID), University of Turku, Turku 20520, Finland

**Teijo Lehtonen**
Business and Innovation Development (BID), University of Turku, Turku 20520, Finland

**Mahmoud A Said**
Center for Wireless Studies, Faculty of Engineering, Cairo University, Cairo, Egypt

**Omar A Nasr**
Center for Wireless Studies, Faculty of Engineering, Cairo University, Cairo, Egypt

**Ahmed F Shalash**
Center for Wireless Studies, Faculty of Engineering, Cairo University, Cairo, Egypt

**Jihyeok Yun**
Department of Electronics and Information, Kyunghee University, Yongin 446-701, South Korea

**Deepak Kumar Singh**
Department of Electronics and Information, Kyunghee University, Yongin 446-701, South Korea

**Doug Young Suh**
Department of Electronics and Information, Kyunghee University, Yongin 446-701, South Korea

**Junsong Liao**
Department of Electrical and Computer Engineering, University of Windsor, Windsor, Ontario, N9B 3P4, Canada

**Brajendra K Singh**
Department of Electrical and Computer Engineering, University of Windsor, Windsor, Ontario, N9B 3P4, Canada

**Mohammed AS Khalid**
Department of Electrical and Computer Engineering, University of Windsor, Windsor, Ontario, N9B 3P4, Canada

**Kemal E Tepe**
Department of Electrical and Computer Engineering, University of Windsor, Windsor, Ontario, N9B 3P4, Canada

**Fahad Moiz**
Computer Science Electrical Engineering Department, University of Missouri-Kansas City, Kansas City, MO 64110, USA

**Sharika Kumar**
Computer Science Electrical Engineering Department, University of Missouri-Kansas City, Kansas City, MO 64110, USA

**Walter D Leon-Salas**
Electrical and Computer Engineering Technology Department, Purdue University, West Lafayette, IN 47907, USA

**Mark Johnson**
Oral and Craniofacial Sciences Department, University of Missouri-Kansas City, Kansas City, MO 64108, USA

**Robert Sobot**
Western University, Electrical and Computer Engineering, London, Ontario, N6A 5B9, Canada

**Philipp K Gentner**
Institute of Telecommunications, Vienna University of Technology, Gusshausstrasse 25/E389, Vienna 1040, Austria

**Robert Langwieser**
Institute of Telecommunications, Vienna University of Technology, Gusshausstrasse 25/E389, Vienna 1040, Austria

**Arpad L Scholtz**
Institute of Telecommunications, Vienna University of Technology, Gusshausstrasse 25/E389, Vienna 1040, Austria

**Günter Hofer**
Infineon Technologies Austria AG, Contactless and RF Exploration, Babenberger Strasse 10, Graz 8020, Austria

**Christoph F Mecklenbräuker**
Institute of Telecommunications, Vienna University of Technology, Gusshausstrasse 25/E389, Vienna 1040, Austria

**Hanan M Hassan**
Center for Wireless Studies, Faculty of Engineering, Cairo University, Giza, Egypt

**Karim Mohammed**
Center for Wireless Studies, Faculty of Engineering, Cairo University, Giza, Egypt

**Ahmed F Shalash**
Center for Wireless Studies, Faculty of Engineering, Cairo University, Giza, Egyp

Printed in the USA
CPSIA information can be obtained
at www.ICGtesting.com
JSHW051429221024
72173JS00006B/1419